A PEOPLE & A NATION

A PEOPLE & A NATION

A HISTORY OF THE UNITED STATES

Third Edition

Volume I: To 1877

Mary Beth Norton
Cornell University

David M. Katzman
University of Kansas

Paul D. Escott
Wake Forest University

Howard P. Chudacoff
Brown University

Thomas G. Paterson
University of Connecticut

William M. Tuttle, Jr.
University of Kansas

HOUGHTON MIFFLIN COMPANY   BOSTON
Dallas   Geneva, Illinois   Palo Alto   Princeton, New Jersey

Mary Beth Norton

Now the Mary Donlon Alger Professor of American History at Cornell University, Mary Beth Norton was born in Ann Arbor, Michigan. She received her B.A. from the University of Michigan (1964) and her Ph.D. from Harvard University (1969). Her dissertation won the Allan Nevins Prize the following year. She has written *The British Americans* (1972) and *Liberty's Daughters* (1980), and she has edited *To Toil the Livelong Day: America's Women at Work, 1790–1980* (with Carol Groneman, 1987), *Women of America* (with Carol Berkin, 1979) and *Major Problems in American Women's History* (1989). Her many articles have appeared in such journals as the *William and Mary Quarterly, Signs,* and the *American Historical Review.* Mary Beth has served on the National Council on the Humanities, and she has been president of the Berkshire Conference of Women Historians and Vice President for Research of the American Historical Association. She has advised many colleges on curriculum development in the areas of women's history and gender studies. She is also one of the organizers of the new International Federation for Research in Women's History. Her scholarship has received assistance from the Shelby Cullom Davis Center, Charles Warren Center, National Endowment for the Humanities, American Antiquarian Society, and Rockefeller Foundation. Siena College, Marymount Manhattan College, and DePauw University have recognized her with honorary degrees.

David M. Katzman

Born in New York City and a graduate of Queens College (B.A., 1963) and the University of Michigan (Ph.D., 1969), David M. Katzman is now a professor of history at the University of Kansas. Known for his work in labor, black, and social history, David has written *Before the Ghetto: Black Detroit in the Nineteenth Century* (1973) and *Seven Days a Week: Women and Domestic Service in Industrializing America* (1978), which won the Philip Taft Labor History Prize. With William M. Tuttle, Jr., he has edited *Plain Folk* (1981). He has contributed to *Three Generations in Twentieth-Century America: Family, Community, and the Nation* (2nd edition, 1981), has written articles for the *Dictionary of American Biography,* and has served as associate editor and editor of *American Studies.* The Guggenheim Foundation, National Endowment for the Humanities, and Ford Foundation have awarded him research assistance. He has been Visiting Professor of Modern History at University College, Dublin, Ireland, and Visiting Professor of Economic and Social History, University of Birmingham, England. David has served as an elected member on the Professional Committee of the American Historical Association. His many activities also include the regional selection panel for the Harry S. Truman Scholarships. At the University of Kansas he has been Director of the Honors Program.

Paul D. Escott

Born and raised in the Midwest (St. Louis, Missouri), Paul D. Escott studied in New England and the South. His interest in southern history and the Civil War/Reconstruction era probably began with southern parents, but it became conscious at Harvard College (B.A., 1969) and matured at Duke University (Ph.D., 1974). Now a professor of history at Wake Forest University, Paul taught for many years at the University of North Carolina, Charlotte. He has written *After Secession: Jefferson Davis and the Failure of Confederate Nationalism* (1978), *Slavery Remembered: A Record of Twentieth-Century Slave Narratives* (1979), *Many Excellent People: Power and Privilege in North Carolina, 1850–1900* (1985), and *Land of the South* (1989, with James Clay, Douglass Orr, and Alfred Stuart). Fellowships from the Rockefeller Foundation, American Philosophical Society, and Whitney M. Young, Jr., Memorial Foundation have aided his research and writing. He has co-edited *Race, Class, and Politics in Southern History* (1989, with Jeffrey J. Crow and Charles L. Flynn, Jr.), and has also collaborated with David Goldfield on two edited works: *Major Problems in the History of the American South* (1990) and *The South for Non-Southerners* (1990). Paul's articles have appeared in *Civil War History* and *Journal of Southern History,* among many others. He has also contributed to Robert W. Twyman and David C. Roller, eds., *The Encyclopedia of Southern History* (1980) and W. Buck Yearns, ed., *The Governors of the Confederacy* (1984).

Howard P. Chudacoff

A professor of history at Brown University, Howard P. Chudacoff was born in Omaha, Nebraska, and earned his degrees from the University of Chicago (A.B., 1965; Ph.D., 1969). Howard has written *Mobile Americans: Residential and Social Mobility in Omaha, 1880–1920* (1972), *The Evolution of American Urban Society* (3rd edition, 1987, with Judith Smith), and *How Old Are You? Age Consciousness in American Culture* (1989). The National Endowment for the Humanities, Ford Foundation, and Rockefeller Foundation have assisted his research. His many articles on topics in urban and social history have appeared in such journals as the *Journal of Family History, Reviews in American History,* and *Journal of American History*. He contributed "Success and Security: The Meaning of Social Mobility in America" to Stanley I. Kutler and Stanley N. Katz, eds., *The Promise of American History* (1982). In this country and in Europe Howard has lectured on many subjects, among them the American family and social mobility. At Brown University, where he has taught since 1970, Howard has co-chaired the American Civilization Program, served on the executive boards of both the Urban Studies Program and the Population Studies and Training Center, and chaired the department of history.

Thomas G. Paterson

Born in Oregon City, Oregon, and graduated from the University of New Hampshire (B.A., 1963) and the University of California, Berkeley (Ph.D., 1968), Thomas G. Paterson is now professor of history at the University of Connecticut. He has written *Meeting the Communist Threat* (1988), *On Every Front* (1979), *Soviet-American Confrontation* (1973), and *American Foreign Policy* (3rd edition, 1988, with J. Garry Clifford and Kenneth J. Hagan). Tom has edited and contributed to *Kennedy's Quest for Victory* (1989) and *Major Problems in American Foreign Policy* (3rd edition, 1989). His many articles have appeared in such journals as the *American Historical Review, Journal of American History,* and *Diplomatic History*. He has served on the editorial boards of the latter two journals. The National Endowment for the Humanities and Institute for the Study of World Politics, among others, have assisted his research and writing. He has been president of the Society for Historians of American Foreign Relations, has directed National Endowment for the Humanities Summer Seminars for College Teachers, and has been a member of the Board of Trustees of Stonehill College. Active in the profession, he has served on committees of the Organization of American Historians and the American Historical Association. Tom has lectured widely in the United States on history of foreign relations topics, as well as in the Soviet Union, Puerto Rico, China, Canada, and New Zealand.

William M. Tuttle, Jr.

A native of Detroit, Michigan, William M. Tuttle, Jr., received his B.A. from Denison University (1959) and his Ph.D. from the University of Wisconsin (1967) before becoming a professor of history at the University of Kansas. Bill has written the award-winning *Race Riot: Chicago in the Red Summer of 1919* (1970) and has edited *W.E.B. Du Bois* (1973) and *Plain Folk* (1982, with David Katzman). His many articles have appeared in such journals as the *Journal of American History, Agricultural History, Journal of Negro History, American Studies, Labor History,* and *Technology and Culture*. His scholarly work has been assisted by the American Council of Learned Societies, Institute of Southern History at Johns Hopkins University, Charles Warren Center at Harvard University, Guggenheim Foundation, and Stanford Humanities Center. From 1986 to 1989 he held a grant from the National Endowment for the Humanities to study the importance of the Second World War in the lives of America's home-front children. As a historical consultant, Bill has helped prepare several public television documentaries and docudramas, including *The Killing Floor,* which appeared on PBS's "American Playhouse." Bill was elected to the Nominating Board of the Organization of American Historians. He has also been active in local politics, having served as a party precinct committeeman for the past ten years.

About the Cover

Spinner Whirligig (folk sculpture), Pennsylvania, maker unknown, late nineteenth century. Wood (pine), metal, polychrome. Courtesy: Shelburne Museum, Shelburne, Vermont.

Cover photograph researched by Rose Corbett Gordon/Corbett Gordon Associates.

Text photographs researched by Pembroke Herbert/Picture Research Consultants.

Printed in the U.S.A.

Library of Congress Catalog Card Number: 89-080952
ISBN: 0-395-43308-8
BCDEFGHIJ-VH-9543210

Brief Contents

Contents

Maps and Charts

Preface

In preparing for the third edition, the authors of *A People and a Nation* met in Boston with Houghton Mifflin editors and art researchers. In several sessions we re-evaluated and discussed every aspect of the book—themes, organization, emphases, coverage, interpretation, scholarship, writing style, and illustrations. In these planning meetings, we analyzed many instructors' reports and profited from their advice. Our goals for this edition were to improve the organization of the book, delineate themes even more sharply, clarify specific passages, and incorporate the best of recent scholarship. Our basic approach to American history as the story of all the people remains the same, and in the third edition we have preserved and strengthened those characteristics of the second edition that students and faculty have found so attractive.

As teachers and students we are always recreating our past, restructuring our memory, rediscovering the personalities and events that have shaped us, inspired us, and bedeviled us. This book is our rediscovery of America's past—its people and the nation they founded and have sustained. This history is sometimes comforting, sometimes disturbing. As with our own personal experiences, it is both triumphant and tragic, filled with injury as well as healing. As a mirror on our lives, it is necessarily revealing—blemishes and all. As memory, it is the way we identify ourselves.

We draw on recent research, authoritative works, and our own teaching experience to offer a comprehensive book that tells the whole story of American history. Politics, government, **Character-** diplomacy, wars, and economic **istics of** patterns have been at the core of **the Book** writing on American history for generations. Into this traditional fabric we weave social history in order to discuss both the public and private spheres of Americans. We investigate the everyday life of the American people, that of the majority of Americans—women—and that of minorities. We explore the many ways Americans have identified and still identify themselves: gender, race, class, ethnicity, religion, work, sexual preference, geographic region, politics.

From the ordinary to the exceptional—the factory worker, the slave, the office secretary, the local merchant, the small farmer, the plantation owner, the ward politician, the president's wife, the film celebrity, the scientist, the army general—Americans have personal stories that have intersected with the public policies of their governments. Whether victors or victims, all have been actors in their own right, with feelings, ideas, and aspirations that have fortified them in good times and bad. All are part of the American story; all speak in *A People and a Nation* through excerpts from letters, diaries, oral histories, and other historical materials that we have integrated into this narrative history.

Several questions guided us in this third edition. On the official, or public, side of American history, we emphasize Americans' expectations of their governments and the practices of **Major** those local, state, and federal in- **Themes** stitutions. We look not only at politics but also at the culture of politics. We identify the mood and mentality of an era, searching for what Americans thought about themselves and their public officials. In our discussion of foreign relations, we ask why negotiations failed to prevent wars, why the United States became an expansionist, interventionist, global power, and how the domestic setting influenced diplomacy and vice versa.

In the social and economic areas, we emphasize patterns of change in the population, geographic and social mobility, and people's adaptation to new environments. We study the often friction-ridden interactions of people of different color, social class, national origin, religious affiliation, sectional identity, and gender, and the efforts made, often in reform movements, to reduce tensions. As well, we focus on the effects of technological development on the economy, the worker and the workplace, and lifestyles.

In the private, everyday life of the family and the home, we pay particular attention to gender roles, childbearing and childrearing, and diet and dress. We ask how Americans have entertained themselves, as participants or spectators, through sports, music, the graphic arts, reading, theater, film, radio, and television. Throughout American history, of course, this private sphere of American life and public policy have interacted and influenced one another.

Students and instructors have commended the book for its discussion of these many topics in clear, concrete language, and they have commented on how enjoyable the book is to read. We have appreciated hearing, too, that we challenged them to think about the meaning of American history, not just to memorize it; to confront one's own interpretations and at the same time to respect the views of others; and to show how the historian's mind works to ask questions and to tease conclusions out of vast amounts of information. We especially welcome these responses because they tell us that we have met our goal: to convey the excitement and fascination we feel as teacher-scholars in recreating and understanding the past.

For this third edition, literally hundreds of changes—major and minor—have been made throughout the book. Among the major changes,

▸ **Changes in the Third Edition**

the third edition is one chapter shorter than the second edition as a result of the merger of two chapters that covered the Hoover and Roosevelt periods. Now the Great Depression and the New Deal are presented in one chapter, 1929–1941. In addition, half of the stories that open chapters are new, and throughout we have provided new examples to illustrate themes.

A number of other revisions deserve special mention. Mary Beth Norton, who had primary responsibility for Chapters 1–7, has introduced new material on the Spanish and French colonies and on the soldiers who fought in colonial wars and the American Revolution. She has also revised the discussion of African migration and slavery and of early political parties. David M. Katzman, who had primary responsibility for Chapters 8–9 and 11–12, has expanded the coverage of the War of 1812, agriculture's adjustment to a market-oriented economy, city and country life, public disorder, Indian removal, abolitionism, and Jacksonian politics. He has reworked the discussion of reform to link it more closely to social and economic changes, religion, and politics. He has also introduced new ma-

terial on how people experienced the market economy, public space, the growing gender divisions in work, asylums, single women, and Hispanics in Texas and California. Paul D. Escott, who had primary responsibilty for Chapters 10 and 13–15, has expanded the treatment of the spread of market relations among southern yeomen and the influence of slavery on national life and, in the chapter on Reconstruction, of black activism in the South, splits among Republicans in Congress, and Supreme Court cases.

Howard P. Chudacoff, who had primary responsibility for Chapters 16–21 and 24, has added new material on Indians and the cultural conflict between their subsistence societies and the market-oriented economy; post–Civil War land policy; child labor; eating habits; and women's history. He has expanded the discussion of immigration and family life, urban reform, the new consumer society, and the origins of feminism. Chapter 20 especially has been reworked to develop the theme of inclusion versus exclusion in politics. Thomas G. Paterson, who had primary responsibility for Chapters 22–23, 26, 29, and 31, and the foreign relations parts of 33 and 34, has sharpened the discussion of expansionism and imperialism and expanded the treatment of the origins of the First World War in Europe and the clash of "systems" before the Second World War. He has added new material on the everyday lives of soldiers, Eisenhower's domestic policies and views on race relations, and the grassroots nature of the civil rights movement. He has also reworked treatment of the world economy, termination policy toward Indians, and the Vietnam War—protest, lessons, and veterans. Paterson served as the coordinating author for *A People and a Nation* and also prepared the Appendix.

William M. Tuttle, Jr., who had primary responsibility for Chapters 25, 27–28, 30, and 32–34, has combined coverage of the Great Depression and the New Deal into one chapter. He has expanded discussion of the Second World War experience of soldiers, McCarthyism, women in higher education, the baby boom, and the 1970s economy. He also reworked treatment of the War on Poverty, the 1968 election, and the fragmentation of the Democratic party. New material on Asian-Americans appears in Chapter 33, and the foreign policy of Jimmy Carter has been relocated there. Finally, Chapter 34 on the Reagan years and the beginnings of the Bush administration has been thoroughly revised; besides carrying the story to the end of the 1980s, the last chapter includes new discussion of Reagan's popularity, AIDS, the Iran-contra scandal, feminization of poverty, and drugs.

We have also revised the "Important Events" lists and moved them toward the front of each chapter. The end-of-chapter bibliographies have been revised to reflect recent scholarship. The Appendix now includes the Articles of Confederation as well as updated information. New illustrations—many of them in color—have been introduced, and new maps have been added and other maps revised.

To make the book as useful as possible for students and instructors, several learning and teaching aids are available, including a *Study Guide* and *MicroGuide* (a computerized study

> **Study and Teaching Aids**

guide), an *Instructor's Manual,* a *Test Items* file, *Diploma III* (test generator and class management software), and *Map Transparencies*. The *Study Guide,* which was prepared by George Warren and Cynthia Ricketson of Central Piedmont Community College, includes an introductory chapter on study techniques for history students, learning objectives and a thematic guide for each chapter in the text, exercises on evaluating and using information and on finding the main idea in passages from the text, map exercises where appropriate, new sections on organizing information for some chapters, and test questions (multiple choice and essay) on the content of each chapter. An answer key tells students not only which response is correct but also why each of the other choices is wrong. The *Study Guide* is available as *MicroGuide,* a computerized, tutorial version that also gives students feedback on incorrect as well as correct answers.

The *Instructor's Manual* contains chapter outlines, suggestions for lectures and discussion, and lists of audio-visual resources. The *Test Items* file, also by Professor Warren, offers more than 1,500 new multiple-choice and essay questions and more than 700 identification terms. The test items are available to adopters for IBM and Macintosh computers. In addition, there is a set of 93 full-color *Map Transparencies* available on adoption.

> **Acknowledgments**

Many instructors have read and criticized the several drafts of our manuscript. Their suggestions have made this a better book. We heartily thank:

John K. Alexander, *University of Cincinnati*
Sara Alpern, *Texas A & M University*
Dee Andrews, *California State University, Hayward*
Robert Asher, *University of Connecticut*
Edward L. Ayers, *University of Virginia*
Len Bailes, *El Paso Community College*
Delmar L. Beene, *Glendale Community College*
Michael Bellesiles, *Emory University*
Sidney R. Bland, *James Madison University*
Frederick J. Blue, *Youngstown State University*
Bill Cecil-Fronsman, *Washburn University*
William F. Cheek, *San Diego State University*
Michael S. Coray, *University of Nevada, Reno*
Donald T. Critchlow, *University of Notre Dame*
Bruce Dierenfield, *Canisius College*
Charles E. Dickson, *Clark State Community College*
Richard W. Etulain, *University of New Mexico*
Owen E. Farley, Jr., *Pensacola Junior College*
Lacy K. Ford, Jr., *University of South Carolina*
Donald E. Green, *Central State University*
L. Ray Gunn, *University of Utah*
Joseph M. Hawes, *Memphis State University*
Gary R. Hess, *Bowling Green State University*
Joseph P. Hobbs, *North Carolina State University*
Alan M. Kraut, *American University*
Monroe H. Little, Jr., *Indiana University, Purdue University at Indianapolis*
Cathy Matson, *University of Tennessee, Knoxville*
Michael N. McConnell, *University of Alabama, Birmingham*
Melissa L. Meyer, *University of Minnesota*
J. Bruce Nelson, *Dartmouth College*
Allan B. Spetter, *Wright State University*
Kathleen Xidis, *Johnson County Community College*
Charles A. Zappia, *San Diego Mesa College*

We also thank the following for their contributions to this third edition: Daniel H. Usner, Jr., Sharyn Brooks Katzman, Theodore A. Wilson, Eric Foner, Phillip Paludan, Nancy Fisher Chudacoff, Elizabeth Mahan, Ellen C. Garber, Kathryn N. Kretschmer, Samuel Watkins Tuttle, David Thelen, and Ronald Schlundt. We owe our special thanks to the many people at Houghton Mifflin who always set high standards, gave this book excellent guidance and care, and have become our friends.

Thomas G. Paterson

A People & A Nation

"*It spread over* the people as great destruction," the old man told the priest. "Some it quite covered [with pustules] on all parts— their faces, their heads, their breasts. . . . There was great havoc. Very many died of it. They could not stir; they could not change position, nor lie on one side, nor face down, nor on their backs. And if they stirred, much did they cry out. Great was its destruction. Covered, mantled with pustules, very many people died of them. And very many starved; there was death from hunger, [for] none could take care of [the sick]; nothing could be done for them."

It was the month of Tepeilhuitl. Four months earlier, Spanish troops led by Hernando Cortés had abandoned their siege of the Aztec capital of Tenochtitlan after failing in their first attempt to gain control of the city. An Aztec chronicler commented, "When the Spaniards thus disappeared, we thought they had gone for good, nevermore to return." The temples, desecrated during the siege, were cleaned and the images of the gods once again clothed with "godly ornaments"—turquoise mosaic masks, parrot and eagle feathers. But the European smallpox germs that would ensure the Spaniards' eventual triumph were already threatening the Aztecs. By the time the invaders returned in the month of Izcalli, the great epidemic described above had fatally weakened Tenochtitlan's inhabitants. Even so, the city held out for months. But in the Aztec year Three House, on the day One Serpent (August 1521), Tenochtitlan finally surrendered. The Spaniards had conquered Mexico, and on the site of the Aztec capital they built what is now Mexico City.

After many millennia of separation, inhabitants of the Americas—the so-called New World—had encountered the residents of the Eastern Hemisphere, with catastrophic results for the former and untold benefits for the latter. By the time Spanish troops occupied Tenochtitlan, the age of European expansion and colonization was already well under way. Over the next 350 years, Europeans would spread their civilization across the globe. Although they began by primarily seeking trade goods, they would eventually come to dominate native peoples in Asia and Africa as well as in the New World of the Western Hemisphere. The history of the tiny colonies in North America that became the United

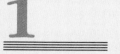

1

THE MEETING OF OLD WORLD AND NEW, 1492–1640

America by Theodor de Bry, 1650. Hand-colored engraving of Columbus arriving in the New World. *John Carter Brown Library, Brown University.*

States must be seen in this broader context of European exploration and exploitation.

After 1400, European nations sought to improve their positions relative to neighboring countries not only by fighting wars on their own continent but also by acquiring valuable colonies and trading posts elsewhere in the world. At the same time, the warring tribes and nations of Asia, Africa, and the Americas attempted to use the alien intruders to their own advantage or, failing that, to adapt successfully to the Europeans' presence in their midst. All the participants in the resulting interaction of divergent cultures were indelibly affected by the process. The contest among Europeans for control of the Americas and Africa changed the course of history in all four continents. Strategies selected by American and African tribes influenced the outcome of the Europeans' contest and determined the fate of their own societies. Although Europeans emerged politically dominant at the end of the long process of interaction among the divergent cultures of the Americas and Africa, they by no means controlled every aspect of it.

Nowhere is that lack of European control shown more clearly than in the early history of the English settlements in North America. England's attempts to establish colonies on the mainland in the sixteenth century failed completely. In the early seventeenth century the English succeeded only because neighboring Indians assisted the newcomers. The English colonists prospered by learning to grow such unfamiliar American crops as corn and tobacco and by developing extensive trading relationships with Native Americans. Eventually, as is seen in Chapter 2, they discovered a third source of prosperity—importing enslaved African laborers to work in their fields.

To achieve the first goal of feeding themselves, they had to adopt agricultural techniques suited both to the new crops and to an alien environment. Their second goal of maintaining lucrative trade networks required them to deal regularly on a more or less equal basis with people who seemed very different from themselves and who were far more familiar with America than they were. The early history of the United States, in short, can best be understood as a series of complex interactions among different peoples and environments rather than as the simple story of a triumph by only one of those groups—the English colonists.

Societies of the Americas and Africa

In the Christian world, it was the year 1400; by the Muslim calendar, 802; by Chinese count, 2896, the year of the hare. To the Maya, who had the most accurate calendar of all, the era started with the date 1 Ahau 18 Ceh. Regardless of the name or reckoning system, the two-hundred-year period that followed changed the course of world history. For thousands of years, human societies had developed largely in isolation from each other. The era that began in the Christian fifteenth century brought that long-standing isolation to an end. As European explorers and colonizers sought to exploit the resources of the rest of the globe, peoples from different races and cultural traditions came into regular contact for the first time and all were changed by the resulting interaction.

The civilizations that had developed separately had several basic characteristics in common. All had political structures governing their secular affairs, kinship customs regulating their social life, economic systems defining their modes of subsistence, and one or more sets of indigenous religious beliefs. In addition, they all organized their work assignments on the basis of the sexual division of labor. Throughout the world, men and women performed different tasks, although the specific definition of those tasks varied from culture to culture. These many societies exhibited basic economic differences. Some were nomadic, surviving by moving continually in search of wild animals and edible plants; others combined regular seasonal movements with a limited reliance on agriculture. In many areas, the cultivation of food crops provided most of the essential food supply. Such agricultural civilizations, assured of steady supplies of meat, grains, and vegetables, did not have to devote all their energies to subsistence. Instead, they were able to accumulate wealth, produce ornamental objects, and create elaborate rituals and ceremonies.

The differences in cultural traditions became the focal point for the interactions that occurred in the fifteenth century and thereafter among the various human societies. Basic similarities were obscured

IMPORTANT EVENTS

1492	Christopher Columbus reaches Bahama islands
1513	Ponce de León reaches Florida
1518–30	Smallpox epidemic decimates Indian population of Central and South America
1521	Tenochtitlan surrenders to Cortés; Aztec empire falls to Spaniards
1533	Henry VIII divorces Catherine of Aragon; English Reformation begins
1534–35	Jacques Cartier explores St. Lawrence River
1539–42	Hernando de Soto explores southeastern United States
1540–42	Francisco Vásquez de Coronado explores southwestern United States
1558	Elizabeth I becomes queen
1565	Establishment of St. Augustine
1587–90	Sir Walter Raleigh's Roanoke colony fails
1603	James I becomes king

1607	Jamestown founded
1611	First Virginia tobacco crop
1619	First blacks arrive in Virginia
1620	First group of English women arrives in Virginia Plymouth colony founded
1622	Powhatan Confederacy attacks Virginia colony
1624	Dutch settle on Manhattan Island (New Amsterdam)
1625	Charles I becomes king
1630	Massachusetts Bay colony founded
1634	Maryland founded
1635	Roger Williams expelled from Massachusetts Bay; founds Providence, Rhode Island
1636	Connecticut founded
1637	Pequot War Anne Hutchinson expelled from Massachusetts Bay colony
1646	Treaty ends hostilities between Virginia and Powhatan Confederacy

by the shock of discovering that not all people were the same color as oneself, that other folk worshiped other gods, or that some people defined the separate roles of men and women differently from the way one's own society did. Because three major human groups—Native Americans, Africans, and Europeans—met and mingled on the soil of the Western Hemisphere during the age of European colonization, their relationships can be examined in that context.

Since the earliest known humanlike remains, about 3 million years old, have been found in what is now Ethiopia, it is likely that human beings originated on the continent of Africa. During many

Paleo-Indians

millennia, the growing human population slowly dispersed to the other continents. Some of the peoples participating in this vast migration crossed a now-submerged stretch of land that joined the Asian and North American continents at the site of the Bering Strait. These forerunners of the Native American population, known as Paleo-Indians, arrived in the Americas more than thirty thousand years ago—about the same time that parts of China and the Soviet Union were also being settled. The Paleo-Indians were nomadic hunters of game and gatherers of wild plants. Over many centuries, they spread through North and South America, probably moving as extended families or "bands." "Tribes" were composed of allied bands. Linguistic and cultural similarities linked tribes into even larger units, described by the name of the language they shared. East of the Mississippi River, the most important linguistic groups were the Algonkians and the Iroquoians, found primarily in the north, and the Muskogeans of the south.

By approximately 5,500 years ago, Indians living in central Mexico had begun to cultivate food crops, the most important of which were maize (corn), squash, beans, and chili peppers. As knowledge of agricultural techniques spread, most Indian groups started to live a more sedentary existence. Some established permanent settlements; others moved several times a year among fixed sites. All the Native American cultures emphasized subsistence. Although they traded goods with each other, no tribe ever became wholly dependent on another group for items vital to its survival. Over the centuries, the North American Indians adapted their once-similar ways of life to specific and very different geographical settings, thus creating the diversity of cultures that the Europeans encountered when they first arrived (see map).

Those Indian bands that lived in environments not well suited to agriculture—because of inadequate rainfall or poor soil, for example—continued the nomadic lifestyle of their ancestors. Within the area of the present-day United States, these tribes included the Paiutes and Shoshones, who inhabited the Great Basin (now Nevada and Utah). Bands of such hunter-gatherers were small, because of the difficulties of finding sufficient food for more than a few people. They were usually composed of one or more related families, with men hunting small animals and women gathering seeds and berries. Where large game was more plentiful and food supplies therefore more certain, as in present-day Canada and the Great Plains, bands of hunters could be somewhat larger.

In more favorable environments, still larger groups of Indians combined agriculture in varying degrees with gathering, hunting, and fishing. Those tribes that lived near the seacoasts, like the Chinooks of present-day Washington and Oregon,

consumed large quantities of fish and shellfish, in addition to growing crops and gathering seeds and berries. Tribes of the interior (for example, the Arikaras of the Missouri River valley) hunted large game animals while also cultivating fields of corn, squash, and beans. So, too, the Algonkian tribes that inhabited much of what is now eastern Canada and the northeastern United States combined hunting and agriculture. The Algonkians commonly moved four or five times during the year. Once the crops were well established, villages would break into small mobile bands and engage in gathering, hunting, and fishing. The village would reassemble for harvest, then once again disperse for the fall hunting season. Finally, the people would spend the harsh winter months together in a protected location before returning to their fields in the spring. Every few years they would alter the site of those fields to ensure their continuing fertility.

Societies that relied primarily on hunting large animals like deer and buffalo for their food supply assigned that task to men, allotting food-processing

▶ **Sexual Division of Labor in America**

and clothing-production chores to women. Before such nomadic bands acquired horses from the Spaniards (see page 20), women —occasionally assisted by dogs —also carried the family's belongings whenever the band relocated. Such a sexual division of labor was universal among hunting tribes, regardless of the linguistic group to which they belonged or their specific location.

Agricultural Indians, by contrast, differed in how they assigned cultivating crops to the sexes. In what is now the southwestern United States, the Pueblo peoples, who lived in sixty or seventy autonomous villages and spoke five different languages, began raising squash and beans about five thousand years ago. They all defined agricultural labor as men's work. In the East, though, Algonkian, Iroquoian, and Muskogean peoples allocated agricultural chores to women. Among these eastern tribes, men's major assignments were hunting and clearing the land. In all the cultures, women gathered wild foods, prepared the food for consumption or storage, and cared for the children.

The southwestern and eastern agricultural Indians had similar social organizations. They lived in villages, sometimes sizable ones with a thousand or more inhabitants. Pueblo villages were large, multistory buildings, constructed on terraces along the

Indian Cultures of North America

The sexual division of labor among the Indians of present-day Florida attracted the attention of the French artist Jacques Le Moyne in 1564–1565. He showed the men breaking up the ground with fish-bone hoes, while the women dropped seeds into holes. Unable to abandon his European vision of how planting should be done, he also erroneously drew plowed furrows in the soil. *John Carter Brown Library, Brown University.*

sides of cliffs or other easily defended sites. Northern Iroquois villages were composed of large, rectangular, bark-covered structures, or long houses; the name *Iroquois* meant "People of the Long House." Muskogeans and southern Algonkians lived in large houses made of thatch. Most of the eastern villages were laid out defensively, often being surrounded by wood palisades and ditches. In these cultures, each dwelling housed an extended family defined matrilineally (through a female line of descent). Mothers, their married daughters, and their daughters' husbands and children all lived together. Matrilineal descent did not imply matriarchy, or the wielding of power by women; it was simply a means of reckoning kinship. The families in such dwellings were linked together into clans, again defined by matrilineal ties. Nomadic bands of the Great Plains, on the other hand, were most of-

ten related patrilineally, through the male line. They lacked settled villages and defended themselves primarily through their ability to move to safer locations when necessary.

In the southwestern and eastern cultures, the village supplied the most important political structures; for the Plains dwellers, bands fulfilled that function. Among Pueblo and Muskogean peoples the village council, composed of ten to thirty men, was the highest political authority; there was no government at the tribal level. That was true, too, of the nomadic hunters. The Iroquois, by contrast, had an elaborate political hierarchy linking villages into tribes and tribes into a widespread confederation. (The Iroquois Confederacy is discussed in detail in Chapter 2.) In all the cultures, political power was divided

> **Indian Politics and Religion**

Chapter 1: The Meeting of Old World and New, 1492–1640

John White, an artist who accompanied the exploratory mission Raleigh sent to America in 1585, sketched Pomeioc, a typical Algonkian village composed of houses made from woven mats stretched over poles, and surrounded by a defensive wooden palisade. *Library of Congress.*

between civil and war leaders, who had authority only so long as they retained the confidence of the people. Consensus rather than autocratic rule characterized the Indians' political systems.

The political position of women varied from tribe to tribe. Women were more likely to assume leadership roles among the agricultural peoples (especially where females were the chief cultivators) than among nomadic hunters. For example, women could become the leaders of certain Algonkian bands, but they never held that position in the hunting tribes of the Great Plains. Iroquois women did not become chiefs, yet tribal matrons nevertheless exercised political power (see page 58). Probably the most powerful female chiefs were found in what is now the southeastern United States. In the mid-sixteenth century a female ruler known as the Lady of Cofitachique governed a large group of villages in present-day western South Carolina. Early English settlers on the Atlantic coast also noted the presence of female chiefs in nearby villages, most of them the wives, sisters, or widows of male leaders.

Indians' religious beliefs varied even more than did their political systems. Yet they were all polytheistic, involving a multitude of gods. One common thread was their integration with nature. Thus the most important rituals related closely to each tribe's chief means of subsistence. The major deities of agricultural Indians like Pueblos and Muskogeans were associated with cultivation, and their chief festivals centered on planting and harvest. The most important gods of hunting tribes (like the Siouan-speakers of the Great Plains), by contrast, were associated with animals, and their major festivals were related to hunting. The tribe's mode of subsistence and women's role in it helped to determine women's potential as religious leaders. Women held the most prominent positions in those agricultural societies (like the Iroquois) in which they were also the chief food producers.

The most highly centralized Indian civilizations

on the North American continent were located in present-day Mexico and Guatemala (Mesoamerica). The major Indian societies that were encountered

Aztec and Maya

by the Spanish explorers in the sixteenth century—the Aztecs and Mayas—were the heirs of earlier civilizations (like the Olmecs), which had also built great empires. Characteristic of these Mesoamerican cultures were large cities, ceremonial sites featuring massive pyramid-shaped temples, rule by a hereditary elite of warrior-priests, primary dependence on agriculture for food, and religious practices that included human sacrifice. The Aztecs, who entered central Mexico in the fourteenth century, were a warlike people who had consolidated their control over the entire region by the time of Cortés's arrival. The Mayas, who lived in what is now Guatemala and Mexico's Yucatan peninsula, were the intellectual leaders of Mesoamerica. They invented systems of writing and mathematics, and their calendar was the most accurate then known.

Thus a wide variety of Indian cultures, comprising perhaps 4 to 6 million people, inhabited North America when Europeans arrived. In modern Mexico, hereditary rulers presided over vast agricultural empires. Along the Atlantic coast of the present-day United States, Indians likewise cultivated crops, but their political systems differed greatly from those of Mesoamerica. To the north and west, in what is now Canada and the Great Plains, lived nomadic and seminomadic societies primarily dependent on hunting large animals. Still farther west were the hunter-gatherer bands of the Great Basin and the agricultural Indians of the Southwest. Finally, on the Pacific coast lived tribes that based their subsistence chiefly on fish. All told, these diverse groups spoke well over one thousand different languages. For obvious reasons, they did not consider themselves as one people, nor did they—for the most part—think of uniting to repel the European invaders. Instead, each tribe or band continued to pursue the same goal it always had: bettering its own circumstances relative to its neighbors, regardless of who those neighbors were.

Fifteenth-century Africa, like fifteenth-century America, housed a variety of cultures adapted to different geographical settings (see map). Many of these cultures were of great antiquity. In the

Africa: Its Peoples

north, along the Mediterranean Sea, lived the Berbers, a Muslim people of Middle Eastern origin. (Muslims are adherents of the Islamic religion founded by the prophet Mohammed in the seventh century.) On the east coast of Africa, city-states dominated by Muslim merchants engaged in extensive trade with India, the Moluccas (part of modern Indonesia), and China. Through these ports passed a considerable share of the trade between the eastern Mediterranean and Far East; the rest followed the long land route across Central Asia known as the Silk Road.

In the African interior, south of the Mediterranean coast, lie the great Sahara and Libyan deserts, huge expanses of nearly waterless terrain that pose a formidable barrier to travel. Below the deserts, much of the continent is divided between tropical rain forests and grassy plains. People speaking a variety of languages and following quite different modes of subsistence lived in a wide belt south of the deserts. Below the Gulf of Guinea (see map), the fertile, forested landscape came to be dominated by Bantu-speaking peoples, who left their homeland in modern Nigeria about two thousand years ago and slowly migrated south and east across the continent, assimilating and conquering other ethnic groups (like the Pygmies and the San) as they went.

Most of the unwilling black migrants to North America came from West Africa, which the Europeans called Guinea, a land of tropical forests and

West Africa (Guinea)

small-scale agriculture that had been inhabited for at least ten thousand years before Europeans set foot there in the fifteenth century. The northern region, or Upper Guinea, was heavily influenced by Islamic culture. As early as the eleventh century, many of its inhabitants had become Muslims; more important, the trans-Saharan trade between Upper Guinea and the Muslim Mediterranean was black Africa's major connection to Europe and the Middle East. In return for salt, dates, and such manufactured goods as silk and cotton cloth, Africans exchanged ivory, gold, and slaves with the northern merchants. (Slaves, who were mostly criminals and wartime captives, were in great demand as household servants in the homes of the Muslim Mediterranean elite.) This commerce was controlled first by the

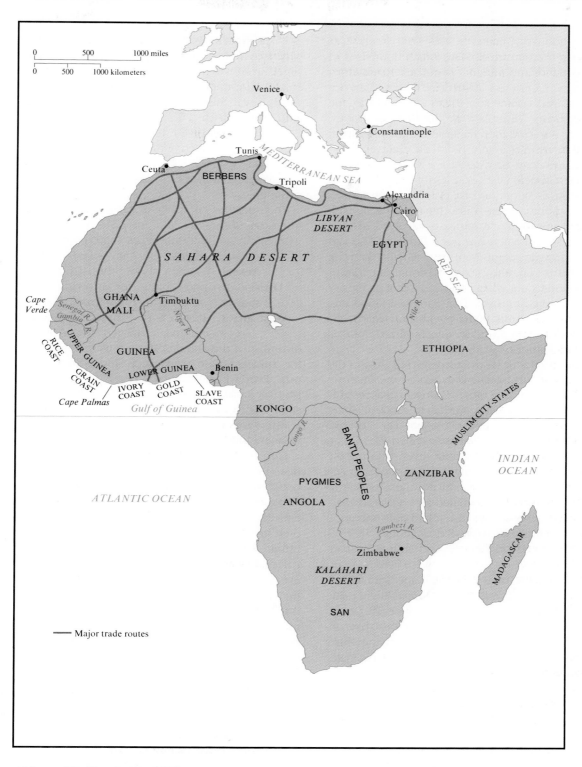

Africa and Its Peoples, ca. 1400

great kingdom of Ghana (ca. 900–1100), then by its successor, the empire of Mali, which flourished in the fourteenth and fifteenth centuries. Black Africa and Islam intersected at the city that was the intellectual and commercial heart of the trade, the near-legendary Timbuktu. A cosmopolitan center, Timbuktu attracted merchants and scholars from all parts of North Africa and the Mediterranean.

Along the coast of West Africa and in the south, or Lower Guinea, Islam had less influence. There, most Africans continued to practice their indigenous religions, which—like those of the agricultural Indians of the Americas—revolved around rituals designed to ensure good harvests. The vast interior kingdoms of Mali and Ghana had no counterparts on the coast. Throughout Lower Guinea, individual villages composed of groups of kin were linked into small, hierarchical kingdoms. At the time of initial contact with Europeans, the region was characterized by decentralized political and social authority.

Just as the political structures varied, so too did the means of subsistence pursued by the different peoples of Guinea. Upper Guinea runs roughly north-south from Cape Verde to Cape Palmas. Its northernmost region (present-day Gambia, Senegal, and Guinea) was the so-called Rice Coast, lying just south of the Gambia River. The people who lived there fished and cultivated rice in coastal swamplands. The Grain Coast, the next region to the south, was thinly populated and not readily accessible from the sea because it had only one good harbor (modern Freetown, Sierra Leone). Its people concentrated on farming and animal husbandry.

South of the Grain Coast, at Cape Palmas, the coastline turns east, and Lower Guinea begins. The Ivory Coast and the Gold Coast were each named by Europeans for the major trade goods they obtained there. The Gold Coast, comprising thirty little kingdoms known as the Akan States, later formed the basis of the great Asante kingdom. Initially many of the slaves destined for sale in the Americas came from the Akan States. By the eighteenth century, though, it was the next section of Lower Guinea, the modern nations of Togo and Benin, that supplied most of the slaves sold in the English colonies. The Adja kings of the region, which became known as the Slave Coast, encouraged the founding of slave-trading posts and served as middlemen in the trade.

The ancient kingdom of Benin (modern Nigeria), which lay east of the Slave Coast and west of the Niger River, was the strongest and most centralized coastal state in Guinea. Long before Europeans arrived, it was, like Mali, a center of trade for West and North Africa. Like the peoples of the Rice Coast, those who lived in Benin along the delta of the Niger made much of their living from the water. They fished, made salt, and used skillfully constructed dugout canoes to carry on a wide-ranging commerce.

The societies of West Africa, like those of the Americas, assigned different tasks to men and women. In general, the sexes shared agricultural **Sexual Division of Labor in West Africa** duties, but in some cultures women bore the primary responsibility for growing crops, whereas in others men assumed that chore. In addition, men hunted, managed livestock, and did most of the fishing. Women were responsible for childcare, food preparation, and cloth manufacture. Everywhere in West Africa women were the primary local traders. They had charge of the extensive local and regional networks through which goods were exchanged among the various families, villages, and small kingdoms.

Despite their different modes of subsistence and deep political divisions, the peoples of West Africa had similar social systems organized on the basis of what anthropologists have called the dual-sex principle. In the societies of West Africa, each sex handled its own affairs: just as male political and religious leaders governed the men, so females ruled the women. In the Dahomean kingdom, every male official had his female counterpart; in the Akan States, chiefs inherited their status through the female line, and each chief had a female assistant who supervised women's affairs. Many West African societies practiced polygyny (one man having several wives, each of whom lived separately with her children). Thus few adults lived permanently in marital households, but the dual-sex system ensured that their actions were subjected to scrutiny by members of their own sex, if not by a spouse.

Religious beliefs likewise stressed the complementary nature of male and female roles. Both women and men served as heads of the cults and secret societies that directed the spiritual life of the villages. Young women were initiated into the Poro

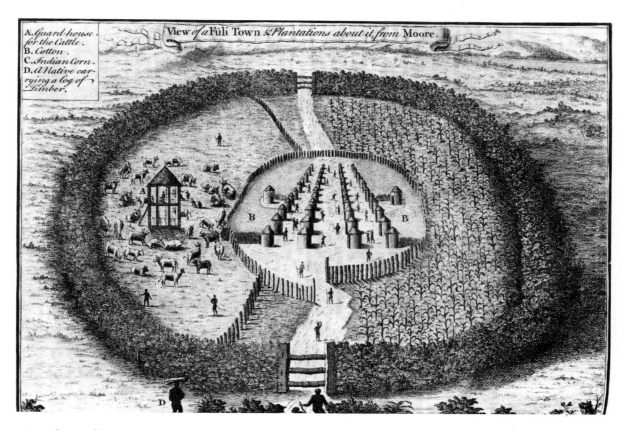

A West African village as drawn by a European observer. A wooden defensive palisade surrounds the circular houses made of woven plant materials. In this the African village resembles Pomeioc, the Indian village pictured on page 9. But note a major difference—a herd of livestock enclosed in a larger fence. Note also that the Africans are growing Indian corn, thus illustrating the exchange of plants between America and Africa (see page 20). *Library of Congress.*

cult, young men into Sandé. Neither cult was allowed to reveal its secrets to the opposite sex. Although African women rarely held formal power over men (unlike some of their Native American contemporaries), they did govern other females in cults and secret societies.

The West Africans brought to the Americas, then, were agricultural peoples, skilled at tending livestock, hunting, fishing, and manufacturing cloth from plant fibers and animal skins. Both men and women were accustomed to working communally, alongside other members of their own sex. They were also accustomed to a relatively egalitarian relationship between the sexes. In the New World, they entered societies that used their labor but had little respect for their cultural traditions. Of the three peoples whose experience intersected in the Americas, their lives were the most disrupted.

Europe and Its Explorations

After 1400, Europe began to recover from centuries of decline. Northern Europe—England and France in particular—had long been an intellectual and economic backwater, far outstripped in importance by the states of the Mediterranean, especially the great Italian city-states like Venice and Florence. The cultural flowering known as the Renaissance began in those city-states in the fourteenth century and spread northward, awakening Europeans' intellectual curiosity. At the same time, the pace of economic activity quickened. Near-constant warfare (for example, the Hundred Years' War between

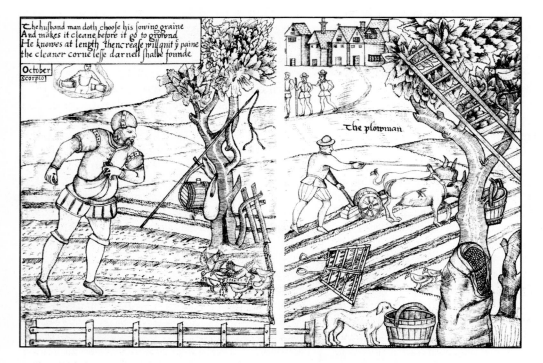

In the illustration:
The husband man doth choose his sowing graine
And makes it cleane before it go to ground
He knowes at length thenc reafe will quit y paine
the cleaner corne leffe darnell fhalbe founde

October
[Scorpio]

The plowman

A 1622 English manuscript illustrated the seasonal cycle of work for ordinary farmers. In October, the month shown here, the wise husbandman (farmer) plowed his fields and sowed a crop of winter wheat (which the English called corn). Note that these scenes contain only men, showing that the sexual division of labor in European agriculture was quite different from that of the Indians illustrated on page 8. *Folger Shakespeare Library.*

England and France, which ended in a French victory in 1453) promoted feelings of nationalism within the combatant countries. All these developments helped to set the stage for extraordinary political and technological change after the middle of the fifteenth century.

Yet in the midst of that change the life of Europe's rural people remained basically untouched for at least another century. European societies were hierarchical, with a few wealthy aristocratic families wielding arbitrary power over the majority of the people. Europe's kingdoms accordingly resembled those of Africa or Mesoamerica but differed greatly from the more egalitarian, consensus-based societies found in America north of Mexico. Most Europeans, like most Africans or Native Americans, lived in small agricultural villages. European farmers, or peasants, had separate land-holdings, but they nevertheless worked their fields communally. Because fields had to lie fallow every second or third year to regain their fertility, a family

could not have ensured itself a regular food supply had not the work and the crop been shared annually by all the villagers.

In European cultures, men did most of the field work, with women helping out chiefly at planting and harvest. At other times, women's duties consisted primarily of childcare and household tasks, including preserving food for the winter, milking cows, and caring for poultry. If a woman's husband was an artisan or storekeeper, she might assist him in business. Since Europeans usually kept domesticated animals (especially pigs, sheep, and cattle) to use for meat, hunting had little economic importance in their cultures. Instead, hunting was a sport engaged in by male aristocrats.

Sexual Division of Labor in Europe

In African or Native American societies women often played major roles in politics and religion. In Europe, however, men were dominant in all areas of life. A few women from noble families—for example, Queen Elizabeth I of England—achieved status or power, but the vast majority of European women were excluded from positions of political authority. In the Roman Catholic church, leadership roles were reserved for men, who alone could become priests and bishops, although women could become nuns. At the familial level, husbands and fathers expected to control the lives of their wives, children, and servants (a patriarchal system of family governance). In short, European women held inferior positions in both public and private realms.

The traditional hierarchical social structure of Europe changed little in the fifteenth century. But the same era witnessed rapid and dynamic political

> **Political and Technological Change**

change, as ruthless monarchs expanded their territories through conquest and marriage and consolidated previously diffuse political power by defeating the nobility. In England, Henry VII in 1485 founded the Tudor dynasty and began uniting a previously divided land. In France, the successors of Charles VII unified the kingdom and gained new sources of revenue. Most successful of all, at least in the short run, were Ferdinand of Aragon and Isabella of Castile. In 1469 they married and combined their kingdoms, thus creating the foundation of a strongly Catholic Spain. In 1492, they defeated the Muslims, who had lived on the Iberian peninsula for centuries, and expelled all Jews from their domain.

The fifteenth century also brought significant technological change to Europe. Movable type and the printing press, invented in Germany in the 1450s, made information more widely and more readily accessible than ever before. Adapting designs from Arab sailors of the eastern Mediterranean, Europeans created more maneuverable ships that could sail against the wind. Of key importance was the perfection of navigational instruments like the astrolabe and the quadrant, which allowed oceanic sailors to estimate their position (latitude) by measuring the relationship of sun, moon, or stars to the horizon. These developments simultaneously stimulated Europeans' curiosity about fabled lands across the seas and enabled them to think about reaching exotic places by ship. For example, Marco Polo's *Travels,* which described a Venetian merchant's adventures in thirteenth-century China and reported that that nation was bordered on the east by an ocean, circulated widely

among Europe's educated elites after it was printed in 1477. This book led many Europeans to believe that they could trade directly with China via ocean-going vessels, instead of relying on the Silk Road or the trade route through East Africa. That would also allow them to circumvent the Muslim and Mediterranean merchants who had hitherto controlled their access to Asian goods.

Thus the European explorations of the fifteenth and sixteenth centuries were made possible by technological advances and by the financial might of newly powerful national rulers.

> **Motives for Exploration**

The primary motivation for the exploratory voyages was a desire for direct access to the wealth of the East. That motive was supported by a secondary concern to spread Christianity around the world. The linking of materialist and spiritual goals might seem contradictory today, but fifteenth-century Europeans saw no necessary conflict between the two. Explorers and colonizers could honestly wish to convert heathen peoples to Christianity. At the same time they could also hope to increase their nation's wealth by establishing direct trade with China, India, and the Moluccas, the sources of spices like pepper, cloves, cinnamon, and nutmeg (needed to season the bland European diet), silk, dyes, perfumes, jewels, and gold.

The seafaring Portuguese people, whose land was located on the southwestern corner of the continent of Europe, began the age of European expansion in 1415 when they seized control of Ceuta, a Muslim city in North Africa (see map, page 11). Prince Henry the Navigator, son of King John I, realized that vast wealth awaited the first European nation to tap the riches of Africa and Asia directly. Each year he dispatched ships southward along the western coast of Africa, attempting to discover a passage to the East. Not until after Prince Henry's death did Bartholomew Dias round the southern tip of Africa (1488) and Vasco da Gama finally reach India (1498).

Although West African states successfully resisted European penetration of the interior, they allowed the Portuguese to establish trading posts along their coasts. Charging the traders rent and levying duties on the goods they imported, the African chiefdoms set the terms of exchange and benefited considerably from their new, easier access to European manufactures. The Portuguese, too, gained a great deal, for they no longer had to rely on the long trans-Saharan trade route. They earned immense profits by transporting African goods swiftly to Europe. Among their most valuable cargoes were slaves. When they carried African Muslim prisoners of war back to the Iberian peninsula, the Portuguese introduced the custom of black slavery into Europe.

Spain, with its reinvigorated monarchy, was the next country to sponsor exploratory voyages. Envious of Portuguese successes, Queen Isabella hoped to gain a foothold in Asia for her nation, and so she agreed to finance a voyage by Christopher Columbus, a Genoese sea captain. Like other experienced sailors, Columbus believed the world to be round. (Only ignorant folk thought it was flat.) But Columbus was regarded as a crackpot because of his estimate of the world's size. He believed that Japan lay only three thousand miles from the southern European coast—the distance is actually twelve thousand miles—and therefore that it would be easier to reach the East by sailing west than by making the difficult voyage around the southern tip of Africa.

> **Christopher Columbus**

On August 3, 1492, with three ships under his command—the *Pinta,* the *Niña,* and the *Santa Maria*—Columbus sailed west from the port of Palos in Spain. On October 12, he landed on an island in the Bahamas, which he named San Salvador and claimed for the king and queen of Spain. Because he thought he had reached the Indies, he called the inhabitants of the region Indians.

Columbus made three more voyages to the west, during which he explored most of the major Caribbean islands and sailed along the coasts of Central and South America. Until the day he died in 1506, Columbus continued to believe that he had reached Asia. Even before his death, others knew better. Because the Florentine Amerigo Vespucci, who explored the South American coast in 1499, was the first to publish the idea that a new continent had been discovered, a mapmaker in 1507 labeled the land America. By then, in 1494, Spain, Portugal, and Pope Alexander VI had signed the Treaty of Tordesillas, which confirmed Portugal's dominance in Africa and Brazil, in exchange for Spanish preeminence in the rest of the New World.

More than five hundred years earlier, Norse explorers had briefly colonized present-day Newfoundland, but the voyages of Columbus and his successors finally brought the Old and New Worlds together. England dispatched John Cabot in 1497 and his son Sebastian in 1507; France financed Giovanni da Verrazzano in 1524 and Jacques Cartier in 1534; and in 1609 and 1610 Henry Hudson explored the North American coast for a Dutch company (see map). All these men were primarily searching for the legendary, nonexistent "Northwest Passage" through the Americas, hoping to find an easy route to the riches of the East. Although they did not attempt to plant colonies in the Western Hemisphere, their discoveries interested European nations in further exploring the New World for its own sake.

Only Spain immediately moved to take advantage of the discoveries. On his first voyage, Columbus had established a base on the island of Hispaniola. From there, Spanish explorers fanned out around the Caribbean basin: in 1513, Juan Ponce de León reached Florida and Vasco Núñez de Balboa crossed the Isthmus of Panama and found the Pacific Ocean. Less than ten years later, the Spaniards' dreams of wealth were realized when Cortés conquered the Aztec empire, killing its ruler, Moctezuma, and seizing a fabulous treasure of gold and silver. Venturing northward, conquistadores like Juan Rodriguez Cabrillo (who sailed along the California coast), Hernando de Soto (who discovered the Mississippi River), and Francisco Vásquez de Coronado (who explored the southwestern portion of what is now the United States) found little of value. By contrast, Francisco Pizarro, who explored the western coast of South America, acquired the richest silver mines in the world by conquering and enslaving the Incas in 1535. Although popular myth would have it that the invaders triumphed because the Indians believed they were gods or because they had horses and guns, the truth is far grimmer: as at Tenochtitlan, deadly germs, not superior technology, won most of the Spaniards' battles for them. Just half a century after Columbus's first voyage, the Spanish monarchs—who treated the American territories as their personal possessions—controlled the richest, most extensive empire Europe had known since ancient Rome.

> **Conquistadores**

Spain established the model of colonization that other countries later attempted to imitate, a model with three major elements. First, the crown main-

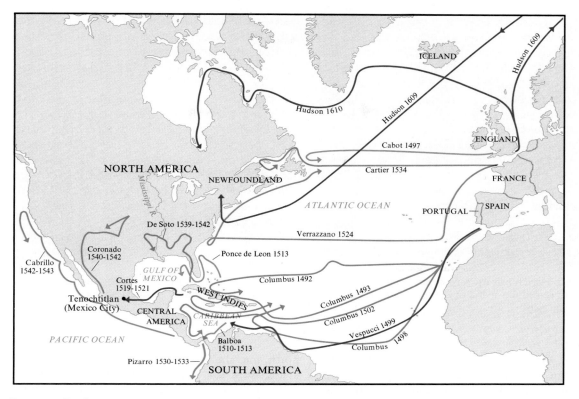

European Explorations in America

tained tight control over the colonies, establishing a hierarchical government that allowed little autonomy to New World jurisdictions. That control included, for example, allowing only selected persons to migrate to America and insisting that the colonies import all their manufactured goods from Spain. Second, most of the colonists sent from Spain were male. They married Indian—and later black—women, thereby creating the racially mixed population that characterizes Latin America to the present day.

Third, the colonies' wealth was based on the exploitation of both the native population and slaves imported from Africa. The Mesoamerican peoples lived in large urban areas and were accustomed to autocratic rule; Spaniards simply took over roles once assumed by native leaders, who had also exacted labor and tribute from their subjects. The *encomienda* system, which granted tribute from Indian villages to individual conquistadores as a reward for their services to the crown, ensured that the conquerors themselves did not have to engage

in field work. Laws adopted in 1542 reformed the system, forbidding Spaniards from enslaving Indians while still allowing them to collect money and goods from their tributary villages. In response, the conquerors, familar with slavery in Spain, began to import Africans in order to increase the labor force under their direct control.

The New World's gold and silver, initially a boon, ultimately brought about the decline of Spain as a major power. The influx of hitherto unprecedented wealth led to rapid inflation, which (among other adverse effects) caused Spanish products to be overpriced in international markets and imported goods to become cheaper in Spain. The once-profitable Spanish textile-manufacturing industry collapsed, as did scores of other businesses. The seemingly endless income from New World colonies emboldened successive Spanish monarchs to spend lavishly on wars against the Dutch and the English. Several times in the late sixteenth and early seventeenth centuries the monarchs repudiated the state debt, thus wreaking havoc on the nation's

In the late sixteenth or early seventeenth century, a Navaho artist used the wall of the Canyon del Muerto (in present-day Arizona) to record the arrival of a Franciscan friar and his escorts. Both the Roman Catholic missionaries and the horses they brought initiated great changes in the lives of the Native Americans. *Richard Erdoes.*

finances. When the South American mines started to give out in the mid-seventeenth century, Spain's economy crumbled and the nation lost its international importance.

American civilizations suffered even more. The Spaniards deliberately leveled Indian cities, building cathedrals and monasteries on sites once occupied by Aztec, Incan, and Mayan temples. Some conquistadores sought to erase all vestiges of the great Indian cultures by burning all the written records they found. With traditional ways of life in disarray, devastated by disease, and compelled to labor for their conquerors, many residents of Mesoamerica accepted the Christian religion brought to New Spain by Franciscan and Dominican missionaries. The friars devoted their initial energies to persuading the Indians to move into new towns and build Roman Catholic churches. There the Indians were exposed to European lifestyles, newly elaborated religious rituals, and attempts to assimilate Christianity and pagan beliefs, such as a deliberate juxtaposition of the cult of the Virgin Mary with that of the corn goddess. These conversion efforts met with remarkable success. Thousands of Indians residing in Spanish territory embraced Catholicism, at least partly because it was the religion of their new rulers, and they were accustomed to obedience.

The Spanish missionaries who ventured farther north, into the territory of the present-day United States, were less able to win Indian converts, for native cultures there remained largely intact despite the European invasion. After several failed attempts to colonize the Atlantic coast, a group of soldiers, settlers, and priests led by Pedro Menendez de Avilés, a Spanish noble, established St. Augustine, Florida, in 1565. Efforts to Christianize the Indians succeeded only after Franciscans forced them to move to mission towns; even then, many resisted the friars' message. Still, by the end of the sixteenth century a chain of Spanish missions stretched across what is now northern Florida.

Unlike the Spanish, other European nations did not immediately start to colonize the coasts their sailors had explored. They were interested in exploiting the natural wealth of **Northern Traders** the region, not in conquering territories. Their mariners, who came to fish in the rich waters off Newfoundland, learned that they could supplement their profits by exchanging cloth and metal goods like pots and knives for the Indians' beaver pelts, which Europeans used to make fashionable felt hats. At first the Europeans conducted their trading from ships sailing along the coast, but later they established permanent outposts on the mainland to centralize and control the traffic in furs. Among the most successful of these were the French trading posts at Quebec (1608) and Montreal (1642), on the St. Lawrence River; the Swedish settlement at Fort Christina (1638) on the Delaware River; and the Dutch forts of New Amsterdam and Fort Orange on the Hudson River, both founded in 1624, which together constituted the colony of New Netherland. All were inhabited primarily by male adventurers, whose chief aim was to send as many pelts as possible home to Europe.

The northern Europeans' trading activities had a significant effect on native societies. The Europeans' insatiable demand for furs, especially beaver, was matched by the Indians' desire for European goods that could make their lives easier and establish their superiority over neighboring tribes. Some tribes concentrated so completely on trapping for the European market that they abandoned their traditional modes of subsistence. The Abenakis of Maine, for example, became partially dependent on food supplied by their neighbors to the south, the Massachusett tribe, because they devoted most of their energies to catching beaver to sell to French traders. The Massachusetts, in turn, intensified their production of foodstuffs, which they traded to the Abenakis in exchange for the European metal tools they preferred to their own handmade stone implements.

The French in particular devoted considerable attention to converting Native Americans to Christianity. Jesuit missionaries in New France, known to the Indians as Black Robes, initially followed the Spaniards' lead. They tried to persuade Native Americans to live near French settlements and to adopt European lifestyles as well as the Europeans' religion. When that effort failed, the Jesuits concluded that they could introduce Roman Catholicism to their new charges without insisting that the Indians alter their customary modes of existence. So the Black Robes learned Indian languages and traveled to remote regions. By the early eighteenth century, they were living as far west as present-day Illinois.

Jesuit Missions in New France

In their pursuit of conversions, the Jesuits sought to undermine the authority of village shamans (the traditional religious leaders) and to gain the confidence of leaders who could influence others. The Black Robes cleverly used a variety of weapons to attain the desired end. Trained in rhetoric, they won admirers for their eloquence. Seemingly immune to smallpox, they explained epidemics among the Native American peoples as God's punishment for sin. Drawing on a knowledge of European science, they predicted solar and lunar eclipses. Perhaps most important of all, they amazed the Indians by being able to communicate with each other over long distances and periods of time by employing marks on pieces of paper. The Indians' desire to learn how to harness the extraordinary power of literacy was probably the most critical factor in making them receptive to the Jesuits' message. Although the process took many years, the Jesuits slowly gained thousands of converts, some of whom moved to reserves set aside for Christian Indians. In those communities they followed Catholic teachings with fervor and piety.

The Europeans' greatest impact on the Americas was unintended. The diseases carried from the Old World to the New by the alien invaders killed millions of Native Americans, who had no immunity to germs that had infested Europe, Asia, and Africa for centuries. The greatest killer was smallpox, which was spread by direct human contact. The epidemic that hit Tenochtitlan in 1520 had begun in Hispaniola two years earlier. Pizarro easily conquered the Incas partly because their society had been devastated by the epidemic shortly before his arrival. Smallpox was not the only villain; influenza, measles, and other diseases added to the destruction.

Killer Diseases

The statistics are staggering. When Columbus landed on Hispaniola in 1492, more than 3 million Indians resided there. Fifty years later, only 500 were still alive.

Even in the north, where smaller Indian populations encountered only a few European explorers, missionaries, traders, and fishermen, disease ravaged the countryside. A great epidemic, most likely chicken pox, swept through the Indian villages along the coast north of Cape Cod in 1616–1618. The mortality rate may have been as high as 90 percent. An English traveler several years later commented that the Indians had "died on heaps, as they lay in their houses," and that bones and skulls covered the remains of their villages. Because of this dramatic depopulation of the area, just a few years later English colonists were able to establish settlements virtually unopposed by native peoples. As one historian has observed, America was more a widowed land than a virgin one when the English arrived there.

The Native Americans, though, took a revenge of sorts. They gave the Europeans syphilis, a virulent venereal disease. The first recorded case of the new disease in Europe occurred in Barcelona, Spain, in 1493, shortly after Columbus's return from the Caribbean. Although less likely to cause immediate death than smallpox, syphilis was extremely dangerous and debilitating. It spread quickly through Europe and Asia, carried by soldiers, sailors, and prostitutes, even reaching China by 1505.

The exchange of diseases was only part of a broader mutual transfer of plants and animals that resulted directly from Columbus's voyages. The two hemispheres had evolved separately over millions of years, developing widely different forms of life. Many large mammals were native to the connected continents of Europe, Asia, and Africa, but the Americas contained no domesticated beasts larger than dogs and llamas. On the other hand, the vegetable crops of the New World—particularly corn, beans, squash, manioc, and potatoes—were more nutritious and produced higher yields than those of the Old, like wheat and rye. In time, Indians learned to raise and consume European domestic animals, and Europeans and Africans became accustomed to planting and eating American crops. As a result, the diets of all three peoples were vastly enriched. One consequence was the doubling of the world's population over the next three hundred years.

> **Exchange of Plants and Animals**

The exchange of two other commodities significantly influenced European and American civilizations. In America, Europeans encountered tobacco, which was at first believed to have beneficial medicinal effects. Smoking and chewing the "Indian weed" became a fad in the Old World. Tobacco cultivation was later to form the basis for the prosperity of the first successful English colonies in North America. Despite the efforts of such skeptics as King James I of England, who in 1604 pronounced smoking to be "loathsome to the eye, hatefull to the Nose, harmfull to the brain, [and] dangerous to the Lungs," tobacco's popularity has continued to the present day.

More important was the impact of the horse on some Indian cultures. Horses brought to America by the Spaniards inevitably fell into the hands of Native Americans. They were traded northward among the tribes and eventually became essential to the life of the nomadic buffalo hunters of the Great Plains. Apaches, Comanches, and Blackfeet, among others, used horses for transportation and hunting, calculated their wealth in the number of horses owned, and waged wars primarily from horseback. Women no longer had to carry the bands' belongings on their backs. Some tribes that had previously cultivated crops abandoned agriculture altogether. As a result of the acquisition of horses, then, a mode of subsistence that had been based on hunting several different animals, combined with some gathering and agriculture, became one focused almost wholly on hunting buffalo.

England Colonizes the New World

English merchants and political leaders watched enviously as Spain's New World possessions enriched Spain immeasurably. In the mid-sixteenth century, English "sea dogs" like John Hawkins and Sir Francis Drake began to raid Spanish treasure fleets. Their actions caused friction between the two countries and helped to foment a war that culminated in the defeat of the Spanish Armada off the English coast in 1588. With the loss of the Armada, Spain's fortunes began to ebb. England started to think about planting its own colonies in the Western Hemisphere, thereby preventing Spain from completely dominating the New World and simultaneously gaining direct access to valuable American commodities.

The first English colonial planners took Spain's possessions in the New World as both a model and a challenge. They hoped to reproduce Spanish successes by dispatching to America men who would similarly exploit the native peoples for their own and their nation's benefit. In the 1580s, a group that included Sir Humphrey Gilbert and his younger half-brother Sir Walter Raleigh promoted a scheme to establish outposts that could trade with the Indians and provide bases for attacks on New Spain. Approving the idea, Queen Elizabeth I authorized Raleigh and Gilbert to colonize North America. Gilbert failed to plant a

> **Raleigh's Roanoke Colony**

TUDOR AND STUART MONARCHS OF ENGLAND, 1509–1649

Monarch	Years of Reign	Relation to Predecessor
Henry VIII	1509–1547	Son
Edward VI	1547–1553	Son
Mary I	1553–1558	Half-sister
Elizabeth I	1558–1603	Half-sister
James I	1603–1625	Cousin
Charles I	1625–1649	Son

colony in Newfoundland, dying in the attempt, and Raleigh was only briefly more successful. In 1587 he sent 117 colonists to the territory he named Virginia (for Elizabeth, the "Virgin Queen"). They established a settlement on Roanoke Island, in what is now North Carolina, but in 1590 a resupply ship could not find them. The colonists had vanished, leaving only the word "Croatoan" (the name of a nearby island) carved on a tree.

The failure of Raleigh's attempt to colonize Virginia ended English efforts at settlement in North America for nearly two decades. When, in 1606, Englishmen decided to try once more, they again planned colonies that imitated the Spanish model. Success came only when they abandoned that model and founded settlements very different from those of other European powers. Unlike Spain, France, or the Netherlands, England eventually sent large numbers of men and women to set up agriculturally based colonies in the New World. Before the history of those colonies is discussed, it is important to examine the two major developments that prompted approximately 200,000 ordinary English men and women to move to North America in the seventeenth century and that led their government to encourage them.

The first development was a significant change in English religious practice, a transformation that eventually led large numbers of English dissenters to leave their homeland. In 1533,

> **English Reformation**

Henry VIII, wanting a male heir and infatuated with Anne Boleyn, sought to annul his marriage to his Spanish-born queen, Catherine of Aragon, despite nearly twenty years of marriage. When the pope refused to approve the annulment, Henry left the Roman Catholic church, founded the Church of England, and—with Parliament's concurrence—proclaimed himself its head. The English people welcomed the schism. Many had little respect for the English Catholic church, which was at the time filled with corrupt bishops and ignorant priests. At first the reformed Church of England differed little from Catholicism in its practices, but under Henry's daughter Elizabeth I (child of his marriage to Anne Boleyn), new currents of religious belief that had originated on the European continent early in the sixteenth century dramatically affected the English church.

The leaders of the continental Protestant Reformation were Martin Luther, a German monk, and John Calvin, a French cleric and lawyer. Combating the Catholic doctrine that priests had to serve as intermediaries between lay people and God, they both insisted that each person could interpret the Bible for himself or herself. One result of that notion was the spread of literacy: to understand and interpret the Bible, people had to learn how to read it for themselves. Both Luther and Calvin rejected Catholic rituals and denied the need for an elaborate church hierarchy. They also asserted that salvation came through faith alone, rather than—as Catholic teaching had it—through a combination of faith and good works. Calvin, though, went further than Luther in stressing God's absolute omnipotence and emphasizing the need for people to submit totally to His will.

Elizabeth I tolerated religious diversity among her subjects as long as they generally acknowledged her authority as head of the Church of

England. Accordingly, during her long reign (1558–1603) Calvin's ideas gained influence within the English church. By the late sixteenth century, many English Calvinists believed that the Reformation had not gone far enough. Henry had simplified the church hierarchy; they wanted to abolish it altogether. Henry had subordinated the church to the interests of the state; they wanted a church free from political interference. And the Church of England, like the Roman Catholic church, continued to define its membership as including everyone in the state. Some Calvinists preferred a more restricted definition; they wanted to confine church membership to persons believed to be "saved." Because these seventeenth-century English Calvinists said they wanted to purify the church, they became known as Puritans.

▶ **Puritans**

Elizabeth I's Stuart successors, her cousin James I (1603–1625) and his son Charles I (1625–1649), were less tolerant of Puritans than she. As Scots, they also had little respect for the traditions of representative government that had developed in England under the Tudors and their predecessors. The wealthy, taxpaying landowners who sat in Parliament had grown accustomed to having considerable influence on government policies, especially taxation. But James I, taking a position later endorsed by his son, publicly declared his adherence to the theory of the divine right of kings. The Stuarts insisted that a monarch's power came directly from God and that his subjects had no alternative but to obey him. A king's authority, they argued, was absolute, just like the authority of a father over his children. Both James I and Charles I believed that their authority included the power to enforce religious conformity among their subjects. Thus they authorized the persecution of Puritans, who were challenging many of the most important precepts of the English church. Consequently, in the 1620s and 1630s a number of English Puritans decided to move to America, where they hoped to put their religious beliefs into practice unmolested by the Stuarts or the church hierarchy.

The second major development that led English folk to move to North America was the onset of dramatic social and economic change caused by the doubling of the English population in the 150-year period after 1530. All those additional people needed food, clothing, and other

▶ **Social Change in England**

goods. The competition for goods led to high inflation, coupled with a fall in real wages as the number of workers increased. In these new economic and demographic circumstances, some English people—especially those with sizable landholdings that could produce food and clothing fibers for the growing population—substantially improved their lot. Others, particularly landless laborers or those with very small amounts of land, fell into unremitting poverty. When landowners raised rents or decided to enclose and combine small holdings into large units, they forced tenant farmers off the land. Geographical as well as social mobility increased, and the population of the cities (especially London) swelled.

Well-to-do English people reacted with alarm to what they saw as the disappearance of traditional ways of life. The streets and highways were filled with steady streams of the landless and the homeless. Officials became obsessed with the problem of maintaining order and came to believe that England was overcrowded. They concluded that colonies established in the New World could siphon off England's "surplus population," thus easing the social strains at home. For similar reasons, many English people decided that they could improve their circumstances by migrating from a small, land-scarce, apparently overpopulated island to a large, land-rich continent. Such economic considerations affected English people's decisions to migrate to the colonies as much as, if not more than, a desire for escape from religious persecution.

The initial impetus for the establishment of what was to become England's first permanent colony in the Western Hemisphere came from a group of merchants and wealthy gentry. In 1606, envisioning the possibility of earning great profits from a New World settlement by finding precious metals and opening new trade routes, they set up a joint-stock company, the Virginia Company, to plant colonies in America.

Joint-stock companies had been developed in England during the sixteenth century as a mechanism for pooling the resources of a large number of small investors. These forerunners of modern corporations were funded through the sale of stock. Until the founding of the Virginia Company, they had been used primarily to finance trading voyages; for that purpose they

▶ **Joint-Stock Companies**

London in 1616, with London Bridge at center right. Overcrowding in the city led many observers to conclude that American colonization could remove "excess" population and provide new employment for poverty-stricken persons. The rapidly growing community of London merchants also sought to develop new sources of overseas profits. *The British Library.*

worked well. No one person risked too much money, and investors usually received quick returns. But joint-stock companies turned out to be a poor way to finance colonies, because the early settlements required enormous amounts of capital and with rare exceptions failed to return much immediate profit. The colonies founded by joint-stock companies accordingly suffered from a chronic lack of capital—for investors did not want to send good money after bad—and from constant tension between stockholders and colonists (who claimed they were not being adequately supported by the joint-stock companies).

The Virginia Company was no exception to this rule. Chartered by King James I in 1606, the company tried but failed to start a colony in Maine and barely succeeded in planting one in Virginia.

> **Founding of Virginia**

In 1607 it dispatched 144 men and boys to North America. Ominously, only 104 of them survived the voyage. In May of that year, they established the settlement called Jamestown on a swampy peninsula in a river they also named for their monarch. The colonists were ill equipped for survival in the unfamiliar environment, and the settlement was afflicted by dissension and disease.

By January 1608, only 38 of the original colonists were still alive. Many of the first migrants were gentlemen unaccustomed to working with their hands and artisans with irrelevant skills like glassmaking. Having come to Virginia expecting to make easy fortunes, most could not adjust to the conditions they encountered. They resisted living "like savages," retaining English dress and casual work habits despite their desperate circumstances. Such attitudes, combined with the effects of chronic mal-

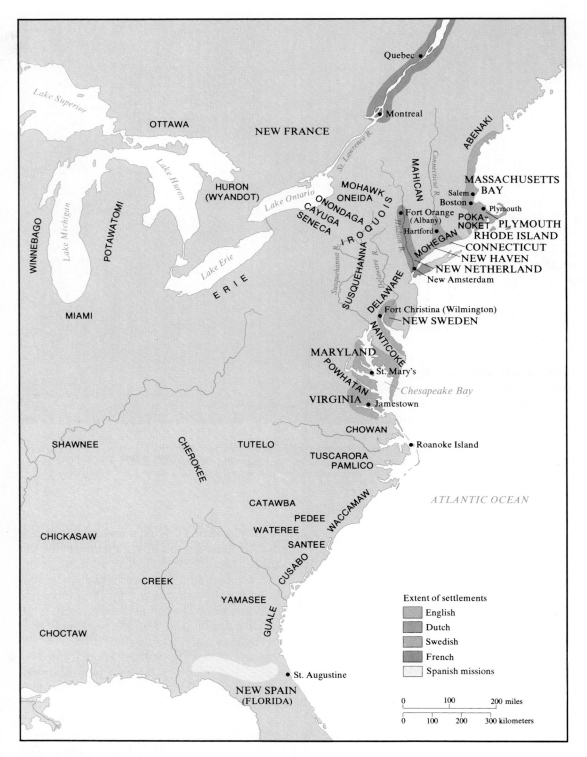

European Settlements and Indian Tribes in America, 1650

◀ Chapter 1: The Meeting of Old World and New, 1492–1640

nutrition and epidemic disease, took a terrible toll. Only when Captain John Smith, one of the colony's founders, imposed military discipline on the colonists in 1608 was Jamestown saved from collapse. But after Smith's departure the colony experienced a severe "starving time" (the winter of 1609–1610), during which some colonists even resorted to cannibalism. Although conditions later improved somewhat, as late as 1624 only 1,300 of approximately 8,000 English migrants to Virginia remained alive.

That the colony survived at all was a tribute not to the English but rather to the Indians within whose territories they settled, a group of six Algonkian tribes known as the Powhatan Confederacy (see map). Powhatan, a powerful figure, was consolidating his authority over some twenty-five other small tribes in the area when the Europeans arrived. Fortunately for the Englishmen, Powhatan at first viewed them as potential allies. He found the English colony a reliable source of such items as steel knives and guns, which gave him a technological advantage over his Indian neighbors. In return, Powhatan's tribes traded their excess corn and other foodstuffs to the starving colonists. The initially cordial relationship soon deteriorated, however. The English colonists kidnaped Powhatan's daughter, Pocahontas, held her as a hostage, and forcibly married her off to one of their number, John Rolfe.

> **Powhatan Confederacy**

Thereafter the relationship between the Jamestown colony and the coastal tribes was an uneasy one. English and Algonkian peoples had much in common: deep religious beliefs, a lifestyle oriented around agriculture, clear political and social hierarchies, and sharply defined sex roles. Yet the English and Indians themselves usually focused on their cultural differences, not their similarities. English men thought that Indian men were lazy because they hunted (hunting was a sport in English eyes) and did not work in the fields. Indian men thought English men effeminate because they did "women's work" of cultivation. In the same vein, the whites believed that Indian women were oppressed since they did heavy field labor.

Other differences between the two cultures caused serious misunderstandings. Although both societies were hierarchical, the nature of the hierarchies differed considerably. Among the east-coast

Pocahontas (1595/96?–1617), here called Matoaka alias Rebecka, portrayed in Elizabethan dress. During her visit to England with her husband, John Rolfe, in 1616, the Indian princess became the toast of London society. She died the following year, just as she was leaving England to return to her homeland, and was buried in the parish church at Gravesend. *National Portrait Gallery, Smithsonian Institution, Washington, D.C.*

> **Algonkian and English Cultural Differences**

Algonkian tribes, people were not born to positions of leadership, nor were political power and social status necessarily inherited through the male line. The English gentry inherited their position from their fathers, and English political and military leaders tended to rule autocratically. By contrast, the authority of Indian leaders rested on the consent of their fellow tribesmen. Accustomed to the European concept of powerful kings, the English sought such figures within the tribes. Often (for example, when negotiating treaties) they willfully overestimated the ability of chiefs to make independent decisions for their people.

Furthermore, the Indians and the English had very different notions of property ownership. In most eastern tribes, land was held communally by the entire group. It could not be bought or sold absolutely, although certain rights to use the land (for example, for hunting or fishing) could be transferred. The English, on the other hand, were accustomed to individual farms and to buying and selling land. In addition, the English refused to accept the validity of Indian claims to traditional hunting territories, insisting that only land intensively cultivated could be regarded as owned or occupied by a tribe.

Above all, the English settlers believed unwaveringly in the superiority of their civilization. Although in the early years of colonization they often harbored thoughts of living peacefully alongside the Indians, they always assumed that they would dictate the terms of such coexistence. They expected the Indians to adopt English customs and to convert to Christianity. They showed little respect for traditional Indian ways of life, especially when they believed their own interests were at stake. That attitude was clearly revealed in the Virginia colony's treatment of the Powhatan Confederacy in subsequent years.

What upset the balance between the English and the Indians was the spread of tobacco cultivation. In tobacco the settlers and the Virginia Company found the salable commodity for

Tobacco: The Basis of Virginia's Success which they had been searching. John Rolfe planted the first crop in 1611. In 1620 Virginians exported 40,000 pounds of cured leaves, and by the end of that decade shipments had jumped dramatically to 1.5 million pounds. The great tobacco boom had begun, fueled by high prices and substantial profits for planters. The price later fell almost as sharply as it had risen, and it fluctuated wildly from year to year in response to increasing supply and international competition. Nevertheless, tobacco became the foundation of Virginia's prosperity, and the colony developed from a small outpost peopled exclusively by males into an agricultural settlement inhabited by both men and women (the first group of English women arrived in 1620).

Successful tobacco cultivation required abundant land, since the crop quickly drained soil of nutrients. Planters soon learned that a field could produce only about three satisfactory crops before it had to lie fallow for several years to regain its fertility. Thus the once-small English settlements began

to expand rapidly: eager planters applied to the Virginia Company for large land grants on both sides of the James River and its tributary streams. Lulled into a false sense of security by years of peace, the planters established farms at some distance from one another along the river banks—a settlement pattern convenient for tobacco cultivation but poorly designed for defense.

Opechancanough, Powhatan's brother and successor, watched the English colonists steadily encroaching on Indian lands and attempting to convert members of the tribes to Christianity. He recognized the danger his brother had overlooked. On March 22, 1622, the confederacy launched coordinated attacks all along the river. By the end of the day 347 colonists (about one-quarter of the total) lay dead, and only a timely warning from two Christianized Indians saved Jamestown itself from destruction.

The Virginia colony reeled from the blow but did not collapse. Reinforced by new shipments of men and arms from England, the settlers launched a series of attacks on Opechancanough's villages. For some years an uneasy peace prevailed, but then in April 1644 Opechancanough tried one last time to repel the invaders. He failed, giving his life in the war that ensued. In 1646, survivors of the Powhatan Confederacy accepted a treaty formally subordinating them to English authority. Although they continued to live in the region, their alliance crumbled and their efforts to resist the spread of white settlement ended.

Life in the Chesapeake: Virginia and Maryland

The 1622 Indian uprising that failed to destroy the colony did succeed in killing its parent. The Virginia Company had never made any profits from the enterprise, for the heavy costs had offset all its earnings. In 1624 James I revoked the charter and made Virginia a royal colony, ruled by the king through appointed officials. At the same time, though, he continued an important policy designed to attract settlers, which the company had adopted in 1617. Under the "headright" system, every new

Advocates of colonization hoped to establish a silk industry in the Chesapeake and published tracts illustrating the production of silk. This one shows a man and a woman working together, but at different tasks. All the attempts to create such industries failed, despite the promoters' efforts. *John Carter Brown Library, Brown University.*

arrival was promised a land grant of fifty acres; those who financed the passage of others received headrights for each. To ordinary English farmers, many of whom had owned little or no land, the headright system offered a powerful incentive to migrate to Virginia. To wealthy gentry, it promised even more: the possibility of establishing vast agricultural enterprises worked by large numbers of laborers.

In 1619, the company had introduced a second policy that James was more reluctant to retain: it had authorized the landowning men of the major Virginia settlements to elect representatives to a legislature called the House of Burgesses. Although England was a monarchy, English landholders had long been accustomed to electing members of Parliament and controlling their own local governments. In accordance with his belief in the absolute power of the monarchy and his distrust of legisla-

tive bodies, James at first abolished the Virginia assembly. But the settlers protested so vigorously that by 1629 the House of Burgesses was functioning once again. Only two decades after the first permanent English settlement had been planted in the New World, the colonists were insisting on governing themselves at the local level. They thus ensured that the political structure of England's American possessions would differ from that of New Spain, which was ruled autocratically by the Spanish monarchs.

By the 1630s, tobacco was firmly established in Virginia as the staple crop and chief source of revenue. It quickly became just as important in the second English colony planted on

Founding of Maryland

Chesapeake Bay: Maryland, chartered by the king in 1632 and given to the Calvert family as a personal possession (proprietorship). (Because

Virginia and Maryland both bordered Chesapeake Bay—see map, page 24—they are often referred to collectively as "the Chesapeake.") The Calverts intended the colony to serve as a haven for their fellow Roman Catholics, who were being persecuted in England. Cecilius Calvert, second Lord Baltimore, became the first colonizer to offer freedom of religion to all Christian settlers; he realized that protecting the Protestant majority was the only way to ensure Catholics' rights.

In everything but religion the two Chesapeake colonies resembled each other. In Maryland as in Virginia, tobacco planters spread out along the river banks, establishing isolated farms instead of towns. The region's deep, wide rivers offered dependable water transportation in an age of few and inadequate roads. Each farm or group of farms had its own wharf, where ocean-going vessels could take on or discharge cargo. As a result, Virginia and Maryland had few towns, for these colonies did not need commercial centers in order to buy and sell goods.

The planting, cultivation, and harvesting of tobacco had to be done by hand; these tasks did not take much skill, but they were repetitious and time-consuming. When the headright system was adopted in Maryland in 1640, a prospective tobacco planter anywhere in the Chesapeake could simultaneously obtain both land and the labor to work it. Good management could make the process self-perpetuating: a planter could use his profits to pay for the passage of more workers and thus gain title to more land.

There were two possible sources of laborers for the growing tobacco farms of the Chesapeake: Africa and England. Nearby tribes could not supply the needed workers, since the region was not densely populated. Further, unlike the hierarchical cultures of Mesoamerica, the fragmented, egalitarian Indian societies could not readily be dominated by Europeans. Beginning in 1619, a few Africans were carried to the Chesapeake. Their numbers were small and their status uncertain; some appear to have been slaves, but others were not. As late as 1670, the black population of Virginia was at most 2,000 and probably no more than 1,500, making up less than 5 percent of the inhabitants. Chesapeake tobacco planters instead looked to England to supply their labor needs. Because men did the agricultural work in European societies, planters and

workers alike assumed that field laborers should be males, preferably young, strong ones. Such laborers migrated to America as indentured servants—that is, in return for their passage they contracted to work for planters for periods ranging from four to seven years.

Indentured servants accounted for 75 to 85 percent of the approximately 130,000 English migrants to Virginia and Maryland during the seventeenth century. Roughly three-quarters of them were men between the ages of fifteen and twenty-four. Most had been farmers and laborers; some had additional skills. They were what their contemporaries called the "common" or "middling" sort. Judging by their youth, though, most had probably not yet established themselves in England.

Migrants to the Chesapeake

Many of the servants came from areas of England that were experiencing severe social disruption. Some had already moved several times within England before they decided to migrate to America. For such people the Chesapeake appeared to offer good prospects. Once they had fulfilled the terms of their indentures, servants were promised "freedom dues" consisting of clothes, tools, livestock, casks of corn and tobacco, and sometimes even land. From a distance at least, America seemed to hold out chances for advancement unavailable in England.

The migrants' lives were difficult. Servants typically worked six days a week, ten to fourteen hours a day, in a climate much warmer than they were accustomed to. Their masters could discipline or sell them, and they faced severe penalties for running away. Even so, the laws did offer them some protection. For example, their masters were supposed to supply them with sufficient food, clothing, and shelter, and they were not to be beaten excessively. Servants who were especially cruelly treated turned to the courts for assistance and sometimes won verdicts directing that they be sold to more humane masters or freed from their indentures.

Conditions of Servitude

Servants and planters alike had to contend with epidemic disease. Migrants first had to survive the process the colonists called "seasoning"—a bout with disease (probably malaria) that usually occurred during their first summer in the Chesapeake. They then had to endure recurrences of malaria, along with dysentery, influenza, typhoid fever, and other diseases. As a result, approximately 40 percent of male servants did not survive long enough to become freedmen. Even young men of twenty-two who had successfully weathered their seasoning could expect to live only another twenty years at best.

For those who survived the term of their indentures, however, the opportunities for advancement were real. Until the last decades of the century, former servants were usually able to become independent planters ("freeholders") and to live a modest but comfortable existence. Some even assumed such positions of political prominence as justice of the peace or militia officer. But in the 1670s tobacco prices entered a fifty-year period of stagnation and decline. At the same time, good land grew increasingly scarce and expensive. In 1681 Maryland dropped its legal requirement that servants receive land as part of their freedom dues, forcing large numbers of freed servants to live as wage laborers or tenant farmers instead of acquiring freeholder status. By 1700 the Chesapeake was no longer the land of opportunity it had once been.

Life in the seventeenth-century Chesapeake was hard for everyone, regardless of sex or status. Farmers (and sometimes their wives) toiled in the fields alongside the servants, laboriously clearing the land of trees, then planting and harvesting not only tobacco but also corn, wheat, and vegetables. Chesapeake households subsisted mainly on pork and corn, a filling but monotonous and not particularly nutritious diet. Thus the health problems caused by epidemic disease were magnified by diet deficiencies and the near-impossibility of preserving food for safe winter consumption. Salting, drying, and smoking, the only methods the colonists knew, did not always prevent spoilage. Few households had many material possessions other than farm implements, beds, and basic cooking and eating utensils. Even their houses were little more than shacks. Planters devoted their income to improving their farms, buying livestock, and purchasing more laborers rather than to improving their standard of living. Instead of making such items as clothing and tools, planter families concentrated their energies solely on growing tobacco, importing necessary manufactured goods from England.

The predominance of males, the incidence of servitude, and the high mortality rates combined to produce unusual patterns of family life. Female servants normally were not allowed to marry during their terms of indenture, since masters did not want pregnancies to deprive them of workers. Many male ex-servants could not marry at all because there were so few women. On the other hand, nearly every adult free woman in the Chesapeake married, and the many widows commonly remarried within a few months of a husband's death. Yet because their marriages were delayed by servitude or broken by death, Chesapeake women bore only one to three children, in contrast to English women, who normally had at least five.

Family Life in the Chesapeake

Thus Chesapeake families were relatively few, small, and short-lived. The migrants could not reproduce the English patriarchal system, even if they wanted to, for they came to America as individuals free of paternal control and tended to die while their own children were still quite young. In one Virginia county, for example, more than three-quarters of the children had lost at least one parent by the time they either married or reached age twenty-one.

As a result of the demographic patterns that led to a low rate of natural increase, migrants made up a majority of the Chesapeake population throughout the seventeenth century. That fact had important implications for politics in Maryland and Virginia. Since migrants dominated the population, they also composed the vast majority of the membership of Virginia's House of Burgesses and Maryland's House of Delegates (established in 1635). So too in each colony they dominated the governor's council, which was simultaneously part of the legislature, the colony's highest court, and executive adviser to the governor.

Chesapeake Politics

English-born colonists naturally tended to look to England for solutions to their problems, and migrants frequently relied on English allies to advance their cause. The seventeenth-century leaders of the Chesapeake colonies engaged in bitter and prolonged struggles for power and personal economic advantage; these struggles then crossed the Atlantic, and decisions made in America were laid

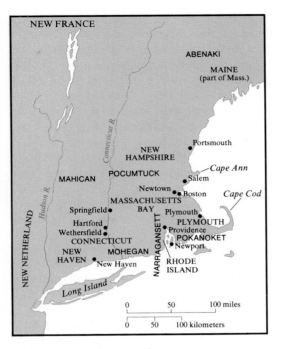

New England Colonies, 1650

and east of the Hudson River soon came to be called (see map). But because Puritans organized the New England colonies, and also because of environmental differences between the two regions, the northern settlements turned out very differently from those in the South. The northern landscape and climate were not suitable for staple-crop production, and so diversified small farms predominated. Except for the Catholics who moved to Maryland, migrants to the Chesapeake seem to have been little affected by religious motives. Yet religion was a primary motivating factor in the minds of many, though certainly not all, of the people who colonized New England. The Puritan church quickly became one of the most important institutions in colonial New England; in the Chesapeake, neither the Church of England nor Roman Catholicism had much impact on the settlers or on the development of these colonies.

Religion was a constant presence in the lives of pious Puritans. As followers of John Calvin, they believed that an omnipotent God predestined souls to heaven or hell before birth and that Christians could do nothing to change their ultimate fate. One of their primary duties as Christians, though, was to assess the state of their own souls. They thus devoted themselves to self-examination and Bible study, and families prayed together each day under the guidance of the husband and father. Yet even the most pious could never be absolutely certain that they were numbered among the saved. Consequently, devout Puritans were filled with anxiety about their spiritual state. Many kept diaries in which they minutely examined their everyday feelings for signs of their status.

Puritan Beliefs

Some Puritans (called Congregationalists) wanted to reform the Church of England rather than abandon it. Another group, known as Separatists, believed the Church of England to be so corrupt that it could not be salvaged. The only way to purify it, they believed, was to start anew, establishing their own religious bodies, with membership restricted to the saved, as nearly as they could be identified.

Separatists were the first to move to New England. In 1609 a group of Separatists migrated to Holland, where they found the freedom of worship denied them in Stuart England. But they were nevertheless troubled by the Netherlands' too-

open to reversal in London. The incessant quarreling and convoluted political tangles thwarted the Virginia and Maryland governments' ability to function effectively.

Representative institutions based on the consent of the governed, it is often argued, are a major source of political stability. In the seventeenth-century Chesapeake, most property-owning white males could vote, and such freeholders chose as their legislators the local elites who seemed to be the natural leaders of their respective areas. But because of the nature of the population, the existence of the assemblies did not lead to political stability. Indeed, the contrary may well have been true. Virginia and Maryland paid a high political price for their unusual demographic patterns.

The Founding of New England

The economic motives that prompted English people to move to the Chesapeake colonies also drew men and women to New England, as the area north

tolerant atmosphere; the nation that tolerated them also tolerated religions and behaviors they abhorred. Hoping to isolate themselves and their children from the corrupting influence of worldly temptations, they received permission from a branch of the Virginia Company to colonize the northern part of its territory.

In September 1620, more than one hundred people, only thirty of them Separatists, set sail from Plymouth, England, on the old and crowded *Mayflower*. Two months later they landed in America, but farther north than they had intended. Still, given the lateness of the season—winter was closing in—they decided to stay where they were. They established their colony on a fine harbor that had been occupied by an Indian village destroyed in the great epidemic of 1616–1618. Their settlement was named after the city from which they had sailed.

> **Founding of Plymouth**

Even before they landed, the Pilgrims had to surmount their first challenge—from the "strangers," or non-Puritans, who had sailed with them to America. Because they landed outside the jurisdiction of the Virginia Company, some of the strangers questioned the authority of the colony's leaders. In response, the Mayflower Compact, signed in November 1620 while everyone was still on board the ship, established a "Civil Body Politic" and a rudimentary legal authority for the colony. The settlers elected a governor and at first made all decisions for the colony at town meetings. Later, after more towns had been founded and the population had increased, Plymouth, like Virginia and Maryland, created an assembly to which the landowning male settlers elected representatives.

A second challenge facing the Pilgrims in 1620 and 1621 was, quite simply, survival. Like the Jamestown settlers before them, they were poorly prepared to survive in the new environment. Their difficulties were compounded by the season of their arrival, for they barely had time to build shelters before winter descended on them. Only half of the *Mayflower*'s passengers were still alive by spring. But, again like the Virginians, the Pilgrims benefited from the political circumstances of their Indian neighbors.

The Pokanokets (also called Wampanoags) controlled the area in which the Pilgrims had settled, yet their villages had suffered terrible losses in the epidemic of 1616–1618. In order to protect themselves from the powerful Narragansett Indians of the southern New England coast (who had been spared the ravages of the disease), the Pokanokets decided to ally themselves with the newcomers. In the spring of 1621, their leader, Massasoit, signed a treaty with the Pilgrims, and during the colony's first difficult years the Pokanokets supplied the English with essential foodstuffs. The settlers were also assisted by Squanto, an Indian whose village had been wiped out by the epidemic. Because he had been captured by traders and held prisoner in England for several years, Squanto spoke English. He served as the Pilgrims' interpreter, as well as their major source of information about the unfamiliar environment.

Before the 1620s had ended, another group of Puritans—this time Congregationalists, not Separatists—launched the colonial enterprise that would come to dominate New England and would absorb Plymouth in 1691. The event that stimulated their interest in the New World was the accession of Charles I to the throne in 1625. Charles was more hostile to Puritan beliefs than his father, and for eleven years after 1629 he refused to call Parliament into session because it was dominated by Puritans. In 1633 he named William Laud, a prominent persecutor of Puritans, as archbishop of Canterbury, thus giving him the most important post in the Church of England. Some non-Separatists therefore began to think about settling in America. A group of Congregationalist merchants sent out a body of settlers to Cape Ann, north of Cape Cod, in 1628. The following year the merchants obtained a royal charter, constituting themselves as the Massachusetts Bay Company.

> **Founding of Massachusetts Bay**

The new company quickly attracted the attention of Puritans of the "middling sort" who were becoming increasingly convinced that they would no longer be able to practice their religion freely in England. They remained committed to the goal of reforming the Church of England but came to believe they should pursue that aim in America rather than at home. In a dramatic move, the Congregationalist merchants boldly decided to transfer the headquarters of the Massachusetts Bay Company to New England. The settlers would then be answerable to no one in the mother country and would be able to handle their affairs, secular and religious, as they pleased.

A colonial Algonkian artist created this wooden bowl in the shape of a beaver, thus commemorating the animal whose valuable fur the tribe traded for desirable European goods like glass, knives, and guns. *Peabody Museum of Archaeology and Ethnology, Harvard University.*

The most important recruit to the new venture was John Winthrop, a pious but practical landed gentleman from Suffolk and a justice of the peace.

> **Governor John Winthrop**

In October 1629, the members of the Massachusetts Bay Company elected the forty-one-year-old Winthrop as their governor. With the exception of isolated years in the mid-1630s and early 1640s, he served in that post until his death in 1649. It thus fell to Winthrop to organize the initial segment of the great Puritan migration to America. In 1630 more than one thousand English men and women came to Massachusetts—most of them to Boston, which soon became the largest town in British North America. By 1643 nearly twenty thousand compatriots had followed them.

On board the *Arbella,* en route to New England in 1630, John Winthrop preached a sermon, "A Modell of Christian Charity," laying out his expecta-

tions for the new colony. Above all, he stressed the communal nature of the endeavor on which he and his fellow settlers had embarked. God, he explained, "hath so disposed of the condition of mankind as in all times some must be rich, some poor, some high and eminent in power and dignity, others mean and in subjection." But differences in status did not imply differences in worth. On the contrary: God had planned the world so that "every man might have need of other, and from hence they might be all knit more nearly together in the bond of brotherly affection." In America, Winthrop asserted, "we shall be as a city upon a hill, the eyes of all people are upon us." If the Puritans failed to carry out their "special commission" from God, "the Lord will surely break out in wrath against us."

Winthrop's was a transcendent vision. The society he foresaw in Puritan America was a true commonwealth, a community in which each person put the good of the whole ahead of his or her private concerns. It was, furthermore, to be a society whose members all lived according to the precepts of Christian charity, loving and aiding friends and enemies alike. Of course, such an ideal was beyond human reach. Early New England had its share of bitter quarrels and unchristian behavior. What is remarkable is how long the ideal prevailed as a goal to be sought, though seldom if ever attained.

The Puritans' communal ideal was expressed chiefly in the doctrine of the covenant. They believed God had made a covenant—that is, an agreement or contract—with them when they were chosen for the special mission to America. In turn they covenanted with each other, promising to work together toward their goals. The founders of churches and towns in the new land often drafted formal documents setting forth the principles on which such institutions would be based. The same was true of the colonial governments of New England. The Pilgrims' Mayflower Compact was a covenant; so too was the Fundamental Orders of Connecticut (1639), which laid down the basic law for the settlements established along the Connecticut River valley in 1636 and thereafter.

> **Ideal of the Covenant**

The leaders of Massachusetts Bay likewise transformed their original joint-stock company charter into the basis for a covenanted community based on mutual consent. Under pressure from the settlers, they gradually changed the General Court, officially merely the company's governing body, into a colonial legislature. They also opened the status of freeman, or voting member of the company, to all property-owning adult male church members residing in Massachusetts. Less than two decades after the first large group of Puritans had arrived in Massachusetts Bay, the colony had a functioning system of self-government composed of a governor and a two-house legislature. The General Court also established a judicial system modeled on England's.

The colony's method of distributing land helped to further the communal ideal. Unlike Virginia and Maryland, where individual applicants sought headrights for themselves and their servants, in Massachusetts groups of families—often from the same region of England—applied together to the General Court for grants of land

> **New England Towns**

on which to establish towns. The men who received the original town grant had the sole authority to determine how the land would be distributed. Understandably, they copied the villages from which they had come. First they laid out town lots for houses and a church. Then they gave each family parcels of land scattered around the town center: pasture here, a woodlot there, an arable field elsewhere. They also reserved the best and largest plots for the most distinguished among them (usually including the minister); people who had been low on the social scale in England were given much smaller and less desirable allotments. Even when migrants began to move beyond the territorial limits of the Bay colony into Connecticut (1636), New Haven (1638), and New Hampshire (1638), the same pattern of town land grants was maintained.

Thus New England settlements initially tended to be more compact than those of the Chesapeake. Town centers grew up quickly, developing in three distinctly different ways. Some, chiefly isolated agricultural settlements in the interior, tried to sustain Winthrop's vision of harmonious community life based on diversified family farms. A second group, the coastal towns like Boston and Salem, became bustling seaports, serving as the places of entry for thousands of new migrants and as focal points for trade. The third category, commercialized agricultural towns, grew up in the Connecticut River valley. There the easy water transportation made it possible for farmers to sell surplus goods readily. In Springfield, Massachusetts, for example, the merchant-entrepreneur William Pynchon and his son John began as fur traders and ended as large landowners with thousands of acres on which tenant farmers produced grain for export. Even in Puritan New England, therefore, the acquisitive, individualistic spirit characteristic of the Chesapeake found some room for expression.

The migration to the Connecticut valley ended the Puritans' relative freedom from clashes with neighboring Indians. The first English settlers in the valley moved there from Newtown (Cambridge), under the direction of their minister, Thomas Hooker. Connecticut was fertile, though remote from the other English towns, and the wide river promised ready access to the ocean. The site had just one problem: it fell within the territory controlled by the Pequot Indians.

John Eliot, painted in 1659 by an unknown artist. Determined to convert the New England Indians to Christianity, Eliot translated the Bible into their language. His *Up-Biblum* was published in 1663, the first Bible printed in the English colonies. *Huntington Library, San Marino, California.*

The Pequots' dominance was based on their role as primary middlemen in the trade between New England Indians and the Dutch in New Netherland.

Pequot War The arrival of English settlers signaled the end of Pequot power over the regional trading networks, for their tributary bands could now trade directly with Europeans. Clashes between the Pequots and the English began even before the Connecticut valley settlements were established, but their founding tipped the balance toward war. The Pequots tried without success to enlist other Indians in resisting English expansion into the interior. After an English raid on their villages, they attacked the new town of Wethersfield in April 1637, killing nine and capturing two of the colonists. In retaliation, a Massachusetts Bay expedition the following month attacked and burned the main Pequot town on the Mystic River. The Englishmen and their Narragansett Indian allies slaughtered at least four hundred people, mostly women and children. The few surviving Pequots were captured and enslaved.

Just five years later the Narragansett leader Miantonomi realized that the Pequots had been correct in assessing the danger posed by the Puritan settlements. He in turn attempted to forge a pan-Indian alliance, telling other bands that "so are we all Indians as the English are . . . so must we be one as they are, otherwise we shall all be gone shortly." But his words fell on deaf ears, and he was killed in 1643 by other Indians acting at the English colonists' behest.

For the next thirty years, the New England Indians tried to accommodate themselves to the spread of white settlement. They traded with the whites and sometimes worked for them, but for the most part they resisted acculturation or incorporation into English society. The Indians clung to their traditional farming methods, which did not employ plows, fertilizer, or fences; and women rather than men continued as the chief cultivators. When Indian men whose hunting territories had been overrun by whites did learn "English" trades in order to survive, they chose those that—like broom making, basket weaving, and shingle splitting—most nearly accorded with their customary occupations and simultaneously ensured both independence and income. The one European practice they did adopt was keeping livestock, for in the absence of game, domesticated animals provided excellent alternative sources of meat.

Although the official seal of Massachusetts Bay showed an Indian crying, "Come over and help us," most whites showed little interest in converting the New England Indians to Christianity. Only a few Puritan clerics, most notably John Eliot, seriously undertook missionary activities. Eliot insisted that converts reside in towns, farm the land in English fashion, assume English names, wear European-style clothing and shoes, cut their hair, and stop observing a wide range of native customs. Since Eliot was demanding a total cultural transformation from his adherents—on the theory that the Indians could not be properly Christianized unless they were also "civilized"—he understandably met with little success. At the peak of Eliot's efforts, only 1,100 Indians lived in the fourteen "Praying Towns" he established, and just 10 percent of those town residents had been formally baptized.

The Jesuits' successful missions in New France contrast sharply with the Puritans' failure to convert many Indians. Three factors account for the difference. First, the small French outposts along the St. Lawrence did not substantially encroach on Indian lands and therefore did not alienate potential converts. Second, Catholicism had several advantages over Puritanism. It employed attractive rituals, instructed converts that through good works they could help to earn their own salvation, and supplied Indian women in particular with inspiring role models—the Virgin Mary and the communities of nuns who resided in Montreal and Quebec. Third, and perhaps most important, the Jesuits understood that Christian beliefs were to some extent compatible with native culture. Unlike the Puritans, they were willing to accept converts who did not wholly adopt European styles of life.

Puritan and Jesuit Missions Compared

But what attracted Indians to these alien religious ideas? Unless entire families or bands converted together, new Christians—both Catholic and Puritan—often found themselves cut off from relatives and native traditions. Surely one primary motive must have been a desire to use the Europeans' religion as a means of coping with the dramatic changes the intruders had wrought on Indian society. The combination of disease, alcohol, new trading patterns, and the loss of territory disrupted customary ways of life to an unprecedented extent. Indian shamans had little success in restoring traditional ways. Many Indians must have concluded that the Europeans' own ideas could provide the key to survival in the new circumstances.

Life in New England

White settlers in New England adopted lifestyles that differed considerably from the lifestyles of both their Indian neighbors and their counterparts in the Chesapeake. Unlike the mobile Algonkians (see page 6), English people lived year-round in the same location. Unlike the residents of the Chesapeake, New Englanders constructed sturdy, permanent dwellings intended to last for many years. (Indeed, some survive to this day.) They used the same fields again and again, believing it was less arduous to employ fertilizer than to clear new fields every few years. Furthermore, they had to fence their croplands to prevent them from being overrun by the cattle, sheep, and hogs that were their chief sources of meat. When New Englanders began to spread out over the countryside, the reason was not so much human crowding as it was animal crowding. All that livestock constantly needed more pasturage.

In contrast to the Chesapeake migrants, Puritans commonly moved to America in family groups. The age range of New Englanders was wide and the sexes were more balanced numerically, so the population could immediately begin to reproduce itself. Moreover, New England's climate was much healthier than the Chesapeake's. Once Puritan settlements had survived the difficult first two or three years and established self-sufficiency in foodstuffs, New England proved to be even healthier than the mother country. Though adult male migrants to the Chesapeake lost about ten years from their English life expectancy of fifty to fifty-five years, their Massachusetts counterparts gained about ten years.

New England and the Chesapeake Compared

Consequently, while Chesapeake population patterns gave rise to families that were few in number, small in size, and transitory, the demographic characteristics of New England made families there numerous, large, and long-lived. In New England most men were able to marry; migrant women married young (at age twenty, on the average); and marriages lasted longer and produced more children, who were more likely to live to maturity. If seventeenth-century Chesapeake women could expect to rear one to three healthy children, New England women could anticipate raising five to seven.

The nature of the population had other major implications for family life. New England in effect created grandparents, since in England people rarely lived long enough to know their children's children. And whereas early southern parents normally died before their children married, northern parents exercised a good deal of control over their adult children. Young men could not marry without

Family Life in New England

Mary Mirick Davie, who died in 1752 at the age of 117, was an extraordinary example of the long lives of some colonial New Englanders. She was widowed three times, bore nine children, and was still able to perform household chores when she was over 100 years old. *Massachusetts Historical Society.*

acreage to cultivate, and because of the communal land-grant system they were dependent on their fathers to supply them with that land. Daughters, too, needed the dowry of household goods that their parents would give them when they married. Yet parents needed their children's labor and were often reluctant to see them marry and start their own households. These needs at times led to considerable conflict between the generations. On the whole, though, children seem to have obeyed their parents' wishes, for they had few alternatives.

Another important difference lay in the influence of religion on New Englanders' lives. The governments of Massachusetts Bay, Plymouth, Connecticut, and the other early northern colonies were all controlled by Puritans. Congregationalism was the only officially recognized religion; mem-

bers of other sects had no freedom of worship except in Rhode Island. Some non-Puritans appear to have voted in town meetings, but with the exception of Connecticut, church membership was a prerequisite for voting in colony elections. All households were taxed to build meetinghouses and pay ministers' salaries. Massachusetts's Body of Laws and Liberties (1641) incorporated regulations drawn from Old Testament scriptures into the legal code of the colony. Penalties were prescribed for expressing contempt for ministers or their preaching and for failing to attend church services regularly.

In the New England colonies, church and state were intertwined. Puritans objected to secular interference in religious affairs but at the same time expected the church to influence the conduct of politics. They also believed that the state had an obligation to support and protect the one true church—theirs. As a result, though they came to America seeking freedom to worship as they wished, they saw no contradiction in their refusal to grant that freedom to others. Indeed, the two most significant divisions in early Massachusetts were caused by religious disputes and by Massachusetts Bay's unwillingness to tolerate dissent.

Roger Williams, a Separatist, migrated to Massachusetts Bay in 1631. Williams soon began to express the eccentric ideas that the king of England

Roger Williams had no right to give away land belonging to the Indians, that church and state should be kept entirely separate, and that Puritans should not impose their religious beliefs on others. Banished from Massachusetts in 1635, Williams founded the town of Providence on Narragansett Bay. Because of his beliefs, Providence and other towns in what became the colony of Rhode Island adopted a policy of tolerating all religions, including Judaism.

The other dissenter, and an even greater challenge to Massachusetts Bay orthodoxy, was Anne Marbury Hutchinson. A skilled midwife popular

Anne Hutchinson with the women of Boston, she was a follower of John Cotton, a minister who stressed the covenant of grace, or God's free gift of salvation to unworthy, helpless human beings. By contrast, most Massachusetts clerics emphasized the need for Puritans to engage in good works, study, and reflection in preparation for receiving God's grace. In 1636 Hutchinson began holding women's meetings in her home to discuss Cotton's sermons. Soon men also started to attend. Hutchinson emphasized the covenant of grace more than did Cotton himself, and she even adopted the belief that the elect could communicate directly with God and be assured of salvation. Such ideas had an immense appeal for Puritans. Anne Hutchinson offered them certainty of salvation instead of a state of constant tension. Her approach also made the institutional church less important.

Hutchinson's ideas were a dangerous threat to Puritan orthodoxy, so in November 1637 she was brought before the General Court of Massachusetts, charged with defaming the colony's ministers. For two days she defended herself cleverly against her accusers, matching scriptural references and wits with John Winthrop himself. Finally, in an unguarded moment, Hutchinson declared that God had spoken to her "by an immediate revelation." That assertion assured her banishment; she and her family, along with some faithful followers, were exiled to Rhode Island. Several years later, after she moved to New Netherland, she and most of her children were killed by Indians. John Winthrop, learning of the tragedy, pronounced it God's judgment on a heretic.

The authorities in Massachusetts Bay perceived Anne Hutchinson as doubly dangerous to the existing order: she threatened not only religious orthodoxy but also traditional gender roles. Puritans believed in the equality before God of all souls, including women, but they also considered women inferior to men, forever tainted by Eve's guilt. Christians had long followed Saint Paul's dictum that women should keep silent in church and be submissive to their husbands. Anne Hutchinson did neither. The magistrates' comments during her trial reveal that they were almost as outraged by her "masculine" behavior as by her religious beliefs. Winthrop charged her with having set wife against husband, since so many of her followers were women. Another judge told her bluntly: "You have stept out of your place, you have rather bine a Husband than a Wife and a preacher than a Hearer; and a Magistrate than a Subject."

The New England authorities' reaction to Anne Hutchinson reveals the depth of their adherence to European gender-role concepts. To them, an orderly society required the submission of wives to husbands as well as the obedience of subjects to rulers. English people intended to change many aspects of their lives by colonizing North America, but not the sexual division of labor or the assumption of male superiority.

In 1630 John Winthrop wrote to his wife Margaret, who was still in England, "my deare wife, we are heer in a paradise." He was, of course, exaggerating. Yet even though America was not a paradise, it was a place where English men and women could free themselves from Stuart persecution or attempt to better their economic circumstances. Many died, but those who lived laid the foundation for subsequent colonial prosperity. That they did so by dispossessing the Indians bothered few besides Roger Williams.

By the middle of the seventeenth century, Europeans had unquestionably come to North America to stay, a fact that signaled major changes for the peoples of both Old and New Worlds. Europeans had indelibly altered not only their own lives but also those of the Native Americans on whose lands they had settled. Europeans killed Indians with their weapons and diseases and had but limited success in converting them to European religions and styles of life. Contacts with the Indians had taught the Europeans to eat new foods, speak new languages, and recognize—however reluctantly—the persistence of native cultural patterns.

European political rivalries, once confined to Europe, now spread around the globe, as the competing nations of England, Spain, Portugal, France, and the Netherlands vied for control of the peoples and resources of Asia, Africa, and the Americas. France and the Netherlands earned their profits from Indian trade rather than imitating the Spanish example and engaging in wars of conquest. Although they too at first relied on trade, the English colonies soon took another form altogether when so many English people of the "common sort" decided to migrate to North America. In the years to come, the European rivalries would grow even fiercer, and residents of the Americas—whites, Indians, and blacks alike—would inevitably be drawn into them. Those rivalries would continue to affect Americans of all races until after France and England fought the greatest war yet known in the mid-eighteenth century and the thirteen Anglo-American colonies won their independence.

Suggestions for Further Reading

General

Charles M. Andrews, *The Colonial Period of American History: The Settlements,* 3 vols. (1934–1937); Leslie Bethel, ed., *The Cambridge History of Latin America,* vol. II: *Colonial Latin America* (1984); D. W. Meinig, *Atlantic America, 1492–1800* (1986); Gary B. Nash, *Red, White, and Black: The Peoples of Early America,* 2nd ed. (1982); John E. Pomfret, *Founding the American Colonies, 1583–1660* (1970); Eric Wolf, *Europe and the People Without History* (1982).

Indians

Harold E. Driver, *Indians of North America,* 2nd ed. (1969); Brian Fagan, *The Great Journey: The Peopling of Ancient America* (1987); Alvin Josephy, Jr., *The Indian Heritage of America* (1968); Alice B. Kehoe, *North American Indians* (1981); Smithsonian Institution, *Handbook of North American Indians,* 6: *Subarctic* (1981), 8: *California* (1978), 9, 10: *The Southwest* (1979, 1983), 15: *The Northeast* (1978).

Africa

Philip Curtin et al., *African History* (1978); J. D. Fage, *A History of Africa* (1978); Robert July, *Precolonial Africa* (1975); Richard Olaniyan, *African History and Culture* (1982); Roland Oliver, ed., *The Cambridge History of Africa,* vol. 3: *c. 1050–c. 1600* (1977).

England

Kenneth Andrews, *Trade, Plunder and Settlement: Maritime Enterprise and the Genesis of the British Empire, 1480–1630* (1984); Carl Bridenbaugh, *Vexed and Troubled Englishmen, 1590–1642,* rev. ed. (1976); Mildred Campbell, *The English Yeoman Under Elizabeth and the Early Stuarts* (1942); Nicholas Canny, *Kingdom and Colony: Ireland in the Atlantic World, 1560–1800* (1988); Peter Laslett, *The World We Have Lost,* 3rd ed. (1984); Wallace Notestein, *The English People on the Eve of Colonization, 1603–1630* (1954); Michael Walzer, *The Revolution of the Saints* (1965); Keith Wrightson, *English Society, 1580–1680* (1982).

Exploration and Discovery

Fredi Chiappelli et al., eds., *First Images of America: The Impact of the New World on the Old,* 2 vols. (1976); Alfred W. Crosby, Jr., *The Columbian Exchange: Biological and Cultural Consequences of 1492* (1972); J. H. Elliott, *The Old World and the New, 1492–1650* (1970); Charles Gibson, *Spain in America* (1966); Samuel Eliot Morison, *The European Discovery of America: The Southern Voyages, A.D. 1492–1616* (1974); *The Northern Voyages, A.D. 1500–1600* (1971); J. H. Parry, *The Age of Reconnaissance* (1963); David B. Quinn, *North America from Earliest Discovery to First Settlements* (1977); John Super, *Food, Conquest, and Colonization in Sixteenth-Century Spanish America* (1988).

Early Contact Between Whites and Indians

James Axtell, *The Invasion Within: The Contest of Cultures in Colonial North America* (1985); James Axtell, *The European and the Indian* (1981); Philip Barbour, *Pocahontas and Her World* (1970); James Bradley, *Evolution of the Onondaga Iroquois* (1987); William Cronon, *Changes in the Land: Indians, Colonists, and the Ecology of New England* (1983); Francis Jennings, *The Invasion of America: Indians, Colonialism, and the Cant of Conquest* (1975); Karen O. Kupperman, *Roanoke, The Abandoned Colony* (1984); Karen O. Kupperman, *Settling with the Indians: The Meeting of English and Indian Cultures in America, 1580–1640* (1980); Kenneth Morrison, *The Embattled Northeast: The Elusive Ideal of Alliance in Abenaki-Euroamerican Relations* (1984); Neal Salisbury, *Manitou and Providence: Indians, Europeans, and the Making of New England, 1500–1643* (1982); Bernard Sheehan, *Savagism and Civility: Indians and Englishmen in Colonial Virginia* (1980); Tzvetan Todorov, *The Conquest of America* (1984); Alden T. Vaughan, *The New England Frontier: Puritans and Indians 1620–1675,* rev. ed. (1979).

Chesapeake

Lois Green Carr and Lorena Walsh, "The Planter's Wife: The Experience of White Women in Seventeenth-Century Maryland," *William and Mary Quarterly,* 3rd ser., 34 (1977), 542–571; Wesley Frank Craven, *White, Red, and Black: The Seventeenth-Century Virginian* (1971); Wesley Frank Craven, *The Southern Colonies in the Seventeenth Century, 1607–1689* (1949); David Galenson, *White Servitude in Colonial America: An Economic Analysis* (1981); Ivor Noël Hume, *Martin's Hundred: The Discovery of a Lost Colonial Virginia Settlement* (1979); Gloria L. Main, *Tobacco Colony: Life in Early Maryland, 1650–1720* (1983); Edmund S. Morgan, *American Slavery, American Freedom: The Ordeal of Colonial Virginia* (1975); Darrett Rutman and Anita Rutman, *A Place in Time: Middlesex County, Virginia, 1650–1750* (1984); Abbot E. Smith, *Colonists in Bondage: White Servitude and Convict Labor in America, 1607–1776* (1947); Thad W. Tate and David L. Ammerman, eds., *The Chesapeake in the Seventeenth Century* (1979); John Van der Zee, *Bound Over: Indentured Servitude and American Conscience* (1985); Alden T. Vaughan, *American Genesis: Captain John Smith and the Founding of Virginia* (1975); *William and Mary Quarterly,* 3rd ser., 30, no. 1 (January 1973): *Chesapeake Society.*

New England

David Grayson Allen, *In English Ways: The Movement of Societies and the Transferral of English Law and Custom to Massachusetts Bay in the Seventeenth Century* (1981); Ben Barker-Benfield, "Anne Hutchinson and the Puritan Attitude Toward Women," *Feminist Studies,* 1 (1972), 65–96; Charles Cohen, *God's Caress: The Psychology of Puritan Religious Experience* (1986); David Cressy, *Coming Over: Migration and Communication Between England and New England in the Seventeenth Century* (1987); John Demos, *A Little Commonwealth: Family Life in Plymouth Colony* (1970); Philip J. Greven, Jr., *Four Generations: Population, Land, and Family in Colonial Andover, Massachusetts* (1970); Philip Gura, *A Glimpse of Sion's Glory: Puritan Radicalism in New England, 1620–1660* (1984); Charles Hambrick-Stowe, *The Practice of Piety* (1982); Stephen Innes, *Labor in a New Land: Economy and Society in Seventeenth-Century Springfield* (1983); Sydney V. James, *Colonial Rhode Island* (1975); Lyle Koehler, *A Search for Power: The "Weaker Sex" in Seventeenth-Century New England* (1980); George Langdon, *Pilgrim Colony: A History of New Plymouth, 1620–1691* (1966); Kenneth A. Lockridge, *A New England Town: The First Hundred Years (Dedham, Massachusetts, 1636–1736)* (1970); Edmund S. Morgan, *The Puritan Family,* rev. ed. (1966); Edmund S. Morgan, *The Puritan Dilemma: The Story of John Winthrop* (1958); Sumner Chilton Powell, *Puritan Village* (1963); Darrett Rutman, *Winthrop's Boston* (1965); Roger Thompson, *Sex in Middlesex: Popular Mores in a Massachusetts County, 1649–1699* (1986).

Olaudah Equiano was eleven years old in 1756 when black raiders seeking slaves for white traders kidnapped him and his younger sister from their village in what is now Nigeria. Until then, he had lived peacefully with his father and mother, his father's other wives, and his seven siblings and half-siblings in a mud-walled compound resembling a small village. Equiano and other members of the Ibo tribe were, he later observed, "habituated to labour from our earliest years." Men, women, and children worked together to cultivate corn, yams, beans, cotton, tobacco, and plantains (a banana-like fruit). Men also herded cattle and goats, and the women spun and wove cotton into clothing. Equiano's family, like others in the region, held prisoners of war as slaves. With what may have been idealizing hindsight, he later recalled that the slaves did "no more work than other members of the community, even their master; their food, clothing, and lodging were nearly the same."

2

AMERICAN SOCIETY TAKES SHAPE, 1640–1720

Equiano's experiences as a captive differed sharply from the life he had led as a child in his father's house. For months he was passed from master to master, finally arriving at the coast, where an English slave ship lay at anchor. Terrified by the light complexions, long hair, and strange language of the sailors, he was afraid that "I had gotten into a world of bad spirits and that they were going to kill me." Equiano was placed below decks, where "with the loathsomeness of the stench and crying together, I became so sick and low that I was not able to eat, nor had I the least desire to taste anything." The whites flogged him to make him eat, and he thought about jumping overboard but was too closely watched. At last some other Ibos told him that they were being taken to the whites' country to work. "I then was a little revived," Equiano remembered, "and thought if it were no worse than working, my situation was not so desperate."

After a long voyage during which many of the Africans died of disease caused by the cramped, unsanitary conditions and poor food, the ship arrived at Barbados, a British island in the West Indies. Equiano and his shipmates feared that "these ugly men" were cannibals, but experienced slaves were brought on board to assure them that they would not be eaten and that many blacks

A Woman by Gerret Duyckinck. Painted between 1690 and 1710 in New Amsterdam. The portrait shows evidence of the sophistication and luxury of the growing colonial metropolis in touch with international taste and markets. *The Henry Francis du Pont Winterthur Museum.*

like themselves lived on the islands. "This report eased us much," Equiano recalled, "and sure enough soon after we landed there came to us Africans of all languages." Everything in Barbados was new and surprising, but Equiano later remarked particularly on two-story buildings and horses, neither of which he had ever seen.

Equiano was not purchased in the West Indies because planters there preferred older, stronger slaves. Instead, he was carried to Virginia along with the other less-valuable Africans. There, on the plantation of his new owner, he was separated from the other Africans and put to work weeding and clearing rocks from the fields. "I was now exceedingly miserable and thought myself worse off than any of the rest of my companions," Equiano reported, "for they could talk to each other, but I had no person to speak to that I could understand. In this state I was constantly grieving and pining and wishing for death rather than anything else."

But Equiano did not remain in Virginia for long. Bought by a sea captain, Olaudah Equiano eventually became an experienced sailor. He learned to read and write English, purchased his freedom at the age of twenty-one, and later actively supported the English antislavery movement. In 1789 Equiano published *The Interesting Narrative of the Life of Olaudah Equiano . . . Written by Himself,* from which this account of his captivity is drawn. Until he was purchased by the sailor, Equiano's experiences differed very little from those of other Africans who were forced into slavery in the English colonies of the New World. Like him, many were sold by black slavers and taken first to the West Indies, then to North America. His *Interesting Narrative,* one of a number of memoirs by former slaves, depicts the captives' terror powerfully and convincingly.

Equiano's life story illustrates one of the major developments in colonial life during the years after 1640: the importation of more than 200,000 unwilling, captive Africans into North America. The introduction of the institution of slavery and the arrival of large numbers of West African peoples dramatically reshaped colonial society. Indeed, the geographic patterns of that migration continue to influence the United States to the present day.

The other important trends in colonial life between 1640 and 1720 were external rather than internal. They involved the English colonists' relationships with others: first, with England itself, and second, with their neighbors in America. Although in the early years of settlement events in England had little direct impact on North America, that situation changed when civil war broke out in the colonists' homeland in 1642. First the Puritan victory in the war, then the restoration of the Stuart monarchy, and finally the Glorious Revolution of 1688–1689 indelibly affected the residents of England's American possessions. By the end of the seventeenth century, the New World colonies were no longer isolated outposts but an integral part of a far-flung mercantile empire. Policies made in distant London then became constant reminders that Americans were tied, willingly or not, to the world of Europe.

The English colonists likewise interacted with their neighbors on the American continent: their Indian trading partners and other transplanted Europeans, with whom they increasingly competed for control of North America. As the English settlements expanded, they came into violent conflict not only with the powerful Indian tribes of the interior but also with the Dutch, the Spanish, and especially the French. By 1720, war—between Europeans and Indians, among Europeans, and among Indians allied with different colonial powers—had become an all-too-frequent feature of American life.

The English Civil War, the Stuart Restoration, and the American Colonies

In 1640, Charles I, who had ruled England arbitrarily for the previous eleven years, called Parliament into session because he needed money and wanted to propose new taxes. But Parliament passed laws limiting his authority, and tensions heightened. In 1642 civil war broke out between royalists and the supporters of Parliament. Four years later, Parliament triumphed, and Charles I was executed in 1649. Oliver Cromwell, the leader of the parliamentary army, then assumed control of the government, taking the title of Lord Protector in 1653. After Cromwell's death in 1658, Parliament decided to restore the monarchy if Charles I's son

IMPORTANT EVENTS

1642–46	English Civil War
1649	Charles I executed
1651	First Navigation Act passed
1660	Stuarts restored to throne; Charles II becomes king
1662	Halfway Covenant drafted
1663	Carolina chartered
1664	English conquer New Netherland; New York founded New Jersey established
1675–76	King Philip's (Metacomet's) War (New England)
1676	Bacon's Rebellion (Virginia)
1680–92	Pueblo revolt (New Mexico)
1681	Pennsylvania chartered
1685	James II becomes king
1686–89	Dominion of New England
1688–89	James II deposed in Glorious Revolution; William and Mary ascend throne
1689–97	King William's War
1692	Witchcraft outbreak in Salem Village
1696	Board of Trade and Plantations established
1701	Iroquois adopt neutrality policy
1702–13	Queen Anne's War
1711–13	Tuscarora War (North Carolina)
1715	Yamasee War (South Carolina)
1732	Georgia chartered

and heir would agree to certain restrictions on his authority. In 1660, Charles II ascended the throne, having promised to seek Parliament's consent for any new taxes and to support the Church of England. Thus ended the tumultuous chapter in English history known as the Interregnum (Latin for "between reigns") or the Commonwealth period.

The Civil War, the Interregnum, and the reign of Charles II (1660–1685) had major significance for the English colonies in the Americas. During the Civil War and the Commonwealth period, Puritans dominated the English government. Therefore the migration to New England largely ceased, and some colonists packed up to return home. During the subsequent reign of Charles II, six of the thirteen colonies that eventually would form the American nation were either founded or came under English rule: New York, New Jersey, Pennsylvania (including Delaware), and North and South Carolina (see map, page 44). All were proprietorships: like Maryland they were granted in their entirety to one man

or a group of men who held title to the soil and controlled the government. Charles II gave these vast American holdings as rewards to men who had supported him during his years of exile. Several of his favorites even shared in more than one grant. Collectively, these became known as the Restoration colonies, because they were created by the restored Stuart monarchy.

One of the first to benefit was Charles's younger brother James, the duke of York. In March 1664, acting as though the Dutch colony of New Netherland did not exist, Charles II gave James the region between the Connecticut and Delaware rivers, including the Hudson valley and Long Island. James immediately organized an invasion fleet. In late August the vessels anchored off Manhattan Island and demanded New Netherland's surrender. The colony's director-general, Peter Stuyvesant, complied without offering resistance. Although the Netherlands briefly regained control of the colony in 1672, the Dutch permanently ceded the province in 1674.

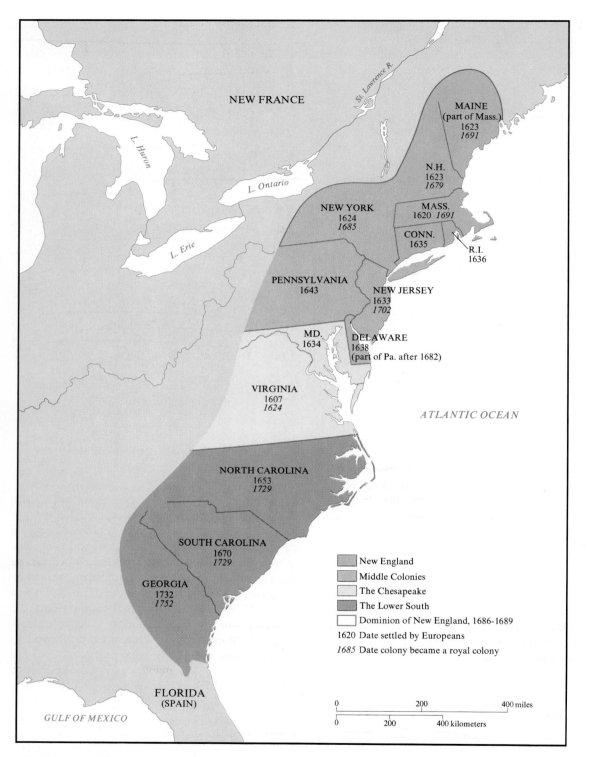

The American Colonies in the Early Eighteenth Century

Thus England acquired a tiny but heterogeneous possession. New Netherland had been founded in 1624 but had remained small in comparison to

> **New Netherland Becomes New York**

its English neighbors. Holland, the world's dominant commercial power in the first half of the seventeenth century, was primarily interested in trade rather than colonization. As the Dutch West India Company's outpost in North America, New Netherland was a relatively unimportant part of a vast commercial empire that included posts in Africa, Brazil, and modern-day Indonesia. Autocratic directors-general ruled the colony for the company; there was no elected assembly, and settlers felt little loyalty to their nominal leaders. Because the Dutch did not experience the economic, demographic, and religious pressures that caused English people to move to the New World, migration was sparse. Even a company policy of 1629 that offered a large land grant, or patroonship, to anyone who would bring fifty settlers to the province failed to attract takers. (Only one such tract—Rensselaerswyck, near modern Albany—was ever fully developed.) In the mid-1660s, when the duke of York assumed control, New Netherland had only about five thousand inhabitants.

The Dutch made up the largest proportion of the population. There was also an appreciable minority of English people, for Puritan New Englanders had begun to settle on Long Island as early as the 1640s. New York, as it was now called, also included sizable numbers of Indians, Germans, French-speaking Walloons (from the southern part of modern Belgium), Scandinavians (New Netherland had swallowed up Swedish settlements on the Delaware River in 1655), and Africans, as well as an additional smattering of other European peoples. The Dutch West India Company, the world's greatest slave-trading power at midcentury (see page 51), actively imported slaves into the colony, some of them intended for resale in the Chesapeake. Many, though, remained in New Netherland as laborers; almost one-fifth of Manhattan's approximately 1,500 inhabitants were black at the time of the English conquest. Slaves thus constituted a higher proportion of New York's urban population than of the Chesapeake's at the same time.

Recognizing the diversity of the population, the duke of York's representatives moved cautiously in

Charles II, who returned from exile to become king in 1660, consolidated England's hold over eastern North America by chartering six new colonies. Moreover, his commercial policies ensured that the economies of the American settlements would be closely linked to that of England. *National Portrait Gallery, London.*

their efforts to establish English authority. The Duke's Laws, a legal code proclaimed in March 1665, at first applied only to the Puritan settlements on Long Island; they were later extended to the rest of the colony. Dutch forms of local government were maintained and Dutch land titles confirmed. Religious toleration was guaranteed through a sort of multiple establishment: each town was permitted to decide which church to support with its tax revenues. Furthermore, the Dutch were allowed to maintain their customary legal practices. Until the 1690s, for example, many Dutch couples wrote joint wills, which were enforced in New York courts even though under English law married women could not draft wills. Much to the chagrin of English residents of the colony, the Duke's Laws made no provision for a representative assembly. Like other Stuarts, James was suspicious of legislative bodies, and so not until 1683 did he agree to

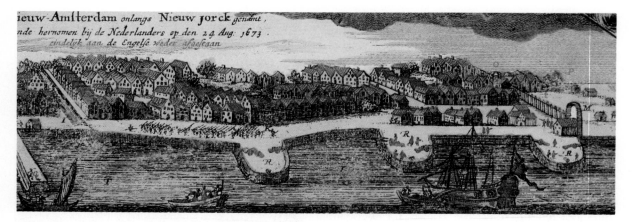

New Amsterdam as it appeared to an artist in 1673, when the city returned to Dutch control for a short period. The inaccuracies in the picture—for example, the exaggerated size of the batteries in the right foreground—may indicate that it was prepared in Europe from sketches made on the scene in America. *John Carter Brown Library, Brown University.*

the colonists' requests for an elected legislature. Before then, New York was ruled by an autocratic governor as it had been under the Dutch.

The English takeover thus had little immediate effect on the colony. Its population grew slowly, barely reaching eighteen thousand by the time of the first English census in 1698. Until the second decade of the eighteenth century, New York City remained a commercial backwater within the orbit of Boston.

One of the chief reasons the English conquest brought so little change to New York was that the duke of York quickly regranted the land between the Hudson and Delaware rivers

Founding of New Jersey

—East and West Jersey—to his friends Sir George Carteret and John Lord Berkeley. That left his own colony confined between Connecticut to the east and the Jerseys to the west and south, depriving it of much fertile land and hindering its economic growth. He also failed to promote migration. Meanwhile the Jersey proprietors acted rapidly to attract settlers, promising generous land grants, limited freedom of religion, and—without authorization from the Crown—a representative assembly. In response, large numbers of Puritan New Englanders migrated southward to the Jerseys, along with some Dutch New Yorkers and a contingent of families from Barbados.

Within twenty years, Berkeley and Carteret sold their interests in the Jerseys to separate groups of investors. Because of the resulting large number of individual proprietary shares, and because the governor of New York had granted lands in the region before learning that the duke had given it away, land titles in northern New Jersey were clouded for many years to come. Nevertheless, New Jersey grew quickly; at the time of its first census as a united colony in 1726, it had 32,500 inhabitants, only 8,000 fewer than New York.

The purchasers of all of Carteret's share (West Jersey) and portions of Berkeley's (East Jersey) were Quakers seeking a refuge from persecution in England. The Quakers, formally known as the Society of Friends, denied the need for an intermediary between the individual and God. Anyone, they believed, could receive the "inner light" and be saved, and all were equal in God's sight. They had no formally trained clergy; any Quaker, male or female, who felt the call could become a "public Friend" and travel from meeting to meeting to discuss God's word. Moreover, any member of the Society could speak in meetings if he or she desired. The Quaker message of radical egalitarianism was not welcome in the hierarchical society of seventeenth-century England—or, for that matter, in Puritan New England. For example, Mary Dyer, who had followed Anne Hutchinson into exile, later became a Quaker, returned to Boston as a missionary, and was hanged for preaching Quaker doctrines.

The Quakers obtained their own colony in 1681, when Charles II granted the region between Mary-

Chapter 2: American Society Takes Shape, 1640–1720

land and New York to William Penn, one of the

sect's most prominent members. The pious yet fun-loving Penn was then thirty-seven years old. Penn's father, Admiral William Penn, had originally served Oliver Cromwell but later joined forces with Charles II and loaned the monarch a substantial sum of money. The younger Penn became a Quaker in the mid-1660s, much to his father's dismay. But despite Penn's radical political and religious beliefs, he and Charles II were close personal friends. Had it not been for their friendship (and the desire of Charles's advisers to rid England of religious dissenters), the despised Quakers would never have won a charter for an American settlement. As it was, the publicly stated reason for the grant—repayment of the loan from Penn's father—was just that, a public rationalization for a private act.

William Penn held the colony as a personal proprietorship, and the vast property holdings earned profits for his descendants until the American Revolution. Even so, Penn, like the Roman Catholic Calverts of Maryland before him, saw the province not merely as a source of revenue but also as a haven for his persecuted coreligionists. Penn offered land to all comers on liberal terms, promised toleration to all religions (though only Christians were given the right to vote), guaranteed such English liberties as the right to bail and trial by jury, and pledged to establish a representative assembly. He also publicized the ready availability of land in Pennsylvania through promotional tracts printed in German, French, and Dutch.

Penn's activities and the natural attraction of his lands for Quakers gave rise to a migration whose magnitude was equaled only by the Puritan exodus to New England in the 1630s. By mid-1683, over three thousand people—among them Welsh, Irish, Dutch, and Germans—had already moved to Pennsylvania, and within five years the population reached twelve thousand. (By contrast, it took Virginia more than thirty years to achieve a comparable population.) Philadelphia, carefully planned to be the major city in the province, drew merchants and artisans from throughout the English-speaking world. From mainland and West Indian colonies alike came Quakers seeking religious freedom; they brought with them years of experience on

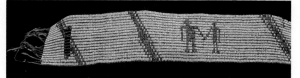

When the Delaware Indians sold land to William Penn, each side recorded the deed in its own way. The English drew up a written document, signed and sealed by all concerned; the Delawares prepared wampum belts portraying the four tribal groups participating in the sale and the peaceful agreement between Indians and whites (shown standing hand in hand). *Deed and top belt: Historical Society of Pennsylvania; bottom belt: Courtesy Museum of the American Indian, Heye Foundation.*

American soil and well-established trading connections. Pennsylvania's lands were both plentiful and fertile, and the colony soon began exporting flour and other foodstuffs to the West Indies. Practically overnight Philadelphia acquired more than two thousand citizens and began to challenge Boston's commercial dominance.

A pacifist with egalitarian principles, Penn was determined to treat the Indians of Pennsylvania fairly. He carefully purchased tracts of land from the Delawares (or Lenni Lenapes), the dominant tribe in the region, before selling them to settlers.

Penn also established strict regulations for the Indian trade and forbade the sale of alcohol to tribesmen. In 1682 he visited a number of Lenni Lenape villages, after taking pains to learn the language. "I must say," Penn commented, "that I know not a language spoken in Europe that hath words of more sweetness in Accent and Emphasis, than theirs."

Penn's Indian policy provides a sterling example of the complexity of the interaction among whites and Indians, because it prompted several tribes to move to Pennsylvania. Indians from western Maryland, Virginia, and North Carolina came northward near the end of the seventeenth century to escape repeated clashes with white settlers. Most important were the Tuscaroras, whose experiences are described later in this chapter. Likewise, Shawnees and Miamis chose to move eastward from the Ohio valley. By a supreme irony, however, the same toleration that attracted Indians to Penn's domains also brought non-Quaker Europeans who showed little respect for Indian claims to the soil. In effect, Penn's policy was so successful that it caused its own downfall. The Scotch-Irish, Palatine Germans, and Swiss who settled in Pennsylvania in the first half of the eighteenth century clashed repeatedly over land with tribes that had also recently migrated to the colony.

The other proprietary colony, granted by Charles II in 1663, encompassed a huge tract of land stretching from the southern boundary of Virginia to Spanish Florida. The area had **Founding of** great strategic importance; a suc-**Carolina** cessful English settlement there would prevent the Spanish from pushing farther north. The semitropical land was also extremely fertile, holding forth the promise of producing such exotic and valuable commodities as figs, olives, wines, and silk. The proprietors named their new province Carolina in Charles's honor (in Latin his name was *Carolus*). The "Fundamental Constitutions of Carolina," which they asked the political philosopher John Locke to draft for them, set forth an elaborate plan for a colony governed by a hierarchy of landholding aristocrats and characterized by a carefully structured distribution of political and economic power. But Carolina failed to follow the course the proprietors laid out. Instead it quickly developed two distinct population centers, which in 1729 permanently split into two separate colonies.

The Albemarle region that became North Carolina was settled by Virginians. They established a society much like their own, with an economy based on tobacco cultivation and the export of such forest products as pitch, tar, and timber. Because North Carolina lacked a satisfactory harbor, its planters continued to rely on Virginia's ports and merchants to conduct their trade, and the two colonies remained tightly linked. Although North Carolina planters held some slaves, they never became as dependent on slave labor as did the other population center in Carolina.

In 1670 Charleston, South Carolina, was founded by a group of settlers from the tiny West Indian island of Barbados, which was already overcrowded less than fifty years after English people had first moved there. The white Barbadians brought with them the slaves who had worked on their sugar plantations and the legal codes that had governed those laborers, thereby irrevocably shaping the future of South Carolina and the subsequent history of the United States.

The Forced Migration of Africans

Since England had no tradition of slavery, why did English settlers in the New World begin to enslave Africans around the middle of the seventeenth century? The answer to that question lies in the combined effect of economics and racial attitudes.

The English were an ethnocentric people. As was seen in Chapter 1, they believed firmly in the superiority of their values and civilization, especially when compared with the native cultures of Africa and North America. Furthermore, they believed that fair-skinned peoples like themselves were superior to the darker-skinned races. Those beliefs alone did not cause them to enslave Indians and Africans, but the idea that other races were inferior to whites helped them to justify slavery and the slave trade.

Although the English had not previously practiced slavery, other Europeans had. The Spanish and Portuguese, for example, had long enslaved African Muslims and other "heathen" peoples. Further, Christian doctrine could be interpreted as al-

Chapter 2: American Society Takes Shape, 1640–1720

lowing enslavement as a means of converting such people to the "true faith." European colonizers needed a large labor force to exploit the riches of the New World, and few free people were willing to work as wage laborers in the difficult and dangerous conditions of South American mines or Caribbean sugar plantations. Needing bound laborers, then, Europeans sought them chiefly in the ranks of dark-skinned non-Christians.

The most obvious source of workers would have been the Indians native to the Americas. But, for a variety of reasons, although some Indians were indeed enslaved (see page 57), they could not supply all the Europeans' labor needs. Alien diseases took a terrible toll of the Native Americans; furthermore, in the Spanish colonies Indian slavery was not only illegal but also actively discouraged by the Catholic church. No such religious motive worked against Indian slavery in the English settlements, but they also had good reason not to enslave too many Indians. For one thing, the native peoples' familiarity with the environment enabled them to escape easily from their white masters. For another, the presence of Indian slaves in a white settlement might provoke retaliatory raids from their fellow tribesmen. Colonial authorities also feared that if they enslaved Indian captives, the tribes might treat captured whites in a similar fashion.

Africans were a different story. Transported far from home and set down in alien surroundings, like Olaudah Equiano they were frequently unable to communicate with their fellow workers. They were also the darkest (and thus, to European eyes, the most inferior) of all peoples. Black Africans therefore seemed to be ideal candidates for perpetual servitude. Furthermore, the English newcomers to the New World had a ready-made model to copy: by the time the English established settlements in the Caribbean and North America, Spanish colonists had already held Africans in slavery for over a century.

The first English colonists in the Americas to utilize slave laborers extensively were those who settled in the Caribbean. In the 1640s the English

Slavery Established

migrants to such islands as Barbados (colonized in 1627), Nevis (1628), and Antigua (1632) discovered that their soil and climate were ideally suited for the cultivation of cane sugar, previously a rare and expensive luxury food item. Caribbean planters imported hundreds of thousands of African slaves to work in the cane fields, making enormous profits for themselves and their home country. Until well into the eighteenth century, England's Caribbean colonies were far more valuable than those on the mainland.

The English colonies to the north did not immediately move to copy the islands' example, largely because their labor needs were still being met by white indentured servants. Lack of evidence makes it difficult to determine the legal status of blacks during the first two or three decades of English settlement, but many of them seem to have been indentured, like whites, which meant that they eventually became free. After 1640, some blacks were being permanently enslaved in each of the English colonies. Massachusetts, in 1641, was the first to mention slavery in its legal code. By the end of the century, the slaves' status was fixed. Barbados adopted a comprehensive slave code in 1661, and the mainland provinces soon did the same. In short, even before the expansion of slavery in North America, the English settlements there had established the legal basis for a slave system.

Between 1492 and 1770 more Africans than Europeans came to the New World. But just 4.5 percent of them (345,000 persons by 1861, or 275,000 during the eighteenth century) were imported into the region that later became the United States. By contrast, 42 percent of the approximately 9.5 million enslaved blacks were carried to the Caribbean, and 49 percent went to South America, mainly to the Portuguese colony of Brazil. The magnitude of this trade in slaves raises three important and related questions. First, what was its impact on West Africa and Europe? Second, how was the trade organized and conducted? Third, what was its effect on the blacks it carried?

The West African coast was one of the most fertile and densely inhabited regions of the continent. Despite the extent of forced migration to the West-

West Africa and the Slave Trade

ern Hemisphere, the area was not seriously depopulated by the trade in human beings. Even so, because American planters preferred to purchase male slaves, the sex ratio of the remaining population was significantly affected by the trade. The relative lack of men increased the work demands on women and simultaneously encouraged polygyny (the practice of one man having several wives). In Guinea, the primary consequences of the trade

In the early eighteenth century, the king of Dahomey formed a women's brigade to help him conquer neighboring kingdoms. This contemporary print, which shows him leading his armed female troops to war, both illustrates the continuing importance in West Africa of dual-sex social organization and shows the significant political changes caused by the slave trade, as rulers sought to extend their power over wider areas. (The women's brigade was not disbanded until 1892.) *The New York Public Library, Astor, Lenox, and Tilden Foundations.*

were political. The coastal kings who served as middlemen in the trade used it as a vehicle to consolidate their power and extend their rule over larger territories. They controlled European traders' access to slaves and at the same time controlled inland peoples' access to desirable European trade goods like cloth, beads, alcohol, tobacco, firearms, and iron bars that could be made into knives and other tools. The centralizing tendencies of the trade thus helped in the formation of such powerful eighteenth-century kingdoms as Dahomey and Asante (created from the Akan States; see page 12).

These West African kings played a crucial role in the functioning of the slave trade. Europeans set up permanent slave-trading posts in Lower Guinea under the protection of local rulers, who then supplied the resident Europeans with slaves to fill the ships that stopped regularly at the coastal forts. In Upper Guinea, the lack of good harbors caused a somewhat different trading pattern: Europeans would sail along the coast, stopping to pick up cargoes when signaled from the shore. Most persons sold into American slavery were wartime captives (including leaders of high status), criminals sentenced to enslavement, or persons seized for nonpayment of debts. A smaller proportion had been kidnaped, like Olaudah Equiano.

Europeans were the chief beneficiaries of this traffic in slaves, despite its importance to some African kings. The expanding network of trade between Europe and its colonies in the seventeenth and eighteenth centuries was fueled by the sale and transportation of slaves, the exchange of commodities produced by slave labor, and the need to

Chapter 2: American Society Takes Shape, 1640–1720

Cape Coast Castle in 1692. Built by the Royal African Company, this fort on the Gold Coast was one of the most important English slave-trading posts in West Africa. *After Greenhill.*

feed and clothe so many bound laborers. The sugar planters of the Caribbean and Brazil, along with the tobacco and rice planters of North America, eagerly purchased slaves from Africa, dispatched shiploads of valuable staple crops to Europe, and bought large quantities of cheap food and clothing, much of it from elsewhere in the Americas. The European economy, previously oriented toward the Mediterranean and the Far East, shifted its emphasis to the Atlantic Ocean. Whereas European merchants' profits had once come primarily from trade with North Africa, the Eastern Mediterranean, and China, by the late seventeenth century commerce in slaves and the products of slave labor constituted the basis of the European economic system. The irony of Columbus's discoveries was thus complete: seeking the wealth of the East, Columbus had found instead the lands that ultimately replaced the East as the source of European prosperity.

Given the economic importance of the slave trade, it is hardly surprising that European nations fought bitterly over control of it. The Portuguese, who initially dominated the trade, were supplanted by the Dutch in the middle of the seventeenth century. The Dutch in turn lost out to the English, who eventually controlled the trade through the Royal African Company, a joint-stock company chartered by Charles II in 1672. Holding a monopoly on all English trade with black Africa, the company built and maintained eight forts, dispatched to West Africa hundreds of ships carrying English manufactured goods, and transported more than 120,000 slaves to England's American colonies. Yet even before the company's monopoly expired in 1712 many individual English traders had illegally entered the market for slaves. By the early eighteenth century, such independent traders were carrying most of the Africans imported into the colonies and

The Forced Migration of Africans

▶ 51

A contemporary print illustrating how slave-ship captains tightly packed their human cargo so as to achieve the greatest possible profits from each voyage. *American Antiquarian Society.*

accordingly earning immense profits from successful voyages.

The experience of the Middle Passage (thus named because it was the middle section of the so-called triangular trade among England, Africa, and the Americas; see pages 62–63)

The Middle Passage was always traumatic and sometimes fatal for the Africans who made up a ship's cargo. An average of 10 to 20 percent of the slaves died en route, but on voyages that were unusually long or were hard hit by epidemic diseases, the mortality rates were much higher. In addition, some slaves usually died either before the ships left Africa or shortly after their arrival in the New World. Their white captors died at the same, if not higher, rates, chiefly through exposure to alien African germs. Just 10 percent of the men sent to run the Royal African Company's forts in Lower Guinea lived to return home to England, and one in every four or five white sailors died on the Middle Passage. Once

again, the exchange of diseases that accompanied the interaction of alien peoples caused unanticipated death and destruction.

On shipboard, men were usually kept shackled in pairs; women and children were released from any bonds once the ship was well out at sea. The slaves were fed a vegetable diet of beans, rice, yams, and corn cooked together in various combinations to create a warm mush. In good weather, they were allowed on deck for fresh air, because only healthy slaves commanded high prices. Many ships also carried a doctor whose primary role was to treat the slaves' illnesses. The average size of a cargo was about 250 slaves, although since the size of ships varied greatly, so too did the number of slaves carried.

Records of slave traders reveal numerous instances of Africans' resistance to captivity. Recall that Olaudah Equiano contemplated suicide; many of his fellow captives took that means of avoiding servitude. Others participated in shipboard revolts;

more than 150 occurred during the three-hundred-year history of the Middle Passage. Yet most of the Africans who embarked on the slave vessels arrived in the Americas alive and still in captivity; the whites saw to that, for only thus could they make a profit.

At first, most of the slaves imported into the English colonies went to the Caribbean islands. But after about 1675 Chesapeake planters could no longer obtain an adequate supply of English workers. A falling birthrate and improved economic conditions in England decreased the number of possible migrants to the colonies. At the same time new English settlements in North America started to compete with the Chesapeake for settlers, both indentured and free. As a result, the number of servant migrants to the Chesapeake leveled off after 1665 and fell in the 1680s. After 1674, when the shortage of servants became acute, imports of Africans increased dramatically. As early as 1690, the Chesapeake colonies contained more black slaves than white indentured servants, and by 1710 one-fifth of the region's population was black. Slaves usually cost about two-and-a-half times as much as servants, but they repaid the greater investment by their lifetime of service.

Slavery in the Chesapeake

Yet not all white planters could afford to devote so much money to purchasing workers. Accordingly, the transition from indentured to enslaved labor increased the social and economic distance between richer and poorer planters. Whites with enough money could acquire slaves and accumulate greater wealth, while less-affluent whites could not even buy indentured servants, whose price had been driven up by scarcity. In addition, the transition to slave labor ended what had become a common way for poorer white planters to earn essential income: renting parts of their property to newly freed servants. Deprived of that source of capital—since there were far fewer ex-servants—many marginal planters sank into landless status. As time passed, white Chesapeake society thus became more and more stratified—that is, the gap between rich and poor steadily widened. The introduction of large numbers of Africans into the Chesapeake had a significant impact on white society, in addition to reshaping the population as a whole.

That impact involved cultural values as well as demographic and economic change. Without realizing it, Chesapeake whites adopted African modes of thought about the use of time and the nature of work. Africans were more accustomed than European migrants to life in a hot climate, and whites soon learned the benefits of following African patterns of time usage—working early and late, taking a long rest in the heat of midday. They also assimilated African attitudes toward work, which were far more casual than those found in New England. There, Puritans emphasized the necessity of "improving" every moment and decried all leisure-time activities. In the Chesapeake, whites, like blacks, came to recognize the importance of recreation and to understand that work could be performed at a leisurely pace on most occasions.

In South Carolina, as has been seen, the first slaves arrived with the first white settlers. Indeed, one-quarter to one-third of South Carolina's early population was black. The Barbados whites quickly discovered that Africans had a variety of skills well suited to the semitropical environment of South Carolina. African-style dugout canoes became the chief means of transportation in the colony, which was crisscrossed by rivers. Fishing nets copied from African models proved to be more efficient than those of English origin. The baskets slaves wove and the gourds they hollowed out came into general use as containers for food and drink. Africans' skill at killing crocodiles equipped them to handle alligators as well. And, finally, slaves adapted African techniques of cattle herding for use in the American context. Since meat and hides, not the exotic products originally envisioned, were the colony's chief exports in its earliest years, blacks contributed significantly to South Carolina's prosperity by utilizing their African heritage.

Blacks in South Carolina

The similarity of South Carolina's environment to West Africa's, coupled with the large number of blacks in the population, ensured that more aspects of West African culture survived in that colony than elsewhere on the mainland of North America. Only in South Carolina did black parents continue to give their children African names; only there did a dialect develop that combined English words with African terms (known as Gullah, it has survived to the present day in isolated areas). African skills remained useful, and so techniques that in other regions were lost when the migrant generation died were instead passed down to their children. And in

Mulberry Plantation, South Carolina, in the late eighteenth century. The mansion house on this indigo and rice plantation (built 1708) is surrounded by slave quarters—African-style huts constructed by Africans and their African-American children. Some of the tiny houses survived into the twentieth century. *Carolina Art Association, Gibbes Art Gallery.*

South Carolina, as in West Africa, black women were the primary traders, dominating the markets of Charleston as they did those of Gambia or Benin. One white observer commented that "these women have such a connection with and influence on the country negroes who come to that market, that they generally find means to obtain whatever they choose, in preference to any white person; thus they forestall and engross many articles, which some hours afterwards you must buy back from them at 100 or 150 per cent advance."

Significantly, the importation of large numbers of Africans near the end of the seventeenth century coincided with the successful introduction of rice as a staple crop in South Carolina. English people knew little about the techniques of growing and processing rice, and their first attempts to raise it were unsuccessful. But slaves from Africa's Rice Coast (see page 12) had spent their lives working with the crop. Although the evidence is circumstantial, it seems likely that the Africans' expertise enabled their English masters to cultivate the crop

profitably. After rice had become South Carolina's major export, 43 percent of the Africans imported into the colony came from rice-producing regions, and blacks' central position in the colony's economy was firmly established. In the mid-eighteenth century a South Carolina merchant commented that "the Slaves from the River Gambia are preferred to all others with us save the Gold Coast."

South Carolina later developed a second staple crop, and it too made use of blacks' special skills. The crop was indigo, much prized in Europe as a blue dye for clothing. In the early 1740s Eliza Lucas, a young white West Indian woman who was managing her father's South Carolina plantations, began to experiment with indigo cultivation. Drawing on the knowledge of white and black West Indians, she developed the planting and processing techniques later adopted throughout the colony. Indigo was grown on high ground, and rice was planted in low-lying swampy areas; rice and indigo also had opposite growing seasons. Thus the two crops complemented each other perfectly. Although South

Carolina indigo never matched the quality of that raised in the West Indies, the indigo industry flourished because Parliament offered Carolinians a bounty on every pound they exported to Great Britain.

After 1700, therefore, white southerners were irrevocably committed to black slavery as their chief source of labor. The same was not true of white northerners. Only a small propor-

Slavery in the North

tion of the blacks brought to the English colonies in America went to the northern mainland provinces, and most of those who did worked as enslaved domestic servants. Lacking large-scale agricultural enterprises, the rural North did not demand many bound laborers. In northern urban areas, though, white domestic servants were hard to find and harder to keep because higher wages were paid for other jobs in the labor-scarce economy. Thus blacks there filled an identifiable need. In some northern colonial cities (notably Newport, Rhode Island, and New York City), black slaves accounted for more than 10 percent of the population.

The introduction of large-scale slavery in the South, coupled with its near-absence in the North, accentuated regional differences that had already begun to develop in England's American colonies. To the distinction between diversified agriculture and staple-crop production was now added a difference in the race and status of most laborers. That difference was one of degree, but it was nonetheless crucial. In the latter years of the seventeenth century, white Southern planters chose a course of action that nearly two centuries later took the future United States into civil war.

Relations Between Europeans and Indians

Everywhere in North America, European colonizers depended heavily on the labor of native peoples. But their reliance on Indians took varying forms in different parts of the continent. In the Northeast, France, England, and the Netherlands competed for the pelts supplied by Indian trappers.

In the Southeast, England, Spain, and later France each tried to control a thriving trade with the tribes in deerskins and Indian slaves. Finally, in the Southwest, Spain attempted to exploit the agricultural and artisan skills of the Pueblo peoples.

In 1598, drawn northward by accounts that rich cities lay in the region, Juan de Oñate, a Mexican-born adventurer, led a group of about five hundred to colonize New Mexico. The emissaries from New Spain had three goals: to acquire personal wealth, preferably by finding precious metals; to claim new territories for their monarch; and to convert the Indians to Catholicism. When it became apparent that New Mexico held little wealth and offered only a hard life, many of the first settlers returned to Mexico. In 1609 Spanish authorities decided to maintain only a small military outpost and a few Christian missions in the area, with the capital at Santa Fé (founded 1610).

Thereafter, Franciscan friars worked energetically to convert the residents of the pueblos, with mixed success. The Pueblo peoples proved

Popé and the Pueblo Revolt

willing to add Christianity to their own religious beliefs but not to give up their indigenous rituals. Friars and secular colonists who held *encomiendas* also placed heavy labor demands on the Indians. As the decades passed, conditions grew worse, for the Franciscans adopted brutal and violent tactics as they tried to wipe out all vestiges of the native religion. Finally, in 1680 the Pueblos revolted under the leadership of Popé, a respected shaman, and successfully drove the Spaniards out of New Mexico (see map, page 56). Although Spanish authority was restored in 1692, Spain had learned its lesson. From that time on Spanish governors stressed cooperation with the Pueblos, rather than confrontation, and no longer attempted to reduce them to bondage or to violate their cultural integrity. The Pueblo revolt was the most successful and longest sustained Indian resistance movement in colonial North America.

When the Spanish expanded their territorial claims to the east (Texas) and the north (California), they followed the strategy they had used in New Mexico, establishing their presence through widely scattered military outposts and Franciscan missions. The army's role was to maintain order among the subject Indians—with the dual aims of

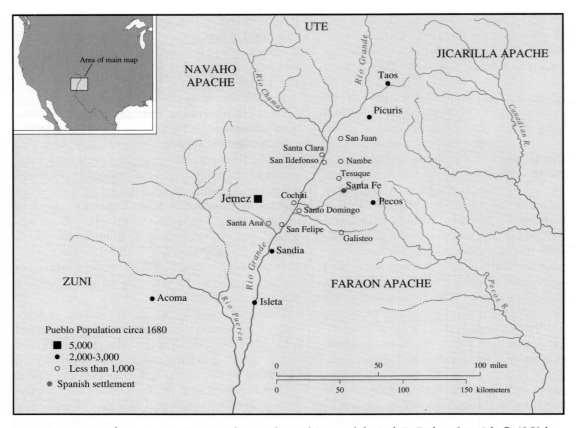

New Mexico, ca. 1680 *Source: From* Apache, Navaho, and Spaniard, *by Jack D. Forbes. Copyright © 1960 by the University of Oklahoma Press. Used by permission.*

Early colonists economy export furs, skins

protecting them from attack by other tribes and ensuring the availability of their labor—and to guard the boundaries of the Spanish empire from possible incursions, especially by the French. The friars, of course, continued to concentrate on conversion efforts. By the late eighteenth century, Spain claimed a vast territory that stretched from California (initially colonized in 1769) through Texas (settled after 1700) to the Gulf Coast. In that region the Spanish presence consisted of a mixture of missions and forts dotting the countryside at considerable distances from each other.

Along the eastern seaboard Europeans valued the Indians as hunters and traders rather than as agricultural workers, but they were no less dependent on Indian labor than were the Spanish. The major Dutch settlements in North America were trading posts; the French settlements were trading posts allied to missions. Although the English colonies eventually began to market their own products, in the earliest phase of each colony's history its primary exports were furs and skins obtained from neighboring Indians.

South Carolina provides a case in point. The Barbadians who colonized the region moved quickly to establish a vigorous trade in deerskins with nearby tribes. During the first decade of the eighteenth century, South Carolina exported to Europe an average of 54,000 skins annually, a number that later climbed to a peak of 160,000. The trade gave rise to other exchanges that reveal the complexity of the economic relationships among Indians and Europeans. For example, white Carolinians carried those deerskins on horses they obtained from the Creek Indians, who had in turn acquired them from the Spaniards through trade and capture.

Another important component of the Carolina trade was traffic in Indian slaves. The warring tribes

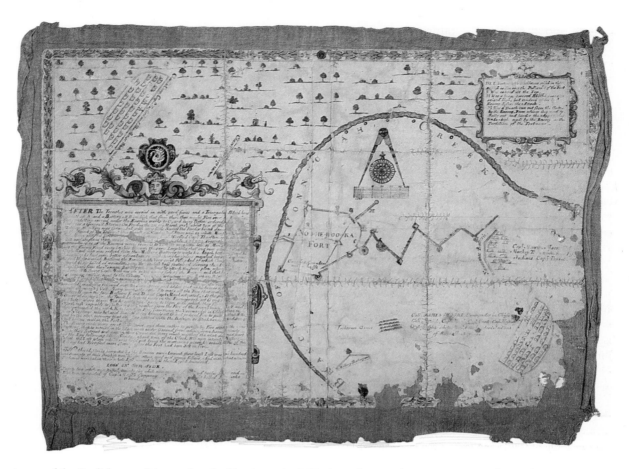

A map of the English expedition against the Tuscaroras in 1713, drawn by an unknown artist. *South Carolina Historical Society, Charleston.*

of South Carolina (especially the Creeks) profited from selling their captive enemies to the whites,

Indian Slave Trade

who then either kept them in the colony as slaves or exported them to other mainland settlements or to the West Indies. There are no reliable statistics on the extent of the trade in Indian slaves, but in 1708 they made up 14 percent of the population of South Carolina. Many were Christians converted by the Spanish missions in northern Florida, then captured by Englishmen and their Indian allies.

A major conflict between white Carolinians and neighboring tribes added to the supply of Indian slaves. In 1711, the Tuscaroras, an Iroquoian people, attacked a Swiss-German settlement at New Bern, which had expropriated their lands without payment. The Tuscaroras had been avid slavers and had sold to the whites many captives from weaker Algonkian tribes. Those tribes seized the opportunity to settle old scores, joining with the English colonists to defeat their enemy in a bloody two-year war. In the end, more than a thousand Tuscaroras were themselves sold into slavery, and the remnants of the tribe drifted northward, where they joined the Five Nations Iroquois in New York.

The abuses of the slave trade led to the most destructive Indian war in Carolina. White traders regularly engaged in corrupt, brutal, and fraudulent practices. They were notorious for cheating the Indians, physically abusing them (including raping the women), and selling friendly tribesmen into slavery when no enemy captives came readily to hand. In the spring of 1715 the Yamasees, aided by

Creeks and a number of other tribes, retaliated by attacking the English colonists. As the raids continued through the summer, white refugees streamed into Charleston by the hundreds. At times the Creek-Yamasee offensive, often guided by information from Indian slaves held by the whites, came close to driving the intruders from the mainland altogether. But then colonial reinforcements arrived from the north, and the Cherokees joined the whites against their ancient enemies, the Creeks. The war pointed up both the difficulty of obtaining unity among the tribes and the Indians' now-critical dependence on European weapons. When the tribal allies ran out of ammunition and could not repair their broken guns, their cause was lost. The Yamasees moved south to seek Spanish protection, and the Creeks retreated to villages in the west. It was years before South Carolina fully recovered from the effects of the Yamasee War.

That the Yamasees could escape by migrating southward exposed the one remaining gap in the line of English coastal settlements, the area between the southern border of South Carolina and Spanish Florida. The gap was plugged in 1732 with the chartering of Georgia, the last of the colonies that would become part of the United States. Intended as a haven for debtors by its founder James Oglethorpe, Georgia was specifically designed as a garrison province. Since all its landholders were expected to serve as militiamen to defend English settlements, the charter prohibited women from inheriting or purchasing land in the colony. The charter also prohibited the use of alcoholic beverages and forbade the introduction of slavery. Such provisions reveal the founders' intention that Georgia should be peopled by sturdy, sober yeoman farmers who could take up their weapons against the Indians or Spaniards at a moment's notice. None of the original conditions of the charter could be enforced, however, and all of them had been abandoned by 1752, when Georgia became a royal colony.

In the Northeast, Indian-white relationships were complicated by the number of European nations and Indian tribes involved in the fur trade. Before the large-scale migration of English people, the Dutch at Fort Orange (Albany) on the upper Hudson River competed for control of the fur trade with the French on the St. Lawrence. In the 1640s the Iroquois, who traded chiefly with the Dutch, went to war against the Hurons, who traded primarily with the French. The Iroquois' object was to become the major supplier of pelts to the Europeans, and they achieved that goal by practically exterminating the Hurons through the use of guns they obtained from their Dutch allies. The Iroquois thus established themselves as a major force in the region, one that Europeans could ignore only at their peril.

The Iroquois nation was not one tribe, but five: Mohawks, Oneidas, Onondagas, Cayugas, and Senecas. (In 1722 the Tuscaroras became the sixth).

Iroquois Confederacy Under the terms of a defensive alliance forged early in the sixteenth century, key decisions of war and peace for the entire Iroquois Confederacy were made by a council composed of tribal representatives. Each tribe retained some autonomy, and no tribe could be forced to comply with a council directive against its will. The Iroquois were unique among Indians not only because of the strength and persistence of their alliance but also because of the role played by their tribal matrons. The older women of each village chose its chief and could either start wars (by calling for the capture of prisoners to replace dead relatives) or stop them (by refusing to supply warriors with necessary foodstuffs).

Before the arrival of the Europeans, the Iroquois had waged wars primarily for the purpose of acquiring captives to replenish their population. Contact with white traders brought ravaging disease as early as 1633 and thus intensified the need for captives. At the same time the arrival of Europeans created an economic motive for warfare: the desire to control the fur trade and gain unimpeded access to European goods. The war with the Hurons was but the first of a series of conflicts with other tribes known as the Beaver Wars, in which the Iroquois fought desperately to maintain a dominant position in the trade. In the mid-1670s, just when it appeared they would be successful, the French stepped in to prevent an Iroquois triumph, for that would have destroyed France's plans to trade directly with the Indians of the Great Lakes and Mississippi valley regions. Over the next twenty years the French launched repeated attacks on Iroquois villages. The English, who replaced the Dutch at Albany after 1664, offered little assistance other than weapons to their trading partners and nominal allies. Their people and resources depleted by constant warfare, the Iroquois in 1701 negotiated neutrality treaties with France, England, and their tribal neighbors. For the next half-century they maintained their power through trade and skillful, often successful diplomacy.

The wars against the Iroquois Confederacy were crucial components of French Canada's plan to penetrate the heartland of North America. In the

> **French Expansion**

1670s Louis de Buade de Frontenac, the governor general of Canada, encouraged the explorations of Father Jacques Marquette, Louis Jolliet, and Robert Cavelier de La Salle in the Great Lakes and Mississippi Valley regions. Officials at home in France approved the expeditions because they wanted to find a route to Mexico. La Salle and Frontenac, by contrast, hoped to make great personal profits by monopolizing the fur trade through establishing trading posts along the Mississippi River.

Unlike the Spanish, these French adventurers did not attempt to subjugate the Indian peoples they encountered or even at first to claim the territory formally for France. Still, when France decided to strengthen its presence near the Gulf of Mexico by founding New Orleans in the early eighteenth century—to counter both the westward thrust of the English colonies and the eastward moves of the Spanish—the Mississippi posts became the glue of empire. *Coureurs de bois* (literally, "woods runners") used the rivers and lakes of the American interior to travel regularly between Quebec and Louisiana, carrying French goods to such outposts as Michilimackinac (at the junction of Lakes Superior and Huron), Cahokia and Kaskaskia (in present-day Illinois), and Fort Rosalie (Natchez), on the lower Mississippi River.

At each post lived a small military garrison and a priest, surrounded by powerful Indian nations like the Choctaws, Chickasaws, Osages, and Illinois (see map, page 60). The tribes permitted the French to remain among them because the traders gave them ready access to precious European goods. The French, for their part, sought political as well as economic ends, attempting to prevent the English from encroaching too far into the interior. Their goals, though, were limited; they did not engage in systematic efforts to convert the Indians of the region to Christianity. Given their geographical isolation, such efforts could very well have been suicidal.

A French settler in Canada made this drawing of an Iroquois about 1700. The artist's fascination with his subject's mode of dress and patterned tattoos is evident. Such pictorial representations of "otherness" help to suggest the cultural gulf that divided the European and Indian residents of North America. *Library of Congress.*

The French learned to live in the midst of powerful tribes with relatively little friction because of the mutual needs of all parties to the arrangement. Matters were very different in the English colonies, where white colonists were interested no longer in trade but rather in acquiring land. In Virginia, the conflict was especially acute because of the colonists' insatiable hunger for land on which to grow still more tobacco.

By the early 1670s, some Virginians were eagerly eyeing the rich lands north of the York River that had been reserved for Indians under earlier treaties. Using as a pretext the July 1675 killing of

> **Bacon's Rebellion**

a white servant by some Doeg Indians, they attacked not only the Doegs but also the Susquehan-

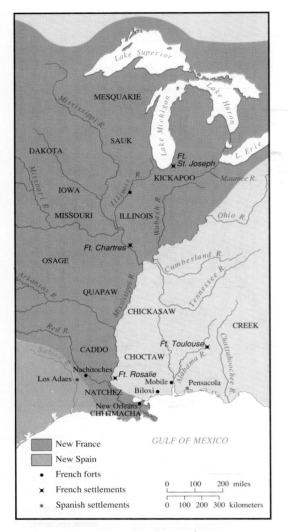

Louisiana, ca. 1720 *Source: Map from* France in America *by William J. Eccles. Copyright © 1972 by William J. Eccles. Reprinted by permission of Harper & Row, Publishers, Inc.*

nocks, a powerful tribe that had recently occupied the region. In retaliation, Susquehannock bands began to raid frontier plantations in the winter of 1676. The land-hungry whites rallied behind the leadership of Nathaniel Bacon, a planter who had arrived in the colony only two years before. Bacon and his followers wanted, in his words, "to ruine and extirpate all Indians in general." Governor William Berkeley, however, hoped to avoid setting off a major war.

Berkeley and Bacon soon clashed. After Bacon forced the House of Burgesses to authorize him to attack the Indians, Berkeley declared Bacon and his men to be in rebellion. As the chaotic summer of 1676 wore on, Bacon alternately pursued Indians and battled with the governor's supporters. In September he marched on Jamestown itself and burned the capital to the ground. But after Bacon died of dysentery the following month, the rebellion collapsed. A new Indian treaty signed in 1677 opened much of the disputed territory to whites.

More than coincidentally, New England, which had also been settled more than fifty years earlier, was wracked by conflict with Indians at precisely the same time. In both areas the whites' original accommodation with the tribes—reached after the defeat of the Pequots in the North and the Powhatan Confederacy in the South—no longer satisfied both parties. In New England, though, it was the Indians, rather than the whites, who felt aggrieved.

In the half-century since the founding of New England, white settlement had spread far into the interior of Massachusetts and Connecticut. In the process the whites had completely surrounded the ancestral lands of the Pokanokets (Wampanoags) on Narragansett Bay. Their chief, Metacomet (known to the whites as King Philip), was the son of Massasoit, who had signed the treaty with the Pilgrims in 1621. Troubled by white encroachments on Pokanoket lands and equally concerned about the impact European culture and Christianity were having on his people, Metacomet in late June 1675 led his warriors in attacks on nearby white communities.

King Philip's War

By the end of the year, two other tribes, the Nipmucks and the Narragansetts, had joined Metacomet's forces. In the fall, the three tribes jointly attacked settlements in the northern Connecticut River valley; in the winter and spring of 1676, they devastated well-established villages and even attacked Plymouth and Providence. Altogether, the alliance totally destroyed twelve of the ninety Puritan towns and attacked forty others. One-tenth of the able-bodied adult white males in Massachusetts were captured or killed. Proportional to population, it was the most costly war in American history. New England's very survival seemed to be at stake.

But the tide turned in the summer of 1676. The Indian coalition ran short of food and ammunition, and whites began to use "praying Indians" as guides and scouts. After Metacomet was killed in an ambush in August, the alliance crumbled. Many surviving Pokanokets, Nipmucks, and Narragansetts, including Metacomet's wife and son, were captured and sold into slavery in the West Indies. The power of New England's coastal tribes was broken. Thereafter they lived in small clusters, subordinated to the whites and often working as servants or sailors. Only on the isolated island of Martha's Vineyard were some surviving Pokanokets able to preserve their tribal identity intact.

New England and the Web of Imperial Trade

By the later years of the seventeenth century the New England settlements had changed in three major ways since the early years of colonization. The population had grown dramatically; the nature of the residents' religious commitment had altered; and the economy had developed in unanticipated ways.

The expansion of the population was the result not of continued migration from England (for that had largely ceased after the outbreak of civil war in
Population Pressures
1640), but rather of natural increase. The original settlers' many children also produced many children, and subsequent generations followed suit. By 1700, New England's population had quadrupled to reach approximately 100,000. Such an increase placed great pressure on the available land, and many members of the third and fourth generations of New Englanders had to migrate—north to New Hampshire or Maine, south to New York, west beyond the Connecticut River—to find sufficient farm land for themselves and their children. Others abandoned agriculture and learned skills like blacksmithing or carpentry so that they could support themselves in the growing number of towns that dotted the countryside.

In addition, second-generation Puritans did not display the same religious fervor that had prompted their ancestors to cross the Atlantic.
Halfway Covenant
Many of them had not experienced the gift of God's grace, or "saving faith," which was required for full membership in the Congregational church. Yet they had been baptized as children, attended church services regularly, and wanted their own infants to be baptized, even though the sacrament of baptism was supposed to be available only to the children of church members. A synod of Massachusetts ministers, convened in 1662 to consider the problem, responded by establishing a category of "halfway" membership in the church. In a statement that has become known as the Halfway Covenant, the clergymen declared that adults who had been baptized as children but were not full church members could have their children baptized. In return, such parents had to acknowledge the authority of the church and live according to moral precepts. As "halfway" members, however, these second-generation Puritans were not allowed to vote in church affairs or take communion.

The Halfway Covenant attempted to deal with one problem of changing religious mores, but it did not touch another: a newly noticeable difference between the experiences of the two sexes. By the end of the seventeenth century, women were more likely than men to experience "saving faith"; thus they made up a majority in many New England congregations. Searching for the cause of this phenomenon, Cotton Mather—the most prominent member of a family of distinguished ministers—speculated that the fear of dying in childbirth made women especially sensitive to their spiritual state. Modern historians have also argued that women were attracted to religion because the church offered them a spiritual equality that offset their secular inferiority. Whatever the explanation, the increasingly female make-up of his audiences prompted Mather to deliver sermons outlining women's proper role in church and society—the first formal examination of that theme in American history. Mather was the first of many men to publish sermons urging American women to be submissive to their husbands, watchful of their children, and attentive to religious duty.

The differential rate of church membership in late seventeenth-century New England suggests a growing division between pious women and their more worldly husbands. That split reflected significant economic changes, which constitute the third major way in which the Puritan colonies were being transformed.

Sea Captains Carousing in Surinam, a scene that could have occurred in any tavern in any Caribbean port. Several recognizable Rhode Island merchants are included among the merrymakers. Painted by John Greenwood (1758), a Bostonian who lived in Surinam (Dutch Guiana), on the northern coast of South America. *The St. Louis Art Museum.*

New England's first commercial system had been based on two pillars: the fur trade and the constant flow of migrants. Together those had allowed New Englanders to acquire the manufactured goods they needed: the fur trade gave them valuable pelts to sell in England, and the migrants were always willing to exchange clothing and other items for the earlier settlers' surplus seed, grains, and livestock. But New England's supply of furs was limited, because the region lacked rivers giving ready access to the interior of the continent, and the migrants stopped coming after the English Civil War began. Thus in 1640 that first economic system collapsed.

The Puritans then began a search for new salable crops and markets. They found such crops in the waters off the coast—fish—and on their own land—grain and wood products.

New England's Trading System By 1643 they had also found the necessary markets: first the so-called Wine Islands (the Azores and Canaries) in the Atlantic and then the English colonies in the Caribbean. All these islands lacked precisely the goods New England could produce in abundance: cheap food (corn and salted fish) to feed to slaves and wood to make barrels that would hold wine and molasses (the form in which sugar was shipped).

Thus developed the series of transactions that has become known, inaccurately, as the triangular trade. Since New England's products duplicated England's, the northern colonists sold their goods in the West Indies and elsewhere to earn the money with which to purchase English products. (Southerners did not have the same problem. Their crops—tobacco, rice, and indigo—could be sold directly to England.) There soon grew up in New England's ports a cadre of merchants who acquired—usually through barter—cargoes of timber and foodstuffs, which they then dispatched to the West Indies for sale. In the Caribbean the ships sailed from island to island, exchanging fish, barrel staves, and grains for molasses, fruit, spices, and slaves.

Once they had a full load, the ships returned to Boston, Newport, or New Haven to dispose of their cargoes. New Englanders then traded those items they did not consume to other colonies or to England. Most important, they distilled West Indian molasses into the more valuable rum, a widely used alcoholic beverage. Rum was a key component of the only part of the trade that could be termed

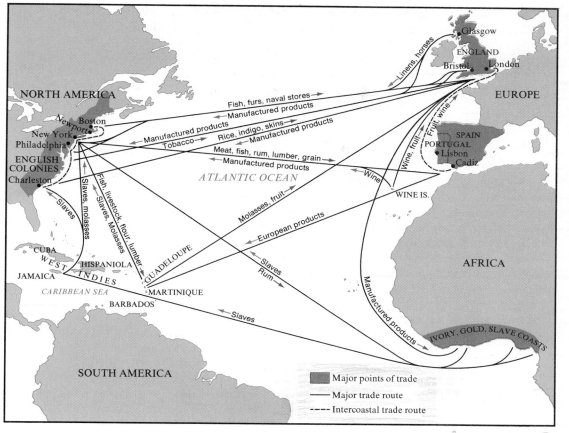

Atlantic Trade Routes

restoration of the Stuarts

triangular: Rhode Islanders took rum to Africa and traded it for slaves, whom they carried to the West Indies to exchange for more molasses to produce still more rum. With that exception, the trading pattern was not a triangle but a shifting set of shuttle voyages (see map). Its sole constant was uncertainty, due to the weather, rapid changes of supply and demand in the small island markets, and the delicate system of credit on which the entire structure depended.

The Puritan New Englanders who ventured into commerce were soon differentiated from their rural counterparts by their ties to a wider transatlantic world and by their preoccupation with material endeavors. As time passed, increasing numbers of Puritans became involved in trade. Small investors who owned shares of voyages soon dominated the field numerically if not

> **Puritans and Anglicans**

monetarily. The gulf between commercial and farming interests widened after 1660, when—with the restoration of the Stuarts to the English throne—Anglican merchants began to migrate to New England to participate directly in the booming trade in slaves and staple crops produced by slaves. Such men had little stake in the survival of Massachusetts Bay and Connecticut in their original form, and some were openly antagonistic to Puritan traditions. As non-Congregationalists they were denied the vote, and they could not practice their religion freely. They resented their exclusion from the governing elite, believing that their wealth and social status entitled them to political power. Congregationalist clergymen returned their hostility in full measure and preached sermons called jeremiads lamenting New England's new commercial orientation. The Reverend Increase Mather (Cotton Mather's father) reminded his congregation in 1676

New England and the Web of Imperial Trade

that "Religion and not the World was that which our Fathers came hither for."

But Mather spoke for the past, not the future or even many of his own contemporaries. By the 1670s, New England and the other American colonies were deeply enmeshed in an intricate international trading network. The seventeenth-century colonies should not be seen as primitive, isolated, self-sufficient communities. Indeed, the early colonies were, if anything, more dependent on overseas markets and imported goods than was eighteenth-century America. During the 1600s the colonies lacked sufficient population to support manufactures or manufacturing. For example, all attempts to establish ironworks or glass factories in the first decades of settlement failed because there simply were not enough colonial customers for their products. Furthermore, the colonies' economic fortunes depended on the sale of their exports in foreign markets: furs, deerskins, sugar, tobacco, rice, fish, and timber products together formed the basis for Anglo-America's prosperity.

The lucrative trade between Europe and its far-flung outposts in this period led to the rise of international piracy. Bands of buccaneers sailed the seas from the Caribbean to the Indian Ocean, seeking treasure ships and merchant vessels. Occasionally they even raided port towns. The pirates found safe havens in places like Port Royal, Jamaica, and Manhattan, where merchants eagerly provisioned their ships and purchased their loot. (Pirates, who had few expenses, usually sold their booty at low prices.) In the last decades of the century, the economy of New York was dependent on the illegal profits gained from aiding and abetting pirates like the infamous Captain William Kidd, who lived in Manhattan when he was not roaming the world in search of rich prizes. For years Kidd and the other pirates could count on the complicity of New York's governors, who ignored their activities in exchange for shares of the bounty, but the cozy relationship ended in 1698 when the earl of Bellomont was named governor. In July 1699 Bellomont ordered Kidd's arrest; he was sent to England, tried, and executed in May 1701.

The valuable American commerce also attracted the attention of English officials seeking a new source of revenue after the disruptions of the Civil War. They realized that the colonies could make important contributions to England's economic well-being. Tobacco from the Chesapeake and sugar from the West Indies had obvious value, but other colonial products also had profitable potential. Additional tax revenues could put the nation back on a sound financial footing, and English merchants wanted to ensure that they—not their Dutch rivals—reaped the benefits of trading with the English colonies. Parliament and the restored Stuart monarchs accordingly began to design a system of laws that would, they hoped, confine the profits of colonial trade primarily to the mother country.

They, like other European nations, based their commercial policy on a series of assumptions about the operations of the world's economic system. Collectively, these assumptions are usually called *mercantilism,* though neither the term itself nor a unified mercantilist theory was formulated until a century later. The economic world was seen as a collection of national states, each government actively competing for shares of a finite amount of wealth. What one nation gained was automatically another nation's loss. Each nation's goal was to become as economically self-sufficient as possible while maintaining a favorable balance of trade with other countries (that is, exporting more than it imported). Colonies had an important role to play in such a scheme. They could supply the mother country with valuable raw materials to be consumed at home or sent abroad, and they could serve as a market for the mother country's manufactured goods.

Parliament applied mercantilist thinking to the American colonies in a series of laws known as the Navigation Acts. The major acts—passed in 1651, 1660, 1663, and 1673—established three main principles. First, only English or colonial merchants and ships could engage in trade in the colonies. Second, certain valuable American products could be sold only in the mother country. At first these "enumerated" goods were wool, sugar, tobacco, indigo, ginger, and dyes; later acts added rice, naval stores (masts, spars, pitch, tar, and turpentine), copper, and furs to the list. Third, all foreign goods destined for sale in the colonies had to be shipped via England and were subject to English import duties. Some years later, a new series of laws declared a fourth principle: the colonies could not make or export items (such as wool cloth-

Navigation Acts

A few women joined the ranks of those seventeenth-century English people who chose to seek their fortunes by becoming pirates. Two of the most notorious, Mary Read and Anne Bonney, are shown here in illustrations taken from a 1724 book that recounted their exploits in semifictional form. *Rare Books Division, New York Public Library, Astor, Lenox, and Tilden Foundations.*

ing, hats, and iron) that competed with English products.

The intention of the Navigation Acts was clear: American trade was to center on England. The mother country was to benefit from colonial imports and exports both. England had first claim on the most valuable colonial exports, and all foreign imports into the colonies had to pass through England first, enriching its customs revenues in the process. Moreover, English and colonial shippers were given a monopoly of the American trade. Even so, the American provinces, especially those in the north, produced many goods that were not enumerated—such as fish, flour, and barrel staves. These products could be traded directly to foreign purchasers as long as they were carried in English or American ships.

The English authorities soon learned that it was easier to write mercantilist legislation than to enforce it. The many harbors of the American coast provided ready havens for smugglers, and colonial officials often looked the other way when illegally imported goods were offered for sale. In ports such as Curaçao in the Dutch West Indies, American merchants could easily dispose of enumerated goods and purchase foreign items on which duty had not been paid. Consequently, Parliament in 1696 enacted another Navigation Act designed to strengthen enforcement of the first four. This law established in America a number of vice-admiralty courts, which operated without juries. In England such courts dealt only with cases involving piracy, vessels taken as wartime prizes, and the like. But since American juries had already demonstrated a tendency to favor local smugglers over customs officers (a colonial customs service was started in 1671), Parliament decided to remove Navigation Act cases from the regular colonial courts.

England took another major step in colonial administration in 1696 by creating the fifteen-member Board of Trade and Plantations, which thereafter served as the chief organ of government con-

STUART MONARCHS OF ENGLAND, 1660–1714		
Monarch	Reign	Relation to Predecessor
Charles II	1660–1685	Son
James II	1685–1688	Brother
Mary	1688–1694	Daughter
William	1688–1702	Son-in-law
Anne	1702–1714	Sister, sister-in-law

Board of Trade cerned with the American colonies. (Previously no one body had had that responsibility.) It gathered information, reviewed Crown appointments in America, scrutinized legislation passed by colonial assemblies, supervised trade policies, and advised successive ministries on colonial issues. Still, the Board of Trade did not have any direct powers of enforcement. It also shared jurisdiction over American affairs not only with the customs service and the navy but also with the secretary of state for the southern department, the member of the ministry responsible for the colonies. In short, although the Stuart monarchs' reforms considerably improved the quality of colonial administration, supervision of the American provinces remained decentralized and haphazard.

Even inefficient enforcement of the Navigation Acts was too much for many colonists, and they resisted the laws in various ways—not only by attempting to circumvent them but also by formally protesting to the government in London. Governor William Berkeley of Virginia was among the most vocal critics of the new laws. Tobacco prices declined significantly after 1660 because of vastly increased production, causing serious economic problems in both Virginia and Maryland. Thus when English officials asked Berkeley about the state of trade in Virginia, he responded unhesitatingly that great hardship had resulted from "that severe act of Parliament which excludes us from having any commerce with any nation in Europe but our own," thereby preventing the development of new markets for tobacco. But such protests had little effect, chiefly because policymakers in England were more concerned about preserving the revenues obtained from colonial trade than about any adverse impact the acts might have on the colonies.

Colonial Political Development and Imperial Reorganization

English officials who dealt with colonial administration in the 1670s and 1680s were confronted not only by resistance to the Navigation Acts but also by a bewildering array of colonial governments. Massachusetts Bay still functioned under its original corporate charter, and its New England neighbors Connecticut and Rhode Island had been granted similar corporate status by Charles II in 1662 and 1663, respectively. Virginia was a royal colony, and New York became one when its proprietor ascended the throne in 1685 as James II. All the other mainland settlements were proprietorships, which had varying political structures, for the royal charters gave the proprietors a great deal of leeway in governing their possessions.

Still, in political structure the colonies shared certain characteristics. Most were ruled by a governor and a two-house legislature. In New England,

Colonial Political Structures the governors were elected by property-holding men or by the legislature; in the Chesapeake, they were appointed by the king or the proprietor. A council, elected in some colonies and appointed in others, advised the governor on matters of policy and sometimes served as the province's highest court. The council also had a legislative function: initially its members met jointly with representatives elected by their districts to debate and vote on laws affecting the colony. But as time passed, the fundamental differences between the two legislative groups' purposes and constituencies led them to separate into two distinct houses. In Virginia that important event occurred in 1663; in Massachusetts Bay it had happened earlier, in 1644. Thus developed the two-house legislature still used in almost all of the states.

While provincial governments were taking shape, so too were local political institutions. In New England, elected selectmen governed the towns at first, but by the end of the century the town meeting, held at least annually and attended by most adult white townsmen, handled most matters of local concern. In the Chesapeake the same function was performed by the judges of the county court and by the parish vestry, a group of laymen charged with overseeing church affairs, whose power also encompassed secular concerns.

By late in the seventeenth century, therefore, the American colonists were accustomed to exercising a considerable degree of local political autonomy. The tradition of consent was especially firmly established in New England. Massachusetts, Connecticut, and Rhode Island were, in effect, independent entities, subject neither to the direct authority of the king nor to a proprietor. Everywhere in the English colonies, white males owning more property than a stated minimum (which varied from province to province) expected to have an influential voice in how they were governed, and especially in how they were taxed.

After James II became king, these expectations clashed with those of the monarch. The new king and his successors sought to bring order to the apparently chaotic state of colonial administration by tightening the reins of government and reducing the colonies' political autonomy. (Simultaneously, they used the Navigation Acts to reduce the colonies' economic autonomy.) They began to chip away at the privileges granted in colonial charters and to reclaim proprietorships for the Crown. New Hampshire (1679), its parent colony Massachusetts

(1691), New Jersey (1702), and the Carolinas (1729) all became royal colonies. The charters of Rhode Island, Connecticut, Maryland, and Pennsylvania were temporarily suspended as well but were ultimately restored to their original status.

The most drastic reordering of colonial administration was attempted in 1686 through 1689, and its chief target was Puritan New England. Reports from

Dominion of New England

America had convinced English officials that New England was a hotbed of smuggling. Moreover, the Puritans refused to allow freedom of religion and insisted on maintaining laws that often ran counter to English practice. New England thus seemed an appropriate place to exert English authority with greater vigor. The charters of all the colonies from New Jersey to Maine (then part of Massachusetts) were revoked and a Dominion of New England was established in 1686 (see map, page 44). Sir Edmund Andros, the governor, was given immense power: all the assemblies were dissolved, and he needed only the consent of an appointed council to make laws and levy taxes.

New Englanders endured Andros's autocratic rule for more than two years. Then came the dramatic news that James II had been overthrown in a bloodless rebellion (known as the Glorious Revolution) and had been replaced on the throne by his daughter Mary and her husband, the Dutch prince William of Orange. Seizing the opportunity to rid themselves of the hated Dominion, New Englanders jailed Andros and his associates, proclaimed their loyalty to William and Mary, and wrote to England for instructions about the form of government they should adopt. Most of Massachusetts Bay's political leaders hoped that the new monarchs would renew their original charter, which had been revoked in 1684 prior to the establishment of the Dominion.

In other American colonies, too, the Glorious Revolution proved to be a signal for revolt. In Maryland the Protestant Association overturned

Glorious Revolution in America

the government of the Catholic proprietor, and in New York Jacob Leisler, a militia officer of German origin, assumed control of the government. Like the New Englanders, the Maryland and New York rebels allied themselves with the supporters of William and

Mary. They saw themselves as carrying out the colonial phase of the English revolt against Stuart absolutism. The problem was that the new monarchs and their colonial administrators did not view American events in the same light.

The Glorious Revolution occurred in the mother country because members of Parliament feared that once again, just as in Charles I's reign, a Stuart king was attempting to seize absolute power. James II, like his father, had levied taxes without parliamentary approval. He had also announced his conversion to Roman Catholicism. The Glorious Revolution affirmed the supremacy of Parliament and of Protestantism when Parliament offered the throne to the Protestants William and Mary. But—and this was the difficulty for the colonists—it did not directly affect English policies toward America. William and Mary, like James II, believed that the colonies were too independent and that England should exercise tighter control over its unruly American possessions.

Consequently, the only American rebellion that received royal sanction was that in Maryland, which was approved primarily because of its anti-Catholic thrust. In New York, Jacob Leisler was hanged for treason, and Massachusetts (including the formerly independent jurisdiction of Plymouth) became a royal colony, complete with an appointed governor. The province was allowed to retain its town meeting system of local government and to elect its council, but the new charter issued in 1691 removed the traditional Puritan religious test for voting. An Anglican parish was even established in the heart of Boston. The "city upon a hill," at least as envisioned by John Winthrop, was no more.

Compounding New England's difficulties in a time of political uncertainty and economic change was a war with the French and their Indian allies. King Louis XIV of France allied himself with the deposed James II, and England declared war on France in the summer of 1689. In Europe, the conflict, which lasted until 1697, was known as the War of the League of Augsburg, but the colonists called it King William's War. The American phase of the war was fought chiefly on the northern frontiers of New England and New York; among the English settlements devastated by enemy attacks in 1690 were Schenectady, New York, and Casco (Falmouth), Maine. Expeditions organized by the colonies against Montreal and Quebec that same year both failed miserably, and throughout the rest of the war New England found itself on the defensive.

In this period of extreme stress there occurred an outbreak of witchcraft accusations in Salem Village (now Danvers), Massachusetts, a rural community adjoining the bustling port of Salem Town. Like their contemporaries elsewhere, seventeenth-century New Englanders believed in the existence of witches, whose evil powers came from the Devil. If people could not find rational explanations for their troubles, they tended to suspect they were bewitched. Before 1689, 103 New Englanders, most of them middle-aged women, had been accused of practicing witchcraft, chiefly by neighbors who had suffered misfortunes they attributed to the suspected witch, with whom they usually had an ongoing dispute. Although most such accusations occurred singly, on occasion a witchcraft panic could result when one charge set off a chain reaction of similar charges (that happened in Hartford, Connecticut, in 1662 and 1663, for example). But nothing else in New England's history ever came close to matching the Salem Village cataclysm.

Witchcraft in Salem Village

The crisis began in early 1692 when a group of adolescent girls accused some older women of having bewitched them. Before the hysteria spent itself ten months later, nineteen people (including several men, most of them related to accused female witches) had been hanged, another pressed to death by heavy stones, and more than one hundred persons jailed. Historians have proposed various explanations for this puzzling episode, but to be understood it must be seen in its proper context—one of political and legal disorder, of Indian war, and of religious and economic change. It must have seemed to Puritan New Englanders as though their entire world was collapsing. At the very least they could have had no sense of security about their future.

Nowhere was that more true than in Salem Village, a farming town torn between old and new styles of life because of its position on the edge of a commercial center. And for no residents of the village was a feeling of insecurity sharper than it was for the girls who issued the initial accusations. Many of them had been orphaned in the recent Indian attacks on Maine; they were living in Salem Village as domestic servants. Their involvement

No seventeenth-century New Englander ever drew a picture of a witchcraft trial or execution, but an artist did record the hanging of several witches in England, ca. 1650. The multiple executions of Salem witches in the summer of 1692 probably resembled this gallows scene. *Essex Institute*.

with witchcraft began when they experimented with fortunetelling as a means of foreseeing their futures, in particular the identity of their eventual husbands. As the most powerless people in a town apparently powerless to affect its fate, they offered their fellow New Englanders a compelling explanation for the seemingly endless chain of troubles afflicting them: their province was under direct attack from the Devil and his legion of witches. Accordingly, it is not perhaps the number of witchcraft prosecutions that seems surprising but rather their abrupt cessation in the fall of 1692.

There were two reasons for the rapid end to the crisis. First, the accusers had grown too bold. When they started to charge some of the colony's most distinguished and respected residents with being in league with the Devil, members of the ruling elite began to doubt their veracity. Second, the new royal charter was fully implemented in late 1692, ending the worst period of political uncertainty and removing a major source of psychological stress. The war continued, and the Puritans were not en-

tirely pleased with the charter, but at least order had formally been restored.

Over the course of the next three decades, Massachusetts and the rest of the English colonies in America accommodated themselves to the new imperial order. Most colonists did not like the class of alien officials who arrived in America determined to implement the policies of king and Parliament, but they adjusted to their demands and to the trade restrictions imposed by the Navigation Acts. They fought another imperial war—the War of the Spanish Succession, or Queen Anne's War—from 1702 to 1713, without enduring the psychological stress of the first, despite the heavy economic burdens the conflict imposed. Colonists who allied themselves with royal government received patronage in the form of offices and land grants and composed "court parties" that supported English officials. Others, who were perhaps less fortunate in their friends, or more principled in defense of colonial autonomy (opinions differ), made up the opposition, or "country" interest. By the end of the first quarter of the eighteenth century, most men in both groups were native-born Americans, members of elite families whose wealth derived from staple-crop production in the South and commerce in the North.

During the eighty years from 1640 to 1720, then, the European colonies in America changed dramatically. From a small outpost in Santa Fé, New Mexico, the Spanish had expanded their influence throughout the region as far east as Texas and—by just after midcentury—as far north as California. The French had moved from a few settlements along the St. Lawrence to dominate the length of the Mississippi River and the entire Great Lakes region. Both groups of colonists lived in close conjunction with Indian nations and were dependent on the Indians' labor and goodwill. The French and Spanish could not fully control their Indian allies—and the French did not even try to do so.

In 1640 there were just two isolated centers of English population, New England and the Chesapeake. In 1720, nearly the entire east coast of mainland North America was in English hands, and Indian power east of the Appalachian Mountains had been broken. What had been a migrant population was now mostly American-born; economies originally based on the fur trade had become far more complex and more closely linked with the mother country; and a wide variety of political structures had been reshaped into a more uniform pattern. Yet at the same time the introduction of large-scale slavery into the Chesapeake and the Carolinas had irrevocably differentiated their societies from those of the colonies to the north. Staple-crop production for the market was not the key distinguishing feature of the southern regional economies; rather, their uniqueness lay in their reliance on a racially based system of perpetual servitude.

By 1720, the essential elements of the imperial structure that would govern the English colonies until 1775 were in place. The regional economic systems originating in the late seventeenth and early eighteenth centuries continued to dominate North American life for another century—until after independence had been won. The period from 1640 to 1720, in other words, established the basic economic and political patterns that were to structure all subsequent changes in colonial American society.

Suggestions for Further Reading

General

Charles M. Andrews, *The Colonial Period of American History,* vol. 4 (1938); C. R. Boxer, *The Dutch Seaborne Empire, 1600–1800* (1965); Carl Bridenbaugh, *Cities in the Wilderness: The First Century of Urban Life in America, 1625–1742* (1938); Nicholas Canny and Anthony Pagden, eds., *Colonial Identity in the Atlantic World, 1500–1800* (1987); Wesley Frank Craven, *The Colonies in Transition, 1660–1713* (1968); W. J. Eccles, *The Canadian Frontier, 1534–1760,* rev. ed. (1983); W. J. Eccles, *France in America* (1972); Jack P. Greene and J. R. Pole, eds., *Colonial British America: Essays in the New History of the Early Modern Era* (1984); John J. McCusker and Russell R. Menard, *The Economy of British America, 1607–1789* (1985); Sidney W. Mintz, *Sweetness and Power: The Place of Sugar in Modern History* (1985); Gary Walton and James Shepherd, *The Economic Rise of Early America* (1979).

New Netherland and the Restoration Colonies

Edwin Bronner, *William Penn's "Holy Experiment": The Founding of Pennsylvania, 1681–1701* (1962); Thomas J. Condon, *New York Beginnings: The Commercial Origins of New Netherland* (1968); Wesley Frank Craven, *New Jersey and the English Colonization of North America* (1964); Mary Maples Dunn, *William Penn: Politics and Conscience* (1967); Michael Kammen, *Colonial New York: A History* (1975); Oliver Rink, *Holland on the Hudson: An Economic and Social History of Dutch New York* (1986); Robert C. Ritchie, *The Duke's Province: A Study of Politics and Society in Colonial New York, 1660–1691* (1977); Robert M. Weir, *Colonial South Carolina: A History* (1983).

Africa and the Slave Trade

Jay Coughtry, *The Notorious Triangle: Rhode Island and the African Slave Trade, 1700–1807* (1981); Philip D. Curtin, *The Atlantic Slave Trade: A Census* (1969); David Brion Davis, *The Problem of Slavery in Western Culture* (1966); David W. Galenson, *Traders, Planters, and Slaves: Market Behavior in Early English America* (1986); Henry Gemery and Jan Hogendorn, eds., *The Uncommon Market: Essays in the Economic History of the Atlantic Slave Trade* (1979); Herbert Klein, *The Middle Passage* (1978); Daniel C. Littlefield, *Rice and Slaves: Ethnicity and the Slave Trade in Colonial South Carolina* (1981); Paul Lovejoy, ed., *Africans in Bondage: Studies in Slavery and the Slave Trade* (1986); James Rawley, *The Transatlantic Slave Trade: A History* (1981).

Blacks in Anglo-America

T. H. Breen and Stephen Innes, *"Myne Owne Ground": Race and Freedom on Virginia's Eastern Shore, 1640–1676* (1980); Richard Dunn, *Sugar and Slaves: The Rise of the Planter Class in the English West Indies, 1624–1713* (1972); Lorenzo J. Greene, *The Negro in Colonial New England* (1942); Allan Kulikoff, *Tobacco and Slaves: The Development of Southern Cultures in the Chesapeake, 1680–1800* (1986); Edgar J. McManus, *Black Bondage in the North* (1973); Edmund S. Morgan, *American Slavery, American Freedom: The Ordeal of Colonial Virginia* (1975); Peter H. Wood, *Black Majority: Negroes in Colonial South Carolina from 1670 Through the Stono Rebellion* (1974).

European-Indian Relations

Henry Bowden, *American Indians and Christian Missions: Studies in Cultural Conflict* (1981); Judith K. Brown, "Economic Organization and the Position of Women Among the Iroquois," *Ethnohistory*, 17 (1970), 151–167; David H. Corkran, *The Creek Frontier, 1540–1783* (1967); Verner W. Crane, *The Southern Frontier, 1760–1732* (1929); Francis Jennings, *The Ambiguous Iroquois Empire* (1984); Elizabeth A. H. John, *Storms Brewed in Other Men's Worlds: The Confrontation of Indians, Spanish, and French in the Southwest, 1540–1795* (1975); Douglas Leach, *Flintlock and Tomahawk: New England in King Philip's War* (1958); Daniel Richter and James Merrell, eds., *Beyond the Covenant Chain: The Iroquois and Their Neighbors in Indian America, 1600–1800* (1987); C. A. Weslager, *The Delaware Indians: A History* (1972); J. Leitch Wright, Jr., *The Only Land They Knew: The Tragic Story of the American Indians in the Old South* (1981).

New England

Bernard Bailyn, *The New England Merchants in the Seventeenth Century* (1955); Paul Boyer and Stephen Nissenbaum, *Salem Possessed: The Social Origins of Witchcraft* (1974); Richard Bushman, *From Puritan to Yankee: Character and the Social Order in Connecticut, 1690–1765* (1967); John Demos, *Entertaining Satan: Witchcraft and the Culture of Early New England* (1982); Christine Heyrman, *Commerce and Culture: The Maritime Communities of Colonial Massachusetts, 1690–1750* (1984); Carol Karlsen, *The Devil in the Shape of a Woman: Witchcraft in Early New England* (1987); Perry Miller, *The New England Mind: From Colony to Province* (1953); Robert Pope, *The Half-Way Covenant: Church Membership in Puritan New England* (1969); Laurel Thatcher Ulrich, *Good Wives: Image and Reality in the Lives of Women in Northern New England, 1650–1750* (1982).

Colonial Politics

Lois Green Carr and David W. Jordan, *Maryland's Revolution of Government, 1689–1692* (1974); Richard P. Johnson, *Adjustment to Empire: The New England Colonies, 1675–1715* (1981); David W. Jordan, *Foundations of Representative Government in Maryland, 1632–1715* (1987); David S. Lovejoy, *The Glorious Revolution in America* (1972); Jack M. Sosin, *English America and Imperial Inconstancy: The Rise of Provincial Autonomy, 1696–1715* (1985); Jack M. Sosin, *English America and the Revolution of 1688: Royal Administration and the Structure of Provincial Government* (1982); Jack M. Sosin, *English America and the Restoration Monarchy of Charles II: Transatlantic Politics, Commerce, and Kingship* (1980).

Imperial Trade and Administration

Lawrence W. Harper, *The English Navigation Laws: A Seventeenth-Century Experiment in Social Engineering* (1939); Michael Kammen, *Empire and Interest: The American Colonies and the Politics of Mercantilism* (1970); Marcus Rediker, *Between the Devil and the Deep Blue Sea: Merchant Seamen, Pirates, and the Anglo-American Maritime World, 1700–1750* (1987); Robert C. Ritchie, *Captain Kidd and the War Against the Pirates* (1986); I. K. Steele, *Politics of Colonial Policy: The Board of Trade in Colonial Administration* (1968); Stephen Saunders Webb, *1676: The End of American Independence* (1984); Stephen Saunders Webb, *The Governors-General: The English Army and the Definition of the Empire, 1569–1681* (1979).

In June 1744, Dr. Alexander Hamilton, a thirty-four-year-old Scottish-born physician living in Annapolis, Maryland, paid his first visit to Philadelphia. There he encountered two quite different worlds. One consisted of men of his own status, the merchants and professionals he called "the better sort." Hamilton mingled with them at the Governor's Club, "a society of gentlemen that met at a tavern every night and converse on various subjects." The night Hamilton attended, the "entertaining" discussion focused on Cervantes and some English poets.

Hamilton reacted differently to the other world of Philadelphia, that composed of people he variously termed "rabble," "a strange medley," or "comicall, grotesque phizzes." Most spoke, he thought, "ignorantly," regardless of the subject. One evening he dined at a tavern with "a very mixed company" of twenty-five men. "There were Scots, English, Dutch, Germans, and Irish; there were Roman Catholics, Church men, Presbyterians, Quakers, Newlightmen, Methodists, Seventh day men, Moravians, Anabaptists and one Jew." Some discussed business, and a few argued about religion, but the "prevailing topick" was politics and the threat of war with France. Hamilton refused to be drawn into any of the conversations. As a gentleman, he consciously set himself apart from ordinary folk, commenting on their behavior but not participating in their exchanges.

And what of the women in Philadelphia? Hamilton met few of them, other than his landlady and one of her friends. "The ladies," he explained, "for the most part, keep at home and seldom appear in the streets, never in publick assemblies except at the churches or meetings." Hamilton was referring to women of "the better sort." He could hardly have walked the streets of the city without seeing many female domestic servants, market women, and wives of ordinary laborers going about their daily chores.

Despite his obvious biases, Dr. Hamilton was an astute observer. The Philadelphians' chief employment, he wrote, "is traffick and mercantile business"; and the richest merchants of all were the Quakers. Members of that sect also controlled the colony's government, but, Hamilton noted, "the standing or falling of the Quakers in the House of Assembly depends upon their mak-

3

GROWTH AND DIVERSITY, 1720–1770

Embroidered silk picture by Lydia Bill, made in Salem, Massachusetts, between 1775 and 1779. *The Henry Francis du Pont Winterthur Museum.*

ing sure the interest of the Palatines [Germans] in this province, who of late have turned so numerous that they can sway the votes which way they please." And Hamilton deplored the impact on the city of the Great Awakening, a religious revival then sweeping the colonies. "I never was in a place so populous where the gout [taste] for publick gay diversions prevailed so little," he remarked. "There is no such thing as assemblys of the gentry among them, either for dancing or musick; these they have an utter aversion to ever since Whitefield preached among them."

Hamilton's comments provide an excellent introduction to mid-eighteenth-century American life, for the patterns he observed in Philadelphia were not unique to that city. Although ethnic diversity was especially pronounced in urban areas, by midcentury non-English migrants were settling in many regions of the mainland colonies. Their arrival not only added to the total population, it also altered political balances worked out before 1720 and affected the religious climate by increasing the number of different sects. The diverse group of men Hamilton encountered in that tavern could have been duplicated in other cities and even in some rural areas.

Hamilton correctly recognized that the Quakers maintained control of Pennsylvania politics because they had managed to win the support of recent German immigrants. The ruling elites in other provinces handled immigrants in a way that eventually was to backfire on them: they ignored the newcomers, refusing to allow them adequate representation and government services. That led to a series of violent clashes after midcentury. Through these tactics such elites, now primarily native-born, established stable political regimes in each of the colonies. They contended with English-born governors and councillors for control of their colonies' government machinery, and in some cases they won. These victories were to serve them well when they began battling for independence later in the century.

In addition, Hamilton accurately assessed the importance of commerce in Americans' lives. The web of imperial trade woven before 1720 became even more complex and all-encompassing during the next fifty years. Americans of all descriptions were tied to an international commercial system that fluctuated wildly for reasons having little to do with the colonies, but with inescapable effects. As

the colonies would learn when they attempted to break their trade ties with Great Britain at the time of the Revolution, they were heavily dependent on England for both imported manufactured goods and markets for their exports.

A well-educated man, Dr. Hamilton was heavily influenced by the Enlightenment, the major European intellectual movement of the day. The Enlightenment stressed reason and empirical knowledge, deliberately discarding superstition and instinct as guides to human behavior. Hamilton, like other enlightened thinkers, believed above all in rationality. To him, God was a distant presence who had ordered the world, setting forth natural laws that humans could discover through careful investigation and logical thought. From this perspective came Hamilton's distaste for the Great Awakening, since that revival drew primarily on the Calvinistic concept of a God that people could never fully comprehend. Moreover, the hallmark of the Great Awakening was emotion, expressed in a conversion experience. To a believer in the primacy of reason, the passions of the newly converted were more than foolish—they were idiotic.

The Enlightenment affected Dr. Hamilton in another way as well, for it helped to create the elite world of which he was a part, a world that seemed so different from the world of ordinary folk. Wealthy, well-read Americans participated in a transatlantic intellectual community, whereas most colonists of "the lesser sort" could neither read nor write. Hamilton and his peers lived in comfortable houses and entertained at lavish parties; most colonists struggled just to make ends meet. Hamilton could take a leisurely four-month journey for his health (his visit to Philadelphia was but one stop on a long trip), but most Americans had to work daily from dawn to dark. The eighteenth century, then, brought an increasing gap between rich and poor. The colonies had always been composed of people of different ranks, but by the last half of the century the social and economic distance between those ranks had widened noticeably.

Above all, after 1720 the colonies present a picture of growth and diversity. Population increased dramatically, and the area settled by whites and blacks expanded until it filled almost all of the region between the Appalachian Mountains and the Atlantic Ocean, displacing the Indians who had previously lived there. At the same time, the colonies became more diverse; the two original re-

1690	Locke's *Essay Concerning Human Understanding*
1720–21	Smallpox inoculation controversy (Boston)
1720–40	Black population of Chesapeake begins to grow by natural increase
1739	Stono Rebellion George Whitefield arrives in America; Great Awakening broadens
1739–48	King George's War
1741	Slave revolt scare (New York City)
1765–66	Hudson River land riots
1767–69	Regulator movement (South Carolina)
1771	North Carolina Regulators defeated at Battle of Alamance

gional economies (the Chesapeake and New England) became four (those two plus the middle colonies and the Lower South). Before 1720, the colonies were still inhabited mainly by English, African, and Indian peoples; just half a century later, a large proportion of the white population was of non-English origin. Many of the colonies were home to a variety of ethnic groups and religious sects. The urban population, though still tiny by today's standards, grew considerably larger after 1720; and in the cities were found the greatest extremes of wealth and poverty. Such changes transformed the character of England's North American possessions. The colonies that revolted in unison against British rule after 1765 were very different from the colonies that revolted separately against Stuart absolutism in 1689.

Population Growth and Ethnic Diversity

One of the most striking characteristics of the mainland colonies in the eighteenth century was their rapid population growth. Only about 250,000 European- and African-Americans resided in the colonies in 1700; thirty years later that number had more than doubled, and by 1775 it had become 2.5 million. Although migration accounted for a considerable share of the growth, most of it resulted from natural increase. Once the difficult early decades of settlement in each colony had passed, the American population doubled approximately every twenty-five years. Such a rate of growth was unparalleled in human history until very recent times. It had a variety of causes, the chief one being the youthful marriage age of women (early twenties for whites, late teens for blacks). Since married women became pregnant every two or three years, women normally bore five to ten children. Because the colonies, especially those north of Virginia, were healthful places to live, a large proportion of the children born reached maturity and began families of their own. As a result, in 1775 about half the American population, white and black, was under sixteen years old. (In 1980, by contrast, only about one-third of the American population was under sixteen.)

Such a dramatic phenomenon did not escape the attention of contemporaries. As early as the 1720s Americans began to point with pride to their fertility, citing population growth as evidence of the advantageous conditions in the colonies. In 1755 Benjamin Franklin published his *Observations Concerning the Increase of Mankind,* which predicted that in another century "the greatest Number of Englishmen will be on this Side the Water. What an

The portrait of an eighteenth-century family shows the typical colonial childbearing pattern in the large number of "stairstep" children, born at approximately two-year intervals. *National Gallery of Art, Washington, D.C., Gift of Edgar William and Bernice Chrysler Garbisch.*

Accession of Power to the British Empire by Sea as well as Land!" he rhapsodized. "What Increase of Trade and Navigation!"

Franklin's purpose in writing his *Observations* was to argue that Britain should prevent Germans from migrating to Pennsylvania. Since the English population in America was increasing so rapidly, he asked, "Why should the Palatine Boors be suffered to swarm into our Settlements? . . . Why should Pennsylvania, founded by the English, become a Colony of Aliens, who will shortly be so numerous as to Germanize us instead of our Anglifying them, and will never adopt our Language or Customs?"

Whether Franklin's fears were shared by a majority of his American-born contemporaries is not known. But the eighteenth-century migration to the English colonies was massive; it comprised approximately 375,000 whites and 275,000 blacks (see maps). Because some of the

▶ **Newcomers from Europe and Africa**

whites (for example, convicts sentenced to exile by English courts) and all the blacks did not choose freely to come to the colonies, nearly half the migrants moved to America against their will. That contrasts sharply with the nineteenth-century pattern of voluntary migration from Europe and Asia discussed later in this book.

Africans made up the largest single racial or ethnic group that came to the colonies during the eighteenth century. More important than the number of black migrants, however, is the fact that in the first half of the century the black population of the Chesapeake began to grow faster through increase than through importation. In the slaveholding societies of South America and the Caribbean, a surplus of males over females and appallingly high mortality rates together produced very different slave population patterns. There, only large, continuing importations from Africa were able to maintain the enslaved work force at adequate levels. South Carolina, where rice cultivation was difficult and unhealthy (chiefly because malaria-carrying mosquitoes bred in the rice swamps), and where planters preferred to purchase males, bore some resemblance to such colonies in that it too required a constant influx of Africans. But in the Chesapeake the black population grew primarily through natural increase after 1740. That increase had significant implications for the society and economy of the region (see pages 83–84).

The largest group of white non-English immigrants to America was the Scotch-Irish, chiefly descended from Presbyterian Scots who had settled

> **Scotch-Irish, Germans, and Scots**

in northern regions of Ireland during the seventeenth century. Perhaps as many as 250,000 Scotch-Irish people moved to the colonies. Fleeing economic distress and religious discrimination—Irish law favored Anglicans over Presbyterians and other dissenters—they were lured as well by hopes of obtaining land. The Scotch-Irish often arrived in Philadelphia. They moved west and south from that city, settling chiefly in the western portions of Pennsylvania, Maryland, Virginia, and the Carolinas. Frequently unable to afford to buy any acreage, they squatted on land belonging to Indian tribes, land speculators, or colonial governments.

The German migrants who so worried Franklin numbered about 100,000. Most of them emigrated from the Rhineland between 1730 and 1755, usually arriving in Philadelphia, like the Scotch-Irish. They became known locally as the Pennsylvania Dutch (a corruption of *Deutsch,* the Germans' word for themselves); late in the century they and their descendants made up one-third of Pennsylvania's residents. But many other Germans moved west and then south along the eastern slope of the Appalachian Mountains, eventually finding homes in western Maryland and Virginia. Others sailed first to Charleston or Savannah and settled in the interior of South Carolina or Georgia. The German immigrants belonged to a wide variety of Protestant sects—primarily Lutheran, German Reformed, and Moravian—and therefore added to the already substantial religious diversity of the middle colonies.

The 50,000 or more Scots who came directly to America from Scotland should not be confused with the Scotch-Irish. Many early Scottish immigrants were supporters of Stuart claimants to the throne of England, or Jacobites (so called because

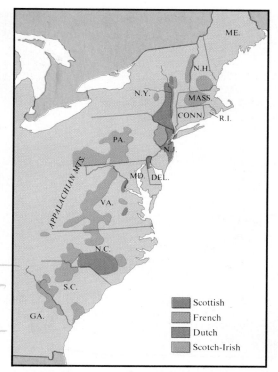

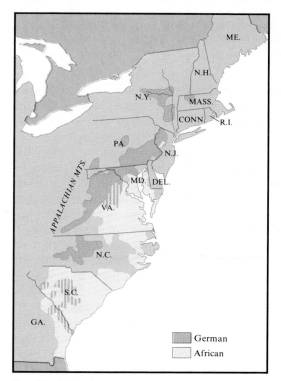

Non-English Ethnic Groups in the British Colonies, ca. 1775

German migrants to England's American colonies maintained many of their traditional customs in their new homeland, among them the production of decorated baptismal certificates like this one. Such documents are called *fraktur* (illuminated writing). *The Henry Francis du Pont Winterthur Museum.*

the Latin name for James was *Jacobus*). After the death of William and Mary's successor Queen Anne in 1714, the British throne passed to the German house of Hanover, in the person of King George I. In 1715 and again in 1745, Jacobite rebels attempted unsuccessfully to capture the Crown for the Stuart pretender, and many were exiled to America as punishment. Most of the Jacobites settled in North Carolina. Ironically, they tended to become loyalists during the Revolutionary War because of their strong commitment to monarchy.

The most concentrated period of immigration to the colonies fell between 1760 and 1775. Tough times in the home country led many to decide to seek a better life in America. In those fifteen years alone arrived more than 220,000 persons—or 10 percent of the entire population of British North America. At least 125,000 of the migrants came from the British Isles: 55,000 Scotch-Irish (2 percent of the population of Ireland), 40,000 Scots (3 percent of the population of Scotland), and over 30,000 English people. To them were added at least 12,000 Germans and 85,000 Africans. Late-arriving

free immigrants had little choice but to remain in the cities or move to the far frontiers of settlement, for land elsewhere was fully occupied. On the frontiers they became the tenants of or bought property from land speculators who had purchased giant tracts in the (usually vain) hope of making a fortune.

Because of the migration patterns of the different ethnic groups and the concentration of slaveholding in the South, half the colonial population south of New England was of non-English origin by 1775. Whether the migrants assimilated readily into Anglo-American culture depended on the patterns of settlement, the size of the group, and the strength of the migrants' ties to their common culture. For example, the Huguenots were French Protestants who fled religious persecution in their homeland after 1685. They settled in tiny enclaves in American cities like Charleston and New York but were unable to sustain either their language or their distinctive religious practices. Within two generations they were almost wholly absorbed into Anglo-American culture. The equally small group of colonial Jews, by contrast, maintained a separate identity. The Jews in early America were Sephardic, most of them descended from persons who had migrated to the Netherlands to escape persecution in Spain and Portugal and then later moved to the Dutch colonies in the New World. In a few cities—most notably New York and Newport, Rhode Island—they established synagogues and worked actively to preserve their culture (for example, by opposing intermarriage with Christians).

Members of the larger groups of migrants (the Germans, Scotch-Irish, and Scots) found it easier to sustain Old World ways if they wished. Countless local areas of the colonies were settled almost exclusively by one group or another. Near Frederick, Maryland, a visitor would have heard more German than English; in Anson and Cumberland counties, North Carolina, that same visitor might have thought she was in Scotland. Where migrants from different countries settled in the same region, ethnic antagonisms often surfaced. One German clergyman, for example, explained his efforts to stop German young people from marrying persons of different ethnic origins by asserting that the Scotch-Irish were "lazy, dissipated and poor" and that "it is very seldom that German and English blood is happily united in wedlock."

Recognizing that it was to their benefit to keep other racial and ethnic groups divided, the dominant white elites on occasion deliberately fostered such antagonisms. When the targets of their policies were European migrants, the goal was the maintenance of political and economic power. When the targets were Indians and blacks, as they were in South Carolina, the stakes were considerably higher. In 1758 one official remarked, "It has been allways the policy of this government to create an aversion in them [Indians] to Negroes." South Carolina whites, a minority of the population, wanted to prevent Indians and blacks from making common cause against them. So that slaves would not run away to join the Indians, whites hired Indians as slave catchers. So that Indians would not trust blacks, whites used blacks as soldiers in Indian wars.

Although the dominant elites probably would have preferred to ignore the colonies' growing racial and ethnic diversity, they could not do so for long and still maintain their power. When such men decided to lead a revolution in the 1770s, they recognized that they needed the support of non-English Americans. Not by chance, then, did they begin to speak of "the rights of man," rather than "English liberties," when they sought recruits for their cause.

Economic Growth and Development

The eighteenth-century American economy was characterized more by sharp fluctuations than by a consistent long-term trend. Those fluctuations had two primary causes: the impact of European wars and variations in the overseas demand for American products. The dramatic increase in colonial population was the only source of stability in the shifting economic climate.

Each year the rising population generated ever-greater demands for goods and services, which led to the development of small-scale colonial manufacturing and to the creation of a complex network of internal trade. As the area of settlement expanded, roads, bridges, mills, and stores were built to serve the new communities. A lively coastal trade developed; by the late 1760s, 54 percent of the vessels leaving Boston harbor were sailing to other mainland colonies rather than to foreign ports. Such ships not only collected goods for export and distributed imports but also sold items made in America. The colonies thus began to move away from their earlier pattern of near-total dependence on Europe for manufactured goods. For the first time, the American population sustained sufficient demand to encourage manufacturing enterprises. The largest indigenous industry was iron making; by 1775, 82 American furnaces and 175 forges were producing more iron than was England itself. Almost all of that iron was for domestic consumption.

The major energizing—yet destabilizing—influence on the colonial economy was foreign trade. Colonial prosperity still depended heavily on overseas demand for American products like tobacco, rice, indigo, fish, and barrel staves, for it was through the sale of such items that the colonists earned the credit they needed to purchase English and European imports. If the demand for American exports slowed, the colonists' income dropped and

Spencer Hall shipyard, Gray's Inn Creek, Kent County, Maryland, about 1760. The earliest known view of a Chesapeake Bay shipyard, this oil painting on a wooden panel shows the wide variety of ships that sailed on the bay, as well as (in the background) lumbermen preparing a supply of timber. *Maryland Historical Society.*

so did their demand for imported goods. Accordingly, even small merchants could be affected by sudden economic downswings they had not anticipated. In 1754, a woman who ran a small dry-goods store in Boston reported that another female merchant had been "obliged to sell all her goods this week" to pay her creditors. "Such things make me double my diligence," she commented, "and endeavor to keep my self as clear [from debt] as is possible."

Despite fluctuations, the economy grew slowly during the eighteenth century. That growth produced higher standards of living for all property-owning Americans. Estate inventories show that in the first two decades of the century households began to acquire amenities like crude earthenware dishes (for eating, food storage, and dairying), chairs, and knives and forks. (Seventeenth-century colonists had used only spoons.) Diet also improved; inventories reveal larger quantities and wider varieties of

Rising Standard of Living

stored foods. After 1750, luxury items like silver plate appeared in the homes of the wealthy, and the "middling sort" started to purchase imported English ceramics and teapots. Even the poorest property owners showed some improvement in the number and type of their household possessions. The rising standard probably resulted from the falling price of British manufactures relative to the income Americans earned from their exports.

Yet the benefits of economic growth were not evenly distributed: wealthy Americans improved their position relative to other colonists. The native-born elite families who dominated American political, economic, and social life by 1750 were those who had begun the century with sufficient capital to take advantage of the changes caused by population growth. They were the urban merchants who exported raw materials and imported luxury goods, the large landowners who rented small farms to immigrant tenants, the slave traders who supplied white planters with their bondspeople, and the owners of rum distilleries. The rise of this group of

Chapter 3: Growth and Diversity, 1720–1770

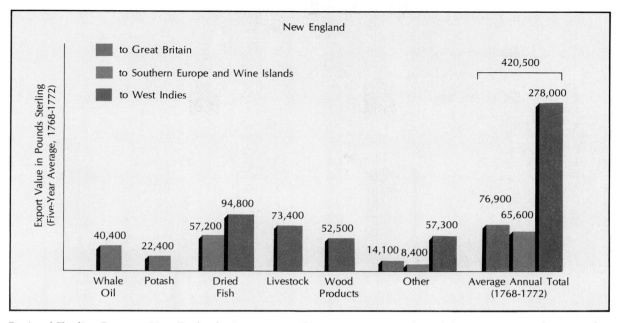

Regional Trading Patterns: New England   *Source: From* Shipping, Maritime Trade, and the Economic Development of Colonial America *by James F. Shepherd and Gary M. Walton. Copyright 1972. Used by permission of Cambridge University Press.*

monied families helped to make the social and economic structure of mid-eighteenth-century America more rigid than before. The new immigrants did not have the opportunities for advancement that had greeted their predecessors. Even so, there seems to have been relatively little poverty among whites in the rural areas in which 90 percent of the colonists lived.

In the cities, however, the story was different. Families of urban laborers lived on the edge of destitution. In Philadelphia, for instance, a male laborer's average annual earnings fell short of the amount needed to supply his family with the bare necessities. Even in a good year, other members of the family (wife or children) had to do wage work; in a bad year, the family could be reduced to beggary. By the 1760s urban poor-relief systems were overwhelmed with applicants for assistance, and some cities began to build workhouses or almshouses to shelter the growing number of poor people. How could that have happened while the lot of the average American family was improving?

> **Urban Poverty**

Three answers to that question suggest themselves. First, although the living standard of property owners was rising, some poor, unskilled colonists were not able to accumulate sufficient resources to acquire property. Such people clustered in the cities, where they could more easily find work. Second, poverty seems to have been a stage that people passed through at certain times in their lives rather than a constant condition. A laborer's family afflicted by disease, a youth not yet established in a trade, a recent immigrant, or an elderly or infirm person would be among the poor at one time but not at another. Again, such people were more likely to be found in a city than in the countryside, and economic conditions in the cities were particularly precarious at midcentury. A third response points to the preponderance of women, mostly widows, among the urban poor. Many married men were killed in colonial wars against European and Indian enemies, thereby creating large numbers of widows. Since women in the eighteenth century, like women today, were paid about half the wages earned by men, it may be that urban poverty was primarily a sex-typed phenomenon, with poor white males being the exception rather than the rule.

Within this overall picture, it is important to distinguish among the various regions: New England,

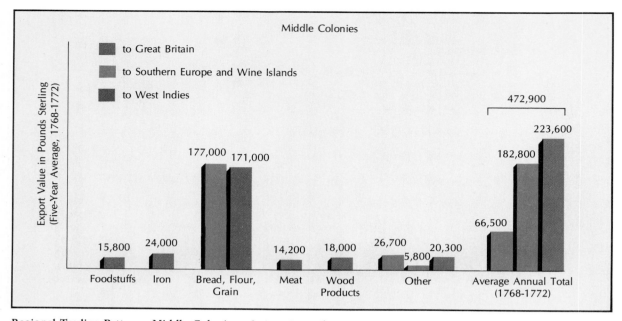

Regional Trading Patterns: Middle Colonies *Source: From* Shipping, Maritime Trade, and the Economic Development of Colonial America *by James F. Shepherd and Gary M. Walton. Copyright 1972. Used by permission of Cambridge University Press.*

the middle colonies, the Chesapeake, and the Lower South (the Carolinas and Georgia). In New England, three elements combined to exert a major influence on economic development: the nature of the landscape, New England's leadership in colonial shipping, and the impact of the imperial wars. New England's soil was rocky and thin, and farmers did not normally produce large surpluses to sell abroad. Farms were worked primarily by family members; the region had relatively few hired laborers. It also had the lowest average wealth per freeholder in the colonies. New England had its share of wealthy men, though; they were the merchants and professionals whose income was drawn from overseas trade, primarily with the West Indies.

Boston's central position in the New England economy and its role as a shipbuilding center ensured that it would be directly affected by any

New England and King George's War

resumption of warfare. In 1739, English vessels began clashing with Spanish ships in the Caribbean, setting off a conflict that would merge with the European War of the Austrian Succession and become known in America as King George's War. Nominally the war was fought to determine who would sit on the Austrian throne,

but one of its causes was European commercial rivalries in the Americas, as the nations jockeyed for position in the lucrative West Indian trade. The war's first impact on Boston's economy was positive. Ships—and sailors—were in great demand to serve as privateers (privately owned vessels authorized by the British to capture the enemy's commercial shipping). Wealthy merchants like Thomas Hancock became even wealthier by profiting from contracts to supply military expeditions.

But Boston suffered heavy losses of manpower both in several Caribbean battles and in forays against the French in Canada after 1744, when France became Spain's ally. The most successful expedition was also the most costly. In 1745 a Massachusetts force captured the French fortress of Louisbourg, which guarded the sea lanes leading to New France, but the colony had to levy heavy taxes on its residents to pay for the expensive effort. For decades Boston's economy felt the continuing effects of King George's War. The city was left with unprecedented numbers of widows and children on its relief rolls, the boom in shipbuilding ended when the war did, and taxes remained high. As a final blow to the colonies, Britain gave Louisbourg back to France in the Treaty of Aix-la-Chapelle (1748).

Chapter 3: Growth and Diversity, 1720–1770

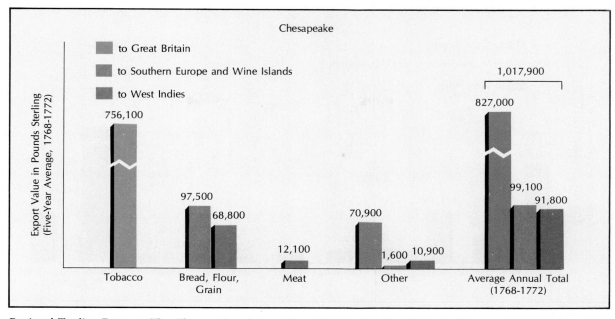

Regional Trading Patterns: The Chesapeake *Source: From* Shipping, Maritime Trade, and the Economic Development of Colonial America *by James F. Shepherd and Gary M. Walton. Copyright 1972. Used by permission of Cambridge University Press.*

Because of one key difference between the northern and middle colonies, the latter were more positively affected by King George's War and its aftermath. That difference was the

> **Prosperity of the Middle Colonies**

greater fertility of the soil in New York and Pennsylvania, where commercial farming was the norm. An average Pennsylvania farm family consumed only 40 percent of what it produced, selling the rest. New York and New Jersey both had many tenant farmers, who rented acreage from large landowners and often paid their rental fees by sharing crops with their landlords. Prosperous property holders were thus in an ideal position to profit from the wartime demand for foodstuffs, especially in the West Indies. After the war a series of poor grain harvests in Europe caused flour prices to rise even more rapidly. Philadelphia and New York, which could draw on large, fertile grain- and livestock-producing areas, took the lead in the foodstuffs trade while Boston, which had no such fertile hinterland, found its economy stagnating.

The increased European demand for grain also had a significant impact on the Chesapeake. After 1745, some Chesapeake planters began to convert tobacco fields to wheat and corn because the price of grain was rising faster than that of tobacco. By diversifying their crops, they could avoid dependency on just one product for their income. But tobacco still ruled the region and remained the largest single export from the mainland colonies. The value of tobacco exports was nearly double that of grain products, the next contender. Thus it is useful to focus briefly on tobacco's continuing impact on the Chesapeake.

Two major results of the region's continuing concentration on tobacco can be discerned in the mid-eighteenth century. The first derived from the

> **Natural Increase of Black Population**

substitution of enslaved for indentured labor. The offspring of slaves were also slaves, whereas the children of servants were free. The consequences of that fact were not clear until the black population of the Chesapeake began to grow through natural increase between 1720 and 1740. It then became evident that a planter who began with only a few slave families could watch the size of his labor force increase steadily without making additional major investments in workers. Not coincidentally, the first truly large Chesapeake plantations appeared in the 1740s. Some years later, the slaveholder Thomas Jefferson indicated that he fully

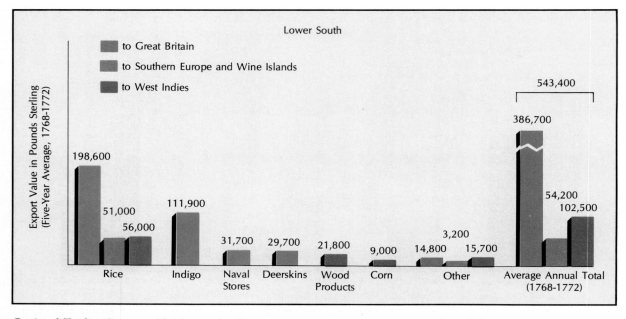

Regional Trading Patterns: The Lower South   *Source: From* Shipping, Maritime Trade, and the Economic Development of Colonial America *by James F. Shepherd and Gary M. Walton. Copyright 1972. Used by permission of Cambridge University Press.*

understood the connections when he declared, "I consider a woman who brings a child every two years more profitable than the best man of the farm. What she produces is an addition to the capital, while his labors disappear in mere consumption."

The second effect of tobacco cultivation on the Chesapeake related to patterns of trade. In the first half of the eighteenth century, wealthy planters served as middlemen in the tobacco trade. They collected and shipped tobacco grown by their less-prosperous neighbors, extended credit to them, and ordered the English imports they wanted. Indeed, they often profited more from fulfilling these functions than from selling their own crops. In the process, though, they went heavily into debt to English merchants, because the entire system operated on credit.

Beginning in the 1740s a major change in the system of marketing tobacco affected all Chesapeake planters, though in varying ways. That change was the entry into the to-

▶ **Scottish Factors**

bacco trade of Scottish merchants, who organized their efforts differently from their London-based competitors. They stationed representatives (called factors) in the Chesapeake to purchase tobacco, ar-

range for shipments, and sell imports. The arrival of the Scottish factors created genuine competition for the first time and thus pushed up tobacco prices. The Scots provided planters with an alternative system for marketing their crops. Large planters could avoid going into debt, and smaller planters could decrease their economic dependence on their wealthier neighbors. When the Chesapeake finally began to develop port towns later in the century, they grew up in centers of Scottish mercantile activity (like Norfolk, Virginia) or in regions that had largely converted to grain production (like Baltimore, Maryland).

The Lower South, like the Chesapeake, depended on staple crops and an enslaved labor force, but its pattern of economic growth was dis-

▶ **Lower South Trade Patterns**

tinctive. In contrast to tobacco prices, which rose slowly through the middle decades of the century, rice prices climbed steeply, doubling by the late 1730s. The sharp rise was caused primarily by a heavy demand for rice in southern Europe. Because Parliament removed rice from the list of enumerated products in 1730, South Carolinians were able to do what colonial tobacco planters never could: trade directly with continental Europe. But dependence on European sales had its drawbacks, as rice growers discovered at the outbreak of King George's War in 1739. Trade with the continent was disrupted, rice prices plummeted, and South Carolina entered a depression from which it did not emerge until the following decade. Still, by the 1760s prosperity had returned because of rapidly rising European demand for South Carolina's exports; indeed, in that period the Lower South experienced more rapid economic growth than the other regions of the colonies. Partly as a result, it had the highest average wealth per freeholder in Anglo-America by the time of the Revolution.

Each region of the colonies, then, had its own economic rhythm derived from the nature of its export trade. King George's War initially helped New England and hurt the Lower South, but in the long run those effects were reversed. In the Chesapeake and the middle colonies, the war initiated a long period of prosperity. The variety of these economic experiences points up a crucial fact about the mainland colonies: they did not compose a unified whole. They were linked economically into regions, but they had few political or social ties beyond or even within those regions. Despite the growing coastal trade, the individual colonies' economic fortunes depended not on their neighbors in America but rather on the shifting markets of Europe and the West Indies. Had it not been for an unprecedented crisis in the British imperial system (which is discussed in Chapter 4), it is hard to see how they could have been persuaded to join in a common endeavor. Even with that impetus they found unity difficult to maintain.

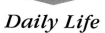

Daily Life

The basic unit of colonial society was the household. Headed by a white male (or perhaps his widow), the household was the chief mechanism of production and consumption. Its members—bound by ties of blood or servitude—worked together to produce goods for consumption or sale. The white male head of the household represented it to the outside world, serving in the militia or political posts, casting the household's sole vote in elections. He managed the finances and held legal authority over the rest of the family—his wife, his

children, and his servants or slaves. (Eighteenth-century Americans used the word *family* for people who lived together in one house, whether or not they were blood kin.) Such households were considerably larger than American families today; in 1790, the average home contained 5.7 whites. Most of those large families were nuclear—that is, they did not include extended kin like aunts, uncles, or grandparents.

The vast majority of colonial families—more than 90 percent of them—lived in rural areas. Therefore nearly all adult white men were farmers and all adult white women farm wives. Though men might work as millers, blacksmiths, or carpenters, and women might sell surplus farm produce to neighbors, they typically did so in addition to their primary agricultural tasks. In colonial America, as in the societies discussed in Chapter 1, household tasks were allocated by sex. The master, his sons, and his male servants or slaves performed one set of chores; the mistress, her daughters, and her female servants or slaves, an entirely different set. So rigid were the gender classifications that when households for some reason lacked a master or mistress, the appropriate jobs were not done. For example, a foreign traveler visiting a Pennsylvania farm remarked that its owner, a bachelor, did not keep poultry or make cheese or clothing because "these domestic farm industries . . . can be carried on well only by women." Only in emergencies and for brief periods of time would women do "men's work" or men do women's.

The mistress of the rural household was responsible for what were termed indoor affairs. She and her female helpers prepared the food, cleaned the house, did the laundry, and often made the clothing. In eighteenth-century America, these basic chores were complex and time-consuming. Preparing food involved planting and cultivating a garden, harvesting and preserving vegetables, salting and smoking meat, drying apples and pressing cider, milking cows and making butter and cheese, not to mention cooking and baking. Making clothes (the chief job of daughters) meant processing raw wool and flax fibers, spinning thread, weaving cloth, dyeing and softening the cloth, and finally cutting out and sewing garments by hand. No wonder one harried Long Island housewife filled her diary in 1768

Sexual Division of Labor Among White Americans

In 1775, a Connecticut woman, Prudence Punderson, created this needlework picture, which she entitled *The First, Second, and Last Scene of Mortality*. At right, she depicted a baby tended by a black servant; at center, a mature woman doing needlework; and at left, a coffin. Thus she summed up a woman's life from birth to the grave, with traditionally female work—like her picture itself—at its core. *Connecticut Historical Society, Hartford.*

and 1769 with such entries as these: "It has been a tiresome day it is now Bedtime and I have not had won minutts rest"; "full of fretting discontent dirty and miserabel both yesterday and today."

The head of the household and his male helpers, responsible for outdoor affairs, also had heavy workloads. They had to plant and cultivate the fields, build fences, chop wood for the fireplace, harvest and market crops, and butcher cattle and hogs to provide the household with meat. Only in the plantation South and in northern cities could even a few adult white males lead lives free from arduous physical labor. Indeed, so extensive was the work involved in maintaining a farm household that a married couple could not do it alone. They had to have help—if not children, then servants or slaves.

Farm households were governed by the seasons and by the hours of daylight. (Candles too had to be manufactured at home; they were too precious to

Rhythms of Rural Life

be wasted, so most people rose and went to bed with the sun.) Men and boys had the most leisure in the winter, when there were no crops that needed care. Women and girls were freest in the summer, before embarking on autumn food preservation and winter spinning and weaving. Other activities, including education, had to be subordinated to seasonal work. Thus farm boys studied in the winter, and their sisters did so in the summer. The seasons also affected travel plans. Because the roads were muddy in spring and fall, most visiting took place in summer and, in the North, in winter, when sleighs could be used.

Because of the isolation and heavy workloads of farm households, rural folk took advantage of every possible opportunity for socializing. Men taking grain to mills would stop at a crossroads tavern for a drink and conversation with friends. Women gathering to assist at childbirth would drink tea and exchange news. Barbecues and week-long house parties were popular among southern planter families. The Reverend Charles Woodmason, an Anglican missionary, found to his consternation that residents of the Carolina backcountry regarded his church services as social events. "No making of them sit still during Service—but they will be in and out—forward and backward the whole Time (Women especially) as Bees to and fro to their Hives," he wrote of one congregation in 1768. And work itself provided opportunities for visiting. Harvest frolics, corn-husking bees, barn raisings, quilting parties, spinning bees, and other communal endeavors brought together neighbors from miles around, often for several days of work followed by feasting, dancing, and singing.

The few colonial cities were nothing but large towns by today's standards. In 1750, the largest, Boston and Philadelphia, had just seventeen thousand and thirteen thousand

> **Rhythms of Urban Life**

inhabitants, respectively. Still, city life differed considerably from rural life. A young Massachusetts man who had moved to Providence described one difference to his farmer father: the city, he remarked, was filled with "Noise and confusion and Disturbance. I must confess, the jolts of Waggons, the rattling of Coaches, the crying of Meat for the Market, the Hollowing of Negros and the ten thousand jingles and Noises, that continually Surround us in every Part almost of the Town, Confuse my thinking." In the cities, lives were likely to be governed by clocks instead of the sun and by work schedules that did not depend so wholly on the seasons. A city wife might preserve a ham in the fall, and a merchant's business might vary according to the weather (which determined sailing schedules), but city dwellers were not inextricably tied to the seasons. Year-round, they could purchase foodstuffs and wood at city markets and cloth at dry-goods stores. They could see friends any time they wished. Wealthy urbanites had plenty of leisure time to read, take walks around town or rides in the countryside, play cards, or attend dances, plays, and concerts, for by midcentury most colonial cities had theaters and assembly halls.

City people also had much more contact with the world beyond their own homes than did their rural compatriots. By the 1750s, every major city had at least one weekly newspaper, and most had two or three. Newspapers printed the latest "advices from

One of the pleasant leisure-time activities of wealthy colonial city-dwellers was attending the theater. A troupe of English actors known as the American Company toured the colonies in the middle years of the eighteenth century. Their performance of William Shakespeare's *Cymbeline* in Annapolis inspired the artist Charles Willson Peale to paint a portrait of their star, Nancy Hallam, playing the role of Imogen, here disguised as a boy, Fidele (1771). *The Colonial Williamsburg Foundation.*

London" (usually two to three months old) and news of events in other English colonies, as well as reports on matters of local interest. The local newspaper was available at taverns and inns, so people who could not afford to buy it could nevertheless read it. Even illiterates could acquaint themselves with the latest news, since the paper was often read aloud by literate customers. However, contact with the outside world also had drawbacks. Sailors sometimes brought exotic and deadly diseases into port with them. Cities like Boston, New York, and Philadelphia endured terrible epidemics of smallpox and yellow fever, which the countryside largely escaped.

Cities attracted many migrants from rural areas. Young men came to learn a skill through an apprenticeship, for cities housed the artisans who

Images of ordinary colonists are rare, and pictures of servants are even rarer. But in 1748 the Boston artist John Greenwood engraved and sold this portrait of Ann Arnold, a wet nurse known locally as "Jersey Nanny," probably a native of the English Isle of Jersey. Compare her rough clothing to that of the women of the better-off family in the illustration on page 76. *Museum of Fine Arts, Boston; gift of Henry Lee Shattuck.*

printed books and newspapers, crafted fine furniture, made shoes, or created expensive gold or silver items. Ordinary laborers too came seeking work, and widows came looking for a means of supporting their families. Without an adult man in the household, a woman had a difficult time running a farm. Consequently, widows tended to congregate in port cities, where they could sell their services as nurses, teachers, seamstresses, servants, or prostitutes, or (if they had some capital) open shops, inns, or boardinghouses. In rural areas, where the economy was based on agriculture and families produced many of their own necessities, there was little demand for the services that landless women and men could perform. In the cities, though, someone always needed another servant, blacksmith, or laundress.

Only widows and the very few never-married women could legally run independent businesses.

An unmarried colonial woman had the same legal rights as a man (with the exception of voting), but an Anglo-American wife was subordinate to her husband in law as well as custom. Under the common-law doctrine of coverture, a married woman became one person with her husband. She could not sue or be sued, make contracts, buy or sell property, or draft a will. Any property she owned prior to marriage became her husband's after the wedding; any wages she earned were legally his; and all children of the marriage fell under his control. Moreover, since divorces were practically impossible to obtain, men and women had little chance to escape from bad marriages.

> **Status of Women**

Anglo-American men expected their wives to defer to their judgment. Most wives seem to have accepted secondary status without murmuring. When girls married, they were commonly advised to devote themselves to their husbands' interests. "Let your Dress your Conversation & the whole Business of your life be to please your Husband & to make him happy & you need not fail of being so your self," a New Yorker told his daughter in the 1730s. That women followed such advice is evident in their diaries. A Virginia woman remarked, for example, that "one of my first resolutions I made after marriage, was never to hold disputes with my husband." It was wives' responsibility, she declared, "to give up to their husbands" whenever differences of opinion arose between them.

The man's legal and customary authority extended to his children as well. Indeed, child rearing was the one task regularly undertaken by both sexes in colonial America. Women cared for infants and toddlers, but thereafter both parents disciplined the children. The father set the general standards by which they were raised and usually had the final word on such matters as education or vocational training. White parents normally insisted on unquestioning obedience from their offspring, and many freely used physical punishment to break a child's will. In the homes of America's elite families, though, more nurturant child-rearing practices prevailed. In such households, the most burdensome chores were performed by white or black servants, freeing parents to spend more time with their offspring and reducing the need for strict disciplinary measures. The relaxed upbringing of these wealthy youngsters foreshadowed nineteenth-century white Americans' greater indulgence of their children.

A white man's authority could include black families as well as his own kin. More than 95 percent of colonial blacks were held in perpetual bondage. In South Carolina, a majority of the population was black; in Georgia, about half; and in the Chesapeake, 40 percent. Although the population of some parts of the southern backcountry was less than one-fifth black, portions of the Carolina low country were nearly 90 percent black by 1790. The trend toward consolidation of landholding and slave ownership after 1740 had a profound effect on the lives of African-Americans. In areas with high proportions of blacks in the population, most slaves resided on plantations with at least nine other bondspeople. Although many southern blacks lived on farms with only one or two other slaves, the majority had the experience of living and working in a largely black setting.

The concentration of the slave population also had a profound effect on whites. One Virginia woman recalled that in her childhood "I believed the world one vast plantation bounded by negro quarters." Whites may have controlled their bondspeople in a formal sense, but living surrounded by blacks affected them in ways they rarely acknowledged. Plantation housing styles, for example, were more African than English in origin, with clusters of small buildings—serving as kitchens, dairies, storage sheds, spinning rooms, and so forth—taking the place of one large structure encompassing all those functions. Just as blacks mimicked the whites' dances in their evening frolics, so too it became customary for whites to perform "Negro jigs" at the end of their cotillions. And words of African origin like "tote" and "okay" were readily incorporated into American English.

The size of such plantations allowed the specialization of labor. Encouraged by planters whose goal was self-sufficiency, African-American men and women became highly skilled at

Sexual Division of Labor Among Black Americans

tasks whites believed appropriate to their sex. Each large plantation had its own male blacksmiths, carpenters, valets, shoemakers, and gardeners, and female dairymaids, seamstresses, cooks, and at least one midwife, who attended pregnant white and black women alike. These skilled slaves—between 10 and 20 percent of the black population—were

Enslaved people in the South pieced quilts from small swatches of fabric. Every plantation had women and men with such skills. *Collection of Gladys-Marie Fry.*

essential to the smooth functioning of the plantation. Whites, though, assigned most slaves, male or female, to work in the fields. Since West African women were accustomed to agricultural labor (see page 12), that task must have coincided with their own cultural expectations. But whites had a different concept of the sexual division of labor. To them, black women's work in the fields connoted inferior status.

The typical Chesapeake tobacco plantation was divided into small "quarters" located at some distance from one another. White overseers supervised work on the distant quarters, while the planter personally took charge of the "home" quarter (which included the planter's house). In the Carolina low country, where planters usually spent months in Charleston to avoid the malaria and yellow fever seasons, blacks often supervised their fellow slaves. Planters commonly assigned "outlandish" (African-born) slaves to do field labor in order to accustom them to plantation work routines and to enable them to learn some English. Artisans, on the other hand, were usually drawn from among the plantation's American-born blacks. In such families skills like carpentry and midwifery were passed down from father to son and mother

An Overseer Doing His Duty, by Benjamin H. Latrobe. Most slave women were field hands like these, sketched in 1798 near Fredericksburg, Virginia. White women were believed to be unsuited for heavy outdoor labor. *Maryland Historical Society.*

to daughter; such knowledge often constituted a slave family's most valuable possession.

All the English colonies legally permitted slavery, so discontented blacks had few places to go to escape bondage. Sometimes recently arrived Africans tried to steal boats to return home or ran off in groups to the frontier, where they joined the Indians or attempted to establish traditional villages. Occasionally slaves from South Carolina tried to reach Spanish Florida. But most slave runaways merely wanted to visit friends or relatives or to avoid their normal work routines for a few days or months. In a society in which blackness automatically connoted perpetual servitude, no black person anywhere could claim free status without being challenged.

From the blacks' perspective, violent resistance had even less to recommend it than running away. Whites may have been in the minority in some areas, but they controlled the guns and ammunition. Even if a revolt succeeded for a time, whites could easily muster the armed force necessary to put it down. Only in very unusual circumstances,

therefore, did colonial blacks attempt to rebel against their white oppressors (see pages 96–97).

African-Americans did try to improve the conditions of their bondage. Their chief vehicle for gaining some measure of control over their lives was the family. Planters' records reveal

Black Families how members of extended-kin groups provided support, assistance, and comfort to each other. They asked to live on the same quarters, protested excessive punishment administered to relatives, and often requested special treatment for children or siblings. On one Virginia plantation, for instance, a mother arranged for her daughter to be treated by a particular black doctor, and a father successfully convinced his master that his daughter should be allowed to live with her stepmother. The extended-kin ties that developed among African-American families who had lived on the same plantation for several generations served as insurance against the uncertainties of existence under slavery. If a nuclear family was broken up by sale, there were always relatives around to help with

Chapter 3: Growth and Diversity, 1720–1770

child rearing and other tasks. Among colonial blacks, the extended family served a more important function than it did among whites.

By a variety of means most black families managed to carve out a small measure of autonomy. On many plantations, slaves were allowed or required to plant their own gardens, hunt, or fish in order to supplement the standard diet of corn and salt pork. Some Chesapeake mistresses permitted their female slaves to raise chickens, which they could then sell or exchange for such items as extra clothing or blankets. In South Carolina, slaves were often able to accumulate personal property because most rice and indigo plantations operated on a task system. Once slaves had completed their assigned tasks for the day, they were free to work for themselves. Occasionally they could cultivate rice or indigo crops of their own. In Maryland and Virginia, where by the end of the century whites had begun to hire out their slaves to others because of a surplus of bound laborers, blacks were sometimes allowed to keep a small part of the wages they earned. In the same era some tobacco planters also began to use a tasking system, thus allowing Chesapeake slaves more freedom from direct supervision by whites. Such advances were slight, but against the bleak backdrop of slavery they deserve to be highlighted.

Yet blacks were always subject to white intrusions into their lives, since they had to serve white families rather than their own. In some households,

Black-White Relations

masters and mistresses enforced their will chiefly through physical coercion. Thus one woman's diary noted matter-of-factly: "December 1: Lucy whippt for getting key of Celler door & stealing apples. December 2: Plato Anthoney & Abraham Pegg's housband whipt for Hog stealing." On other plantations, masters were more lenient and respectful of slaves' property and their desire to live with other members of their families. But even in households where whites and blacks displayed genuine affection for one another, there were inescapable tensions. Such tensions were caused not only by whites' uneasiness about the slave system, but also by the dynamics of day-to-day relationships in which a small number of whites wielded arbitrary power over the lives of many blacks.

Thomas Jefferson was deeply concerned about that issue. In 1780 he observed, "The whole commerce between master and slave is a perpetual exercise of the most boisterous passions, the most unremitting despotism on the one part, and degrading submission on the other. Our children see this, and learn to imitate it. . . . The man must be a prodigy who can retain his manners and morals undepraved by such circumstances." What troubled Jefferson most was the impact of the system on whites, not on the people they held in bondage. Before the Revolution, only a tiny number of Quakers (most notably John Woolman in his *Some Considerations on the Keeping of Negroes,* published in 1754) took a different approach, criticizing slavery out of sympathy for blacks. The other white colonists who questioned slavery took Jefferson's approach, stressing the institution's adverse effect on whites. Even they were extremely few in number. A labor system so essential to the functioning of the colonial economy met with little open challenge.

By the third quarter of the eighteenth century, the daily work routines of most Americans had changed little from those of their Old World ancestors. Ordinary white folk lived in farm households, their lives governed by the sexual division of labor. Most African-Americans were held in perpetual bondage, but their work was performed as it had been in West Africa, communally in the fields. Even in colonial cities life differed little from European cities in previous centuries. Yet if the routines of daily life seemed fixed and unchanging, the wider context in which those routines occurred did not. In both Europe and America the eighteenth century was a time of great cultural and intellectual ferment. The movement known as the Enlightenment at first primarily influenced the educated elites. Ordinary people seemed little touched by it. But since enlightened thinking played a major part in the ideology of the American Revolution, it was eventually to have an important impact on the lives of all Americans.

Colonial Culture

The traditional form of colonial culture was oral, communal, and—for at least the first half of the eighteenth century—intensely local. The newer culture of the elite was print-oriented, individualized, and self-consciously cosmopolitan. Although the two are discussed separately here, they mingled in a variety of ways, for people of both descriptions lived side by side in small communities.

A majority of the residents of British America (almost all the blacks, half the white women, and at least one-fifth of the white men) could neither read nor write. That had important consequences for the transmission and development of American culture. In the absence of literacy, the primary means of communication was face-to-face conversation. Information tended to travel slowly and within relatively confined regions. Different locales developed divergent cultural traditions, and those differences were heightened by racial or ethnic variations.

Oral Culture

When Europeans or Africans migrated to the colonies, they left familiar environments behind but brought with them assumptions about how society should work and how their own lives fitted into the broader social context. In North America, those assumptions influenced the way they organized their lives. Yet Old World customs usually could not be recreated intact in the New World, because people from different origins now resided in the same communities. Accordingly, the colonists had to forge new cultural identities for themselves, and they did so through the vehicle of public rituals.

Attendance at church was perhaps the most important such ritual in the colonies. In Congregational (Puritan) churches, seating was assigned by church leaders to reflect standing in the community. In early New England, men and women sat on opposite sides of a central aisle, arranged in ranks according to age, wealth, and church membership. By the middle of the eighteenth century, wealthy men and their wives sat in privately owned pews, with their children, servants, and the less fortunate still seated in sex-segregated fashion at the rear or sides of the church. In eighteenth-century Virginia, seating in Anglican parishes also revealed the local status hierarchy. Planter families purchased their own pews, and in some parishes the landed gentlemen customarily strode into church as a group just before the service, deliberately drawing attention to their exalted position. Quite a different message came from the entirely egalitarian, but sex-segregated, seating system used in Quaker meetinghouses. Where one sat

Religious Rituals

in colonial churches, in other words, symbolized one's place in society and the values of the local community.

Other aspects of the service also reflected communal values. In most colonial churches, trained clergymen delivered formal sermons, but in Quaker services members of the meeting spoke informally to each other. Communal singing in Congregational churches added an egalitarian element to an otherwise status-conscious experience. The first book printed in the colonies was the *Bay Psalm Book* (1640), consisting of Old Testament psalms recast in short, rhyming, metrical lines so they could be easily learned and sung even by people who could not read. Such singing helped to reduce the ritual significance of hierarchical seating arrangements, bringing a kind of crude democracy into the church. Everyone had an equal voice in deciding which version of the psalms to use and whether instruments should accompany the singing.

Communal culture also centered on the civic sphere. In New England in particular, colonial governments proclaimed official days of thanksgiving (for good harvests, victories in war, and so forth) or days of fasting and prayer (when the colony was experiencing difficulties). Everyone in the community was expected to participate in the public rituals held on such occasions. Militia musters (known as training days), normally scheduled once a month, were similar moments that brought the community together, since all able-bodied men between the ages of sixteen and sixty were members of the militia.

Civic Rituals

In the Chesapeake, some of the most important cultural rituals occurred on court and election days. When the county court was in session, men would come from miles around to file suits, appear as witnesses, serve as jurors, or simply observe the goings-on. Attendance at court functioned as a method of civic education; from watching the proceedings men learned what behavior their neighbors expected of them. Elections served the same purpose, for freeholders voted in public. An election official, often flanked by the candidates for the office in question, would call each man forward to declare his preference. The voter would then be thanked politely by the gentleman for whom he had cast his oral ballot. Traditionally, the candidates treated their supporters to rum at nearby taverns.

In such settings as church and courthouse, then, elite and ordinary folk alike participated in the oral culture that served as the cement holding their communities together. But the genteel residents of the colonies also took part in a newer kind of culture, one organized through the world of print and the message conveyed by reading as well as by observing one's neighbors.

Literacy was certainly less essential in eighteenth-century America than it is today. People—especially women—could live their entire lives without ever being called upon to read a book or write a letter. Thus education beyond the bare rudiments of reading, writing, and "figuring" was usually regarded as a frill for either sex. Men might have to know how to read a contract or keep rough accounts, and women might need or want to read the Bible, but beyond that, little learning appeared necessary. Teaching slaves to read or write was forbidden as too subversive of the social order. Education accordingly was a sign of status. Only parents who wanted their children to be distinguished from less-fortunate peers (perhaps for reasons of piety, or a desire for upward mobility or maintenance of status) were willing to forgo their children's valuable labor to allow them to attend school. And when parents did so, the education they gave their sons differed from that given their daughters. Girls ordinarily received little intellectual training beyond the rudiments, though they might learn music, dancing, or fancy needlework (since those skills all connoted genteel status). Elite boys, on the other hand, studied with tutors or attended grammar schools that prepared them to enter college at age fourteen or fifteen.

> **Attitudes Toward Education**

The colonial system of higher education for males was therefore more fully developed than was basic instruction for either sex. The first American colleges were designed to train young men for the ministry. Following the earlier examples of Harvard (1636), William and Mary (chartered 1693, but not a functioning entity until 1726), and Yale (1701), the colleges founded in the mid-eighteenth century—those now known as Princeton (1747), Columbia (1754), Brown (1764), and Rutgers (1766)—were intended to supply clergymen to fill the pulpits of Presbyterian, Anglican, Baptist, and Dutch Reformed churches, respectively. (Dartmouth College, founded 1769, though not explicitly aimed at

Nabby Martin, an eighteenth-century girl living in Providence, depicted in her needlework sampler buildings representing higher education (University Hall at Brown University) and politics (the Rhode Island State House). Ironically, she was excluded from participating in both on account of her sex. *Museum of Art, Rhode Island School of Design, Providence, R.I.*

educating clerics, also had a religious purpose, that of Christianizing the Indians.) But during the eighteenth century the curriculum and character of all these colleges changed considerably. Their students, the sons of the colonial elite, were now interested in careers in medicine, law, and business instead of the ministry. And the learned men who headed the colleges, though ministers themselves, were deeply affected by the Enlightenment.

In the seventeenth century, some European thinkers began to analyze nature in an effort to determine the laws that govern the universe. They employed experimentation and abstract reasoning to discover general prin-

> **The Enlightenment**

ciples behind such everyday phenomena as the motions of the planets and stars, the behavior of falling objects, and the characteristics of light and sound. Above all, Enlightenment philosophers emphasized acquiring knowledge through reason, taking particular delight in challenging previously unquestioned assumptions. John Locke's *Essay Concerning Human Understanding* (1690), for example, disputed the notion that human beings were born already imprinted with innate ideas. All knowledge, Locke asserted, came instead from one's observations of the external world.

The Enlightenment had an enormous impact on well-to-do, educated people in Europe and America. It supplied them with a common vocabulary and a unified view of the world, one that insisted that the enlightened eighteenth century was better than all previous ages. It joined them in a common endeavor, the effort to make sense of God's orderly creation. Thus American naturalists like John and William Bartram supplied European scientists with information about New World plants and animals, so that they could be fitted into newly formulated universal classification systems. So too Americans interested in astronomy took part in 1769 in an international effort to learn about the workings of the solar system by studying a rare occurrence, the transit of Venus across the face of the sun.

Enlightenment rationalism affected politics as well as science. Locke's *Two Treatises of Civil Government* (1691) and other works by French and Scottish philosophers challenged previous concepts of an unchanging and unchangeable political order. Government, declared Locke, was created by men and so could be altered by them. If a ruler broke his agreement with the people and refused to protect their rights, he could legitimately be ousted from power by peaceful—or even violent—means. Enlightenment theorists proclaimed that the aim of government was the good of the people, that a proper political order could prevent the rise of tyrants, and that even the power of monarchs was subject to God's natural laws.

These intellectual currents had a dramatic effect on the curriculum of the colonial colleges. Whereas in the seventeenth century Harvard courses had focused on the study of the ancient languages and theology, after the 1720s colleges began to introduce courses in mathematics (including algebra, geometry, and calculus), the natural sciences, law,

and medicine (including anatomy and physiology). The young men educated in such colleges—and their sisters at home, with whom they occasionally shared their books and ideas—developed a rational outlook on life that differentiated them from their fellow colonists. This was the world of Dr. Alexander Hamilton and his associates. When he left Annapolis in 1744, he carried letters of introduction to "the better sort" in all the places he intended to visit. Such people had learned the value of reading, of regular correspondence with like-minded friends, of convivial gatherings at which the conversation focused on recent books imported from Europe, and of attendance at plays performed by touring companies of English actors.

Well-to-do graduates of American colleges, along with others who like Hamilton had obtained their education in Great Britain, formed the core of genteel culture in the colonies. Men

▶ **Elite Culture** and women from these families wanted to set themselves apart from ordinary folk. Beginning in the 1720s they constructed grandiose residences furnished with imported carpets, silver plate, and furniture. They entertained their friends at elaborate dinner parties and balls at which all present dressed in the height of fashion. They cultivated polite manners and saw themselves as part of a transatlantic and intercolonial network.

In what ways did this genteel, enlightened culture affect the lives of the majority of colonists? Certainly no resident of the colonies could have avoided some contact with members of the elite. Ordinary folk were expected to doff their hats and behave in a deferential fashion when conversing with their "betters." Many besides employees and tenants were economically dependent on genteel folk; for example, the elite's demand for consumer goods of all kinds led to the growth of artisan industries like silversmithing or fine furniture-making in the colonies. But the Enlightenment's most immediate impact on all Americans was in the realm of medicine.

The key figure in the drama was the Puritan clergyman, Reverend Cotton Mather, who was a member of England's Royal Society, an

▶ **Smallpox Inoculations** organization of the intellectual elite. In a Royal Society publication Mather read about the benefits of inoculation (deliberately infecting a person with a mild case of a disease) as a protection against the dreaded smallpox. In 1720 and 1721, when Boston suffered a major smallpox epidemic, Mather and a doctor ally urged people to be inoculated despite fervent opposition from Boston's leading physician. When the epidemic ended, the statistics bore out Mather's opinion: of those inoculated, fewer than 3 percent died; of those who became ill without inoculation, nearly 15 percent perished. Although it was midcentury before inoculation was generally accepted as a preventive procedure, enlightened methods had provided colonial Americans with protection from the great killer disease.

If the lives of genteel and ordinary folk in the eighteenth-century colonies seemed to follow different patterns, there was one man who in his person appeared to combine their traits; appropriately enough, he later became for Europeans the symbolic American. That man was Benjamin Franklin. Born in Boston in 1706, he was the perfect example of a self-made, self-educated man. Apprenticed at an early age to his older brother James, a Boston printer and newspaper publisher, Franklin ran away to Philadelphia in 1723. There he worked as a printer and eventually started his own publishing business, printing books, a newspaper, and *Poor Richard's Almanack*. The business was so successful that Franklin was able to retire from active control in 1748, at forty-two. He thereafter devoted himself to intellectual endeavors and public service, as deputy postmaster general for the colonies, as an agent representing colonial interests in London, and finally as a diplomat during the Revolution. Franklin's *Experiments and Observations on Electricity* (1751) was the most important scientific work by a colonial American; it established the terminology and basic theory of electricity still in use today.

In 1749 and 1751 Franklin published pamphlets proposing the establishment of a new educational institution in Pennsylvania. The purpose of Franklin's "English School" was not to produce clerics or scholars but to prepare young men "for learning any business, calling or profession." He wanted to enable them "to pass through and execute the several offices of civil life, with advantage and reputation to themselves and country." The College of Philadelphia (now the University of Pennsylvania), which he founded in 1755, was intended to graduate youths who would resemble Franklin himself—

> **Benjamin Franklin, the Symbolic American**

talented, practical men of affairs competent in a number of different fields.

Franklin and the student he envisioned thus fused the conflicting tendencies of colonial culture. Free of the Old World's traditions, the ideal American would achieve distinction through hard work and the application of common-sense principles. Like Franklin he would rise from an ordinary family into the ranks of the genteel, thereby transcending the cultural boundaries that divided the colonists. He would be unpretentious but not unlearned, simple but not ignorant, virtuous but not priggish. The American would be a true child of the Enlightenment, knowledgeable about European culture yet not bound by its fetters, advancing through reason and talent alone. To him all things would be possible, all doors open.

The contrast with the original communal ideals of the early New England settlements could not have been sharper. Franklin's American was an individual, free to make choices about his future, able to contemplate a variety of possible careers. John Winthrop's American, outlined in his "Modell of Christian Charity" (see pages 32–33), had been a component of a greater whole that required his unquestioning submission. But the two visions had one point in common: both described only white males. Blacks, Indians, and females played no part in them. Not until many years later would America formally recognize what had been true all along: that females and nonwhites had participated in the creation of the nation's cultural tradition.

Politics and Religion: Stability and Crisis at Midcentury

In the first decades of the eighteenth century, colonial political life developed a new stability. Despite the large migration from overseas, most residents of the mainland colonies were now native-born. Men from genteel families dominated the political structures in each province, for voters (white men who met property-holding requirements) tended to defer to their well-educated "betters" on election days. The most noticeable consequence of such deferential behavior was a declining rate of turnover among elected officials in most of the colonies.

Colonial political leaders sought to increase the powers of the elected assemblies relative to those of the governors and other appointed officials. Assemblies began to claim privileges associated with the British House of Commons, such as the right to initiate all tax legislation and to control the militia. The assemblies also developed effective ways of influencing British appointees, especially by threatening to withhold their salaries. In some colonies (like Virginia and South Carolina), the elite members of the assemblies usually presented a united front to royal officials, but in others (like New York), they fought with each other long and bitterly. The latter province took the first steps on the road to modern American democracy. In their attempts to win hotly contested elections, New York's genteel leaders began to appeal to "the people," competing openly for the votes of ordinary freeholders.

> **Rise of the Assemblies**

Yet eighteenth-century assemblies bore little resemblance to twentieth-century state legislatures. Much of their business was what today would be termed administrative; only on rare occasions did they formulate new policies or pass laws of major importance. Members of the assemblies also saw their roles differently from modern legislators. Instead of believing that they should act positively to improve the lives of their constituents, eighteenth-century assemblymen saw themselves as acting negatively to prevent encroachments on the people's rights. In their minds, their primary function was to stop the governors or councils from enacting (for example) oppressive taxes, rather than to pass laws that would actively benefit their constituents.

By the middle of the century, politically aware colonists commonly drew analogies between their governments and the balance between king, lords, and commons found in Great Britain—a combination that had been thought to produce a stable polity since the days of ancient Greece and Rome. Although the analogy was not exact, political leaders equated their governors with the monarch, their councils with the aristocracy, and their assemblies with the House of Commons. All three were thought essential to good government, but Americans did not regard them with the same degrees of approval. They saw the governors and appointed councils as aliens who posed a potential threat to colonial freedoms and customary ways of life. As representatives of England rather than America, the governors and councils were to be feared rather than trusted. Colonists saw the assemblies, on the other hand, as the people's protectors. And for their part, the assemblies regarded themselves as representatives of the people.

But again, such beliefs should not be equated with modern practice. The assemblies, firmly controlled by dominant families whose members were re-elected year after year, rarely responded to the concerns of their poorer constituents. Although settlement continually spread westward, assemblies failed to reapportion themselves to provide adequate representation for newer communities—a lack of action that led to serious grievances among frontier dwellers, especially those from non-English ethnic groups. Thus it is important to distinguish between the colonial ideal, which placed the assembly to the forefront in the protection of people's liberties, and the reality, in which the people protected tended chiefly to be the wealthy and the assembly members themselves.

At midcentury, the political structures that had stabilized in a period of relative calm confronted a series of crises. None affected all the mainland provinces, but on the other hand no colony escaped wholly untouched by at least one. The crises were of various sorts—ethnic, racial, economic, religious—and they exposed the internal tensions building in the pluralistic American society. They foreshadowed the greater disorder of the revolutionary era. Most important, they demonstrated that the political accommodations arrived at in the aftermath of the Glorious Revolution were no longer adequate to govern Britain's American empire. Once again, changes appeared necessary.

One of the first—and greatest—of the crises occurred in South Carolina. Early one morning in September 1739, about twenty South Carolina slaves gathered near the Stono River south of Charleston. After seizing guns and ammunition from a store, they killed the storekeepers and some nearby planter families. Then, joined by other slaves from the area, they headed south toward Florida in hopes of finding refuge in that Spanish colony. By midday, however, the alarm had been sounded among whites in the

> **Stono Rebellion**

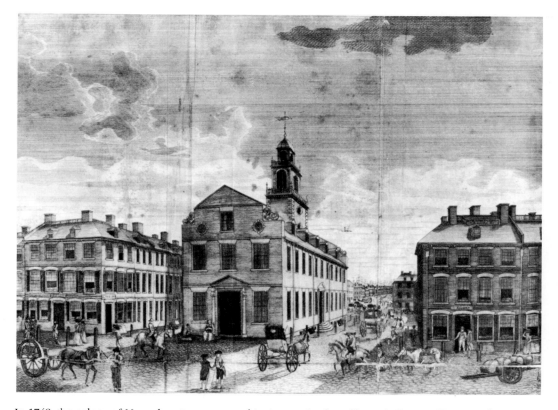

In 1748, the colony of Massachusetts constructed its impressive State House in Boston. Here met the Assembly and the Council. The solidity and imposing nature of the building must have symbolized for its users the increasing consolidation of power in the hands of the Massachusetts legislature. *The Bostonian Society.*

district. In the late afternoon a troop of militia caught up with the fugitives, then numbering about a hundred, and attacked them, killing some and dispersing the rest. More than a week later, the whites finally captured most of the remaining conspirators. Those not killed on the spot were later executed, but for more than two years afterward renegades were rumored to be still at large.

The Stono Rebellion shocked white South Carolinians and residents of other colonies as well. Laws governing the behavior of blacks were stiffened throughout British America. But the most immediate response came in New York, which itself had suffered a slave revolt in 1712. There the news from the South, coupled with fears of Spain generated by the outbreak of King George's War, set off a reign of terror in the summer of 1741. Hysterical whites transformed a biracial gang of thieves and arsonists into malevolent conspirators who wanted to foment a slave uprising under the guidance of a supposed priest in the pay of Spain. By summer's end, thirty-one blacks and four whites had been executed for participating in the "plot." Not only did the Stono Rebellion and the New York conspiracy expose and confirm whites' deepest fears about the dangers of slaveholding, they also revealed the assemblies' inability to prevent serious internal disorder. Events of the next two decades confirmed that pattern.

By midcentury, much of the fertile land east of the Appalachians had been purchased or occupied. As a result, conflicts over land titles and conditions of landholding grew in number

Land Riots and frequency as colonists competed for control of land good for farming. In 1746, for example, New Jersey farmers holding land under grants from the governor of New York (dating from the brief period when both provinces were owned by the duke of York) clashed violently with agents of the East Jersey proprietors. The proprietors claimed the land as theirs and demanded annual payments, called quitrents, for the use of the property. Similar violence occurred in the 1760s in the region that later became Vermont. There, farmers (many of them migrants from eastern New England) holding land grants issued by New Hampshire battled with speculators claiming title to the area through grants from New York authorities.

The most serious land riots of the period took place along the Hudson River in 1765 and 1766. Late in the seventeenth century, Governor Benjamin Fletcher of New York had granted several huge tracts in the lower Hudson valley to prominent colonial families. The proprietors in turn divided these estates into small farms, which they rented chiefly to poor Dutch and German migrants who regarded tenancy as a step on the road to independent freeholder status. By the 1750s some proprietors were earning as much as £1,000 to £2,000 annually from quitrents and other fees.

After 1740, though, increasing migration from New England brought conflict to the great New York estates. The mobile New Englanders, who had moved in search of land, did not want to become tenants. Many squatted on vacant portions of the manors and resisted all attempts to evict them. In the mid-1760s the Philipse family brought suit against the New Englanders, some of whom had lived on Philipse land for twenty or thirty years. New York courts upheld the Philipse claim and ordered the squatters to make way for tenants with valid leases. Instead of complying, the farmers organized a rebellion against the proprietors. For nearly a year the insurgent farmers controlled much of the Hudson Valley. They terrorized proprietors and loyal tenants, freed their friends from jail, and on one occasion battled a county sheriff and his posse. The rebellion was put down only after British troops dispatched from New York City captured its most important leaders.

Violent conflicts of a different sort erupted just a few years later in the Carolinas. The Regulator movements of the late 1760s (South Carolina) and early 1770s (North Carolina)

The Regulators

pitted backcountry farmers against the wealthy eastern planters who controlled their provinces' governments. The frontier dwellers, most of whom were Scotch-Irish, protested their lack of an ade-

quate voice in colonial political affairs. The South Carolinians for months policed the countryside in vigilante bands, contending that law enforcement in the region was too lax and was biased against them. The North Carolinians, many of whose grievances had their origin in heavy taxation, fought and lost a battle with eastern militiamen at Alamance in 1771. Regional, ethnic, and economic tensions thus combined to create these disturbances, which ultimately arose from frontier people's dissatisfaction with the Carolina governments.

The most widespread crisis occurred not in politics but in religion. From the late 1730s through the 1760s, waves of religious revivalism—known col-

First Great Awakening

lectively as the Great Awakening—swept over various parts of the colonies, primarily New England (1735–1745) and Virginia (1750s and 1760s). America was ripe for religious renewal at midcentury. Orthodox Calvinists were eager to combat Enlightenment rationalism, which denied innate human depravity. The economic and political uncertainty accompanying King George's War made colonists—especially genteel New Englanders whose wealth rested on commerce—receptive to the spiritual certainty offered by evangelical religion. In addition, many recent immigrants and residents of the backcountry had no prior religious affiliation, thus presenting evangelists with a likely source of converts.

The first signs of what was to become the Great Awakening appeared in western Massachusetts, in the Northampton Congregational Church led by the Reverend Jonathan Edwards, a noted preacher and theologian. During 1734 and 1735, Edwards noticed a remarkable response among the youthful members of his flock to a message based squarely on Calvinist principles. Individuals, Edwards argued, could attain salvation only through recognition of their own depraved natures and the need to surrender completely to God's will. Such surrender brought an intensely emotional release from sin and came to be seen as a single identifiable moment of conversion.

The effects of such conversions remained isolated until 1739, when an English Methodist named George Whitefield arrived in America. For

George Whitefield

fifteen months he toured the colonies, preaching to large audiences from Georgia to New England and concentrating his efforts in the major cities: Boston, New York, Philadelphia, and Charleston. An effective orator, Whitefield was the chief generating force behind the Great Awakening. Everywhere he traveled, his fame preceded him. Thousands turned out to listen—and to experience conversion. At first, regular clerics welcomed Whitefield and the native itinerant evangelist preachers who sprang up to imitate him. Soon, however, many clergymen began to realize that "revived" religion, though it filled their churches, ran counter to their own approach to matters of faith. They disliked the emotional style of the revivalists, whose itinerancy also disrupted normal patterns of church attendance because it took church-goers away from the services they usually attended.

Opposition to the Awakening heightened rapidly, and large numbers of churches splintered in its wake. "Old Lights"—traditional clerics and their followers—engaged in bitter disputes with the "New Light" evangelicals. American religion, already characterized by numerous sects, became further divided as the major denominations split into Old Light and New Light factions and as new evangelical sects—Methodists and Baptists—quickly gained adherents. Paradoxically, the angry fights and the rapid rise in the number of distinct denominations eventually led to an American willingness to tolerate religious diversity. No one sect could make an unequivocal claim to orthodoxy, so they all had to coexist if they were to exist at all.

The most important effect of the Awakening was its impact on American modes of thought. The revivalists' message directly challenged the colonial tradition of deference. Itinerant preachers, many of whom were not ordained clergymen, claimed they understood the will of God better than orthodox clerics. The Awakening's emphasis on emotion rather than learning undermined the validity of received wisdom, and New Lights questioned not only religious but also social and political orthodoxy. For example, New Lights began to defend the rights of groups and individuals to dissent from a community consensus, thereby challenging one of the most fundamental tenets of colonial political life up to that time.

Nowhere was this trend more evident than in Virginia, where the plantation gentry and their os-

Impact of the Awakening

George Whitefield (1714–1770), the spell-binding evangelical preacher who made several tours of the American colonies and was largely responsible for the spread of the Great Awakening. *Courtesy of The Trustees of the Boston Public Library.*

tentatious lifestyle dominated society. By the 1760s Baptists had gained a major foothold in Virginia, and their beliefs and behavior were openly at odds with the way most gentry families lived. They rejected as sinful the horse racing, gambling, and dancing that occupied much of the gentry's leisure time. Like the Quakers before them, they dressed plainly and simply, in contrast to the fashionable opulence of the gentry. By attending monthly "great meetings" that attracted hundreds of people, they introduced new public rituals that rivaled the more conventional weekly Anglican services. They addressed each other as "brother" and "sister" and organized their congregations—more than ninety of them by 1776—on the basis of equality.

Strikingly, almost all the Virginia Baptist congregations included both black and white members. When the Dan River Baptist Church was founded in 1760, for example, eleven of its original seventy-four members were black, and some congregations had black majorities. Church rules governed the behavior of both blacks and whites; interracial sexual relationships, divorce, and adultery were forbidden to all. In addition, whites were directed not to break up slave marriages through sale. Complaints about church members' misbehavior were investigated by biracial committees. If churches excommunicated blacks for stealing from their masters, they also excommunicated whites for physically abusing their slaves. One white slaveowner who was so treated in 1772 experienced a true conversion. Penalized for "burning" one of his slaves, Charles Cook apologized to the congregation and became a preacher in a largely black church. Other white Baptists decided that slaveowning was "unrighteous" and took the logical step of freeing their bondspeople.

At midcentury the Great Awakening thus injected an egalitarian strain into American life and further disrupted traditional structures of existence. Although primarily a religious movement, the Awakening also had important social and political consequences, calling into question habitual modes of behavior in the secular as well as the religious realm. The Great Awakening, in short, helped to break Americans' ties to their limited seventeenth-century origins. So too did the newcomers from Germany, Scotland, Ireland, and Africa, who brought their languages, customs, and religions to North America. Also important were the changes in the economy that linked the colonies tightly to international markets, drawing them irrevocably into European wars and creating the wealthy class of merchants and landowners who dominated colonial political and social life.

A century and a half after English people had first settled in North America, the colonies were only nominally English. Rather, they mixed diverse European, American, and African traditions into a novel cultural blend. That culture owed much to the Old World but just as much, if not more, to the New. In the 1760s Americans began to recognize that fact. They realized that their interests were not necessarily identical to those of Great Britain or its monarch. For the first time, they offered a frontal challenge to British authority.

Suggestions for Further Reading

General

Wayne Craven, *Colonial American Portraiture* (1986); Jack P. Greene, *Pursuits of Happiness: The Social Development of the Early Modern British Colonies and the Formation of American Culture* (1988); Jack P. Greene and J. R. Pole, eds., *Colonial British America* (1984); Richard Hofstadter, *America at 1750: A Social Portrait* (1971); Stephen Innes, ed., *Work and Labor in Early America* (1988); D. W. Meinig, *Atlantic America, 1492–1800* (1986); Robert V. Wells, *The Population of the British Colonies in America Before 1776* (1975).

Rural Society

T. H. Breen, *Tobacco Culture* (1985); Lois Green Carr et al., eds., *Colonial Chesapeake Society* (1988); Rhys Isaac, *The Transformation of Virginia, 1740–1790* (1982); Christopher Jedrey, *The World of John Cleaveland: Family and Community in Eighteenth-Century New England* (1979); Sung Bok Kim, *Landlord and Tenant in Colonial New York: Manorial Society, 1664–1775* (1978); James T. Lemon, *The Best Poor Man's Country: A Geographical Study of Early Southeastern Pennsylvania* (1972); Kenneth A. Lockridge, *The Diary, and Life, of William Byrd II of Virginia, 1674–1744* (1987); Jackson Turner Main, *Society and Economy in Colonial Connecticut* (1985); Michael Zuckerman, *Peaceable Kingdoms: New England Towns in the Eighteenth Century* (1970).

Urban Society

Carl Bridenbaugh, *Cities in Revolt: Urban Life in America, 1743–1776* (1955); Christine L. Heyrman, *Commerce and Culture: The Maritime Communities of Colonial Massachusetts, 1690–1750* (1984); Gary B. Nash, *The Urban Crucible: Social Change, Political Consciousness, and the Origins of the American Revolution* (1979); Frederick B. Tolles, *Meeting House and Counting House: The Quaker Merchants of Colonial Philadelphia, 1682–1763* (1948); Stephanie G. Wolf, *Urban Village: Population, Community, and Family Structure in Germantown, Pennsylvania, 1683–1800* (1976).

Economic Development

Paul Clemens, *The Atlantic Economy and Colonial Maryland's Eastern Shore: From Tobacco to Grain* (1980); Alice Hanson Jones, *Wealth of a Nation to Be: The American Colonies on the Eve of the Revolution* (1980); John J. McCusker and Russell R. Menard, *The Economy of British America,*

1607–1789 (1985); Edwin J. Perkins, *The Economy of Colonial America* (1980); James F. Shepherd and Gary M. Walton, *Shipping, Maritime Trade and the Economic Development of Colonial North America* (1972); Gary M. Walton and James F. Shepherd, *The Economic Rise of Early America* (1979).

Politics

Bernard Bailyn, *The Origins of American Politics* (1968); Patricia U. Bonomi, *A Factious People: Politics and Society in Colonial New York* (1971); Richard Bushman, *King and People in Provincial Massachusetts* (1985); Edward M. Cook, Jr., *The Fathers of the Towns: Leadership and Community Structure in Eighteenth-Century New England* (1976); Jack P. Greene, *The Quest for Power: The Lower Houses of Assembly in the Southern Royal Colonies, 1689–1776* (1963).

Immigration

Bernard Bailyn, *The Peopling of British North America* (1986); Bernard Bailyn, *Voyagers to the West* (1986); Jon Butler, *The Huguenots in America* (1983); R. J. Dickson, *Ulster Immigration to Colonial America, 1718–1775* (1966); A. Roger Ekirch, *Bound for America: The Transportation of British Convicts to the Colonies, 1718–1775* (1987); Ian C. C. Graham, *Colonists from Scotland: Emigration to North America, 1701–1783* (1956); Ned Landsman, *Scotland and Its First American Colony* (1985); James G. Leyburn, *The Scotch-Irish* (1962); Sharon Salinger, *To Serve Well and Faithfully: Labor and Indentured Servants in Pennsylvania, 1682–1800* (1988).

Blacks

Ira Berlin, "Time, Space, and the Evolution of Afro-American Society in British Mainland America," *American Historical Review,* 85 (1980), 44–78; Thomas J. Davis, *A Rumor of Revolt: The "Great Negro Plot" in Colonial New York* (1985); Herbert Gutman, *The Black Family in Slavery and Freedom, 1750–1925* (1976); Allan Kulikoff, *Tobacco and Slaves: The Development of Southern Cultures in the Chesapeake, 1680–1800* (1986); Gerald W. Mullin, *Flight and Rebellion: Slave Resistance in Eighteenth-Century Virginia* (1972); William Pierson, *Black Yankees: The Development of an Afro-American Subculture in Eighteenth-Century New England* (1988); Mechal Sobel, *The World They Made Together: Black and White Values in Eighteenth-Century Virginia* (1987).

Women and Family

J. William Frost, *The Quaker Family in Colonial America* (1972); Philip J. Greven, *The Protestant Temperament: Patterns of Child-rearing, Religious Experience, and the Self in Early America* (1977); Barry J. Levy, *Quakers and the American Family* (1988); Mary Beth Norton, *Liberty's Daughters:* *The Revolutionary Experience of American Women, 1750–1800* (1980); Marylynn Salmon, *Women and the Law of Property in Early America* (1986); Daniel Blake Smith, *Inside the Great House: Planter Family Life in Eighteenth-Century Chesapeake Society* (1980).

Colonial Culture and the Enlightenment

Daniel J. Boorstin, *The Americans: The Colonial Experience* (1958); Richard Beale Davis, *Intellectual Life in the Colonial South, 1585–1763,* 2 vols. (1978); Howard Mumford Jones, *O Strange New World. American Culture: The Formative Years* (1964); Henry F. May, *The Enlightenment in America* (1976); Louis B. Wright, *The Cultural Life of the American Colonies, 1607–1763* (1957).

Education

James Axtell, *The School upon a Hill: Education and Society in Colonial New England* (1974); Bernard Bailyn, *Education in the Forming of American Society* (1960); Patricia Cline Cohen, *A Calculating People: The Spread of Numeracy in Early America* (1982); Lawrence A. Cremin, *American Education: The Colonial Experience, 1607–1783* (1970); Kenneth A. Lockridge, *Literacy in Colonial New England* (1974).

Science and Medicine

Jane Donegan, *Women and Men Midwives: Medicine, Morality, and Misogyny in Early America* (1978); John Duffy, *Epidemics in Colonial America* (1953); Brooke Hindle, *The Pursuit of Science in Revolutionary America* (1956); Raymond P. Stearns, *Science in the British Colonies of America* (1970).

Religion and the Great Awakening

Patricia U. Bonomi, *Under the Cope of Heaven: Religion, Society, and Politics in Colonial America* (1986); Carl Bridenbaugh, *Mitre and Sceptre: Transatlantic Faiths, Ideas, Personalities, and Politics, 1689–1775* (1962); J. M. Bumstead and John E. Van de Wetering, *What Must I Do to Be Saved? The Great Awakening in Colonial America* (1976); Alan E. Heimert, *Religion and the American Mind: From the Great Awakening to the Revolution* (1966); David S. Lovejoy, *Religious Enthusiasm in the New World* (1985); Harry S. Stout, *The New England Soul: Preaching and Religious Culture in Colonial New England* (1986); Patricia Tracy, *Jonathan Edwards, Pastor* (1980).

In late October 1769, the young Boston shopkeeper Betsy Cuming was visiting a sick friend when outside the house she heard "a voilint Skreeming Kill him Kill him." Betsy ran to the window and saw John Mein, a bookseller and newspaper publisher, being chased by "a larg Croud of those who Call themselves Gentleman but," she added, "in reality they ware no other then Murderers for there disigne was certainly on his life." Later that evening a crowd of at least a thousand men and boys passed the door, "& on a Kart a Man was Exibited as we thought in a Gore of blood." Betsy concluded that the mob had caught Mein, but she was mistaken. She learned the next day that the victim was a customs informer seized by the crowd after Mein had taken shelter in a British army guardhouse. That same night, Mein fled to a vessel anchored in the harbor. He later sailed to England and never returned to the city.

4

SEVERING THE BONDS OF EMPIRE, 1754–1774

What had John Mein done to arouse the antagonism of the "gentlemen" of Boston? He published a newspaper, the *Boston Chronicle,* which generally supported the British side in the current disputes with the colonies. The offense that led to the mobbing, though, was more specific: he had printed several lists of names of local merchants who had recently cleared imports through the Boston customs house. The Mein incident thus involved one of the first recorded examples in American history of a carefully orchestrated political "leak" from official sources. Some administrator had given the printer access to the supposedly private customs records. Why was the information Mein revealed so explosive? In the fall of 1769 many American merchants had signed an agreement not to import goods from Great Britain; Mein's lists indicated that some of the most vocal supporters of nonimportation (including the patriot leader John Hancock) had been violating the agreement. That was why the "gentlemen" of Boston had to silence the outspoken publisher.

John Mein was not the first, and he would be far from the last, resident of the colonies who found his life wholly disrupted by the growing political antagonism between England and her American possessions. Indeed, even Betsy Cuming was eventually forced into exile in Nova Scotia because she opposed the trend of

A Perspective View of Part of the Commons (detail) engraved by Sidney Smith in 1770, based on a watercolor by Christin Remick of an event that took place on the Boston Common, October 1, 1768. *The Concord Antiquarian Society.*

A LIST of the Names of *those*
who AUDACIOUSLY continue to counteract the UNIT-
ED SENTIMENTS of the BODY of Merchants thro'out
NORTH-AMERICA ; by importing British Goods
contrary to the Agreement.

John Bernard,
    (In King-Street, almost opposite Vernon's Head.

James McMasters,
    (On Treat's Wharf.

Patrick McMasters,
    (Opposite the Sign of the Lamb.

John Mein,
    (Opposite the White-Horse, and in King-Street.

Nathaniel Rogers,
    (Opposite Mr. Henderson Inches Store lower End
    King-Street.

William Jackson,
    At the Brazen Head, Cornhill, near the Town-House.

Theophilus Lillie,
    (Near Mr. Pemberton's Meeting-House, North-End.

John Taylor,
    (Nearly opposite the Heart and Crown in Cornhill.

Ame & Elizabeth Cummings,
(Opposite the Old Brick Meeting House, all of Boston.

Israel Williams, Esq; & Son,
    (Traders in the Town of Hatfield.

And, *Henry Barnes,*
    (Trader in the Town of Marlboro'.

*The following Names should have been inserted in
the List of Justices.*

County of Middlesex.	County of Lincoln.
Samuel Hendley	
John Borland	John Kingsbury
Henry Barnes	
Richard Cary	County of Berkshire.
County of Bristol.	Mark Hopkins
George Brightman	Elijah Dwight
County of Worcester.	Israel Stoddard
Daniel Bliss	

A blacklist printed in the *North American Almanac* for 1770 identified those Boston merchants who had ignored the nonimportation agreement. Among their number were both John Mein, the object of the mob's wrath the previous October, and Betsy (Elizabeth) Cuming, the narrator of the story, who—with her sister Anne—ran a small dry-goods store. *Library of Congress.*

American resistance to Great Britain. Long afterward, John Adams identified the years between 1760 and 1775 as the period in which the true American Revolution had occurred. The Revolution, Adams declared, was completed before the fighting started, for it was "in the Minds of the people," involving not the actual winning of independence but rather a shift of allegiance from England to America. Today, not all historians would agree with Adams's assertion that that shift constituted the Revolution. But none would deny the importance of the events of those crucial years, which led to the division of the American population along political lines and started the colonies on the road to independence.

The story of the 1760s and early 1770s is one of an ever-widening split between England and America, and among their respective supporters in the colonies. In the long history of British settlement in the Western Hemisphere, there had at times been considerable tension in the relationship between individual provinces and mother country. Still, that tension had rarely been sustained for long, nor had it been widespread, except in 1688 and 1689. The primary divisions affecting the colonies had been internal rather than external. In the 1750s, however, a series of events began to change all that, shifting the colonists' attention from domestic matters to their relations with Great Britain. It all started with the Seven Years' War (1754–1763).

Britain's overwhelming victory in that war forever altered the balance of power in North America. France was ousted from the continent, an event with major consequences for both the Indian tribes of the interior and the residents of the British colonies. Northern Indians could no longer play European powers off against one another, and so they lost one of their major diplomatic tools. Anglo-Americans, for their part, no longer had to fear a French threat on their borders. Some historians have argued that if the colonies had had to worry about the continuing presence of France on the North American mainland, the Revolution could never have occurred. The British colonies would never have dared to break with their mother country, it is said, if an enemy nation and its Indian allies had controlled the interior of the continent.

The British victory in 1763, then, constituted a major turning point in American history because of its direct effect on white and Indian residents of North America. It also had a significant impact on Great Britain, one that soon affected the colonies as well. To win the war, Britain had gone heavily into debt. To reduce the debt, Parliament for the first time laid revenue-raising taxes on the colonies. That decision exposed differences in the political thinking of Americans and Britons—differences that had until then been obscured by the use of a common political vocabulary.

During the 1760s a broad coalition of white Americans, men and women alike, resisted new tax levies and attempts by British officials to tighten

1754	Albany Congress Seven Years' War begins	1767	Townshend Acts
1756	War officially declared	1770	Lord North becomes prime minister
1760	American phase of war ends George III becomes king		Repeal of the Townshend duties except the tea tax Boston Massacre
1763	Treaty of Paris Pontiac's uprising Proclamation of 1763	1772	Boston Committee of Correspondence formed
1764	Sugar Act	1773	Tea Act Boston Tea Party
1765	Stamp Act Sons of Liberty formed	1774	Coercive Acts
1766	Repeal of the Stamp Act Declaratory Act		

controls over the provincial governments. America's elected leaders became ever more suspicious of Britain's motives as the years passed. They laid aside intercolonial antagonisms to coordinate their response to the new measures, and they slowly began to reorient their political thinking. As late as the summer of 1774, though, most were still seeking a solution within the framework of the empire; few harbored thoughts of independence. When independence, as opposed to loyal resistance, did become the issue, the coalition of the 1760s broke down. That, however, did not happen until after the battles of Lexington and Concord in April 1775. Before then, only a few Americans closely connected to colonial administration or the Church of England opposed the trend of resistance.

Renewed Warfare Among Europeans and Indians

The English colonies along the Atlantic seaboard were surrounded by hostile—or potentially hostile—neighbors: Indians everywhere, the Spanish in Florida and along the coast of the Gulf of Mexico, the French along the great inland system of rivers and lakes that stretched from the St. Lawrence to the Mississippi (see pages 55–61). The Spanish outposts posed little threat to the English, for Spain's days as a major power had passed, but the French were another matter. Their long chain of forts and settlements dominated the North American interior, facilitating trading partnerships and alliances with the tribes of the region. In none of the three wars fought between 1689 and 1748 was England able to shake France's hold on the American frontier. Under the Peace of Utrecht, which ended Queen Anne's War in 1713, the English won control of such peripheral northern areas as New-foundland, Hudson's Bay, and Nova Scotia (Acadia). But Britain made no additional territorial gains in King George's War (see map, page 106).

During both Queen Anne's War and King George's War, the Iroquois Confederacy adhered to the policy of neutrality it first developed in 1701 (see page 59). While English and French forces fought for nominal control of the North American continent, the confederacy, which actually dominated a large portion of that continent,

Iroquois Neutrality

European Settlements and Indian Tribes, 1750

A colonial soldier in 1758 etched onto his powder horn images of Indians and English troops fighting in the Seven Years' War. *The New-York Historical Society.*

skillfully played the Europeans off against one another, refusing to commit its warriors fully to either side despite being showered with presents by both. Instead, the Iroquois fought only their traditional southern enemies, the Catawbas. Since France repeatedly urged them to attack the Catawbas, who were allied with England, the Iroquois achieved three desirable goals. They kept the French happy and simultaneously consolidated their control over the entire interior region north of Virginia. In addition, these southern wars (by identifying a common enemy) enabled the confederacy to cement its alliance with its weaker tributaries, the Shawnees and Delawares, and to ensure the continued subordination of those tribes.

But even the careful Iroquois diplomats could not prevent the region inhabited by the Shawnees and Delawares (now western Pennsylvania and eastern Ohio) from providing the spark that set off a major war. That conflict spread from America to Europe (a significant reversal of previous patterns) and proved decisive in the contest for North America. Trouble began in 1752 when English fur traders ventured into the area known as the Ohio country. The French could not permit their English rivals to gain a foothold in the region, for it contained the source of the Ohio River, which offered direct access by water to their posts on the Mississippi. A permanent English presence in the Ohio country could challenge France's control of the western fur trade and even threaten its prominence in the Mississippi valley. Accordingly, in 1753 the French pushed southward from Lake Erie, building fortified outposts at strategic points along the rivers of the Ohio country.

In response to the threat posed by the French to their western frontiers, delegates from seven northern and middle colonies gathered in Albany, New York, in June 1754. With the backing of administrators in London, they sought two goals: to persuade the Iroquois to abandon their traditional neutrality and to coordinate the defenses of the colonies. In neither aim were they successful. The Iroquois, while listening politely to the colonists' arguments, saw no reason to change a policy that had served them well for half a century. And although the Albany Congress delegates adopted a Plan of Union (which would have established an elected intercolonial legislature with the power to tax), the plan was uniformly rejected by their provincial governments—primarily because those governments feared a loss of autonomy.

> **Albany Congress**

The delegates to the Albany Congress did not know that, while they deliberated, the war they sought to prepare for was already beginning. Governor Robert Dinwiddie of Virginia had sent a small militia force westward to counter the French moves. Virginia claimed ownership of the Ohio country, and Dinwiddie was eager to prevent the

On the night of September 13, 1759, British forces under General James Wolfe scaled the heights of Quebec and defeated the French army led by General Louis Joseph Montcalm. Both generals died on the battlefield. *Library of Congress.*

French from establishing a permanent post there. But the Virginia militiamen arrived too late. The French had already taken possession of the strategic point—now Pittsburgh—where the Allegheny and Monongahela rivers meet to form the Ohio, and they were busily engaged in constructing Fort Duquesne. The foolhardy and inexperienced young colonel who commanded the Virginians attacked a French detachment, then allowed himself to be trapped by the French in his crudely built Fort Necessity at Great Meadows, Pennsylvania. After a day-long battle (on July 3, 1754), during which more than one-third of his men were killed or wounded, twenty-two-year-old George Washington surrendered. He signed a document of capitulation, and he and his men were allowed to return to Virginia.

Washington had blundered grievously. He had started a war that would eventually encompass nearly the entire world. He had also ensured that the tribes of the Ohio valley, many of whom had moved west to escape Iroquois domination and to trade directly with the French, would for the most part support France in the coming conflict. The Indians took Washington's mistakes as an indication of Britain's inability to win the war, and nothing that occurred in the next four years made them change their minds. In July 1755 a combined force of French and Indians ambushed General Edward Braddock, two regiments of British regulars, and some colonial troops a few miles south of Fort Duquesne. Braddock was killed and his men demoralized by their complete defeat. After news of the debacle reached London, Britain declared war on France in 1756, thus formally beginning the conflict that is known as the Seven Years' War.

> **Seven Years' War**

For three more years one disaster followed another for Great Britain. The war went so badly that Britain began to fear France would attempt to retake Newfoundland and Nova Scotia. Trying to solidify their hold on that area, the British administrators of Nova Scotia forced its French residents to leave the homes they had occupied for generations. After years of wandering, many of these Acadian exiles eventually made their way to Louisiana, where they then became known as Cajuns.

At last, under the leadership of William Pitt, who was named secretary of state in 1757, the British mounted the effort that won them the war in North America. Pitt encouraged cooperation between the colonists and Great Britain, agreeing to reimburse the colonies for their military expenditures and placing troop recruitment wholly in local hands. He thereby gained wholehearted American support for the war effort. By contrast, in the early years of the Seven Years' War—the years of England's many defeats—British officers had usually tried to coerce the colonies into supplying men and materiel to the army.

In July 1758, British forces recaptured the fortress at Louisbourg, winning control of the entrance to the St. Lawrence and breaking the Canadians' major supply route to France. Then, in a surprise night attack in September 1759, General James Wolfe's soldiers defeated the French on the Plains of Abraham and broke down the defenses of Quebec. Sensing a British victory, the Iroquois abandoned their policy of neutrality and allied themselves with the British, hoping thereby to gain some diplomatic leverage. A year later the British took Montreal, the last French stronghold on the continent, and the American phase of the war had ended.

When the Treaty of Paris was signed in 1763, France ceded its major North American holdings to Britain. Spain, an ally of France toward the end of the war, gave Florida to the victorious English. And since Britain feared the presence of France on its western borders, it forced the French to cede the region west of the Mississippi (Louisiana) to Spain. No longer would the English seacoast colonies have to worry about the threat to their existence posed by France's extensive North American territories, and the British gained control of the fur trade of the entire continent (see maps).

BEFORE 1754

- English
- New France
- New Spain
- Russian

NOVA SCOTIA (Acadia)

AFTER 1763

- English
- New France
- New Spain
- Russian

NOVA SCOTIA (Acadia)

European Claims in North America

Because most of the fighting had been in the Northeast, the war had especially pronounced effects on New Englanders. As many as one-third of all Massachusetts men between the ages of sixteen and twenty-nine served for a time in the provincial army. Wartime service left a lasting impression on these soldiers. For the first time, ordinary Americans came into extended contact with Britons—and they did not like what they saw. The provincials thought the redcoats haughty, profane Sabbath-breakers who arbitrarily imposed overly harsh punishments on anyone who broke the rules. Nearly sixty years later a veteran still vividly recalled an incident in 1762 when hundreds of lashes were inflicted on three men for "some trifling offense." "I felt at the time as though I could have taken summary vengeance on those who were the authors of it," he wrote in his memoirs.

> **American Soldiers**

The New England soldiers also learned that British regulars did not share their adherence to principles of contract and consensus—the values that had governed their lives at home. Colonial regiments mutinied or rebelled en masse if they believed they were being treated unfairly, as happened, for example, when they were not allowed to leave at the end of their formal enlistments. One private in these circumstances grumbled in his journal in 1759, "Although we be Englishmen born, we are debarred Englishmen's liberty. . . . [The British soldiers] are but little better than slaves to their officers. And when I get out of their [power] I shall take care how I get in again." Such men would later draw on their personal experience of British "tyranny" when they were deciding to support the Revolution.

The overwhelming British triumph stimulated some Americans to think expansively about the colonies' future. Persons like Benjamin Franklin, who had long touted the colonies' wealth and potential, predicted a new, glorious future for British North America—a future that included not just further geographical expansion but also large-scale economic and demographic development. Such men were to form the core of the leadership of resistance to British measures in the years after 1763. They uniformly opposed any laws that would retard America's growth and persistently supported steps to increase Americans' control over their own destiny.

1763: A Turning Point

The great victory over France had an irreversible impact on North America, the effects of which were felt first by the interior tribes. With France excluded from the continent altogether and Spanish territory now confined to the area west of the Mississippi, the diplomatic strategy that had served the tribes well for so long could no longer be employed. The consequences were immediate and devastating.

Even before the Treaty of Paris, southern Indians had to adjust to the new circumstances. After the British gained the upper hand in the American war in 1758, the Creeks and Cherokees lost their ability to force concessions from them by threatening to turn instead to the French or the Spanish. In desperation and in retaliation for British atrocities, the Cherokees attacked the Carolina and Virginia frontiers in 1760. Although initially victorious, the tribesmen were defeated the following year by a force of British regulars and colonial militia. Late in 1761 the two sides concluded a treaty under which the Cherokees allowed the construction of English forts in tribal territories and also opened a large tract of land to white settlement.

The fate of the Cherokees in the South was a portent of things to come in the Ohio country. There, the Ottawas, Chippewas, and Potawatomis became angry when Great Britain, no longer facing French competition, raised the price of trade goods and ended the practice of paying rent for forts. In addition, the British allowed settlers to move into the Monongahela and Susquehanna valleys, onto Delaware and Iroquois lands.

Pontiac, the war chief of an Ottawa village near Detroit, understood the implications of such British actions. Only unity among the western tribes, he realized, could possibly prevent total dependence on and subordination to the victorious British.

> **Pontiac's Uprising**

Using his considerable powers of persuasion, in the spring of 1763 he forged an unprecedented alliance among Hurons, Chippewas, Potawatomis, Delawares, and Shawnees, even gaining the participation of some Mingoes (Pennsylvania Iroquois). Pontiac laid seige to the fort at Detroit while his war parties attacked other British outposts in the Great Lakes region. Detroit with-

Benjamin West, the first well-known American artist, engraved this picture of a prisoner exchange at the end of Pontiac's uprising, with Colonel Henry Bouquet supervising the return of whites captured during the war. In the foreground, a white child resists leaving the Indian parents he had grown to love. Many whites were fascinated by the phenomenon West depicted—the reluctance of captives to abandon their adoptive Indian families. *Rare Book Division, New York Public Library, Astor, Lenox, and Tilden Foundations.*

stood the siege, but by the end of June all the other forts west of Niagara and north of Fort Pitt (old Fort Duquesne) had fallen to the Indian alliance.

That was the high point of the uprising. The tribes raided the Virginia and Pennsylvania frontiers at will throughout the summer, killing at least two thousand whites. But they could not take the strongholds of Niagara, Fort Pitt, or Detroit. In early August, a combined force of Delawares, Shawnees, Hurons, and Mingoes was soundly defeated at Bushy Run, Pennsylvania, by troops sent from the coast. Conflict ceased when Pontiac broke off the siege of Detroit in late October, after most of his warriors had returned to their villages. A treaty ending the war was finally negotiated in 1766.

In the aftermath of the bloody summer of 1763, Scotch-Irish frontiersmen from Paxton Township, Pennsylvania, sought revenge on the only Indians within reach, a peaceful band of Christian converts living at Conestoga. In December the whites raided the Indian village twice, killing twenty people. Two months later hundreds of frontier dwellers known to history as the Paxton Boys marched on Philadelphia to demand military protection against future Indian attacks. City officials feared violence and mustered the militia to repel the westerners, but the protesters presented their request in an orderly fashion and returned home.

Pontiac's uprising and the march of the Paxton Boys showed that Great Britain would not find it

King George III in his coronation robes, 1760, painted by Allan Ramsay. *The Colonial Williamsburg Foundation.*

Other decisions made in London in 1763 and thereafter had a wider impact in British North America. The victory in the Seven Years' War both posed problems for and offered opportunities to the British government. The most pressing problem was Britain's immense war debt. The men who had to solve that problem were King George III and his new prime minister, George Grenville.

In 1760 George III, then twenty-two years old, succeeded his grandfather, George II, on the English throne. The young king, a man of mediocre intellect and even more mediocre education, was unfortunately a poor—or, more accurately, an erratic—judge of character. During the crucial years between 1763 and 1770, when the rift between England and the colonies was growing ever wider, he replaced ministries with bewildering rapidity. The king, though determined to assert the power of the monarchy, was immature and unsure of himself. He often substituted stubbornness for intelligence, and he regarded adherence to the status quo as the hallmark of patriotism.

> **George III**

The man he selected as prime minister in 1763, George Grenville, believed that the American colonies should be more tightly administered than in the past. Grenville confronted a financial crisis: England's burden of indebtedness had nearly doubled since 1754, from £73 million to £137 million. Annual expenditures before the war had amounted to no more than £8 million; now the yearly interest on the debt alone came to £5 million. Obviously, Grenville's ministry had to find new sources of funds, and the English people themselves were already heavily taxed. Since the colonists had been major beneficiaries of the wartime expenditures, Grenville concluded that the Americans should be asked to pay a greater share of the cost of running the empire.

It did not occur to Grenville to question Great Britain's right to levy taxes on the colonies. Like all his countrymen, he believed that the government's legitimacy derived ultimately from the consent of the people, but he defined consent far more loosely than did the colonists. Americans had come to believe that they could be represented only by men for whom they or their property-holding neighbors had actually voted; otherwise, they could not count on legis-

> **Theories of Representation**

easy to govern the huge territory it had just acquired from France. The central administration in London had had no prior experience in managing such a vast tract of land, particularly one inhabited by two hostile peoples—the remaining French settlers along the St. Lawrence and the many Indian tribes. In October, in a futile attempt to assert control over the interior, the ministry issued the Proclamation of 1763, which declared the headwaters of rivers flowing into the Atlantic from the Appalachian Mountains to be the temporary western boundary for colonial settlement. The proclamation was intended to prevent clashes between Indians and colonists by forbidding whites to move onto Indian lands until the tribes had given up their land by treaty. But many whites had already established farms or purchased property west of the proclamation line, and as a result, the policy was doomed to failure from its outset.

> **Proclamation of 1763**

lators to protect them from oppression. To Grenville and his English contemporaries, Parliament—king, lords, and commons acting together—by definition represented all English subjects, wherever they resided (even overseas) and whether or not they could vote. According to this theory of government, called *virtual representation,* the colonists were said to be virtually, if not actually, represented in Parliament. Thus their consent to acts of Parliament could be presumed.

The Americans and the English began at the same theoretical starting point but arrived at different conclusions in practice. In England, members of Parliament saw themselves as *collectively* representing the entire nation, composed of nobility and common folk. Only members of the House of Commons were elected, and the particular constituency that chose a member had no special claim on his vote. In the colonies, by contrast, members of the lower houses of the assemblies were viewed as *individually* representing the voters who had elected them. Before Grenville proposed to tax the colonists, the two notions existed side by side without apparent contradiction. But the events of the 1760s pointed up the difference between the English and colonial definitions of representation.

The same events threw into sharp relief Americans' attitudes toward political power. The colonists had become accustomed to a government that wielded only limited authority over them and affected their daily lives very little. In consequence, they believed that a good government was one that largely left them alone, a view in keeping with the theories of a group of British writers known as the Real Whigs. Drawing on a tradition of English dissenting thought that reached back to John Locke and even the Civil War (see pages 42–43), the Real Whigs stressed the dangers inherent in a powerful government, particularly one headed by a monarch. They warned the people to guard constantly against government's attempts to encroach on their liberty and to seize their property. Political power was always to be feared, wrote John Trenchard and Thomas Gordon in their essay series *Cato's Letters* (originally published in England in 1720–1723 and reprinted many times thereafter in the colonies). Rulers would try to corrupt and oppress the people. Only the perpetual vigilance of the people and their elected representatives could preserve their fragile yet precious liberty, which

was closely linked to their right to hold private property.

Britain's attempts to tighten the reins of government and raise revenues from the colonies in the 1760s and early 1770s convinced many Americans that the Real Whigs' reasoning applied to their circumstances, especially because of the connection between liberty and property rights. Excessive and unjust taxation, they believed, could destroy their freedoms. They began to interpret British measures in light of the Real Whigs' warnings and to see evil designs behind the actions of Grenville and his successors. Historians disagree over the extent to which those perceptions were correct, but by 1775 a large number of colonists unquestionably believed they were. In the mid-1760s, however, colonial leaders did not immediately accuse Grenville of an intent to oppress them. They at first simply questioned the wisdom of the laws Grenville proposed.

The first such measures, the Sugar and Currency Acts, were passed by Parliament in 1764. The Sugar Act (also known as the Revenue Act) revised the

Sugar and Currency Acts existing system of customs regulations; laid new duties on certain foreign imports into the colonies; established a vice-admiralty court at Halifax, Nova Scotia; and included special provisions aimed at stopping the widespread smuggling of molasses, one of the chief commodities in American trade. Although the Sugar Act appeared to resemble the Navigation Acts, which the colonies had long accepted as legitimate (see page 64), it broke with tradition because it was explicitly designed to raise revenue, not to channel American trade through Britain. The Currency Act in effect outlawed colonial issues of paper money. Americans could accumulate little hard cash, since they imported more than they exported; thus the act seemed to the colonists to deprive them of a useful medium of exchange.

The Sugar and Currency Acts were visited upon an economy already in the midst of depression. A business boom had accompanied the Seven Years' War, but the brief spell of prosperity ended abruptly in 1760 when the war shifted overseas. Urban merchants could not sell all their imported goods to colonial customers alone, and without the military's demand for foodstuffs, American farmers found fewer buyers for their products. The bottom dropped out of the European tobacco market, threatening the livelihood of Chesapeake planters. Sailors were thrown out of work, and artisans found few employers to hire them. In such circumstances, the prospect of increased customs duties and inadequate supplies of currency aroused merchants' hostility.

Unsurprisingly, both individual colonists and colonial governments decided to protest the new policies. But, lacking any precedent for a united campaign against acts of Parliament, Americans in 1764 took only hesitant and uncoordinated steps. Eight colonial legislatures sent separate petitions to Parliament requesting repeal of the Sugar Act. They argued that the act placed severe restrictions on their commerce (and would therefore hurt Britain as well), and they said that they had not consented to its passage. The protests had no effect. The law remained in force, and Grenville proceeded with another revenue plan.

The Stamp Act Crisis

The Stamp Act, Grenville's most important proposal, was modeled on a law that had been in effect in England for nearly a century. It touched nearly every colonist by requiring tax stamps on most printed materials, but it placed the heaviest burden on merchants and other members of the colonial elite, who used printed matter more frequently than ordinary folk. Anyone who purchased a newspaper or pamphlet, made a will, transferred land, bought dice or playing cards, needed a liquor license, accepted a government appointment, or borrowed money would have to pay the tax. Never before had a revenue measure of such scope been proposed for the colonies. The act also required that tax stamps be paid for with hard money, which was scarce, and that violators be tried in vice-admiralty courts, which were presided over by judges alone and had no juries. Previously such courts had only heard cases involving violations of maritime law; Americans feared the loss of their right to trial by a jury of their peers. Finally, such a law would break decisively with the colonial tradition of self-imposed taxation.

The most important colonial pamphlet protest-ing the Sugar Act and the proposed Stamp Act was *The Rights of the British Colonies Asserted and Proved*, by James Otis, Jr., a brilliant young Massachusetts attorney. Otis starkly exposed the ideological dilemma that was to confound the colonists for the next decade. How could they justify their opposition to certain acts of Parliament without questioning Parliament's authority over them? On the one hand, Otis asserted that Americans were "entitled to all the natural, essential, inherent, and inseparable rights" of Britons, including the right not to be taxed without their consent. "No man or body of men, not excepting the parliament . . . can take [those rights] away," he declared. On the other hand, Otis was forced to admit that, under the British system established after the Glorious Revolution of 1688 and 1689, "the power of parliament is uncontrollable but by themselves, and we must obey. . . . Let the parliament lay what burthens they please on us, we must, it is our duty to submit and patiently bear them, till they will be pleased to relieve us."

> Otis's *Rights of the British Colonies*

Otis's first contention, drawing on colonial notions of representation, implied that Parliament could not constitutionally tax the colonies because Americans were not represented in its ranks. Yet his second point both acknowledged political reality and accepted the prevailing theory of British government—that Parliament was the sole, supreme authority in the empire. Even unconstitutional laws enacted by Parliament had to be obeyed until Parliament decided to repeal them. According to orthodox British political theory, there could be no middle ground between absolute submission to Parliament and a frontal challenge to its authority. Otis tried to find such a middle ground by proposing colonial representation in Parliament, but his idea was never taken seriously on either side of the Atlantic. The British believed that the colonists were already virtually represented in Parliament, and the Americans quickly realized that a handful of colonial delegates to London would simply be outvoted.

Otis wrote his pamphlet before the Stamp Act was passed. When Americans learned of its adoption in the spring of 1765, they did not at first know how to react. Few colonists—even appointed government officials—publicly favored the law. But

Chapter 4: Severing the Bonds of Empire, 1754–1774

colonial petitions had already failed to prevent its adoption, and further lobbying appeared futile. Perhaps Otis was right, and the only course open to Americans was to pay the stamp tax, reluctantly but loyally. Acting on that assumption, colonial agents in London sought the appointment of their American friends as stamp distributors so that the law would at least be enforced equitably.

Not all the colonists were resigned to paying the new tax. Among them was a twenty-nine-year-old lawyer serving his first term in the Virginia House of Burgesses. Patrick Henry later recalled that he was "young, inexperienced, unacquainted with the forms of the house and the members that composed it"—and appalled by his fellow legislators' unwillingness to oppose the Stamp Act. Henry decided to act. "Alone, unadvised, and unassisted, on a blank leaf of an old law book," he wrote the Virginia Stamp Act Resolves.

> **Patrick Henry and the Virginia Stamp Act Resolves**

Little in Henry's earlier life foreshadowed his success in the political arena he entered so dramatically. The son of a prosperous Scottish immigrant to western Virginia, Henry had had little formal education. After marrying at eighteen, he failed at both farming and storekeeping before turning to the law as a means of supporting his wife and their six children. Henry lacked legal training, but his oratorical skills made him an effective advocate, first for his clients and later for his political beliefs. A prominent Virginia lawyer observed, "He is by far the most powerful speaker I ever heard. Every word he says not only engages, but commands the attention; and your passions are no longer your own when he addresses them."

Patrick Henry introduced his seven proposals in late May, near the end of the legislative session, when many members of the House of Burgesses had already departed for home. Henry's fiery speech in support of his resolutions led the Speaker of the House to accuse him of treason. (Henry quickly denied the charge, contrary to the nineteenth-century myth that had him exclaiming in reply, "If this be treason, make the most of it!") The small number of burgesses remaining in Williamsburg adopted five of Henry's resolutions by a bare majority. Although they repealed the most radical resolution the next day, their action had far-reaching effects. Some colonial newspapers printed Henry's seven original resolutions as if they had been uniformly passed by the House, even though one had been rescinded and two others evidently were never debated or voted on at all.

The four propositions adopted by the burgesses repeated the arguments James Otis had already advanced. The colonists had never forfeited the rights of British subjects, they declared, and consent to taxation was one of the most important such rights. The other three resolutions went much further. The one that was repealed claimed for the burgesses "the only exclusive right" to tax Virginians. The final two asserted that residents of the colony did not have to obey tax laws passed by other legislative bodies (namely Parliament) and termed any opponent of that opinion "an Enemy to this his Majesty's Colony."

The burgesses' decision to accept only the first four of Henry's resolutions anticipated the position most Americans would adopt throughout the following decade. Though willing to contend for their rights, the colonists did not seek independence. They merely wanted some measure of self-government. Accordingly, they backed away from the assertions that they owed Parliament no obedience and that only their own assemblies could tax them. Indeed, declared the Maryland lawyer Daniel Dulany, whose *Considerations on the Propriety of Imposing Taxes on the British Colonies* was the most widely read pamphlet of 1765, "The colonies are dependent upon Great Britain, and the supreme authority vested in the king, lords, and commons, may justly be exercised to secure, or preserve their dependence." But, warned Dulany, a superior did not have the right "to seize the property of his inferior when he pleases"; there was a crucial distinction between a condition of "dependence and *inferiority*" and one of "absolute *vassalage* and slavery."

During the next ten years, America's political leaders searched for a formula that would enable them to control their internal affairs, especially taxation, but remain within the British Empire. The chief difficulty lay in British officials' inability to compromise on the issue of parliamentary power. The notion that Parliament could exercise absolute authority over all colonial possessions was basic to the British theory of government. Even the harshest British critics of the ministries of the 1760s and 1770s questioned only the wisdom of specific

Paul Revere produced this engraving, showing the hanging in effigy of John Huske, an American-born member of Parliament who allegedly supported the Stamp Act. Note the sign, which symbolically designates "Liberty Tree" and includes the date August 14, 1765—the time of the first major anti-Stamp Act demonstration in Boston. *American Antiquarian Society.*

policies, not the principles on which they were based. In effect, the Americans wanted British leaders to revise their fundamental understanding of the workings of their government. That was simply too much to expect, given the circumstances.

The ultimate effectiveness of Americans' opposition to the Stamp Act rested on more than ideological arguments over parliamentary power. What gave the resistance its primary force were the decisive and inventive actions of some colonists during the late summer and fall of 1765.

In August the Loyal Nine, a Boston social club of printers, distillers, and other artisans, organized a demonstration against the Stamp Act. Hoping to

> **Loyal Nine**

show that people of all ranks opposed the act, they approached the leaders of the city's rival laborers' associations, based in the North End and the South End. The two gangs, composed of unskilled workers and poor tradesmen, often battled with each other, but the Loyal Nine convinced them to lay aside their differences and participate in the demonstration. After all, the stamp taxes would have to be paid by all colonists, not just affluent ones.

Early in the morning of August 14, the demonstrators hung an effigy of Andrew Oliver, the province's stamp distributor, from a tree on Boston Common. That night a large crowd led by a group of about fifty well-dressed tradesmen paraded the effigy around the city. The crowd tore down a small building they thought was intended as the stamp office and built a bonfire near Oliver's house with the wood from the destroyed building. They then beheaded the effigy and added it to the flames. Members of the crowd broke most of Oliver's windows and threw stones at officials who tried to disperse them. In the midst of the melee, the North End and the South End leaders drank a toast to their successful union. The Loyal Nine's demonstration achieved its objective when Oliver publicly promised not to fulfill the duties of his office. One Bostonian jubilantly told a relative, "I believe people never was more Universally pleased not so much one could I hear say he was sorry, but a smile sat on almost every ones countinance."

But another crowd action twelve days later, aimed this time at Oliver's brother-in-law, Lieutenant Governor Thomas Hutchinson, drew no praise from the respectable citizens of Boston. On the night of August 26, a mob reportedly led by the South End leader, Ebenezer MacIntosh, attacked the homes of several customs officers. The crowd then completely destroyed Hutchinson's elaborately furnished townhouse in one of Boston's most fashionable districts. The lieutenant governor reported that by the next morning "one of the best finished houses in the Province had nothing remaining but the bare walls and floors." His trees and garden were ruined, his huge library lost, and the mob had "emptied the house of every thing whatsoever except a part of the kitchen furniture." But Hutchinson took some comfort in the fact that "the encouragers of the first mob never intended matters should go this length and the people in general express the utmost detestation of this unparalleled outrage."

The differences between the two Boston mobs of August 1765 exposed divisions that would continue to characterize colonial protests in the years that

> **Americans' Divergent Interests**

followed. Although few residents of the colonies sided with Great Britain during these early years of protest, the various colonial groups often had divergent goals that caused splits in their ranks. The skilled craftsmen who composed the Loyal Nine and members of the educated elite like merchants and lawyers preferred orderly demonstrations confined to political issues. For the city's laborers, by contrast, economic grievances may have been paramount. Certainly, their "hellish Fury" as they wrecked Hutchinson's house suggests a resentment against his ostentatious display of wealth.

Colonists, like Britons, had a long tradition of crowd action in which disfranchised people took to the streets to redress deeply felt local grievances. But the Stamp Act controversy drew ordinary urban folk into the vortex of imperial politics for the first time. Matters that had previously been of concern only to genteel folk or to members of colonial legislatures were now discussed on every street corner. Sally Franklin observed as much when she wrote to her father, Benjamin, who was then serving as a colonial agent in London, that "nothing else is talked of, the Dutch [Germans] talk of the stompt act the Negroes of the tamp, in short every body has something to say."

The entry of lower-class whites, blacks, and women into the realm of imperial politics both threatened and afforded an opportunity to the elite white men who wanted to mount effective opposition to British measures. On the one hand, crowd action could have a stunning impact. Anti–Stamp Act demonstrations occurred in cities and towns

stretching from Halifax, Nova Scotia, in the north, to the Caribbean island of Antigua (see maps, page 118). They were so successful that by November 1, when the law was scheduled to take effect, not a single stamp distributor was willing to carry out the duties of his office. Thus the act could not be enforced. But at the same time, since the goals of the crowd were not always identical to the goals of its nominal leaders (as the Boston experience showed), wealthy men recognized that mobs composed of the formerly powerless could endanger their own dominance of the society. What would happen, they wondered, if the "hellish Fury" of the crowd were turned against them?

Therefore, they attempted to channel resistance into acceptable forms by creating an intercolonial association, the Sons of Liberty. The first such

> **Sons of Liberty**

group was created in New York in early November, and branches spread rapidly through the coastal cities. Composed of merchants, lawyers, prosperous tradesmen, and the like, the Sons of Liberty linked protest leaders from Charleston, South Carolina, to Portsmouth, New Hampshire, by early 1766.

The Sons of Liberty could influence but not control events. In Charleston in late October 1765 an organized crowd shouting "Liberty Liberty and stamp'd paper" forced the resignation of the South Carolina stamp distributor. The event was celebrated a few days later in the largest demonstration the city had ever known, at which was displayed a British flag with the word "LIBERTY" written across it. But white resistance leaders were horrified when in January 1766 local slaves paraded through the streets similarly crying "Liberty." The local militia was mustered; messengers were sent to outlying areas with warnings of a possible plot; and one black was banished from the colony.

In Philadelphia, resistance leaders were dismayed when an angry mob threatened to attack Benjamin Franklin's house. The city's laborers believed Franklin to be partly responsible for the Stamp Act, since he had obtained the post of stamp distributor for a close friend. But Philadelphia's artisans—the backbone of the opposition movement there and elsewhere—were fiercely loyal to Franklin, one of their own who had made good. They gathered to protect his home and family from the crowd. The house was saved, but the resulting split

The Stamp Act Crisis

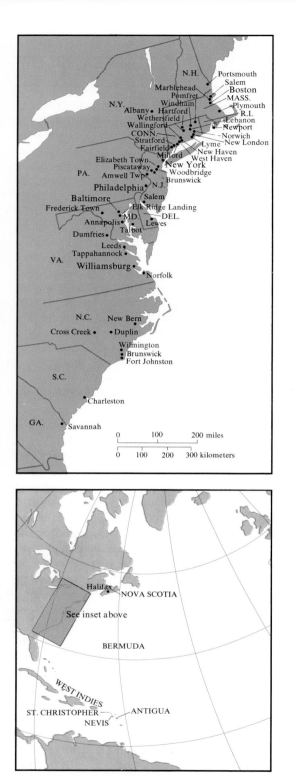

Sites of Major Demonstrations Against the Stamp Act

between the better-off tradesmen and the common laborers prevented the establishment of a successful workingmen's alliance like that of Boston.

During the fall and winter of 1765 and 1766, opposition to the Stamp Act proceeded on three separate fronts. Colonial legislatures petitioned Parliament to repeal the hated law and sent delegates to an intercolonial congress, the first since the Albany Congress of 1754. In October the Stamp Act Congress met in New York to draft a unified but conservative statement of protest. At the same time, the Sons of Liberty held mass meetings in an effort to win public support for the resistance movement. Finally, American merchants organized nonimportation associations to put economic pressure on British exporters. By the 1760s one-quarter of all British exports were being sent to the colonies, and American merchants reasoned that London merchants whose sales suffered severely would lobby for repeal. Since times were bad and American merchants were finding few customers for imported goods in any case, a general moratorium on future purchases would also help to reduce their bloated inventories.

In March 1766, Parliament repealed the Stamp Act. The nonimportation agreements had the anticipated effect, creating allies for the colonies among

> **Repeal of the Stamp Act**

wealthy London merchants. But boycotts, formal protests, and crowd actions were less important in winning repeal than was Grenville's replacement as prime minister in summer 1765. Lord Rockingham, the new head of the ministry, had opposed the Stamp Act, not because he believed Parliament lacked power to tax the colonies but because he thought the law unwise and divisive. Thus, although Rockingham proposed repeal, he linked it to passage of the Declaratory Act, which asserted Parliament's ability to tax and legislate for Britain's American possessions "in all cases whatsoever."

News of the repeal arrived in Newport, Rhode Island, in May, and the Sons of Liberty quickly transmitted the welcome tidings to all parts of the colonies. They also organized many celebrations commemorating the glorious event, all of which stressed the Americans' unwavering loyalty to Great Britain. Their goal achieved, the Sons of Liberty dissolved. Few colonists saw the ominous implications of the Declaratory Act.

BRITISH MINISTRIES AND THEIR AMERICAN POLICIES

Head of Ministry	Major Acts
George Grenville	Sugar Act (1764)
	Currency Act (1764)
	Stamp Act (1765)
Lord Rockingham	Stamp Act repealed (1766)
	Declaratory Act (1766)
William Pitt/Charles Townshend	Townshend Acts (1767)
Lord North	Townshend duties repealed (all but tea tax) (1770)
	Coercive Acts (1774)
	Quebec Act (1774)

Resistance to the Townshend Acts

The colonists had accomplished their immediate aim, but the long-term prospects were unclear. Another change in the ministry, in the summer of 1766, revealed how fragile their victory had been. Charles Townshend, a Grenvillite, was named chancellor of the exchequer in a new administration headed by the ailing William Pitt. Pitt was ill much of the time, and Townshend became the dominant force in the ministry. He decided to renew the attempt to obtain additional funds from the colonies.

The taxes proposed by Townshend in 1767 were to be levied on trade goods like paper, glass, and tea, and thus seemed on the surface to be nothing more than extensions of the existing Navigation Acts. But the Townshend duties differed from previous customs taxes in two ways. First, they were levied on items imported into the colonies from Britain, not from foreign countries. Thus they were at odds with mercantilist theory (see page 64). Second, they were designed, like the Sugar Act, to raise money. The receipts, moreover, would pay the salaries of royal officials in the colonies. That posed a direct challenge to the colonial assemblies, which derived considerable power from threatening to withhold officials' salaries. In addition, Townshend's scheme provided for the establish-

ment of an American Board of Customs Commissioners and for the creation of vice-admiralty courts at Boston, Philadelphia, and Charleston. Both moves angered merchants, whose profits would be threatened by more vigorous enforcement of the Navigation Acts. Lastly, Townshend proposed the appointment of a secretary of state for American affairs and the suspension of the New York legislature for refusal to comply with the Quartering Act of 1765, which required colonial governments to supply certain items (like firewood and candles) to British troops who were stationed permanently in America.

Unlike 1765, when months had passed before the colonists began to protest the Stamp Act, the passage of the Townshend Acts drew a quick response. One series of essays in particular, *Letters from a Farmer in Pennsylvania* by the prominent lawyer John Dickinson, expressed a broad consensus. Eventually all but four colonial newspapers printed Dickinson's essays; in pamphlet form they went through seven American editions. Dickinson contended that Parliament could regulate colonial trade but could not exercise that power for the purpose of raising revenues. By drawing a distinction between the acceptable regulation of trade and unacceptable commercial taxation, Dickinson avoided the sticky issue of consent and how it affected the extent of colonial subordination to Parliament. But his argument created a different, and equally knotty, problem. In effect it forced the colonies to assess Parliament's motives in passing any

Paul Revere's punchbowl commemorating the 92 members of the Massachusetts Assembly who voted against rescinding the circular letter. *Courtesy, Museum of Fine Arts, Boston, Gift by Subscription and Francis Bartlett Fund.*

law pertaining to imperial trade before deciding whether to obey it. That was clearly an unworkable position.

The Massachusetts assembly responded to the Townshend Acts by drafting a circular letter to the other colonial legislatures, calling for unity and suggesting a joint petition of protest. Not the letter itself but the ministry's reaction to it united the colonies. When Lord Hillsborough, the first secretary of state for America, learned of the circular letter, he ordered Governor Francis Bernard of Massachusetts to insist that the assembly recall it. He also directed other governors to prevent their assemblies from discussing the letter. Hillsborough's order gave the colonial assemblies the incentive they needed to forget their differences and join forces to meet the new threat to their prerogatives. In late 1768 the Massachusetts legislature met, debated, and resoundingly rejected recall by a

> **Massachusetts Assembly Dissolved**

vote of 92 to 17. Bernard immediately dissolved the assembly, and other governors followed suit when their legislatures debated the circular letter.

The number of votes cast against recalling the circular letter—92—assumed ritual significance for the supporters of resistance to Great Britain. The figure 45 already carried such symbolism because John Wilkes, a radical Englishman sympathetic to the American cause, had been jailed for libel early in the decade for publishing an essay entitled *The North Briton No. 45*. In Boston, the silversmith Paul Revere made a punchbowl weighing 45 ounces that held 45 gills (half-cups) and was engraved with the names of the 92 legislators; James Otis, John Adams, and others publicly drank 45 toasts from it. In Charleston, the city's tradesmen decorated a tree with 45 lights and set off 45 rockets. Carrying 45 candles, they adjourned to a tavern, where 45 tables were set with 45 bowls of wine, 45 bowls of punch, and 92 glasses.

> **Rituals of Resistance**

Pleasant social occasions though they were, such public rituals served important educational functions. Just as the pamphlets by Otis, Dulany, Dickinson, and others acquainted literate colonists with the issues raised by British actions, so the public rituals taught illiterate Americans about the reasons for resistance and familiarized them with the terms of the argument. When Boston's revived Sons of Liberty invited hundreds of the city's residents to dine with them each August 14 to commemorate the first Stamp Act uprising, and the Charleston Sons of Liberty held their meetings in public, crowds gathered to watch and listen. Likewise, the composing and public singing of songs supporting the American cause helped to spread the word. The participants in such events were openly expressing their commitment to the cause of resistance and encouraging others to join them.

During the two-year campaign against the Townshend duties, the Sons of Liberty and other American leaders made a deliberate effort to involve ordinary folk in the formal resistance movement, not just in occasional crowd actions. In a June 1769 Maryland nonimportation agreement, for instance, the signers (who were identified as "Merchants, Tradesmen, Freeholders, Mechanics [artisans], and other Inhabitants") agreed not to import or consume items of British origin. Such tactics helped to increase the number of colonists who were publicly aligned with the protest movement.

Women, who had previously regarded politics as outside their proper sphere, now took a part in resisting British policy. In towns throughout America, young women calling themselves Daughters of Liberty met to spin in public in an effort to spur other women to make homespun and end the colonies' dependence on English cloth. These symbolic displays of patriotism served the same purpose as the male rituals involving the numbers 45 and 92. When young ladies from well-to-do families sat publicly at spinning wheels all day, eating only American food and drinking local herbal tea, and afterward listening to patriotic sermons, they were serving as political instructors. Many women took great satisfaction in their new-found role. When a New England satirist hinted that women discussed only "such triffling subjects as Dress, Scandal and Detraction" during their spinning bees, three Boston women replied

Daughters of Liberty

MADE at the Subscriber's Glass-Works, and now on Hand, to be sold at his House in Market-Street, opposite the Meal-Market, either wholesale or retail, between Three and Four Hundred BOXES of WINDOW GLASS, consisting of the common Sizes, 10 by 12, 9 by 11, 8 by 10, 7 by 9, 6 by 8, &c. Lamp Glass, or any uncommon Sizes, under 16 by 18, are cut upon a short Notice. Where also may be had, most Sorts of Bottles, Gallon, Half Gallon, and Quart, full Measure Half Gallon Case Bottles, Snuff and Mustard, Receivers and Retorts of various Sizes; also electrifing Globes and Tubes, &c, As the abovementioned Glass is of American Manufactory, it is consequently clear of the Duties the Americans so justly complain of, and at present it seems peculiarly the Interest of America to encourage her own Manufactories, more especially those upon which Duties have been imposed, for the sole Purpose of raising a Revenue,
N B. He also continues to make the Philadelphia Brass Buttons, well noted for their Strength, such as were made by his deceased Father, and are warranted for seven Years.
Philadelphia, August 10. RICHARD WISTAR.

At the peak of the nonimportation movement in the summer of 1769, the Philadelphia glassmaker Richard Wistar placed this advertisement in the *New York Journal.* In addition to listing his wares, he appealed for customers by arguing that Americans should patronize local glassmakers instead of paying the hated Townshend duties on imported glass. Thus could patriotic pleas serve to increase an artisan's business at the expense of merchants dealing in imported goods. *The Historical Society of Pennsylvania.*

angrily: "Inferior in abusive sarcasm, in personal invective, in low wit, we glory to be, but inferior in veracity, sincerity, love of virtue, of liberty and of our country, we would not willingly be to any."

Women also took the lead in promoting nonconsumption of tea. In Boston more than three hundred matrons publicly promised not to drink tea, "Sickness excepted." The women of Wilmington, North Carolina, burned their tea after walking through town in a solemn procession. Housewives throughout the colonies exchanged recipes for tea substitutes or drank coffee instead. The best known of the protests (because it was satirized by a British cartoonist), the so-called Edenton Ladies Tea Party, actually had little to do with tea; it was a meeting of prominent North Carolina women who pledged formally to work for the public good and to support resistance to British measures.

But the colonists were by no means united in support of nonimportation. If the Stamp Act protests had occasionally (as in Boston and Philadelphia) revealed a division between artisans and merchants, on the one hand, and

Divided Opinion over Boycotts

A Society of Patriotic Ladies, 1775, attributed to Philip Dawes, an English printmaker. This grotesque caricature of female patriots shows the women emptying their tea into a chamber pot (at left) and flirting with their male counterparts (at center), while a neglected child sits below the table. The cartoon bears no resemblance to the actual event, the signing of an anti-British petition by female residents of Edenton, North Carolina. *Library of Congress.*

common laborers, on the other, resistance to the Townshend Acts exposed new splits in the American ranks. The most important divided the former allies of 1765 and 1766, the urban artisans and merchants, and it arose from a change in economic circumstances. The Stamp Act boycotts had helped to revive a depressed economy. In 1768 and 1769, by contrast, merchants were enjoying boom times and had no financial incentive to support a boycott. As a result, merchants signed the agreements only reluctantly. And, as John Mein revealed, they often secretly violated those agreements. Artisans, on the other hand, supported nonimportation enthusiastically, recognizing that the absence of British goods would create a ready market for their own manufactures. Thus tradesmen formed the core of the crowds that coerced both importers and their

customers by picketing stores, publicizing offenders' names, and sometimes destroying property.

Such tactics were effective: colonial imports from England dropped dramatically in 1769, especially in New York, New England, and Pennsylvania. But they also aroused significant opposition, creating a second major division among the colonists. Some Americans who supported resistance to British measures began to question the use of violence to force others to join the boycott. In addition, wealthier and more conservative colonists were frightened by the threat to private property inherent in the campaign. Moreover, political activism by ordinary colonists challenged the ruling elite's domination, just as they had feared in 1765. Thus a Charleston essayist warned in 1769 that "the industrious mechanic [is] a useful and essential part of society . . . in his own sphere," but "when he steps out of it, and sets up for a statesman! believe me he is in a fair way to expose himself to ridicule, and his family to distress, by neglecting his private business." Pretending concern for tradesmen's welfare, the author obviously feared for his own position.

Americans were relieved when the news arrived in April 1770 that a new prime minister, Lord North, had persuaded Parliament to repeal the

> **Repeal of the Townshend Duties**

Townshend duties, except the tea tax, on the grounds that duties on trade within the empire were bad policy. Although some political leaders argued that nonimportation should be continued until the tea tax was repealed, merchants quickly resumed importing. The rest of the Townshend Acts remained in force, but repeal of the taxes made the other laws appear less objectionable. In addition, John Mein's widely circulated disclosure that leading patriots like John Hancock were violating the nonimportation agreement caused dissension in the ranks of the boycotting merchants. That too hastened the end of nonimportation.

Growing Rifts

At first the new ministry did nothing to antagonize the colonists. Yet on the very day Lord North proposed repeal of the Townshend duties, a clash between civilians and soldiers in Boston led to the death of five Americans. The origins of the event patriots called the Boston Massacre lay in repeated clashes between customs officers and the people of Massachusetts. The Townshend Acts' creation of an American Board of Customs Commissioners had been error enough, but a decision to base the board in Boston severely compounded the mistake.

From the day of their arrival in November 1767, the customs commissioners were frequent targets of mob action. In June 1768, their seizure of the patriot leader John Hancock's sloop *Liberty* on suspicion of smuggling caused a riot in which prominent customs officers' property was destroyed. The riot in turn helped to convince the ministry in London that troops were needed to maintain order in the unruly port. The assignment of two regiments of regulars to their city confirmed Bostonians' worst fears; the redcoats were a constant reminder of the oppressive potential of British power.

Bostonians, accustomed to leading their lives with a minimum of interference from government, now found themselves hemmed in at every turn. Guards on Boston Neck, the entrance to the city, checked all travelers and their goods. Redcoat patrols roamed the city day and night, questioning and sometimes harassing passers-by. Military parades were held on Boston Common, accompanied by martial music and often the public whipping of deserters and other violators of army rules. Parents began to fear for the safety of their daughters, who were subjected to the soldiers' sexual insults when they ventured out on the streets. But the greatest potential for violence lay in the uneasy relationship between the soldiers and Boston laborers. Many redcoats sought employment in their off-duty hours, competing for unskilled jobs with the city's ordinary workingmen, and members of the two groups brawled repeatedly in taverns and on the streets.

On March 2, 1770, workers at a ropewalk (a ship-rigging factory) attacked some redcoats seeking jobs; a pitched battle resulted when both groups acquired reinforcements. Three **Boston** days later the tension exploded. **Massacre** Early on the evening of March 5, a crowd began throwing hard-packed snowballs at sentries guarding the Customs House. Goaded beyond endurance, the sentries fired on the crowd against express orders to the contrary, killing four and wounding eight, one of whom died a few days later. Resistance leaders idealized the dead rioters as martyrs for the cause of liberty, holding a solemn funeral three days later and commemorating March 5 annually with patriotic orations. The best-known engraving of the massacre, by Paul Revere, was part of the propaganda campaign. It depicts a peaceful crowd, an officer ordering the soldiers to fire, and shots coming from the window of the Customs House.

The leading patriots wanted to make certain the soldiers did not become martyrs as well. Despite the political benefits the patriots derived from the massacre, it is unlikely that they approved of the crowd action that provoked it. Ever since August 1765 the men allied with the Sons of Liberty had supported orderly demonstrations and expressed distaste for uncontrolled riots, of which the Boston Massacre was a prime example. Thus when the soldiers were tried for the killings in November, they were defended by John Adams and Josiah Quincy, Jr., both unwavering patriots. All but two of the accused men were acquitted, and those convicted were released after having been branded on the thumb. Undoubtedly the favorable outcome of the trials prevented London officials from taking further steps against the city.

For more than two years after the Boston Massacre and the repeal of the Townshend duties, a superficial calm descended on the colonies. Local incidents, like the burning of the customs vessel *Gaspée* in 1772 by Rhode Islanders, marred the relationship of individual colonies and the mother country, but nothing caused Americans to join in a unified protest. Even so, the resistance movement continued to gather momentum. The most outspoken colonial newspapers, such as the *Boston Gazette,* the *Pennsylvania Journal,* and the *South Carolina Gazette,* published essays drawing on Real Whig ideology and accusing Great Britain of a deliberate plan to oppress America. After repeal of the Stamp Act, the patriots had praised Parliament; following repeal of the Townshend duties, they warned of impending tyranny. What had seemed to be an isolated mistake, a single ill-chosen stamp tax, now appeared to be part of a plot against American liberties. Among other things, essayists pointed to Parliament's persecution of the English radical John Wilkes, the stationing of troops in Boston, and the growing number of vice-admiralty courts as evi-

Paul Revere's engraving of the Boston Massacre, a masterful piece of propaganda. At right, the British officer seems to be ordering the soldiers to fire on a peaceful, unresisting crowd. The Customs House has been labeled Butcher's Hall, and smoke drifts up from a gun barrel sticking out of the window. *Library of Congress.*

dence of plans to enslave the colonists. Indeed, patriot writers played repeatedly on the word *enslavement*. Most white colonists had direct knowledge of slavery (either being slaveholders themselves or having slaveowning neighbors), and the threat of enslavement by Britain must have hit them with peculiar force.

Still, no one yet advocated complete independence from the mother country. Though the patriots were becoming increasingly convinced that they should seek freedom from parliamentary authority, they continued to acknowledge their British identity and to pledge their allegiance to George III. They began, therefore, to try to envision a system that would enable them to be ruled by their own elected legislatures while remaining loyal to the king. But any such scheme was totally alien to Britons' conception of the nature of their government, which was that Parliament held sole undivided sovereignty over the empire. Furthermore, in the British mind, Parliament encompassed the king as well as lords and commons, and so separating the monarch from the legislature was impossible.

Conservative colonists recognized the dangers inherent in the patriots' new mode of thinking. The former stamp distributor Andrew Oliver, for example, predicted in 1771 that "serious consequences" would follow from the fact that "the leaders of the people were never [before] so open in asserting our independence of the British Legislature," even though "there is an intermission of Acts of violence at present."

Oliver's prediction proved correct when, in the fall of 1772, the North ministry began to implement the portion of the Townshend Acts that provided for governors and judges to be paid from customs revenues. In early November, voters at a Boston town meeting established a Committee of Correspondence to publicize the decision by exchanging letters with other Massachusetts towns. Heading the committee was the man who had proposed its formation, Samuel Adams. A year earlier, Adams had described the benefits of organizing an official communications network within and among the separate colonies. "If conducted with a proper spirit," Adams had asked, "would it not afford reason for the Enemies of our common Liberty, to tremble?"

> **Committees of Correspondence**

Samuel Adams was fifty-one years old in 1772, thirteen years the senior of his distant cousin John and a decade older than most other leaders of American resistance. He had been a Boston tax collector, a member and clerk of the Massachusetts assembly, and an ally of the Loyal Nine (though evidently not a member). Unswerving in his devotion to the American cause, Adams drew a sharp contrast between a corrupt Britain and the virtuous colonies. His primary forum was the Boston town meeting. An experienced political organizer, Adams continually stressed the necessity of prudent collective action. His Committee of Correspondence thus undertook the task of creating an informed consensus among all the citizens of Massachusetts.

Such committees, which were soon established throughout the colonies, represented the next logical step in the organization of American resistance. Until 1772, the protest movement was largely confined to the seacoast and primarily to major cities and towns (see map, page 118). Adams realized that the time had come to widen the movement's geographic scope, to attempt to involve the residents of the interior in the struggle that had hitherto enlisted chiefly the residents of urban areas. Accordingly, the Boston town meeting directed the Committee of Correspondence "to state the Rights of the Colonists and of this Province in particular," to list "the Infringements and Violations thereof that have been, or from time to time may be made," and to send copies to the other towns in the province. In return, Boston requested "a free communication of their Sentiments on this Subject."

Samuel Adams, James Otis, Jr., and Josiah Quincy, Jr., prepared the statement of the colonists' rights. Declaring that Americans had absolute rights to life, liberty, and property, the committee asserted that the idea that "a British house of commons, should have a right, at pleasure, to give and grant the property of the colonists" was "irreconcileable" with "the first principles of natural law and Justice . . . and of the British Constitution in particular." The list of grievances, drafted by another group of prominent patriots, was similarly sweeping. It complained of taxation without representation, the presence of unnecessary troops and customs officers on American soil, the use of imperial revenues to pay colonial officials, the expanded jurisdiction of vice-admiralty courts, and even the nature of the instructions given to American governors by their superiors in London.

The entire document, which was printed as a pamphlet for distribution to the towns, exhibited none of the hesitation that had characterized colonial claims against Parliament in the 1760s. No longer were patriots—at least in Boston—concerned about defining the precise limits of parliamentary authority. No longer did they mention the necessity of obedience to Parliament. They were committed to a course that placed American rights first, loyalty to Great Britain a distant second.

The response of the Massachusetts towns to the committee's pamphlet must have caused Samuel Adams to rejoice. Some towns disagreed with Boston's assessment of the state of affairs, but most aligned themselves with the city. From Braintree came the assertion that "all civil officers are or ought to be Servants to the people and dependent upon them for their official Support, and every instance to the Contrary from the Governor downwards tends to crush and destroy civil liberty." The town of Holden declared that "the People of New England have never given the People of Britain any Right of Jurisdiction over us." The citizens of Petersham commented that resistance to tyranny was "the first and highest social Duty of this people." And Pownallborough warned, "Allegiance is a relative Term and like Kingdoms and commonwealths is local and has its bounds." It was beliefs like these that made the next crisis in Anglo-American affairs the final one.

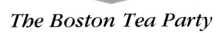

The Boston Tea Party

The only one of the Townshend duties still in effect by 1773 was the tax on tea. In the years since 1770 some Americans had continued to boycott English tea, while others had resumed drinking it either openly or in secret. Tea had long been an important component of the Anglo-American diet, and the possession of tea-drinking equipment (teapots and matched sets of cups) indicated high status (see page 80). Well-to-do Americans, women and men alike, socialized frequently at private tea parties, so that observing the tea boycott required colonial elites not only to change the beverage they habitually drank but also to alter their lifestyles. Tea thus retained an explosively symbolic character even though the boycott was less than fully effective after 1770.

In May 1773, Parliament passed an act designed to save the East India Company from bankruptcy. The company, which held a legal monopoly on British trade with the East Indies, **Tea Act** was of critical importance to the British economy and to the financial well-being of many prominent British politicians who had invested in its stock. Resistance leaders were immediately suspicious. Under the Tea Act, certain duties paid on tea were to be returned to the company. Tea was to be sold only by designated agents, which would enable the East India Company to avoid colonial middlemen and undersell any competitors, even smugglers. The net result would be cheaper tea for American consumers. But many colonists interpreted the new measure as a pernicious device to make them admit Parliament's right to tax them, since the less-expensive tea would still be taxed under the Townshend law. Others saw the Tea Act as the first step in the establishment of an East India Company monopoly of all colonial trade. Residents of the four cities singled out to receive the first shipments of tea accordingly prepared to respond to what they perceived as a new threat to their freedom.

In New York City, the tea ships failed to arrive on schedule. In Philadelphia, the captain was per-suaded to turn around and sail back to England. In Charleston, the tea was unloaded, stored under the direction of local tradesmen, and later destroyed. The only confrontation occurred in Boston, where both sides—the town meeting, joined by participants from nearby towns, and Governor Thomas Hutchinson, two of whose sons were tea agents—rejected compromise.

The first of three tea ships, the *Dartmouth,* entered Boston harbor on November 28. Under the customs laws, a cargo had to be landed and the appropriate duty paid within twenty days of a ship's arrival. If that was not done, the cargo would be seized by customs officers. After a series of mass meetings, Bostonians voted to prevent the tea from being unloaded and to post guards on the wharf. Hutchinson, for his part, refused to permit the vessels to leave the harbor.

On December 16, 1773, one day before the cargo would have to be confiscated, more than five thousand people (nearly a third of the city's population) crowded into Old South Church. The meeting, chaired by Samuel Adams, made a final attempt to persuade Hutchinson to send the tea back to England. But Hutchinson remained adamant. At about 6 P.M. Adams reportedly announced "that he could think of nothing further to be done—that they had now done all they could for the Salvation of their Country." As if his statement were a signal, cries rang out from the back of the crowd: "Boston harbor a tea-pot tonight! The Mohawks are come!" Small groups pushed their way out of the meeting. Within a few minutes, about sixty men crudely disguised as Indians assembled at the wharf, boarded the three ships, and dumped the cargo into the harbor. By 9 P.M. their work was done: 342 chests of tea worth approximately £10,000 floated in splinters on the ebbing tide.

Among the "Indians" were many representatives of Boston's artisans. Five masons, eleven carpenters and builders, three leatherworkers, a blacksmith, a hatter, three coopers, two barbers, a coachmaker, a silversmith, and twelve apprentices have been identified as participants. Their ranks also included four farmers from outside Boston, ten merchants, two doctors, a teacher, and a bookseller, thus illustrating the widespread support for the resistance movement. The next day John Adams exulted in his diary that the Tea Party was "so bold, so daring, so firm, intrepid and inflexible" that "I can't but consider it as an epocha in history."

After the Boston tea party, some patriots gathered up tea from the harbor as souvenirs of the event. This flask contains some of those leaves. *Massachusetts Historical Society.*

The North administration reacted with considerably less enthusiasm when it learned of the Tea Party. In March 1774, the ministry proposed the first of the four laws that became known as the Coercive, or Intolerable, Acts. It called for closing the port of Boston until the tea was paid for and prohibiting all but coastal trade in food and firewood. Colonial sympathizers in Parliament were easily outvoted by those who wished to punish the city that had been the center of opposition to British policies. Later in the spring, Parliament passed three other punitive measures. The Massachusetts Government Act altered the province's charter, substituting an appointed council for the elected one, increasing the powers of the governor, and forbidding special town meetings. The Justice Act provided that a person accused of committing murder in the course of suppressing a riot or enforcing the laws could be tried outside the colony where the incident had occurred. Finally, a new Quartering Act gave broad authority to military commanders seeking to house their troops in private dwellings.

Coercive and Quebec Acts

After passing the last of the Coercive Acts in early June, Parliament turned its attention to much-needed reforms in the government of Quebec. The Quebec Act, though unrelated to the Coercive Acts, thus became linked with them in the minds of the patriots. Intended to ease the strains that had arisen since the British conquest of the formerly French colony, the Quebec Act granted greater religious freedom to Catholics—alarming the Protestant colonists, who regarded Roman Catholicism as a mainstay of religious and political despotism. It also reinstated French civil law, which operated without juries and which had been replaced by British procedures in 1763, and it established an appointed council (rather than an elected legislature) as the governing body of the colony. Finally, in an attempt to provide the northern Indian tribes some protection against white settlement, the act annexed to Quebec the area east of the Mississippi River and north of the Ohio River. Thus that region, parts of which were claimed by individual seacoast colonies, was removed from their jurisdiction.

Members of Parliament who voted for the punitive legislation believed that the acts would be obeyed, that at long last they had solved the problem posed by the troublesome Americans. But the patriots showed little inclination to bow to the wishes of Parliament. In their eyes, the Coercive Acts and the Quebec Act proved what they had feared since 1768: that Great Britain had embarked on a deliberate plan to oppress them. If the port of Boston could be closed, why not those of Philadelphia or New York? If the royal charter of Massachusetts could be changed, why not that of South Carolina? If certain people could be removed from their home colonies for trial, why not all violators of all laws? If troops could be forcibly quartered in private houses, did not that pave the way for the occupation of all of America? If the Roman Catholic church could receive favored status in Quebec, why

The Boston Tea Party

not everywhere? It seemed as though the full dimensions of the plot against American rights and liberties had at last been revealed.

The Boston Committee of Correspondence urged all the colonies to join in an immediate boycott of British goods. But the other provinces were not yet ready to take such a drastic step. Instead, they suggested that another intercolonial congress be convened to consider an appropriate response to the Coercive Acts. Few people wanted to take hasty action; even the most ardent patriots still hoped for reconciliation with Great Britain. Despite their objections to British policy, they continued to see themselves as part of the empire. Americans were approaching the brink of confrontation, but they had not committed themselves to an irrevocable break. And so the colonies agreed to send delegates to Philadelphia in September.

Over the preceding decade, momentous changes had occurred in the ways politically aware colonists thought about themselves and their allegiance. Once linked unquestioningly to Great Britain, they had begun to develop a sense of their own identity as Americans. They had started to realize that their concept of the political process differed from that held by people in the mother country. They also had come to understand that their economic interests did not necessarily coincide with those of Great Britain. Colonial political leaders reached such conclusions only after a long train of events, some of them violent, had altered their understanding of the nature of their relationship with the mother country. Parliamentary acts such as the Stamp Act and the Townshend Acts had elicited colonial responses—both ideological and practical—that produced further responses from Britain. Tensions escalated until they climaxed in the Tea Party. From that point on, there was to be no turning back.

In the late summer of 1774, the Americans were committed to resistance but not to independence. Even so, they had started to sever the bonds of empire. During the next decade, they would forge the bonds of a new American nationality to replace those rejected Anglo-American ties.

Suggestions for Further Reading

General

Ian R. Christie, *Crisis of Empire: Great Britain and the American Colonies, 1754–1783* (1966); Ian R. Christie and Benjamin W. Labaree, *Empire or Independence, 1760–1776: A British-American Dialogue on the Coming of the American Revolution* (1976); Edward Countryman, *The American Revolution* (1985); Marc Egnal, *A Mighty Empire: The Origins of the American Revolution* (1988); Merrill Jensen, *The Founding of a Nation: A History of the American Revolution, 1763–1776* (1968); Robert Middlekauff, *The Glorious Cause: The American Revolution, 1763–1783* (1982); Edmund S. Morgan, *The Birth of the Republic, 1763–1789* (1956); Robert W. Tucker and David C. Hendrickson, *The Fall of the First British Empire: Origin of the War of American Independence* (1982).

Colonial Warfare and the British Empire

Fred Anderson, *A People's Army: Massachusetts Soldiers and Society in the Seven Years' War* (1984); Lawrence Henry Gipson, *The British Empire Before the American Revolution,* 15 vols. (1936–1970); Douglas Leach, *Roots of Conflict: British Armed Forces and Colonial Americans, 1677–1763* (1986); Robert C. Newbold, *The Albany Congress and Plan of Union of 1754* (1955); Howard H. Peckham, *The Colonial Wars, 1689–1762* (1963); William Pencak, *War, Politics, and Revolution in Provincial Massachusetts* (1981); Alan Rogers, *Empire and Liberty: American Resistance to British Authority, 1755–1763* (1974); John Shy, *Toward Lexington: The Role of the British Army in the Coming of the American Revolution* (1965).

British Politics and Policy

Colin Bonwick, *English Radicals and the American Revolution* (1977); John Brewer, *Party Ideology and Popular Politics at the Accession of George III* (1976); John Brooke, *King George III* (1972); John L. Bullion, *A Great and Necessary Measure: George Grenville and the Genesis of the Stamp Act, 1763–1765* (1981); Bernard Donoughue, *British Politics and the American Revolution: The Path to War, 1773–1775* (1965); Michael Kammen, *A Rope of Sand: The Colonial Agents, British Politics, and the American Revolution* (1968); Lewis B. Namier, *England in the Age of the American Revolution,* 2nd ed. (1961); P. D. G. Thomas, *The Townshend Duties Crisis* (1987); P. D. G. Thomas, *British Politics and the Stamp Act Crisis* (1975); Carl Ubbelohde, *The Vice-Admiralty Courts and the American Revolution* (1960).

Indians and the West

Thomas P. Abernethy, *Western Lands and the American Revolution* (1959); John R. Alden, *John Stuart and the Southern Colonial Frontier: A Study of Indian Relations, War, Trade, and Land Problems in the Southern Wilderness, 1754–1775* (1944); Richard Aquila, *The Iroquois Restoration: Iroquois Diplomacy on the Colonial Frontier, 1701–1754* (1983); David H. Corkran, *The Cherokee Frontier: Conflict and Survival, 1740–1762* (1962); Francis Jennings, *Empire of Fortune: Crowns, Colonies and Tribes in the Seven Years' War in America* (1988); Georgiana C. Nammack, *Fraud, Politics, and the Dispossession of the Indians: The Iroquois Land Frontier in the Colonial Period* (1969); Howard H. Peckham, *Pontiac and the Indian Uprising* (1947); Jack M. Sosin, *Whitehall and the Wilderness: The Middle West in British Colonial Policy, 1760–1775* (1961).

Political and Economic Thought

Bernard Bailyn, *The Ideological Origins of the American Revolution* (1967); J. E. Crowley, *This Sheba, Self: The Conceptualization of Economic Life in Eighteenth-Century America* (1974); Jay Fliegelman, *Prodigals and Pilgrims: The American Revolution Against Patriarchal Authority, 1750–1800* (1982); J. G. A. Pocock, *The Machiavellian Moment: Florentine Political Thought and the Atlantic Republican Tradition* (1975); Caroline Robbins, *The Eighteenth-Century Commonwealthman: Studies in the Transmission, Development, and Circumstance of English Liberal Thought from the Restoration of Charles II Until the War with the Thirteen Colonies* (1959); Clinton Rossiter, *Seedtime of the Republic: The Origin of the American Tradition of Political Liberty* (1953).

American Resistance

David Ammerman, *In the Common Cause: American Response to the Coercive Acts of 1774* (1974); Richard Beeman, *Patrick Henry: A Biography* (1974); Richard D. Brown, *Revolutionary Politics in Massachusetts: The Boston Committee of Correspondence and the Towns, 1772–1774* (1970); Joseph Albert Ernst, *Money and Politics in America, 1755–1775: A Study in the Currency Act of 1764 and the Political Economy of Revolution* (1973); Paul Gilje, *The Road to Mobocracy: Popular Disorder in New York City, 1763–1834* (1987); Dirk Hoerder, *Crowd Action in Revolutionary Massachusetts, 1765–1780* (1977); Rhys Isaac, *The Transformation of Virginia, 1740–1790* (1982); Benjamin W. Labaree, *The Boston Tea Party* (1964); Pauline R. Maier, *The Old Revolutionaries: Political Lives in the Age of Samuel Adams* (1980); Pauline R. Maier, *From Resistance to Revolution: Colonial Radicals and the Development of American Opposition to Britain, 1765–1776* (1972); Edmund S. Morgan and Helen M. Morgan, *The Stamp Act Crisis: Prologue to Revolution* (1953); Gary B. Nash, *The Urban Crucible: Social Change, Political Consciousness, and the Origins of the American Revolution* (1979); Richard Ryerson, *The Revolution Has Now Begun: The Radical Committees of Philadelphia, 1765–1776* (1978); Peter Shaw, *American Patriots and the Rituals of Revolution* (1981); John W. Tyler, *Smugglers and Patriots: Boston Merchants and the Advent of the American Revolution* (1986); Richard Walsh, *Charleston's Sons of Liberty: A Study of the Artisans, 1763–1789* (1959); Alfred F. Young, ed., *The American Revolution: Explorations in the History of American Radicalism* (1976); Hiller B. Zobel, *The Boston Massacre* (1970).

On November 20, 1837, Sarah Benjamin, then eighty-one years old, appeared before the county clerk in Wayne, Pennsylvania, to apply for a pension as the widow of a Revolutionary War soldier. She declared that she had married Aaron Osborn, a blacksmith, in Albany in 1780. After he enlisted without her knowledge, he insisted that she accompany him to the army. The narrative she dictated in 1837 is the only known autobiographical account left by one of the thousands of women who traveled with the revolutionary army as "camp followers."

For the first eighteen months of their service, Sarah and Aaron Osborn were stationed at West Point, on the Hudson River, where she did washing and sewing for the soldiers. Three other women were also attached to the company—an unmarried black woman and the wives of a sergeant and a lieutenant. This orderly existence changed abruptly in the fall of 1781, when their unit joined others marching hurriedly to Yorktown under the command of General George Washington.

5

A REVOLUTION, INDEED, 1775–1783

There, she reported, she "busied herself washing, mending, and cooking for the soldiers, in which she was assisted by the other females." At intervals she carried beef, bread, and coffee to the front lines, and she reported that she "heard the roar of the artillery for a number of days." Once she met Washington himself, who asked whether she was afraid of the cannonballs; Osborn staunchly replied, "It would not do for the men to fight and starve too." One day she heard the British drums "beat excessively" and inquired what had happened. "The British have surrendered," she was told. Sarah then watched the redcoats' ceremonial capitulation: the army "marched out beating and playing a melancholy tune, their drums covered with black handkerchiefs and their fifes with black ribbands tied around them." In an abandoned house on the edge of the recaptured town she found a piece of pewter. The house's owner—Virginia's governor—soon appeared and told her he would give it to her; she carried it home "and sold it for old pewter, which she has a hundred times regretted."

The Osborns returned north with the army and stayed until the troops were disbanded in early 1784. Soon thereafter, Aaron Osborn deserted his wife, leaving her with two young children. After

The Battle of Bunker's Hill (detail) by John Trumbull, 1786. Oil on canvas. *Copyright Yale University Art Gallery.*

he contracted a bigamous second marriage, she decided she too was free to remarry. Her second husband, John Benjamin, was also an army veteran, and in response to her 1837 petition the government awarded her a double pension in honor of her two husbands. Her own service earned her nothing. Still, her remarkably clear memories of her Revolutionary War exploits suggest their impact on her consciousness. Obviously, these were the most important experiences of her life.

The Revolution was more than just a series of clashes between British and patriot armies. It uprooted thousands of families like the Osborns, disrupted the economy, reshaped society by forcing many colonists into permanent exile, led Americans to develop new conceptions of politics, and created a nation from thirteen separate colonies. Thus it marked a significant turning point in Americans' collective history.

The struggle for independence required revolutionary leaders to accomplish three separate but closely related tasks. The first was political and ideological: they had to transform the 1760s consensus favoring loyal resistance into a coalition supporting independence. They adopted a variety of steps ranging from persuasion to coercion to enlist all whites in the patriot cause. From blacks and Indians, America's elected leaders hoped for cooperation at best, neutrality at worst, for they had good reason to fear that Indians and blacks would unite with the English against them.

The second task involved foreign relations. To win their independence, the patriot leaders knew they needed international recognition and aid, particularly assistance from France. Thus they dispatched to Paris Benjamin Franklin, the most experienced American diplomat (he had served for years as a colonial agent in London). Franklin skillfully negotiated the Franco-American alliance of 1778, which was to prove crucial to the winning of independence.

Only the third task directly involved the British. George Washington, commander-in-chief of the American army, quickly realized that his primary goal should be not to win battles but rather to avoid losing them decisively. He understood that, as long as his army survived to fight another day, the outcome of any individual battle was more or less irrelevant (although at times victories were necessary, if only to bolster morale). Accordingly, the story of the Revolutionary War reveals British action and American reaction, British attacks and American defenses. The American war effort was aided by the failure of British military planners to analyze accurately the problem confronting them. Until it was too late, they treated the war against the colonists as they did wars against other Europeans—that is, they concentrated on winning battles and did not consider the difficulties inherent in achieving their main goal, retaining the colonies' allegiance. In the end, the Americans' triumph owed more to their own endurance and to Britain's mistakes than to their military prowess.

Government by Congress and Committee

When the fifty-five delegates to the First Continental Congress convened in Philadelphia in September 1774, they knew that any measures they adopted were likely to enjoy support among many of their fellow countrymen and countrywomen. During the summer of 1774, open meetings held throughout the colonies had endorsed the idea of another nonimportation pact. Participants in such meetings had promised (in the words of the freeholders of Johnston County, North Carolina) to "strictly adhere to, and abide by, such Regulations and Restrictions as the Members of the said General Congress shall agree to and judge most convenient." The committees of correspondence that had been established in many communities publicized these popular meetings so effectively that Americans everywhere knew about them. Most of the congressional delegates were selected by extralegal provincial conventions whose members were chosen at such local gatherings, since the royal governors had forbidden the regular assemblies to conduct formal elections. Thus the very act of designating delegates to attend the Congress involved Americans in open defiance of British authority.

The colonies' leading political figures—most of them lawyers, merchants, or planters—were sent to the Philadelphia Congress. The Massachusetts delegation included both Samuel Adams, the experienced organizer of the Boston resistance, and his younger cousin John, an ambitious lawyer. Among others New York sent John Jay, a

First Continental Congress

1774	First Continental Congress	**1778**	French alliance with the United States
1775	Battles of Lexington and Concord		British evacuate Philadelphia
	Second Continental Congress	**1779**	Sullivan expedition against Iroquois villages
	Lord Dunmore's Proclamation		
1776	Thomas Paine, *Common Sense*	**1780**	British take Charleston
	British evacuate Boston	**1781**	Cornwallis surrenders at Yorktown
	Declaration of Independence		
	New York campaign	**1782**	Peace negotiations begin
1777	British take Philadelphia	**1783**	Treaty of Paris
	Burgoyne surrenders at Saratoga		

talented young attorney. From Pennsylvania came the conservative Joseph Galloway, speaker of the assembly, and his long-time rival John Dickinson. Virginia elected Richard Henry Lee and Patrick Henry, both noted for their patriotic zeal, as well as the stolid and reserved George Washington. Most of these men had never met, but in the weeks, months, and years that followed they were to become the chief architects of the new nation.

The congressmen faced three tasks when they convened at Carpenters Hall on September 5, 1774. The first two were explicit: defining American grievances and developing a plan for resistance. The third—outlining a theory of their constitutional relationship with England—was implicit and proved troublesome. The most radical congressmen, like Lee of Virginia, argued that the colonists owed allegiance only to George III and that Parliament was nothing more than a local legislature for Great Britain with no authority over the colonies. The conservatives—Joseph Galloway and his allies—by contrast proposed a formal plan of union that would have required the joint consent of Parliament and a new general American legislature to all laws pertaining to the colonies. After a heated debate, the delegates rejected Galloway's proposal, but they were not prepared to accept the radicals' position either.

Finally, they accepted a compromise position worked out by John Adams. The crucial clause that

Adams drafted in the Congress's Declaration of Rights and Grievances read in

> **Declaration of Rights and Grievances**

part: "From the necessity of the case, and a regard to the mutual interest of both countries, we cheerfully consent to the operation of such acts of the British parliament, as are bona fide, restrained to the regulation of our external commerce." Note the key phrases. "From the necessity of the case" declared that Americans had decided to obey Parliament only because they had decided that doing so was in the best interest of both countries. "Bona fide, restrained to the regulation of our external commerce" made it clear to Lord North that they would continue to resist taxes in disguise, like the Townshend duties. Most striking of all was that such language, which only a few years before would have been regarded as irredeemably radical, could be presented and accepted as a compromise in the fall of 1774. The Americans had come a long way since their first hesitant protests against the Sugar Act ten years earlier (see page 114).

With the constitutional issue resolved, the delegates readily agreed on a list of the laws they wanted repealed (notably the Coercive Acts) and decided to implement an economic boycott while petitioning the king for relief. They adopted the Continental Association, which called for nonimportation of British goods (effective December 1,

1774), nonconsumption of British products (effective March 1, 1775), and nonexportation of American goods to Britain and the British West Indies (effective September 10, 1775, so that southern planters would have a chance to market their 1774 tobacco crop, which had to be dried and cured before it could be sold).

To enforce the Continental Association, Congress recommended the election of committees of observation and inspection in every county, city, and town in America. Since Congress specified that committee members be chosen by all persons qualified to vote for members of the lower house of the colonial legislatures, the committees were guaranteed a broad popular base. In some places the committeemen were former local officeholders; in other towns they were obscure men who had never before held office. Everywhere, however, these committeemen—perhaps seven to eight thousand of them in the colonies as a whole—became the local leaders of American resistance.

> **Committees of Observation**

Such committees were officially charged only with overseeing the implementation of the boycott, but over the next six months they became de facto governments. They examined merchants' records and published the names of those who continued to import British goods. They also promoted home manufactures and encouraged Americans to adopt simple modes of dress and behavior. Since expensive leisure-time activities were symbols of vice and corruption, Congress urged Americans to forgo dancing, gambling, horse racing, cock fighting, and other forms of "extravagance and dissipation." Some committees accordingly forbade dancing, extracted apologies from people caught gambling or racing, prohibited the slaughter of lambs (because of the need for wool), and offered prizes for the best locally made cloth. The Baltimore County committee even advised citizens not to attend the upcoming town fair because it was nothing more than an occasion for "riots, drunkenness, gaming, and the vilest immoralities."

Thus the committees gradually extended their authority over many aspects of American life. In particular, they attempted to identify opponents of American resistance, developing elaborate spy networks, circulating copies of the Continental Association for signatures, and investigating reports of dissident remarks and activities. Suspected dissenters were first urged to convert to the colonial cause; if they failed to do so, the committees had them watched, restricted their movements, or tried to force them to leave the area. People engaging in casual political exchanges with friends one day could find themselves charged with "treasonable conversation" the next. One Massachusetts man, for example, was called before his local committee for calling the Congress "a Pack or Parcell of Fools" that was "as tyrannical as Lord North and ought to be opposed & resisted." When he refused to recant, the committee ordered him watched.

Those who dissented more openly received harsher treatment, as was demonstrated by the experiences of the Reverend John Agnew of Virginia. Agnew, an Anglican, insisted on warning his congregation of "the danger and sin of rebellion." He rejected the committee's summons and was thereafter ostracized by its order. Millers would not grind his corn, and doctors would not treat his sick wife and children. The committee tried to intimidate him by sending armed men to his church to beat drums and practice the manual of arms during services. When that failed, the patriots nailed shut the church's doors and windows. Finally Agnew and his oldest son fled, but the persecution of his wife and younger children continued. She was, she later recalled, "daily insulted and robbed . . . [and] searched under various pretense."

While the committees of observation were expanding their power during the winter and early spring of 1775, the established governments of the colonies were collapsing. Only in Connecticut, Rhode Island, Delaware, and Pennsylvania did regular assemblies continue to meet without encountering patriot challenges to their authority. In every other colony, popularly elected provincial conventions took over the task of running the government, sometimes entirely replacing the legislatures and at other times holding concurrent sessions. In late 1774 and early 1775, these conventions approved the Continental Association, elected delegates to the Second Continental Congress (scheduled for May), organized militia units, and gathered arms and ammunition. The British-appointed governors and councils, unable to stem the tide of resistance, watched helplessly as their authority crumbled.

> **Provincial Conventions**

The frustrating experience of Governor Josiah Martin of North Carolina is a case in point. When a provincial convention was called to meet at New Bern on April 4, 1775—the day the legislature was to convene—Martin proclaimed that "the Assembly of this province duly elected is the only true and lawful representation of the people." He asked all citizens to "renounce disclaim and discourage all such meetings cabals and illegal proceedings . . . which can only tend to introduce disorder and anarchy." Martin's proclamation had no visible effect, and when the convention met at New Bern its membership proved to be virtually identical to that of the colonial legislature. The delegates proceeded to act alternately in both capacities and even passed some joint resolves. Continuing the farce, the exasperated Martin delivered a speech to the assembly denouncing the election of the convention. On April 7, Martin admitted to Lord Dartmouth, secretary of state for America in North's ministry, that his government was "absolutely prostrate, impotent, and that nothing but the shadow of it is left."

Royal officials in the other colonies suffered the same frustrations. Courts were prevented from holding sessions; taxes were paid to agents of the conventions rather than to provincial tax collectors; sheriffs' powers were questioned; and militiamen refused to muster except by order of the local committees. In short, during the six months preceding the battles at Lexington and Concord, independence was being won at the local level, but without formal acknowledgment and for the most part without shooting or bloodshed. Not many Americans fully realized what was happening. The vast majority still proclaimed their loyalty to Great Britain and denied that they sought to leave the empire. Among the few who did recognize the trend toward independence were those who opposed it.

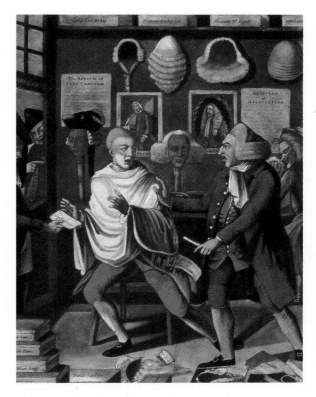

The Patriotic Barber of New-York, a satirical cartoon, commemorates the legendary barber who supported the rebel cause by half-shaving a British officer, then sending him out onto the street to be ridiculed by passersby. *Courtesy of the Boston Public Library, Print Department.*

Choosing Sides: Loyalists, Blacks, and Indians

The first protests against British measures, in the mid-1760s, had won the support of most colonists. Only in the late 1760s and early 1770s did a significant number of Americans begin to question both the aims and the tactics of the resistance movement. In 1774 and 1775 such people found themselves in a difficult position. Like their more radical counterparts, most of them objected to parliamentary policies and wanted some kind of constitutional reform. Joseph Galloway, for instance, was a conservative by American standards, but his plan for restructuring the empire was too novel for Britain to accept. Nevertheless, if forced to a choice, these colonists sympathized with Great Britain rather than with an independent America. The events of the crucial year between the passage of the Coercive Acts and the outbreak of fighting in Massachusetts crystallized their thinking. Their doubts about violent protest, their desire to uphold the legally constituted colonial governments, and their fears of anarchy combined to make them especially sensitive to the dangers of resistance.

In 1774 and 1775 some conservatives began to publish essays and pamphlets critical of the Congress and its allied committees. In New York City, a group of Anglican clergymen jointly wrote pamphlets and essays arguing the importance of maintaining a cordial connection between England and America. In Pennsylvania, Joseph Galloway published *A Candid Examination of the Mutual Claims of Great Britain and the Colonies*, attacking the Continental Congress for rejecting his plan of union. In Massachusetts, the young attorney Daniel Leonard, writing under the pseudonym Massachusettensis, engaged in a prolonged newspaper debate with Novanglus (John Adams). Leonard and the others realized that what had begun as a dispute over the extent of American subordination within the empire had now raised the question of whether the colonies would remain linked to Great Britain at all. "Rouse up at last from your slumber!" the Reverend Thomas Bradbury Chandler of New Jersey cried out to Americans. "There is a set of people among us . . . who have formed a scheme for establishing an independent government or empire in America."

Some colonists heeded the conservative pamphleteers' warnings. About one-fifth of the white American population remained loyal to Great Britain, actively opposing independence. Unlike their fellow countrymen and countrywomen, loyalists remained true to the colonial self-conception once held by most eighteenth-century white Americans. In other words, it was the patriots who changed their allegiance, not the loyalists. What is therefore surprising is that there were so few active loyalists, not that there were so many.

> **Loyalists, Patriots, and Neutrals**

With notable exceptions, most people of the following types remained loyal to the Crown: British-appointed government officials; merchants whose trade depended on imperial connections; Anglican clergy everywhere and lay Anglicans in the North—where their denomination was in the minority—since the king was the head of their church as well as head of state; former officers and enlisted men from the British army, many of whom had settled in America after 1763; non-English ethnic minorities, especially Scots; tenant farmers, particularly those whose landlords sided with the patriots; members of persecuted religious sects; and many of the backcountry southerners who had rebelled against eastern rule in the 1760s and early 1770s. All these people had one thing in common: the patriot leaders were their long-standing enemies,

though for different reasons. Local and provincial disputes thus helped to determine which side a person chose in the imperial conflict.

The active patriots, who accounted for about two-fifths of the population, came chiefly from the groups that had dominated colonial society, either numerically or politically. Among them were yeoman farmers, members of dominant Protestant sects (both Old and New Lights), Chesapeake gentry, merchants dealing mainly in American commodities, city artisans, elected officeholders, and people of English descent. Wives usually but not always adopted their husbands' political beliefs. Although all these patriots supported the Revolution, many pursued different goals within the broader coalition, as they had in the 1760s. Some sought limited political reform, others extensive political change, and still others social and economic reforms. (The ways in which their concerns interacted are discussed in Chapter 6.)

There remained in the middle perhaps two-fifths of the white population. Some of those who tried to avoid taking sides were sincere pacifists, such as Pennsylvania Quakers. Others opportunistically shifted their allegiance depending on which side happened to be winning at the time. Still others simply wanted to be left alone to lead their lives; they cared little about politics and normally obeyed whichever side controlled their area. But such colonists also resisted the British and the Americans alike when the demands made on them seemed too heavy—when taxes became too high, for example, or when calls for militia service came too often. Their attitude might best be summed up in the phrase "a plague on both your houses." Such persons made up an especially large proportion of the population in the southern backcountry, where the Scotch-Irish settlers had little love for either the patriot gentry or the English authorities.

To American patriots, that sort of apathy or neutrality was a crime as heinous as loyalism. Those who were not for them were against them; in their minds, there could be no conscientious objectors. By the winter of 1775–1776, less than a year after the battles of Lexington and Concord, the Second Continental Congress was recommending to the states that all "disaffected" persons be disarmed and arrested. The state legislatures quickly passed laws prescribing severe penalties for suspected loyalists. Many began to require all voters (or, in some cases, all free adult males) to take oaths of allegiance; the punishment for refusal was usually banishment or extra taxes. After 1777, many states confiscated the property of banished loyalists and used the proceeds for the war effort.

During the war, loyalists tended to congregate in cities held by the British army. When those posts were evacuated at the end of the war, the loyalists scattered to different parts of the British Empire— England, the West Indies, and especially Canada. In the provinces of Nova Scotia, New Brunswick, and Ontario they recreated their lives as colonists, laying the foundations of British Canada. All told, perhaps as many as 100,000 white Americans preferred to leave their homeland rather than to live in a nation independent of British rule. That fact speaks volumes about the depth of their loyalty to an Anglo-American definition of their identity.

The patriots' policies helped to ensure that the weak, scattered, and persecuted loyalists could not band together to threaten the revolutionary cause. But loyalists were not the patriots' only worry. They had reason to believe that Indians and slaves might join the forces arrayed against them. Early in the war, free blacks from New England enlisted in local patriot militias, but the revolutionaries could not assume that enslaved African-Americans would also support the struggle for independence.

Slaves faced a dilemma at the beginning of the Revolution: how could they best achieve their goal of escaping perpetual servitude? Should they fight with or against their white masters? The correct choice was not immediately apparent, and so blacks made different decisions. Some indeed joined the revolutionaries, but to most an alliance with the British appeared more promising. Thus news of slave conspiracies surfaced in different parts of the colonies in late 1774 and early 1775. All shared a common element: a plan to assist the British in return for freedom. A group of blacks petitioned General Thomas Gage, the commander-in-chief of the British army in Boston, promising to fight for the redcoats if he would liberate them. The governor of Maryland authorized the issuance of extra guns to militiamen in four counties where slave uprisings were expected. The most serious incident occurred during the summer of 1775 in Charleston, where Thomas Jeremiah, a free black harbor pilot, was brutally executed after being convicted of attempting to foment a slave revolt.

The Blacks' Dilemma

Peter Oliver, named chief justice of Massachusetts in 1771, was one of the most prominent New England loyalists. Brother-in-law of Thomas Hutchinson, he and the rest of the Hutchinson-Oliver family went into exile in England, where he lived quietly in Birmingham until his death in 1791. His acerbic history, *Origin and Progress of the American Rebellion,* was finally published in 1961. *The Henry Francis du Pont Winterthur Museum.*

A fear of acts such as these made white residents of the British West Indian colonies far more cautious in their opposition to parliamentary policies than their counterparts on the mainland. On most of the Caribbean islands, blacks outnumbered whites by six or seven to one. The planters simply could not afford to risk opposing Britain, their chief protector, with the ever-present threat of black revolt hanging over their heads. The Jamaica assembly agreed with the mainland colonial legislatures that citizens should not be bound by laws to which they had not consented. Nevertheless its members assured the king in 1774 that "it cannot be supposed, that we now intend, or ever could have intended Resistance to Great Britain." They cited as reasons Jamaica's "weak and feeble" condition, "its very small number of white inhabitants, and . . . the

RUN away from *Hampton,* on *Sunday* laft, a lufty Mulatto Fellow named ARGYLE, well known about the Country, has a Scar on one of his Wrifts, and has loft one or more of his fore Teeth; he is a very handy Fellow by Water, or about the Houfe, &c. loves Drink, and is very bold in his Cups, but daftardly when fober. Whether he will go for a Man of War's Man, or not, I cannot fay; but I will give 40 s. to have him brought to me. He can read and write.
NOVEMBER 2, 1775. JACOB WRAY.

An advertisement for a runaway slave suspected of joining Lord Dunmore—a common sight in Virginia and Maryland newspapers during the fall and winter of 1775 and 1776. *Virginia State Library.*

incumbrance of more than Two hundred thousand Slaves."

Racial composition affected politics in the continental colonies as well. In the North, where whites greatly outnumbered blacks, revolutionary fervor was at its height. In Virginia and Maryland, where whites constituted a safe majority of the population, there was occasional alarm over potential slave revolts but no disabling fear. But in South Carolina, which was over 60 percent black, and Georgia, where the racial balance was nearly even, whites were noticeably less enthusiastic about resistance. Georgia sent no delegates to the First Continental Congress and reminded its representatives at the Second Continental Congress to consider its circumstances, "with our blacks and tories within us," when voting on the question of independence.

> **Racial Composition and Patriotic Fervor**

The whites' worst fears were realized in November 1775, when Lord Dunmore, the governor of Virginia, offered to free any slaves and indentured servants who would leave their patriot masters to join the British forces. Dunmore hoped to use blacks in his fight against the revolutionaries and to disrupt the economy by depriving white Americans of their labor force. But fewer blacks than expected rallied to the British standard in 1775 and 1776 (there were at most two thousand), and many of them perished in a smallpox epidemic. Even so, Dunmore's proclamation led Congress in January 1776 to modify an earlier policy that had prohibited the enlistment of blacks in the Continental Army.

Although black Americans did not pose a serious threat to the revolutionary cause in its early years, the patriots managed to turn rumors of slave uprisings to their own advantage. In South Carolina, they won adherents by promoting white unity under the revolutionary banner. The Continental Association was needed, they argued, to protect whites from blacks at a time when the royal government was unable to muster adequate defense forces. Undoubtedly many wavering Carolinians were drawn into the revolutionary camp by fear that an overt division among the colony's whites would encourage a slave revolt.

A similar factor—the threat of Indian attacks—helped to persuade some reluctant westerners to support the struggle against Great Britain. In the years since the Proclamation of 1763, British officials had won the trust of the interior tribes by attempting to protect them from land-hungry whites. The British-appointed superintendents of Indian affairs, John Stuart in the South and Sir William Johnson in the North, lived among and understood the Indians. In 1768, Stuart and Johnson negotiated separate agreements modifying the proclamation line and attempting to draw realistic, defensible boundaries between tribal holdings and white settlements. The two treaties—signed at Hard Labor Creek, South Carolina, in October and at Fort Stanwix, New York, in November—supposedly established permanent western borders for the colonies. But just a few years later, in the treaties of Lochaber (1770) and Augusta (1773), the British pushed the southern boundary even

Chapter 5: A Revolution, Indeed, 1775–1783

farther west to accommodate the demands of whites in western Georgia and Kentucky.

By the time of the Revolution, the Indians were impatient with white Americans' aggressive pressure on their lands. The relationship of the tribes and frontier whites was filled with bitterness, misunderstanding, and occasional bloody encounters. In combination with the tribes' confidence in Stuart and Johnson, such grievances predisposed most Indians toward an alliance with the British. Even so, the latter hesitated to make full and immediate use of their potential Indian allies. The superintendents were aware that tribal war aims and the Indians' style of fighting were not necessarily compatible with those of the British. Accordingly, Stuart and Guy Johnson (who became northern superintendent following his uncle's death) sought nothing more from the tribes than a promise of neutrality. The superintendents even helped to prevent a general Indian uprising in the summer of 1774. Through clever maneuvering they ensured that the Shawnees attracted few Indian allies for an attack on frontier villages in Kentucky. Lord Dunmore's War, between the Shawnees and the Virginia militia, ended with Kentucky being opened to white settlement but with hunting and fishing rights still being reserved to the Shawnees.

> **The Indians' Grievances**

The patriots, recognizing that their standing with the tribes was poor, also sought the Indians' neutrality. In 1775 the Second Continental Congress sent a general message to the tribes describing the war as "a family quarrel between us and Old England" and requesting that they "not join on either side," since "you Indians are not concerned in it." A branch of the Cherokee tribe, led by Chief Dragging Canoe, nevertheless decided that the whites' "family quarrel" would allow them to settle some old scores. They attacked white settlements along the western borders of the Carolinas and Virginia in the summer of 1776. But a coordinated campaign by Carolina and Virginia militia destroyed many Cherokee towns, along with crops and large quantities of supplies. Dragging Canoe and his diehard followers fled west to the Tennessee River, where they established new outposts; the rest of the Cherokees agreed to a treaty that ceded more of their land to the whites.

The fate of the Shawnees and Cherokees—each forced to fight alone without other Indian allies, and each more easily defeated as a result—foreshadowed the history of Indian involvement in the American Revolution. During the eighteenth century the Iroquois had forcefully established their dominance over neighboring tribes. But the basis of their power started to disintegrate with the British victory over France in 1763, and their subsequent friendship with Sir William Johnson could not prevent the erosion of their position during the years before 1775. Tribes long resentful of Iroquois power (and of the similar status of the Cherokees in the South) saw little reason to ally themselves with those from whose dominance they had just escaped, even to prevent white encroachment on their lands. Consequently, during the Revolution most tribes pursued a course that aligned them with neither side and (as the American leaders wanted) kept them out of active involvement in the war.

> **Lack of Unity Among Indians**

Thus, although the patriots could never completely ignore the threats posed by loyalists, blacks, neutrals, and Indians, only rarely did fear of these groups seriously hamper the revolutionary movement. Occasionally militia on the frontier refused to turn out for duty on the seaboard because they feared Indians would attack in their absence. Sometimes southern troops refused to serve in the North because they (and their political leaders) were unwilling to leave the South unprotected against a slave insurrection. But the practical impossibility of a large-scale slave revolt, coupled with tribal feuds and the patriots' successful campaign to disarm and neutralize loyalists, ensured that the revolutionaries would remain firmly in control as they fought for independence.

War Begins

On January 27, 1775, Lord Dartmouth, secretary of state for America, addressed a fateful letter to General Thomas Gage in Boston. Expressing his belief that American resistance was nothing more than the response of a "rude rabble without plan," Dartmouth ordered Gage to arrest "the principal actors and abettors in the provincial congress." If such a

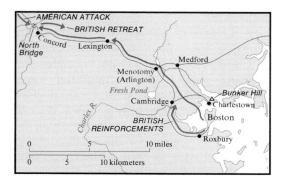

Lexington and Concord, April 19, 1775.

step were taken swiftly and silently, Dartmouth observed, no bloodshed need occur. Opposition could not be "very formidable," Dartmouth wrote, and even if it were, "it will surely be better that the Conflict should be brought on, upon such ground, than in a riper state of Rebellion."

Because of poor sailing weather, Dartmouth's letter did not reach Gage until April 14. The major patriot leaders had by then already left Boston, and

Battles of Lexington and Concord

in any event Gage did not believe that arresting them would serve a useful purpose. The order nevertheless spurred him to action: he decided to send an expedition to confiscate provincial military supplies stockpiled at Concord. Bostonians dispatched two messengers, William Dawes and Paul Revere (later joined by a third, Dr. Samuel Prescott), to rouse the countryside. Thus when the British vanguard of several hundred men approached Lexington at dawn on April 19, they found a straggling group of seventy militiamen—approximately half the adult male population of the town—drawn up before them on the town common. The Americans' commander, Captain John Parker, ordered his men to withdraw, realizing they could not halt the redcoat advance. But as they began to disperse, a shot rang out; the British soldiers then fired several volleys. When they stopped, eight Americans lay dead and another ten had been wounded. The British moved on to Concord, five miles away (see map).

There the contingents of militia were larger; the men of Concord had been joined by groups from Lincoln, Acton, and other nearby towns. The Americans allowed the British to enter Concord unopposed, but later in the morning they attacked the British infantry companies guarding the North

Bridge. The brief exchange of gunfire there spilled the first British blood of the Revolution: three men were killed and nine (including four officers) wounded. On their retreat to Boston, the British were attacked by thousands of militiamen, firing from behind trees, bushes, and houses along the road. By the end of the day, the redcoats had suffered 272 casualties, including 70 deaths. Only the arrival of reinforcements from the city and the militia's lack of coordination prevented much heavier British losses. The patriots suffered just 93 casualties.

By the evening of April 20, perhaps as many as twenty thousand American militiamen had gathered around Boston, summoned by local committees that spread the alarm across the New England countryside. Many did not stay long, since they were needed at home for spring planting, but those who remained dug in along siege lines encircling the city. For nearly a year the two armies sat and stared at each other across those lines. During that period the redcoats attacked their besiegers only once, on June 17, when they drove the Americans from trenches atop Breed's Hill in Charlestown. In that misnamed Battle of Bunker Hill, the British incurred their greatest losses of the entire war: over 800 wounded and 228 killed. The Americans, though forced to abandon their position, lost less than half that number. During the same eleven-month period, the patriots captured Fort Ticonderoga, a British fort on Lake Champlain, acquiring much-needed cannon. In the hope of bringing Canada into the war on the American side, they also mounted an uncoordinated northern campaign that ended in disaster at Quebec in early 1776. But the chief significance of the first year of the war lay in the long lull in fighting between the main armies at Boston. The delay gave both sides a chance to regroup, organize, and plan their strategies.

Lord North and his new American secretary, Lord George Germain, made three major assumptions about the war they faced. First, they con-

British Strategy

cluded that patriot forces could not withstand the assaults of trained British regulars. They and their generals were convinced that the campaign of 1776 would be the first and last of the war. Accordingly, they dispatched to America the largest single force Great Britain had ever assembled anywhere: 370 transport ships carrying 32,000 troops and tons of supplies, accompanied by 73 naval vessels and 13,000 sailors. Such an extraordinary effort would, they thought, ensure a quick victory. Among the troops were thousands of mercenaries from the German state of Hesse; eighteenth-century armies were often composed of such professional soldiers who hired out to the highest bidder.

Second, British officials and army officers persisted in comparing this war to wars they had fought successfully in Europe. Thus they adopted a conventional strategy of capturing major American cities and defeating the rebel army decisively without suffering serious casualties themselves. Third, they assumed that a clear-cut military victory would automatically bring about their goal of retaining the colonies' allegiance.

All these assumptions proved false. North and Germain, like Lord Dartmouth before them, vastly underestimated the Americans' commitment to armed resistance. Defeats on the battlefield did not lead the patriots to abandon their political aims and sue for peace. The ministers also failed to recognize the significance of the American population's dispersal over an area 1,500 miles long and more than 100 miles wide. Although at one time or another during the war the British would control each of the most important American ports, less than 5 percent of the population lived in those cities, and the coast offered so many excellent harbors that essential commerce was easily rerouted. In other words, the loss of the cities did little to damage the American cause, while the desire for such ports repeatedly led redcoat generals astray.

Most of all, the British did not at first understand that a military victory would not necessarily bring a political victory. Securing the colonies permanently would require hundreds of thousands of Americans to return to their original allegiance. The conquest of America was thus a far more complicated task than the defeat of France twelve years earlier. The British needed not only to overpower the patriots but also to convert them. After 1778, they adopted a strategy designed to achieve that goal through the expanded use of loyalist forces and the restoration of civilian authority in occupied areas. But the new policy came too late. The British never fully realized that they were fighting not a conventional European war but rather an entirely new kind of conflict: the first modern war of national liberation.

The British at least had a bureaucracy ready to supervise the war effort. The Americans had only the Second Continental Congress, originally intended merely as a brief gathering of colonial representatives to consider the British response to the Continental Association. Instead, the delegates who convened in Philadelphia on May 10, 1775, found that they had to assume the mantle of intercolonial government. "Such a vast Multitude of objects, civil, political, commercial and military, press and crown upon us so fast, that we know not what to do first," John Adams wrote a close friend early in the session. Yet as the summer passed, Congress slowly organized the colonies for war. It authorized the printing of money with which to purchase necessary goods, established a committee to supervise relations with foreign countries, and took steps to strengthen the militia. Most important of all, it created the Continental Army and appointed its generals.

> **Second Continental Congress**

Until Congress met, the Massachusetts provincial congress had taken responsibility for organizing the massive army of militia encamped at Boston. But that army, composed of men from all the New England states, was a heavy drain on limited local resources. Consequently, on May 16, Massachusetts asked the Continental Congress to assume the task of directing the army. First, the Congress had to choose a commander-in-chief. Since the war had thus far been a wholly northern affair, many delegates recognized the importance of naming someone who was not a New Englander. There seemed only one obvious candidate: they unanimously selected their fellow delegate, the Virginian George Washington.

Washington was no fiery radical, nor was he a reflective political thinker. He had not played a prominent role in the prerevolutionary agitation, but his devotion to the American cause was unquestioned. He was dignified, conservative, and respectable—a man of unimpeachable integrity. The younger son of a Virginia planter, Washington had not expected to inherit substantial property and had planned to make his living as a surveyor. But the early death of an older brother and his marriage to the wealthy widow Martha Custis had made him a rich man. Though unmistakably an aristocrat, Washington was unswervingly committed to repre-

> **George Washington: A Portrait of Leadership**

Thomas Paine, the English radical who wrote *Common Sense*. James Watson prepared this 1783 engraving from a portrait by Charles Willson Peale, who depicted his subject accompanied by the tools of the writer's trade—several sheets of paper and a quill pen. *National Portrait Gallery, Smithsonian Institution, Washington, D.C.*

sentative government, and he had other desirable traits as well. His stamina was remarkable: in more than eight years of war Washington never had a serious illness and took only one brief leave of absence. Moreover, he both looked and acted like a leader. Six feet tall in an era when most men were five inches shorter, his presence was stately and commanding. Other patriots praised his judgment, steadiness, and discretion, and even a loyalist admitted that Washington could "atone for many demerits by the extraordinary coolness and caution which distinguish his character."

Washington needed all the coolness and caution he could muster when he took command of the army outside Boston in July 1775. It took him months to impose hierarchy and discipline on the unruly troops and to bring order to the supply system. But by March 1776, when the arrival of cannon from Ticonderoga enabled him at last to put direct pressure on the redcoats in the city, the army was prepared to act. As it happened, an assault on Boston proved unnecessary. Sir William Howe, who had replaced Gage, had been considering an evacu-

ation for some time; he wanted to transfer his troops to New York City. The patriots' bombardment of Boston early in the month decided the matter. On March 17, the British and more than a thousand of their loyalist allies abandoned Boston forever.

That spring of 1776, as the British fleet left Boston for the temporary haven of Halifax, Nova Scotia, the colonies were moving inexorably toward the act the Massachusetts loyalists on board the ships feared most: a declaration of independence. Even months after fighting had begun, American leaders still denied they sought a break with the empire. But in January 1776 there appeared a pamphlet by a man who both thought the unthinkable and advocated it.

Thomas Paine's *Common Sense* exploded on the American scene like a bombshell. Within three months of publication, it sold 120,000 copies. The author, a radical English printer who had lived in America only since 1774, called stridently and stirringly for independence. More than that: Paine challenged many common American assumptions about government and the colonies' relationship to England. Rejecting the notion that a balance of monarchy, aristocracy, and democracy was necessary to preserve freedom, he advocated the establishment of a republic, a government by the people with no king or nobility. Instead of acknowledging the benefits of a connection with the mother country, Paine insisted that Britain had exploited the colonies unmercifully. In place of the frequently heard assertion that an independent America would be weak and divided, he substituted an unlimited confidence in America's strength when freed from European control.

Thomas Paine's Common Sense

These striking statements were clothed in equally striking prose. Scorning the polite, rational style of his classically educated predecessors, Paine adopted a furious, raging tone. Although a printed work, the pamphlet reflected the oral culture of ordinary folk. It was couched in everyday language and relied heavily on the Bible—the only book familiar to most Americans—as a primary source of authority. No wonder the pamphlet had a wider distribution than any other political publication of its day.

There is no way of knowing how many people were converted to the cause of independence by reading *Common Sense*. But by late spring 1776 independence had clearly become inevitable. On May 10, the Second Continental Congress formally recommended that individual colonies "adopt such governments as shall, in the opinion of the representatives of the people, best conduce to the happiness and safety of their constituents in particular, and America in general." From that source grew the first state constitutions. Perceiving the trend of events, the few loyalists still connected with Congress severed their ties to that body.

Then on June 7 came confirmation of the movement toward independence. Richard Henry Lee of Virginia, seconded by John Adams of Massachusetts, introduced the crucial resolution: "that these United Colonies are, and of right ought to be, free and independent States, that they are absolved of all allegiance to the British Crown, and that all political connection between them and the State of Great Britain is, and ought to be, totally dissolved." Congress debated but did not immediately adopt Lee's resolution. Instead, it postponed a vote until early July, to allow time for consultation and public reaction. In the meantime, a committee composed of Thomas Jefferson, John Adams, Benjamin Franklin, Robert R. Livingston of New York, and Roger Sherman of Connecticut was directed to draft a declaration of independence.

The committee in turn assigned primary responsibility for writing the declaration to Jefferson, who was well known for his apt and eloquent style. Years later John Adams recalled that Jefferson had modestly protested his selection, suggesting that Adams prepare the initial draft. The Massachusetts revolutionary recorded his frank response: "You can write ten times better than I can."

Thomas Jefferson was at the time thirty-four years old, a Virginia lawyer educated at the College of William and Mary and in the law offices of the prominent attorney George Wythe. He had read widely in history and political theory and had been a member of the House of Burgesses. His broad knowledge was evident not only in the declaration but also in his draft of the Virginia state constitution, completed just a few days before his appointment to the committee. Jefferson, an intensely private man, loved his home and family deeply. This early stage of his political career was marked by his beloved wife Martha's repeated difficulties in childbearing. While he wrote and debated in Philadelphia during the summer of 1776, she suffered a miscarriage at their home, Monticello. Not until after her death in 1782, from complications following the birth of their sixth (but only third surviving) child in ten years of marriage, did Jefferson fully commit himself to public service.

The draft of the declaration was laid before Congress on June 28. The delegates officially voted for independence four days later, then debated the wording of the declaration for two more days, adopting it with some changes on July 4. Since Americans had long since ceased to see themselves as legitimate subjects of Parliament, the Declaration of Independence concentrated on George III (see the Appendix). That focus also provided a single identifiable villain on whom to center the charges of misconduct. The document accused the king of attempting to destroy representative government in the colonies and of oppressing Americans through the unjustified use of excessive force.

> **Declaration of Independence**

The declaration's chief long-term importance, however, did not lie in its lengthy catalogue of grievances against George III (including, in a section omitted by Congress, Jefferson's charge that the British monarchy had introduced slavery into America). It lay instead in the ringing statements of principle that have served ever since as the ideal to which Americans aspire. "We hold these truths to be self-evident: That all men are created equal; that they are endowed by their Creator with certain unalienable rights; that among these are life, liberty and the pursuit of happiness; that, to secure these rights, governments are instituted among men, deriving their just powers from the consent of the governed; that whenever any form of government becomes destructive of these ends, it is the right of the people to alter or to abolish it, and to institute new government." These phrases have echoed down through American history like no others.

The delegates in Philadelphia who voted to accept the Declaration of Independence did not have the advantage of our two hundred years of hindsight. When they adopted the declaration, they risked their necks: they were committing treason. Thus when they concluded the declaration with the assertion that they "mutually pledge[d] to each other our lives, our fortunes, and our sacred honor," they spoke no less than the truth. The real struggle still lay before them, and few of them had Thomas Paine's boundless confidence in success.

After listening to the first formal reading of the Declaration of Independence in New York City on July 9, 1776, a crowd of American soldiers and civilians pulled down a statue of George III that stood on the Bowling Green in the heart of the city. Most of the statue was later melted down into bullets, but a British officer rescued the head (below), which was later taken to London. *Library of Congress; below: McCord Museum of Canadian History, McGill University, Montreal.*

The Long Struggle in the North

In late June 1776, the first of the ships carrying Sir William Howe's troops from Halifax appeared off the coast of New York. On July 2, the day Congress voted for independence, the redcoats landed on Staten Island. But Howe waited until mid-August, after the arrival of troop transports from England, to begin his attack on the city. The delay gave Washington sufficient time to march his army south to meet the threat. To defend New York, Washington had approximately seventeen thousand soldiers: ten thousand Continentals who had promised to serve until the end of the year, and seven thousand militiamen who had enlisted for shorter terms. Neither he nor most of his men had ever fought a major battle against the British, and their lack of experience led to disastrous mistakes. The difficulty

Chapter 5: A Revolution, Indeed, 1775–1783

of defending New York City only compounded the errors.

Washington's problem was as simple as the geography of the region was complex (see map). To protect the city adequately, he would have to divide his forces among Long Island, Manhattan Island, and the mainland. But the British fleet under Admiral Lord Richard Howe, Sir William's brother, controlled the harbors and rivers that divided the American forces. The patriots thus constantly courted catastrophe, for swift action by the British navy could cut off the possibility of retreat and perhaps even communication. But despite these dangers, Washington could not afford to surrender New York to the Howes without a fight. Not only did the city occupy a strategic location, but the region that surrounded it was known to contain many loyalist sympathizers. A show of force was essential if the revolutionaries were to retain any hope of persuading waverers to join them.

Battle for New York City

On August 27, Sir William Howe's forces attacked the American positions on Brooklyn Heights, pushing the untried rebel troops back into their defensive entrenchments. But Sir William failed to press his advantage, even neglecting to send his brother's ships into the East River to cut off a retreat. Consequently, the Americans were able to escape. A troop of fishermen from Marblehead, Massachusetts, ferried nine thousand men to the southern tip of Manhattan Island in less than twelve hours on the night of August 29. Washington then moved north on the island, retreating onto the mainland but leaving behind nearly three thousand men in supposedly impregnable Fort Washington on the west shore of Manhattan. Howe slowly followed him into Westchester County, then turned back to focus his attention on the fort. Its defenses collapsed, and the large garrison surrendered in early November. Only when Charleston fell to the British in May 1780 did the Americans lose more men on a single occasion.

George Washington had defended New York, but badly. He had repeatedly broken a basic rule of military strategy: never divide your force in the face of a superior enemy. In the end, though, the Howe brothers' failure to move quickly prevented a decisive defeat of the Americans. Although Washington's army had been seriously reduced by casualties, the surrender of Fort Washington, and

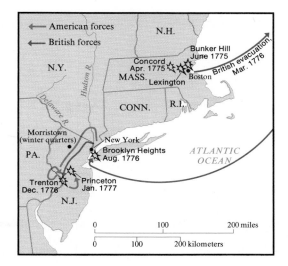

The War in the North, 1775–1777

the loss of most of the militiamen (who had returned home for the harvest), its core remained. Through November and December, Washington led his men in a retreat across New Jersey. Howe followed at a leisurely pace, setting up a string of outposts manned mostly by Hessian mercenaries. After Washington crossed the Delaware River into Pennsylvania, the British commander turned back and settled into comfortable winter quarters in New York City.

The British controlled most of New Jersey, and hundreds of Americans accepted the pardons offered by the Howes. Among them were Joseph Galloway, a delegate to the First Continental Congress, and Richard Stockton, a signer of the Declaration of Independence. Occupying troops met little opposition, and the Revolutionary cause appeared to be in disarray. "These are the times that try men's souls," wrote Thomas Paine in his pamphlet *The Crisis*. "The summer soldier and the sunshine patriot will, in this crisis, shrink from the service of his country; . . . yet we have this consolation with us, that the harder the conflict, the more glorious the triumph."

In the aftermath of battle, as at its height, the British generals let their advantage slip away. The redcoats stationed in New Jersey went on a rampage of rape and plunder. Because loyalists and patriots were indistinguishable to the British and Hessian troops, families on both sides suffered nearly equally. Livestock, crops, and firewood were

At the battle of Princeton in early 1777, American forces under George Washington cemented the victory they had won a few days earlier at Trenton. This view was painted in 1787 by William Mercer, whose father was killed in the battle. *Princeton University Library.*

seized for use by the army. Houses were looted and burned, churches and public buildings desecrated. But nothing was better calculated to rally doubtful Americans to the cause than the wanton murder of innocent civilians and the rape of women.

The soldiers' marauding alienated potentially loyal New Jerseyites and Pennsylvanians whose allegiance the British could ill afford to lose. It also spurred Washington's determination to strike back. The enlistments of most of the Continental troops were to expire on December 31, and Washington also wanted to take advantage of short-term Pennsylvania militiamen who had recently joined him. He moved quickly and attacked the Hessian encampment at Trenton early in the morning of December 26, while the redcoats were still reeling from their Christmas celebration. The patriots captured more than nine hundred Hessians and killed another thirty; only three Americans were wounded. A few days later, after persuading many of his men to stay on beyond the term of their enlistments, Washington attacked again at Princeton. Having gained command of the

> **Battle of Trenton**

field and buoyed American spirits with the two swift victories, Washington set up winter quarters at Morristown, New Jersey.

The campaign of 1776 established patterns that were to persist throughout much of the war, despite changes in British leadership and strategy. British forces were usually more numerous and often better led than the Americans. But their ponderous style of maneuvering, lack of familiarity with the terrain, and inability to live off the land without antagonizing the populace helped to offset those advantages. Furthermore, although Washington always seemed to lack regular troops—the Continental Army never numbered more than 18,500 men— he could usually count on the militia to join him at crucial times. American militiamen did not like to sign up for long terms of service or to fight far from home, but when their homes were threatened they would rally to the cause. Washington and his officers frequently complained about the militia's habit of disappearing during planting or harvesting. But time and again their presence, however brief, enabled the Americans to launch an attack or counter an important British thrust.

Chapter 5: A Revolution, Indeed, 1775–1783

As the war dragged on, the Continental Army and the militia took on decidedly different characters. State governments, responsible for filling military quotas, discovered that most

The American Army

men willing to enlist for long periods in the regular army were young, single, and footloose. Farmers with families tended to prefer short-term militia duty. As the supply of whites willing to sign up with the Continentals diminished, recruiters in the northern states turned increasingly to blacks, both slave and free. (White southerners continued to resist this approach.) Perhaps as many as five thousand blacks eventually served in the Revolutionary army, and most of them won their freedom as a result. They commonly served in racially integrated units, often being assigned tasks that whites wanted to avoid, such as cooking, foraging for food, or driving wagons.

Also attached to the American forces were a number of women, who like Sarah Osborn were the wives and widows of poor soldiers. Such camp followers worked as cooks, nurses, and launderers, performing vital services for the army in return for rations and low wages. The presence of women, as well as militiamen who floated in and out of the American camp at irregular intervals, made for an unwieldy army that officers found difficult to manage. Yet the army's shapelessness also reflected its greatest strength: an almost unlimited reservoir of man and woman power.

The officers of the Continental Army—those who enlisted for long periods or for the war's duration—developed an intense sense of pride and commitment to the revolutionary cause. The hardships they endured, the battles they fought, the difficulties they overcame all helped to forge an esprit de corps that was to outlast the war. The realities of warfare were often dirty, messy, and corrupt, but the officers drew strength from a developing image of themselves as professionals who sacrificed personal gain for the good of the entire nation. When one of their number, Benedict Arnold, violated that virtuous self-image by defecting to the British in exchange for a promise of £20,000, they excoriated him in overwrought prose that unconsciously revealed the fear that they might succumb to the same temptations. "How black, how despised, loved by none, and hated by all," wrote one. "I cannot get Arnold out of my head," said another.

Deborah Sampson (1760–1827), who disguised herself as a man and enlisted in the Continental Army as Robert Shurtleff. She served from May 1782 to October 1783, when her sex was discovered and she was discharged. In later years she gave public lectures describing her wartime experiences. After her death her husband became the only man to receive a pension as the "widow" of a revolutionary soldier. *Courtesy of The Rhode Island Historical Society.*

In 1777, the chief British effort was planned by the flashy "Gentleman Johnny" Burgoyne, a playboy general as much at home at the gaming tables of London as on the battlefield. Burgoyne, a subordinate of Howe, had spent the winter of 1776–1777 in London, where he gained the ear of Lord George Germain. Burgoyne convinced Germain that he could lead an invading force of redcoats and Indians down the Hudson River from Canada, cutting off New England from the rest of the states. He proposed to rendezvous near Albany with a similar force that would move east from Niagara along the Mohawk River valley. The combined forces would then presumably link up with Sir William Howe's troops in New York City.

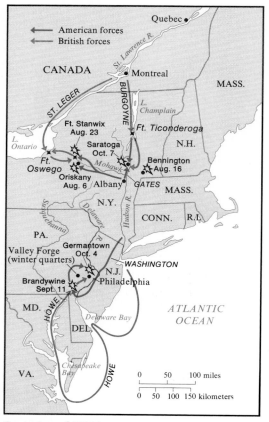

Campaign of 1777

neuver cost him at least a month, debilitated his men, and depleted his supplies. Incredibly, he was only forty miles closer to Philadelphia at the end of the lengthy voyage than when he started. Two years later, when Parliament formally inquired into the conduct of the war, Howe's critics charged that his errors were so extraordinary that he must have deliberately committed treason. Even today, historians have not been able to explain his motives adequately. In any event, by the time Howe was ready to move on Philadelphia, Washington had had time to prepare its defenses. Twice, at Brandywine Creek and again at Germantown, the two armies clashed near the patriot capital. Although the British won both engagements, the Americans handled themselves well. The redcoats took Philadelphia in late September, but to little effect. The campaign season was nearly over; the Revolutionary army had gained confidence in itself and its leaders; few welcoming loyalists had materialized; and, far to the north, Burgoyne was going down to defeat.

Burgoyne and his men set out from Montreal in mid-June 1777, floating down Lake Champlain into New York in canoes and flat-bottom boats. They easily took Fort Ticonderoga from its outnumbered and outgunned patriot defenders. Trouble began, however, as Burgoyne started his overland march. His clumsy artillery carriages and baggage wagons foundered in the heavy forests and ravines. Patriot militia felled giant trees across the army's path. As a result, Burgoyne's troops took twenty-four days to travel the twenty-three miles to Fort Edward, on the Hudson River. Short of supplies, the general dispatched eight hundred German mercenaries to forage the countryside. On August 16, American militia companies nearly wiped out the Germans near Bennington. Yet Burgoyne failed to recognize the seriousness of his predicament and continued to dawdle, giving the Americans more than enough time to prepare for his coming. By the time he finally crossed the Hudson in mid-September, bound for Albany, Burgoyne's fate was sealed. After several bloody clashes with the American force commanded by Horatio Gates, Burgoyne was surrounded near Saratoga, New York. On October 17, 1777, he surrendered his entire force of more than six thousand men.

Two months before, the 1,400 redcoats and Indians marching along the Mohawk River from Ni-

> **Burgoyne's Campaign in New York**

That Burgoyne's scheme would give "Gentleman Johnny" all the glory and relegate Howe to a supporting role did not escape Sir William's notice. While Burgoyne was plotting in London, Howe was laying his own plans in New York City. Joseph Galloway and other Pennsylvania loyalists persuaded Howe that Philadelphia could be taken easily and that his troops would be welcomed by many residents of the region. Just as Burgoyne left Howe out of his plans, Howe left Burgoyne out of his. Thus the two major British armies in America would operate independently in 1777, and the result would be a disaster (see map).

Howe accomplished his objective: he captured Philadelphia. But he did so in inexplicable fashion, delaying for months before beginning the campaign, then taking six weeks to transport his troops by sea to the head of Chesapeake Bay instead of marching them overland. That ma-

> **Howe Takes Philadelphia**

agara toward Albany had also been turned back. Under the command of Colonel Barry St. Leger, they had advanced easily until they reached the isolated American outpost at Fort Stanwix in early August. After they had laid siege to the well-fortified structure, they learned that a patriot relief column was en route to the fort. Leaving only a small detachment at Fort Stanwix, the British ambushed the Americans at Oriskany on August 6. The British claimed victory in the ensuing battle, one of the bloodiest of the war, but they and their Indian allies lost their taste for further fighting. The Americans tricked them into believing that another large patriot force was on the way, and in late August the British abandoned the siege and returned to Niagara.

The Battle of Oriskany marked a split of the Iroquois Confederacy (see pages 58–59). In 1776 the Six Nations had formally pledged to remain neutral in the Anglo-American struggle. But two influential Mohawk leaders, Joseph Brant and Mary Brant, worked tirelessly to persuade their fellow Iroquois to join the British. Mary Brant, a powerful tribal matron, was also the widow of the Indian superintendent Sir William Johnson. Her younger brother Joseph, a renowned warrior, was convinced that the Six Nations should ally themselves with the British in order to prevent American encroachment on their lands. As an observer said of Mary, "One word from her goes farther with them [the Iroquois] than a thousand from any white man without exception." The Brants won over to the British the Senecas, Cayugas, and Mohawks, all of whom contributed warriors to St. Leger's expedition. But the Oneidas preferred the American side, bringing the Tuscaroras with them. The Onondagas split into three factions, one on each side and one supporting neutrality. At Oriskany, some Oneidas and Tuscaroras joined the patriot militia to fight their Iroquois brethren; thus a league of friendship that had survived over three hundred years was torn apart by the whites' family quarrel.

Split of the Iroquois Confederacy

The collapse of Iroquois unity and the confederacy's abandonment of neutrality had important consequences for both whites and Indians in subsequent years. In 1778, Iroquois warriors allied with the British raided the frontier villages of Wyoming, Pennsylvania, and Cherry Valley, New York; to retaliate, in the late summer of 1779 the whites dis-

The Mohawk chief Joseph Brant (1742–1807), painted in London in 1786 by Gilbert Stuart. *New York State Historical Society, Cooperstown, N.Y.*

patched an expedition under General John Sullivan to burn Iroquois crops, orchards, and settlements. The destruction was so thorough that many bands had to leave their ancestral homeland to seek food and shelter with the British north of the Great Lakes during the winter of 1779–1780. A large number of Iroquois people never returned to New York but settled permanently in British Canada.

For the Indians, Oriskany was the most significant battle of the northern campaign; for the whites, Saratoga was. The news of Burgoyne's surrender brought joy to patriots, discouragement to loyalists and Britons. In exile in London, Thomas Hutchinson wrote of the "universal dejection" among loyalists there. "Everybody in a gloom," he commented; "most of us expect to lay our bones here." The disaster prompted Lord North to authorize a peace commission to offer the Americans everything they had requested in 1774—in effect, a return to the imperial system of 1763. It was, of course, far too late for that: the patriots rejected the overture, and the peace commission sailed back to England empty-handed in mid-1778.

Most important of all, the American victory at Saratoga drew France formally into the conflict.

Ever since 1763, the French had sought to avenge their defeat in the Seven Years' War, and the American Revolution gave them that opportunity. Even before Benjamin Franklin arrived in Paris in late 1776, France was covertly supplying the revolutionaries with military necessities. Indeed, 90 percent of the gunpowder that was used by the Americans during the first two years of the war came from France.

Franklin worked tirelessly to strengthen ties between the two nations. Although he was not a Quaker, he deliberately affected a plain style of dress that made him stand out amid the luxury of the court of King Louis XVI. He cleverly presented himself as a representative of American simplicity, playing on the French image of Americans as virtuous yeomen. Franklin's effort culminated in February 1778 when the countries signed two treaties. In the Treaty of Amity and Commerce, France recognized American independence and established trade ties with the new nation; the second treaty provided for a formal alliance between the two nations. In this Treaty of Alliance, France and the United States promised—assuming that France would go to war with Britain, which it soon did—that neither country would negotiate peace with the enemy without consulting the other. France also abandoned all its claims to North American territory east of the Mississippi River and to Canada. The most visible symbol of Franco-American cooperation in the years that followed was the Marquis de Lafayette, a young nobleman who had volunteered for service with George Washington in 1777 and fought with the American forces until the conflict ended.

> **Franco-American Alliance of 1778**

The French alliance had two major benefits for the patriot cause. First, France began to aid the Americans openly, sending troops and naval vessels in addition to arms, ammunition, clothing, and blankets. Second, the British could no longer focus their attention on the American mainland alone, for they had to fight the French in the West Indies and elsewhere. Spain's entry into the war in 1779 as an ally of France (but not the United States) further magnified Britain's problems. Throughout the war, French assistance was important to the Americans, but in the last years of the conflict that aid was especially vital.

The Long Struggle in the South

In the aftermath of the Saratoga disaster, Lord George Germain and the military officials in London reassessed their strategy. Maneuvering in the North had done them little good; perhaps shifting the field of battle southward would bring success. The many loyalist exiles in England encouraged this line of thinking. They argued that loyal southerners would welcome the redcoat army as liberators and that once the region had been pacified and returned to civilian control it could serve as a base for attacking the North.

In early 1778 Sir William Howe was replaced by Sir Henry Clinton. As commander-in-chief, Clinton was also afflicted with sluggishness and lack of resolution. Still, he oversaw the regrouping of British forces in America, ordering the evacuation of Philadelphia in June 1778 and dispatching a small expedition to Georgia at the end of the year. When Savannah and then Augusta fell easily into British hands, Clinton became convinced that a southern strategy would work. In late 1779 he sailed down the coast from New York with 8,500 troops to attack Charleston, the most important American city in the South (see map).

Although the Americans worked hard to bolster Charleston's defenses, the city fell to the British on May 12, 1780. General Benjamin Lincoln surrendered the entire southern army—5,500 men—to the invaders. In the weeks that followed, the redcoats spread through South Carolina, establishing garrisons at key points in the interior. As in New Jersey in 1776, hundreds of South Carolinians renounced allegiance to the United States and proclaimed their loyalty to the Crown. Clinton organized loyalist regiments, and the process of pacification began.

> **Fall of Charleston**

Yet the British triumph was less complete than it appeared. The success of the southern campaign depended on British control of the seas, for only by sea could the widely dispersed British armies remain in communication with one another. For the moment the Royal Navy safely dominated the American coastline, but French naval power posed a threat to the entire southern enterprise. Moreover, the redcoats never managed to establish full control of the areas they seized. As a result, patriot bands operated freely throughout the state, and loyalists could not be guaranteed protection against their enemies. Last but not least, the fall of Charleston did not dishearten the patriots; instead, it spurred them to greater exertions. As one Marylander declared confidently, "The Fate of America is not to be decided by the Loss of a Town or Two." Patriot women in four states formed the Ladies Association, which collected money to purchase shirts for needy soldiers. Recruiting efforts were stepped up.

Nevertheless, throughout most of 1780, the war in South Carolina went badly for the patriots. In August, a reorganized southern army under the command of Horatio Gates was crushingly defeated at Camden by the forces of Lord Cornwallis, who had been placed in charge of the southern campaign. The British army was joined wherever it went by hundreds, even thousands, of blacks seeking freedom on the basis of Lord Dunmore's proclamation (see page 138). Slaves ran away from their patriot masters individually and as families in such numbers that they seriously disrupted planting and harvesting in 1780 and 1781. More than fifty-five thousand blacks were lost to their owners as a result of the war. Not all of them joined the British or won their freedom if they did, but their flight had just the effect Dunmore wanted. Many served the British well as scouts, guides, and laborers.

After the defeat at Camden, Washington (who had to remain in the North to oppose the British army occupying New York) gave command of

> **Greene Rallies South Carolina**

the southern campaign to General Nathanael Greene of Rhode Island. Greene was appalled by what he found in South Carolina. As he wrote to a friend, "The word difficulty when applied to the state of things here . . . is almost without meaning, it falls so far short" of reality. His troops needed clothing, blankets, and food, but "a great part of this country is already laid waste and in the utmost danger of becoming a desert." The constant guerrilla warfare had, he commented, "so corrupted the principles of the people that they think of nothing but plundering one another." Under such circumstances, Greene had to move cau-

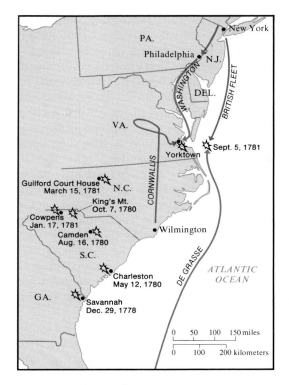

The War in the South

tiously. He adopted a conciliatory policy toward loyalists and neutrals, persuading the governor of South Carolina to offer complete pardons to those who had fought for the British if they would join the patriot militia. He also ordered his troops not to loot loyalist property and to treat captives fairly. Greene recognized that the patriots could win only by convincing the people that they could bring stability to the region. He thus helped the shattered provincial congresses of Georgia and South Carolina to begin re-establishing civilian authority in the interior—a goal the British were never able to accomplish, even along the coast.

Greene also took a conciliatory approach to the southern Indians. With his desperate need for soldiers, he could not afford to have frontier militia companies occupied in defending their homes against Indian attacks. Since he had so few regulars (only 1,600 when he took command), Greene had to rely on western volunteers. Therefore, he negotiated with the Indians.

His policy eventually met with success, although at first royal officials cooperating with the British invasion forces won allies among a number of southern tribes, especially Dragging Canoe's Cherokee band. But the southern Indians, recalling the disastrous defeat the Cherokees had suffered in 1776, never committed themselves wholeheartedly to the British. In 1781 the Cherokees began negotiations with the patriots, and the next year the other tribes too sued for peace. By the end of the war only the Creeks remained British allies. A group of Chickasaw chiefs explained their reasoning to American agents in July 1782, after Greene's battlefield successes had forced the redcoats to withdraw into Savannah and Charleston: "The English put the Bloody Tomahawk into our hands, telling us that we should have no Goods if we did not Exert ourselves to the greatest point of Resentment against you, but now we find our mistake and Distresses. The English have done their utmost and left us in our adversity. We find them full of Deceit and Dissimulation."

Even before Greene took command of the southern army in December 1780, the tide had begun to turn. In October, at King's Mountain, near the North Carolina–South Carolina border, a force of "overmountain men" from the settlements west of the Appalachians defeated a large party of redcoats and loyalists. Then in January 1781 Greene's trusted aide Brigadier General Daniel Morgan brilliantly defeated the crack British regiment Tarleton's Legion at Cowpens, also near the border of the Carolinas. Greene himself confronted the main body of British troops under Lord Cornwallis at Guilford Court House, North Carolina, in March. Cornwallis controlled the field at the end of the day, but most of his army had been destroyed. He had to retreat to Wilmington, on the coast, to receive supplies and fresh troops from New York by sea. In the meantime Greene returned to South Carolina, where, in a series of swift strikes, he forced the redcoats to abandon their posts in the interior and quickly retire to Charleston.

Cornwallis had already ignored explicit orders not to leave South Carolina unless the state was safely in British hands. Evidently bent on his own destruction, he headed north into Virginia, where he joined forces with a detachment of redcoats commanded by the American traitor Benedict Arnold. (Arnold had fought heroically with the patriots early in the war but defected to the

Surrender at Yorktown

British in 1780, believing his talents were not sufficiently appreciated by the Americans.) Instead of acting decisively with his new army of 7,200 men, Cornwallis withdrew to the edge of the peninsula between the York and James rivers; there he fortified Yorktown and in effect waited for the end. Seizing the opportunity, Washington quickly moved over 7,000 troops south from New York City. When a French fleet under the Comte de Grasse arrived from the West Indies in time to defeat the Royal Navy vessels sent to rescue Cornwallis, the British general was trapped (see map, page 151). On October 19, 1781, four years and two days after Burgoyne's defeat at Saratoga, Cornwallis surrendered to the combined American and French forces.

When news of the surrender reached England, Lord North's ministry fell. Parliament voted to cease offensive operations in America and authorized peace negotiations. But guerrilla warfare between patriots and loyalists continued to ravage the Carolinas and Georgia for more than a year, and in the North vicious retaliatory raids by Indians and whites kept the frontier aflame. Indeed, the single most brutal massacre of the war occurred in March 1782, at Gnadenhuetten in the Ohio country. A group of white militiamen, seeking the Indians who had killed a frontier family, encountered a peaceful band of Delawares. The Indians, who had been converted to both Christianity and pacifism by Moravian missionaries, were slaughtered. Ninety-six men, women, and children died that day, some burned at the stake, others tomahawked. Two months later, hostile members of the Delaware tribe captured three white militiamen and subjected them to gruesome tortures in reprisal. The persistence of conflict between whites and Indians after the Battle of Yorktown, all too often overlooked in accounts of the Revolution, serves to underline the degree to which the Indians were the real losers in the war initiated by whites.

The fighting finally ended when Americans and Britons learned of the signing of a preliminary peace treaty at Paris in November 1782. The American negotiators—Benjamin Franklin, John Jay, and John Adams—ignored their instructions from the Congress to be guided by France and instead struck a separate agreement with Great Britain. Their instincts were sound: the French government was more an enemy to Britain

Treaty of Paris

In 1781 Charles Wilson Peale traveled to Yorktown to commemorate the great victory by the combined American and French forces. That he was present in the immediate aftermath of the battle is indicated by his portrayal of sunken ships in the river and dead horses on the beach. On the right stands Washington with (from left to right) the Marquis de Lafayette, Count Rochambeau, and Tench Tilghman, one of Washington's aides. *Maryland Historical Society.*

than a friend to the United States. In fact, French ministers worked secretly behind the scenes to try to prevent the establishment of a strong, unified, independent government in America. That Spain, which was allied to France but not to the United States during the war, wanted to lay claim to the region between the Appalachian Mountains and the Mississippi River further complicated the issues. But the American delegates proved adept at playing the game of power politics and gained their main goal: independence as a united nation. The new British ministry, headed by Lord Shelburne (formerly a persistent critic of Lord North's harsh American policies), was weary of war and made numerous concessions—so many, in fact, that Parliament ousted the ministry shortly after the peace terms were approved.

Under the treaty, signed formally on September 3, 1783, the Americans were granted unconditional independence and unlimited fishing rights off New-foundland. The boundaries of the new nation were generous: to the north, approximately the present-day boundary with Canada; to the south, the 31st parallel (about the modern northern border of Florida); to the west, the Mississippi River. Florida, which the British had acquired in 1763, was returned to Spain. In ceding so much land unconditionally to the Americans, the British entirely ignored the territorial rights of their Indian allies. Once again, the tribes' interests were sacrificed to the demands of European power politics. Loyalists and British merchants were also poorly served by the British negotiators. The treaty's ambiguously worded clauses pertaining to the payment of pre-war debts and the postwar treatment of loyalists caused trouble for years to come and proved impossible to enforce.

The long war finally over, the victorious Americans could look back on their achievement with satisfaction and awe. In 1775, with an inexperienced, ragtag army, they had taken on the greatest military power in the world—and eight years later they had won. They had accomplished their goal more through persistence and commitment than through brilliance on the battlefield. Actual victories had been few, but their army had always survived defeats and stand-offs to fight again. Ultimately, the Americans had simply worn their enemy down.

Achieving independence in military terms, however, was only half the battle. The Americans also faced perhaps even greater challenges: establishing stable republican governments at the state and national levels to replace the monarchy they had rejected so resoundingly, and ensuring their governments' continued existence in a world filled with bitter rivalries among the major powers—England, France, and Spain. Those European rivalries had worked to the Americans' advantage during the war, but in the decades to come they would pose significant threats to the survival of the new nation.

Suggestions for Further Reading

General

Edward Countryman, *The American Revolution* (1985); Larry Gerlach, ed., *Legacies of the American Revolution* (1978); *Journal of Interdisciplinary History,* 6, no. 4 (Spring 1976), *Interdisciplinary Studies of the American Revolution;* Stephen G. Kurtz and James H. Hutson, eds., *Essays on the American Revolution* (1973); Library of Congress, *Symposia on the American Revolution,* 5 vols. (1972–1976); Edmund S. Morgan, *The Challenge of the American Revolution* (1976); *William and Mary Quarterly,* 3rd ser., 33, no. 3 (July 1976), *The American Revolution;* Alfred F. Young, ed., *The American Revolution: Explorations in the History of American Radicalism* (1976).

Military

John Richard Alden, *The American Revolution, 1775–1783* (1964); E. Wayne Carp, *To Starve the Army at Pleasure: Continental Army Administration and American Political Culture, 1775–1783* (1984); John C. Dann, ed., *The Revolution Remembered: Eyewitness Accounts of the War for Independence* (1980); Don Higginbotham, *The War of American*

Independence: Military Attitudes, Policies, and Practice, 1763–1789 (1971); Ronald Hoffman and Peter Albert, eds., *Arms and Independence: The Military Character of the American Revolution* (1984); Piers Mackesy, *The War for America, 1775–1783* (1964); James K. Martin and Mark Lender, *"A Respectable Army": The Military Origins of the Republic, 1763–1789* (1982); Charles Royster, *A Revolutionary People at War: The Continental Army and American Character, 1775–1783* (1980); John Shy, *A People Numerous and Armed: Reflections on the Military Struggle for American Independence* (1976).

Local and Regional

Richard Buel, *Dear Liberty: Connecticut's Mobilization for the Revolutionary War* (1980); Edward Countryman, *A People in Revolution: The American Revolution and Political Society in New York, 1760–1790* (1981); Elaine F. Crane, *A Dependent People: Newport, R.I., in the Revolutionary Era* (1985); Jeffrey Crow and Larry Tise, eds., *The Southern Experience in the American Revolution* (1978); Thomas Doerflinger, *A Vigorous Spirit of Enterprise: Merchants and Economic Development in Revolutionary Philadelphia* (1986); Robert A. Gross, *The Minutemen and Their World* (1976); Ronald Hoffman, *A Spirit of Dissension: Economics, Politics, and the Revolution in Maryland* (1973); Ronald Hoffman, Thad W. Tate, and Peter Albert, eds., *An Uncivil War: The Southern Backcountry During the American Revolution* (1985); Stephen Rosswurm, *Arms, Country, and Class: The Philadelphia Militia and the "Lower Sort" During the American Revolution* (1988); John Selby, *The Revolution in Virginia, 1775–1783* (1988).

Indians and Blacks

Barbara Graymont, *The Iroquois in the American Revolution* (1972); Isabel T. Kelsey, *Joseph Brant, 1743–1807: Man of Two Worlds* (1984); Duncan J. MacLeod, *Slavery, Race, and the American Revolution* (1974); James H. O'Donnell III, *Southern Indians in the American Revolution* (1973); Benjamin Quarles, *The Negro in the American Revolution* (1961); Anthony F. C. Wallace, *The Death and Rebirth of the Seneca* (1969).

Loyalists

Bernard Bailyn, *The Ordeal of Thomas Hutchinson* (1974); Robert McCluer Calhoon, *The Loyalists in Revolutionary America, 1760–1781* (1973); William H. Nelson, *The American Tory* (1961); Mary Beth Norton, *The British-Americans: The Loyalist Exiles in England, 1774–1789* (1972); Janice Potter, *The Liberty We Seek: Loyalist Ideology in Colonial New York and Massachusetts* (1983); Paul H. Smith, *Loyalists and Redcoats: A Study in British Revolutionary Policy* (1964); James W. St. G. Walker, *The Black Loyalists: The Search for a Promised Land in Nova Scotia and Sierra Leone, 1783–1870* (1976).

Women

Richard Buel and Joy Buel, *The Way of Duty: A Woman and Her Family in Revolutionary America* (1984); Linda Grant DePauw and Conover Hunt, *"Remember the Ladies": Women in America, 1750–1815* (1976); Linda K. Kerber, *Women of the Republic: Intellect and Ideology in Revolutionary America* (1980); Mary Beth Norton, *Liberty's Daughters: The Revolutionary Experience of American Women, 1750–1800* (1980).

Foreign Policy

Jonathan Dull, *A Diplomatic History of the American Revolution* (1985); Felix Gilbert, *To the Farewell Address* (1961); Ronald Hoffman and Peter Albert, eds., *Peace and the Peacemakers: The Treaty of 1783* (1986); Ronald Hoffman and Peter Albert, eds., *Diplomacy and Revolution: The Franco-American Alliance of 1778* (1981); Lawrence Kaplan, ed., *The American Revolution and a "Candid World"* (1977); Richard B. Morris, *The Peacemakers: The Great Powers and American Independence* (1965); Jan Willem Schulte Nordholt, *The Dutch Republic and American Independence* (1982); Richard W. Van Alstyne, *Empire and Independence: The International History of the American Revolution* (1965).

Patriot Leaders

Fawn M. Brodie, *Thomas Jefferson: An Intimate History* (1974); Verner W. Crane, *Benjamin Franklin and a Rising People* (1954); Marcus Cunliffe, *George Washington: Man and Monument* (1958); Noble Cunningham, *In Pursuit of Reason: The Life of Thomas Jefferson* (1987); James T. Flexner, *George Washington,* 4 vols. (1965–1972); Eric Foner, *Tom Paine and Revolutionary America* (1976); Claude A. Lopez and Eugenia Herbert, *The Private Franklin: The Man and His Family* (1975); Dumas Malone, *Jefferson and His Time,* 6 vols. (1948–1981); Peter Shaw, *The Character of John Adams* (1976).

On January 25, 1787, an army of 1,500 farmers drawn from the hills and valleys of western Massachusetts advanced on the federal armory at Springfield, which housed 450 tons of military supplies, including 7,000 muskets and 1,300 barrels of gunpowder. Inside the arsenal, General William Shepard prepared his group of 1,000 militiamen to resist the assault. First, though, he dispatched two aides to warn the farmers that they would soon "inevitably" draw the fire of men who had been their officers during the Revolutionary War. "That is all we want, by God!" replied one of the rebels. The farmers moved toward the armory, urged on by the commands of Daniel Shays, one of their leaders. "March, God Damn you, March!" he shouted. Shepard fired two cannons over the heads of the farmers, then—when that did not frighten them—directed his men to shoot directly at the straggling ranks. Four men died; twenty were wounded; and the rebels withdrew from the field.

6

FORGING A NATIONAL REPUBLIC, 1776–1789

What had caused this violent clash between former comrades in arms, just six short years after the victory at Yorktown? The Massachusetts farmers were angered by high taxes and the scarcity of money. Since the preceding summer they had used committees and crowd actions—adopting the tactics used so successfully in the 1760s and early 1770s—to halt court proceedings in which the state was trying to seize property for nonpayment of taxes. Many of the insurgents were respected war veterans, described as "gentlemen" in contemporary accounts of the riots. Daniel Shays, their nominal leader (he disclaimed the title, declaring that decisions were made collectively), had been a captain in the Continental Army. Clearly the episode could not be dismissed as the work of an unruly rabble. What did the uprising mean for the future of the republic? Was it a sign of impending anarchy?

The protesters explained their position in an address to the governor and council of Massachusetts. They proclaimed their loyalty to the nation but objected to the state's fiscal policies, which, they said, prevented them from providing adequately for their families. Referring to their experience as revolutionary soldiers, they asserted that they "esteem[ed] one moment of Liberty to be worth an eternity of Bondage." One rebel sympathizer ex-

The John Cadwalader Family by Charles Wilson Peale, 1772. Oil on canvas. *Philadelphia Museum of Art. The Cadwalader Collection. Purchased with funds contributed by the Pew Memorial Trust and gift of the Cadwalader Family.*

A woodcut of Daniel Shays and one of his chief officers. Job Shattuck, in 1787. *National Portrait Gallery, Smithsonian Institution, Washington, D.C.*

plained, "Whenever any encroachments are made either upon the liberties or properties of the people, if redress cannot be had without, it is virtue in them to disturb government." The Massachusetts government, Shays asserted, was "tyrannical" and, like that of Great Britain, deserved to be overthrown.

To the state's elected leaders, the most frightening aspect of the uprising was the rebels' attempt to forge direct links with the earlier struggle for independence. The state legislature issued an address to the people, asserting that "in a republican government the majority must govern. If the minor part governs it becomes aristocracy; if every one opposed at his pleasure, it is no government, it is anarchy and confusion." Thus Massachusetts officials insisted that the crowd actions that had once been a justifiable response to British tyranny were no longer legitimate. In a republic, reform had to come about through the ballot box rather than by force. If the nation's citizens refused to submit to legitimate authority, the result would be chaos and the collapse of the government.

The confrontation at the Springfield armory symbolized for many Americans the trials facing the new nation. That the rebels were dispersed easily, that their leaders (including Shays) were forced to flee to neighboring states for asylum, that two of the insurgents were hanged, and that a newly elected Massachusetts legislature adopted conciliatory measures—all those facts were almost irrelevant to American political leaders' interpretation of the events in western Massachusetts. In Shays's Rebellion they thought they discerned the first signs of disintegration of the republic they had worked so hard to establish.

Republicanism—the idea that governments should be based wholly on the consent of the people—had first been discussed by political theorists in ancient Greece and Rome. Republics, such writers declared, were desirable yet fragile forms of government. Unless their citizens were especially virtuous and largely in agreement on key issues, republics were doomed to failure. When they left the British Empire, Americans abandoned the idea that the best system of government balanced monarchy, aristocracy, and democracy—or, to put it another way, that a stable polity required participation by a king, the nobility, and the people. Instead they substituted a belief in the superiority of repub-

Chapter 6: Forging a National Republic, 1776–1789

1776	Second Continental Congress directs states to draft constitutions	**1787**	Northwest Ordinance Constitutional Convention
1777	Articles of Confederation sent to states for ratification	**1788**	Hamilton, Jay, and Madison, *The Federalist* Constitution ratified
1781	Articles of Confederation ratified	**1794**	Battle of Fallen Timbers
1786	Annapolis Convention	**1795**	Treaty of Greenville
1786–87	Shays's Rebellion	**1800**	Weems, *Life of Washington*

licanism, in which the people, not Parliament, were sovereign. Now they had to deal with the potentially unwelcome consequences of that decision. How could they best ensure political stability? How could they create a virtuous republic?

America's political and intellectual leaders worked hard to inculcate virtue in their fellow countrymen and countrywomen. After 1776, American literature, theater, art, architecture, and education all had explicitly moral goals. The education of women was particularly important, for as the mothers of the republic's children, they were primarily responsible for ensuring their nation's future. On such matters Americans could agree, but they disagreed on many other critical issues. Although almost all white men concurred that women, Indians, and blacks should be excluded from formal participation in politics, they found it very difficult to reach a consensus on how many of their own number should be included. And when should consent be sought: semiannually? annually? at intervals of two or more years? Further, how should governments be structured so as to reflect the people's consent most accurately? Americans replied to these questions in different ways.

Republican citizens had to answer many other questions as well. Should a republic conduct its dealings with Indian tribes and foreign countries any differently from other types of governments? Did republics, in other words, have an obligation to negotiate fairly and honestly at all times? And then there were Thomas Jefferson's words in the Declaration of Independence: "all men are created equal." Given that bold statement of principle, how could white republicans justify holding African-Americans in perpetual bondage? Some answered that question by freeing their slaves or by voting for state laws that abolished slavery. Others responded by denying that blacks were "men" in the same sense as whites.

The most important task facing Americans in these years was the construction of a *national* government. Before 1765, the English mainland colonies had rarely cooperated on common endeavors. Many things separated them: their diverse economies, varying religious traditions and ethnic compositions, competing land claims (especially in the West), and differences in their political systems (see Chapters 2 and 3). But fighting the Revolutionary War brought them together and created a new nationalistic spirit, especially in the ranks of those men who served in the Continental Army or the diplomatic corps. Wartime experiences broke down at least some of the boundaries that had previously divided Americans, replacing loyalties to state and region with loyalties to the nation.

Still, forging a national republic (as opposed to a set of loosely connected state republics) was neither easy nor simple. America's first such government, the Articles of Confederation, proved to be inadequate. But some of the nation's political leaders learned from their experiences and tried another approach when they drafted the Constitution in 1787. Some historians have argued that the Articles of Confederation and the Constitution reflected opposing political philosophies, the Constitution representing an "aristocratic" counter-revolution against the "democratic" Articles. The two documents are more accurately viewed as separate and successive attempts to solve the same problems. Both in part applied theories of republicanism to practical problems of governance; neither was entirely successful in resolving those difficulties.

Creating a Virtuous Republic

Many years after the Revolution, John Dickinson recalled that in 1776, when the colonies declared their independence from Great Britain, "there was no question concerning forms of Government, no enquiry whether a Republic or a limited Monarchy was best. . . . We knew that the people of this country must unite themselves under some form of Government and that this could be no other than the republican form." But how could that goal be implemented?

Three different definitions of *republicanism* emerged in the new United States. The first, held chiefly by members of the educated elite (for example, the Adamses of Massachu-

Varieties of Repub- licanism setts), was based directly on ancient history and political theory. The histories of popular governments in Greece and Rome seemed to prove that republics could succeed only if they were small in size and homogeneous in population. Furthermore, unless the citizens of a republic were willing to sacrifice their own private interests for the good of the whole, the government would inevitably collapse. In return for sacrifices, though, a republic offered its citizens equality of opportunity. Under such a government, rank would be based on merit rather than inherited wealth and status. Society would be ruled by members of a "natural aristocracy," men of talent who had risen from what might have been humble beginnings to positions of power and privilege. Rank would not be abolished but instead would be placed on a different footing.

A second definition, also advanced by members of the elite but in addition by some skilled craftsmen, drew more on economic than political thought. Instead of perceiving the nation as an organic whole composed of people sacrificing to the common good, this version of republicanism followed the English theorist Adam Smith in emphasizing individuals' pursuit of rational self-interest. The relevance of such an approach was underlined by the huge profits some men reaped from their patriotic participation in the war effort by selling supplies to the army. The nation could only benefit from aggressive economic expansion, argued such men as Alexander Hamilton (see page 193). When republican men sought to improve their own economic and social circumstances, the entire nation would benefit. Republican virtue would be achieved through the advancement of private interests, rather than through their subordination to some communal ideal.

The third notion of republicanism was less influential because it was popular primarily with people who were illiterate or barely literate and who thus wrote little to promote their beliefs. But it involved a more egalitarian approach to governance than did either of the other two, both of which contained considerable potential for inequality. Some late-eighteenth-century Americans (like Thomas Paine) emphasized the importance of widespread participation in political activities, wanted government to be responsive to their needs, and openly questioned the gentry's ability to speak for them. They can, in fact, be termed democrats in more or less the modern sense.

Despite the differences, it is important to recognize that the three strands of republicanism were part of a unified whole and shared many of the same assumptions. For example, all three contrasted a virtuous, industrious America to the corrupt luxury of England and Europe. In the first version, that virtue manifested itself in frugality and self-sacrifice; in the second, it would prevent self-interest from becoming vice; in the third, it was the justification for including even propertyless white men in the ranks of voters. "Virtue, Virtue alone . . . is the basis of a republic," asserted Dr. Benjamin Rush of Philadelphia, an ardent patriot, in 1778. His fellow Americans concurred, even if they defined virtue in divergent ways.

As the citizens of the United States set out to construct their republic, they believed they were embarking on an unprecedented enterprise. With great pride in their new nation, they expected to

Virtue and the Arts

exchange the vices of monarchical Europe for the virtues of republican America. They wanted to embody republican principles not only in their governments (see page 168) but also in their society and their culture. They looked to painting, literature, drama, and architecture to convey messages of nationalism and virtue to the public.

But Americans faced a crucial contradiction at the very outset of their efforts. To some republicans, the fine arts themselves were manifestations of vice. Their appearance in a virtuous society, many contended, signaled the arrival of luxury and corruption. What need did a frugal yeoman have for a painting—or, worse yet, a novel? Why should anyone spend hard-earned wages to see a play in a lavishly decorated theater? The first American artists, playwrights, and authors were thus trapped in a dilemma from which escape was nearly impossible. They wanted to produce works embodying virtue, but those very works, regardless of their content, were viewed by many as corrupting.

Still, they tried. William Hill Brown's *The Power of Sympathy* (1789), the first novel written in the United States, was a lurid tale of seduction intended as a warning to young women, who made up a large proportion of America's fiction readers. In Royall Tyler's *The Contrast* (1787), the first successful American play, the virtuous conduct of Colonel Manly was contrasted (hence the title) with the reprehensible behavior of the fop Billy Dimple. The most popular book of the era, Mason Locke Weems's *Life of Washington,* published in 1800 shortly after George Washington's death, was, the author declared, designed to "hold up his great Virtues . . . to the imitation of Our Youth." Weems could hardly have been accused of being subtle. The famous tale he invented—six-year-old George bravely admitting cutting down his father's favorite cherry tree—ended with George's father exclaiming, "Run to my arms, you dearest boy. . . . Such an act of heroism in my son, is worth more than a thousand trees, though blossomed with silver, and their fruit of purest gold."

Painting, too, was expected to embody high moral standards. The major artists of the republican period—Gilbert Stuart and John Trumbull—studied in London under Benjamin West and John Singleton Copley, the first great American-born painters, both of whom had emigrated to England before the Revolution. Stuart and Charles Willson

A scene from Royall Tyler's *The Contrast,* as performed in New York City in 1787. The play both satirized English aristocrats and celebrated the virtuous simplicity of its American hero and heroine. *Harvard Theatre Collection.*

Peale (an American-trained artist) painted innumerable portraits of upstanding republican citizens—the political, economic, and social leaders of the day. Trumbull's vast canvases depicted such milestones of American history as the Battle of Bunker Hill, Burgoyne's surrender at Saratoga, and Cornwallis's capitulation at Yorktown. Both portraits and historical scenes were intended to instill patriotic virtues in their viewers.

Architects likewise hoped to convey in their buildings a sense of the young republic's ideals, and most of them consciously rejected British models. When the Virginia government asked Thomas Jefferson, then ambassador to France, for advice on the design of a state capitol in Richmond, Jefferson unhesitatingly recommended copying a Roman building, the Maison Carrée at Nîmes. "It is very simple," he explained, "but it is noble beyond expression." Jefferson set forth ideals that would guide American architecture for a generation to come: simplicity of line, harmonious proportions, a feeling of grandeur. Nowhere were these rational goals of republican art manifested more clearly than in Benjamin H. Latrobe's plans for the majestic, domed United States Capitol in Washington, built shortly after the turn of the century.

Despite the artists' efforts, or perhaps, some would have said, because of them, some Americans were beginning to detect signs of luxury and corruption by the mid-1780s. The end of the war and resumption of European trade brought a return to fashionable clothing styles for both men and women and abandonment of the simpler homespun garments patriots had once worn with pride. Balls and concerts were attended by well-dressed elite families. Parties no longer seemed complete without gambling and card playing. Social clubs for young people multiplied; Samuel Adams worried in print about the possibilities for corruption lurking behind innocent plans for tea drinking and genteel conversation among Boston youths. Especially alarming to fervent republicans was the establishment in 1783 of the Society of the Cincinnati, a hereditary organization of Revolutionary War officers and their descendants. Many feared that the group would become the nucleus of a native-born aristocracy. All these developments directly challenged the United States's image as a virtuous republic.

Their deep-seated concern for the future of the infant republic focused Americans' attention on their children, the "rising generation." Education acquired new significance in the

> **Educational Reform**

context of the republic. Since the early days of the colonies, education had been seen chiefly as a private means to personal advancement, of concern only to individual families. Now, though, it would serve a public purpose. If young people were to resist the temptation of vice, they would have to learn the lessons of virtue at home and at school. In fact, the very survival of the nation depended on it. The early republican period was thus a time of major educational reform.

The 1780s and 1790s brought two significant changes in American educational practice. First, some northern states began to be willing to use tax money to support public elementary schools. Nearly all education in the colonies had been privately financed. In the republic, though, schools could lay claim to tax dollars. In 1789, Massachusetts became one of the first states to require towns to supply their citizens with free public elementary education.

Second, schooling for girls was improved. Americans' recognition of the importance of the rising generation led to the realization that mothers would have to be properly educated if they were to be able to instruct their children adequately. Therefore Massachusetts insisted in its 1789 law that town elementary schools be open to girls as well as boys. Throughout the United States, private academies were founded to give teenage girls from well-to-do families an opportunity for advanced schooling. No one yet proposed opening colleges to women, but a few fortunate girls could study history, geography, rhetoric, and mathematics. The academies also trained female students in fancy needlework—the only artistic endeavor open to women.

The chief theorist of women's education in the early republic was Judith Sargent Murray of Gloucester, Massachusetts. In a series of essays published in the 1780s and 1790s,

> **Judith Sargent Murray on Education**

Murray argued that women and men had equal intellectual capacities, though women's inadequate education might make them seem to be less intelligent. "We can only reason from what we know," she declared, "and if an opportunity of acquiring knowledge hath been denied us, the inferiority of our sex cannot fairly be deduced from thence." Therefore, concluded Murray, boys and girls should be offered equivalent scholastic training. She further contended that girls should be taught to support themselves by their own efforts: "Independence should be placed within their grasp." Because she rejected the prevailing notion that a young woman's chief goal in life should be finding a husband, Judith Sargent Murray deserves the title of the first American feminist. (That distinction is usually accorded to better-known nineteenth-century women like Margaret Fuller or Sarah Grimké.)

Murray's direct challenge to the traditional colonial belief that (as one man put it) girls "knew quite enough if they could make a shirt and a pudding" was part of a general rethinking of women's position that occurred as a result of the Revolution. Male patriots who enlisted in the army or served in Congress were away from home for long periods of time. In their absence their wives, who had previously handled only the "indoor affairs" of the household, had to shoulder the responsibility for "outdoor affairs" as well. As the wife of a Connecticut militiaman later recalled, her husband "was out more or less during the remainder of the war [after 1777], so much so as to be unable to do anything on our farm. What was done, was done by myself."

In many households, the necessary shift of responsibilities during the war taught men and women that their notions of proper gender roles had to be rethought. Both John and Abigail Adams took great pride in Abigail's developing skills as a "farmeress," and John praised her courage repeatedly. "You are really brave, my dear, you are an Heroine," he told her in 1775. Abigail Adams, like her female contemporaries, stopped calling the farm "yours" in letters to her husband and began referring to it as "ours"—a revealing change of pronoun. Both men and women realized that female patriots had made a vital contribution to winning the war through their work at home. Thus, in the years after the Revolution, Americans began to develop new ideas about the role women should play in a republican society.

The best-known example of those new ideas came in a letter Abigail Adams addressed to her husband in March 1776. "In the new Code of Laws

> **Abigail Adams: "Remember the Ladies"**

which I suppose it will be necessary for you to make I desire you would Remember the Ladies," she wrote. "Remember all Men would be tyrants if they could. . . . If perticuliar care and attention is not paid to the Laidies we are determined to foment a Rebelion, and will not hold ourselves bound by any Laws in which we have no voice, or Representation."

With these words, Abigail Adams took a step that was soon to be duplicated by other disfranchised Americans. She deliberately employed the ideology that had been developed to combat Great Britain's claims to political supremacy, but she applied it to purposes white male leaders had never intended. Since men were "Naturally Tyrannical," she argued, America's new legal code should "put it out of the power of the vicious and the Lawless to use us with cruelty and indignity." Thus she called

Judith Sargent (1751–1820), later Mrs. John Murray, painted by John Singleton Copley when she was in her late teens. Although her steady gaze suggests clear-headed intelligence, there is little in the stylized portrait—typical of Copley's work at the time—to suggest her later emergence as the first notable American feminist theorist. *Frick Art Reference Library.*

for reformation of the American law of marriage, which made wives wholly subordinate to their husbands. John Adams did not take his wife's suggestion seriously. Two weeks later he replied, "As to your extraordinary Code of Laws, I cannot but Laugh." Women, he insisted, had little cause for complaint. "In Practice you know We are subjects. We have only the Name of Masters, and rather than give up this, which would compleatly subject Us to the Despotism of the Peticoat, I hope General Washington and all our brave Heroes would fight."

Abigail Adams did not ask that women be allowed to vote. But other women wanted to claim that right, as events in New Jersey proved. The men who drafted the state constitution in 1776 defined voters loosely as "all free inhabitants" who met certain property qualifications. They thereby unintentionally gave the vote to property-holding white

Creating a Virtuous Republic

spinsters and widows, as well as to free blacks. In the 1780s and 1790s qualified women regularly voted in New Jersey's local and congressional elections. They continued to exercise that right until 1807, when women and blacks were disfranchised by the state legislature on the grounds that their votes could be easily manipulated. Yet the fact that they had voted at all was evidence of their altered perception of their place in political life.

Such dramatic episodes were unusual. On the whole the re-evaluation of women's position had its greatest impact on private life. The traditional colonial view of marriage had stressed the subordination of wife to husband. But in 1790 a female "Matrimonial Republican" asserted that "marriage ought never to be considered as a contract between a superior and an inferior, but a reciprocal union of interest. . . . The obedience between man and wife is, or ought to be mutual." This new understanding of the marital relationship seems to have contributed to a rising divorce rate after the war. Dissatisfied wives proved less willing to remain in unhappy marriages than they had been previously. At the same time, state judges became more sympathetic to women's desires to be freed from abusive or unfaithful husbands. Even so, divorces were still rare; most marriages were for life, and married women continued to suffer serious legal disabilities. Like John Adams, most political leaders failed to heed calls for reform. Not until the 1830s did legislators begin to change the statutes governing the legal status of married women.

Women's Role in the Republic

After the war, then, Americans still viewed woman's role in traditional terms. Most eighteenth-century white Americans assumed that women's place was in the home and that their primary function was to be good wives and mothers. They accepted the notion of equality, broadly defined, but within the context of men's and women's separate roles in life. Seeing such differences between the male and female characters eventually enabled Americans to resolve the conflict between the two most influential strands of republican thought. Because married women could not own property or participate directly in economic life, women in general came to be seen as the embodiment of self-sacrificing, disinterested republicanism. Through female-run charitable and other social welfare groups, they assumed responsibility for the welfare of the community as a whole. Yet because they worked chiefly with women and children in familial settings, women continued to be seen primarily as private beings. Thus men were freed from any naggings of conscience as they pursued their economic self-interest (that other republican virtue), secure in the knowledge that their wives and daughters were fulfilling the family's obligation to the common good. The ideal republican man, therefore, was an individualist, seeking advancement for himself and his family; the ideal republican woman, by contrast, always put the well-being of others ahead of her own.

Together white men and women established the context for the creation of a virtuous republic. But nearly 20 percent of the American population was black. How did approximately 700,000 African-Americans fit into the developing national plan?

Emancipation and the Growth of Racism

Revolutionary ideology exposed one of the primary contradictions in American society. Both blacks and whites saw the irony in slaveholding Americans' claims that one of their aims in taking up arms was to prevent Britain from "enslaving" them.

As early as 1764, James Otis, Jr., had identified the basic problem in his pamphlet *The Rights of the British Colonies Asserted and Proved* (see page 114). If according to natural law all people were born free and equal, that meant all humankind, black and white. "Does it follow that 'tis right to enslave a man because he is black?" Otis asked. "Can any logical inference in favor of slavery be drawn from a flat nose, a long or short face?" The same theme was later voiced by other revolutionary leaders. In 1773 the Philadelphia doctor Benjamin Rush called slavery "a vice which degrades human nature," warning ominously that "the plant of liberty is of so tender a nature that it cannot thrive long in the neighborhood of slavery." Common folk too saw the contradiction. When Josiah Atkins, a Connecticut soldier marching south, saw Washington's plantation, he observed in his journal: "Alas!

Liberty Displaying the Arts and Sciences, by Samuel Jennings, 1792. The directors of the Library Company of Philadelphia commissioned this painting, an allegory intended to demonstrate the importance of learning in the young republic. They asked the artist to portray a group of freed blacks "in some attitude expressive of Ease & Joy," and so the painting symbolizes the connection between republican education and antislavery ideals. *The Henry Francis du Pont Winterthur Museum.*

That persons who pretend to stand for the rights of mankind for the liberties of society, can delight in oppression, & that even of the worst kind!"

African-Americans themselves were quick to recognize the implications of revolutionary ideology. In 1779 a group of slaves from Portsmouth, New Hampshire, asked the state legislature "from what authority [our masters] assume to dispose of our lives, freedom and property," and pleaded "that the name of slave may not more be heard in a land gloriously contending for the sweets of freedom." That same year several black residents of Fairfield, Connecticut, petitioned the legislature for their freedom, characterizing slavery as a "dreadful Evil" and "flagrant Injustice." Surely, they declared pointedly, "your Honours who are nobly contending in the Cause of Liberty, whose Conduct excited

the Admiration, and Reverence, of all the great Empires of the World; will not resent, our thus freely animadverting, on this detestable Practice."

Both legislatures responded negatively. But the postwar years did witness the gradual abolition of slavery in the North. Vermont abolished slavery in its 1777 constitution. Massachusetts courts decided in the 1780s that the clause in the state constitution declaring that "all men are born free and equal, and have certain natural, essential, and unalienable rights" prohibited slavery in the state. Pennsylvania passed an abolition law in 1780; four years later Rhode Island and Connecticut provided for gradual emancipation, followed by New York (1799) and New Jersey (1804). Although New Hampshire did not

Gradual Emancipation

formally abolish slavery, only eight slaves were reported on the 1800 census and none remained a decade later.

No southern state adopted similar general emancipation laws, but the legislatures of Virginia (1782), Delaware (1787), and Maryland (1790 and 1796) did decide to change laws that had restricted masters' ability to free their slaves. South Carolina and Georgia never considered adopting such acts, and North Carolina insisted that all manumissions (emancipations of individual slaves) be approved by county courts.

Thus revolutionary ideology had limited impact on the well-entrenched economic interests of large slaveholders. Only in the North, where there were few slaves and where little money was invested in human capital, could state legislatures vote to abolish slavery with relative ease. Even there, legislators' concern for property rights—the Revolution, after all, was fought for property as well as life and liberty—led them to favor gradual emancipation over immediate abolition. Most states provided only for the freeing of children born after passage of the law, not for the emancipation of adults. And even those children were to remain slaves until ages ranging from eighteen to twenty-eight. Still, by 1840 in only one northern state—New Jersey—were black persons legally held in bondage.

Despite the slow progress of abolition, the free black population of the United States grew dramatically in the first years after the Revolution. Before the war there had been few free **Growth of** blacks in America. According to a **the Free** 1755 Maryland census, for example, only 4 percent of the African-**Black** Americans in the colony were **Population** free. Most prewar free blacks were mulattos, born of unions between white masters and enslaved black women. But wartime disruptions radically changed the size and composition of the free black population. Slaves who had escaped from plantations during the war, others who had served in the American army, and still others who had been emancipated by their owners or by state laws were now free. Because most of them were not mulattos, dark skin was no longer an automatic sign of slave status. By 1790 there were nearly 60,000 free people of color in the United States; ten years later they numbered more than 108,000, nearly 11 percent of the total black population.

The effects of postwar manumissions were felt most sharply in the Chesapeake, where they were fostered by such economic changes as declining soil fertility and the shift from tobacco to grain production. Since grain cultivation was less labor-intensive than tobacco growing, planters began to complain about "excess" slaves. They often solved that problem by freeing the most favored or least productive of their bondspeople. The free black population of Virginia more than doubled between 1790 and 1810, and by the latter year nearly one-quarter of Maryland's black population was no longer in legal bondage.

In the 1780s and thereafter, freed people often made their way, as had landless colonists decades before them, to the port cities of the North. Boston and Philadelphia, where slavery was abolished sooner than it was in New York City, were particularly popular destinations. Women outnumbered men among the migrants by a margin of three to two. Like female whites, black women found more opportunities for employment, particularly as domestic servants, in the cities than in the countryside. Some black men also worked in domestic service, but larger numbers were employed as unskilled laborers or seamen. A few of the women and a sizable proportion of men (nearly one-third of those in Philadelphia in 1795) were skilled workers or retailers. These freed people chose new names for themselves, exchanging the surnames of former masters for names like Newman or Brown, and as soon as possible they established independent two-parent nuclear families instead of continuing to live in white households. They also began to cluster their residences in certain neighborhoods, probably as a result of both discrimination by whites and a desire for black solidarity.

Emancipation did not bring equality, though. Even whites who recognized African-Americans' right to freedom were unwilling to accept them as equals. Laws discriminated against **Discrimina-** emancipated blacks as they had **tion Against** against slaves—South Carolina, **Blacks** for example, did not permit free blacks to testify against whites in court. Public schools often refused to educate the children of free black parents. Freedmen found it difficult to purchase property and find good jobs. And though in many areas African-Americans were accepted as members—even ministers—of evangelical churches, whites rarely allowed them an equal voice in church affairs.

Gradually free blacks developed their own separate institutions, often based in the neighborhoods in which they lived. In Charleston, mulattos formed the Brown Fellowship Society, which provided insurance coverage for its members, financed a school for free children, and helped to support black orphans. In 1794, blacks in Philadelphia and Baltimore founded societies that eventually became the African Methodist Episcopal (AME) denomination. AME churches later sponsored schools in a number of cities and, along with African Baptist, African Episcopal, and African Presbyterian churches, became cultural centers of the free black community. Freed people quickly learned that if they were to survive and prosper they would have to rely on their own collective efforts rather than on the benevolence or goodwill of their white compatriots.

Their endeavors were all the more important because the postrevolutionary years ironically witnessed the development of a coherent racist theory in the United States. Whites had

Development of Racist Theory

long regarded blacks as inferior, but the most influential writers on race had attributed that inferiority to environmental rather than hereditary factors. They argued that blacks' seemingly debased character derived from their enslavement, instead of enslavement being the consequence of genetic inferiority. In the aftermath of the Revolution, white southerners needed to defend their holding other human beings in bondage against the notion that "all men are created equal." Consequently, they began to argue that blacks were less than fully human, that the principles of republican equality applied only to whites. To avoid having to confront the contradiction between their practice and the egalitarian implications of revolutionary theory, they redefined the theory, making it inapplicable to blacks.

Their racism had several intertwined elements. First was the insistence that, as Thomas Jefferson suggested in 1781, blacks were "inferior to the whites in the endowments both of body and mind." Second came the belief that blacks were congenitally lazy, dishonest, and uncivilized (or uncivilizable). Third, and of crucial importance, was the notion that all blacks were sexually promiscuous

A woodcut portrait of Benjamin Banneker adorned the cover of his almanac for 1795. *Maryland Historical Society*.

and that black men lusted after white women. The specter of interracial sexual intercourse involving black men and white women haunted early American racist thought. The reverse situation, which occurred with far greater frequency (as white masters sexually exploited their female slaves), aroused little comment.

African-Americans did not allow these developing racist notions to pass unnoticed. Benjamin Banneker, a free black surveyor, astronomer, and mathematical genius, directly challenged Thomas Jefferson's belief in blacks' intellectual inferiority. In 1791 Banneker sent Jefferson a copy of his latest almanac (which included his astronomical calculations) as an example of blacks' mental powers. Jefferson's response admitted Banneker's capability but implied that he regarded Banneker as an exception. The future president insisted that he needed more evidence before he would abandon his previous position.

At its birth, then, the republic was defined by whites as an exclusively white enterprise. Indeed, some historians have argued that the subjection of

> **A Republic for Whites Only**

blacks was a necessary precondition for equality among whites. They have pointed out that identifying a common racial antagonist helped to create white solidarity and to lessen the threat to gentry power posed by the enfranchisement of poorer whites. It was less dangerous to allow whites with little property to participate formally in politics than to open the possibility that they might combine with freed blacks to question the rule of the "better sort." That was one reason why, in the postrevolutionary years, the division of American society between slave and free was transformed into a division between blacks—some of whom were free—and whites. The white male wielders of power ensured their continued dominance in part by making certain that race replaced enslavement as the primary determinant of African-Americans' status.

Designing Republican Governments

On May 10, 1776, even before passage of the Declaration of Independence, the Second Continental Congress directed the states to devise new republican governments to replace the provincial congresses and committees that had met since 1774. Thus Americans initially concentrated on drafting state constitutions and devoted little attention to their national government—an oversight they were later forced to remedy. At the state level, they immediately faced the problem of defining just what a constitution was. The British Constitution could not serve as a model because it was an unwritten mixture of law and custom; Americans wanted tangible documents specifying the fundamental structures of government. Several years passed before the states agreed that their constitutions, unlike ordinary laws, could not be drafted by regular legislative bodies. Following the lead established by Massachusetts in 1780, they began to call conventions for the sole purpose of drafting constitutions. Thus the states sought direct authorization from the people—the theoretical sovereigns in a republic—before establishing new governments. After the new constitutions had been drawn up, delegates submitted them to the voters for ratification.

Those who wrote the state constitutions concerned themselves primarily with outlining the distribution of and limitations on government power.

> **Drafting of State Constitutions**

Both questions were crucial to the survival of republics. If authority was improperly distributed among the branches of government or not confined within reasonable limits, the states might become tyrannical, as Britain had. Indeed, Americans' experience with British rule affected every provision of their new constitutions.

Under their colonial charters, Americans had learned to fear the power of the governor—in most cases the appointed agent of the king or the proprietor—and to see the legislature as their defender. Accordingly, the first state constitutions typically provided for the governor to be elected annually (usually by the legislature), limited the number of terms any one governor could serve, and gave him little independent authority. At the same time the constitutions expanded the powers of the legislature. All the states except Pennsylvania retained the two-house organization common in the colonial years and provided that members of the upper house would have longer terms and be required to meet higher standards of property holding. But they also redrew the lines of electoral districts to reflect population patterns more accurately and increased the numbers of members in both the upper and the lower houses. Finally, most states lowered property qualifications for voting. As a result the legislatures came to include some men who before the war would not have been eligible to vote. Thus the revolutionary era witnessed the first deliberate attempt to broaden the base of American government, a process that has continued into our own day.

But the authors of the state constitutions knew that governments designed to be responsive to the people would not necessarily provide sufficient protection if tyrants were elected to office. Consequently, they included limitations on government authority in the documents they composed. Seven of the constitutions contained formal bills of rights, and the others had similar clauses. Most of them guaranteed citizens freedom of the press and of religion, the right to a fair trial, the right of consent to taxation, and protection against general search warrants. An independent judiciary was charged with upholding such rights.

In sum, the constitution makers put far greater emphasis on preventing state governments from becoming tyrannical than on making them effective wielders of political authority. Their approach to the process of shaping governments was understandable, given the American experience with Great Britain. But establishing such weak political units, especially in wartime, practically ensured that the constitutions would soon need revision. As early as the 1780s some states began to rewrite the constitutions they had drafted in 1776 and 1777. Invariably, the revised versions increased the powers of the governor and reduced the scope of the legislature's authority. Only then, a decade after the Declaration of Independence, did Americans start to develop a formal theory of checks and balances as the primary means of controlling government power. Once they realized that legislative supremacy did not in itself guarantee good government, Americans attempted to achieve that goal by balancing the powers of the legislative, executive, and judicial branches against one another. The national constitution they drafted in 1787 embodied that principle.

But the constitutional theories that Americans applied at the state level did not at first influence their conception of the nature of a national government. The powers and structure of the Continental Congress evolved by default early in the war, since Americans had little time to devote to legitimizing their de facto government while organizing the military struggle against Britain. Not until late 1777, after Burgoyne's defeat at Saratoga, did Congress send the Articles of Confederation to the states for ratification.

The Articles by and large wrote into law the arrangements that had developed, unplanned and largely unheeded, in the Continental Congress. The chief organ of national government was a unicameral (one-house) legislature in which each

Articles of Confederation

state had one vote. Its powers included the conduct of foreign relations, the settlement of disputes between states, control over maritime affairs, the regulation of Indian trade, and the valuation of state and national coinage. The Articles did not give the national government the ability to tax effectively or to enforce a uniform commercial policy. The United States of America was described as "a firm league of friendship" in which each state "retains its sovereignty, freedom and independence, and every Power, Jurisdiction and right, which is not by this confederation expressly delegated to the United States, in Congress assembled."

The Articles required the unanimous consent of the state legislatures for ratification or amendment, and a clause concerning western lands turned out to be troublesome. The draft accepted by Congress allowed the states to retain all land claims derived from their original colonial charters. But states with definite western boundaries in their charters (like Maryland, Delaware, and New Jersey) wanted the other states to cede the lands west of the Appalachian Mountains to the national government. Otherwise, they feared, states with large claims could expand and overpower their smaller neighbors. Maryland absolutely refused to accept the Articles until 1781, when Virginia finally promised to surrender its western holdings to national jurisdiction (see map, page 170). Other states followed suit, establishing the principle that western lands would be held by the nation as a whole.

The fact that a single state could delay ratification for three years was a portent of the fate of American government under the Articles of Confederation. The unicameral legislature, whether it was called the Second Continental Congress (until 1781) or the Confederation Congress (thereafter), was too inefficient and unwieldy to govern effectively. The authors of the Articles had not given adequate thought to the distribution of power within the national government or to the relationship between the Confederation and the states. The Congress they created was simultaneously a legislative body and a collective executive, but it had no independent income and no authority to compel the states to accept its rulings. What is surprising, in other words, is not how poorly the Confederation functioned in the following years, but rather how much the government was able to accomplish.

Western Land Claims and Cessions, 1782–1802

The map legend reads:

N.Y. cedes to Congress, 1782

Va. cedes to Congress, 1784

Ga. cedes to Congress, 1802

Mass. cedes to Congress, 1785

Mass. relinquishes sovereignty and jurisdiction to N.Y., 1786 (Hartford Agreement); Mass. retains title to land

Mass. relinquishes all claims to N.Y., 1786 (Hartford Agreement)

Conn. relinquishes claims to Pa., 1782 (Congressional arbitration)

Conn. cedes to Congress, 1786

Conn. cedes Western Reserve to Congress, 1800

N.C. cedes to Congress, 1790

S.C. relinquishes claims to Ga., 1787 (Beaufort Convention)

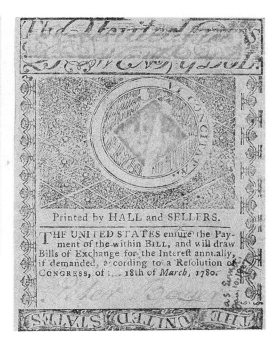

Examples of pieces of paper money issued by the state of Massachusetts and by the United States in the 1780s. *Massachusetts Historical Society.*

Trials of the Confederation

During and after the war the most persistent problem faced by the American governments, state and national, was finance. Because legislators at all levels were reluctant to levy taxes on their fellow countrymen, both Congress and the states tried to finance the war by printing currency. Even though the money was backed by nothing but good faith, it circulated freely and without excessive depreciation during 1775 and most of 1776. Demand for military supplies and civilian goods was high, stimulating trade (especially with France) and local production. Indeed, the amount of money issued in those years was probably no more than what a healthy economy required as a medium of exchange.

Financial Problems

But in late 1776, as the American army suffered major battlefield reverses in New York and New Jersey, prices began to rise and inflation set in. The value of the currency rested on Americans' faith in their government, a faith that was sorely tested in the years that followed, especially during the dark days of the early British triumphs in the South (1779 and 1780). Some state governments fought inflation by controlling wages and prices, requiring acceptance of paper currency on an equal footing with hard money, borrowing, and even levying taxes. Their efforts were futile. So too was Congress's attempt to stop printing currency altogether and to rely solely on state contributions. By early 1780 it took forty paper dollars to purchase one silver dollar. A year later, Continental currency was worthless.

The severe wartime inflation seriously affected people on fixed incomes, including many soldiers and civilian leaders of the Revolution. Common laborers, small farmers, clergymen, and poor folk in general could do nothing to stop the declining value of their incomes. Yet there were people who benefited from such economic conditions. Military contractors could make sizable profits. Farmers who produced surpluses of meat, milk, and grains could sell their goods at high prices to the army or to civilian merchants. People with money could invest in lucrative trading voyages. More risky, but potentially even more profitable, was privateering against enemy shipping, which attracted venturesome sailors and wealthy merchants alike.

Such accumulations of private wealth did nothing to help Congress with its financial problems. In

1781, faced with the total collapse of the monetary system, the delegates undertook major reforms. After establishing a department of finance under the wealthy Philadelphia merchant Robert Morris, they asked the states to amend the Articles of Confederation to allow Congress to levy a duty of 5 percent on imported goods. Morris put national finances on a solid footing, but the customs duty was never adopted. First Rhode Island, then New York refused to agree to the tax. The states' resistance reflected genuine fear of a too-powerful central government. As one worried citizen wrote in 1783, "If permanent Funds are given to Congress, the aristocratical Influence, which predominates in more than a major part of the United States, will fully establish an arbitrary Government."

Congress also faced major diplomatic problems at the close of the war. Chief among them were issues involving the peace treaty itself. Article 4, which promised the repayment of prewar debts (most of them owed by Americans to British merchants), and Article 5, which recommended that states allow loyalists to recover their confiscated property, aroused considerable opposition. States passed laws denying British subjects the right to sue for recovery of debts or property in American courts, and town meetings decried the loyalists' return. As residents of Norwalk, Connecticut, put it, few Americans wanted to permit the "Tory Villains" to return "while filial Tears are fresh upon our Cheeks and our Murdered Brethren scarcely cold in their Graves." The state governments also had reason to oppose enforcement of the treaty. Sales of loyalists' land, houses, and other possessions had helped to finance the later stages of the war; since most of the purchasers were prominent patriots, the states had no desire to raise questions about the legitimacy of their property titles.

The failure of state and local governments to comply with Articles 4 and 5 gave Britain an excuse to maintain military posts on the Great Lakes long after its troops were supposed to have been withdrawn. Furthermore, Congress's inability to convince the states to implement the treaty pointed up its lack of power, even in an area—foreign affairs—in which it had been granted specific authority by the Articles of Confederation. Concerned nationalists argued publicly that enforcement of the treaty, however unpopular, was a crucial test for the re-

Weakness in Foreign Affairs and Commerce

public. "Will foreign nations be willing to undertake anything with us or for us," asked Alexander Hamilton, "when they find that the nature of our governments will allow no dependence to be placed on our engagements?"

Congress's weakness was especially evident in the realm of trade because the Articles of Confederation specifically denied it the power to establish a national commercial policy. Immediately following the war, Britain, France, and Spain restricted American trade with their colonies. Americans, who had hoped independence would bring about free trade with all nations, were outraged but could do little to change matters. Members of Congress watched helplessly as British manufactured goods flooded the United States while American produce could no longer be sold in the British West Indies, once its prime market. The South Carolina indigo industry, deprived of the British bounty that had supported it, suffered a setback. Although Americans reopened trade with northern European countries like the Netherlands and started a profitable trade with China in 1784, neither substituted for access to closer and larger markets.

Congress also had difficulty dealing with the threat posed by Spain's presence on the southern and western borders of the United States. Determined to prevent the new nation's expansion, Spain in 1784 closed the Mississippi River to American navigation. It thus deprived the growing settlements west of the Appalachians of their major access route to the rest of the nation and the world. If Spain's policy were not reversed, westerners might have to accept Spanish sovereignty as the necessary price for survival. Congress opened negotiations with Spain in 1785, but even John Jay, one of the nation's most experienced diplomats, could not win the necessary concessions on navigation. The talks collapsed the following year after Congress divided sharply on the question of whether agreement should be sought on other issues. Southerners, voting as a bloc, insisted on navigation rights on the Mississippi; northerners were willing to abandon that claim in order to win commercial concessions. The impasse raised doubts about the possibility of a national consensus on foreign affairs.

Diplomatic problems of another sort confronted congressmen when they considered the status of the land on the United States's western borders. Although tribal claims were not discussed by Brit-

**Encroach-
ment on
Indian Lands**

ish and American diplomats at the end of the war, the United States assumed that the Treaty of Paris (1783) cleared its title to all land east of the Mississippi except the areas still held by Spain. But recognizing that some sort of land cession should be obtained from the major tribes, Congress initiated negotiations with both northern and southern Indians. At Fort Stanwix, New York, in 1784, and at Hopewell, South Carolina, in late 1785 and early 1786, American representatives signed separate treaties of questionable legality with the Iroquois and with Choctaw, Chickasaw, and Cherokee chiefs (see map). The United States took the treaties as final confirmation of its sovereignty over the Indian territories and authorized white settlers to move onto the land. Whites soon poured over the southern Appalachians, provoking the Creek tribe—which had not agreed to the Hopewell treaties—to defend its territory by declaring war. Only in 1790, when the Creek chief Alexander McGillivray traveled to New York to negotiate a treaty, did the tribe finally come to terms with the United States.

In the North, meanwhile, the Iroquois Confederacy was in disarray. The members of the Six Nations who had not fled to Canada in 1779 soon found that they had little bargaining power left. In 1786 they formally repudiated the Fort Stanwix treaty and threatened new attacks on frontier settlements, but both whites and Indians knew the threat was an empty one. The flawed treaty was permitted to stand by default. At intervals during the remainder of the decade the state of New York purchased large amounts of land from individual Iroquois tribes. By 1790 the once-proud Iroquois Confederacy was confined to a few scattered reservations.

Western tribes like the Shawnees, Chippewas, Ottawas, and Potawatomis had once allowed the Iroquois to speak for them. After the collapse of Iroquois power, they formed their own confederacy and demanded direct negotiations with the United States. Their aim was to present a united front, so as to avoid the piecemeal surrender of land by individual tribes.

At first the national government ignored the western Indian confederacy. Shortly after the state land cessions were completed, Congress began to organize the Northwest Territory, bounded by the Mississippi River, the Great Lakes, and the Ohio

**Northwest
Ordinances**

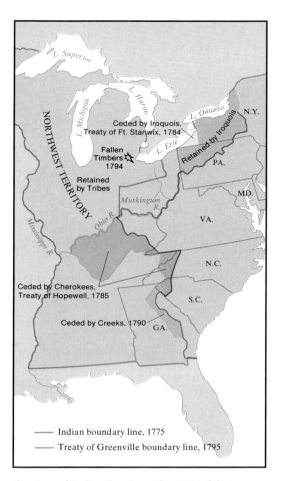

**Cession of Indian Lands to the United States,
1775–1790** *Source: From Lester J. Cappon et al.,
eds., Atlas of Early American History: The Revolutionary Era, 1760–1790. Copyright © 1976 by
Princeton University Press. Reprinted by permission
of Princeton University Press.*

River. Ordinances passed in 1784, 1785, and 1787 outlined the process through which the land could be sold to settlers and formal governments organized. To ensure orderly development, Congress in 1785 directed that the land be surveyed into townships six miles square, each divided into thirty-six sections of 640 acres (one square mile). Revenue from the sale of the sixteenth section of each township was to be reserved for the support of public schools—the first instance of federal aid to education in American history. The minimum price per acre was set at one dollar, and the minimum sale was to be 640 acres. Congress was not especially concerned about helping the small farmer: the

A contemporary map of the first land (in what is now Ohio) surveyed under the terms of the Land Ordinance of 1785. Each square encompasses one section, or 640 acres. *The National Archives.*

twentieth-century Americans were to be less generous in their attitudes toward residents of later territories, many of whom were nonwhite or non-Protestant. But the nation never fully lost sight of the egalitarian principles of the Northwest Ordinance.

In a sense, though, the ordinance was purely theoretical at the time it was passed. The Miamis, Shawnees, and Delawares refused to acknowledge American sovereignty and insisted on their right to the land. They opposed white settlement violently, attacking unwary pioneers who ventured too far north of the Ohio River. In 1788 the Ohio Company, to which Congress had sold a large tract of land at reduced rates, established the town of Marietta at the juncture of the Ohio and Muskingum rivers. But the Indians prevented the company from extending settlement very far into the interior. After General Arthur St. Clair, the first governor of the Northwest Territory, failed to negotiate a meaningful treaty with the tribes in early 1789, it was apparent that the United States could not avoid a clash with a western confederacy composed of eight tribes and led by the Miamis.

Little Turtle, the able war chief of the Miami Confederacy, defeated first General Josiah Harmar (1790) and then St. Clair himself (1791) in major battles near the present border

War in the Northwest between Indiana and Ohio. More than six hundred of St. Clair's men were killed and scores more wounded; it was the whites' worst defeat in the entire history of the American frontier. In 1793 the Miami Confederacy declared that peace could be achieved only if the United States recognized the Ohio River as the boundary between white and Indian lands. But the national government refused to relinquish its claim to the Northwest Territory. A new army under the command of General Anthony Wayne, a Revolutionary War hero, attacked and defeated the tribesmen in August 1794 at the Battle of Fallen Timbers (near Toledo, Ohio). This victory made it possible for serious negotiations to begin.

By the summer of 1795, Wayne had reached agreement with delegates from the Miami Confederacy. The Treaty of Greenville gave each side a portion of what it wanted. The United States gained the right to settle much of what was to become the state of Ohio, the tribes retaining only the northwest corner of the region. The Indians received the acknowledgment they had long sought: American

minimum outlay of $640 was beyond the reach of most Americans (except of course, veterans who had received part of their army pay in land warrants). The proceeds from the land sales were the first independent revenues available to the national government.

The most important ordinance was the third, passed in 1787. The Northwest Ordinance contained a bill of rights guaranteeing settlers in the territory freedom of religion and the right to a jury trial, prohibiting cruel and unusual punishments, and abolishing slavery. It also specified the process by which residents of the territory could eventually organize state governments and seek admission to the Union "on an equal footing with the original States." Early in the nation's history, therefore, Congress laid down a policy of admitting new states on the same basis as the old and assuring residents of the territories the same rights as citizens of the original states. Having suffered under the rule of a colonial power, congressmen understood the importance of preparing the United States's first "colony" for eventual self-government. Nineteenth- and

Chapter 6: Forging a National Republic, 1776–1789

After the Battle of Fallen Timbers in August 1794, General Anthony Wayne accepted the surrender of the Indian leader Little Turtle (painting). The following summer, the United States and the Miami Confederacy signed the Treaty of Greenville (below), bringing an end to open conflict after several years of warfare. *Painting: Chicago Historical Society; below: The National Archives.*

recognition of their rights to the soil. At Greenville, the United States formally accepted the principle of Indian sovereignty, by virtue of residence, over all lands the tribes had not yet ceded. Never again would the United States government claim that it had acquired Indian territory solely through negotiation with a European or American country.

The problems the United States encountered in ensuring safe settlement of the Northwest Territory pointed up, once again, the basic weakness of the Confederation government. Not until after the Articles of Confederation were replaced with a new constitution could the United States muster sufficient force to implement all the provisions of the Northwest Ordinance. Thus, although the ordinance is often viewed as one of the few major accomplishments of the Confederation Congress, it must be seen within a context of political impotence.

Trials of the Confederation

From Crisis to a Constitution

The Americans most deeply concerned about the inadequacies of the Articles of Confederation were those involved in overseas trade and foreign affairs. In those areas the Articles were obviously deficient: Congress could not impose its will on the states to establish a uniform commercial policy or to ensure the enforcement of treaties. The problems involving trade were particularly serious. Less than a year after the end of the war, the American economy slid into a depression. Exporters of staple crops (especially tobacco and rice) and importers of manufactured goods were adversely affected by the postwar restrictions European powers imposed on American commerce. Although recovery had begun by 1786, the war's effects proved impossible to erase entirely, particularly in the Lower South. Some estimates suggest that between 1775 and 1790 America's per capita gross national product declined by nearly 50 percent.

Economic Change

The war, indeed, had wrought permanent change in the American economy. The near-total cessation of commerce in nonmilitary items during the war years proved a great stimulus to domestic manufacturing. Consequently, despite the influx of European goods after 1783, the postwar period witnessed the stirrings of American industrial development—for example, the first American textile mill began production in Pawtucket, Rhode Island, in 1793. Because of continuing population growth, the domestic market assumed greater relative importance in the overall economy. Moreover, foreign trade patterns shifted from Europe and toward the West Indies, continuing a trend that had begun before the war. Foodstuffs shipped to the French and Dutch Caribbean islands became America's largest single export, replacing tobacco (thus accelerating the Chesapeake's conversion from tobacco to grain production; see page 83).

Recognizing the Confederation Congress's inability to deal with commercial matters, Virginia invited the other states to a convention at Annapolis, Maryland, to discuss trade policy. Although eight states named representatives to the meeting in September 1786, only five delegations attended. Those present realized that they were too few in number to have any real impact on the political system. They issued a call for another convention, to be held in Philadelphia in nine months, "to devise such further provisions as shall . . . appear necessary to render the constitution of the federal government adequate to the exigencies of the Union."

The other states did not respond immediately to the summons to another general meeting. But then Shays's Rebellion (see pages 157–158) convinced many of the critical state of affairs. Of the major American political thinkers, only Thomas Jefferson could view the incidents in western Massachusetts without alarm. "What country can preserve its liberties, if its rulers are not warned from time to time that their people preserve the spirit of resistance?" Jefferson wrote from Paris, where he was serving as American ambassador. "What signify a few lives lost in a century or two? The tree of liberty must be refreshed from time to time, with the blood of patriots and tyrants. It is its natural manure."

Jefferson was exceptional. The reaction to Shays's Rebellion hastened the movement toward comprehensive revision of the Articles of Confederation. In February 1787, after most of the states had already appointed delegates, the Confederation Congress belatedly endorsed the convention. In mid-May, fifty-five men, representing all the states but Rhode Island, assembled in Philadelphia to begin their deliberations.

The vast majority of the delegates to the Constitutional Convention were men of property and substance, and they all favored reform; otherwise they would not have come to Philadelphia. Most wanted to invigorate the national government, to give it new authority to solve the problems besetting the United States. Among their number were merchants, planters, physicians, generals, governors, and especially lawyers—twenty-three had studied the law. Most had been born in America, and many came from families that had arrived in the seventeenth century. In an era when only a tiny proportion of the population had any advanced education, more than half of the delegates had attended college. A few had been educated in Britain, but most were graduates of American institutions: Princeton (ten), William and Mary (four), Yale (three), Harvard and Colum-

Constitutional Convention

bia (two each). The youngest delegate was twenty-six, the oldest—Benjamin Franklin—eighty-one. Like George Washington, whom they elected chairman, most were in their vigorous middle years. A dozen men did the bulk of the convention's work: Oliver Ellsworth and Roger Sherman of Connecticut; Elbridge Gerry and Rufus King of Massachusetts; William Paterson of New Jersey; Gouverneur Morris of New York; James Wilson of Pennsylvania; John Rutledge and Charles Pinckney of South Carolina; and Edmund Randolph, George Mason, and James Madison of Virginia. Of those leaders, Madison was by far the most important; he truly deserves the title Father of the Constitution.

The frail, shy, slightly built James Madison was thirty-six years old in 1787. Raised in the Piedmont country of Virginia, he had attended Princeton, served on the local Committee of Safety, and been elected successively to the Virginia provincial convention, the state's lower and upper houses, and the Continental Congress (1780–1783). Although Madison returned to Virginia to serve in the state legislature in 1784, he remained in touch with national politics, partly through his continuing correspondence with his close friend Thomas Jefferson. A promoter of the Annapolis Convention, he strongly supported its call for further reform.

James Madison

Madison was unique among the delegates in his systematic preparation for the Philadelphia meeting. Through Jefferson in Paris he bought more than two hundred books on history and government and carefully analyzed their accounts of past confederacies and republics. In April 1787, a month before the Constitutional Convention began, he summed up the results of his research in a lengthy paper entitled "Vices of the Political System of the United States." After listing the eleven major flaws he perceived in the current structure of the government (among them "encroachments by the states on the federal authority" and "want of concert in matters where common interest requires it"), Madison revealed the conclusion that would guide his actions over the next few months. What the government most needed, he declared, was "such a modification of the sovereignty as will render it sufficiently neutral between the different interests and factions, to controul one part of the society from invading the rights of another, and at the same time sufficiently controuled itself, from

THE FEDERAL ALMANACK.

THE GRAND CONVENTION.

BEHOLD conven'd in firm debate,
Of high importance to each State;
    Our honour'd fathers fit.
And knowledge ruling at the helm,
They wifely point to every realm;
    The rocks on which they've fplit.
Aloud they cry, that Luxury's charms,
Are worfe than Indians cloath'd in arms;
    And deeper wound the whole.
Then high they rais'd, a godlike mound,
The STATES in FEDERAL virtue bound;
    And BID their FAME fublime to roll.

Only members were allowed to attend the Constitutional Convention. Thus this view of the deliberations, which appeared on the cover of *Weatherwise's Federal Almanack for 1788,* was based primarily on its creator's imagination. *Rare Books Division, New York Public Library, Astor, Lenox, and Tilden Foundations.*

setting up an interest adverse to that of the whole Society."

Thus Madison set forth the principle of checks and balances. The government, he believed, had to be constructed in such a way that it could not become tyrannical or fall wholly under the influence of a particular interest group. He regarded the large size of a potential national republic as an advantage in that respect. Rejecting the common assertion that republics had to be small to survive, Madison argued that a large, diverse republic was in fact to be preferred. Because the nation would include many

James Madison (1751–1836), the youthful scholar and skilled politician who earned the title Father of the Constitution. *Library of Congress.*

different interest groups, no one of them would be able to control the government. Political stability would result from compromises among the contending parties.

Madison's conception of national government was embodied in the so-called Virginia Plan, introduced on May 29 by his colleague Edmund Randolph. The plan provided for a

Virginia and New Jersey Plans

two-house legislature, one house elected directly by the people and the other selected by the first, with proportional representation in both houses, an executive elected by Congress, a national judiciary, and congressional veto over state laws. The Virginia Plan gave Congress the broad power to legislate "in all cases to which the separate states are incompetent." Had it been adopted intact, it would have created a government in which national authority reigned unchallenged and state power was greatly diminished.

But the convention included many delegates who, while recognizing the need for change,

believed that the Virginians had gone too far in the direction of national consolidation. After Randolph's proposal had been debated for several weeks, the disaffected delegates united under the leadership of William Paterson. On June 15 Paterson presented an alternative scheme, the New Jersey Plan, calling for modifications in the Articles of Confederation rather than a complete overhaul of the government. Paterson proposed retaining the unicameral Confederation Congress but giving it new powers of taxation and trade regulation. Even before introducing his proposals, Paterson had made his position clear in debate. On June 9 he asserted that the Articles were "the proper basis of all the proceedings of the convention," and he warned that if the delegates did not confine themselves to amending the Articles they would be charged with "usurpation" by their constituents. All that was needed, Paterson contended, was "to mark the orbits of the states with due precision and provide for the use of coercion" by the national government. Although the delegates rejected Paterson's narrow interpretation of their task, he and his allies won a number of major victories in the months that followed.

The delegates began their work by discussing the structure and functions of Congress. They readily agreed that the new national government should have a two-house (bicameral) legislature. But then they discovered that they differed widely in their answers to three key questions: Should representation in both houses of Congress be proportional to population? How was representation in either or both houses to be apportioned among the states? And, finally, how were the members of the two houses to be elected?

The last issue was the easiest to resolve. In the words of John Dickinson, the delegates thought it "essential" that members of one branch of Congress be elected directly by the people and "expedient" that members of the other be chosen by the state legislatures. Since the legislatures had selected delegates to the Confederation Congress, they would expect a similar privilege in the new government. If the convention had not agreed to allow state legislatures to elect senators, the Constitution would have aroused significant opposition among political leaders at the state level.

Considerably more difficult was the matter of proportional representation in the Senate. The delegates accepted without much debate the principle of proportional representation in the lower house. But the smaller states, through their spokesman Luther Martin of Maryland, argued for equal representation in the Senate, while large states like Pennsylvania supported a proportional plan for the upper house. Martin argued that "an equal vote in each state was essential to the federal idea," but James Wilson responded with the query, are we forming a government "for *men,* or for the imaginary beings called *states*?" For weeks the convention was deadlocked on the issue, neither side being able to obtain a majority. A committee appointed to work out a compromise recommended equal representation in the Senate, coupled with a proviso that all appropriation bills had to originate in the lower house. But not until the convention accepted Roger Sherman's suggestion that a state's two senators vote as individuals rather than as a unit was a breakdown averted.

Another critical question remained, one that divided the nation along sectional lines rather than by size of state: how was representation in the lower house to be apportioned among the states? Delegates from states with large numbers of slaves wanted all people, black and white, to be counted equally; delegates from states with few slaves wanted only free people to be counted. So the inescapable question of the role of slavery in the nation became inextricably bound up in the fundamental foundation of the new government. The issue was resolved by using a formula developed by the Confederation Congress in 1783 to allocate financial assessments among the states: three-fifths of the slaves would be included in the population totals. (The formula reflected the delegates' judgment that slaves were less efficient producers of wealth than free people, not that they were 60 percent human and 40 percent property.) The three-fifths compromise was unanimously accepted by the convention. Only two delegates, Gouverneur Morris and George Mason, spoke out against the institution of slavery.

Although the words "slave" and "slavery" do not appear in the Constitution (the framers used euphemisms like "other persons"), direct and indirect protections for slavery were deeply embedded in the document. The three-fifths clause, for example, ensured not only that white southern voters would be represented in Congress out of all proportion to their numbers, but also that they would

Slavery and the Constitution

have a disproportionate influence in the selection of the president, since the number of each state's electoral votes was determined by the size of its congressional delegation. Congress was prevented from outlawing the slave trade for at least twenty years, and the fugitive slave clause (Article IV, Section 2, Paragraph 3) required all states to return runaways to their masters. By guaranteeing that the national government would aid any states threatened with "domestic violence," the Constitution promised aid in putting down future slave revolts.

Once agreement was reached on the knotty, conjoined problems of slavery and representation, the delegates readily achieved consensus on the other major issues confronting them. Instead of giving Congress the nearly unlimited scope proposed in the Virginia Plan, the delegates enumerated congressional powers and then provided for flexibility by granting all authority "necessary and proper" to carry out those powers. Discarding the legislative veto contained in the Virginia Plan, the convention implied a judicial veto instead. The Constitution plus national laws and treaties would constitute "the supreme law of the land; and the judges in every state shall be bound thereby." As another means of circumscribing state powers, the delegates drafted a long list of actions—such as "impair[ing] the obligation of contracts"—forbidden to the states.

The convention placed primary responsibility for the conduct of foreign affairs in the hands of the president, who was also designated commander-in-chief of the armed forces. He could appoint judges and other federal officers. The delegates established an elaborate mechanism, the electoral college—the members of which would be chosen in each state by legislatures or qualified voters—to select the president. This, they hoped, would ensure that the executive would be independent of the national legislature—and of the people. They also agreed that the chief executive should serve a four-year term but be eligible for re-election.

The final document still showed signs of its origins in the Virginia Plan, but compromises had created a system of government less powerful at the national level than Madison and Randolph had originally envisioned, partly because Madison realized during the convention that the states, properly curbed, could be contributors to, not opponents of, effective gov-

Separation of Powers

ernment. The key to the Constitution was the distribution of political authority—separation of powers among the executive, legislative, and judicial branches of the national government, and division of powers between states and nation. The branches were balanced against one another, their powers deliberately entwined to prevent them from acting independently. The president was given a veto over congressional legislation, but his treaties and major appointments required the consent of the Senate. Congress could impeach the president and the federal judges, but the courts appeared to have the final say on the interpretation of the Constitution. The system of checks and balances would make it difficult for the government to become tyrannical. At the same time, though, the elaborate system would sometimes prevent the government from acting quickly and decisively. Furthermore, the line between state and national powers was so ambiguously and vaguely drawn that the United States had to fight a civil war in the next century before the issue was fully resolved. (See the Appendix for the full text of the Constitution.)

The convention held its last session on September 17, 1787. Of the forty-two delegates present, only three refused to sign the Constitution. (Two of the three, George Mason and Elbridge Gerry, declined in part because of the lack of a bill of rights.) Benjamin Franklin had written a speech calling for unity; because his voice was too weak to be heard, James Wilson read it for him. "I confess that there are several parts of this constitution which I do not at present approve," Franklin admitted. Yet he urged its acceptance "because I expect no better, and because I am not sure, that it is not the best." Only then was the Constitution made public. The convention's proceedings had been entirely secret—and remained so until the delegates' private notes were published in the nineteenth century.

Opposition and Ratification

Later that same month the Confederation Congress submitted the Constitution to the states but did not formally recommend approval. The ratification clause of the Constitution provided for the new system to take effect once it was approved by special conventions in at least nine states. The delegates to each state convention were to be elected by the qualified voters. Thus the national Constitution, unlike the Articles of Confederation, would rest directly on popular authority (and the presumably hostile state legislatures would be circumvented).

As the states began to elect delegates to the special conventions, discussions of the proposed government grew more heated. Federalists—supporters of the Constitution—and Antifederalists, its opponents, wrote newspaper essays and pamphlets vigorously defending or attacking the convention's decisions. The extent of the debate was unprecedented. Every newspaper in the country printed the full text of the Constitution, and most newspapers supported its adoption. Even so, it quickly became apparent that the disputes within the Constitutional Convention had been minor compared with the divisions of opinion within the country as a whole. After all, the delegates at Philadelphia had agreed on the need for basic reforms in the American political system. Many citizens not only rejected that conclusion but also believed that the proposed government, despite its built-in safeguards, held the potential for tyranny.

The Antifederalists fell into two main groups: those who emphasized the threat to the states embodied in the new national government and those who stressed the dangers to individuals posed by the lack of a bill of rights. Ultimately, however, the two positions were one. The Antifederalists saw the states as the chief protectors of individual rights and their weakening as the onset of arbitrary power. Unlike the document's supporters, Antifederalists did not fear such democratic "excesses" as state laws protecting debtors or providing for the issuance of paper currency, both of which were prohibited by the proposed Constitution.

Fundamentally, the Antifederalists feared a too-powerful central government. They rejected the Federalists' emphasis on the need for national leadership by a disinterested elite and trusted the rough-and-tumble politics at the state level to protect their interests. Their arguments against the Constitution often consisted of lists of potential abuses of the national government's authority. They were the heirs of the Real Whig ideology of the late 1760s and early 1770s, which stressed the need for

Antifederalists

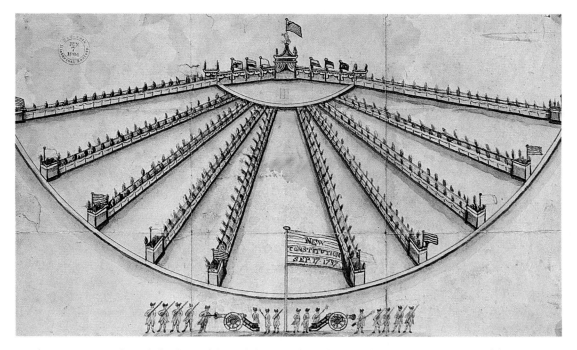

In July 1788, New York City's leaders celebrated their state's ratification of the Constitution at an elaborate banquet served in a pavilion erected for the occasion. Their hopes for an orderly government were symbolized by the orderly arrangement of the tables, separate but linked into a semicircle by the central structure displaying flags and banners. *The New-York Historical Society.*

the people's constant vigilance to avert oppression (see page 113). Indeed, some of the Antifederalists were the very men who had originally promulgated those ideas; for example, Samuel Adams and Richard Henry Lee were both leaders of the opposition to the Constitution. Antifederalist ranks were heavily peopled not only by such older Americans (whose political opinions had been shaped prior to the more centralizing, nationalistic Revolution) but also by small farmers, who jealously guarded their property against excessive taxation, and by ambitious, upwardly mobile men who knew they would reap many financial benefits from a less tightly controlled economic and political system than the Constitution promised to establish.

As the months passed and public debate continued, the Antifederalists focused more sharply on the Constitution's lack of a bill of rights. Even if the states were weakened by the new system, they believed, the people could still be protected from tyranny if their rights were specifically guaranteed. The Constitution did contain some prohibitions on congressional power. For example, the writ of habeas corpus, which prevented arbitrary impris-

onment, could not be suspended except in dire emergencies. But the Antifederalists found such provisions inadequate. Nor were they reassured by the Federalists' assertion that, since the new government was one of limited powers, it had no authority to violate the people's rights. *Letters of a Federal Farmer,* perhaps the most widely read Antifederalist pamphlet, listed the rights that should be protected: freedom of the press and of religion, the right to trial by jury, and guarantees against unreasonable search warrants.

From Paris, Thomas Jefferson added his voice to the chorus. Replying to Madison's letter conveying a copy of the Constitution, Jefferson wrote: "I like much the general idea of framing a government which should go on of itself peaceably, without needing continual recurrence to the state legislatures." He also approved of the separation of powers among the three branches of government and declared himself "captivated" by the compromise between the large and small states. Nevertheless, he added, he did not like "the omission of a bill of rights. . . . A bill of rights is what the people are entitled to against every government on earth, general or particular, and what no just government should refuse, or rest on inference."

As the state conventions met to consider ratification, the lack of a bill of rights loomed larger and larger as a flaw in the new form of government.

> **Ratification of the Constitution**

Four of the first five states to ratify did so unanimously, but serious disagreement then began to surface. Massachusetts, in which Antifederalist forces had been bolstered by a backlash against the heavy-handed way the state government had dealt with the Shays rebels, ratified by a majority of only 19 votes out of 355 cast. In New Hampshire the Federalists won by a majority of 57 to 47. When New Hampshire ratified, in June 1788, the requirement of nine states had been satisfied. But New York and Virginia had not yet voted, and everyone realized the new Constitution could not succeed unless those key states accepted it.

In Virginia, despite a valiant effort by the Antifederalist Patrick Henry, the pro-Constitution forces won 89 to 79. In New York, James Madison, John Jay, and Alexander Hamilton campaigned for ratification by publishing *The Federalist,* a political tract that explained the theory behind the Constitution and masterfully answered its critics. Their reasoned arguments, coupled with the promise that a bill of rights would be added to the Constitution, helped win the battle. On July 26, 1788, New York ratified the Constitution by the slim margin of 3 votes. The new government was a reality, even though the last state (Rhode Island, which had not participated in the convention) did not formally join the Union until 1790.

The experience of fighting a war and of struggling for survival as an independent nation in the 1780s had altered the political context of American life. Whereas at the outset of the war most politically aware Americans believed that "that government which governs best governs least," by the late 1780s many had changed their minds. These were the drafters and supporters of the Constitution, who had concluded from the republic's vicissitudes under the Articles of Confederation that the United States needed a more powerful central government. They won their point when the Constitution was adopted, however narrowly. They contended during the ratification debates that their proposed solution to the nation's problems was just as "republican" in conception (if not more so) as the Articles. Both sides concurred in a general adherence to republican principles, but they emphasized different views of republicanism. The Federalists adhered to a vision of a virtuous, self-sacrificing republic vigorously led by a disinterested aristocracy of talent. By contrast, the Antifederalists distrusted strong central governments, fearing the motives of political leaders and advocating a loosely regulated economy. They also stressed the need for the formal protection of individual rights.

Leading Federalists and Antifederalists did share one key common characteristic: they were all white males. The era of the formation of the Union was also the age of the systematic formulation of American racist thought, and the two processes were intimately linked. One way to preserve the freedom of all whites was to ensure the continued subjection of all blacks, slave or free. Likewise, one way to preserve the unchallenged economic independence of white men was to ensure the economic and political dependence of white women. Independence had been fought for and won by many Americans—white, black, and red, male and female—but in the new republic only white males would hold political power. In the decades ahead they would make the crucial decisions that would mold the nation under the newly ratified Constitution.

Suggestions for Further Reading

General

Richard Beeman et al., eds., *Beyond Confederation: Origins of the Constitution and American National Identity* (1987); Staughton Lynd, *Class Conflict, Slavery, and the United States Constitution: Ten Essays* (1967); Forrest McDonald, *Novus Ordo Seclorum: The Intellectual Origins of the Constitution* (1985); Forrest McDonald, *E Pluribus Unum: The Formation of the American Republic, 1776–1790* (1965); Edmund S. Morgan, *Inventing the People: The Rise of Popular Sovereignty in England and America* (1988); Robert R. Palmer, *The Age of the Democratic Revolution: A Political History of Europe and America, 1760–1800,* 2 vols. (1959, 1964); *William and Mary Quarterly,* 3rd ser., 44, no. 3 (July 1987), *The Constitution of the United States;* Gordon S. Wood, *The Creation of the American Republic, 1776–1787* (1969); Rosemary Zagarri, *The Politics of Size: Representation in the United States, 1776–1850* (1988).

Chapter 6: Forging a National Republic, 1776–1789

Continental Congress and Articles of Confederation

E. James Ferguson, *The Power of the Purse: A History of American Public Finance, 1776–1790* (1961); H. James Henderson, *Party Politics in the Continental Congress* (1974); Merrill Jensen, *The Articles of Confederation,* 2nd ed. (1959); Merrill Jensen, *The New Nation: A History of the United States During the Confederation, 1781–1789* (1950); Jerrilyn G. Marston, *King and Congress: The Transfer of Political Legitimacy, 1774–1776* (1987); Peter S. Onuf, *The Origins of the Federal Republic: Jurisdictional Controversies in the United States, 1775–1787* (1983); Jack N. Rakove, *The Beginnings of National Politics: An Interpretive History of the Continental Congress* (1979).

State Politics

Willi Paul Adams, *The First American Constitutions: Republican Ideology and the Making of the State Constitutions in the Revolutionary Era* (1980); Edward Countryman, *A People in Revolution: The American Revolution and Political Society in New York, 1760–1790* (1981); Ronald Hoffman and Peter Albert, eds., *Sovereign States in an Age of Uncertainty* (1981); Donald Lutz, *Popular Consent and Popular Control: Whig Political Theory in the Early State Constitutions* (1980); Jackson Turner Main, *Political Parties Before the Constitution* (1973); Jackson Turner Main, *The Sovereign States, 1775–1783* (1973); Stephen E. Patterson, *Political Parties in Revolutionary Massachusetts* (1973); J. R. Pole, *Political Representation in England and the Origins of the American Republic* (1966); David P. Szatmary, *Shays' Rebellion: The Making of an Agrarian Insurrection* (1980).

The Constitution

Douglass Adair, *Fame and the Founding Fathers* (1974); Charles A. Beard, *An Economic Interpretation of the Constitution of the United States* (1913); Forrest McDonald, *We the People: The Economic Origins of the Constitution* (1958); Jackson Turner Main, *The Anti-Federalists: Critics of the Constitution, 1781–1788* (1961); Frederick W. Marks III, *Independence on Trial: Foreign Affairs and the Making of the Constitution* (1973); Clinton Rossiter, *1787: The Grand Convention* (1973); Robert A. Rutland, *The Ordeal of the Constitution: The Antifederalists and the Ratification Struggle of 1787–88* (1966); Abraham Sofaer, *War, Foreign Affairs, and Constitutional Power,* vol. 1: *The Origins* (1976); Carl Van Doren, *The Great Rehearsal: The Story of the Making and Ratifying of the Constitution of the United States* (1948).

Education and Culture

Lawrence A. Cremin, *American Education: The National Experience, 1783–1876* (1981); Joseph M. Ellis, *After the Revolution: Profiles of Early American Culture* (1979); Carl F. Kaestle, *Pillars of the Republic: Common Schools and American Society, 1780–1860* (1983); Russell B. Nye, *The Cultural Life of the New Nation: 1776–1803* (1960); Kenneth Silverman, *A Cultural History of the American Revolution* (1976).

Women

Charles Akers, *Abigail Adams: An American Woman* (1980); Joan Jensen, *Loosening the Bonds: Mid-Atlantic Farm Women, 1750–1850* (1984); Linda K. Kerber, *Women of the Republic: Intellect and Ideology in Revolutionary America* (1980); Mary Beth Norton, *Liberty's Daughters: The Revolutionary Experience of American Women, 1750–1800* (1980); Lynn Withey, *Dearest Friend: A Life of Abigail Adams* (1980).

Blacks and Slavery

Ira Berlin, *Slaves Without Masters: The Free Negro in the Antebellum South* (1974); Ira Berlin and Ronald Hoffman, eds., *Slavery and Freedom in the Age of the American Revolution* (1983); David Brion Davis, *The Problem of Slavery in the Age of Revolution, 1770–1823* (1975); Carol V. R. George, *Segregated Sabbaths: Richard Allen and the Emergence of Independent Black Churches, 1760–1840* (1973); Winthrop Jordan, *White over Black: American Attitudes Toward the Negro, 1550–1812* (1968); Duncan J. Macleod, *Slavery, Race, and the American Revolution* (1974); Gary Nash, *Forging Freedom: The Formation of Philadelphia's Black Community, 1720–1840* (1988); Donald L. Robinson, *Slavery in the Structure of American Politics, 1765–1820* (1971); Arthur Zilversmit, *The First Emancipation: The Abolition of Slavery in the North* (1967).

Indians

Harvey L. Carter, *The Life and Times of Little Turtle* (1987); Dorothy Jones, *License for Empire: Colonialism by Treaty in Early America* (1982); Francis Paul Prucha, *American Indian Policy in the Formative Years: The Indian Trade and Intercourse Acts, 1790–1834* (1962); Bernard Sheehan, *Seeds of Extinction: Jeffersonian Philanthropy and the American Indian* (1973); Anthony F. C. Wallace, *The Death and Rebirth of the Seneca* (1969).

Abigail Adams was furious. "I am at a loss to know how the people who were formerly so much alive to the usurpation of one Nation can crouch so tamely to a much more dangerous and dareing one," she wrote to her sister Mary Cranch in January 1798. France, she asserted, "aims not only at our independance and libe[r]ty, but a total annihilation of the Christian Religion." Yet every state except one—Connecticut—had inexplicably elected French sympathizers to Congress. "Virginia has but two Feder-ilists, North Carolina but one," she la-mented. "Can we expect such measures to be adopted as the safety and security of the Country require?"

Abigail Adams's anger stemmed from the way in which American opinion had divided over the French Revolution, which had begun in 1789. She and her husband, along with many others, viewed the violent tactics of the French revolutionaries with deep alarm and saw the United States's for-mer ally as the major threat to freedom in the world, even though other Americans continued to sympathize with the French. "There is no end to their audaciousness," she informed her sister in the spring of 1798; "French emissaries are in every corner of the union sowing and spreading their Sedition. We have renewed information that their System is, to calumniate the President, his family, his administration, untill they oblige him to resign." Her husband's critics were "vile liars," spreading "malice & falshood" in their newspapers. Yet ultimately she had faith that the people's good sense would prevail. "They cannot suppose that their President can have any object in view for himself or Family, from the whole course & tennor of his Life, incompatable with the honour, dignity and independance of his Country," she concluded.

Opinionated and fiercely loyal to her husband John, elected president of the United States in 1796, Abigail Adams found her-self in the middle of an unprecedented situation: the first truly heated partisan battle in the new republic. No wonder she was both angry and concerned. She knew her husband had devoted his life to the nation's welfare. What then could be the source of the bitter invective directed at him by his opponents, the political faction now called Republicans? For her and her husband there

7

POLITICS AND SOCIETY IN THE EARLY REPUBLIC, 1789–1800

This flag of the New York Society of Pewterers was carried in the New York City Constitution ratification parade in July 1788. *The New-York Historical Society.*

was only one answer: the criticism must have been instigated by France, whose revolutionary government saw the Adams administration as its enemy. Indeed, she told Mrs. Cranch, her husband's opponents were "so Criminal they ought to be Presented [indicted] by the grand jurors."

The failure of Americans' quest for unity and unqualified independence during the 1790s was nowhere more evident than in the political battles that absorbed Abigail Adams's attention. The fight over the Constitution had been but the precursor of an even wider division over the major political, economic, and diplomatic questions confronting the young republic. To make matters worse, Americans had not anticipated the political disagreements that characterized the decade. Believing that the Constitution would resolve the problems that had arisen during the Confederation period, they expected the new government to rule by consensus. Accordingly, like Abigail Adams many Americans found it difficult to understand the partisan tensions that developed out of disputes over such fundamental issues as the extent to which authority

(especially fiscal authority) should be centralized in the national government, the formulation of foreign policy in an era of continual warfare in Europe, and the limits of dissent within the republic. They could not understand or fully accept the division of America's political leaders into two factions—not yet political parties—known as Federalists and Republicans. As the decade closed, they still had not come to terms with the implications of partisan politics.

Prosperity and expansion too were not easily attained. The United States economy still depended on the export trade, as it had throughout the colonial era. When warfare between England and France resumed in 1793, Americans found their commerce disrupted once again, with consequent fluctuations in their income and profits. Moreover, the strength of the Miami Confederacy blocked the westward expansion of white settlement north of the Ohio River until after the Treaty of Greenville in 1795. South of the Ohio, settlements were established west of the mountains as early as the 1770s, but the geographical barrier of the Appalachians

Chapter 7: Politics and Society in the Early Republic, 1789–1800

IMPORTANT EVENTS

1789	George Washington inaugurated Judiciary Act of 1789 French Revolution begins
1790	Alexander Hamilton's *Report on Public Credit*
1791	First ten amendments (Bill of Rights) ratified
1793	France declares war on Britain, Spain, and Holland Neutrality Proclamation Democratic-Republican societies founded
1794	Whiskey Rebellion
1795	Jay Treaty
1796	First contested presidential election: John Adams elected president, Thomas Jefferson vice president
1798	XYZ affair Alien and Sedition Acts Virginia and Kentucky resolutions
1798–99	Quasi-War with France
1800	Franco-American Convention Jefferson elected president, Aaron Burr vice president Second Great Awakening begins Gabriel's Rebellion

tended to isolate them from the eastern seaboard. Not until the first years of the nineteenth century did the frontier settlements become more fully integrated into American life through the vehicle of the Second Great Awakening, a religious revival that swept both east and west.

Building a Workable Government

In 1788, Americans celebrated the ratification of the Constitution with a series of parades, held in many cities on the Fourth of July. The processions were carefully planned to symbolize the unity of the new nation and to recall its history to the minds of the watching throngs. The parades, like pre-revolutionary protest meetings, served as political educators for literate and illiterate Americans alike. Men and women who could not read were thereby informed of the significance of the new Constitution in the life of the nation. They were also instructed about political leaders' hopes for industry and frugality on the part of a virtuous American public.

The Philadelphia parade, planned by the artist Charles Willson Peale, was filled with symbols related to those goals. About five thousand people participated in the procession, which stretched for a mile and a half and lasted three hours. Twelve costumed "axemen" representing the first pioneers were followed by a mounted military troop and a group of men carrying flags symbolizing independence, the peace treaty, the French alliance, and other revolutionary events. A band played a "Federal March" composed for the occasion. There followed a Constitution float displaying a large, framed copy of the Constitution and a thirteen-foot-high eagle. A number of local dignitaries marched in front of the next float, "The Grand Federal Edifice," a wooden, domed structure supported by thirteen columns (three of which were left unfinished to signify the states that had not yet ratified the Constitution).

The remainder of the parade consisted of groups of artisans and professionals marching together and dramatizing their work. One of the farmers scattered seed in the streets. On the manufacturers' float, cloth was being made. The printers operated a press, distributing copies of a poem written to honor the Constitution. More than forty other groups of tradesmen, such as barbers, hatters, and clockmakers, sponsored similar floats. The artisans were followed by lawyers, doctors, clergymen of all denominations, and congressmen. Bringing up the rear was a symbol of the nation's future, students from the University of Pennsylvania and other city schools. Marching with their teachers, they carried a flag labeled "The Rising Generation."

The nationalistic spirit expressed in the ratification processions carried over into the first session of Congress. In the congressional elections held late in 1788, only a few Anti-federalists ran for office, and even fewer were elected. Thus the First Congress consisted chiefly of men who supported a strong national government. Since the Constitution had deliberately left many key issues undecided, the nationalists' domination of Congress meant that their views on those points quickly prevailed.

> **First Congress**

Congress faced four immediate tasks when it convened in April 1789: raising revenue to support the new government, responding to the state ratification conventions' call for the addition of a bill of rights to the Constitution, setting up executive departments, and organizing the federal judiciary. The last task was especially important. The Constitution established a Supreme Court but left it to Congress to decide whether to have other federal courts as well.

James Madison, who had been elected to the House of Representatives, soon became as influential in Congress as he had been at the Constitutional Convention. Only a few months into the first session, he persuaded Congress to impose a 5 percent tariff on certain imported goods. Thus, the First Congress quickly achieved what the Confederation Congress never had: an effective national tax law. The new government would have problems, but lack of revenue in its first years was not one of them.

Madison also took the lead on the issue of constitutional amendments. At the convention and thereafter, he had consistently opposed additional limitations on the national government because he believed it unnecessary to guarantee the people's rights when the government was one of delegated powers. But Madison recognized that public opinion, as expressed by the

> **Bill of Rights**

state ratifying conventions, was against him. Accordingly, he placed nineteen proposed amendments before the House. Congress eventually sent twelve amendments to the states for ratification. Two, having to do with the number of congressmen and their salaries, were not accepted by a sufficient number of states. The other ten amendments officially became part of the Constitution on December 15, 1791. Not for many years, though, did they become known collectively as the Bill of Rights (see the Appendix).

The First Amendment specifically prohibited Congress from passing any law restricting the people's right to freedom of religion, speech, press, peaceable assembly, or petition. The next two arose directly from the former colonists' fear of standing armies as a threat to freedom. The Second Amendment guaranteed the people's right "to keep and bear arms" because of the need for a "well-regulated Militia." Thus the constitutional right to bear arms was based on the expectation that most able-bodied men would serve the nation as citizen soldiers and there would be no need for a standing army. The Third Amendment defined the circumstances in which troops could be quartered in private homes. The next five pertained to judicial procedures. The Fourth Amendment prohibited "unreasonable searches and seizures"; the Fifth and Sixth established the rights of accused persons; the Seventh specified the conditions for jury trials in civil, as opposed to criminal, cases; and the Eighth forbade "cruel and unusual punishments." Finally, the Ninth and Tenth Amendments reserved to the people and the states other unspecified rights and powers. In short, the authors of the amendments made clear that in listing some rights explicitly they did not mean to preclude the exercise of others.

While debating the proposed amendments, Congress also concerned itself with the organization of the executive branch. It readily agreed to continue the three administrative departments established under the Articles of Confederation: War, Foreign Affairs (renamed State), and Treasury. Congress also instituted two lesser posts: the attorney general—the nation's official lawyer—and the postmaster general, who would oversee the Post Office. The only serious controversy arose over whether the president alone could dismiss officials whom he had originally appointed with the consent of the Senate. After some debate, the House and Senate agreed that he had such authority. Thus was established the important principle that the heads of the executive departments are responsible to the president. Though it could not have been foreseen at the time, that precedent paved the way for the development of the president's cabinet.

Aside from the constitutional amendments, the most far-reaching piece of legislation enacted by the First Congress was the Judiciary Act of 1789.

▶ **Judiciary Act of 1789**

That act was largely the work of Senator Oliver Ellsworth of Connecticut, a veteran of the Constitutional Convention who in 1796 would become the third chief justice of the United States. The Judiciary Act provided for the Supreme Court to have six members: a chief justice and five associate justices. It also defined the jurisdiction of the federal judiciary and established thirteen district courts and three circuit courts of appeal.

The act's most important provision may have been Section 25, which allowed appeals from state courts to the federal court system when certain types of constitutional issues were raised. This section was intended to implement Article VI of the Constitution, which stated that federal laws and treaties were to be considered "the supreme Law of the Land." If Article VI was to be enforced uniformly, the national judiciary clearly had to be able to overturn state court decisions in cases involving the Constitution, federal laws, or treaties. Yet nowhere did the Constitution explicitly permit such action by federal courts. The nationalistic First Congress accepted Ellsworth's argument that the right of appeal from state to federal courts was implied in the wording of Article VI. In the nineteenth century, however, judges and legislators committed to the ideal of states' rights were to challenge that interpretation.

During the first decade of its existence, the Supreme Court handled few cases of any importance. Indeed, for its first three years it heard no cases at all. John Jay, the first chief justice, served only until 1795, and only one of the first five associate justices remained on the bench in 1799. But in a significant 1796 decision, *Ware* v. *Hylton,* the Court—acting on the basis of Section 25 of the Judiciary Act of 1789—for the first time declared a state law unconstitutional. That same year it also reviewed the constitutionality of an act of Congress, upholding its validity in the case of *Hylton* v. *U.S.* The most important case of the decade, *Chisholm* v. *Georgia* (1793), established that states could be freely sued in federal courts by citizens of other states. This decision, unpopular with the state governments, was overruled five years later by the Eleventh Amendment to the Constitution. (See the Appendix for the text of the Constitution and all amendments.)

Domestic Policy Under Washington and Hamilton

George Washington did not seek the presidency. When in 1783 he returned to Mount Vernon, his plantation on the Potomac River, he was eager for

▶ **Election of the First President**

the peaceful life of a Virginia planter. He rebuilt his house, redesigned his gardens, experimented with new agricultural techniques, improved the breeding of his livestock, and speculated in western lands. Yet his fellow countrymen never regarded Washington as just another private citizen. He was unanimously elected the presiding officer of the Constitutional Convention. As such, he did not participate in debates, but he consistently voted for a strong national government. Once the proposed structure of the government was presented to the public, Americans agreed that only George Washington had sufficient prestige to serve as the republic's first president. The unanimous vote of the electoral college was just a formality.

Washington was reluctant to return to public life but knew he could not ignore his country's call. Awaiting the summons to New York City, the nation's capital, he wrote to an old friend, "My movements to the chair of Government will be accompanied by feelings not unlike those of a culprit who is going to the place of his execution. . . . I am sensible, that I am embarking the voice of my Countrymen and a good name of my own, on this voyage, but what returns will be made for them, Heaven alone can foretell."

During his first months in office Washington acted cautiously, knowing that whatever he did would set precedents for the future. He held weekly receptions at which callers could pay their respects, and he toured different areas of the country in turn. When the title by which he should be

John Trumbull painted "Washington at Verplanck's Point" in the spring of 1790, when George Washington was completing his first year as president. Washington's stepgrandson later wrote that this portrait was "the most perfect extant" of its subject, whom Trumbull depicted wearing a Continental Army uniform. *The Henry Francis du Pont Winterthur Museum.*

addressed aroused a good deal of controversy (Vice President John Adams favored "His Highness, the President of the United States of America, and Protector of their Liberties"), Washington said nothing; the accepted title soon became a plain "Mr. President." He used the heads of the executive departments collectively as his chief advisers and thus created the cabinet. As the Constitution required, he sent Congress an annual State of the Union message. Washington also concluded that he should exercise his veto power over congressional legislation very sparingly—only, indeed, if he was convinced a bill was unconstitutional.

Washington's first major task as president was to choose the men who would head the executive departments. For the War Department he selected an old comrade-in-arms, Henry Knox, who had been his reliable general of artillery during much of the Revolution. His choice for the State Department was his fellow Virginian Thomas Jefferson, who had just returned to the United States from his post as minister to France. For the crucial position of secretary of the treasury, the president chose the brilliant, intensely ambitious Alexander Hamilton.

The illegitimate son of a Scottish aristocrat and a woman divorced by her husband for adultery and desertion, Hamilton was born in the British West Indies in 1757. His early years were spent in poverty; after his mother's death when he was eleven, he worked as a clerk for a mercantile firm. In 1773 Hamilton enrolled in King's College (later Columbia University) in New York City; only eighteen months later the precocious seventeen-year-old contributed a major pamphlet to the prerevolutionary publication wars of late 1774. Devoted to the patriot cause, Hamilton volunteered for service in the American army, where he came to the attention of George Washington. In 1777 Washington appointed the young man as one of his aides, and the two developed great affection for one another. Indeed, in some respects Hamilton became the son Washington never had.

> **Alexander Hamilton**

The general's patronage enabled the poor youth of dubious background to marry well. At twenty-three he took as his wife Elizabeth Schuyler, the daughter of a wealthy New York family. After the war, Hamilton practiced law in New York City and served as a delegate first to the Annapolis Convention in 1786 and the following year to the Constitutional Convention. Though he exerted little influence at either meeting, his contributions to *The Federalist* in 1788 revealed him to be one of the chief political thinkers in the republic.

In his dual role as secretary of the treasury and one of Washington's major advisers, two traits distinguished Hamilton from most of his contemporaries. First, he displayed an undivided, unquestioning loyalty to the nation as a whole. As a West Indian who had lived on the mainland only briefly before the war, Hamilton had no ties to an individual state. He showed little sympathy for, or understanding of, demands for local autonomy. Thus the aim of his fiscal policies was always the consolidation of power at the national level. Further, he never feared the exercise of centralized executive authority, as did his older counterparts who had clashed repeatedly with colonial governors.

Second, he regarded his fellow human beings with unvarnished cynicism. Perhaps because of his difficult early life and his own overriding ambition, Hamilton believed people to be motivated primarily, if not entirely, by self-interest—particularly economic self-interest. He placed absolutely no reliance on people's capacity for virtuous and self-sacrificing behavior. That outlook set him apart from those republicans who foresaw a rosy future in which public-spirited citizens would pursue the common good rather than their own private advantage. Although other Americans (like Madison) also stressed the role of private interests in a republic, Hamilton went beyond them in his nearly exclusive emphasis on self-interest as the major motivator of human behavior. And those beliefs significantly influenced the way in which he tackled the monumental task before him: straightening out the new nation's tangled finances.

In 1789, Congress ordered the new secretary of the treasury to study the state of the public debt and to submit recommendations for supporting the government's credit. Hamilton discovered that the country's remaining war debts fell into three categories: those owed by the national government to foreign governments and investors, mostly to France (about $11 million); those owed by the national government to merchants, former soldiers, holders of revolutionary bonds, and the like (about $27 million); and, finally, similar debts owed by state governments (roughly estimated at $25 million). With respect to the national debt, there was little disagreement: politically aware Americans recognized that if their new government was to succeed it would have to repay at full face value the financial obligations the nation had incurred while winning independence.

National Debt

The state debts were quite another matter. Some states—notably Virginia, Maryland, North Carolina, and Georgia—had already paid off most of their war debts. They would oppose the national government's assumption of responsibility for other states' debts, since their citizens would be taxed to pay such obligations. Massachusetts, Connecticut, and South Carolina, on the other hand, still had sizable unpaid debts and would welcome a system of national assumption. The possible assumption of state debts also had political implications. Consolidation of the debt in the hands of the national government would help to concentrate economic and political

Alexander Hamilton (1737–1804), painted by John Trumbull in 1792. Hamilton was then at the height of his influence as secretary of the treasury, and his haughty, serene expression reveals his supreme self-confidence. Trumbull, an American student of the English artist Benjamin West, painted the portrait at the request of John Jay. *National Gallery of Art, Gift of the Avalon Foundation.*

power at the national level. A contrary policy would reserve greater independence of action for the states.

Hamilton's first *Report on Public Credit*, sent to Congress in January 1790, reflected both his national loyalty and his cynicism. He proposed that Congress assume outstanding state debts, combine them with national obligations, and issue new securities covering both principal and accumulated unpaid interest.

Hamilton's First *Report* on *Public Credit*

Current holders of state or national debt certificates would have the option of taking a portion of their payment in western lands. Hamilton's aims were clear: he wanted to expand the financial reach of the United States government and reduce the economic power of the states. He also wanted to ensure that the holders of public securities—many of them wealthy merchants and speculators—would have a significant financial stake in the survival of the national government.

Domestic Policy Under Washington and Hamilton

Hamilton's plan stimulated lively debate in Congress. The opposition coalesced around his former ally James Madison. Madison opposed the assumption of state debts, since his own state of Virginia had already paid off most of its obligations. As a congressman tied to agrarian rather than moneyed interests, he opposed the notion that only current holders of public securities should receive payments. Well aware that speculators had purchased large quantities of debt certificates at a small fraction of their face value, Madison proposed that the original holders of the debt also be compensated by the government. Madison's plan, though more fair than Hamilton's—because it would have directly repaid those people who had actually supplied the revolutionary governments with goods or services—would have been difficult, perhaps impossible, to administer. The House of Representatives rejected it.

At first, the House also rejected the assumption of state debts. The Senate, by contrast, adopted Hamilton's plan largely intact, and a series of compromises followed. Hamilton agreed to changes in the assumption plan that would benefit Virginia in particular. The assumption bill also became linked in a complex way to the other major controversial issue of that congressional session: the location of the permanent national capital. Both northerners and southerners wanted the capital in their region. The traditional story that Hamilton and Madison agreed over Jefferson's dinner table to exchange assumption of state debts for a southern site is not supported by the surviving evidence, but a political deal was undoubtedly struck. The Potomac River was designated as the site for the capital. Simultaneously, the four congressmen from Maryland and Virginia whose districts contained the most likely locations for the new city switched from opposition to support for assumption. The first part of Hamilton's financial program became law in August 1790.

Four months later Hamilton submitted to Congress a second report on public credit, recommending the chartering of a national bank. Like his proposal for assumption of the **First Bank of the United States** debt, this recommendation too aroused considerable opposition. Unlike the earlier debate, which involved matters of policy, this one focused on constitutional issues. It arose primarily after Congress had already adopted the bank proposal.

Hamilton modeled his bank on the Bank of England. The Bank of the United States was to be capitalized at $10 million, of which only $2 million would come from public funds. Private investors would supply the rest. The bank's charter was to run for twenty years, and one-fifth of its directors were to be named by the government. Its bank notes would circulate as the nation's currency; it would also act as the collecting and disbursing agent for the Treasury and would lend money to the government. Most political leaders recognized that such an institution would benefit the country, especially because it would solve the problem of America's perpetual shortage of an acceptable medium of exchange. But there was another issue: did the Constitution give Congress the power to establish such a bank?

James Madison, for one, answered that question with a resounding no. He pointed out that the delegates at the Constitutional Convention had specifically rejected a clause authorizing Congress to issue corporate charters. Consequently, he argued, that power could not be inferred from other parts of the Constitution.

Washington was sufficiently disturbed by Madison's contention that he decided to request other opinions before signing the bill. Edmund Randolph, the attorney general, and Thomas Jefferson, the secretary of state, agreed with Madison that the bank was unconstitutional. Jefferson referred to Article I, Section 8, of the Constitution, which gave Congress the power "to make all Laws which shall be necessary and proper for carrying into Execution the foregoing Powers." The key word, Jefferson argued, was "necessary": Congress could do what was needed, but it could not do what was merely desirable without specific constitutional authorization. Thus Jefferson formulated the strict-constructionist interpretation of the Constitution.

Washington asked Hamilton to reply to these negative assessments of his proposal. Hamilton's *Defense of the Constitutionality of the Bank,* presented to Washington in February 1791, was a brilliant exposition of what has become known as the broad-constructionist view of the Constitution. Hamilton argued forcefully that Congress could choose any means not specifically prohibited by the Constitution to achieve a constitutional end. In short, if the end was constitutional and the means was not unconstitutional, then the means was also constitutional.

Washington was convinced. The bill became law; the bank proved successful. So did the scheme for funding the national debt and assuming the states' debts: the new nation's securities became desirable investments for its own citizens and for wealthy foreigners. Two other aspects of Alexander Hamilton's wide-ranging financial scheme did not fare so well.

In December 1791, Hamilton presented to Congress his *Report on Manufactures,* the third and last of his prescriptions for the American economy. In it he outlined an ambitious plan for encouraging and protecting the United States's infant industries, like shoemaking and textile manufacturing. Hamilton argued that the nation could never be truly independent as long as it had to rely heavily on Europe for its manufactured goods. He thus urged Congress to promote the immigration of technicians and laborers, enact protective tariffs, and support industrial development. Although many of Hamilton's ideas were implemented in later decades, few congressmen in 1791 could see much merit in his proposals. They firmly believed that America's future lay in agriculture and commerce. The mainstay of the republic was the virtuous yeoman farmer; therefore, Congress rejected the report.

That same year Congress did accept another part of Hamilton's financial program, an excise tax on whiskey. Congressmen both recognized the need

Whiskey Rebellion for additional government revenues and hoped to reduce the national consumption of distilled spirits. (Eighteenth-century Americans were notorious for their heavy drinking; annual per capita consumption of alcohol then was about double today's rate.) Import duties adopted in 1789 had raised the price of rum (which was made from imported molasses); the excise tax increased the price of domestically produced whiskey. The new tax most directly affected western farmers, who sold their grain crops in the form of distilled spirits as a means of avoiding the high costs of transporting wagonloads of bulky corn over the mountains.

News of the excise law set off protests in frontier areas of Pennsylvania, where residents were already dissatisfied with the army's as yet unsuccessful attempts to defeat the Miami Confederacy (see pages 174–175). To their minds, the same government that was offering them inadequate protection

A lady's dressing table, made in Baltimore about 1800. The mirror is topped by an American eagle, and the decorative medallions on the sides contain republican symbols. American furniture-makers, like the craftsman who created this fine object, had difficulty competing with European manufacturers. Patriotic motifs helped to make their products more salable. *Maryland Historical Society.*

was now proposing to tax them disproportionately. Still, matters did not come to a head until July 1794, when western Pennsylvania farmers resisted a federal marshal and a tax collector who were trying to enforce the law. Three rioters were killed in the disturbances and several militiamen wounded. About seven thousand rebels convened on August 1 to plot the destruction of Pittsburgh but decided not to face the heavy guns of the fort guarding the town. Unrest nevertheless continued for months on the frontiers of Pennsylvania, Maryland, and Virginia. Crowds of men drafted petitions protesting the excise, raised liberty poles (in deliberate imitation of the 1760s), and occasionally harassed tax collectors. But the Whiskey Rebellion remained largely leaderless and unorganized.

Nevertheless, President Washington took decisive action to prevent a recurrence of events like those during Shays's Rebellion. On August 7, he issued a proclamation calling on the insurgents to disperse by September 1, and he summoned nearly thirteen thousand militia from Pennsylvania and neighboring states. By the time the federal forces marched westward in October and November (headed some of the time by Washington himself), the disturbances had long since ended. The troops met little resistance and arrested only twenty suspects. Two, neither of them prominent leaders of the rioters, were convicted of treason, but Washington pardoned both. The rebellion, such as it was, ended almost without bloodshed.

The chief importance of the Whiskey Rebellion was not military victory over the rebels—for there was none—but rather the message it forcefully conveyed to the American public. The national government, Washington had demonstrated, would not allow violent organized resistance to its laws. In the new republic, change would be effected peacefully, by legal means. Those who were dissatisfied with the law should try to amend or repeal it, not take extralegal action.

By 1794, a group of Americans were already beginning to seek change systematically within the confines of electoral politics, even though traditional political theory regarded organized opposition—especially in a republic—as illegitimate. The leaders of the opposition were Thomas Jefferson and James Madison, who became convinced as early as 1792 that Hamilton and his supporters intended to impose a corrupt, aristocratic government on the United States. Jefferson and Madison justified their opposition to Hamilton and his policies by contending that they were the true heirs of the Revolution and that Hamilton was plotting to subvert republican principles. To emphasize their point, they and their followers in Congress began calling themselves Republicans. Hamilton in turn accused Jefferson and Madison of the same crime: attempting to destroy the republic. To legitimize their claim to being the rightful interpreters of the Constitution, Hamilton and his supporters called themselves Federalists. In short, each group accused the other of being an illicit faction that was working to destroy the republican principles of the Revolution. (In the traditional sense of the term, a *faction* was by definition opposed to the public good.)

At first, President Washington tried to remain aloof from the political dispute that divided his chief advisers, Hamilton and Jefferson. Even so, the controversy helped persuade him to seek a second term of office in 1792 in hopes of promoting political unity. But in 1793 and thereafter, a series of developments in foreign affairs magnified the disagreements.

Partisan Politics and Foreign Policy

The first years under the Constitution were blessed by international peace. Eventually, however, the French Revolution, which began in 1789, brought about the resumption of hostilities between France, America's wartime ally, and Great Britain, America's most important trading partner.

At first Americans welcomed the news that France was turning toward republicanism. The French people's success in limiting, then overthrowing, the monarchy seemed to vindicate the United States's own revolution. Americans saw themselves as being in the vanguard of an inevitable historical trend that would reshape the world for the better. But by the early 1790s the reports from France were disquieting. Outbreaks of violence continued; ministries succeeded each other with bewildering rapidity; and executions were commonplace. The king himself was beheaded in early 1793. Although many Americans, including Jefferson and Madison, retained their sympathy for the French revolutionaries, others began to view France as a prime example of the perversion of republicanism. As might be expected, Alexander Hamilton fell into the latter group.

At that juncture, France declared war on Britain, Spain, and Holland. The Americans thus faced a dilemma. The 1778 Treaty of Alliance with France bound them to that nation "forever," and a mutual commitment to republicanism created ideological bonds. Yet the United States was connected to Great Britain as well. Aside from sharing a common history and language, America and England were economic partners. Americans still purchased most of their manufactured goods from Great Britain and sold much of their own produce in British and British colonial markets. Indeed, since the nation's financial system depended heavily on import tariffs as a source of revenue, and America's imports came primarily from Britain, the United States's economic health in effect required uninterrupted trade with the former mother country.

The political and diplomatic climate was further complicated in April 1793, when Citizen Edmond Genêt, a representative of the French government, landed in Charleston. As Genêt made his leisurely way northward to New York City, he was wildly cheered and lavishly entertained at every stop. En route, he recruited Americans for expeditions against British and Spanish possessions in the Western Hemisphere and distributed privateering commissions with a generous hand. Genêt's arrival raised a series of key questions for President Washington. Should he receive Genêt, thus officially recognizing the French revolutionary government? Should he acknowledge an obligation to aid France under the terms of the 1778 Treaty of Alliance? Or should he proclaim American neutrality in the conflict?

▶ **Citizen Genêt**

For once, Hamilton and Jefferson saw eye to eye. Both told Washington that the United States could not afford to ally itself firmly with either side. Washington agreed. He received Genêt officially but also issued a proclamation informing the world that the United States would adopt "a conduct friendly and impartial toward the belligerent powers." In deference to Jefferson's continued support for France, the word *neutrality* did not appear in the declaration, but the meaning of the declaration was nevertheless clear.

Genêt himself was removed as a factor in Franco-American relations at the end of the summer. His faction fell from power in Paris, and instead of returning home to face almost-certain execution he sought political asylum in the United States. But his disappearance from the diplomatic scene did not lessen the continuing impact of the French Revolution in America. The domestic divisions Genêt helped to widen were perpetuated by clubs called Democratic-Republican societies, formed by Americans sympathetic to the French Revolution and worried about policies pursued by the Washington administration. These societies thus expressed a growing grassroots concern about the same developments that were troubling Jefferson and Madison during this time.

More than forty Democratic-Republican societies were organized between 1793 and 1800, in both rural and urban areas. Their members saw themselves as heirs of the Sons of Liberty, seeking the same goal as their predecessors: protection of the people's liberties against encroachments by corrupt and evil rulers. To that end, they publicly protested government policies and published "addresses to the people" warning of impending tyranny. The societies repeatedly proclaimed their belief in "the equal rights of man," stressing in particular the rights to free speech, free press, and assembly. Like the Sons of Liberty, the Democratic-Republican societies were composed chiefly of artisans and craftsmen of various kinds, although professionals, farmers, and merchants also joined.

▶ **Democratic-Republican Societies**

The rapid growth of such groups, outspoken in their criticism of the Washington administration for its failure to come to the aid of France and for its domestic economic policies, deeply disturbed Hamilton and eventually Washington himself. Newspapers sympathetic to the Federalists charged that the societies were subversive agents of a foreign power. Their "real design," one asserted, was "to involve the country in war, to assume the reins of government and tyrannize over the people." The climax of the attack came in the fall of 1794, when Washington accused the societies of having fomented the Whiskey Rebellion.

In retrospect, Washington's and Hamilton's reaction to the Democratic-Republican societies seems hysterical, overwrought, and entirely out of proportion to whatever challenge they may have posed to the administration. But it must be kept in mind that factional disputes were believed to be dangerous to the survival of a republic. In a monarchy, opposition groups were to be expected, even encouraged. In a government of the people, serious and sustained disagreement was taken as a sign of corruption and subversion. The Democratic-Republican societies were the first formally organized political dissenters in the United States. As such, they aroused the fear and suspicion of elected officials who had not yet accepted the idea that one component of a free government was an organized loyal opposition.

That same year George Washington decided to send Chief Justice John Jay to England to try to reach agreement on four major unresolved ques-

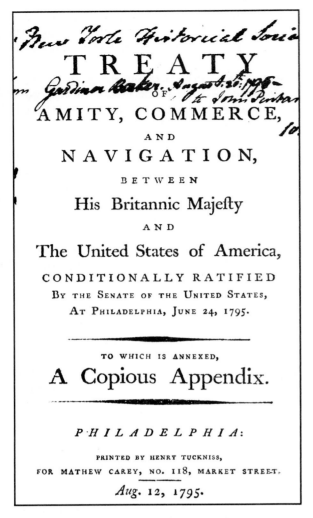

Title page of the Jay Treaty. Publication of the document after its secret ratification by the Senate aroused widespread protest against its terms. The House of Representatives tried but failed to halt its implementation. *The New-York Historical Society.*

Jay Treaty

tions affecting Anglo-American affairs. Jay's diplomatic mission had important domestic consequences. The first point at issue was recent British seizures of American merchant ships trading in the French West Indies. The United States wanted to establish the principle of freedom of the seas and to assert its right, as a neutral nation, to trade freely with both sides. Second, Great Britain had not yet carried out its promise in the Treaty of Paris (1783) to evacuate its posts in the American Northwest.

Western settlers believed that the British were responsible for the renewed Indian warfare in the region (see pages 171–175), and they wanted that threat removed. Third and fourth, the Americans hoped for a commercial treaty and sought compensation for the slaves who had left with the British army at the end of the war.

The negotiations in London proved difficult, since Jay had little to offer Britain in exchange for the concessions he wanted. In the end, Britain did agree to evacuate the western forts and ease the restrictions on American trade to England and the West Indies. (Some limitations were retained, however, violating the Americans' stated commitment to open commerce.) No compensation for lost slaves was agreed to, but Jay accepted a provision establishing an arbitration commission to deal with the matter of prewar debts owed to British creditors. A similar commission was to handle the question of compensation for the seizures of American merchant ships. Under the circumstances, Jay did remarkably well: the treaty averted war with England at a time when the United States, which lacked an effective navy, could not have hoped to win a conflict with its former colonial ruler. Nevertheless, most Americans, including the president, were dissatisfied with at least some parts of the treaty.

At first, potential opposition was blunted because the Senate debated and ratified the treaty in secret. Not until after it was formally approved by a vote of 20 to 10 on June 24, 1795, was the public informed of its provisions. The Democratic-Republican societies led protests against the treaty, which were especially intense in the South. Planters criticized Jay's failure to obtain compensation for runaway slaves as well as the commitment to repay prewar debts. Once President Washington had reluctantly signed the treaty, though, there seemed to be little the Republicans could do to prevent it from taking effect. Just one opportunity remained: Congress had to appropriate funds to carry out the treaty provisions, and according to the Constitution money bills had to originate in the House of Representatives.

When the House took up the issue in March 1796, opponents of the treaty tried to prevent approval of the appropriations. To that end, they called on Washington to submit to the House all documents pertinent to the negotiations. In successfully resisting the House's request, Washington established the doctrine of executive privilege—that is, the power of the president to withhold information from Congress if he believes circumstances warrant doing so. Although the treaty's opponents initially appeared to be in the majority, pressure for approval built as time passed. Frontier residents were eager for evacuation of the British posts, fearing a new outbreak of Indian war despite the signing of the Treaty of Greenville the previous year. Merchants wanted to reap the benefits of widened trade with the British Empire. Furthermore, Thomas Pinckney of South Carolina had negotiated a treaty with Spain giving the United States navigation privileges on the Mississippi, which would be an economic boost to the West and South. Its popularity (the Senate ratified Pinckney's Treaty unanimously) helped to overcome opposition to the Jay Treaty. For all these reasons the House on April 30, 1796, voted the necessary funds by the narrow margin of 51 to 48.

Analysis of the vote reveals both the regional nature of the division and the growing cohesion of the Republican and Federalist factions in Congress.

> **Republicans and Federalists** Voting in favor of the appropriations were 44 Federalists and 7 Republicans; voting against were 45 Republicans and 3 Federalists. The final tally was also split by region. The vast majority of votes against the bill were cast by southerners (including the three Federalists, who were Virginians). The bill's supporters were from New England and the middle states, with the exception of two South Carolina Federalists. The seven Republicans who voted for the appropriations were from commercial areas in New York, Pennsylvania, and Maryland.

The small number of defectors revealed a new force at work in American politics: partisanship. Voting statistics from the first four Congresses show the ever-increasing tendency of members of the House of Representatives to vote as coherent groups, rather than as individuals. If factional loyalty is defined as voting together at least two-thirds of the time on national issues, the percentage of nonaligned congressmen dropped from 42 percent in 1790 to just 7 percent in 1796. Significantly, this trend toward party cohesion occurred even though Congress experienced extremely heavy turnover. Most congressmen served only one or two terms in office, and fewer than 10 percent were re-elected more than three times. During the 1790s the majority slowly shifted from Federalist to Republican. Federalists controlled the first three Congresses, through spring 1795. Republicans gained the ascendancy in the Fourth Congress. Federalists returned to power with slight majorities in the Fifth and Sixth Congresses, and the Republicans took over in the Seventh Congress in 1801.

To describe these shifts is easier than to explain them. The growing division cannot be accurately explained in the terms used by Jefferson and Madison (aristocrats versus the people) or by Hamilton and Washington (true patriots versus subversive rabble). Simple economic differences between agrarian and commercial interests do not provide the answer either, since more than 90 percent of Americans in the 1790s lived in rural areas. Moreover, Jefferson's vision of a prosperous agrarian America was based on commercial, not self-sufficient, farming. Nor did the Federalist-Republican division simply repeat the Federalist-Antifederalist debate of 1787–1788. Even though most Antifederalists became Republicans, the party's leaders, Madison and Jefferson, had supported the adoption of the Constitution.

Yet certain distinctions can be made. Republicans, who were especially prominent in the southern and middle states, tended to be self-assured, confident, and optimistic about both politics and the economy. Southern planters, firmly in control of their region and of a class of enslaved laborers, did not fear instability, at least among the white population. They foresaw a prosperous future based partly on continued westward expansion, which they expected to dominate. They sought to widen the people's participation in government and employed democratic rhetoric to win the allegiance of small farmers south of New England. Members of non-English ethnic groups, especially Irish, Scots, and Germans, found their words attractive. Also included in the Republican coalition were artisans, who saw themselves as the urban equivalent of yeomen farmers and valued their independence from domineering bosses. Republicans of all descriptions emphasized developing the United States's own resources and were less concerned about its position in the world. Republicans also remained sympathetic to France in international affairs.

By contrast, Federalists, who were concentrated in New England, came mostly from English stock. They drew considerable support from commercial interests and were insecure, uncertain of the future. They stressed the need for order, authority, and regularity in the political world. Unlike Republicans, they had no grassroots political organization and put little emphasis on involving ordinary people in government. Not all Federalists were wealthy merchants; many were ordinary farmers who, lacking the ability to expand agricultural production because of New England's poor soil, gravitated toward the more conservative party. Like Republicans, Federalists assumed that southern interests would dominate the lands west of the mountains, so they had little incentive to work actively to develop that potentially rich territory. The nation was, in Federalist eyes, perpetually threatened by potential enemies, both internal and external, and best protected by a continuing alliance with Great Britain. Their vision of international affairs may have been more accurate than that of the Republicans, given the warfare in Europe, but it was also narrow and unattractive. Since it held out little hope of a better future to the voters of any region, it is not surprising that the Republicans eventually became dominant.

The presence of the two organized groups, not yet parties in the modern sense but nonetheless active contenders for office, made the presidential election of 1796 the first that was seriously contested. George Washington, tired of the criticism to which he had been subjected, decided to retire from office. (Presidents had not yet been limited to two terms by constitutional amendment.) In September Washington published his famous Farewell Address, most of which was written by Hamilton. Washington outlined two principles that guided American foreign policy at least until the late 1940s: maintain commercial but not political ties to other nations and enter no permanent alliances. He also drew a sharp distinction between the United States and Europe, stressing America's uniqueness and the need for unilateralism (independent action in foreign affairs).

Domestically, Washington lamented the existence of factional divisions among his fellow countrymen. His call for an end to partisan strife has often been interpreted by historians as the state-

> **Washington's Farewell Address**

ment of a man who could see beyond political affiliations to the good of the whole. But it is more accurately read in the context of its day as an attack on the legitimacy of the Republican opposition. What Washington wanted was unity behind the Federalist banner, which he saw as the only proper political stance. The Federalists (like the Republicans) continued to see themselves as the sole guardians of the truth, the only true heirs of the Revolution, and they perceived their opponents as misguided, unpatriotic troublemakers who were undermining the ideals of the Revolution.

To succeed Washington, the Federalists in Congress put forward Vice President John Adams, with the diplomat Thomas Pinckney of South Carolina

> **Election of 1796**

as his vice-presidential running mate. Congressional Republicans caucused and chose Thomas Jefferson as their presidential candidate; the lawyer, Revolutionary War veteran, and active Republican politician Aaron Burr of New York agreed to run for vice president.

That the election was contested did not mean that its outcome was decided by the people. Voters could cast their ballots only for electors, not for the candidates themselves. Many voters did not even have that opportunity, because in 1796 more than 40 percent of the members of the electoral college were chosen by state legislatures, some even before the presidential candidates had been selected. Moreover, the method of voting in the electoral college tended to work against the new parties. The authors of the Constitution had not foreseen the development of opposing national political organizations, and so the Constitution required members of the electoral college to vote for two persons without specifying the office. There was no way an elector could explicitly support one person for president and another for vice president. The man with the highest total became president; the second highest, vice president.

This procedure proved to be the Federalists' undoing. Adams won the presidency with 71 votes, but a number of Federalist electors (especially those from New England) did not cast ballots for Pinckney. Thomas Jefferson won 68 votes, 9 more than Pinckney, and became vice president. The incoming administration was thus politically divided. The next four years were to see the new president and vice president, once allies and close friends, become bitter enemies.

John Adams
and Political Dissent

John Adams took over the presidency peculiarly blind to the partisan developments of the previous four years. As president he never abandoned an outdated notion discarded by George Washington as early as 1794: that the president should be above politics, an independent and dignified figure who did not seek petty factional advantage. Thus Adams kept Washington's cabinet intact, despite its key members' allegiance to his chief rival, Alexander Hamilton. Adams often adopted a passive posture, letting others (usually Hamilton) take the lead, when he should have acted decisively. As a result his administration gained a reputation for inconsistency. When Adams's term ended, the Federalists were severely divided and the Republicans had won the presidency. But Adams's detachment from Hamilton's maneuverings enabled him to weather the greatest international crisis the republic had yet faced: the so-called Quasi-War with France.

The Jay Treaty improved America's relationship with England, but it provoked retaliation from France. Angry that the United States had reached agreement with its enemy, the Directory (the coalition then in power in Paris) ordered French vessels to seize American ships carrying British goods. In response, Adams appointed three special commissioners to try to reach a settlement with France: Elbridge Gerry, an old friend from Massachusetts; John Marshall, a Virginia Federalist; and Charles Cotesworth Pinckney of South Carolina, Thomas Pinckney's older brother. At the same time Congress increased military spending, authorizing the building of ships and the stockpiling of weapons and ammunition.

For months, the American commissioners futilely sought to open negotiations with Talleyrand, the French foreign minister. But Talleyrand's

▶ **XYZ Affair**

agents demanded a bribe of $250,000 before talks could begin. The Americans retorted, "No, no; not a sixpence," and reported the incident in dispatches that President Adams received in early March 1798. Adams informed Congress of the impasse and recommended increased appropriations for defense.

Convinced that Adams had deliberately sabotaged the negotiations, congressional Republicans insisted that the dispatches be turned over to Congress. Aware that releasing the reports would work to his advantage, Adams complied. He withheld only the names of the French agents, referring to them as X, Y, and Z. The revelation that the Americans had been treated with utter contempt by the Directory stimulated a wave of anti-French sentiment in the United States. A journalist's version of the commissioners' reply, "Millions for defense, but not a cent for tribute," became the national slogan. Cries for war filled the air. Congress formally abrogated the Treaty of Alliance and authorized American ships to seize French vessels.

Thus began an undeclared war with France. The so-called Quasi-War was fought in the West Indies, between French privateers seeking to capture American merchant vessels and warships of the United States Navy. Although initial American losses of merchant shipping were heavy, by early 1799 the navy had established its superiority in Caribbean waters. Its ships captured a total of eight French privateers and naval vessels, easing the threat to America's vital West Indian trade.

The Republicans, who opposed war and continued to sympathize with France, could do little to stem the tide of anti-French feelings. Since Agent Y had boasted of the existence of a "French party in America," Federalists flatly accused the Republicans of traitorous designs. A New York newspaper declared that anyone who remained "lukewarm" after reading the XYZ dispatches was a "criminal— and the man who does not warmly reprobate the conduct of the French must have a soul black enough to be *fit* for *treason Strategems* and *spoils.*" John Adams wavered between calling the Republicans traitors and acknowledging their right to oppose administration measures. As was demonstrated at the beginning of this chapter, his wife was less tolerant. "Those whom the French boast of as their Partizans," Abigail Adams told Mary Cranch, deserved to be "adjudged traitors to their country." If Jefferson had been president, "we should all have been sold to the French."

The Federalists saw this climate of opinion as an opportunity to deal a death blow to their Republican opponents. Now that the

▶ **Alien and Sedition Acts**

country seemed to see the truth of what they had been saying ever since the Whiskey Rebellion in

Matthew Lyon, the congressman convicted of violating the Sedition Act, had a fiery temper. In January 1798, before his arrest and trial, he engaged in this brawl with a congressman from Connecticut in the chamber of the House of Representatives. *Library of Congress.*

1794—that the Republicans were subversive foreign agents—the Federalists sought to codify that belief into law. In the spring and summer of 1798, the Federalist-controlled Congress adopted a set of four laws known as the Alien and Sedition Acts, intended to suppress dissent and prevent further growth of the Republican party.

Three of the acts were aimed at immigrants, whom the Federalists quite correctly suspected of being Republican in their sympathies. The Naturalization Act lengthened the residency period required for citizenship from five to fourteen years and ordered all resident aliens to register with the federal government. The Alien Enemies Act provided for the detention of enemy aliens in time of war. The Alien Friends Act, to be in effect for two years, gave the president almost unlimited authority to deport any alien he deemed dangerous to the nation's security. (Adams never used that authority. The Alien Enemies Act was not implemented either, since war was never formally declared.)

The fourth law, the Sedition Act, sought to control both citizens and aliens. It outlawed conspiracies to prevent the enforcement of federal laws and set the maximum punishment for such offenses at five years in prison and a $5,000 fine. The act also tried to control speech. Writing, printing, or uttering "false, scandalous and malicious" statements "against the government of the United States, or the President of the United States, with intent to defame . . . or to bring them or either of them, into contempt or disrepute" became a crime punishable by as much as two years' imprisonment and a fine of $2,000. Today the Supreme Court would declare unconstitutional any such law punishing speech alone. But in the eighteenth century, when organized political opposition was regarded with suspicion, the restrictions that the Sedition Act placed on free speech were acceptable to many.

In all, there were fifteen indictments and ten convictions under the Sedition Act. Most of the accused were outspoken Republican newspaper editors

Chapter 7: Politics and Society in the Early Republic, 1789–1800 who failed to mute their criticism of the administration in response to the law. But the first victim—whose story may serve as an example of the rest—was a hot-tempered Republican congressman from Vermont, Matthew Lyon. The Irish-born Lyon, a former indentured servant who had purchased his freedom and fought in the Revolution, was indicted for declaring in print that John Adams had displayed "a continual grasp for power" and "an unbounded thirst for ridiculous pomp, foolish adulation, and selfish avarice." Though convicted, fined $1,000, and sent to prison for four months, Lyon was not silenced. He conducted his re-election campaign from jail, winning an overwhelming majority. The fine, which he could not afford, was ceremoniously paid by contributions from leading Republicans around the country.

Faced with the prosecutions of their major supporters, Jefferson and Madison sought an effective means of combating the Alien and Sedition Acts.

> **Virginia and Kentucky Resolutions**

Petitioning the Federalist-controlled Congress to repeal the laws would clearly do no good. Furthermore, Federalist judges refused to allow accused persons to question the Sedition Act's constitutionality. Accordingly, the Republican leaders turned to the only other mechanism available for protest: the state legislatures. Carefully concealing their own role (it would hardly have been desirable for the vice president to be indicted for sedition), Jefferson and Madison each drafted a set of resolutions. Introduced into the Kentucky and Virginia legislatures respectively in the fall of 1798, the resolutions differed somewhat, but their import was the same. Since the Constitution was created by a compact among the states, they contended, the people speaking through their states had a legitimate right to judge the constitutionality of actions taken by the federal government. Both sets of resolutions pronounced the Alien and Sedition Acts null and void and asked other states to join in the protest.

Although no other state replied positively to the Virginia and Kentucky resolutions, they nevertheless had major significance. In the first place, they were superb political propaganda, rallying Republican opinion throughout the country. They placed the opposition party squarely in the revolutionary tradition of resistance to tyrannical authority. Second, the theory of union they proposed was expanded on by southern states' rights advocates in the 1830s and thereafter. Jefferson and Madison had identified a key constitutional issue: how far could the states go in opposing the national government? How could a conflict between the two be resolved? These questions were not to be definitively answered until the Civil War.

Ironically, just as the Sedition Act was being implemented and northern state legislatures were rejecting the Virginia and Kentucky resolutions, Federalists split badly over the course of action the United States should take toward France. Hamilton and his supporters still called for a declaration legitimizing the undeclared naval war the two nations had been waging for months. But Adams had received a number of private signals that the Directory regretted its treatment of the three American commissioners. Acting on these assurances, he dispatched the envoy William Vans Murray to Paris. The United States asked two things of France: nearly $20 million in compensation for ships the French had seized since 1793, and abrogation of the treaty of 1778. The Convention of 1800, which ended the Quasi-War, included the latter but not the former. Still, it freed the United States from its only permanent alliance, thus allowing it to follow the independent diplomatic course George Washington had outlined in his Farewell Address (see page 198).

The results of the negotiations were not known in the United States until after the presidential election of 1800. Even so, Adams's decision to seek a peaceful settlement probably cost him re-election because of the divisions it caused in Federalist ranks.

In sharp contrast, the Republicans entered the 1800 presidential race firmly united behind Jefferson and Burr. Although they won the election, their lack of foresight almost cost them dearly.

> **Election of 1800**

The problem was caused by the system of voting in the electoral college, which the Federalists understood more clearly than the Republicans. The Federalists arranged in advance for one of their electors to fail to vote for Charles Cotesworth Pinckney, their vice-presidential candidate. John Adams thus received the higher number of Federalist votes (65 to Pinckney's 64). The Republicans failed to make the same distinction between their candidates, and all 73 cast ballots for both Jefferson and Burr (see map, page 203). Because neither Republican had a plurality, the Constitution required

This handpainted banner, ca. 1800, celebrating Thomas Jefferson's victory over John Adams, was found in the early 1960s in Massachusetts. The eagle carries a streamer that reads, "T. Jefferson/President of the United States of America/John Adams no more." *Ralph E. Becker Collection, Smithsonian Institution.*

that the contest be decided in the House of Representatives, with each state's congressmen voting as a unit. Since the new House, dominated by Republicans, would not take office for some months, Federalist congressmen decided the election. It took them thirty-five ballots to decide that Jefferson would be a lesser evil than Burr. As a result of the tangle, the twelfth amendment to the Constitution (1804) changed the method of voting in the electoral college to allow for a party ticket.

Westward Expansion, Social Change, and Religious Ferment

In the postrevolutionary years, the United States experienced a dramatic increase in internal migration. As much as 5 to 10 percent of the population moved each year, half of the movers relocating to another state. Young white men were the most mobile segment of the populace, but all groups moved with approximately equal frequency. The major population shifts were from east to west (see map, page 204): from New England to upstate New York and Ohio, from New Jersey to western Pennsylvania, from the Chesapeake to the new states of Kentucky and Tennessee, which entered the union in 1792 and 1796, respectively. Very few people moved north or south, but some southerners (perhaps yeomen farmers escaping the expansion of slavery) did seek new homes farther north.

Some of these migrants moved west of the Appalachian Mountains. The first permanent white settlements beyond the mountains were established in

> **White Settlement in the West**

western North Carolina in 1771, along the Holston and Wautauga rivers. But not until after the defeat of the Shawnees in 1774 and the Cherokees in 1776 (see pages 138–139) was the way cleared for a more general migration. Small groups of families filtered through the Cumberland Gap into Kentucky, following the Wilderness Road carved out by Daniel Boone in 1775. Once the war had ended, Americans

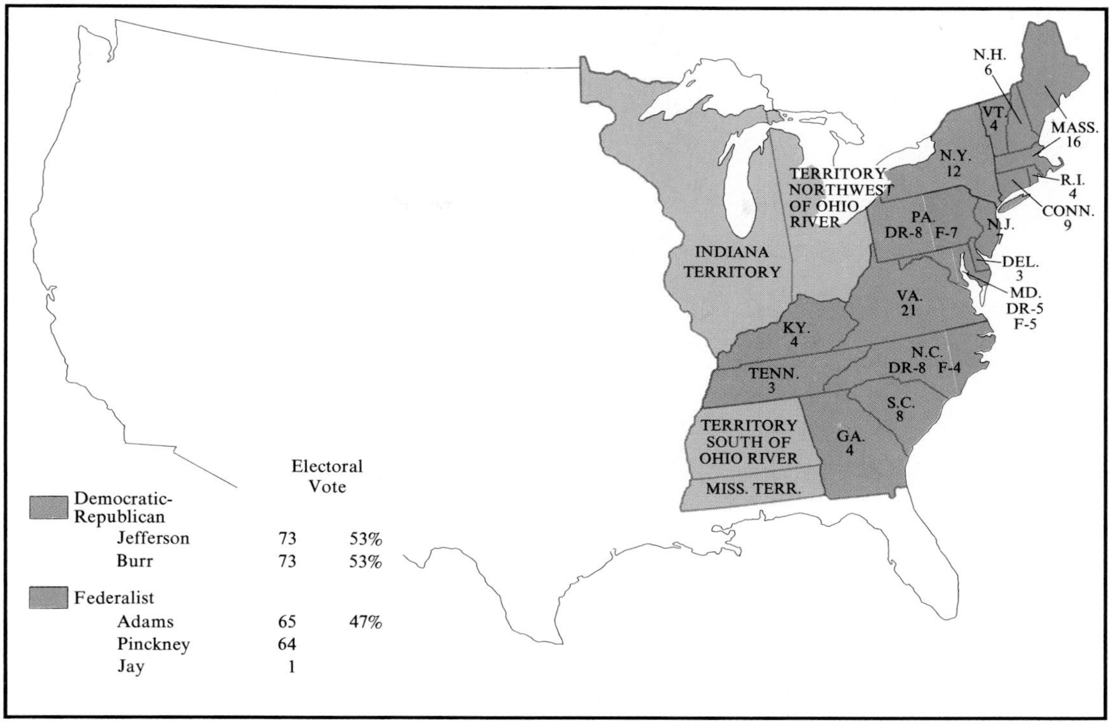
N.H.
6
VT.
4
MASS.
16
N.Y.
12
R.I.
4
CONN.
9
TERRITORY
NORTHWEST
OF OHIO
RIVER
PA.
DR-8 F-7
N.J.
7
DEL.
3
MD.
DR-5
F-5
INDIANA
TERRITORY
VA.
21
KY.
4
N.C.
DR-8 F-4
TENN.
3
S.C.
8
GA.
4
TERRITORY
SOUTH OF
OHIO RIVER
MISS. TERR.
Electoral
Vote
Democratic-Republican
Jefferson 73 53%
Burr 73 53%
Federalist
Adams 65 47%
Pinckney 64
Jay 1

Presidential Election, 1800

streamed over the mountains in considerably larger numbers. In 1783, only about 12,000 people lived west of the mountains and south of the Ohio River; less than a decade later, the 1790 census counted more than 100,000 residents of the future states of Kentucky and Tennessee.

North of the Ohio River, white settlements grew more slowly because of the strength of the Miami Confederacy. But once the Treaty of Greenville was signed in 1795, the Ohio country too grew rapidly. Many whites traveled by land to Pittsburgh, then floated down the Ohio River on flatboats and rafts to Marietta. Others settled along Lake Erie, on land Connecticut had once claimed under its colonial charter—the so-called western reserve.

The transplanted New Englanders did their best to recreate the societies they had left behind, laying out farms and towns in neat checkerboard patterns, founding libraries and Congregational churches. Early arrivals recruited others to join them through enthusiastic letters describing Ohio's rich soil and potential for growth, setting off a phenomenon known in New England as "Ohio Fever." The New Englanders, proud of their literate, orderly culture, viewed their neighbors with disdain. Ohioans, said one, were "intelligent, industrious, and thriving," whereas the Virginians who had settled across the river in Kentucky were "ignorant, lazy, and poor." He continued the contrast: "Here the buildings are neat, . . . there the habitations are miserable cabins. Here the grounds are laid out in a regular manner . . . ; there the fields are surrounded by a rough zigzag log fence." His characterization accurately forecast the cultural clash that would occur when southern Republicans moved across the Ohio and contended with New England Federalists for political control of the region, which became a state in 1803.

Blacks in the West

The westward migration of slaveholding whites, first to Kentucky and Tennessee and then later into the rich lands of western Georgia and eventually the Gulf Coast, had a major adverse impact on African-Americans. The web of family connections built up over several generations of residence in the Chesapeake was torn apart by the population movement. Even those few large planters who moved their entire slave

Western Expansion, 1785–1805

Around 1790, an unknown artist painted Benjamin Hawkins, an Indian trader, and a group of Creeks at his trading post in northern Florida. Such commerce with the Indians, long a part of American life, continued to play an important role in the national economy during the early years of the republic. *Courtesy of Priddy and Beckerdite.*

force west could not have owned all the members of every family on their plantations. Far more commonly the white migrants were younger sons of eastern slaveholders, whose inheritance included only a portion of the family's slaves, or small farmers who owned just one or two blacks. In the early years of American settlement in the West, the population was widely dispersed; accordingly, Chesapeake blacks who had been raised in the midst of large numbers of kin had to adapt to lonely lives on isolated farms, far from their parents, siblings, or even spouses and children. The approximately 100,000 African-Americans forcibly moved west by 1810 had to begin to build new families there to replace those unwillingly left behind in the East. They succeeded well, as is shown in Chapter 10.

The mobility of both blacks and whites created a volatile population mix in southern frontier areas. Everyone was new to the region and few had rela-

tives nearby. Since most of the migrants were young single men just starting to lead independent lives, western society was at first unstable. Like the seventeenth-century Chesapeake (see page 29), the late-eighteenth-century American West was a society in which single women married quickly. One genteel Connecticut girl, reluctantly moving to Ohio with relatives in 1810 after the death of her parents, was dismayed to find that other travelers assumed she was going west to find a husband after failing to wed in the East. (She did marry within a year.) The other side of the same coin was that the few women among the migrants lamented their lack of congenial female friends. Isolated, far from familiar surroundings, women and men both strove to create new communities to replace those they had left behind.

Perhaps the most meaningful of the new communities was the community supplied by evangelical religion. Among the migrants to Kentucky and

In the early nineteenth century, a French artist traveling in America drew this picture of Methodists en route to a camp meeting. They carry bundles of food and clothing with them. Note the large proportion of women in the crowd. *Library of Congress.*

Second Great Awakening

Tennessee were clergymen and committed lay members of the evangelical sects that arose in America after the First Great Awakening: Baptists, Presbyterians, and Methodists. The Awakening had flourished in the southern backcountry much later than it had in New England (see pages 98–99), and therefore the Second Great Awakening, which began around 1800 in the West and continued into the 1840s (see pages 343–345), can in one sense be seen as simply an extension of the first colonial revival. Laymen and clerics alike spread the doctrine of evangelical Christianity through the countryside, carrying the message of salvation to the rootless and mostly uneducated frontier folk.

At camp meetings, sometimes attended by thousands of people and usually lasting from three days to a week, clergymen exhorted their audiences to repent their sins and become genuine Christians. They stressed that salvation was open to all, downplaying the doctrine of predestination that

had characterized orthodox colonial Calvinism. The emotional nature of the conversion experience was emphasized far more than the need for careful study and preparation. Such preachers thus brought the message of religion to the people in more ways than one. They were in effect democratizing American religion, making it available to all rather than to a preselected and educated elite.

The most famous camp meeting took place at Cane Ridge, Kentucky, in 1801. At a time when the largest settlement in the state had no more than two thousand inhabitants, attendance at Cane Ridge was estimated at between ten and twenty-five thousand. One witness, a Presbyterian cleric, marveled that "no sex nor color, class nor description, were exempted from the pervading influence of the spirit; even from the age of eight months to sixty years." He went on to recount how people responded to the preaching with "loud ejaculations of prayer, . . . some struck with terror, . . . others, trembling, weeping and crying out . . . fainting and swooning away, . . . others surrounding them with melodious songs, or fervent prayers for their happy resurrection, in the love of Christ." Such scenes were to be repeated many times in the decades that followed. Revivals swept across different regions of the country until nearly the middle of the century, leaving an indelible legacy of evangelism to many American Protestant churches.

The sources of the Second Great Awakening, which revitalized Protestant Christianity in the United States, were embedded in late-eighteenth-century American society in the East as well as the West. From the 1760s through the 1780s, religious concerns had been subordinated to secular affairs, as clergymen and lay people of all denominations had concentrated their energies on war and politics. Indeed, clerics had created a "civil religion" for the nation, in which the fervor of the veneration for the public sometimes surpassed the fervor of religious worship. Most churches, influenced by Enlightenment thought, had for decades stressed reason more than revelation. Circumstances were thus ripe for a movement of spiritual renewal that would appeal to the emotional side of people's natures.

In addition, America's largest Protestant denominations had to find new sources of financial and membership support after the Revolution. In the

Disestablishment of Religion

colonial period, most of the provinces had had established, or state-supported, churches. In Massachusetts, for example, the Congregational church had been financed by taxes levied on all residents of the colony, not just the members of that church. The same was true of the Church of England in such southern colonies as Virginia and South Carolina. Before the war, the protests of religious dissenters, like Baptists, had fallen on deaf ears. Yet they learned to use revolutionary ideology for their own purposes. Isaac Backus, a New England Baptist, pointed out forcefully that "many, who are filling the nation with the cry of LIBERTY and against *oppressors* are at the same time themselves violating that dearest of all rights, LIBERTY OF CONSCIENCE." Legislators could not resist the logic of such arguments. Many states dissolved their ties to churches during or immediately after the war, and others vastly reduced state support for established denominations.

These changes meant that congregations could no longer rely on tax revenues and that all

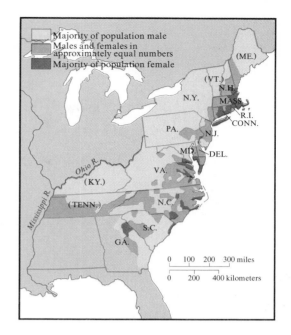

Sex Ratio of White Population, 1790

churches were placed on the same footing with respect to the government. Church membership became entirely voluntary, as did monetary contributions from members. If congregations were to survive, they had to generate new sources of support and increase the size of their membership. Revivals proved a convenient means of doing so. The revivals represented genuine outpourings of religious sentiment, but their more mundane function must not be overlooked.

An analysis of secular society can help to explain the conversion patterns of the Second Awakening. Unlike the First Great Awakening, when converts

Women and the Second Awakening

were evenly divided by sex, more women than men—particularly young women—answered the call of Christianity during the Second Awakening. The increase in female converts seems to have been directly related to major changes in women's circumstances at the end of the eighteenth century. In some areas of the country, especially New England (where the revival movement flourished), women outnumbered men after 1790, for many young men had migrated westward (see map). Thus eastern girls could no longer count on finding marital partners. The uncertainty of their social and familial position seems to have led them to seek spiritual certainty in the church.

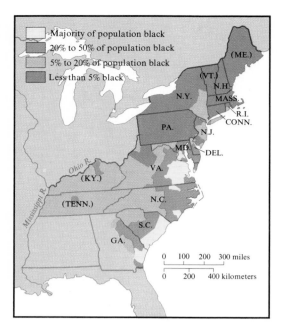

Black Population, 1790: Proportion of Total Population *Source: From Lester J. Cappon et al., eds.,* Atlas of Early American History: The Revolutionary Era, 1760–1790. *Copyright © 1976 by Princeton University Press. Reprinted by permission of Princeton University Press.*

Young women's domestic roles changed dramatically at the same time, as cloth production began to move from the household to the factory (see page 260). Deprived of their chief household role as spinners and weavers, New England daughters found in the church a realm where they could continue to make useful contributions to society. Church missionary societies and charitable associations provided an acceptable outlet for their talents. One of the most striking developments of the early nineteenth century was the creation of hundreds of female associations to aid widows and orphans, collect money for foreign missions, or improve the quality of maternal care. Thus American women collectively assumed the role of keepers of the nation's conscience, taking the lead in charitable enterprises and freeing their husbands from concern for such moral issues.

The religious ferment among blacks and whites in frontier regions of the Upper South contributed to racial ferment as well. People of both races attended the camp meetings to hear black and white preachers. When revivals spread eastward into

Blacks and the Second Awakening more heavily slaveholding areas, white planters became fearful of the egalitarianism implied in the evangelical message of universal salvation and harmony. At the same time, revivals created a group of respected black leaders—preachers—and provided them with a ready audience for a potentially revolutionary doctrine.

Events in the West Indies gave whites ample reason for apprehension. In 1793, mulattos and blacks in the French colony of Saint Domingue (Haiti) overthrew European rule under the leadership of a mulatto, Toussaint L'Ouverture. The revolt was bloody, vicious, prolonged, and characterized by numerous atrocities committed by both sides. In an attempt to prevent the spread of such unrest to their own slaves, southern state legislators passed laws forbidding white Haitian refugees from bringing their slaves with them. But North American blacks learned about the revolt anyway. And the preconditions for racial upheaval did not have to be imported into the South from the West Indies: they already existed on the spot.

The Revolution had caused immense destruction in the South, especially in the states south of Virginia. The heavy losses of slaves and constant guerrilla warfare, not to mention the changes in American trading patterns brought about by withdrawal from the British Empire, wreaked havoc on the southern economy. The expansion of cotton production after the invention of the cotton gin in 1793 and the beginnings of large-scale westward migration led to increased demands for slaves. After the war, Lower South planters rushed to purchase new black laborers; the postwar decades therefore witnessed the single most massive influx of Africans into North America since the beginnings of the slave trade. Before the legal trade was halted in 1808, more than ninety thousand new Africans had been imported into the United States (see map).

The vast postwar increase in the number of free blacks severely challenged the system of race relations that had evolved during the eighteenth century. Color, caste, and slave status no longer coincided, as they had when the few free blacks were all mulattos. Furthermore, like their white compatriots, blacks (both slave and free) had become familiar with notions of liberty and equality. They had also witnessed the benefits of fighting collectively for freedom, rather than resisting indi-

The Destrehan plantation house in St. Charles Parish, Louisiana, was originally constructed between 1787 and 1790 (and remodeled in 1840). Its primary builder was Charles, a "free Mulatto" who was described as "carpenter, wood worker and mason" in the construction contract. In Virginia, skilled blacks like Charles, both slave and free, formed the core of the support for Gabriel's Rebellion. *Gene Cizek.*

vidually or running away. The circumstances were ripe for an explosion, and the Second Awakening was the match that lit the fuse in both Virginia and North Carolina.

The Virginia revolt was planned by Gabriel Prosser, a blacksmith who argued that blacks should fight to obtain the same rights as whites and who explicitly placed himself in the tradition of the French and Haitian revolutions. At revival meetings led by his brother Martin, a preacher, Gabriel recruited other blacks like himself—artisans who moved easily in both black and white circles and who lived in semifreedom under minimal white supervision. The artisan leaders then enlisted rural blacks in the cause. The conspirators planned to attack Richmond on the night of August 30, 1800, setting fire to the city, seizing the state capitol, and capturing the governor. Their plan showed considerable political sophistication, but heavy rain made it impossible to execute the plot as scheduled. Several whites then learned of the plan from their slaves and spread the alarm. Gabriel avoided capture for some weeks, but most

> **Gabriel's Rebellion**

of the other leaders of the rebellion were quickly arrested and interrogated. The major conspirators, including Prosser himself, were hanged, but in the months that followed other insurrectionary scares continued to frighten Virginia slaveowners.

Two years later a similar wave of fear swept North Carolina and the bordering counties of Virginia. A slave conspiracy to attack planters' homes, kill all whites except small children, and seize the land was uncovered in Bertie County. Similar plots were rumored elsewhere. Again, slave artisans and preachers played prominent roles in the planned uprisings. Nearly fifty blacks were executed as a result of the whites' investigations of the rumors. Some were certainly innocent victims of the planters' hysteria, but there can be no doubt about the existence of most of the plots. In the wake of these disturbances, southern state legislatures increased the severity of the slave codes. Before long, all talk of emancipation (gradual or otherwise) ceased, and slavery became even more firmly entrenched as an economic institution and way of life.

Significantly, the Iroquois were affected by a religious revival at the same time as American whites and blacks were experiencing the Second Great Awakening. Led by their prophet,

▶ **Handsome Lake** Handsome Lake, the remaining American Iroquois, who were scattered on small reservations, embraced the traditional values of their culture and renounced such destructive white customs as drinking alcohol and playing cards. At the same time, though, they began abandoning their ancient way of life. With Handsome Lake's approval, Quaker missionaries taught the Iroquois Anglo-American styles of agricultural subsistence; men were now to be cultivators rather than hunters and women housekeepers rather than cultivators. Since the tribes had lost their hunting territories to white farmers, Iroquois men accepted the changes readily. But many women, especially the powerful tribal matrons, resisted the shift in the gender division of labor. They realized that when they surrendered control over food production they would jeopardize their status in the tribe. But Handsome Lake branded as "witches" any women who opposed the changes too vigorously, and eventually he triumphed. A division of work by sex continued to characterize Iroquois economic organization, but the specific tasks assigned to men and women changed completely. In order to maintain some cultural autonomy, the Iroquois had to adopt an economic system resembling that of the dominant whites.

The plight of the Iroquois may be taken as symbolic of the plight of tribes located west of the Appalachians, for they too would have to find ways of accommodating themselves to the dominant Anglo-American culture. Although most had yet to feel the full force of the whites' westward thrust, the weapon that had served the Iroquois and other interior tribes so well—the countervailing presence of England, France, and Spain—was not available to them. Since the United States had established its independence, western tribes had no alternative but to confront directly the problems posed by land-hungry whites. They would delay but not halt the expansion of the United States.

As the new century began, white, red, and black inhabitants of the United States were moving toward an accommodation to their new circumstances. Indians east of the Mississippi learned they would have to give up some parts of their traditional culture to preserve others. Blacks and whites tried to create new lives in the West and, in the East,

to adjust to changed economic circumstances. Building on successful negotiations with both Britain (the Jay Treaty) and France (the Convention of 1800), the United States charted its own diplomatic course, striving to avoid dependence on the European powers. The 1790s spawned vigorous debates over foreign and domestic policy and saw the beginnings of a system of political parties. Religious revivals again swept portions of the countryside, and again those revivals contributed to social unrest.

At the end of the decade, after years of struggle, the Jeffersonian interpretation of republicanism finally prevailed over Hamilton's approach. As a result, in the years to come the country would be characterized by a decentralized economy, minimal government (especially at the national level), and maximum freedom of action and mobility for individual white men. Jeffersonian Republicans, like white male Americans before them, failed to extend to white women, Indians, and blacks the freedom and individuality they recognized as essential for themselves.

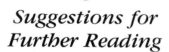

Suggestions for Further Reading

National Government and Administration

Ralph Adams Brown, *The Presidency of John Adams* (1975); John R. Howe, *The Changing Political Thought of John Adams* (1966); Richard H. Kohn, *Eagle and Sword: The Federalists and the Creation of the Military Establishment in America, 1783–1802* (1975); Forrest McDonald, *Alexander Hamilton* (1979); Forrest McDonald, *The Presidency of George Washington* (1974); John C. Miller, *The Federalist Era, 1789–1801* (1960); John R. Nelson, Jr., *Liberty and Property: Political Economy and Policymaking in the New Nation, 1789–1812* (1987); Merrill D. Peterson, *Thomas Jefferson and the New Nation* (1970); Garry Wills, *Cincinnatus: George Washington and the Enlightenment* (1984).

Partisan Politics

Lance Banning, *The Jeffersonian Persuasion: Evolution of a Party Ideology* (1978); Richard Buel, Jr., *Securing the Revolution: Ideology in American Politics, 1789–1815* (1972); William Nisbet Chambers, *Political Parties in a New Nation: The American Experience, 1776–1809* (1963); Joseph Charles, *The Origins of the American Party System* (1956);

Noble E. Cunningham, *The Jeffersonian Republicans: The Formation of Party Organization, 1789–1801* (1957); Manning J. Dauer, *The Adams Federalists* (1953); Ronald Formisano, *The Transformation of Political Culture: Massachusetts Parties, 1790s–1840s* (1983); Richard Hofstadter, *The Idea of a Party System: The Rise of Legitimate Opposition in the United States, 1780–1840* (1970); Adrienne Koch, *Jefferson and Madison: The Great Collaboration* (1950); Eugene P. Link, *Democratic-Republican Societies, 1790–1800* (1942); Norman K. Risjord, *Chesapeake Politics, 1781–1800* (1978); Patricia Watlington, *The Partisan Spirit: Kentucky Politics, 1779–1792* (1972); Alfred F. Young, *The Democratic-Republicans of New York: The Origins, 1763–1797* (1967); John Zvesper, *Political Philosophy and Rhetoric: A Study of the Origins of American Party Politics* (1977).

Foreign Policy

Harry Ammon, *The Genêt Mission* (1973); Samuel F. Bemis, *Jay's Treaty,* 2nd ed. (1962); Samuel F. Bemis, *Pinckney's Treaty,* 2nd ed. (1960); Jerald A. Combs, *The Jay Treaty* (1970); Alexander DeConde, *The Quasi-War: Politics and Diplomacy of the Undeclared War with France, 1797–1801* (1966); Alexander DeConde, *Entangling Alliance: Politics and Diplomacy Under George Washington* (1958); Felix Gilbert, *To the Farewell Address: Ideas of Early American Foreign Policy* (1961); Reginald Horsman, *The Diplomacy of the New Republic, 1776–1815* (1985); Lawrence Kaplan, *"Entangling Alliances with None": American Foreign Policy in the Age of Jefferson* (1987); Bradford Perkins, *The First Rapprochement: England and the United States, 1795–1805* (1967); William Stinchcombe, *The XYZ Affair* (1981); Paul A. Varg, *Foreign Policies of the Founding Fathers* (1963).

Civil Liberties

Leonard W. Levy, *Emergence of a Free Press* (1985); Leonard W. Levy, *Origins of the Fifth Amendment* (1968); Robert A. Rutland, *The Birth of the Bill of Rights, 1776–1791,* rev. ed. (1983); James Morton Smith, *Freedom's Fetters: The Alien and Sedition Laws and American Civil Liberties* (1956).

Women, Blacks, and the Family

Ira Berlin and Ronald Hoffman, eds., *Slavery and Freedom in the Age of the American Revolution* (1983); Nancy F. Cott, *The Bonds of Womanhood: "Woman's Sphere" in New England, 1780–1835* (1977); Toby Ditz, *Property and Kinship: Inheritance in Early Connecticut, 1750–1820* (1986); Gerald W. Mullin, *Flight and Rebellion: Slave Resistance in Eighteenth-Century Virginia* (1972); Christine Stansell, *City of Women: Sex and Class in New York, 1789–1860* (1986).

Social Change and Westward Expansion

Andrew Cayton, *The Frontier Republic: Ideology and Politics in the Ohio Country, 1789–1812* (1986); Reginald Horsman, *The Frontier in the Formative Years, 1783–1815* (1970); Howard Rock, *Artisans of the New Republic: The Tradesmen of New York City in the Age of Thomas Jefferson* (1979); Malcolm Rohrbough, *The Trans-Appalachian Frontier: Peoples, Societies, and Institutions, 1775–1850* (1979); W. J. Rorabaugh, *The Alcoholic Republic: An American Tradition* (1979); Thomas Slaughter, *The Whiskey Rebellion* (1986); Charles G. Steffen, *The Mechanics of Baltimore: Workers and Politics in the Age of Revolution, 1763–1812* (1984); Sean Wilentz, *Chants Democratic: New York City and the Rise of the American Working Class, 1788–1850* (1984).

Religion

Sydney Ahlstrom, *A Religious History of the American People* (1972); Catharine Albanese, *Sons of the Fathers: The Civil Religion of the American Revolution* (1976); Ruth Bloch, *Visionary Republic: Millennial Themes in American Thought* (1985); Fred J. Hood, *Reformed America, 1783–1837* (1980); William McLoughlin, *Revivals, Awakenings, and Reform* (1978).

"*I have this* morning witnessed one of the most interesting scenes a free people can ever witness," Margaret B. Smith, a Philadelphian, wrote on March 4, 1801, to her sister-in-law. "The changes of administration, which in every government and in every age have most generally been epochs of confusion, villainy and bloodshed, in this our happy country take place without any species of distraction, or disorder." On that day, Thomas Jefferson strolled from his New Jersey Avenue boardinghouse in the new federal capital of Washington, D.C., to take the oath as president at the Capitol building. The precedent of an orderly and peaceful change of government had been established.

8

THE EMPIRE OF LIBERTY, 1801–1824

Jefferson's inauguration marked a change of style in government, at the beginning of a period when Americans were struggling to assert and define their nationalism amid challenges, both foreign and domestic. Almost overnight the formality of the Federalist presidencies of Washington and Adams disappeared as Jefferson set the tone for the Republican government. Gone were the aristocratic wigs and breeches (knee-length trousers) the first two presidents had favored; Jefferson wore plainer garb. Though personally richer and with more luxurious tastes than Adams, Jefferson rejected the aristocratic and wealthy pretensions he associated with the Federalists. Republican virtue would be restored.

Ordinary folk who had come to celebrate Jefferson's inaugural overran Washington, causing Federalists to shudder at the seeming collapse of authority and order. For two weeks following the inauguration, Jefferson still lived and worked at his modest lodgings a few blocks from the Capitol. He ran the presidency from the parlor next to his bedroom and continued to eat at the communal dining table. His first cabinet meetings were held in Conrad and McMunn's rooming house. Not until March 19 did he move to the president's mansion.

The government had moved to Washington from Philadelphia in November 1800, and its unfinished federal buildings symbolized the unfinished nation. Augustus John Foster, a British diplomat, lamented the move. The diplomatic corps, he reported, found it "difficult to digest" moving "to what was then scarce any

Liberty, 1804, embroidered picture by Mary Green of Massachusetts after a print of the same title by Edward Savage. *Worcester Art Museum.*

better than a mere swamp." Abigail Adams found it "the very dirtyest Hole," its streets "a quagmire after every rain." On the other hand, Washington offered amusements unlike any other Atlantic capital. "Excellent snipe shooting and even partridge shooting was to be had on each side of the main [Pennsylvania] avenue and even close under the wall of the capitol," Foster recalled. The new city suited the newcomers as the government changed from the formality of the Federalists to the less-pretentious Republicans.

The new district, carved out of Maryland and Virginia, had been chosen because of its central location. Washington was thus beholden neither to the colonial past nor to any single state. Few buildings were needed to house the government, which essentially collected tariffs, delivered mail, and defended the nation's borders. A small government suited the republic. Even for the Federalists, the adoption of the Constitution had been more a result of dissatisfaction with the Articles of Confederation than a sign of confidence in central government. In an age when it took some congressmen more than a week to reach the capital, most Americans favored government closer to home. Though President Thomas Jefferson, after his inauguration in 1801, cut the federal budget and operations, he and his Republican successors (James Madison and James Monroe) invigorated the federal government over the next two decades.

The transfer of power to the Republicans from the Federalists intensified political conflict and voter interest. Republican presidents, in the Revolutionary War tradition, sought to restrain government. Federalists prized a stronger national government with more centralized order and authority. With both factions competing for adherents and popular support, the basis was laid for the evolution of democratic politics. But factionalism, personal disputes, and suspicion of partisanship within each group prevented the development of modern political parties, and the Federalists, unable to build a popular base, slowly faded away.

Events abroad and on the frontier encouraged and threatened the expansionism of the young nation. Seizing one opportunity, the United States purchased the Louisiana Territory, pushing the frontier farther west. But then from the high seas came war. Caught between the British and the French, the United States found itself a victim of European conflict with its shipping rights as a neu-

tral, independent nation ignored and violated. When the humiliation became too great, Americans took up arms in the War of 1812 both to defend their rights as a nation and to expand farther to the west and north. Although unprepared for combat, the United States fought Great Britain to a standstill and routed Indian resistance and unity. The peace treaty restored the prewar status quo, but together the war and the treaty reaffirmed American independence, strengthened American determination to steer clear of European conflicts, and fostered accommodation with Great Britain.

The War of 1812 unleashed a wave of nationalism and self-confidence. War promoted the development of domestic manufacturing and internal transportation. After the war, the federal government championed business and promoted road and canal building. The new spirit encouraged economic growth and western expansion at home and assertiveness throughout the Western Hemisphere. By the 1820s the United States was no longer an experiment; a new nation had emerged. Free of its colonial past, the country began energetically shaping its own identity.

Growth and expansion, however, generated new problems. In 1819 a financial panic brought hardship and conflict that sowed the seeds for the Jacksonian movement in the 1820s and 1830s. More ominously, sectional differences and the presence of slavery created divisions that would widen in the wake of further westward expansion during the 1840s and 1850s.

Jefferson in Power

Jefferson delivered his inaugural address in the Senate chamber, the only part of the Capitol that had been completed. Nearly a thousand people strained to hear his barely audible voice. "We are all Republicans, we are all Federalists," he told the assembly in an appeal for unity. Confidently addressing those with little faith in the people's ability to govern themselves, he called America's republican government "the world's best hope." If "man cannot be trusted with the government of himself," Jefferson argued,

> **Jefferson's Inaugural Address**

IMPORTANT EVENTS

1801	John Marshall becomes chief justice Jefferson inaugurated
1801–05	Tripoli War
1803	*Marbury* v. *Madison* Louisiana Purchase
1804	Jefferson re-elected
1804–06	Lewis and Clark expedition
1805	Prophet emerges as Shawnee leader
1807	*Chesapeake* affair Embargo Act
1808	Madison elected president
1808–13	Prophet and Tecumseh: Indian resistance
1812–15	War of 1812
1813	Death of Tecumseh
1814	Treaty of Ghent
1814–15	Hartford Convention
1815	Battle of New Orleans
1816	Monroe elected president Second Bank of the United States chartered
1817	Rush-Bagot Treaty
1819	*McCulloch* v. *Maryland* Adams-Onís Treaty
1819–23	Financial panic; depression
1820	Missouri Compromise Monroe re-elected
1823	Monroe Doctrine

"can he, then, be trusted with the government of others? Or have we found angels in the forms of kings to govern him? Let history answer this question."

The new president went on to outline his goals:

> A wise and frugal government, which shall restrain men from injuring one another, which shall leave them otherwise free to regulate their own pursuits. . . . Equal and exact justice to all men, of whatever state or persuasion, religious or political. . . . The support of the state governments in all their rights, as the most competent administrators for our domestic concerns and the surest bulwarks against antirepublican tendencies.

At the same time, he assured Federalists that he shared some of their concerns as well:

> The preservation of the general government in its whole constitutional vigor. . . . The honest payment of our debts and sacred preservation of the public faith. . . . Encouragement of agriculture and of commerce as its handmaid.

Still, the Federalists and Republicans distrusted each other. The outgoing president, John Adams, left Washington before dawn on inaugural day to avoid witnessing the Republican triumph. Republicans considered the Federalists antidemocratic and antirepublican at heart and accused them of imitating the court society of England.

One of Jefferson's first acts was to extend the grasp of Republicanism over the federal government. Virtually all of the six hundred or so officials appointed under Washington and Adams were loyal Federalists: only six were known Republicans. To counteract Federalist power and restore government to those who shared his vision of an agrarian republic and individual liberty, Jefferson refused to recognize Adams's last-minute "midnight appointments" to local offices in the District of Columbia. He dismissed Federalist customs collectors from New England ports, and awarded vacant treasury and judicial offices to Republicans. By July 1803 only 130 of 316 presidentially controlled offices were held by Federalists. In restoring political balance in government, Jefferson used patronage to reward his friends, to build a party organization, and to compete with the Federalists.

Rembrandt Peale's 1805 portrait of President Thomas Jefferson. Charles Wilson Peale and his five sons helped establish the reputation of American art in the new nation. Rembrandt Peale was most famous for his presidential portraits; here he captures Jefferson in a noble pose without the usual symbols of office or power, befitting the Republican age.   *The New-York Historical Society.*

The Republican Congress similarly proceeded to affirm its republicanism. Limited government would check authoritarianism and undermine deference to elites; Republicans placed a greater emphasis on individual initiative and an involved citizenry. Secretary of the Treasury Albert Gallatin and John Randolph of Virginia, Jefferson's ally in the House, translated ideology into policy and put the federal government on a diet. Congress repealed all internal taxes, including the whiskey tax. Gallatin cut the army budget in half, to just under $2 million, and reduced the 1802 navy budget from $3.5 to $1 million. Moreover, Gallatin planned to reduce the national debt—Alexander Hamilton's engine of economic growth—from $83 million to $57 million, as part of a plan to retire it altogether by 1817. Jefferson even closed two of the nation's five diplomatic missions abroad—at The Hague and Berlin—to save money.

More than frugality, however, separated Republicans from Federalists. Opposition to the Alien and Sedition laws of 1798 had helped unite Republicans before Jefferson's election (see pages 199–202). Now as president, Jefferson declined to use the acts against his opponents, as President Adams had done, and pardoned those convicted; Congress let the acts expire in 1801 and 1802. Congress also repealed the Naturalization Act of 1798, which had required fourteen years of residency for citizenship. The 1802 act that replaced it required only five years of residency, acceptance of the Constitution, and the forsaking of foreign allegiance and titles. The new act would remain the basis of naturalized American citizenship into the twentieth century.

The Republicans turned next to the judiciary, the last stronghold of unchecked Federalist power. During the 1790s not a single Republican had been appointed to the federal bench.

> **Attacks on the Judiciary**

Moreover, the Judiciary Act of 1801, passed in the last days of the Adams administration, had created fifteen new judgeships (which Adams filled in his midnight appointments, signing appointments until his term was just hours away from expiring) and would reduce by attrition the number of justices on the Supreme Court from six to five. Since that reduction would have denied Jefferson any Supreme Court appointments until two vacancies had occurred, the new Republican-dominated Congress, in one of its first moves, repealed the 1801 act.

Republicans also targeted opposition judges for removal. Federalist judges had refused to review the Sedition Act, and Federalists had prosecuted critics of the administration under the act. At Jefferson's suggestion, the House impeached (indicted) Federal District Judge John Pickering of New Hampshire, and in 1804 the Senate removed him from office. Pickering had not committed any crime, although he was an alcoholic and was emotionally disturbed.

The day Pickering was convicted, the House impeached Supreme Court Justice Samuel Chase for judicial misconduct. Chase, an arch-Federalist and leader in pressing for convictions under the Sedition Act, had repeatedly denounced Jefferson's administration from the bench. Jefferson had initially suggested action against Chase; the Republicans, however, failed to muster the necessary two-thirds majority of senators to convict him. Their failure to remove Chase preserved the Court's independence by establishing the precedent that criminal actions, not political disagreements, were the proper grounds for impeachment. Time soon cured Republican grievances; in his tenure as president, Jefferson appointed three new Supreme Court justices. Nonetheless, under Chief Justice John Marshall, the Court remained a Federalist stronghold.

Marshall was an astute lawyer with keen political sense. A Virginia Federalist who had served under George Washington in the Revolutionary War, he had been minister to France and then secretary of state under President Adams before being named chief justice. Jefferson considered Marshall a midnight appointment, believing that any appointment made after Adams learned of his defeat in the electoral college on December 12, 1800, was wrong and immoral, if not illegal. But Congress approved the appointment in January 1801 before Jefferson was sworn in as president.

> **John Marshall**

Although he was an autocrat by nature, Marshall possessed a grace and openness of manner well suited to the new Republican political style. Under Marshall's domination, the Supreme Court retained a Federalist viewpoint even after Republican justices achieved a majority in 1811. Throughout his tenure (from 1801 until 1835), the Court upheld federal supremacy over the states and protected the interests of commerce and capital.

More important, Marshall made the Court an equal branch of government in practice as well as theory. First, he made service on the Court a coveted honor. Prior to Marshall it had been difficult to keep the Court filled. During its first twelve years, fifteen justices served on the six-member Court; after Marshall's appointment, it took forty years for fifteen new members to be appointed. Marshall's presence made the Court worthy of ambitious and talented men. Second, he unified the Court, influencing the justices to issue single majority opinions rather than individual concurring judgments. Marshall himself became the voice of the majority. From 1801 through 1805 he wrote 24 of the Court's 26 decisions; through 1810 he wrote 85 percent of the 171 opinions, including every important decision.

Marshall also increased the Court's power. *Marbury* v. *Madison* (1803) was the landmark case that enabled Marshall to strengthen the Court. William

John Marshall (1755–1835), chief justice of the Supreme Court from 1801 to 1835. This portrait shows the strength of personality that enabled Marshall to make the Court into a Federalist stronghold. *Washington and Lee University, Virginia.*

> **Marbury v. Madison**

Marbury had been designated a justice of the peace in the District of Columbia as part of Adams's midnight appointments of March 2, 1801. Marbury sued the new secretary of state, James Madison, for failing to certify his appointment so that Jefferson could appoint a Republican. In his suit Marbury requested a writ of mandamus (a court order forcing Madison to appoint him).

At first glance, the case presented a political dilemma. If the Supreme Court ruled in favor of Marbury and issued a writ of mandamus, the president might not comply. After all, why should the president, sworn to uphold the Constitution, allow the Court to decide for him what was constitutional? However, if the Court refused to issue the writ, it would be handing the Republicans a victory. Marshall avoided both alternatives. Speaking for the Court, he ruled that Marbury had a right to his commission but that the Court could not compel Madison to honor it, because the Constitution did not grant the Court power to issue a writ of mandamus. Thus Marshall declared unconstitutional Section 13 of the Judiciary Act of 1789, which authorized the Court to issue such writs. Marbury lost his job and the justices denied themselves the power to issue writs of mandamus, but the Supreme Court established its great power to judge the constitutionality of laws passed by Congress.

In succeeding years Marshall fashioned the theory of judicial review. Since the Constitution was the supreme law, he reasoned, any act (federal or state) contrary to the Constitution must be null and void. And since the Supreme Court was responsible for upholding the law, the Court had a duty to decide whether a conflict existed between a legislative act and the Constitution. If such a conflict existed, the Court would declare the act unconstitutional.

Marshall's decision rebuffed Republican criticism of the Court as a partisan instrument. He avoided a confrontation with the Republican-dominated Congress by not ruling on its repeal of the 1801 Judiciary Act. And he enhanced the Court's independence by claiming the power of judicial review.

While President Jefferson fought with the Federalist judiciary and struggled to reduce federal spending, he kept watch on the Louisiana Territory.

Louisiana Purchase Louisiana, France's largest colony in the New World, defined the western United States border along the Mississippi from the Gulf of Mexico to present-day Minnesota. It had been ceded to Spain in 1763 at the end of the Seven Years' War (see page 109). Jefferson shared with other Americans the belief that the United States was destined to expand its "empire of liberty." Since the first days of American independence, Louisiana had held a special place in the young nation's expansionist dreams. By 1800, hundreds of thousands of Americans in search of land had trekked into the rich Mississippi and Ohio valleys to settle, intruding on Indian lands. Down the Mississippi and Ohio rivers to New Orleans they floated their farm goods for export. Thus, whoever controlled the port of New Orleans had a hand on the throat of the American economy. As long as Spain owned Louisiana, Americans did not fear.

Rumors of the transfer of Louisiana to Napoleonic France proved true in 1802, and France threatened to rebuild its empire in the New World. The acquisition, moaned Jefferson, "works most sorely" on the United States. "Every eye in the United States," Jefferson wrote the American minister in Paris Robert R. Livingston, "is now focused on the affairs of Louisiana." Fears intensified even more in October 1802, when Spanish officials, on the eve of ceding control to the French, violated Pinckney's Treaty (see page 197) by denying Americans the privilege of storing their products at New Orleans prior to transshipment to foreign markets. Western farmers and eastern merchants thought a devious Napoleon had closed the port; they grumbled and talked war. "The Mississippi," Secretary of State James Madison wrote, "is to them everything. It is the Hudson, the Delaware, the Potomac and all navigable rivers of the Atlantic States formed into one stream."

To relieve the pressure for war and to prevent westerners from joining Federalists in opposition to his administration, Jefferson simultaneously prepared for war and accelerated talks with the French. In January 1803 he sent James Monroe to France to join Robert Livingston in negotiating to buy New Orleans. Meanwhile, Congress authorized the call-up of eighty thousand militia if it proved necessary. Arriving in Paris in April, Monroe was astonished to learn that France had already offered to sell all 827,000 square miles of Louisiana to the United States for $15 million. On April 30 Monroe and Livingston signed a treaty to purchase the vast territory, whose borders were undefined and whose land was uncharted (see map).

The Louisiana Purchase doubled the size of the nation and opened the way for westward expansion across the continent. The acquisition was the single most popular achievement of Jefferson's presidency. Yet for Jefferson, the purchase presented a dilemma. It promised fulfillment of his dream of a continental nation reaching to the Pacific coast, "with room enough for our descendants to the hundredth and thousandth generation." It offered to resolve Indian-settler conflict on the frontier by providing land to which eastern tribes, North and South, could be removed. But its legality was questionable. The Constitution gave him no clear authority to acquire new territory and incorporate it into the nation. Jefferson considered requesting a constitutional amendment to allow the purchase, but finally he justified it on the grounds that he was exercising the president's implied powers to pro-

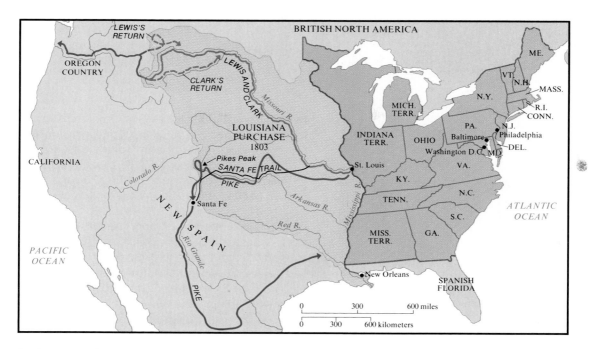

Louisiana Purchase

tect the nation. The people, he knew, would accept or reject the purchase on election day in 1804.

The president had a long-standing interest in Louisiana and the West. As early as 1782, as an American envoy in France, Jefferson had suggested sending an exploratory mission across the continent to California. As secretary of state ten years later he commissioned a French emigré, André Michaux, to explore the Missouri River. Allegations of Michaux's complicity in the Genêt Affair (see page 195) aborted this mission. In 1803 Jefferson renewed Michaux's instructions when he sent Meriwether Lewis and William Clark to the Pacific Ocean via the Missouri and Columbia rivers. Lewis and Clark, from 1804 to 1806, headed the nearly fifty-strong "Corps of Discovery," which was aided by trappers and American Indians along the way. A French-Canadian trader and his young Shoshoni wife, Toussaint Charbonneau and Sacagawea, joined the expedition. Sacagawea interpreted both the terrain and the languages of the West to the wanderers. Lewis and Clark knew that this wilderness was a crowded one. They carried twenty-one bags of gifts for Indian leaders both to establish goodwill and to advertise the potential for trade using American manufactured goods.

> **Lewis and Clark**

The Lewis and Clark expedition, planned in secrecy before the Louisiana Purchase, reflected Jefferson's scientific curiosity and his interest in western commercial development, especially the fur and China trades. Other explorers soon followed Lewis and Clark, led in 1805 and 1806 by Lieutenant Zebulon Pike in search of the source of the Mississippi. Pike attempted to find a navigable water route to the Far West and sought the headwaters of the Arkansas River. He reached the Rocky Mountains in present-day Colorado, though he never made it to the top of the peak that bears his name. Pike and his men wandered into Spanish territory to the south, where the Spanish arrested them and held them captive for several months in Santa Fe. After his release, Pike wrote an account of his experiences that set commercial minds spinning. He described a potential commercial market in southwestern Spanish cities as well as the bounty of furs and precious minerals to be had. The vision of the road to the Southwest became a reality with the opening of the Santa Fe Trail in the 1820s. Over the next few decades Americans avidly read published accounts of western exploration; expansion caught their imagination. Jefferson considered Louisiana and the opening of the West among his greatest presidential accomplishments.

Jefferson in Power

Buffalo-skin shirt and compass of William Clark used on the Lewis and Clark expedition, 1804–1806. With courage, daring, and the assistance of Indians throughout the territory, Lewis and Clark's fifty-strong "Corps of Discovery" traversed the newly acquired Louisiana Territory, mapping its terrain and recording the people, fauna, and flora they encountered. *Hunting shirt: Peabody Museum of Archeology and Ethnology, Harvard University; compass: Smithsonian Institution.*

Republicans Versus Federalists

In 1804, campaigning for re-election on his record, Jefferson claimed credit for western expansion and the restoration of republican values. He had removed the Federalist threat to liberty by ending the Alien and Sedition and Judiciary Acts. He had reduced the size and cost of government by cutting spending. Despite his opponents' charges, he had proved that Republicans supported commerce and promoted free trade. He had removed major obstacles to American commercial growth by purchasing the Louisiana Territory, including New Orleans, and by having Congress repeal Federalist excise and property taxes. American trade with Europe was flourishing. Unwisely, Federalists who had earlier criticized Jefferson for not seizing Louisiana now attacked the president for paying too much for the territory and for exceeding his powers.

> **Election of 1804**

Charles Cotesworth Pinckney, a wealthy South Carolina lawyer and former Revolutionary War aide to General George Washington, carried the opposition standard against Jefferson. Pinckney had been Adams's vice-presidential candidate in 1800 and inherited the Federalist leadership. Jefferson dumped Aaron Burr from the 1804 ticket, and he and his running mate, George Clinton of New York, swamped Pinckney and Rufus King in the electoral college by 162 votes to 14, carrying fifteen of the seventeen states.

Jefferson's re-election was both a personal and an organizational triumph. The political dissenters of the 1790s had used their Democratic-Republican societies to win elections. More than anything else, opposition to the Federalists had molded and unified them. Indeed, in areas where the Federalists were strongest—in commercial New York and Pennsylvania in the 1790s and in New England in the 1800s—the Republicans had organized most effectively.

Until the Republican successes in 1800 and 1804, most Federalists had disdained popular campaigning. They believed in government by the "best" people—those whose education, wealth, and experience marked them as leaders. For candidates to

John Lewis Krimmel, *Election Day in Philadelphia* (1815). Citizens crowded outside the State House in Philadelphia on election day in 1815 to whip up support for their candidates and to await the results. The painting suggests the overwhelmingly white, male composition of the electorate. *The Henry Francis du Pont Winterthur Museum.*

debate their qualifications before their inferiors—the voters—was unnecessary and undignified. The direct appeals of the Republicans struck the Federalists as a subversion of the natural political order.

After the resounding Federalist defeat in 1800, a younger generation of Federalists began to imitate the Republicans. They organized statewide and, led by men like Josiah Quincy, a young congressman from Massachusetts, campaigned for popular support. Quincy cleverly identified the Federalists as the people's party, attacking Republicans as autocratic planters. "Jeffersonian Democracy," Quincy satirized in 1804, was "an Indian word, signifying *'a great tobacco planter who had herds of black slaves.'*" In attacking frugal government, the self-styled Younger Federalists played on fears of a weakened army and navy. Merchants depended on a strong navy to protect ocean trade

> **Younger Federalists**

while westerners, encroaching on Indian tribes, looked for federal support.

In the states where both factions organized and ran candidates, participation in elections increased markedly. In some states more than 90 percent of the eligible voters—nearly all of whom were white males—cast ballots between 1804 and 1816. People became more interested in politics generally, especially at the local level; and as participation in elections increased, the states expanded suffrage. Nevertheless, the popular base remained restricted. Property qualifications for voting and holding office persisted, and in six states the legislatures still selected presidential electors in 1804. Even Republicans restrained their organization; fearing the divisiveness of partisanship, most leaders shied away from cohesive political movements.

Yet political competition, spurred on by a vigorous press that saw its primary role as partisan advocacy, prompted grassroots campaigning. The political barbecue symbolized the new style as the factions responded to increasing voter involvement in politics. In New York they roasted oxen; on the New England coast they baked clams; in Maryland they served oysters. The guests washed down their meals with beer and punch and sometimes competed in corn shuckings or horse pulls. During the barbecue, candidates and party leaders spoke from the stump. Oratory was a popular form of entertainment, and the speakers delivered lengthy and uninhibited speeches. They often made wild accusations, which—given the slow speed of communications—might not be answered until after the election. In 1808, for example, a New England Republican accused the Federalists of causing the Boston Massacre.

Soon both factions used barbecues to rally voters. But although the Younger Federalists adopted the political barbecue, the Federalist party never fully mastered the art of wooing voters. Older Federalists still opposed such blatant campaigning. And though they were strong in a few states like Connecticut and Delaware, the Federalists never offered the Republicans sustained competition. Divisions between Older and Younger Federalists often hindered them, and the extremism of some Older Federalists tended to discredit the organization. A case in point was Timothy Pickering, a Massachusetts congressman and former secretary of state who opposed the Louisiana Purchase, feared Jefferson's re-election, and urged the secession of New England in 1803 and 1804. Pickering won some support among the few Federalists in Congress, but others opposed his plan for a northern confederacy. When Vice President Aaron Burr lost his bid to become governor of New York in 1804, the plan collapsed. Burr, more an opportunist than a loyal Republican, was to have led New York into secession, with the other states to follow.

Both political groups suffered from divisions and individuals' personal ambitions, which undermined cohesiveness. For a long time, for instance, Aaron Burr and Alexander Hamilton had crossed swords in political conflict. Burr had an affinity for conspiracies, and it seemed to him that Hamilton always blocked his path. Hamilton had thwarted Burr's attempt to steal the election of 1800 from Jefferson (see page 201), and in the 1804 New York gubernatorial race the Federal-

Hamilton-Burr Duel

ist Hamilton backed a rival Republican faction against Burr. Again a loser, Burr turned his resentment on Hamilton and challenged him to a duel. Hamilton had been so outspoken in charging Burr as too dangerous and unfit to hold office that Burr could choose from among insults. With his honor at stake, Hamilton accepted Burr's challenge, although he found dueling repugnant. They withdrew to New Jersey because New York had outlawed dueling. On July 11, 1804, at Weehawken, New Jersey, Hamilton deliberately fired astray. He paid for that decision with his life. Burr was indicted for murder in New York and New Jersey and faced immediate arrest if he returned to either state.

His political career in ruins, Burr plotted to create a new empire in the Southwest, using the Louisiana Territory as a base. With the collusion of General James Wilkinson, the United States commander in the Mississippi Valley, Burr planned to raise a private army in the territory to grab land either from the United States or from Spain (his exact plans remain uncertain). Wilkinson switched sides and informed President Jefferson of Burr's ambitions. Jefferson personally assisted the prosecution in Burr's 1807 trial for treason. Chief Justice Marshall, the presiding judge, was sympathetic to Burr. The jury acquitted Burr, who then fled to Europe to avoid further prosecution. The conflict between Jefferson and Marshall in the trial made Burr seem incidental at times.

The controversies surrounding Burr highlight some of the limitations of the emerging political system. Personal animosities were as strong a force as ideology and political differences, and new, temporary factions flourished. Moreover, although politicians appealed for voter support and participation in politics broadened, the electoral base remained narrow. As the election of 1804 revealed, the Federalists could offer only weak competition at the national level. And where Federalists were too weak to be a threat, Republicans succumbed to the temptation to fight among themselves.

Thus, although this period is commonly called the era of the first party system, parties as such were not fully developed. Competition encouraged party organization, but personal ambition, personality clashes, and local, state, and regional loyalties worked against it. Increasingly, external events intruded and would occupy most of Jefferson's time in his second administration.

Preserving
American Neutrality
in a World at War

"Peace, commerce, and honest friendship with all nations, entangling alliance with none," President Jefferson had proclaimed in his first inaugural address. Jefferson's efforts to stand clear of European conflict were successful until 1805. Thereafter he found peace and undisturbed commerce an elusive goal, though pursuit of it occupied nearly his entire second administration.

After the Senate ratified the Jay Treaty in 1795 (see pages 196–197), the United States and Great Britain appeared to reconcile their differences. Britain withdrew from its western forts and interfered less in American trade with France. More importantly, trade between the United States and Britain increased: the republic became Britain's best customer, and the British Empire in turn bought the bulk of American exports.

But renewal of the Napoleonic wars in May 1803—two weeks after Napoleon sold Louisiana to the United States—again trapped the nation between the two unfriendly European powers. For two years American commerce benefited from the conflict. As the world's largest neutral carrier, the United States became the chief supplier of food to Europe. American merchants also gained control of most of the West Indian trade, which was often transshipped though American ports to Europe.

Meanwhile, the United States victory over Tripolitan pirates on the north coast of Africa (the Barbary states) provided Jefferson with his one clear success in protecting American trading rights. In 1801 Jefferson had refused the demands of the sultan of Tripoli for payment to exempt American ships and sailors from being taken hostage. Instead he sent a naval squadron to the Mediterranean to protect American merchant ships. In 1803–1804, under Lieutenant Stephen Decatur, the navy blockaded Tripoli harbor while marines marched overland from Egypt to seize the port of Derna. The United States signed a peace treaty with Tripoli in 1805 but continued to pay tribute to other Barbary states until 1815, when the navy, under Decatur (by then a captain), forced Algiers and Tunis to renounce attacks against Americans.

American merchants were more concerned about Anglo-French interference with trade. In October 1805 Britain tightened its control of the high seas with its victory over the French and Spanish fleets at the Battle of Trafalgar. Two months later Napoleon defeated the Russian and Austrian armies at Austerlitz. Stalemated, France and Britain waged commercial war, blockading and counterblockading each other's trade. As a trading partner of both countries, the United States paid a high price.

The British navy stepped up impressments of American sailors. Britain, whose navy was the world's largest, was suffering a severe shortage of sailors. Few men enlisted, and those already in service frequently deserted, discouraged by poor food and living conditions and brutal discipline. The Royal Navy resorted to stopping American ships and forcibly removing British deserters, British-born naturalized American seamen, and other unlucky sailors suspected of being British. It is estimated that six to eight thousand Americans were drafted in this manner between 1803 and 1812.

Impressment of American Sailors

Americans saw impressment as a direct assault on their new republic. The British principle of "once a British subject, always a British subject" ignored United States citizenship and sovereignty and insulted Americans. Moreover, the practice exposed the weakness of the new nation: the United States was in effect unable to protect its citizens from impressment. Alleged British deserters—American citizens—faced British court martial, and some, like Jenkin Ratford, taken off the U.S.S. *Chesapeake* in 1807, were hanged.

In February 1806 the Senate denounced British impressment as aggression and a violation of neutral rights. To protest the insult Congress passed the Non-Importation Act, prohibiting importation from Great Britain of a long list of cloth and metal articles. In November, Jefferson suspended the act temporarily while William Pinckney, a Baltimore lawyer, joined James Monroe in London in an attempt to negotiate a settlement. The treaty Monroe and Pinckney carried home violated their instructions—it did not mention impressment—and Jefferson never submitted it to the Senate for ratification.

Less than a year later, the *Chesapeake* affair exposed American military weakness and revealed

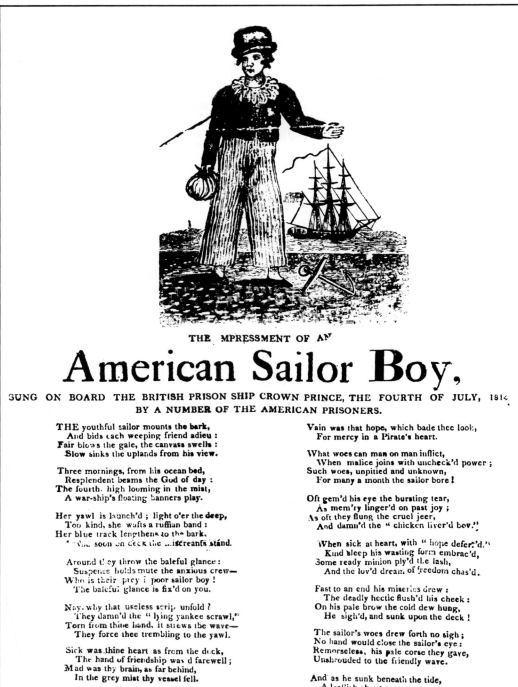

Ballad of an American sailor impressed by the British during the War of 1812. References to the British captain as a "pirate" and the British crew as "demons" reveal the intense indignation felt by the American public. *The New-York Historical Society.*

the emotional impact of impressment on the public. In June 1807 the forty-gun frigate U.S.S. *Chesapeake* left Norfolk, Virginia, on a mission to protect American ships trading in the Mediterranean. About ten miles out, still inside American territorial waters, it met the fifty-gun British frigate *Leopard*. When the *Chesapeake* refused to be searched for deserters, the *Leopard* repeatedly emptied its guns broadside into the American ship. Three Americans were killed and eighteen wounded, including the ship's captain, Commodore James Barron. The British impressed four sailors—three of them American citizens, all of them deserters from the Royal Navy. Wounded and humiliated, the *Chesapeake* crept back into port.

► **Chesapeake Affair**

Had the United States been better prepared militarily, the howl of public indignation that resulted might have brought about a declaration of war. But the United States was ill equipped to defend its neutral rights with force; it was no match for the British navy. Fortunately, with Congress not in session at the time of the *Chesapeake* affair, Jefferson was able to avoid hostilities. The president responded instead by strengthening the military and putting economic pressure on Great Britain. In July, Jefferson closed American waters to British warships to prevent similar incidents, and soon thereafter he increased military and naval expenditures. On December 14, 1807, Jefferson again invoked the Non-Importation Act, and it was followed eight days later by a new measure, the Embargo Act.

Intended as a short-term measure, the Embargo Act forbade virtually all exports from the United States to any country. Imports came to a halt as well, since foreign ships delivering goods had to leave American ports with empty holds. Smuggling blossomed overnight.

► **Embargo Act**

Few American policies were as well intentioned but as unpopular and unsuccessful as Jefferson's embargo. Although the notion of "peaceable coercion" was an enlightened concept in international affairs, some Republicans felt uneasy about using coercive federal power. Federalists felt no unease; commercially minded and generally pro-British, they opposed the embargo vociferously. Some feared its impact abroad. "If England sink," Rufus King said in 1808, "her fall will prove the grave of our liberties." For mercantile New Englanders, the embargo dug another grave. Their region, the heart of Federalist opposition to the Virginian presidents (Jefferson, Madison, and Monroe), felt the brunt of the resulting depression. Shipping collapsed as exports fell by 80 percent from 1807–1808. In the winter of 1808–1809, talk of secession spread through New England port cities.

Although unemployment soared, some benefited from the embargo. Merchants with ships abroad at the time of the embargo or those willing to trade illegally and risk the weak and lax enforcement could garner enormous profits. Similarly, United States manufacturers received a boost, since the domestic market was theirs exclusively.

Great Britain, in contrast, was only mildly affected by the embargo. The British citizens hurt most—West Indians and English factory workers—had no voice in policy. English merchants actually gained, since they took over the Atlantic carrying trade from the stalled American merchant marine. Moreover, because the British blockade of Europe had already ended most trade with France, the embargo had little practical effect on the French. Indeed, it gave France an excuse to set privateers against American ships that had managed to escape the embargo by avoiding American ports. The French argued that such ships must be British ships in disguise, since the embargo barred American ships from the seas.

In the election of 1808, the Republicans faced the Federalists, the embargo, and internal factional dissent. Although nine state legislatures passed resolutions urging Jefferson to accept another term, Jefferson followed Washington's example in renouncing a third term and supported James Madison, his secretary of state, as the Republican standard-bearer. Madison won the endorsement of the congressional caucus, but Virginia Republicans put forth James Monroe (who later withdrew), and some eastern Republicans supported Vice President George Clinton. This was the first time the Republican nomination was contested.

Charles Cotesworth Pinckney and Rufus King again headed the Federalist ticket, but with new vigor. The Younger Federalists, led by Harrison Gray Otis and other Bostonians, pounded away at the widespread disaffection with Republican policy, especially with the embargo. Although Pinckney received only 47 electoral votes to Madison's 122, the Federalists did manage to make the election a race.

Pinckney carried all of New England except Vermont, and he won Delaware and some electoral votes in two other states as well. Federalists also gained seats in Congress and captured the New York state legislature. For the Younger Federalists, the future looked promising.

The embargo eventually collapsed under the pressure of domestic opposition. Jefferson felt the weight of his failure; "never did a prisoner, released from his chains," Jefferson wrote on leaving office, "feel such relief as I in shaking off the shackles of power." In his last days in office he had tried to lighten the burden by working to replace the embargo with the Non-Intercourse Act of 1809. The act reopened trade with all nations except Britain and France and authorized the president to resume trade with either country if it ceased to violate neutral rights. But the new act solved only the problems that had been created by the embargo; it did not convince Britain and France to change their policies. For one brief moment it appeared to work; President Madison reopened trade with England in June 1809 after the British minister to the United States assured him that Britain would offer the concessions he sought. His Majesty's government in London, however, repudiated the minister's assurances, and Madison reverted to nonintercourse.

> **Non-Intercourse Act**

When the Non-Intercourse Act expired in spring 1810, Congress created a variant, labeled Macon's Bill Number 2. The bill reopened trade with both Great Britain and France, but it provided that if either nation ceased to violate American rights, the president could shut down American commerce with the other. Madison, eager to use the bill rather than go to war, was tricked at his own game. When Napoleon declared that French edicts against United States shipping would be lifted, Madison declared nonintercourse against Great Britain in March 1811. But Napoleon did not keep his word. The French continued to seize American ships, and nonintercourse failed a second time.

Britain, not France, was the main target of American hostility because the Royal Navy controlled the Atlantic. New York harbor was virtually blockaded by the British, so reopening trade with any nation had little practical effect. Angry American leaders tended to blame even Indian resistance in the West on British agitation, ignoring the Indians' legitimate protests against white encroachment and treaty violations. Frustrated and having exhausted all efforts to alter British policy, the United States in 1811 and 1812 drifted into war with Great Britain.

Meanwhile, unknown to the president and Congress, Great Britain was changing its policy. The Anglo-French conflict had ended much of British commerce with the European continent, and exports to the United States had fallen 80 percent. Depression had hit the British Isles. On June 16, 1812, Britain opened the seas to American shipping. But two days later, before word had crossed the Atlantic, Congress declared war.

The War of 1812 was the logical outcome of United States policy after the renewal of war in Europe in 1803. The grievances enumerated in President Madison's message to Congress on June 1, 1812, were old ones: impressment, interference with neutral commerce, and British alliances with western Indians. Unmentioned was the resolve to defend American independence and honor—and the thirst of expansionists for British Canada.

Congress and the country were divided. Much of the sentiment for war came from the War Hawks, land-hungry southerners and westerners led by Henry Clay of Kentucky and John C. Calhoun of South Carolina. Westerners had increased their numbers in Congress following reapportionment after the 1810 census, and the enlarged delegation was concerned equally with national honor and expansion. Most representatives from the coastal states, which included the Federalists, opposed war, since armed conflict with the great naval power threatened to close down all American shipping. The vote for war—79 to 49 in the House, 19 to 13 in the Senate—reflected these sharp regional differences. The split would also be reflected in the way Americans fought the war.

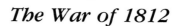

The War of 1812

War was a foolish adventure for the United States in 1812; despite six months of preparation, American forces remained ill equipped. Because the army had neither an able staff nor an adequate force of enlisted men, the burden of fighting fell on the state militias, and not all the states cooperated. The navy did have a corps of well-trained, experienced officers who had proven their mettle in protecting

American merchantmen from Mediterranean pirates. But next to the Royal Navy, the ruler of the seas, the United States Navy was minuscule. Jefferson's warning that "our constitution is a peace establishment—it is not calculated for war" proved a wise one. Fortunately for the United States, the war consisted mostly of scuffles and skirmishes; full-scale battles were rare.

For the first time the United States waged a general land war. It had an ill-equipped regular army, with only a few professionally trained soldiers;

> **Recruiting an Army**

West Point had produced only eighty-nine regular officers by 1812. The army expanded by appointing political leaders to organize volunteer companies and by depending upon state militia. The government offered enlistees a $16 sign-up bonus, $5 monthly pay, a full set of clothes, and a promise of three months' pay and 160 acres of land upon discharge. Recruiting officers received a $2 premium for each enlistee. Among those who joined, 42 percent were illiterate.

On the frontier, recruitment went well, at first. Civic spirit and even stronger anti-Indian sentiment led thousands of volunteers from the Old Northwest (Ohio, Indiana, Illinois, Michigan, and Wisconsin), from Kentucky and Tennessee, and from the southern frontier to enlist. The army adjusted to the new recruits by abolishing flogging in 1812. Within a year, however, frontier enlistments declined. Word spread that the War Department was often slow in meeting its payroll and supplying clothing. Even success could dampen enlistments; after General William Henry Harrison's victory at Tippecanoe Creek (see page 231), regular army enlistments stopped.

Conditions in the army could be dismal. The Kentucky volunteers who constituted the majority of General Harrison's command at the Battle of the Thames were a ragtag group. Recruited as volunteers in the Kentucky militia, they were drafted into the regular army and sent to fight against Lower Canada. They marched twenty to thirty miles a day from Kentucky to join Harrison's forces in Ohio. They received no training, carried only swords and knives on the march, and were undisciplined. The generals complained that the citizens of Ohio overcharged them for food and other purchases.

In the South, Andrew Jackson's Tennessee volunteers were no better organized in their first fifteen

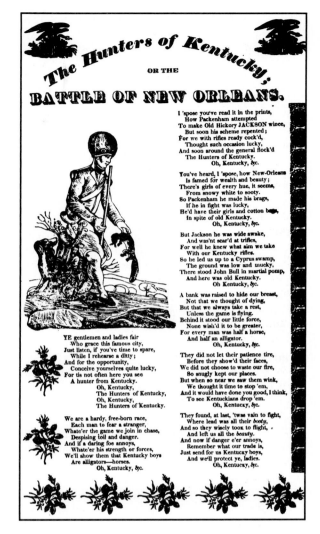

The volunteer frontiersmen who fought in the Kentucky militia during the War of 1812 became legendary for their achievements under General Andrew Jackson's command. This broadside of the popular verse "The Hunters of Kentucky" extolled their victory at the end of the war. *The Historic New Orleans Collection.*

months of service. Jackson had raised his militia in December 1812 with the promise that they would serve one year. By the late fall of 1813 his anti-Creek campaign was stalled because of a lack of supplies, and his men were talking of disbanding and going home. Jackson refused to discharge the men; they could not, he claimed, leave their posts on enemy ground. The officers repeatedly threatened to shoot any man who sought to leave. In March 1814, Jackson executed John Woods, a militiaman, for disobedience and mutiny. This broke the opposition in the ranks, and his men defeated the Creek nation at the Battle of Horseshoe Bend.

In New England, raising an army proved even more difficult. Many viewed the conflict as a Republican war ("Mr. Madison's War"), and Federalists discouraged enlistments. Some Republican officials in New England declined invitations to raise volunteer companies. Those who accepted promised their men that they would serve only a defensive role, as in Maine where they guarded the coastline. Indeed the inability of the United States to mount a successful invasion of Canada was due, in part, to the army's failure to assemble an effective force. State militias in New England and New York often declined to fight outside the borders of their own state.

Canada was important because it offered the United States the only readily available battlefront on which to confront Great Britain. The mighty

Invasion of Canada

Royal Navy was useless on the waters separating the United States and Canada, since no river afforded it access from the sea. Canada, thousands of miles from British supply sources, was vulnerable. And England, preoccupied with fighting Napoleon on the European continent, was unlikely to reduce its continental forces to defend Canada.

Begun with high hopes, the invasion of Canada ended as a disaster. The American strategy was to concentrate on the West, splitting Canadian forces and isolating the Shawnees, Potawatomis, and other tribes who supported the British. General William Hull, governor of Michigan Territory, marched his troops into Lower Canada, near Detroit. More experienced as a politician than as a soldier, Hull surrounded himself with newly minted colonels who were as politically astute and militarily ignorant as he was. The British anticipated the invasion, mobilized their Indian allies, moved troops into the area, and demanded Hull's surrender. When a pro-British, mostly Potawatomi, contingent captured Fort Dearborn, near Detroit, Hull capitulated (see map). Farther to the west, other American forts surrendered. By the winter of 1812–1813, the British controlled about half of the Old Northwest.

The United States had no greater success on the Niagara front, where New York borders Canada. At the Battle of Queenstown, north of Niagara, the United States regular army met defeat because the New York state militia refused to leave the state. This scene was repeated near Lake Champlain, where American plans to attack Montreal were foiled when the militia declined to cross the border. To a great extent the American offensive in the far north—the attempts to expand into Canada—were doomed to fail; the United States lacked the means to hold permanently any part of Canada.

The navy provided the only bright note in the first year of the war: the U.S.S. *Constitution,* the U.S.S. *Wasp,* and the U.S.S. *United States* all bested British warships on the Atlantic. But their victories gave the United States only a brief advantage. In defeat the British lost just 1 percent of their strength; in victory the Americans lost 20 percent. The British admiralty simply shifted its fleet away from the American ships, and by 1813 the Royal Navy again commanded the seas.

In 1813 the two sides also vied for control of the Great Lakes, the key to the war in the Northwest. The contest was largely a shipbuilding race. Under Master Commandant Oliver

Great Lakes Campaign

Hazard Perry and shipbuilder Noah Brown, the United States outbuilt the British on Lake Erie and defeated them at the bloody Battle of Put-in-Bay on September 10. The ships fought fiercely and at close range; of 103 men on duty on the U.S.S. *Lawrence,* 21 were killed and 63 wounded. With this costly victory, the Americans gained control of Lake Erie.

General William Henry Harrison then began the march that proved to be the United States's most successful moment in the war. Harrison's 4,500-man force, mostly Kentucky volunteers, crossed Lake Erie and pursued the British, Shawnee, and Chippewa forces into Canada, defeating them on October 5 at the Battle of the Thames, which gave the United States control of the Old Northwest.

An important by-product of the war at this stage was the defeat of effective Indian resistance to American expansion. In the decade before the War of 1812, the Shawnee leaders Prophet and Tecumseh had attempted to build a pan-Indian federation, taking advantage of Anglo-American friction, but in the end they failed. With their failure died the most significant resistance to the federal government's treaty-making tactics.

Prophet's early experiences mirror the fate that befell many frontier tribes. Born in 1775, a few

Major Campaigns of the War of 1812

months after his father had died in battle, Prophet
was raised by his sister and called
Lalawethika (Noisemaker) as a
young man. Among the Shawnees
who were defeated at the Battle of Fallen Timbers
and expelled to Ohio under the 1795 Treaty of
Greenville (see page 174), Lalawethika later moved
to Indiana. Within the shrunken territory granted to
the Shawnees under the treaty, game became
scarce. Encroachment by whites and the periodic
ravages of disease brought further misery to Indian

> **Prophet**

villages and tribes. Like other Indians, Lalawethika
turned to whiskey. He also turned to traditional folk
knowledge and remedies, and in 1804 he became a
tribal medicine man. But Lalawethika was a failure;
his medicine could not stop the white man's viral
illness from ravaging his village.

Lalawethika emerged from his own battle with
illness in 1805 as a new man, called Prophet. Claiming to have died and been resurrected, he told a
visionary tale of this experience and warned of
damnation for those who drank whiskey. In the

The Shawnee Chiefs Prophet (left) and Tecumseh (right). The two brothers led a revival of traditional Shawnee culture and preached Indian federation against white encroachment. In the War of 1812, they allied themselves with the British, but Tecumseh's death at the Battle of Thames (1813) and British indifference thereafter caused Indian resistance and unity to collapse. *Prophet: National Museum of American Art, Smithsonian Institution, Gift of Mrs. Joseph Harrison, Jr.; Tecumseh: Field Museum of Natural History, FMNH Neg. #A93851.*

following years, Prophet traveled widely in the Northwest as a religious leader, attacking the decline of moral values among Indians, condemning intertribal battles, and stressing harmony and respect for elders. In essence he preached the revitalization of traditional Shawnee culture. Return to the old ways, he told the Indians of the Old Northwest, abandon white customs. Hunt with bows and arrows, he said, not guns; release domestic animals and discard the wearing of hats; refrain from eating bread and cultivate corn and beans.

Prophet's message was a reassuring one to the Shawnees, Potawatomis, and other Indians of the Old Northwest who felt unsettled and threatened by whites. Prophet won converts by performing miracles—he seemed to darken the sun by coinciding his activities with a solar eclipse—and used opposition to federal Indian policy to draw others into his camp. His message spread to southern tribes as well.

The government and white settlers were alarmed by the religious revival led by Prophet. With his brother, Tecumseh, who was seven years older, he refused to leave lands claimed by the government. In 1808, Prophet and his brother began to turn from a message of spiritual renewal to one of resistance to American aggression. They were encouraged by the British, who looked to alliances with Indian tribes after renewed Anglo-American hostilities following the *Chesapeake* affair of 1807. In repudiating land cessions to the government under the Treaty of Fort Wayne (1809), Tecumseh told Indiana's Governor William Henry Harrison at Vincennes in 1810 that "the only way to check and stop this evil is, for all the red men to unite in claiming a common and equal right in the land, as it was at first, and should be yet; for it never was divided, but belongs to all, for the use of each. . . . No part has a right to sell, even to each other, much less to strangers."

Tecumseh

At that point Tecumseh, the towering six-foot warrior and magnetic orator, replaced Prophet as Shawnee leader. Because Prophet's religious vision could not stop the whites, young warriors looked to Tecumseh for political leadership. Convinced that only a federation of tribes could stop the advance of white settlement, Tecumseh sought to unify northern and southern Indians. He warned Harrison that the Indians would resist white occupation of the 2.5 million acres on the Wabash that they had ceded in the Treaty of Fort Wayne.

A year later, using a Potawatomi raid on an Illinois settlement as an excuse, Harrison attacked and demolished Tecumseh's headquarters on Tippecanoe Creek in Indiana Territory. Losses on both sides were heavy. Indian warriors throughout the Midwest came to Tecumseh's side; Harrison appealed for help to President Madison. When the War of 1812 started, Tecumseh joined the British in return for a promise of an Indian country in the Great Lakes region. Tecumseh's position was strengthened by the death in July 1812 of Little Turtle, chief of the Miami tribe, who led defenders of the 1795 Treaty of Greenville drawn from the Miami, Delaware, and divided Kickapoo tribes. Tecumseh, however, was killed in the Battle of the Thames in October 1813, and with his death Indian unity collapsed.

The American success against the Shawnees in the West and on Lake Erie could not be repeated on Lake Ontario. After the Battle of the Thames, both sides seemed to favor petty victories over strategic goals in the Northwest. The Americans razed York (now Toronto), the Canadian capital, and looted and burned the Parliament building before withdrawing, too few in number to hold the city.

Outside the Old Northwest the British set Americans back. In December 1812 the Royal Navy blockaded the Chesapeake and Delaware bays. By **British Naval Blockade** May 1813 the blockade closed nearly all southern and Gulf of Mexico ports, and by November it reached north to Long Island Sound. By 1814 all New England ports were closed. American trade had declined nearly 90 percent since 1811, and the decline in revenues from customs duties threatened to bankrupt the federal government.

Impressment continued during the war, and American naval victories reminded Americans of the threat. When the U.S.S. *Constitution,* for instance, defeated H.M.S. *Java* off the coast of South America in December 1812, thirteen impressed American seamen came home. The story of Richard Thompson was publicized in a congressional investigation. A native of New York, Thompson and two other Americans had been impressed on the H.M.S. *Peacock.* When they learned that the United States and Great Britain were at war, the three went to the captain to demand to be treated as prisoners of war. Instead they were put in chains for twenty-four hours, lashed, and "put to duty." They were forced to fight for the British until the U.S.S. *Hornet* bested the *Peacock* and liberated the Americans.

After their defeat of Napoleon in April 1814, the British stepped up the land campaign against the United States, concentrating their efforts in the Chesapeake Bay region. In retaliation for the burning of York—and to divert American troops from Lake Champlain, where the British planned a new offensive—royal troops occupied Washington in August and set it ablaze, leaving the presidental mansion scarred by fire. The attack on the capital, however, was only a raid. The major battle occurred at Baltimore, in September, where the Americans held firm. Francis Scott Key, witnessing the British fleet's bombardment of Fort McHenry in Baltimore harbor, was inspired to write the verses of "The Star-Spangled Banner." (In 1931 it became the national anthem.) Although the British inflicted heavy damage both materially and psychologically, they achieved no more than a stalemate. The British offensive at Lake Champlain proved equally unsuccessful. An American fleet forced a British flotilla to turn back at Plattsburgh on Lake Champlain, and the offensive was discontinued.

The last campaign of the war was waged in the South, along the Gulf of Mexico. It began when Tennessee militia general Andrew Jackson defeated the Creek Indians at the Battle of Horseshoe Bend in March 1814. The battle ended the year-long Creek War, which began after the Shawnee leaders had ignited religious revival among the Creeks following Tecumseh's visit in late 1811. The Creek prophets and their followers—known as the Red Sticks—sparked Indian resistance in the South. President Madison, however, left suppression of Creeks to the southern states and territories; he lacked the regular troops to fight them. Andrew Jackson defeated the Creek nation and began his rise to power; the Creeks had to cede two-thirds of their land and withdraw to southern and western Alabama. Jackson became a major general in the regular army and continued south toward the Gulf. To forestall a British invasion at Pensacola Bay, which guarded an overland route to New Orleans, Jackson seized Pensacola—in Spanish Florida—on November 7, 1814. After securing Mobile, he marched on to New Orleans and prepared for a British attempt to capture the city.

The Battle of New Orleans was the final military engagement. Early in December the British fleet landed 1,500 men east of New Orleans, hoping to gain control of the Mississippi

> **Battle of New Orleans**

River. They faced an American force of regular army troops, plus a larger contingent of Tennessee and Kentucky frontiersmen and two companies of free black volunteers from New Orleans. For three weeks the British under Sir Edward Pakenham and the Americans under Jackson played cat-and-mouse, each trying to gain a major strategic position. Finally, on January 8, 1815, the two forces met head-on. In fortified positions, Jackson and his mostly untrained army held their ground against two suicidal frontal assaults and a reinforced British contingent of 6,000. At day's end, more than 2,000 British soldiers lay dead or wounded. The Americans suffered only 21 casualties. Andrew Jackson emerged a national hero. Ironically, the Battle of New Orleans was fought two weeks after the end of the war; unknown to Jackson, a treaty had been signed in Ghent, Belgium, on December 24, 1814.

The United States government had gone to war reluctantly and during the conflict had continued to probe for a diplomatic end to hostilities. In 1813, for instance, President Madison had eagerly accepted a Russian offer to mediate, but Great Britain had refused it. Three months later, British Foreign Minister Lord Castlereagh suggested opening peace talks. It took over ten months to arrange meetings, but in August 1814 a team of American negotiators, including John Quincy Adams and Henry Clay, began talks with the British in Ghent.

The Ghent treaty made no mention of the issues that had led to war. The United States received no satisfaction on impressment, blockades, or other maritime rights for neutrals. Like-

> **Treaty of Ghent**

wise, British demands for an Indian buffer state in the Northwest and territorial cessions from Maine to Minnesota were not satisfied. Essentially, the Treaty of Ghent restored the prewar status quo. It provided for an end to hostilities with the British and with Indian tribes, release of prisoners, restoration of conquered territory, and arbitration of boundary disputes. Other questions—notably compensation for losses and fishing rights—would be negotiated by joint commissions.

Why did the negotiators settle for so little? Events in Europe had made peace and the status quo acceptable at the end of 1814, as they had not been in 1812. Napoleon's fall from power allowed the United States to abandon its demands, since peace in Europe made impressment and interference with American commerce moot questions. Similarly, war-weary Britain, its treasury nearly depleted, stopped pressing for a military victory.

The War of 1812 reaffirmed the independence of the young American republic. Although conflict with Great Britain continued, it never again led to war. The experience strengthened

> **Results of War of 1812**

America's resolve to steer clear of European politics, for it had been the British-French conflict that had drawn the United States into war. For the rest of the century the United States would shun involvement in European political issues and wars.

The war had disastrous results for most Indian tribes. Although Indians were not a party to the Treaty of Ghent, the ninth article pledged the United States to end hostilities and to restore "all the possessions, rights, and privileges" that the tribes had enjoyed before the war. More than a dozen treaties were signed in 1815 with midwestern tribal leaders, but they had little meaning. Restoration was moot. With the death of Tecumseh, the Indians lost their most powerful political and military leader; with the withdrawal of the British, they lost their strongest ally. The Shawnees, Potawatomis, Chippewas, and other midwestern tribes had lost the resources with which they could have resisted American expansion.

Domestically, the war exposed weaknesses in defense and transportation, which were vital for westward expansion. American generals had found American roads inadequate to move an army and its supplies among widely scattered fronts. In the Northwest, General Harrison's troops had depended on homemade cartridges and gifts of clothing from Ohio residents, and in Maine, troops had melted down spoons to make bullets. Clearly, improved transportation and a well-equipped army were major priorities. In 1815, President Madison responded by centralizing control of the military, and Congress voted a standing army of 10,000 men, one-third of the army's wartime strength but three

The Battle of New Orleans, 1815. American troops decisively routed a larger British contingent at the Battle of New Orleans, fought two weeks after the Treaty of Ghent had officially ended the war but before word could reach the armies. This idealistic painting of the battle highlights General Andrew Jackson (on horseback), whose victory made him a national hero. *The Historic New Orleans Collection.*

times the size of the army during Jefferson's administration.

Possibly most important of all, the war stimulated economic change. The embargo, the Non-Importation and Non-Intercourse Acts, and the war itself spurred the production of manufactured goods—cloth and metal—to replace banned imports. In the absence of commercial opportunities abroad, New England capitalists began to invest in manufactures. The effects of these changes were to be far-reaching (see Chapter 9).

And, finally, the war sealed the fate of the Federalist party. Realizing that their chances of wining a presidential election in wartime were slight, the Federalists joined dissatisfied Republicans in supporting De Witt Clinton of New York in 1812. This was the high point of Federalist organization at the state level, and the Younger Federalists campaigned hard. Clinton nevertheless lost to President Madison by 128 to 89 electoral votes. Areas that favored the war (the South and West) voted solidly

Republican. The Federalists, however, did gain some congressional seats, and they carried many local elections.

Once again extremism undermined the Federalists. During the war Older Federalists had revived talk of secession, and from December 15, 1814, to January 5, 1815, Federalist delegates from New England met in Hartford, Connecticut. With the war in a stalemate and trade in ruins, they plotted to revise the national compact or pull out of the republic. Moderates prevented a resolution of secession, but convention members condemned the war and the embargo and endorsed radical changes in the Constitution. In particular, they wanted constitutional amendments restricting the presidency to one term and requiring a two-thirds congressional vote to admit new states. They also hoped to abolish the three-fifths compromise, whereby slaves were counted in the apportionment of congressional representatives

Hartford Convention

This print of a road accident shows the primitive state of American roads in the early part of the nineteenth century. *Print Collection, Miriam and Ira D. Wallach Division of Art, Prints, and Photographs, The New York Public Library, Astor, Lenox, and Tilden Foundations.*

of revival as opponents of war flocked to the Federalist banner, helped kill the faction.

Postwar Nationalism and Diplomacy

With peace came a new sense of American nationalism. Self-confidently, the nation asserted itself at home and abroad as Republicans aped Federalists in encouraging economic development and commerce. In his message to Congress in December 1815, President Madison embraced Federalist doctrine by recommending military expansion and a program to stimulate economic growth. Wartime experiences, he said, had demonstrated the need for a national bank (the charter of the first Bank of the United States had expired) and for better transportation. To raise government revenues and perpetuate the wartime growth in manufacturing, Madison called for a protective tariff—a tax on imported goods. Though straying from Jeffersonian Republicanism, Madison did so within limits. Only a constitutional amendment, he argued, could give the federal government authority to build roads and canals that were less than national in scope.

The congressional leadership pushed Madison's nationalist program energetically. Congressman John C. Calhoun and Speaker of the House Henry Clay, who named the program **American System** the American System, believed it would unify the country. They looked to the tariff on imported goods to stimulate industry. New mills would purchase raw materials; new millworkers would buy food from the agricultural South and West. New roads would make possible the flow of produce and goods, and tariff revenues would provide the money to build them. A national bank would facilitate all these transactions.

Fundamental to the new Republican policy was Hamilton's original plan for the first Bank of the United States. Fearing the concentration of economic power in a central bank, the Republicans had allowed the charter of the first Bank of the United States to expire in 1811. State banks, how-

(see page 179), and to forbid naturalized citizens from holding office. These proposals were aimed at the growing West and South—the heart of Republican electoral strength—and at Irish immigrants.

The timing of the Hartford Convention proved fatal. The victory at New Orleans and news of the peace treaty made the convention, with its talk of secession and proposed constitutional amendments, look ridiculous, if not treasonous. Rather than harassing a beleaguered wartime administration, the Federalists retreated before a rising tide of nationalism. Though Federalism remained strong in a handful of states until the 1820s, the Federalists began to dissolve. The War of 1812, at first a source

ever, proved inadequate to the nation's needs. Their resources were insufficient to assist the government in financing the War of 1812. Moreover, people distrusted currency issued by banks in distant localities. Because many banks issued notes without gold to back them up, and counterfeit notes were common, merchants hesitated to accept strange currency. Republicans therefore came to favor a national bank. In 1816 Congress chartered the Second Bank of the United States for twenty years. Its headquarters, like those of the first Bank of the United States, were in Philadelphia. The government provided $7 million of the $35 million capital and appointed one-fifth of the directors, and the bank opened its doors on January 1, 1817.

Congress did not share Madison's reservations about the constitutionality of using federal funds to build local roads. "Let us, then, bind the republic together," Calhoun declared, "with a perfect system of roads and canals." But Madison vetoed Calhoun's internal improvements bill, which provided for the construction of roads of mostly local benefit, insisting that it was unconstitutional. Internal improvements were the province of the states and of private enterprise. (Madison did, however, approve funds for the continuation of the National Road, which began in Maryland, to Ohio, on the grounds that it was a military necessity.)

Protective tariffs completed Madison's nationalist program. The embargo and the war had stimulated domestic industry, especially the manufacturing of cloth and iron, but the resumption of trade after the war brought competition from abroad. Americans charged that British firms were dumping their goods below cost on the American market to stifle American manufacturing. To aid the new industries, Madison recommended and Congress passed the Tariff of 1816, the first substantial protective tariff in American history. The act levied taxes on imported woolens and cottons, especially inexpensive ones, and on iron, leather, hats, paper, and sugar. In effect it raised the cost of these imported goods. Some New England representatives viewed the tariff as interference in free trade, and southern representatives (except Calhoun and a few others) opposed it because it raised the cost of imported goods to southern families. But the western and Middle Atlantic states backed it, and the tariff passed.

James Monroe, Madison's successor as president, retained Madison's domestic program, supporting the national bank and tariffs and vetoing internal improvements on constitutional grounds. Monroe was the third Virginian to hold the presidency between 1801 and 1825. A former United States senator, twice governor of Virginia, and an experienced diplomat, he served under Madison as secretary of state and of war. While heading the State Department, he accepted the presidential nomination of the Republican congressional caucus in 1816 and easily defeated the last Federalist nominee, Rufus King, sweeping all the states except the Federalist strongholds of Massachusetts, Connecticut, and Delaware. Monroe optimistically declared that "discord does not belong to our system." The American people were, he said, "one great family with a common interest." A Boston newspaper dubbed the one-party period the "Era of Good Feelings." And for Monroe's first term that label seemed appropriate.

Under Chief Justice John Marshall, the Supreme Court during this period became the bulwark of a nationalist point of view. In *McCulloch* v. *Maryland*

MuCulloch v. Maryland

(1819), the Court struck down a Maryland law taxing a branch of the federally chartered Second Bank of the United States. Maryland had adopted the tax in an effort to destroy the bank's Baltimore branch. The issue was thus one of state versus federal power. Speaking for a unanimous Court, Marshall asserted the supremacy of the federal government over the states. "The Constitution and the laws thereof are supreme," he declared; "they control the constitution and laws of the respective states and cannot be controlled by them."

Having established federal supremacy, the Court in *McCulloch* v. *Maryland* went on to consider whether Congress could issue a bank charter. No such power was specified in the Constitution. But Marshall noted that Congress had the authority to pass "all laws which shall be necessary and proper for carrying into execution" the enumerated powers of the government (Article I, Section 8). Therefore Congress could legally exercise "those great powers on which the welfare of the nation essentially depends." If the ends were legitimate and the means were not prohibited, Marshall ruled, a law was constitutional. The Constitution was, in Marshall's words, "intended to endure for ages to come, and consequently, to be adapted to the various causes of human affairs." The bank charter was declared legal.

In *McCulloch* v. *Maryland* Marshall combined Federalist nationalism with Federalist economic views. By asserting federal supremacy, he was protecting the commercial and industrial interests that favored a national bank. This was federalism in the tradition of Alexander Hamilton. The decision was only one in a series. In *Fletcher* v. *Peck* (1810), the Court voided a Georgia law that violated individuals' right of contract. Similarly, in *Dartmouth College* v. *Woodward* (1819), the Court nullified a New Hampshire act altering the charter of Dartmouth College, which Marshall ruled constituted a contract. In protecting such contracts, Marshall thwarted state interference in commerce and business. *Gibbons* v. *Ogden* confirmed federal supremacy in interstate commerce (see page 252).

John Quincy Adams, Monroe's secretary of state, matched the self-confident Marshall Court in nationalism and assertiveness. From 1817 to 1825 he managed the nation's foreign policy brilliantly. The son of John and Abigail Adams, he was an experienced diplomat who had served abroad and negotiated the Treaty of Ghent. Adams stubbornly pushed for expansion, fishing rights for Americans in Atlantic waters, political distance from the Old World, and peace. An ardent expansionist, he nonetheless placed limits on expansion, believing that it must come through negotiations, not war, and that newly acquired territories must not permit slavery. In appearance a small, austere man, once described by a British official as a "bulldog among spaniels," Adams was a superb diplomat who knew six languages.

> **John Quincy Adams as Secretary of State**

Despite being an Anglophobe, Adams worked to strengthen the peace with Great Britain. In April 1817 the two nations agreed in the Rush-Bagot Treaty to limit their Great Lakes naval forces to one ship each on Lakes Ontario and Champlain and two vessels each on the other lakes. The first disarmament treaty of modern times led to the demilitarization of the United States–Canadian border.

Adams then pushed for the Convention of 1818, which fixed the United States–Canadian border from the Lake of the Woods in Minnesota west to the Rockies along the 49th parallel. When agreement could not be reached on the territory west of the mountains, Britain and the United States settled on joint occupation of Oregon for ten years (it was renewed for another ten years in 1827). Adams wanted to fix the border along the 49th parallel right through to the Pacific Ocean and thereby gain the important inland waterways of Juan de Fuca Strait and Puget Sound. He hoped for a better negotiating position when the treaty lapsed.

Adams's next move was to settle long-term disputes with Spain. Although the 1803 Louisiana Treaty had omitted reference to Spanish-ruled West Florida, the United States claimed the territory as far as the Perdido River (the present-day Florida-Alabama border) but occupied only a small finger of that area. During the War of 1812 the United States seized Mobile and the remainder of West Florida. Afterward it took advantage of Spain's preoccupation with domestic and colonial troubles to negotiate for the purchase of East Florida. Talks took place in 1818, while General Andrew Jackson's troops occupied much of present-day Florida on the pretext of suppressing Seminole raids against American settlements across the border. Adams was furious with Jackson but defended his brazen act.

> **Adams-Onís Treaty**

The following year, Don Luís de Onís, Spanish minister to the United States, on behalf of Spain agreed to cede Florida to the United States without payment. In this Transcontinental, or Adams-Onís Treaty, the United States also defined the southwestern boundary of the Louisiana Purchase. The border zigzagged across the West from Texas to the Pacific Ocean (see map, page 219). In return, the United States government assumed $5 million worth of claims by American citizens against Spain and gave up its dubious claim to Texas. Expansion was thus achieved at little cost and without war, and American territorial claims stretched from the Atlantic to the Pacific.

While the Rush-Bagot Treaty, the Convention of 1818, and the Adams-Onís Treaty temporarily resolved conflict between the United States and European nations, events to the south still threatened United States interests. John Quincy Adams's desire to insulate the United States and the Western Hemisphere from European conflict led to his greatest achievement: the Monroe Doctrine.

The thorny issue of the recognition of new governments in Latin America had to be confronted. Between 1808 and 1822, the United Provinces of the Río de la Plata (present-day northern Argentina, Paraguay, and Uruguay), Chile, Peru, Colombia, and Mexico had all broken free from Spain. Many Americans wanted to recognize the independence of these former colonies because they seemed to be following in the United States's revolutionary tradition. Monroe and Adams moved cautiously. They sought to avoid conflict with Spain and its allies and to assure themselves of the stability of the revolutionary regimes. But in 1822, shortly after the Adams-Onís Treaty with Spain was safely signed and ratified, the United States became the first nation outside Latin America to recognize the new states.

Soon events in Europe again threatened the stability of the New World. Spain suffered a domestic revolt, and France occupied Spain in an attempt to bolster the weak Spanish monarchy against the rebels. The United States feared that France would seek to restore the new Latin American states to Spanish rule. Similarly distrustful of France, Great Britain proposed a joint United States–British declaration against European intervention in the hemisphere and a joint disavowal of British and American territorial ambitions in the region. Adams rejected the British overture; he insisted that the United States act independently in accordance with the principle of avoiding foreign entanglements.

Determined to thwart joint action with Great Britain, the unbending Adams tenaciously outargued other cabinet members. Those who favored joint action believed that the United States needed British naval power to prevent French or Russian intervention. They were supported by former president Jefferson, then in retirement at Monticello. Adams, however, won. "It would be more candid, as well as more dignified," he argued, "to avow our principles explicitly to Russia and France, than to come in as a cockboat in the wake of the British man-of-war." Moreover, he rejected the British proposal to disavow territorial ambitions as a deliberate attempt at preventing further American expansion.

President Monroe presented the American position—the Monroe Doctrine—in his message to Congress on December 2, 1823. He called for, first,

John Quincy Adams (1767–1848), secretary of state from 1817 to 1825 and architect of the Monroe Doctrine, in a Pieter Van Huffel painting of 1815. Van Huffel's portrait makes Adams appear formal but friendly; it does not show the sternness and stubbornness others found in him. *National Portrait Gallery.*

Monroe Doctrine *noncolonization* of the Western Hemisphere by European nations, a principle that expressed American anxiety not only about Latin America but also about Russian expansion on the West Coast. Second, he demanded *nonintervention* by Europe in the affairs of independent New World nations. Finally, Monroe pledged *noninterference* by the United States in European affairs, including those of Europe's existing New World colonies.

The Monroe Doctrine proved popular at home as an anti-British, anti-European assertion of American nationalism, and it eventually became the foundation of American policy in the Western Hemisphere. Monroe's words, however, carried no force. Indeed, the policy could not have succeeded without the support of the British, who were already committed to keeping other European nations out of the New World. Europeans ignored the doctrine; it was the Royal Navy they respected, not American policy.

The Panic of 1819 and Renewed Sectionalism

Monroe's domestic achievements could not match the diplomatic successes that John Quincy Adams brought to his administration. In 1819, financial panic interrupted the postwar nationalism and confidence and stimulated sectional loyalties. Neither panic nor the resurgence of sectionalism hurt Monroe politically; without a rival political party to rally opposition, he won a second term in 1820 unopposed.

But hard times spread. The postwar expansion was built on loose money and widespread speculation. State banks extended credit and printed notes too freely, fueling a speculative

Hard Times western land boom. When expansion slowed, the manufacturing depression that had begun in 1818 deepened and prices spiraled downward. The Second Bank of the United States, in order to protect its assets, reduced loans, thus accelerating the contraction in the economy. Distressed urban workers lobbied for relief and began to take a more active role in politics. Farmers clamored for lower tariffs on manufactured goods. Hurt by a sharp decline in the price of cotton, southern planters railed at the protective Tariff of 1816, which had raised prices while their incomes were falling sharply. The Virginia Agricultural Society of Fredericksburg, for example, argued that the tariff violated the very principles on which the nation had been founded. In a protest to Congress in January 1820, the society called the tariff an unequal tax that awarded exclusive privileges to "oppressive monopolies, which are ultimately to grind both us and our children after us 'into dust and ashes.'" Manufacturers, on the other hand, demanded greater tariff protection—and eventually got it in the Tariff of 1824.

Western farmers suffered too. Those who had purchased public land on credit could not repay their loans. To avoid mass bankruptcy, Congress delayed payment of the money, and western state legislatures passed "stay laws" restricting mortgage foreclosures. Many westerners blamed the panic on the Second Bank of the United States for tightening the money supply. Many state banks, in debt to the national bank, folded, and westerners bitterly accused the bank of saving itself while the nation went to ruin. Although the economy recovered in the mid-1820s, resentment against the bank contributed to the rise of the Jacksonian movement (see pages 353–357).

Even more divisive was the question of slavery. Ever since the drafting of the Constitution, most political leaders had avoided the issue. The one

Slavery Question exception was the 1807 act closing the foreign slave trade after January 1, 1808, which passed without much opposition. Those for and those against slavery took it for granted that once the constitutional ban (Article I, Section 9) on closing the slave trade expired in 1808, Congress would act. In February 1819, however, slavery finally crept onto the political agenda when Missouri residents petitioned Congress for admission to the Union as a slave state. For the next two-and-a-half years the issue dominated all congressional action. "This momentous question," Thomas Jefferson wrote, fearful for the life of the Union, "like a fire bell in the night, awakened and filled me with terror."

The debate transcended slavery in Missouri. At stake was the undoing of the compromises that had kept the issue quarantined since the Constitutional Convention. Five new states had joined the Union since 1812—Louisiana (1812), Indiana (1816), Mississippi (1817), Illinois (1818), and Alabama (1819)—and of these, Louisiana, Mississippi, and Alabama were slave states. Missouri was on the same latitude as free Illinois, Indiana, and Ohio (a state since 1803), and its admission as a slave state would thus thrust slavery farther northward. It would also tilt the political balance in the Senate toward the states committed to slavery. In 1819 the Union consisted of an uneasy balance of eleven slave and eleven free states. If Missouri entered as a slave state, the slave states would have a two-vote edge in the Senate.

What made the issue so deeply felt was not the politics of admission to statehood but the debates over the morality of slavery and white people's emotional attitudes toward slavery. The settlers of Missouri, mostly Kentuckians and Tennesseeans, had grown up with slavery. But in the North, slavery was slowly dying out, and many northerners had come to the conclusion that it was evil. During the Second Great Awakening, there arose a ground-

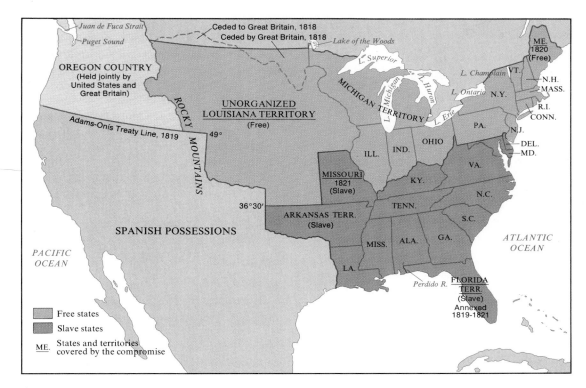

The Missouri Compromise and the State of the Union, 1820

swell for reform, including abolition, especially among women (see Chapter 12). Thus when Representative James Tallmadge, Jr., of New York introduced an amendment providing for gradual emancipation in Missouri, it led to passionate and sometimes violent debate over moral and political concerns. The House, which had a northern majority, passed the Tallmadge amendment, but the Senate rejected it. The two sides were deadlocked.

A compromise emerged in 1820 under pressure from House Speaker Henry Clay: the admission of free Maine, carved out of Massachusetts, was linked with that of slave Missouri. In the

▶ **Missouri Compromise** rest of the Louisiana Territory north of 36°30′ (Missouri's southern boundary), slavery was prohibited forever (see map). The compromise carried, but the agreement almost came apart in November when Missouri submitted a constitution that barred free blacks from settling in the state. Opponents contended that the proposed state constitution violated the federal Constitution's provision that "the citizens of each State shall be entitled

to all privileges and immunities of citizens in the several States." Advocates argued that restrictions on free blacks were common in state law in both North and South. In 1821, Clay produced a second compromise: Missouri guaranteed that none of its laws would discriminate against citizens of other states. (Once admitted to the Union, however, Missouri twice adopted laws banning free blacks.)

Although political leaders had successfully removed slavery from the congressional agenda, sectional issues undermined Republican unity and ended the reign of the Virginia dynasty. The Republican party would come apart in 1824 as presidential candidates from different sections of the country scrambled for caucus support (see pages 353–354).

Sectionalism and the question of slavery would ultimately threaten the Union itself. Still, the first decades of the nineteenth century were a time of nationalism and growth for the young republic. Political parties increased white, male involvement in government and channeled and limited partisan divisions, and a tradition of peaceful transition of

ENUMERATION OF THE INHABITANTS OF THE STATE OF MISSOURI.

COUNTIES	Free males	Free females	Free persons of color	Slaves	Persons bound to service for a term of years	Total	Memorandums
Boone,	1679	1456	1	576		3693	3
Cooper,	1612	1419	12	440		3483	3
Callaway,	712	642		443		1797	1
Cole	532	444		52		1028	1
Chariton,	583	541	7	290	5	1416	1
Cape Girardeau	3526	3200	44	1082		7852	6
Franklin	880	853	9	186		1928	2
Gasconade	650	463	1	60		1174	1
Howard	3219	2690	2	1400	3	7321	5
Jefferson	875	749	4	200	1	1833	2
Lincoln	823	636	2	211	2	1674	1
Lillard	695	515		180		1540	1
Montgomery	928	802		502		2032	2
Madison	858	715	7	344	3	1907	1
New madrid	1155	972	7	310		2444	2
Pike	1286	1014	2	405		2677	2
Perry	740	623	1	929	6	1592	1
Ralls	749	581	1	358	2	1694	1
Ray	912	730	2	141	2	1732	2*
St. Louis	3564	2858	141	1608	24	8190	3
St. Charles	1856	1453	11	733	5	4055	3
St. Genevieve	1317	1081	62	717	4	3181	2
Saline	519	476	2	128	1	1126	1
Washington	1816	1362	2	560		3740	3
Wayne	720	645		246	2	1614	1
	32129	26003	321	11224	60	70647	54

*County divided.   County of St. Francois   1

55

With the Missouri Compromise of 1820, Missouri and Maine joined the Union as slave and free states respectively. The first census of the new state (1821) enumerated the large slave population and the small number of free blacks whom many Missourians wished to bar from settlement. *Library of Congress.*

power through presidential elections was established. A second war with Britain—the War of 1812—had to be fought to reaffirm American independence and to thwart Indian opposition to United States expansion; thereafter the nation was able to settle many disputes at the bargaining table.

The foreign policy problems confronting the infant republic from the turn of the century through the mid-1820s strikingly resemble those faced today by the newly established nations of the Third World. Mother countries often treat their former colonies as if they had not won their independence. Like Third World nations today, the young United States steered clear of alliances with the great powers, preferring neutrality and unilateralism. The War of 1812 and diplomatic assertiveness brought a sense of national security and confidence.

After the war, all branches of the government, responding to the popular mood, pursued a vigorous national policy. The Supreme Court further advanced national unity by extending federal power over the states and encouraging commerce and economic growth. In spite of Jefferson's vision of an agrarian society of independent farmers and artisans, the country was gradually changing to a market economy in which people produced goods not just for their own use but to sell to others (see Chapter 9). Disruption of trade during the war had promoted the manufacturing of goods in the United States, instead of dependence on imports from Europe. Developments in transportation further stimulated the economy, and old cities expanded in the market-oriented North as new ones sprouted up in the West on trade and transportation routes.

Along with nationalism and geographic expansion came the problem of sectionalism. While the manufacturers and commercial interests in the North were becoming increasingly connected with the agricultural producers in the West through transportation and trade, the South was developing its own economy and culture based on cotton crops, export markets, a plantation system, and slavery (see Chapter 10). Politicians kept the question of slavery off the national agenda as long as possible and worked out the Missouri Compromise as a stopgap measure. But new land acquisitions and further westward expansion in the 1840s and 1850s combined with a rising tide of reform and made the question of slavery unavoidable (see Chapters 12 and 13).

Suggestions for Further Reading

General

Henry Adams, *History of the United States of America During the Administration of Thomas Jefferson and of James Madison,* 9 vols. (1889–1891); George Dangerfield, *The Awakening of American Nationalism, 1815–1828* (1965); George Dangerfield, *The Era of Good Feelings* (1952); John Mayfield, *The New Nation, 1800–1845* (1981); Glover Moore, *The Missouri Compromise, 1819–1821* (1953); Murray N. Rothbard, *The Panic of 1819* (1962); Marshall Smelser, *The Democratic Republic, 1801–1815* (1968).

Party Politics

Joyce Appleby, *Capitalism and a New Social Order: The Republican Vision of the 1790s* (1984); James M. Banner, *To the Hartford Convention: The Federalists and the Origins of Party Politics in the Early Republic, 1789–1815* (1967); James Broussard, *The Southern Federalists, 1800–1816* (1978); Noble E. Cunningham, Jr., *The Jeffersonian Republicans in Power: Party Operations, 1801–1809* (1963); David Hackett Fischer, *The Revolution of American Conservatism: The Federalist Party in the Era of Jeffersonian Democracy* (1965); Linda K. Kerber, *Federalists in Dissent* (1970); Shaw Livermore, *Twilight of Federalism: The Disintegration of the Federalist Party, 1815–1830* (1962); Milton Lomask, *Aaron Burr,* 2 vols. (1979, 1983); Richard P. McCormick, *The Presidential Game: The Origins of American Presidential Politics* (1982); Drew McCoy, *The Elusive Republic* (1980); James Sterling Young, *The Washington Community, 1800–1828* (1966).

The Virginia Presidents

Harry Ammon, *James Monroe: The Quest for National Identity* (1971); Irving Brant, *James Madison,* 6 vols. (1941–1961); Noble E. Cunningham, Jr., *In Pursuit of Reason: The Life of Thomas Jefferson* (1987); Noble E. Cunningham, Jr., *The Process of Government Under Jefferson* (1978); Ralph Ketcham, *Presidents Above Party: The First American Presidency, 1789–1829* (1984); Forrest McDonald, *The Presidency of Thomas Jefferson* (1976); Dumas Malone, *Jefferson and His Time,* 6 vols. (1948–1981); Merrill D. Peterson, *Thomas Jefferson and the New Nation* (1970); Merrill D. Peterson, *The Jefferson Image in the American Mind* (1960); Robert Allen Rutland, *James Madison: The Founding Father* (1987).

The Supreme Court and the Law

Leonard Baker, *John Marshall: A Life in Law* (1974); Albert Beveridge, *The Life of John Marshall,* 4 vols. (1916–1919); Richard E. Ellis, *The Jeffersonian Crisis: Courts and Politics in the Young Republic* (1971); Charles G. Haines, *The Role of the Supreme Court in American Government and Politics, 1789–1835* (1944); Morton J. Horowitz, *The Transformation of American Law, 1780–1860* (1977); R. Kent Newmyer, *The Supreme Court Under Marshall and Taney* (1968); Francis N. Stites, *John Marshall: Defender of the Constitution* (1981).

Expansion and the War of 1812

Roger H. Brown, *The Republic in Peril: 1812* (1964); A. L. Burt, *The United States, Great Britain, and British North America* (1940); Harry L. Coles, *The War of 1812* (1965); Alexander De Conde, *This Affair of Louisiana* (1976); R. David Edmunds, *Tecumseh and the Quest for Indian Leadership* (1984); R. David Edmunds, *The Shawnee Prophet* (1983); Clifford L. Egan, *Neither Peace nor War: Franco-American Relations, 1803–1812* (1983); Reginald Horsman, *The War of 1812* (1969); Donald Jackson, ed., *Letters of the Lewis and Clark Expedition with Related Documents, 1783–1854* (1962); Bradford Perkins, *Prologue to War: England and the United States, 1805–1812* (1961); Julius W. Pratt, *Expansionists of 1812* (1925); James P. Ronda, *Lewis and Clark Among the Indians* (1984); J. C. A. Stagg, *Mr. Madison's War: Politics, Diplomacy, and Warfare in the Early Republic, 1783–1830* (1983).

The Monroe Doctrine

Samuel F. Bemis, *John Quincy Adams and the Foundations of American Foreign Policy* (1949); Walter LaFeber, ed., *John Quincy Adams and American Continental Empire* (1965); Ernest R. May, *The Making of the Monroe Doctrine* (1976); Dexter Perkins, *Hands Off: A History of the Monroe Doctrine* (1941); Dexter Perkins, *The Monroe Doctrine, 1823–1826* (1927).

John Jervis suffered from canal and railroad fever nearly all his life. He first contracted the disease in 1817, when at age twenty-two he left his father's upstate New York farm to clear a cedar swamp for the Erie Canal. Like the other laborers, as well as the men directing the project, Jervis had no experience in canal construction. Indeed, he had never built anything according to a plan or diagram.

Together the directors and workers learned enough on the job to construct 363 well-engineered miles of canal. Jervis's education began his first day. Although he was an expert axeman, he had never downed a line of trees along an exact path; now he learned to hew with precision. Jervis learned new skills each year, advancing from axeman to surveyor to engineer to superintendent of a division. He was the most famous engineer to receive his training from the Erie Canal "School of Engineering."

When the Erie Canal was completed in 1825, Jervis signed on as second-in-command of the Delaware and Hudson Canal project. To reduce costs, he substituted a railroad line for the last seventeen miles of the canal. Since there was not a single locomotive in the United States in 1828, Jervis had one sent from England. The engine that was delivered, however, was heavier than the one he had ordered, and it crushed the hemlock rails.

Undaunted, the self-trained engineer left the Delaware canal company to supervise construction of another early rail experiment, the Mohawk and Hudson Railroad from Albany to Schenectady. In building the railroad, Jervis redesigned the locomotive's wheel assembly, and his design became standard throughout America.

Jervis spent the next two decades building the 98-mile Chenango Canal and the freshwater system for New York City—consisting of the Croton Reservoir, a 33-mile aqueduct, and pumps. Later he helped build other railroads, including the Michigan Southern, the Rock Island, and the Nickel Plate. In 1864, at age sixty-nine, Jervis returned home to Rome, New York, and organized an iron mill. He had spent his life constructing the mechanisms—canals and railroads—that would change America and connect its far-flung regions.

9

RAILS, MARKETS, AND MILLS: THE NORTH AND WEST, 1800–1860

John Jervis's life bridged the old and the new. His roots lay in the rural farm country typical of the United States at the beginning of the nineteenth century. Born at Huntington, Long Island, in 1795, he was taken to western New York in 1798 by his carpenter father, who moved to the frontier to farm. John learned to read and write during occasional attendance at common school. His father taught him to farm and handle an axe. In 1817 he acquired skills not used on the farm: the ability to follow and create construction plans, to calculate weight stresses, and to work precisely in tandem with others. A religious man, he extolled the pioneer virtues of hard work and independence, and he prided himself on his rise from farm boy to world-class engineer. Yet by the time of his death in 1885, engineering leadership had passed to the university-trained.

The canals and railroads that John Jervis and others built were the most visible signs of economic development and the best-known links in the growing national economy from 1800 through 1860. The canal boat, the steamboat, the locomotive, and the telegraph helped to open up the frontier and to expand farm production for markets at home and abroad. They made it possible for New England mill girls to turn slave-produced southern cotton into factory-made cloth that was purchased by women from New York to San Francisco and in thousands of smaller towns across America. And they made it possible for ready-made men's garments, manufactured in New York and Cincinnati, to be purchased everywhere. Increasingly, farmers grew more for market and urban producers worked for wages. Thus, if transportation was the most visible change, less tangible but equally significant was the increased specialization in agriculture, manufacturing, and finance that fostered a national, capitalist market-oriented economy.

The dramatic transformation of the United States in the nineteenth century began in the first decades of the century and spread nearly everywhere. In 1800 most of the 5.3 million Americans earned a living working the land or serving those who did. Except in Kentucky and Tennessee, settlement had not stretched far to the west. By 1860, 31.4 million Americans had spread across the continent; in the Midwest some farms were 1,500 miles from the Atlantic; and on the Pacific Slope, settlement boomed. A continental nation had been forged. Though still primarily agricultural, the economy was being transformed by an enormous commercial and industrial expansion.

Promotion of economic growth became the hallmark of government, especially in the nationalist mood after the War of 1812. Government sought to encourage individual freedom and choice by promoting an environment in which farming and industry could flourish. New financial institutions amassed the capital for large-scale enterprises like factories and railroads. Mechanization took root; factories and precision-made machinery successfully competed with home workshops and handmade goods, while reapers and sowers revolutionized farming.

New problems and tensions accompanied the rewards of economic expansion. Not everyone profited, as John Jervis did, in wealth and opportunity. The journeyman tailor who was replaced by new retailers and cheaper labor had a far different experience from the new merchant princes. New England farm daughters found their world changing no less radically as many became wage workers. Farmers everywhere experienced the tensions between farming as a traditional way of life and the opportunities and demands of market-oriented production. Moreover, the cycles of boom and bust became part of the fabric of ordinary life. Whatever the benefits and drawbacks, however, economic development and change were irreversible.

Transportation and Regionalization

From 1800 through 1860 the North, South, and West followed distinctly different economic paths. Everywhere agriculture remained the foundation of the American economy. Nevertheless, industry, commerce, and finance came to characterize the North, plantations and subsistence farms the South, and commercialized family farms, agricultural processing, and implement manufacturing the West. This tendency toward regional specialization made the sections at once more different and more dependent on each other. All looked to transportation to link the nation.

The revolution in transportation and communications was probably the single most important

1807	Fulton's steamboat, *Clermont*
1812–15	War of 1812
1813	Boston Manufacturing Company founded
1818	National Road reaches Wheeling, Virginia
1819	*Dartmouth College* v. *Woodward*
1819–23	Hard times
1820s	New England textile mills expand
1824	*Gibbons* v. *Ogden*
1825	Erie Canal completed
1830	Baltimore and Ohio Railroad begins operation
1831	McCormick invents the reaper
1834	Mill women strike at Lowell
1837	*Charles River Bridge* v. *Warren Bridge*
1839–43	Hard times
1844	Baltimore-Washington telegraph line
1848	Regularly scheduled steamship passage between Liverpool and New York City
1849	California gold rush
1853	British study of American system of manufacturing
1854	Railroad reaches the Mississippi
1857	Hard times

cause of these changes. The North's heavy investment in canals and railroads made it the center of American commerce; its growing seaboard cities distributed western produce and New England textiles. New York financial and commercial houses linked the southern cotton-exporting economy to the North and Europe. The South, with most of its capital invested in slave labor, built fewer canals, railroads, and factories and remained mostly rural and undeveloped (see Chapter 10).

Before the canal fever of the 1820s and 1830s and the railroad fever of the 1830s and after became epidemic, it was by no means certain that New England and the Middle Atlantic states would dominate American economic life. Indeed, the natural orientation of the 1800 frontier—Tennessee, Kentucky, and Ohio—was to the South. The southward-flowing Ohio and Mississippi rivers were the life lines of early western settlement. Flatboats transported western grain and hogs southward for consumption or transfer to ocean-going vessels at New Orleans. Southern products—first tobacco, then lumber and cotton—flowed directly

> **Change in Trade Routes**

to Europe. The steamboat, successfully introduced in 1807 when Robert Fulton's *Clermont* paddled up the Hudson River from New York City, soon plied western rivers. In 1815 the *Enterprise* first carried cargo upstream on the Mississippi and Ohio rivers, further strengthening southern and western ties.

But the pattern changed in the 1820s. New arteries opened up east-west travel. The National Road, a stone-based, gravel-topped highway beginning in Cumberland, Maryland, reached Wheeling (then in Virginia) in 1818 and Columbus, Ohio, in 1833. (In the twentieth century, U.S. 40 and I-70 would follow that route.) More important, the Erie Canal, completed in 1825, forged an east-west axis from the Hudson River to Lake Erie, linking the Great Lakes with New York City and the Atlantic Ocean. The canal carried easterners and then immigrants to settle the Old Northwest and the frontier beyond; in the opposite direction, it bore western grain to the large and growing eastern markets. Railroads and later the telegraph would solidify these east-west links. By contrast, only at one place—Bowling Green, Kentucky—did a northern railroad connect with a southern one. Al-

Watercolor view of the Erie Canal by John William Hill, 1829. The 363-mile-long Erie Canal linked the Great Lakes with New York City and the Atlantic Ocean. Its completion in 1825 opened up the Midwest for settlement and brought western grain and dairy products to eastern and world-wide markets. *Print Collection, Miriam and Ira D. Wallach Division of Art, Prints, and Photographs, The New York Public Library, Astor, Lenox, and Tilden Foundations.*

though trade still continued southward along the Ohio and Mississippi rivers, the bulk of western trade flowed eastward by 1850. Thus, by the eve of the Civil War, the northern and Middle Atlantic states were closely tied to the former frontier of the Old Northwest.

Construction of the 363-mile-long Erie Canal was a visionary enterprise. When the state of New York authorized it in 1817, the longest existing American canal was only 28 miles long.

▶ **Canals** Vigorously promoted by Governor De Witt Clinton, the Erie cost $7 million, much of it raised by loans from British investors. The canal shortened the journey between Buffalo and New York City from twenty to six days and reduced freight charges from $100 to $5 a ton. By 1835, traffic was so heavy that the canal had to be widened from forty to seventy feet and deepened from four to seven feet. Skeptics who had called the canal "Clinton's big ditch" had long since been silenced by the success of the enterprise.

The Erie Canal triggered an explosion of canal building. Other states and cities, sensing the advantage New York had gained, rushed to follow suit. By 1840, canals crisscrossed the Northeast and Midwest, and canal mileage in the United States reached 3,300—an increase of more than 2,000 miles in a single decade. Unfortunately for investors, none of these canals enjoyed the financial success achieved by the Erie. The high cost of construction and economic contraction after 1837 lowered profitability. As a result, investment in canals began to slump in the 1830s. By 1850 more miles were being abandoned than built, and the canal era had ended.

Meanwhile, railroad construction boomed, and visionaries like John Jervis left canals for railroads. The railroad era in the United States began in 1830 when Peter Cooper's locomotive

▶ **Railroads** Tom Thumb first steamed along 13 miles of track constructed by the Baltimore and Ohio Railroad. In 1833 a second

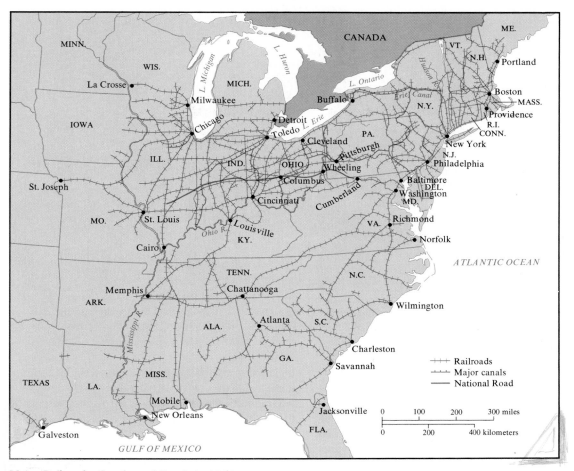

Major Railroads, Canals, and Roads in 1860

railroad ran 136 miles from Charleston to Hamburg, South Carolina. By 1850 the United States had nearly 9,000 miles of railroad; by 1860, roughly 31,000 (see map). Canal fever stimulated this early railroad construction. Promoters of the Baltimore and Ohio believed that railroads would compete successfully with canals. Similarly, the line between Boston and Worcester, Massachusetts, was intended as the first link in a line to Albany, at the eastern end of the Erie Canal.

Visitors thought that the country had gone railroad crazy. Before French traveler Chevalier de Gerstier sailed from Europe in 1837, he saw his first American newspaper: *The Railroad Journal.* On board ship he recalled only conversations about the railroad. In New York he saw a "Marine Railroad" for hauling ships in drydock; in Pennsylvania he saw railroads in mines; and after he visited a

Philadelphia prison, the overseer said, "But you have not seen my Railroad." Indeed, if we can believe the Chevalier, he scarcely saw anything else but railroads.

The earliest railroads connected two cities or one city and its surrounding area. Not until the 1850s did railroads offer long-distance service at reasonable rates. The early lines had technical problems to overcome. As John Jervis had discovered, locomotives heavy enough to climb steep grades and pull long trains required strong rails and resilient roadbeds. Engineers met those needs by replacing wooden track with iron rails and by supporting the rails with ties embedded in gravel. John Jervis's wheel alignment—called the swivel truck—removed another major obstacle by enabling engines to hold the track on sharp curves. Other problems persisted: the use of hand brakes

In Providence, Rhode Island, locomotives replaced horses in transporting freight and people. In Atlantic ports the rail lines extended to the water's edge to meet the steamers and sailing ships. *Museum of Art, Rhode Island School of Design.*

severely restricted speed, and the lack of a standard gauge for the width of track thwarted development of a national system. Pennsylvania and Ohio railroads, for instance, had no fewer than seven different track widths. A journey from Philadelphia to Charleston, South Carolina, involved eight changes in gauge.

In the 1850s technological improvements, competition, economic recovery, and a desire for national unity prompted the development of regional and, eventually, national rail networks. By 1853 rail lines linked New York to Chicago, and a year later track had reached the Mississippi River. In 1860 the rails stretched as far west as St. Joseph, Missouri—the edge of the frontier. In 1853 seven short lines combined to form the New York Central system, and the Pennsylvania Railroad was unified from Philadelphia to Pittsburgh. Most lines, however, were still independently run, separated by gauge, scheduling, differences in car design, and a commitment to serve their home towns first and foremost.

Railroads did not completely replace water transportation. By midcentury steamships still carried bulk cargo more cheaply than railroads except during freezing weather. The sealike Great Lakes permitted the construction of giant ships with propellers in place of paddle wheels; these leviathans carried heavy bulk cargoes like lumber, grain, and ore.

Gradually steamships replaced sailing vessels on the high seas. In days gone by, sailing ships—whalers, sleek clippers, and square-rigged packets—had been the pride of American commerce. But sailing ships were dependent on prevailing winds and thus could not easily schedule regular crossings. In 1818 steam-powered packets made four round trips a year between New York and Liverpool, sailing on schedule rather than waiting for a full cargo as ships had done before then. The breakthrough came in 1848, though, when Samuel Cunard introduced regularly scheduled steamships to the Atlantic run between Liverpool and New York, reducing travel time from twenty-five days eastbound and forty-nine days westbound to between ten and fourteen days each way. Sailing ships quickly lost first-class passengers and light cargo to these swift steamships. Over the next decade sailing ships continued to carry immigrants and bulk cargo, but by 1860 only the freight trade remained to them.

By far the fastest-spreading technological advance of the era was the magnetic telegraph. Samuel F. B. Morse's invention freed long-distance messages from the restraint of traveling no faster

> **Steamboats**

> **Telegraph** than the messenger; instantaneous communication became possible even over long distances. By 1853, only nine years after construction of the first experimental line, 23,000 miles of telegraph wire spread across the United States; by 1860, 50,000. In 1861 the telegraph bridged the continent, connecting the east and west coasts. The new invention revolutionized news gathering, provided advance information for railroads and steamships, and altered patterns of business and finance. Rarely has innovation had so great an impact so quickly.

The changes in transportation and communications from 1800 to 1860 were revolutionary. Railroads reduced the time of travel, were cheap to build over difficult terrain, and remained in use all year, unlike water transport, which was frozen out in winter. But time was the key. In 1800 it took four days to travel by coach from New York City to Baltimore and nearly four weeks to reach Detroit. By 1830 Baltimore was only a day-and-a-half away, and Detroit, via the Erie Canal, was only a two-week journey. By 1857 Detroit was but an overnight train ride from New York City; in a week one could reach Texas, Kansas, or Nebraska. The reduction in travel time saved money and facilitated commerce. During the first two decades of the century, wagon transportation cost 30 to 70 cents per ton per mile. By 1860, railroads in New York State carried freight at an average charge of 2.2 cents per ton per mile; wheat moved from Chicago to New York for 1.2 cents per ton-mile. In sum, the transportation revolution had transformed the economy.

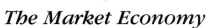

The Market Economy

Prior to the transportation revolution, most farmers in the early nineteenth century had geared production to family needs. They lived in interdependent communities and kept detailed account books of labor and goods exchanged with neighbors. Farm families tended to produce much of what they needed—foodstuffs, clothing, candles, soap, and the like—but they traded agricultural surpluses for or purchased items they could not produce, such as cooking pots, horseshoes, coffee, tea, and white sugar. On most such farms, men selling cordwood and women selling eggs, butter, cheese, and poultry produced the family's only cash. By the Civil War, however, the United States had an industrializing economy in which an increasing number of men and women worked for wages and in which most people outside the South—farmers and workers alike—increasingly purchased store-bought goods produced in workshops and factories.

In the market economy, men and women grew crops and produced goods for sale in the marketplace, at home or abroad. The money received in
> **Definition of a Market Economy** market transactions, whether from the sale of goods or of a person's labor, purchased items produced by other people—such as candles and soap no longer made at home. Such a system encouraged specialization. Formerly self-sufficient farmers began to grow just one or two crops or to concentrate on raising only cows, pigs, or sheep for market. Farm women gave up spinning and weaving at home and purchased fabric produced by wage-earning farm girls in Massachusetts textile mills.

The United States experienced enormous economic growth. Improvements in transportation and technology, the division of labor, and new methods of financing, all fueled expansion of the economy—that is, the multiplication of goods and services. In turn, this growth prompted new improvements. The effect was cumulative; by the 1840s the economy was growing more rapidly than in the previous four decades. Per capita income doubled between 1800 and 1860 while the price of manufactured goods and food fell between 1809 and 1860. An expanding economy provided greater opportunities for wage labor.

Despite the great economic change and growth, the pace was uneven. Prosperity reigned during two long periods, from 1823 to 1835 and from 1843
> **Boom-and-Bust Cycles** to 1857. But there were long stretches of economic contraction as well. During the time from Jefferson's 1807 embargo through the War of 1812, the interruption in trade contributed to a negative growth rate—that is, fewer goods and services were produced. Contraction and deflation occurred again during the hard times of 1819 through 1823, 1839 through 1843, and 1857. These periods were characterized by the collapse of banks, business bankruptcies, and a decline in wages and prices. Workers faced increasing insecurity as a result of these boom-and-bust cycles; on

the down side, they suffered not only lower incomes but also unemployment.

Working people in 1819, a Baltimore physician noted, felt hard times "a thousand fold more than the merchants." Yet even during good times wage earners could not build up sufficient financial reserves to get them through the next hard times; often they could not make it through the winter without drawing on charity for food, clothing, and firewood. In the 1820s and 1830s, free laborers in Baltimore found steady work from March through October and unemployment and hunger from November through February.

If good times were hard on workers and their families, hard times devastated them. In 1839 in Baltimore, small manufacturers for the local market closed their doors; tailors, shoemakers, milliners, and shipyard and construction workers lost their jobs. Ninety miles to the north, Philadelphia took on an eerie aura. "The streets seemed deserted," Sidney George Fisher observed in 1842; "the largest [merchant] houses are shut up and to rent, there is no business . . . no money, no confidence." Only auctions boomed, as the sheriff sold off seized property at a quarter of predepression prices. Elsewhere in the city, soup societies fed the hungry. In New York, bread lines and beggars crowded the sidewalks. In smaller cities like Lynn, Massachusetts, the poor who did not leave became scavengers, digging for clams and harvesting dandelions.

In 1857 hard times struck again. The Mercantile Agency—the forerunner of Dun and Bradstreet—recorded 5,123 bankruptcies in 1857—nearly double the number in the previous year. The bankrupt firms had a total debt of $300 million, only half of which would be paid off. Contemporary reports estimated 20,000 to 30,000 unemployed in Philadelphia, and 30,000 to 40,000 in New York City. Female benevolent societies expanded their soup kitchens and distributed free firewood to the needy. In Chicago, charities reorganized to meet the needs of the poor; in New York, the city hired the unemployed to fix streets and develop Central Park. And in Fall River, Massachusetts, a citizens' committee disbursed public funds on a weekly basis to nine hundred families. The soup kitchen, the bread line, and public aid had become fixtures in urban America.

What caused the cycles of boom and bust that brought about such suffering? In general, they were a direct result of the new market economy. Prosperity stimulated greater demand for staples and finished goods. Increased demand led in turn to higher prices and still higher production, to speculation in land, and to the flow of foreign currency into the country. Eventually production surpassed demand, leading to lower prices and wages; and speculation inflated land and stock values. The inflow of foreign money led first to easy credit and then to collapse when unhappy investors withdrew their funds.

> **Cause of Boom-and-Bust Cycles**

Some early economists considered this process beneficial—a self-adjusting cycle in which unprofitable economic ventures were eliminated. In theory, people concentrated on the activities they did best, and the economy as a whole became more efficient. Advocates of the system argued also that it furthered individual freedom, since ideally each seller, whether of goods or labor, was free to determine the conditions of the sale. But in fact the system put workers on a perpetual roller coaster; they became dependent on wages—and the availability of jobs—for their very existence.

People experienced the market economy in different ways. Many women found their lives altered. In traditional agriculture, women contributed to the family farm as unpaid labor. Increasingly in the nineteenth century, however, farm women contributed money to the family. They added the selling of eggs, butter, cheese, and poultry to their unpaid domestic work and unpaid production of cloth, clothing, and dairy products for family use. In New England and the Middle Atlantic states farm women did industrial work at home, weaving cloth and sewing shoes for contractors who paid them for each piece finished. Many New England daughters left home to work in textile mills. By midcentury the earnings of many women not only supplemented family income but also maintained the women and their families.

Many people felt a distinct loss of status in the market economy. For Joseph T. Buckingham, foreman of the Boston printing shop of West and Richardson, wage labor represented failure. Buckingham had been a master printer, running the shop of Thomas and Andrews on commission and doing some publishing of his own. In 1814 he purchased the shop but did not get enough work to pay his debts. Without the capital to sustain his losses or to compete with larger shops, Buckingham had to sell his presses at auction. He became a wage earner, albeit a foreman. Although his wages were about the equal of an ordinary printer's income, Buckingham was unhappy. In his own words, he was "nothing more than a journeyman, except in responsibility."

Government Promotes Economic Growth

The eighteenth-century political ideas that had captured the imagination of the Revolutionary War generation and found expression in the ideal of republican virtue were paralleled in economic thought by the writings of Adam Smith, a Scottish political economist. Smith's *The Wealth of Nations* first appeared in 1776, the year of the Declaration of Independence. Both works emphasized individual liberty, one economic, the other political. Both were reactions against forceful government: Jefferson attacked monarchy and distant government; Smith attacked mercantilism (government regulation of the economy to benefit the state; see page 64). They believed that virtue was lodged in individual freedom and that the entire community would benefit most from individuals pursuing their own self-interest. As president, Jefferson put these political and economic beliefs into action by reducing the role of government.

Jefferson, influenced by the economic and egalitarian ideas of republicanism (see pages 160–161), recognized that government was nonetheless a necessary instrument in promoting individual freedom. Freedom, he believed, thrived where individuals had room for independence, creativity, and choices; individuals fettered by government, monopoly, or economic dependence could not be free. Committed to the idea that a republican democracy would flourish best in a nation of independent farmers and artisans and in an atmosphere of widespread political participation, Jefferson worked to realize those ideals. Beginning with the purchase of Louisiana in 1803, Republican policy, no less than that of the Federalists, turned to using the federal government to promote economic growth. Belief in limited government was not an end in itself, but only a means to greater individual freedom. The result was faith in a market economy in which government also played an active role.

Once Louisiana had been acquired, the federal government facilitated economic growth and geographic expansion by encouraging westward exploration and settlement and by promoting agriculture. The Lewis and Clark expedition from 1804 to 1806 (see page 219) was the beginning of a continuing federal interest in geographic and geologic surveying and the first step in the opening of western lands to exploitation and settlement.

New steps followed quickly. In 1817 and 1818 Henry Rowe Schoolcraft explored the Missouri and Arkansas region, reporting on its geologic features and mineral resources. In 1819 and 1820 Major Stephen Long explored the Great Plains, mapping the area between the Platte and Canadian rivers. Between 1827 and 1840 the government surveyed about fifty railroad routes. The final door to western settlement was opened in 1843 and 1844 by John C. Frémont's expedition, which followed the Oregon Trail to the Pacific, then traveled south to California and returned east by way of the Great Salt Lake. Frémont, later a California senator and in 1856 the first Republican presidential candidate, gained fame as a soldier-surveyor of the West. His report of his journey dispelled a long-standing myth that the center of the continent was a desert.

To encourage western agriculture, the federal government offered public lands for sale at reasonable prices (see page 271) and evicted Indian tribes from their traditional lands (see Chapter 11). And because transportation was crucial to the development of the frontier, the government first financed roads and then canals and later subsidized railroad construction through land grants. Even the State Department aided agriculture: its consular offices overseas collected horticultural information, seeds, and cuttings and published technical reports in an effort to improve American farming.

The federal government played a key role in technological and industrial growth. Federal arsenals pioneered new manufacturing techniques and helped to develop the machine-tool industry. The United States Military Academy at West Point, founded in 1802, emphasized technical and scientific subjects in its curriculum. The U.S. Post Office stimulated interregional trade and played a brief

The Marshall Court enouraged business competition by ending the state-licensed monopolies on inland waterways. *Gibbons* v. *Ogden* (1824) opened up the New York–New Jersey trade to new lines, and within a short time dozens of steamboats ferried passengers and freight across the Hudson River. *The New-York Historical Society.*

but crucial role in the development of the telegraph: the first telegraph line, from Washington to Baltimore, was constructed in 1844 under a government grant, and during 1845 the Post Office ran it, employing inventor Samuel F. B. Morse as superintendent. Finally, to create an atmosphere conducive to economic growth and individual creativity, the government protected inventions and domestic industries. Patent laws gave inventors a seventeen-year monopoly on their inventions, and tariffs protected American industry from foreign competition.

The federal judiciary validated government promotion of the economy and encouraged business enterprise. In *Gibbons* v. *Ogden* (1824), the Supreme Court overturned a New York state law that had given Robert Fulton and Robert Livingston a monopoly on the New York–New Jersey steamboat trade. Ogden, their successor, lost his monopoly when

> **Legal Foundations of Commerce**

Chief Justice John Marshall ruled that existing congressional licensing took precedence over New York's grant of monopoly rights to Fulton and Livingston. Marshall declared that Congress's power under the commerce clause of the Constitution extended to "every species of commercial intercourse," including the transportation systems. Within a year, forty-three steamboats were plying Ogden's route.

In defining interstate commerce broadly, the Marshall Court expanded federal powers over the economy while limiting the ability of states to control economic activity within their borders. Its action was consistent with its earlier decision in *Dartmouth College* v. *Woodward* (1819), which protected the sanctity of contracts against interference by the states (see page 236). "If business is to prosper," Marshall wrote, "men must have assurance that contracts will be enforced."

Federal and state courts, in conjunction with state legislatures, also encouraged the proliferation of corporations—groups of investors that could hold property and transact business as one person with limited liability for the owners. In 1800 the United States had about 300 incorporated firms; in 1817, about 2,000. By 1830 the New England states alone had issued 1,900 charters, one-third to manufacturing and mining firms. At first each firm needed a special legislative act to incorporate, but after the 1830s applications became so numerous that incorporation was authorized by general state laws. Though legislative action created corporations, the courts played a crucial role in defining their status, extending their powers, and protecting them.

A further encouragement to economic development, corporate development, and free enterprise was the Supreme Court's ruling in *Charles River Bridge* v. *Warren Bridge* (1837) that new enterprises could not be restrained by implied privileges under old charters. The case involved issues of great importance. Should a new interest be able to compete against existing, older privileges, and should the state protect existing privilege or encourage innovation and the growth of commerce through competition?

In 1785 the Massachusetts legislature chartered the Charles River Bridge Company and in 1791 extended its charter to a seventy-year term. In return for assuming the risk of building the bridge between Charlestown and Boston, the owners received the privilege of collecting tolls. In 1828 the legislature chartered another company to build the Warren Bridge across the Charles, with the right to collect tolls for six years, after which the bridge would be turned over to the state and be toll-free. With the terminus of the new span only ninety yards away from its own bridge, the Charles River Bridge Company sued in 1829, claiming that the new bridge breached the earlier charter and contradicted the principles in *Dartmouth College* v. *Woodward*. Roger Taney, Marshall's successor as chief justice, speaking for the Court majority, noted that the original charter did not confer the privilege of monopoly and therefore exclusivity could not be implied. Focusing on the question of corporate privilege rather than the right of contracts, Taney ruled that charter grants should be interpreted narrowly and that ambiguities would be decided in favor of the public interest. New enterprises should not be restricted under old charters, and economic growth would best be served by narrowing the application of the *Dartmouth College* decision. Thus, the judiciary supported economic expansion and individual economic opportunity.

State governments far surpassed the federal government in promoting the economy. From 1815 through 1860, for example, 73 percent of the $135 million invested in canals was government money, mostly from the states. In the 1830s the states started to invest in rail construction. Even though the federal government played a larger role in constructing railroads than in building canals, state and local governments provided more than half of southern rail capital. State governments also invested in corporation and bank stocks, providing those institutions with much-needed capital. Pennsylvania, probably the most active of the states in promoting its economy, invested a total of $100 million in canals, railroads, banks, and manufacturing firms; its appointees sat on more than 150 corporate boards of directors.

> **State Promotion of the Economy**

States actually equaled or surpassed private enterprise in their investments. But they did more than invest in industry. By establishing bounties for agricultural prizes, they stimulated commercial agriculture, especially sheep raising and wool manufacture (see page 266). Through special acts and general incorporation laws, states regulated the nature and activities of corporations and banks. They also used their licensing capacity to regulate industry; in Georgia, for example, the grading and marketing of tobacco were regulated by the state.

From the end of the War of 1812 until 1860 the United States experienced uneven but sustained economic growth largely as a result of these government efforts. Although political controversy raged over questions of state versus federal activity—especially with regard to internal improvements and banking—all parties agreed on the general goal of economic expansion (see Chapters 8 and 12). Indeed, the major restraint on government action during these years was not philosophical but financial: both the government and the public purse were small. As the private sector grew stronger, entrepreneurs looked less to government for financial support and states played less of an investment role. In either case, government provided an atmosphere conducive to business and economic growth.

The Rise of Manufacturing and Commerce

The McCormick reaper, ridiculed in the London *Times*, looked like "a cross between a flying-machine, a wheelbarrow, and an Astly chariot." In one continuous motion, the horse-drawn reaper used a revolving drum to position the stalks before a blade; the cut grain fell onto a platform. Put to a competitive test through rain-soaked wheat, the Chicago-made reaper alone passed, to the cheers of the skeptical English spectators. The reaper, invented by Cyrus McCormick in 1831, and hundreds of other American products made their international debut at the 1851 London Crystal Palace Exhibition, the first modern world's fair. There the design and quality of American machines and wares—from familiar farm tools to such exotic devices as an ice-cream freezer and the reaper—astonished observers. American manufacturers returned home with dozens of medals, including all three prizes for piano making. Most impressive to the Europeans were three simple machines: Alfred C. Hobb's unpickable padlocks, Samuel Colt's revolvers, and Robbins and Lawrence's six rifles with completely interchangeable parts. All were machine- rather than hand-tooled, products of what the British called the American system of manufacturing.

So impressed were the British—the leading industrial nation of the time—that in 1853 they sent a parliamentary commission to study the American system. A year later a second committee, skeptical of American claims, returned to examine the firearms industry in detail. In their report, the committee described an astonishing experiment performed at the federal armory in Springfield, Massachusetts. To test the interchangeability of machine-made musket parts, the committee selected rifles made in each of the previous ten years. While the committee watched, the guns were dismantled "and the parts placed in a row of boxes, mixed up together." The Englishmen "then requested the workman, whose duty it is to 'assemble' the arms, to put them together, which he did—the Committee handing him the parts, taken at hazard—with the use of a turnscrew only, and as

quickly as though they had been English muskets, whose parts had carefully been kept separate." Britain's Enfield arsenal subsequently converted to American equipment. Within the next few years other nations followed Great Britain's lead, sending delegations across the Atlantic to bring back American machines.

The American system of manufacturing used precision machinery to produce interchangeable parts that needed no filing or fitting. In 1798, Eli Whitney promoted the idea of

> **American System of Manufacturing**

interchangeable parts when he contracted with the federal government to make ten thousand rifles in twenty-eight months. By the 1820s the U.S. Ordnance Department, through the national armories at Springfield, Massachusetts, and Harpers Ferry, Virginia, and through contracts with private firms, introduced machine-made interchangeable parts for firearms. From the arsenals the American system spread, giving birth to the machine-tool industry—the mass manufacture of specialized machines for other industries. One by-product was an explosion in consumer goods: since the time and skill involved in manufacturing had been greatly reduced, the new system permitted mass production at low cost. Waltham watches and Yale locks became household items, inexpensive yet of uniformly high quality.

Interchangeable parts and the machine-tool industry were uniquely American contributions to the industrial revolution. Both paved the way for America's swift industrialization after the Civil War. The process of industrialization began, however, in a simple and traditional way, like that of other nations. In 1800, manufacturing was relatively unimportant to the American economy. What manufacturing there was took place mostly in small workshops or homes. Journeymen and apprentices worked with and under master craftsmen; women working alone at home spun thread and wove cloth. Tailors, shoemakers, and blacksmiths made articles by hand for a specific customer.

The clothing trades illustrate well the nineteenth-century changes in manufacturing and distribution and the reliance on the market economy. The ma-

> **Clothing Trades**

chine-tool industry produced new machinery that transferred textile and clothing production from kitchens and home workshops to mills and factories. Production, which had been

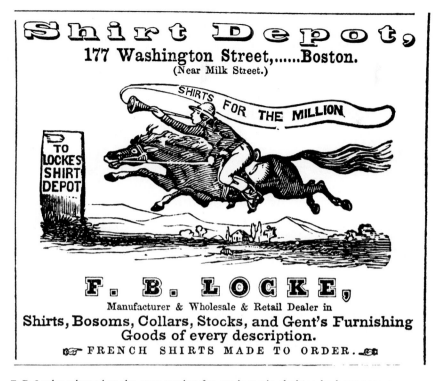

F. B. Locke adapted to the new market for ready-made clothing by becoming a manufacturer, wholesaler, and retailer of men's shirts. Though continuing to make shirts to order, the Shirt Depot's staple was mass-produced shirts, as this advertisement from the *Boston Directory, 1848–49* indicates. *Warshaw Collection of Business Americana, Smithsonian Institution.*

based on artisan shops and mostly unpaid female family labor, now depended upon workers who were paid by the piece or by the hour. The manufactured product, first cloth then cloth and finished clothing, was sold throughout the United States.

In the eighteenth century, most men had worn clothes made by their mothers, wives, or daughters, or they occasionally bought used clothing. Wealthy men had clothing made by tailors who cut and sewed unique garments to fit them. A tailor was a master craftsman whose journeymen and apprentices worked with him to produce goods made to order. By the 1820s and 1830s, clothiers and clothing manufacturers replaced most, though not all, of the old system. Typically, a journeyman cut the fabric panels in the factory, and the sewing was put out at piece rates to unskilled or semiskilled labor, often women working in their own homes. In 1832, Boston manufacturers employed 300 journeymen tailors at $2 per day and 100 boys and 1,300 women at 50 cents a day. Most of the women sewed straight seams at home. Apprentices, if used at all, were no longer learning a trade but were a permanent source of cheap labor. Women learned sewing skills within a different type of master-apprentice system; skills were passed down from mother to daughter. Previously women often had sewn an entire garment, but by the late 1850s as many as seventeen different pairs of hands were involved in making a single pair of pants.

Most of the early mass-produced clothes, crude and limited to a variety of loose-fitting sizes, were produced for men. They were purchased by men who lived in city boarding and rooming houses, away from the female kin who previously would have made their clothes. Most women made their own clothes, since nearly all girls were expected to acquire sewing skills, but women who could afford to do so employed seamstresses to make their tailored garments.

Improvements in fitting and changes in men's fashion made ready-to-wear apparel more acceptable to white-collar and professional men. The embroidered waistcoat and tailored, tight trousers competed in the 1830s and 1840s with the frock or cutaway coat. By the 1850s the short sack coat, without an indentation at the waist, replaced the more tailored coats. This forerunner of the modern suit jacket fit loosely, making hand tailoring less necessary. Now even upper-class men felt free to purchase ready-made apparel. Henry Sands Brooks opened a New York City store in 1818, and in 1855 it became Brooks Brothers, offering tailoring services and ready-made apparel to wealthy patrons—the carriage trade.

Merchants adapted to the changes in production. In the 1820s clothiers appeared with stocks of ready-made clothes. T. S. Whitmarsh of Boston advertised in 1827 that "he keeps constantly for Sale, from 5 to 10,000 Fashionable ready-made Garments." In 1830, J. T. Jacobs of New York boasted that "Gentlemen can rely upon being as well fitted from the shelves as if their measures were taken—their stock being very extensive and their sizes well assorted."

Upon entering Whitmarsh's or Jacobs's emporium, a customer found row after row of ready-made apparel without a sign of tailors or a workshop. The merchant often bought the goods wholesale, though many merchants manufactured garments in their own factories apart from the retail stores. Lewis and Hanford of New York City boasted of cutting more than 100,000 garments in the winter of 1848–1849. The New York firm sold most of its clothing in the South and owned its own retail outlet in New Orleans. A New Orleans competitor, Paul Tulane, owned a New York factory that made goods for his Louisiana store. In the West, Cincinnati became the center of the new men's clothing industry. By midcentury, Cincinnati's ready-to-wear apparel industry employed 1,500 men and 10,000 women. As in Boston, most of the women did outwork.

The rise of cotton textile mills made possible the changes in the clothing industry. First in England, then in the United States, mills processed the increasing supply of cotton grown in the slave South. At the same time, the expanding market economy, fed by the population boom, bought the manufactured cotton goods. The first American textile mill, built in Pawtucket, Rhode Island, in 1790, used water-powered spinning machines constructed from British models by the English immigrant

Samuel Slater. Slater employed women and children as cheap labor and sold thread from Maine to Maryland. Soon other mills sprang up, stimulated by the embargo on British imports from 1807 through 1815. From 1809 through 1813 alone, 151 cotton and woolen companies incorporated.

Early mills also used the "putting-out" system. Traditionally women had spun their own thread and woven it into cloth for their own families; now many women received thread from the mills and returned finished cloth. The change was subtle but significant: although the work itself was familiar, women operated their looms for piece-rate wages and produced cloth for the market, not for their own use.

Textile manufacturing was radically transformed in 1813 by the construction of the first American power loom and the chartering of the Boston Manufacturing Company. The

Waltham (Lowell) System corporation was capitalized at $400,000—ten times the amount behind the Rhode Island mills—by Francis Cabot Lowell and other Boston merchants. Its goal was to eliminate problems of timing, shipping, coordination, and quality control inherent in the putting-out system. The owners erected their factories in Waltham, Massachusetts, combining all the manufacturing processes at a single location. They also employed a resident manager to run the mill, thus separating ownership from management. The company produced cloth so inexpensively that women began to purchase rather than make their own cloth. Nonetheless, spinning and weaving remained women's work in many rural homes. Not until the end of the century would a majority of women purchase ready-made clothing (see page 560).

In the rural setting of Waltham not enough hands could be found to staff the mill, so the managers recruited New England farm daughters, accepting responsibility for their living conditions. To persuade young women to come, they offered cash wages, company-run boarding houses, and such cultural events as evening lectures—none of which was available on the farm. This paternalistic approach, called the Waltham (or Lowell) system, was adopted in other mills erected alongside New England rivers. The Hamilton Corporation (1825), the Appleton and Lowell corporations (1828), and the Suffolk, Tremont, and Lawrence firms (1831) all followed.

By 1860 a cotton mill resembled a modern factory. A majority of the mill work force by this time were immigrant Irish women who lived at home; the mills did not provide subsidized housing for them. New England farm girls continued to stay in the remaining boarding houses, but they had become few in number. Technological improvements in the looms and other machinery made the work tasks less skilled and more alike. The mills could thus pay lower wages, and because of increased immigration during the nineteenth century, mill owners always had a reservoir of unskilled labor to draw from. The factory radically altered work relationships in America.

Textile manufacturing changed New England. Lowell, the "city of spindles," symbolized early American industrialization while growing from 2,500 people in 1826 to 33,000 in 1850. The textile industry became the most important in the nation before the Civil War, employing 115,000 workers in 1860, more than half of whom were women and immigrants. The key to its success was that the machines, not the women, spun the thread and wove the cloth. The workers watched the machines and intervened to maintain smooth operation. When a thread broke, the machine stopped automatically; the worker would find the break, piece the ends together, and restart the machine. The mills used increasingly specialized machines, relying heavily on advances in the machine-tool industry. Technology enabled American firms to compete successfully with British cotton mills. Here was the American system of manufacturing applied.

Outside of New England, as in Pennsylvania's Delaware Valley, the textile industry grew more slowly, combining traditional ways with technology. In Rockdale, Pennsylvania, partnerships not corporations led the way. A decade after the Waltham mills first appeared, entrepreneurs converted paper mills to cotton manufacturing. Lacking the large sums available to the Lowell mills, they raised money from friends and relatives. The owners lived and worked in mill villages. Small factories employed families to work in the mills, and unmarried workers boarded in workers' homes. The textile workers sought to save money to buy western land, and many were successful. Growth and change occurred at a modest pace; not until the 1850s would a major manufacturing center arise in that once-rural corner of Southeastern Pennsylvania.

Textile mills were in the vanguard of industrialization, but manufacturing grew in many areas. The manufacture of woolen textiles, farm implements, machine tools, iron, glass, and finished consumer goods all became major industries. "White coal"—water power—was widely used to run the machines. In 1860, manufacturing accounted for one-third of total production and had doubled in twenty years.

To a great extent, industrialization in this period, rather than being the agent of change, flowed from changes in American life. Ever since Alexander Hamilton's *Report on Manufactures* (see page 193), national self-consciousness and pride had spurred the development of American industry. Contrary to Hamilton's hopes, however, between 1789 and 1808 more money flowed into the merchant marine than into industry. In the early republic, greater profits could be made by transporting British products to the United States than by producing the same items at home. But the embargo and the War of 1812 reversed the situation, and merchants began to shift their capital from shipping to manufacturing (see pages 225–233). It was in this new economic environment that the Waltham system took root.

Other factors also helped to stimulate industry. Population growth, especially in urban areas and the Old Northwest, created a large domestic market for finished goods (see maps, page 258). The rise of commercial agriculture brought farmers more fully into the market economy. Specialty merchants and new modes of transportation speeded up the development of these new markets. And the relative scarcity of skilled craftsmen encouraged mechanization: as more workers moved westward than entered the factories, merchants had to find ways to produce more goods with less labor. Finally, beginning with the Tariff of 1816 and culminating in the Tariff of Abominations of 1828, Congress passed tariffs more to protect the market for domestic manufactures than to increase government revenue.

Commercial growth and expansion accompanied the rise of manufacturing. Cotton, for instance, had once been traded by plantation agents who handled all the goods produced and bought by the

Specialization of Commerce

owners, extending credit where needed. As cotton became a great staple export following the invention of the cotton gin in 1793, ex-

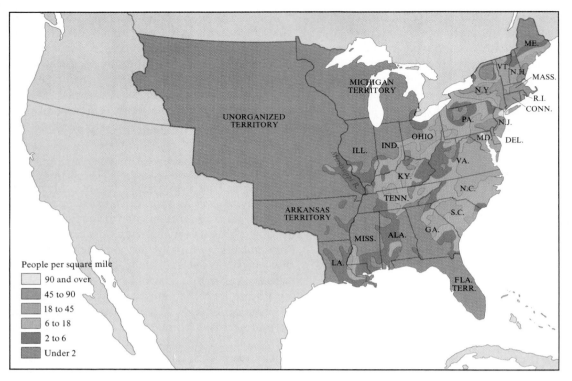

People per square mile
- 90 and over
- 45 to 90
- 18 to 45
- 6 to 18
- 2 to 6
- Under 2

United States Population, 1820

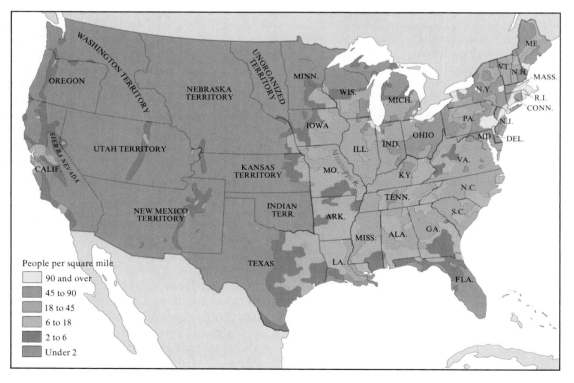

People per square mile
- 90 and over
- 45 to 90
- 18 to 45
- 6 to 18
- 2 to 6
- Under 2

United States Population, 1860

Chapter 9: Rails, Markets, and Mills: The North and West, 1800–1860

ports rose from half a million pounds in that year to 83 million pounds in 1815. Gradually, some agents came to specialize in finance alone: cotton brokers appeared, men who for a commission brought together buyers and sellers. Similarly, wheat and hog brokers sprang up in the West—in Cincinnati, Louisville, and St. Louis. The supply of finished goods also became more specialized. Wholesalers bought large quantities of a particular item from manufacturers, and jobbers broke down the wholesale lots for retail stores and country merchants.

In small towns the general merchant persisted for a longer time. Such merchants continued to sell some goods through exchange with farm women—trading flour or pots and pans for eggs or other local produce. They left the sale of finished goods, such as shoes and clothing, to local craftsmen. In rural areas and on the frontier, peddlers acted as general merchants. But as transportation improved and towns grew, even small-town merchants began to specialize.

Commercial specialization made some traders in the big cities, especially New York, virtual merchant princes. New York had emerged as the dominant port in the late 1790s, outstripping Philadelphia and Boston. When the Erie Canal opened, the city became a standard stop on every major trade route—from Europe, the ports of the South, and the West. New York traders were the middlemen in southern cotton and western grain trading; in fact, New York was the nation's major cotton-exporting city. Merchants in other cities played a similar role within their own regions.

Newly rich traders invested their profits in processing and then manufacturing, further stimulating the growth of northern cities. Some cities became leaders in specific industries: Rochester became a milling center and Cincinnati—"Porkopolis"—the first meat-packing center.

To support their complex commercial transactions, many merchants required large office staffs. In an age before word processors and photocopiers, much of the office staff—all male—worked on high stools, laboriously copying business forms and correspondence. At the bottom of the office hierarchy were messenger boys, often preteens, who delivered documents. Above them were the ordinary copyists, who hand-copied documents in ink as many times as needed. Clerks handled such assignments as customs-house clearances and duties,

shipping papers, and translations. Above them were the bookkeeper and the confidential chief clerk. Those seeking employment in such an office, called a counting house, could take a course from a writing master to acquire a "good hand." All hoped to rise to the status of partner.

Banking and other financial institutions played a significant role in the expansion of commerce and manufacturing and were also an important industry. Financial institutions (banks, insurance companies, and corporations) linked savers—those who deposited money in banks—with producers or speculators—those who wished to borrow money for equipment. The expiration of the first Bank of the United States in 1811 after Congress refused to renew its charter acted as a stimulus to state-chartered banks, and in the next five years the number of banks more than doubled. Nonetheless, state banks proved inadequate to spur national growth, and in 1816 Congress chartered the Second Bank of the United States (see page 235). Many farmers, local bankers, and politicians, however, denounced the bank as a monster and in 1836 finally succeeded in killing it (see pages 359–360).

> **Banking and Credit Systems**

The closing of the Second Bank in 1836 caused a nationwide credit shortage that, along with the Panic of 1837, stimulated major reforms in banking. Michigan and New York introduced charter laws promoting what was called *free banking*. Previously every new bank had required a special legislative charter, and thus each bank incorporation was in effect a political decision. Under the new laws, any proposed bank that met certain minimum conditions—capital invested, notes issued, and types of loans to be made—would automatically receive a state charter. Although banks in Michigan and New York were thus freer to incorporate, restrictions were placed on their practices, slightly reducing the risk of bank failure. Many other states soon followed suit.

Free banking proved a significant stimulus to the economy in the late 1840s and 1850s. New banks sprang up everywhere, providing merchants and manufacturers with the credit they needed. The free banking laws also served as a precedent for general incorporation statutes, which allowed manufacturing firms to receive state charters without special acts of the state legislature. Investors in corporations, called shareholders, were granted *limited liability,* or freedom from responsibility for the company's debts. An attractive feature to potential investors, limited liability encouraged people to back new business ventures.

Changes in insurance firms also promoted industrialization. In the course of business, insurance companies accumulated large amounts of money as reserves against future claims. Then as now, their greatest profits came from investing those reserves. Beginning in the 1840s and 1850s, insurance companies lent money for longer periods than banks, and they bought shares in corporations. They introduced new, more popular policies and took advantage of improvements in communications to establish networks of local agencies, thus expanding the number of customers they served.

In the 1850s, with credit and capital both easily obtainable, the pace of industrialization increased. In the North, industry began to rival agriculture and commerce in dollar volume. Meanwhile, commercial farming, financed by the credit boom, integrated the early frontier into the northern economy. By 1860 six northern states—Massachusetts, New York, Pennsylvania, Connecticut, Rhode Island, and Ohio—were highly industrialized. The clothing, textile, and shoe industries employed more than 100,000 workers each, lumber 75,000, iron 65,000, and woolens and leather 50,000. Although agriculture still predominated even in these states, industrial employment would soon surpass it.

Mill Girls and Mechanics

Oh, sing me the song of the Factory Girl!
So merry and glad and free!
The bloom in her cheeks, of health how it speaks,
Oh! a happy creature is she!
She tends the loom, she watches the spindle,
And cheerfully toileth away,
Amid the din of wheels, how her bright eyes kindle,
And her bosom is ever gay.

Oh, sing me the song of the Factory Girl!
Whose fabric doth clothe the world.
From the king and his peers to the jolly tars
With our flag o'er all seas unfurled.
From the California's seas, to the tainted breeze
Which sweeps the smokened rooms,
Where "God save the Queen" to cry are seen
The slaves of the British looms.

This idyllic portrait of factory work appeared in the Chicopee, Massachusetts, *Telegraph* in 1850. It was a fitting song for the teenage, single women who first left the villages and farms of New England to work in the mills. The mill owners, believing that the degradation of English factory workers arose from their living conditions and not from the work itself, designed a model community offering airy courtyards and river views, secure dormitories, prepared meals, and cultural activities. Housekeepers enforced strict curfews, banned alcohol, and reported to the corporations on workers' behavior and church attendance.

Kinship ties, the promise of steady work, and good pay at first lured rural young women into the mills. Many pairs of sisters and cousins worked in the same mills and lived in the same boarding houses. They helped each other adjust, and letters home brought other kin to the mills. Girls then had few opportunities for work outside their own homes, and at the same time their families had less need for their labor. The commercial production of thread and cloth had reduced a good part of the work done in farm households by New England daughters, who averaged sixteen and one-half years of age when they entered the mills and usually stayed there only about five years. Few intended to stay longer. Mill earnings brought a special satisfaction: feelings of independence and freedom of choice in deciding whether to spend or save their earnings. That satisfaction was not sufficient, however, to change their life's ambitions to be wives and mothers, not mill girls. Most left the mills to marry and were replaced by other women interested in earning a wage.

In the 1840s factory girls rebelled against the mill and mill town. They expressed their feelings in many ways, as in the song "The Factory Girl's Come-All-Ye" (about 1850):

No more I'll take my bobbins out,
No more I'll put them in,
No more the overseer will say
"You're weaving your cloth too thin!"

No more will I eat cold pudding,
No more will I eat hard bread,
No more will I eat those half-baked beans,
For I vow! They're killing me dead!

I'm going back to Boston town
And live on Tremont Street;
And I want all you fact'ry girls
To come to my house and eat!

The young mill women who worked in this New England textile mill stopped work to pose for this early view, ca. 1850. New England farm daughters, and later Irish immigrants, comprised much of the nation's first factory workforce. *International Museum of Photography, George Eastman House.*

What happened to dash the hopes of these young women? The corporation's goal of building an industrial empire and maximizing profits had taken precedence over its concern for workers' living conditions. In the race for profits, owners lengthened hours, cut wages, and tightened discipline. Eliza R. Hemingway, a six-year veteran of the Massachusetts mills, told an 1845 state House of Representatives committee that the workers' hours were too long, "her time for meals too limited. In the summer season, the work is commenced at 5 o'clock, A.M., and continued 'til 7 o'clock, P.M., with half an hour for breakfast and three quarters of an hour for dinner." When Hemingway worked evenings—doing so was compulsory—lamps provided dim light in the room. There was no bloom of health in her cheeks. The demands of increased production took precedence over the protective paternalism of the early mills.

New England millworkers responded to their deteriorating working conditions by organizing and striking. In 1834, in reaction to a 25 percent wage cut, they unsuccessfully "turned out" (struck) against the Lowell mills. Two years later, when boarding-house rates were raised, they turned out again. Following the period from 1837 to 1842, when most mills ran only part-time because of a decline in demand for cloth, managers applied still greater pressures on workers. The speed-up, the stretch-out, and the premium system became common methods of increasing production. The speed-up increased the speed of the machines; the stretch-out increased the number of machines each worker had to operate. Premiums were paid to overseers whose departments produced the most cloth. The result was that in Lowell, between 1836 and 1850, the number of spindles and looms increased 150 and 140 percent respectively, while the number of workers increased by only 50 percent. Some millworkers began to think of themselves as slaves.

> **Mill Girl Protests**

As conditions worsened, workers changed their methods of resistance. In the 1840s, strikes gave way to a concerted effort to shorten the workday. Massachusetts mill women joined forces with other workers to press for legislation mandating a ten-hour day. They aired their complaints in worker-run newspapers. In 1842 the *Factory Girl* appeared in New Hampshire, the *Wampanoag and Opera-tives' Journal* in Massachusetts. Two years later the *Factory Girl's Garland* and the *Voice of Industry,* nicknamed "the factory girl's voice," were founded. Even the *Lowell Offering,* the owner-sponsored paper that was the pride of millworkers and managers alike, became embroiled in controversy when some workers charged that articles critical of working conditions had been suppressed.

Not all the militant native-born millworkers stayed on to fight the managers and owners, and gradually fewer New England daughters entered the mills. The immigrant women, mostly Irish, who constituted a majority of millworkers by the end of the 1850s were driven to the mills by the need to support their families. Most could not afford to complain about their working conditions.

What happened in the New England mills occurred in less-dramatic fashion throughout the nation. Work tasks and workplaces changed, as did relations between workers and supervisors. In the traditional workshops and households, work relationships were intensely personal. People worked within family settings and shared a sense of unity and purpose; men and women had a feeling of control over the quality, value (wages), and conditions of their labor.

One important change, especially in the textile, clothing, and shoemaking industries, was the growing gender division in work. Although women and

Gender Divisions in Work

men tended to do different tasks in traditional agricultural and artisan households, they worked as a family unit. In the nineteenth century, however, as wage work came to dominate, men's and women's work cultures became more separate. Women and girls left home to work in textile mills; they worked and lived in Lowell and other towns in a mostly female world. In the clothing and shoemaking industries, male artisans had once worked in households, assisted by unpaid family labor. But both industries changed radically as men worked outside the home while women continued to work at home through the putting-out

system. The tasks and wages too were different: women did sewing at home while men received higher wages for shaping the materials and finishing the final product in shops employing men only. These new work patterns contributed to social and economic differences between men and women (see Chapter 11).

New work patterns produced other changes as well. The new textile mills, insurance companies, wholesale stores, and railroads were the antithesis of the old workshop and household production tradition. Large factories lacked the reciprocity that had characterized earlier relationships. Factory workers lost their sense of autonomy, and impersonal market forces seemed to dominate. Stiff competition among mills in the growing textile industry of the 1820s and 1830s led to layoffs and replacement of operatives with cheaper, less-skilled workers or children. The formal rules of the factory contrasted sharply with the conditions in artisan or farm households. Supervisors separated the workers from the owners. The division of labor and the use of machines reduced the skills required of workers. And the coming and going of the large work forces was governed by the bell, the steam whistle, or the clock. In 1844 the *Factory Girl's Garland* published a poem describing how the ringing of the factory bell controlled when the workers awoke, ate, began and ended work, and went to sleep. The central problem, of course, was the quickening pace of the work between the bells. Since owners and managers no longer shared the workers' tasks, it was easy for them to expect faster and faster performance.

Changes in the Workplace

Like the mill women, many workers at first welcomed the new manufacturing methods; new jobs and higher wages seemed adequate compensation. But wage reductions, speed-ups, and stretch-outs later changed their minds. Other adjustments were difficult too. Young women in the mills had to tolerate the roar of the looms, and all workers on power machines risked accidents that could kill or maim. Most demoralizing of all, they had to accept that their future was relatively fixed. Opportunities to become an owner or manager in the new system were virtually nil.

Changes in the workplace transformed workers. Initially, mill girls used kinship, village, and gender ties to build supportive networks in factories. In the

1840s and after, as Irish women came to predominate, more workers were strangers to each other before they entered the mills. Once employed, what they had in common—the bases for friendship and mutual support—were their work and job experiences. As a sense of distance from their employers increased, so did deep-seated differences among workers. Nationality, religion, education, and future prospects separated Irish and Yankee millworkers. For many Irish women, mill work was not a stage in their lives; it was permanent employment. Unlike their Yankee sisters, they could not risk striking and losing their jobs; they and their families were dependent upon their earnings. With legions of unskilled immigrants looking for work, Irish mill girls and women considered themselves fortunate to hold on to their jobs, even though the mills cut wages three times in the 1850s and continued the speed-ups and stretch-outs. Many New England women resented the immigrants who came to the mill villages, and management set one group against the other through selective hiring and promotions. The Irish workers assisted one another as much as possible, but formal action was limited.

Eroded too were the republican virtues that artisans shared with the Revolutionary War generation. Thomas Jefferson had hoped to preserve these values with the purchase of the Louisiana Territory and the encouragement of a market economy, but factory work and cycles of boom and bust did not enhance individual freedom. Those who stayed in the master-journeyman-apprentice system or remained on farms after the 1830s saw themselves as distinct from the new wage workers. So too did many Yankee millworkers, for whom factory work remained a stage in the life cycle before marriage.

While women textile workers and shoemakers organized and protested, male workers responded to changes in work by actively participating in reform politics (direct political participation was closed to women). In the 1820s labor parties arose in Pennsylvania, New York, and Massachusetts; they eventually spread to a dozen states. These parties advocated free public education, abolition of imprisonment for debt, revision of the militia system (in which workers bore the greatest burden), and opposition to banks and monopolies. Workers' reform often coincided with middle-class benevolent movements. The two groups shared a concern not only for public education but also for public mor-

This 1853 timetable from the Lowell Mills illustrates the regimentation workers had to submit to in the new environment of the factory. Note that workers frequently began before daylight, finished after sunset, and were given only half an hour for meals. *Museum of American Textile History.*

als: temperance, observance of the Sabbath, and suppression of vice (see Chapter 12). Ironically, however, reform politics tended to divide workers. Many of the reforms—moral education, temperance, Sabbath closings—served merchants and industrialists seeking a more disciplined work force. Others broadened the divisions between native-born and immigrant workers. Anti-immigrant and anti-Catholic movements spread.

Many journeymen recognized that the new manufacturing threatened them. Because many masters in shoemaking, textiles, and apparel manufacturing attempted to keep up with change by turning workshops into small factories with themselves as managers, the gap between master and journeymen threatened to become insurmountable. The market economy, if it freed masters, seemed to make journeymen dependent. Masters stressed the freedom of the individual to produce and contract for their labor; journeymen sought out the mutual protection of their fellow workers.

Organized labor's greatest achievement during this period was gaining relief from the threat of conspiracy laws. When journeymen shoemakers or-

Emergence of a Labor Movement

ganized in the first decade of the century, employers turned to the courts, charging criminal conspiracy. The cordwainers' (shoemakers') cases, which involved six trials from 1806 through 1815, left labor organizations in a tenuous position. Although the journeymen's right to organize was recognized, the courts ruled unlawful any coercive action that harmed other businesses or the public. In effect strikes were illegal. Eventually a Massachusetts case, *Commonwealth* v. *Hunt* (1842), effectively reversed the decision when Chief Justice Lemuel Shaw ruled that Boston journeymen bootmakers could combine and strike "in such manner as best to subserve their own interests." Conspiracy laws no longer thwarted unionization.

Yet permanent organizations were difficult to maintain. Most workers were unskilled or semiskilled at best, outside the crafts. Moreover religion, race, and ethnicity divided workers. The early labor unions tended to be local in nature; the strongest resembled medieval guilds. The first unions arose among urban journeymen in printing, woodworking, shoemaking, and tailoring. These craftsmen sought to protect themselves against the competition of inferior workmen by regulating apprenticeship and establishing minimum wages. In the 1820s and 1830s craft unions—unions organized by skilled occupations—forged larger umbrella organizations in the cities, including the National Trades Union (1834). But in the hard times of 1839–1843, the movement fell apart amid wage reductions and unemployment. In the 1850s the deterioration of working conditions strengthened the labor movement again. Workers won a reduction in hours, and the ten-hour day became standard. Though the Panic of 1857 wiped out the umbrella organizations, some of the new national unions for specific trade groups—notably printers, hat finishers, and stonecutters—survived. By 1860 five more national unions had been organized by the painters, cordwainers, cotton spinners, iron molders, and machinists.

The impact of economic and technological change, however, fell more heavily on individual workers than on their organizations. As a group, the workers' share of the national wealth declined after the 1830s. Individual producers—craftsmen, factory workers, and farmers—had less economic power than they had had a generation or two before. And workers were increasingly losing control over their own work.

Commercial Farming

Beyond the town and city limits, agriculture remained the backbone of the economy. Although urban areas were growing quickly, so too were rural districts. America was still overwhelmingly rural; even in 1860 rural residents far outnumbered urban dwellers. Indeed, it was rural population growth that transformed so many farm villages into bustling small cities. And it was the market orientation of farm families and their ability to feed the growing town and village populations that made possible the concentration of population and the development of commerce and industry.

New England and Middle Atlantic farmers in 1800 worked as their fathers and mothers had. Life centered around a household economy in which the needs of the family and the labor it supplied mostly determined what was produced and in what amounts. Most of their implements were homemade—wooden plows, rakes, shovels, and yokes. For iron parts, they turned to the local blacksmith.

But then canals and railroads began transporting grains, especially wheat, eastward from the fertile Old Northwest. And at the same time, northeastern

North-eastern Agriculture

agriculture developed some serious problems. Northeastern farmers had already cultivated all the land they could; expansion was impossible. Moreover, small New England farms with their uneven terrain did not lend themselves to the new labor-saving farm implements introduced in the 1830s—mechanical sowers, reapers, threshers, and balers. Many northeastern farms also suffered from soil exhaustion: the worn-out land produced lower yields while requiring a greater investment in seed.

In response to these problems and to competition from the West, many northern farmers either

Women making butter, early nineteenth century. Women's production and earnings in cheese and other areas were an essential part of farm families' adaptation to the market economy. *The Sinclair Hamilton Collection of American Illustrated Books, Princeton University Library.*

went west or gave up farming for jobs in the merchant houses and factories. For eastern farm sons and daughters, western New York was the first frontier. After the Erie Canal was completed, these Yankees and New Yorkers settled on more fertile, cheaper land in Ohio and Indiana and then in Michigan, Illinois, and Wisconsin. Farm daughters who did not go west flocked to the early textile mills. Still other New Englanders—urban, better educated, and often experienced in trade—entered the counting houses of New York and other cities. Between 1820 and 1860 the percentage of people in the North living on farms declined from 71 to 40 percent.

Neither the counting house nor the factory, however, depleted New England agriculture. The farmers who remained proved as adaptable at farming as their children were at copy desks and water-powered looms. By the 1850s New England and Middle Atlantic farm families were successfully adjusting to competition from western agricultural products. Many abandoned the commercial production of wheat and corn and stopped tilling poor land. Instead they improved their livestock, especially cattle, and specialized in vegetable and fruit production and dairy farming. They financed these changes through land sales or borrowing. In fact, their greatest potential profit was from increasing land values, not from farming itself.

Increasingly farm families everywhere adjusted to market conditions. In 1820 about one-third of food produced was intended for market; by 1860, about two-thirds. The passing of the pioneer stage in any farm district was marked by the appearance of merchants who specialized as middlemen in the grain and food trades. They replaced country storekeepers who had handled everything for local farmers during settlement, acting as both retailer and marketing and purchasing agents.

The increased role of women in earning income through wages or market sales was another important element in the market economy and in the growth of consumers' markets.

Women's Paid Labor As agriculture became commercialized, women's production and earnings were essential to the survival of the family farm. In New England, women did "put-out" work for income. In the Middle Atlantic states, especially near towns and cities, and in Ohio, women's dairy production was crucial to family income. Butter and cheese making for local and regional markets replaced spinning and weaving as a major activity, especially since cloth could be purchased so cheaply. The work was physically demanding, especially when production for market was added to regular home and farm chores. Yet women took pride in their work; it gave many a sense of independence on the farm. Esther Lewis, a widow who sent 75 to 100 pounds of butter monthly to Philadelphia in the 1830s, even used hired women to expand production.

The success of women in butter and cheese making led some farms to specialize as dairy farms and some entrepreneurs to expand production. In northeastern Ohio and New England in the 1840s men joined the work. Beginning in 1847 in Ohio, entrepreneurs built cheese factories in rural towns and contracted to buy curd from local dairy farmers. In 1852 one such factory in Gustavus, Ohio, produced daily 5,000 pounds of cheese from the milk of 2,500 cows. The cheese was shipped by canal and railroad to cities and eastern ports. In Boston and New York, some merchants turned to handling cheese and other diary products exclusively, selling to consumers as far away as California, England, and China. By 1860 Ohio dairies were producing 21.6 million pounds of cheese a year for market.

Most farm families seemed to welcome the opportunities offered by the market economy. Although they took pride in self-sufficiency and rural serenity, they shifted toward specialization and market-oriented production. The rewards in this period for such flexibility were great; produce sold at market financed land and equipment purchases and made credit arrangements possible. Many farm families flourished.

Nonetheless there was a growing division in commercial agriculture between hired hands or tenants and farm owners. Not all farmers were yeomen; not all managed to buy land. Given the high cost of land and of farming, hired hands had little opportunity to acquire farms of their own. By the 1850s it took from ten to twenty years for a rural laborer to save enough money to farm for himself. Thus the number of tenant farmers increased. Farm laborers, once scarce in the United States, became commonplace. In the North in 1860 there was one hired hand for every 2.3 farms.

Americans saw great promise in railroads and industry, but they still valued agrarian life. State governments energetically promoted commercial agriculture in order to spur economic growth and sustain the values of an agrarian-based republic. Massachusetts in 1817 and New York in 1819 subsidized agricultural prizes and county fairs. New York required contestants to submit written descriptions of how they grew their prize crops; the state then published the best essays to encourage the use of new methods and to promote specialization. Farm journals also helped to familiarize farmers with developments in agriculture. By 1860 there were nearly sixty journals with a combined circulation of from 250,000 to 300,000.

Even so, the Old Northwest gradually and inevitably replaced the northeastern states as the center of American family agriculture. Farms in the Old Northwest were much larger than

**Mechaniza-
tion of Agri-
culture**

northeastern ones and better suited to the new mechanized farming implements. The farmers of the region bought machines such as the McCormick reaper on credit and paid for them with the profits from their high yields. By 1847 Cyrus McCormick was selling a thousand reapers a year. Using interchangeable parts, he expanded production to five thousand a year, but demand still outstripped supply. Similarly, John Deere's steel plow, invented in 1837, replaced the inadequate iron plow; steel blades kept the soil from sticking and were tough enough to break the roots of prairie grass. By 1856, Deere's sixty-five employees were making 13,500 plows a year.

Mechanized farming was the basis of expanded production. In the 1850s alone wheat production surged 70 percent. By that time the area that had been the western wilderness in 1800 had become one of the world's leading agricultural regions. Midwestern farm families fed an entire nation and a generation of immigrants—and had food to export.

The Western Frontier

Integral to the development of the market economy was the steady expansion of the United States. In 1800 the edge of settlement had formed an arc from western New York through the new states of Kentucky and Tennessee, south to Georgia. By 1820 it had shifted to Ohio, Indiana, and Illinois in the North and Louisiana, Alabama, and Mississippi in the South. By 1860 settlement reached the Southwest and the West Coast; the 1800 frontier was long-settled; and once-unexplored regions were dotted with farms and mines, towns and villages. Unsettled land remained—mostly between the Mississippi River and the Sierra Nevada—but the old frontier and its native inhabitants, the Indians, had given way to white settlement (see pages 328–334). Still the plains and mountain territories were only sporadically settled by whites.

The legal boundaries of the country also changed rapidly during this period. Between 1803 and 1853 the United States pushed its original boundaries to their present continental limits (except for Alaska). The Louisiana Purchase roughly doubled the nation's size, and the acquisition of Florida from Spain in 1819 secured the Southeast. In the 1840s the United States annexed the Republic of Texas, defined America's northern border with Canada, and acquired through war California, Nevada, Utah, and most of Arizona from Mexico (see pages 368, 373–376). In 1853 the Gadsden Purchase added southern Arizona and New Mexico.

The lore of the frontier and pioneers form a part of the mythology of America. James Fenimore Cooper used the frontier setting and ordinary peo-

Legends of Pioneers ple in his Leatherstocking tales, a series of novels first appearing in 1823 whose hero, Hawkeye (Natty Bumppo), was the first popular fictional hero in America. At heart a romantic, Hawkeye preferred the freedom of the virgin forest to domesticated society. Popular legends, songs, and dime novels in the nineteenth century, like movies, television, and paperbacks in the twentieth century, glorified fur trappers, explorers and scouts, and pioneers. Major themes included pioneers crossing the arid plains and snow-covered Rockies by Conestoga wagon to bring civilization to the wilderness; frontiersmen and settlers defeating both the environment and the Indians to earn their right to make the land productive; Mormons finding Zion in the Great American Desert; and gold seekers sailing on clipper ships to California.

Americans have only recently come to recognize that there are other sides to these familiar stories. Women, Indians, and blacks as well as white men were pioneers. Explorers and pioneers did not discover North America by themselves, nor did the wagon trains fight their way across the plains—Indians guided them along traditional paths and led them to food and water. And rather than civilizing the frontier, settlers at first brought a rather primitive economy and society, which did not compare favorably with the well-ordered Indian civilizations. In many midwestern settlements Indians introduced pioneers to raising corn, harvesting berries and nuts, and tapping maples for sugar. The Mormons who sought a new Jerusalem by the Great Salt Lake were fleeing the gehenna (hell) imposed on them by intolerant, violent frontier folk farther east (see page 310). And all those who sought furs, gold, and lumber spoiled the natural landscape in the name of progress and development.

This was the ironic contrast between the ideal and the reality of the frontier. If pioneers were attracted by the beauty and bounty of the American wilderness, if they were lured by the opportunity to live a simple, rewarding life close to the soil, they were also destroying the natural ecology in the process. It was almost as if the vast forests, prairies, and lakes were enemies to be conquered and bent to their will. Settlers felled millions of trees to make way for farms, while lumbermen in Michigan denuded the land. Farther west, miners in search of gold leveled the hills. And even those who sought to escape civilization, like fur trappers, were linking economically the wilderness and the market economy.

No figure has come to symbolize the frontier more aptly than the footloose, rugged fur trapper, who roamed the wilderness in search of pelts. The

Fur Trade trapper, with his backpack, rifle, and kegs of whiskey, spearheaded America's manifest destiny (see page 365), extending the United States presence to the Pacific Slope. Fur trading, especially for beaver, had been economically important since the early colonial period. Traders were the link in an elaborate network that reached from beyond the settled frontier to sophisticated European shops. But after 1800, American investors organized to compete with foreign trading companies such as Hudson's Bay. The German immigrant John Jacob Astor, for instance, became a millionaire through his American Fur Trading Company. Americans also changed the method by which furs were acquired. In 1825 the St. Louis merchant William Henry Ashley pioneered the rendezvous system. Instead of buying beaver furs from Indians, Ashley sent out non-

Spring rendezvous at Green River, Wyoming, painted by William Henry Jackson. With oils and a camera, Jackson and a small group of other artists and photographers created visions of the Far West for millions of Americans who would never cross the Mississippi. *United States Department of the Interior, National Park Service.*

Indian trappers to roam the Rockies and farther west; at a meeting on the Green River, in present-day Wyoming, at season's end, the trappers exchanged their pelts for goods Ashley had brought in from St. Louis. This annual spring rendezvous was the hallmark of the American fur-trading system through the late 1830s, when silk hats replaced beaver ones and trapping declined. In many areas the beaver had been virtually trapped out of existence.

Throughout the West, trappers sought the cooperation of neighboring tribes in their territory, and nearly 40 percent wed Indian women. Most often the trapper or trader followed the tribe's custom, negotiating with the Indian bride's parents for the match. When a chief's daughter wed a fur merchant, separate cultures convened to celebrate, as when Archibald McDonald of Hudson's Bay Company and Koale-xoa, daughter of a Chinook chief, were married in traditional ceremonies at the mouth of the Columbia River. Since in Indian and white frontier societies there was little distinction between public and private spheres, an Indian wife played an important "public" role in bridging trapper cul-

ture and economy and Indian society. Moreover, Indian women brought special trading privileges as well as family ties and experiences of life on the frontier. Over time, Metís, or mixed bloods (Indian-white offspring), and white women replaced Indian women as trappers' wives; not only did this change trapper culture, but in itself it was a sign of the decline of the fur trade. It signaled the coming of settled, agrarian society.

Ironically, the history of trapping is in essence the history of the passing of the frontier. Early fur traders exploited friendly Indian tribes; then pioneers (mountain trappers) monopolized the trade through the systematic organization and financial backing of trading companies. Soon settlements and towns sprang up along the trappers' routes. With the decline in the fur trade, some trappers settled down. In Oregon in 1843, former trappers helped organize the first provisional government and pressured for United States statehood. In the mountain states the mining and cattle frontiers were to continue for another half-century, following the development of the fur-trading frontier.

But not all regions followed that pattern. Anglos settled newly acquired California almost overnight. In January 1848 James Marshall, a carpenter,

California Gold Rush spotted a few goldlike particles in the millrace at Sutter's Mill (now Coloma, California). Word of the discovery spread, and other Californians rushed to garner instant fortunes. When John C. Frémont reached San Francisco in June 1848, he found that "all, or nearly all, its male inhabitants had gone to the mines." The town, "which a few months before was so busy and thriving, was then almost deserted."

By 1849 the news had spread eastward; hundreds of thousands of fortune seekers flooded in. Success in the market economy required capital, hard labor, and time; by contrast, gold mining seemed to promise instant riches. Most forty-niners never found enough gold to pay their expenses. "The stories you hear frequently in the States," one gold seeker wrote home, "are the most extravagant lies imaginable—the mines are a humbug. . . . the almost universal feeling is to get home." But many stayed, unable to afford the passage back home or tempted by the growing labor shortage in California's cities and agricultural districts. San Francisco, the gateway from the West Coast to the interior, became an instant city, ballooning from 1,000 people in 1848 to 35,000 just two years later.

Although those who came produced almost nothing, they had to be fed. Thus began the great California agricultural boom. Wheat was the great staple; it required minimal investment, was easily planted, and offered a quick return at the end of a relatively short growing season. California farmers became eager importers of machinery, since wages were high in the labor-scarce district and the extensive flat, treeless plains were well suited to horse-drawn machines. By the mid-1850s, California was exporting wheat. In its growing cities, merchant princes arose to supply, feed, and clothe the new settlers. One such merchant was the German Jew Levi Strauss, whose tough mining pants became synonymous with American jeans.

Still, food had to be cooked and clothes washed. In the western frontier, women were relatively few in number. Unlike the Midwest, where family farms were the basic unit of production and life, in California gold and ore mining, graz-

Frontier Women ing, and large-scale wheat farming were overwhelmingly male occu-

The gold rush brought treasure seekers—black and white, men and women, native and foreign born—to California. Few found their fortune in gold, but most stayed to settle the West Coast. *California State Library.*

pations. Women, who constituted about one-seventh of the travelers on the overland trails, found their domestic skills in great demand. They received high fees for cooking, laundering, and sewing. Inevitably boarding houses and hotels were run by women, as men shunned domestic work. Not all women were entrepreneurs, however. Some wives, at their spouses' commands, cooked for and served their husbands' friends. The women did the work while their husbands built reputations as hosts. Abigail Scott Duniway, a leading western crusader for women's suffrage and a veteran of the Overland Trail to Oregon, wrote of one woman's experience. She lived in a "neighborhood composed chiefly of bachelors," Duniway wrote in 1859, "who found comfort in mobilizing at meal time at the homes of the few married men of the township, and seemed especially fond of congregating at the hospitable cabin home of my good husband, who was never quite so much in his glory as when entertaining men at this fireside, while I, if not washing, scrubbing, churning, or nursing the

Sarah Snelling Tandy and her wagon chair. In 1851, Tandy and her children traveled the Oregon trail west. Suffering from arthritis, she sat on the chair in the back of a covered wagon, which served as the family home and shelter during the five-month journey. *Lane County Historical Museum, Oregon.*

baby, was preparing their meals in our lean-to kitchen."

Gold altered the pattern of settlement along the entire Pacific coast. Before 1848 most overland traffic flowed north over the Oregon Trail; few pioneers turned south to California or used the Santa Fe Trail. By 1849 a pioneer observed that the Oregon Trail "bore no evidence of having been much traveled this year." Traffic was instead flowing south, and California was becoming the new population center of the Pacific Slope. One measure of the shift was the overland mail routes. In the 1840s the Oregon Trail had been the major communications link between the Pacific and the Midwest. But the Post Office officials who organized mail routes in the 1850s terminated them in California, not in Oregon; there was no route farther north than Sacramento.

By 1860 California, like the Great Plains and prairies farther east, had become a farmers' and merchants' frontier linked to the market economy.

Farming Frontier Although the story of these settlers is less dramatic than that of the trappers and forty-niners, it is nevertheless the story of the overwhelming majority of westerners before 1860. The farming frontier started first on the western fringes of the eastern seaboard states and in the Old Northwest, then moved to the edge of the Great Plains and California. Pioneer families cleared the land of trees or prairie grass, hoed in corn and wheat, fenced in animals, and constructed cabins of logs or sod. If they were successful—and many were not—they slowly cleared more land. As settled areas expanded, farmers built roads to carry their stock and produce to market and bring back supplies they could not produce themselves. Growth brought specialization; as western farmers shifted from self-sufficiency to commercial farming, they too tended to concentrate on one crop. By this time the area was no longer a frontier, and families seeking new land had to go farther west. In John Jervis's time a farmer from Rome, New York, might have gone to Michigan via the Erie Canal and Lake Erie. A later generation would go farther west to Iowa, Nebraska, or even California.

Though most often thought of as the result of individualism, many frontier settlements depended upon family and kinship networks and communal cooperation. Sugar Creek on the Sangamon River in central Illinois exemplified the cooperative spirit. White settlers came in 1817 and named the settlement for the sugar maples first tapped by the Kickapoos and then by the American settlers. Although the settlement was based on private land ownership, life and work were infused with a cooperative spirit. Most of the newcomers who moved in over the next decade were part of kin networks, and they assisted each other in clearing land and turning the temporary dwellings of their first years into permanent cabins. Whether raising hogs or children, Sugar Creek families depended upon kin and friends for support. And in a crisis, they rose to the occasion. When someone "would be sick with chills or jaundice, or something else," Sugar Creek farmer James Megredy recalled, "his neighbors would meet and take care of his harvest, get up wood, or repair his cabin, or plant his corn." Neighbors used a "borrowing system" in which scarce tools and labor constantly circulated through the neighborhood. Settlers who came without previous ties, if they stayed, did not remain strangers.

What made possible such settlements as Sugar Creek was the availability of land and credit. Some public lands were granted as a reward for military service: veterans of the War of **Land Grants and Sales** 1812 received 160 acres; veterans of the Mexican War (see Chapter 13) could purchase land at reduced prices. And until 1820, civilians could buy government land at $2 an acre (a relatively high price) on a liberal four-year payment plan. More important, from 1800 to 1817 the government successively reduced the minimum purchase from 640 to 80 acres. However, when the availability of land prompted a flurry of land speculation that ended in the Panic of 1819, the government discontinued credit sales. Instead it reduced the price further, to $1.25 an acre.

Some eager pioneers settled land before it had been surveyed and put up for sale. Such illegal settlers, or squatters, then had to buy the land they lived on at auction, and they faced the risk of being unable to purchase it. Often neighbors protected the squatters; in Sugar Creek, Illinois, they assisted them in acquiring the land. In 1841, to facilitate settlement, simplify land sales, and end property disputes, Congress passed the Pre-emption Act, which legalized settlement prior to surveying.

Since most settlers, squatters or not, needed to borrow money, private credit systems arose. Banks, private investors, country storekeepers, and speculators all extended credit to farmers. Railroads also sold land on credit—land they had received from the government as construction subsidies. (The Illinois Central, for example, received 2.6 million acres in 1850.) Indeed, nearly all economic activity in the West involved credit, from land sales to the shipping of produce to railroad construction. In 1816, 1836, and 1855 easy credit helped to boost land prices. When the speculative bubbles burst, much land fell into the hands of speculators, and as a consequence tenancy became more common in the West than it had been in New England.

Towns and cities were the life lines of the agricultural West. Cities along the Ohio and Mississippi rivers—Louisville, Cincinnati, and St. Louis— **Frontier Cities** preceded most of the settlement of the early frontier. A generation later the lake cities of Cleveland, Detroit, and Chicago spearheaded settlement farther west. Steamboats connected eastern markets and ports with these river and lake cities, carrying grain east and returning with finished goods. As in the Northeast, these western cities eventually developed into manufacturing centers when merchants shifted their investments from commerce to industry. Chicago became a center for the manufacture of farm implements, Louisville of

The greatest wealth was to be found in supplying, feeding, and clothing the gold seekers. Men and women opened stores for and provided services to the miners; towns like Stockton, California, sprang up overnight. W. H. Creasy's watercolor of the 1849 Stockton waterfront captures the energy of the expanding city—its tents and boats housing people and the wooden buildings under construction. *Collection of The Haggin Museum, Stockton, California.*

textiles, and Cleveland of iron. Smaller cities specialized in flour mills, and all produced consumer goods for the hinterlands.

Urban growth in the West was so spectacular that by 1860 Cincinnati, St. Louis, and Chicago had populations exceeding 100,000, and Buffalo, Louisville, San Francisco, Pittsburgh, Detroit, Milwaukee, and Cleveland had surpassed 40,000. Thus commerce, urbanization, and industrialization overtook the farmers' frontier, wedding western areas to the Northeast.

For the North and the West the period from 1800 through 1860 was one of enormous growth. Population increased sixfold. Settlement, once restricted to the Atlantic seaboard and the eastern rivers, extended beyond the Mississippi by 1860 and was spreading east from the Pacific Ocean as well. Whereas agriculture had completely dominated the nation at the turn of the century, by midcentury farming was being challenged by a booming manufacturing sector. And agriculture itself was becoming more market-oriented as well as mechanized.

Economic development changed the American landscape and the way people lived. Canals, railroads, steamboats, and telegraph lines linked economic activities hundreds and thousands of miles apart. The market economy brought sustained growth and cycles of boom and bust. Hard times and unemployment became frequent occurrences.

At the same time, commercial and industrial growth altered production and consumption. The market economy changed farm work as farmers began to purchase goods produced formerly by wives and daughters and farm families geared production to faraway markets. Farm women increasingly contributed wages and income from market sales to the family farm. In New England many farm daughters left to become the first factory workers in the new textile industry. As workshops and factories replaced household production, and as the master-journeyman-apprentice system faded away, workplace relations became more impersonal and conditions harsher. And men's and women's work became more distinctly different. Immigrants began to form a new industrial group, and some workers organized labor unions.

The American people too were changing. Immigration and western expansion made the population and society more diverse. Urbanization, commerce, and industry produced significant divisions among Americans. And their reach extended deeply into the home as well as the workshop. The South was not totally insulated from these changes, but its dependence upon slave rather than free labor set it apart. Above all else, slavery defined the South.

Suggestions for Further Reading

General

Stuart Bruchey, *The Roots of American Economic Growth, 1607–1861: An Essay in Social Causation* (1965); David Klingaman and Richard Vedder, eds., *Essays in Nineteenth-Century History* (1975); Susan Previant Lee and Peter Passell, *A New Economic View of American History* (1979); Otto Mayr and Robert C. Post, eds., *Yankee Enterprise: The Rise of the American System of Manufactures* (1981); Douglass C. North, *Economic Growth of the United States, 1790–1860* (1966); Nathan Rosenberg, *Technology and American Economic Growth* (1972).

Transportation

Robert G. Albion, *The Rise of New York Port, 1815–1860* (1939); Albert Fishlow, *American Railroads and the Transformation of the Ante-Bellum Economy* (1965); Carter Goodrich, *Government Promotion of American Canals and Railroads, 1800–1890* (1960); Louis C. Hunter, *Steamboats on the Western Rivers* (1949); Harry N. Scheiber, *Ohio Canal Era: A Case Study of Government and the Economy, 1820–1861* (1969); Ronald E. Shaw, *Erie Water West: Erie Canal, 1797–1854* (1966); George R. Taylor, *The Transportation Revolution, 1815–1860* (1951); James A. Ward, *Railroads and the Character of America, 1820–1887* (1986).

Commerce and Manufacturing

Alfred D. Chandler, Jr., *The Visible Hand: Managerial Revolution in American Business* (1977); Thomas C Cochran, *Frontiers of Change: Early Industrialization in America* (1981); Robert F. Dalzell, Jr., *Enterprising Elite: The Boston Associates and the World They Made* (1987); Louis Hartz, *Economic Policy and Democratic Thought: Pennsylvania, 1776–1860* (1954); David A. Hounshell, *From the American System to Mass Production, 1800–1932: The Development of Manufacturing Technology in the United States* (1984); David J. Jeremy, *Transatlantic Industrial Revolution: The Diffusion of Textile Technologies Between Britain and America, 1790s–1830s* (1981); Stanley I. Kutler, *Privilege and Creative Destruction: The Charles River Bridge Case* (1971); Merritt Roe Smith, *Harpers Ferry Armory and the New Technology* (1977); Barbara M. Tucker, *Samuel Slater and the Origins of the American Textile Industry, 1790–1860* (1984); Anthony F. C. Wallace, *Rockdale: The Growth of an American Village in the Early Industrial Revolution* (1978).

Agriculture

"American Agriculture, 1790–1840, A Symposium," *Agricultural History* 46 (January 1972); Jeremy Atack and Fred Bateman, *To Their Own Soil: Agriculture in the Antebellum North* (1987); Allen G. Bogue, *From Prairie to Corn Belt: Farming on the Illinois and Iowa Prairies in the Nineteenth Century* (1963); Clarence Danhof, *Change in Agriculture: The Northern United States, 1820–1870* (1969); John Mack Faragher, *Sugar Creek: Life on the Illinois Prairie* (1986); Paul W. Gates, *The Farmer's Age: Agriculture, 1815–1860* (1962); Benjamin H. Hibbard, *A History of Public Land Policies* (1939); Joan M. Jensen, *Loosening the Bonds: Mid-Atlantic Farm Women, 1750–1850* (1986); Robert Leslie Jones, *History of Agriculture in Ohio to 1880* (1983); Edward C. Kendall, *John Deere's Steel Plow* (1959).

The Western Frontier

Ray A. Billington, *The Far Western Frontier, 1830–1860* (1956); Ray A. Billington and Martin Ridge, *Westward Expansion*, 5th ed. (1982); John Mack Faragher, *Women and Men on the Overland Trail* (1979); William H. Goetzmann, *Exploration and Empire: The Explorer and the Scientist in the Winning of the American West* (1966); Leroy R. Hafen, ed., *The Mountain Men and the Fur Trade of the Far West*, 10 vols. (1965–1972); Julie Roy Jeffrey, *Frontier Women: The Trans-Mississippi West, 1840–1880* (1979); Theodore J. Karamanski, *Fur Trade and Exploration: Opening the Far Northwest, 1821–1852* (1983); John D. Unruh, Jr., *The Overland Emigrants and the Trans-Mississippi West, 1840–1860* (1979); David J. Wishart, *The Fur Trade of the American West, 1807–1840* (1979).

Workers

Mary H. Blewett, *Men, Women, and Work: Class, Gender, and Protest in the New England Shoe Industry, 1780–1910* (1988); Alan Dawley, *Class and Community: The Industrial Revolution in Lynn* (1977); Thomas Dublin, *Women at Work: The Transformation of Work and Community in Lowell, Massachusetts, 1826–1860* (1979); Alice Kessler-Harris, *Out to Work: A History of Wage-earning Women in the United States* (1982); Jonathan Prude, *The Coming of Industrial Order: Town and Factory Life in Rural Massachusetts, 1810–1860* (1983); W. J. Rorabaugh, *The Craft Apprentice: From Franklin to the Machine Age in America* (1986); Steven J. Ross, *Workers on the Edge: Work, Leisure, and Politics in Industrializing Cincinnati, 1788–1890* (1985); Norman Ware, *The Industrial Worker, 1840–1860* (1924); Sean Wilentz, *Chants Democratic: New York City and the Rise of the American Working Class, 1788–1850* (1984).

He was weeping, sobbing. In a humble voice he had begged his master not to give him to Mr. King, who was going away to Alabama, but it had done no good. Now his voice rose and he uttered "an absolute cry of despair." Raving and "almost in a state of frenzy," he declared that he would never leave the Georgia plantation that was home to his father, mother, wife, and children. He twisted his hat between clenched fists and flung it to the ground; he would kill himself, he said, before he lost his family and all that made life worth living.

To Fanny Kemble, watching from the doorway, it was a horrifying and disorienting scene. One of the most famous British actresses ever to tour America, Fanny had grown up breathing England's antislavery tradition as naturally as the air. In New England she had become friends with such enlightened antislavery thinkers as William Ellery Channing, the liberal Boston minister who founded Unitarianism; Catharine Maria Sedgwick, America's foremost woman novelist; and Elizabeth Dwight Sedgwick, an educator and Catharine's sister-in-law. Amid such company, Fanny understandably assumed that attitudes in America were advanced and civilized. Then the man she married took her away from New England to a Georgia rice plantation, where hundreds of dark-skinned slaves produced the white grain that was his source of wealth.

Pierce Butler, Fanny's husband, was everything that a cultured Philadelphia gentleman should be. He had lived all his life in the North, though part of his family's fortune had always sprung from southern slavery. When Fanny chose him from dozens of suitors, he had seemed an attractive exemplar of American culture. Yet now he shattered his slave's hopes without hesitation. Quietly "leaning against a table with his arms folded," Butler advised the distraught black man not to "make a fuss about what there was no help for."

Fanny wondered what America was really like. In the South, the northerner she thought she knew seemed a different man. Only with tears and vehement pleas was she able to convince Butler to keep the slave family together. He finally agreed as a favor to her, not on principle or because she had a right to be consulted.

10

SLAVERY AND THE GROWTH OF THE SOUTH, 1800–1860

Southern Plantation (detail) ca. 1860, anonymous artist. From *The Civil War: Brother Against Brother.* *Photograph by John Miller from a Private Collection* © *1983 Time-Life Books, Inc.*

One force behind the South's growth was soaring world demand for cotton. John Stobart's painting shows a steam packet, heavily laden with bales of cotton, arriving in New Orleans. *Courtesy Maritime Heritage Prints.*

This incident, which occurred in 1839, illustrates both the similarities between South and North and the differences that were beginning to emerge. Although racism existed in the North, its influence was far more visible on southern society. And although some northerners, like Pierce Butler, were undisturbed by the idea of human bondage, a growing number considered it shocking and backward. In the years after the Revolution, these northerners, possessing few slaves and influenced by the revolutionary ideal of natural rights, had adopted gradual emancipation laws (see page 165). At the same time they developed a widening market economy and embarked on an industrial revolution. These changes increased production, spurred mechanization, and rendered forced labor obsolete.

In the South too, the years from 1800 to 1860 were a time of growth and prosperity; new lands were settled and new states peopled. But as the North grew and changed, economically the South merely grew; change there only reinforced existing economic patterns. Steadily the South emerged as the world's most extensive and vigorous slave economy. Its people were slaves, slaveholders, and nonslaveholders rather than farmers, merchants, mechanics, and manufacturers. Its well-being depended on agriculture alone, rather than on agriculture plus commerce and manufacturing. Its population was almost wholly rural rather than rural and urban.

These facts meant that the social lives of southerners were unavoidably distinct from those of northerners. Nonslaveholders operated their family farms in a society dominated by slaveholding planters. A handful of planters developed an aristocratic lifestyle, while slaves—one-third of the South's people—lived without freedom, struggling to develop a culture that sustained hope. The influence of slavery spread throughout the social system, affecting not just southern economics but southern values, customs, and laws. It created a society that was noticeably different from the society of the North.

Migration, Growth, and the Cotton Boom

Between 1800 and 1860 the South grew dramatically. Small farmers and slaveowning planters migrated westward and brought new territory under cultivation. Farms and plantations spread across the landscape as human labor, both voluntary and coerced, built a vastly larger, slaveholding society.

The attraction of rich, new lands drew thousands of southerners across the Appalachian Mountains. Early settlers told those back east about "dark, heavy forests, . . . wide, thick canebrakes, [and] clear running river[s], full of fish." This news created in many an irresistible urge to move. Both small farmers and ambitious slaveowners poured across the mountains, pushing the Indians off their lands in the Gulf region (see pages 329–334). The floodtide of migration reached Alabama and Mississippi in the 1830s, then spilled into Texas in the 1850s.

The earliest settlers in the swelling stream of migration often were yeomen—small farmers who generally owned no slaves. Yeomen pioneered the southern wilderness, moving into undeveloped regions and building their log cabins. They came first as herders of livestock and then as farmers. After the War of 1812 they moved in successive waves down the southern Appalachians into new Gulf lands. The herdsmen, who fattened their cattle and pigs on the abundant natural vegetation in the woods, generally moved on as farmers filled up an area and broke ground for crops. These yeoman farmers forced many herdsmen farther west and eventually across the Mississippi.

Migration became almost a way of life for some yeoman families. Lured by stories of good land over the horizon, men uprooted their wives and children repeatedly. Each new land seemed "like a paradise" to many eager settlers. The Alabama Territory, wrote one new arrival, had "the greatest prospect of corn and cotton I ever saw." Writing to friends in older parts of the South, he asked, "Why will you stay . . . and work them poor stony ridges when one half of the labor and one third of the ground heare will bring you more?" Most migrants agreed that "every young man should emigrate if he is poor," and thousands of poor men did just

that. The excitement over new lands alarmed one North Carolinian, who wrote, "The *Alabama Fever* rages here with great violence. . . . I am apprehensive if it continues to spread as it has done, it will almost depopulate the country."

The men worked hard on the frontier to clear fields and establish a farm, while their wives labored in the household economy and patiently recreated the social ties—to relatives, neighbors, church members—that enriched experience. "We have been [moving] all our lives," lamented one woman. "As soon as ever we git comfortably settled, it is time to be off to something new." Maria Lides's father took the family from South Carolina to Alabama, but "his having such a good crop" there, lamented Maria, "seems to make him more anxious to move." She almost wished he would decide on California, because "he would be obliged to stop then for he could go no farther."

Some yeomen acquired large tracts of level land and became wealthy planters. Others clung to the beautiful mountainous areas they loved or pressed farther into the wilds because they "couldn't stand the sound of another man's axe." As they moved, they tended to stick to the climate and soils they knew best. Yeomen could not afford the richest bottomlands, which were swampy and required expensive draining, but they acquired land almost everywhere else.

For slaveholding southerners another powerful motive impelled westward movement: the chance to profit from a spectacular cotton boom. Southern

Rise of the Cotton South

planters were not sentimentalists who held onto their slaves for noneconomic reasons even in the face of the industrial revolution. Like other Americans, they were profit-oriented. But the cotton boom caused nonmechanized, slave-based agriculture to remain highly profitable in the South, sustaining the plantation economy.

This had not always seemed likely. At the time of the Revolution, slave-based agriculture was not very profitable in the Upper South, where most southerners then lived. Persistent debt hung heavily over Virginia's extravagant and aristocratic tobacco growers. Farther south, slaves grew rice and some indigo, but cotton was a profitable crop only for sea-island planters, who grew the luxurious long-staple variety. The short-staple cotton that grew readily in the interior was unmarketable because its sticky seeds lay tangled in the fibers. Yet, in spite of the limited usefulness of slavery, much wealth was tied up in it. Ingrained social forces and fear of slave revolts prevented its abolition.

Then England's burgeoning textile industry changed the southern economy. English mills consumed more and more cotton. Sea-island cotton was so profitable between 1785 and 1795 that thousands of farmers in the interior tried growing the short-staple variety; by the early 1790s southern farmers were growing 2 to 3 million pounds of it each year, despite their inability to remove the seeds. Some of this cotton was meant for domestic use, but most was grown in the hope that some innovation would make the crop salable to the English. In such circumstances the invention of a cotton gin was almost inevitable, and Eli Whitney responded in 1793 with a simple machine that removed the seeds from the fibers. By 1800 cotton was spreading rapidly westward from the seaboard states.

The voracious appetite of English mills caused a meteoric rise in cotton production (see maps). From 1800 to the Civil War, British demand for cotton multiplied rapidly, and southern planters rushed to increase their acreage of the white fiber. Despite occasional periods of low prices, the demand for cotton surged ahead every decade. This inspired southerners with capital to buy more land, buy more slaves, and plant ever more cotton. Cotton growers boosted production so successfully that by 1825 the South was the world's dominant supplier of cotton; by the 1850s the South sent Britain over 70 percent of all the cotton it imported.

Thus the antebellum South, or Old South before the Civil War, became primarily a cotton South. Tobacco continued to be grown in Virginia and North Carolina, and rice and sugar were very important in certain coastal areas, especially in South Carolina, Georgia, and Louisiana. But cotton was the largest crop, the most widespread, and it was a force behind the South's hunger for new territory.

Small slaveowners and planters (those who owned at least twenty bondsmen) sought out alluvial bottomland and other fertile soils, eager to grasp the opportunity for wealth that came with the cotton boom. As demand for cotton increased, slaveowners pushed feverishly to grow more. A Virginian who came to Vicksburg in 1836 marveled at the atmosphere. "They do business in a kind of frenzy," he wrote, but that frenzy produced many brand-new aristocrats. Some old Virginia and South Carolina families were represented among the proud new "cotton snobs," but most of the wealthy were newly rich.

Their desire to plant more cotton and buy more slaves often caused men with new wealth to postpone the enjoyment of luxuries. Many first-generation planters lived for decades in their original log cabin, improved only by clapboards or a frame addition. A Mississippi gentleman admitted, "If you wish to see people worth millions living as [if] they were not worth hundreds, come down here." Yet the planters' wealth put ease and refinement within their grasp, and for the lucky, riches and high social status could come quickly.

A good example is the family of Jefferson Davis. Like Abraham Lincoln, Davis was born in humble circumstances. His father was one of the thousands of American farmers on the frontier who moved frequently, unwisely buying land when prices were high and selling when they were low, never making his fortune. Luckily for Davis, his older brother migrated to Mississippi and became successful. Settling on rich bottomlands next to the Mississippi River, Joseph Davis made profits, expanded his holdings of land and slaves, and made more profits. Soon he was an established figure in society, and he used his position to arrange an education at West Point for his younger brother. A large plantation awaited Jefferson's resignation from the army. Thus the Davis family became aristocrats in one generation.

Jefferson Davis: His Early Life

The rise of new aristocrats in the Gulf and the migration of thousands of aspiring slaveholders across the Appalachians meant another kind of migration—involuntary movement—for black southerners. Cotton planters in the Gulf region generated a steady demand for more slaves, but Congress had closed the international slave trade in 1808. Despite some smuggling, slave labor from abroad was essentially unavailable. Thus new slaves for the Lower South had to come from the older states of the Upper South.

As it happened, slaveowners there often had more slaves than they needed. Their slave population had grown, but tobacco prices had fallen and soil exhaustion had become a serious problem. Thus planters in Virginia and North Carolina were shifting toward wheat and corn, crops that were

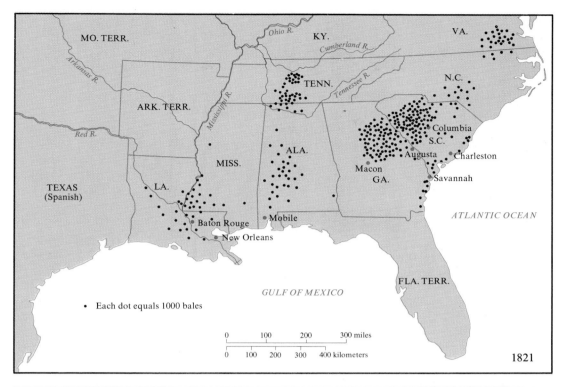

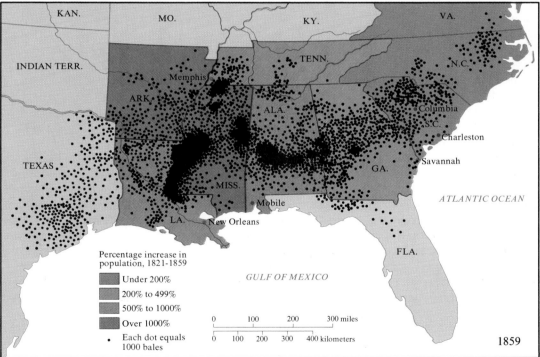

Cotton Production in the South

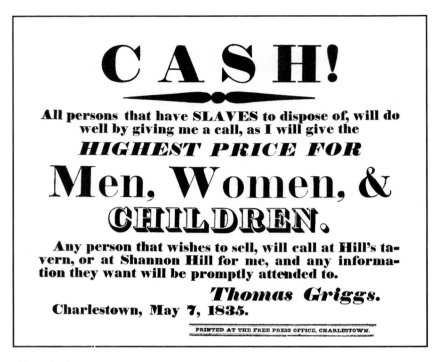

CASH!

All persons that have SLAVES to dispose of, will do well by giving me a call, as I will give the

HIGHEST PRICE FOR

Men, Women, & CHILDREN.

Any person that wishes to sell, will call at Hill's tavern, or at Shannon Hill for me, and any information they want will be promptly attended to.

Thomas Griggs.

Charlestown, May 7, 1835.

PRINTED AT THE FREE PRESS OFFICE, CHARLESTOWN.

Although slave traders were not admired in the South, the market in human beings remained strong because it served vital functions in an economy based on slave labor. *Library of Congress.*

less labor-intensive. Slaveowners on worn-out tobacco lands were glad to sell excess slaves to the expanding black belt areas of the cotton South.

Consequently, the expansion of slaveholding across the Appalachians caused a large interregional movement of the black population. Between 1810 and 1820 alone, 137,000 slaves were forced to move from North Carolina and the Chesapeake states to Alabama, Mississippi, and other western regions. Interregional sales and transfers continued thereafter, as the cotton boom kept demand high for slave laborers in the Lower South. An estimated 2 million persons were sold between 1820 and 1860 to satisfy the need for slave labor. Thousands of black families were disrupted every year to serve the needs of the cotton economy.

Thus the South was growing and expanding, driven by excitement over new lands and energies related to the cotton boom. To white southerners the period from 1800 to 1860 was a time of great change and progress, no less so than in the North. But the South's growth was different. Despite the change that characterized an expanding South, common patterns were putting a special impress upon the social system: the distinguishing features of an agricultural and a slave society.

An Agrarian Society

Agriculture and slavery dominated southern development. It is true that the South shared some of the diversity of the bustling, urbanizing, commercial North. There were merchants, artisans, and craftsmen in the larger cities and men of commerce who promoted railways and transportation improvements. Immigrants from Ireland and other parts of Europe arrived in Savannah and other southern ports in dramatically increasing numbers during the 1840s and 1850s. But these developments were only faint shadows of the northern phenomena, and they had relatively little impact on the South overall. The largest patterns of southern development reflected the dominance of agriculture and slavery and the prominence of rural slaves, slaveholders, and yeomen farmers in the population.

This painting of Franklin College (later the University of Georgia) at Athens, Georgia, suggests the way that rural settings predominated in southern life. *University of Georgia Libraries.*

In the South population distribution remained thin. Cotton growers spread out over as large an area as possible in order to maximize production and income. Because farms were far apart, rather than clustered around villages, southern society remained predominantly rural. Population growth fell behind the North's because most immigrants sought urban, not rural, locations. Population density, low even in the older plantation states, was extremely low in the frontier areas being brought under cultivation. In 1860 there were only 2.3 people per square mile in Texas, 15.6 in Louisiana, and 18.0 in Georgia. By contrast, population density in the nonslaveholding states east of the Mississippi River was almost three times higher. The Northeast had an average of 65.4 persons per square mile, and in some places the density was much higher. Massachusetts had 153.1 people per square mile, and New York City, where overcrowding reached epic proportions, compressed 86,400 people into each square mile.

> **Population Distribution**

Even in the 1850s, much of the South seemed almost uninhabited, a virtual wilderness. Frederick Law Olmsted, a northerner who later became famous as a landscape architect, made several trips through the South in the 1850s as a reporter. He found that the few trains and stagecoaches available to travelers offered only rough accommodations and kept their schedules poorly. Indeed, he had to do most of his traveling on horseback along primitive trails. Passing from Columbus, Georgia, to Montgomery, Alabama, Olmsted observed "a hilly wilderness, with a few dreary villages, and many isolated cotton farms." Alabama, of course, had been frontier as recently as 1800, but Olmsted encountered the same conditions in parts of eastern Virginia: "For hours and hours one has to ride through the unlimited, continual, all-shadowing, all-embracing forest, following roads in the making of which no more labor has been given than was necessary to remove the timber which would obstruct the passage of wagons; and even for days and days he may sometimes travel and see never two dwellings of mankind within sight of each other."

Society in such rural areas was characterized by relatively weak institutions, for it takes people to create and support organized activity. Where the concentration of people was low, it was difficult to finance and operate schools, churches, libraries, or even hotels, restaurants, and other urban amenities. Southerners were strongly committed to their churches, and some believed in the importance of universities, but all such institutions were far less developed than those in the North.

The South's cities were likewise smaller and less developed than those in the North. As exporters, southerners did not need large cities; a small group of merchants working in connection with northern brokers sufficed to ship their cotton overseas and to import necessary supplies and luxuries. As planters, southerners invested most of their capital in slaves; they had little money left to build factories—another source of urban growth. A few southerners did invest in iron or textiles on a small scale. But the largest southern "industry" was lumbering, and the largest factories were cigar factories, where slaves finished tobacco products.

Weak Urban Sector

More importantly, the South did not develop a unified market economy or regional transportation network, as the North did. Far less money was spent on canals, turnpikes, or railroads. In 1850 the South had only 26 percent of the nation's railroad mileage and, despite major efforts, only 35 percent in 1860. As a result, urban growth after 1820 was far less vigorous than in the North, and metropolitan centers were almost nonexistent. In 1860 only 49,000 out of 704,000 South Carolinians lived in towns with 2,500 or more residents. Less than 3 percent of Mississippi's population lived in places of comparable size. In 1860 the population of Charleston was only 41,000, Richmond 38,000, and Mobile 29,000. New Orleans, by far the largest southern city, had only 169,000 residents, and it was being left behind because it was not part of the national railroad network.

Thus, although it was economically attuned to an international market, the South was only semideveloped in comparison with other sections of the country. Its white people were prospering but neither as rapidly nor as independently as residents of the North. There, commerce and industry brought unprecedented advances in productivity, widening the range of affordable goods and services and raising the average person's standard of living. In the South, change was quantitative rather than qualitative; farming techniques remained essentially the same. To prosper, southern planters increased their acreage and hoped for continued high demand from foreign customers—decisions that worked to the ultimate disadvantage of the region. Subsistence farmers merely worked harder and hoped to grow a bit more.

Farmers, Planters, and Free Blacks

A large majority of white southern families (three-quarters in 1860) owned no slaves. Some of them lived in towns and ran stores or businesses, but most were yeoman farmers who owned their own land and grew their own food. They were the typical whites, but typical in a society of extremes. The social distance between different groups of whites could be great; still greater was the distance between whites and blacks.

Although they were the most numerous group of southern whites, subsistence farmers, as a rule, did not set the direction of the slave society. Normally they occupied a relatively autonomous position within the slavery-based, staple-crop economy that was expanding around them. Independent and motivated by a hearty share of frontier individualism, they provided for themselves in the traditional way of American farm families, prospering slowly from improvements on their acreage or the settlement of new and better land. And this meant steady progress for thousands of yeomen as the South expanded.

But the lives of most southern yeomen, as compared to northern farmers, had not been transformed by improvements in transportation. Because few railroads penetrated the southern interior, yeomen generally had little connection with the market or its type of progress. Families might raise a small surplus to trade for needed items or spending cash, but they were far from major market networks and therefore not particularly concerned about larger cash income. They valued instead their self-reliance and freedom from others' control. Absorbed in an isolated but demanding rural life, they formed an important, though sometimes silent, part of southern society. If their rights were threatened, however, they could react strongly.

The thatched log house in this 1820 watercolor was located on the left bank of the Mississippi River. The scene reveals the pioneering lifestyles of many yeoman families. *Art Collection, Tulane University, New Orleans.*

The yeomen enjoyed a folk culture based on family, church, and community. They spoke with a drawl, and their inflections were reminiscent of their Scottish and Irish backgrounds. Once a year they flocked to religious revivals called protracted meetings or camp meetings, and in between they enjoyed events such as house-raisings, logrollings, quilting bees, and corn-shuckings. These combined work with fun, offered food in abundance, and usually included liquor. Such community events provided a fellowship that was especially welcome to isolated rural dwellers.

> **Folk Culture of the Yeoman**

Beyond these basic facts, historians know little about the yeomen. Because their means were modest, they did not generate the voluminous legal papers—contracts, wills, and inventories of estates—that document the activities of the rich. Only a few letters have found their way into libraries and archives. It is reasonable to suppose, though, that yeomen held a variety of opinions and pursued individual goals.

Among the yeomen were many who aspired to wealth, who were eager to join the race for slaves, land, and profits from cotton. An example of this kind of individual was a North Carolinian named John F. Flintoff, whose diary reveals that the road to wealth was not always easy. Flintoff was born in 1823 and at age eighteen went to Mississippi to seek his fortune. Like other aspiring yeomen, he worked as an overseer but often found it impossible to please his employers. At one time he gave up and returned to North Carolina, where he married and lived in his parents' house. But Flintoff was "impatient to get along in the world," so he tried Louisiana next and then Mississippi again.

For Flintoff, the fertile Gulf region had its disadvantages. "My health has been very bad here," he noted; "chills and fever occasionally has hold of me." "First rate employment" alternated with "very low wages." Moreover, as a young man working on isolated plantations, Flintoff often felt "all alone." Even a revival meeting in 1844 proved "an extremely cold time" with "little warm feeling." His uncle and other employers found fault with his work, and in 1846 Flintoff concluded in despair that "managing negroes and large farms is soul destroying."

Still, a desire to succeed kept him going. At twenty-six, before he owned a foot of land, Flintoff bought his first slave, "a negro boy 7 years old."

Soon he had purchased two more children, the cheapest slaves available. Conscious of his status as a slaveowner, Flintoff resented the low wages he was paid and complained that his uncle offered him *"hand pay,"* the wages of a day laborer rather than a slaveowner and a manager. In 1853, with nine young slaves and a growing family, Flintoff faced "the most unhappy time of my life." He was fired by his uncle, "treated shamefully." Finally he said, "I will have to sell some of my negroes to buy land. This I must have. I want *a home.*"

Returning to North Carolina, Flintoff purchased 124 acres with help from his in-laws. He grew corn, wheat, and tobacco and earned extra cash hauling wood in his wagon. By 1860 he owned 3 horses, 26 hogs, 10 cattle, and several slaves and was paying off his debts. As the Civil War approached, he could look forward to acquiring more land and slaves, freeing his wife from much of the labor of yeoman women, and possibly sending his sons to college. Flintoff achieved success, but the struggle upward had not been easy, and he never became the cotton planter he had aspired to be.

Probably more typical of the southern yeoman was Ferdinand L. Steel. As a young man Steel moved from North Carolina to Tennessee to work as a hatter and river boatman, but he eventually settled down to farming in Mississippi. He rose every day at five and worked until sundown. With the help of his family he raised corn, wheat, pork, and vegetables for the family table. Cotton was his cash crop: like other yeomen he sold five or six bales a year to obtain money for sugar, coffee, salt, calico, gunpowder, and a few other store-bought goods.

Steel picked his cotton himself (never exceeding 120 pounds per day—less than many slaves averaged) and regretted that cotton cultivation was so arduous and time-consuming. He was not tempted to grow more of it. The market fluctuated, and if cotton prices fell, a small grower like himself could be driven into debt and lose his farm. Steel, in fact, wanted to grow less cotton. "We are too weak handed" to manage it, he noted in his diary. "We had better raise small grain and corn and let cotton alone, raise corn and keep out of debt and we will have no necessity of raising cotton."

Steel's life in Mississippi in the 1840s retained much of the flavor of the frontier. He made all the family's shoes; his wife and sister sewed dresses, shirts, and "pantiloons." The Steel women also rendered their own soap, and spun and wove cotton

into cloth; the men hunted for game. House-raisings and corn-shuckings provided entertainment, and Steel doctored his illnesses with boneset tea and other herbs.

The focus of Steel's life was his family and his religion. The family prayed together every morning and night, and he prayed and studied Scripture for an hour after lunch. Steel joined a temperance society and looked forward to church and camp meetings. "My Faith increases, & I enjoy much of that peace which the world cannot give," he wrote in 1841. Seeking to improve himself and be "ready" for judgment, Steel borrowed histories, Latin and Greek grammars, and religious books from his church. Eventually he became a traveling Methodist minister. "My life is one of toil," he reflected, "but blessed be God that it is as well with me as it is."

Toil, with even less security, was the lot of two other groups of free southerners: landless whites and free blacks. From 25 to 40 percent of the white

> **Landless Whites**

workers in the South were laborers who owned no land. Their property consisted of a few household items and some animals—usually pigs—that could feed themselves on the open range. These animals were a major economic asset, for good, steady employment was uncertain in a region whose large producers relied on slave labor. In addition to unskilled laborers in the countryside and towns, the landless included some immigrants, especially Irish, who did heavy and dangerous work such as building railroads and digging ditches.

The white farm laborers were people struggling to become yeomen. They faced low wages or, if they rented, were dependent on the unpredictable market price for their crops. Some fell into debt and were frequently sued; others, by scrimping and saving and finding odd jobs, managed to climb into the ranks of yeomen. When James and Nancy Bennitt of North Carolina succeeded in their ten-year struggle to buy land, they decided to avoid the unstable market in cotton as much as possible; thereafter they raised extra corn and wheat as sources of cash.

There were nearly a quarter of a million free blacks in the South in 1860, people whose conditions generally were worse than the yeoman's and often little better than the slave's.

> **Free Blacks**

The free blacks of the Upper South were usually descendants of

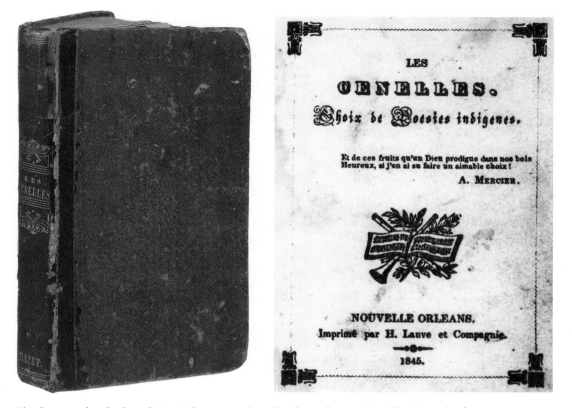

The free people of color of New Orleans carved out for themselves a status, identity, and culture separate from both the black and the white worlds. *Les Cennelles*, published in 1845, was a book of Romantic poetry written in French by seventeen free men of color. *The Historic New Orleans Collection.*

men and women emancipated by their owners in the 1780s and 1790s, a period of postrevolutionary idealism that coincided with a decline in tobacco prices. Some achieved substantial progress in towns or cities, but most lived in rural areas and had few material advantages. Usually they did not own land and had to labor in someone else's field, frequently beside slaves. By law they could not own a gun or liquor, violate curfew, assemble except in church, testify in court, or (everywhere after 1835) vote. Despite these obstacles, a minority bought land, and others found jobs as artisans, draymen, boatmen, and fishermen. A few owned slaves, who were almost always their wives and children, purchased from bondage.

Farther south, in the cotton and Gulf regions, a large proportion of free blacks were mulattos, the privileged offspring of wealthy planters. Some received good educations and financial backing from their fathers, who recognized a moral obligation to them. In a few cities such as New Orleans and Mobile, extensive interracial sex had produced a mulatto population that was recognized as a distinct class. These mulattos formed a society of their own and sought a status above slaves and other freedmen, if not equal to planters. But outside New Orleans, Mobile, and Charleston such groups were rare, and most mulattos encountered disadvantages more frequently than they enjoyed benefits from their light skin tone. (For a more detailed discussion of free blacks during this period, see Chapter 11.)

At the opposite end of the spectrum from free blacks were the slaveholders. As a group slaveowners lived well, on incomes that enabled them to enjoy superior housing, food, clothing, and luxuries. But most did not live on the opulent scale that legend suggests. A few statistics tell the story: 88 percent of southern slaveholders had fewer than twenty slaves; 72 percent had fewer than ten; 50 percent had fewer than five. Thus the average slaveholder was not a man of great wealth but an aspiring farmer. Nor was he a polished aristocrat but more usually a person of humble origins, with little formal education and many rough edges to his manner. In fact, he probably had little beyond a degree of wealth and a growing ambition to distinguish him from a nonslaveholder.

A Louisiana planter named Bennet Barrow can serve as an example. Barrow had gained considerable wealth from growing cotton, yet he remained neither especially polished nor unusually coarse. Barrow's wealth was new, and he was habitually preoccupied with moneymaking. He worried constantly over his cotton crop, filling his diary with tedious weather reports and gloomy predictions of his yields. Yet Barrow also strove to appear above such worries, and in boom times he grandly endorsed notes for men who left him saddled with debt.

Barrow hunted frequently, and he had a passion for racing horses and raising hounds. Each year he set aside several weeks to attend the races in New Orleans, where he entered stallions brought from as far away as Tennessee. Barrow could report the loss of a slave without feeling, but emotion shattered his laconic manner when misfortune struck his sporting animals. "Never was a person more unlucky than I am," he complained; "My favorite pup never lives." His strongest feelings surfaced when his horse Jos Bell—equal to "the best Horse in the South"—"broke down running a mile . . . ruined for Ever." That same day the distraught Barrow gave his field hands a "general Whipping." Barrow was rich, but his wealth had not softened his rough, direct style of life.

The wealth of the greatest planters gave ambitious men like Barrow something to aspire to. Most planters lived in spacious, comfortable farmhouses, but some did live in mansions. Most slaveowners sat down at mealtimes to an abundance of tempting country foods—pork and ham, beef and game, fresh vegetables and fruits, tasty breads and biscuits, cakes and jams—but the sophisticated elite consumed such delights as "gumbo, ducks and olives, *supreme de volaille,* chickens in jelly, oysters, lettuce salad, chocolate cream, jelly cake, claret cup, etc." On formal and business occasions such as county court days, a traveler in Mississippi would see gentlemen decked out in "black cloth coats, black cravats and satin or embroidered silk waistcoats; all, too, sleek as if just from a barber's hands, and redolent of perfumes."

The ladies wore the latest fashions to parties and balls and made many other occasions sources of merriment. Relations and friends often visited each other for several days or weeks at a time, enjoying good food and good company. Courtship was a major attraction at the larger parties or dances. Between social occasions women and many men kept up their close friendships through constant letter-writing.

Slaveholding men held the dominant position in society and, especially among the wealthiest and oldest families, they justified their dominance through a paternalistic ideology.

Southern Paternalism Instead of stressing the acquisitive aspects of commercial agriculture, they focused on *noblesse oblige.* They saw themselves as custodians of the welfare of society as a whole and of the black families who depended on them. The paternalistic planter saw himself not as an oppressor but as the benevolent guardian of an inferior race. He developed affectionate feelings toward his slaves (as long as they kept in their place) and was genuinely shocked at outside criticism of his behavior.

The letters of Paul Carrington Cameron, North Carolina's largest slaveholder, illustrate this mentality. After a period of sickness among his one thousand North Carolina slaves (he had hundreds more in Alabama and Mississippi), Cameron wrote, "I fear the Negroes have suffered much from the want of proper attention and kindness under this late distemper . . . no love of lucre shall ever induce me to be cruel, or even to make or permit to be made any great exposure of their persons at inclement seasons." On another occasion he described to his sister the sense of responsibility he felt: "I cannot better follow the example of our venerated Mother than in doing my duty to her faithful old slaves and their descendants. Do you remember a cold & frosty morning, during her illness, when she said to me 'Paul my son the people ought to be shod' this is ever in my ears, whenever I see any ones shoes in bad order; and in my ears it will be, so long as I am master."

There is no doubt that the richest southern planters saw themselves in this way. It was comforting to do so, and slaves, accommodating themselves to the realities of power, encouraged their masters to think their benevolence was appreciated. Paternalism also provided a welcome defense against abolitionist criticism. Still, for most planters, pater-

The North Carolina planter Duncan Cameron (1776–1853) built this spacious and comfortable farmhouse for his bride, Rebecca Bennehan, in 1804. The house, called Fairntosh, is more typical of the average planter's home than the elaborate Greek-revival-style mansions of popular legend. *Library of Congress.*

nalism affected the manner and not the substance of their behavior. It was a matter of style. Its softness and warmth covered harsher assumptions: blacks were inferior; planters should make money. As discussion of owners' duties increased, theories about the complete and permanent inferiority of blacks also multiplied.

Even Paul Cameron's concern vanished with changed circumstances. After the Civil War, he bristled at blacks' efforts to be free and made sweeping economic decisions without regard to their welfare. Writing on Christmas Day 1865, Cameron showed little Christian charity (but a healthy profit motive) when he expressed his desire to get "free . . . of the negro. I am convinced that the people who gets rid of the free negro first will be the first to advance in improved agriculture. Have made no effort to retain any of mine [and] will not attempt a crop beyond the capacity of 30 hands." With that he turned out nearly a thousand black agriculturalists, rented his lands to several white farmers, and invested in industry, which he evidently considered more promising economically.

Relations between men and women in the planter class were similarly paternalistic. An upper-class southern woman typically was raised and educated to be the subordinate companion of men. Her proper responsibility was home management. She was not to venture into politics and other worldly affairs. In a social system based on the coercion of an entire race, no women could be allowed to challenge society's rules, on sexual or racial relations. If she defied or questioned the status quo, she risked universal condemnation.

Elite Women's Role

Within the domestic circle the husband reigned supreme. For the fortunate women, like North Carolina diarist Catherine Devereux Edmondston, whose marriage joined two people of shared tastes and habits, the husband's authority weighed lightly or not at all. But other women, even some who considered themselves happily married, were acutely conscious of that authority. "He is master of the house," wrote South Carolina's Mary Boykin Chesnut. "To hear is to obey . . . all the comfort of

Elizabeth Ridgely of Baltimore was fifteen when Thomas Sully created this portrait in 1818. Her hair style, clothing, and the European pedal harp, which she knew how to play, bear witness to her family's wealth and status. *National Gallery of Art, Washington, Gift of Maude Monell Vetlesen.*

girls and received an education that emphasized grammar, composition, penmanship, geography, literature, and languages, but little science and mathematics. As she developed some sense of herself, the young woman typically maintained dutiful and affectionate ties with her parents. But very soon she had to commit herself for life to a man whom she generally had known for only a brief time.

Once married, she lost most of her legal rights to her husband, became part of his family, and was expected to get along with numerous in-laws during extended visits. Most of the year, she was isolated on a large plantation, where she had to learn a host of new duties. Although free from much of the labor of yeoman women, the plantation mistress was not free from care. She had to supervise many tasks: overseeing the cooking and preserving of food, managing the house, caring for the children, and attending sick slaves. As a woman she was forbidden to travel and visit unless accompanied by a man. All the circumstances of her future life depended on the man she chose.

It is not surprising that the intelligent and perceptive young woman sometimes approached marriage with a feeling akin to dread. Lucy Breckinridge, a wealthy Virginia girl, sensed how much autonomy she would have to surrender on her wedding day. She realized that thereafter her life would depend on men, who though chivalrous in manner, expected to be the center of attention. In her diary she recorded this unvarnished observation on marriage: "If [husbands] care for their wives at all it is only as a sort of servant, a being made to attend to their comforts and to keep the children out of the way. . . . A woman's life after she is married, unless there is an immense amount of love, is nothing but suffering and hard work."

Lucy loved young children but knew that childbearing often involved grief and sorrow. On learning of a relative's death, Lucy said, "It is a happy release for her, for her married life has been a long term of suffering. She has been married about seven years and had five children." This case was not too unusual, for in 1840 the birthrate for southern women in their fertile years was almost 20 percent higher than the national average. At the beginning of the nineteenth century, the average southern woman could expect to bear eight children; by 1860 the figure had decreased only to six, and one or more miscarriages were likely among so many pregnancies. The high birthrate took a toll

my life depends upon his being in a good humor." In a darker mood Chesnut once observed that "there is no slave . . . like a wife." Unquestionably there were some, possibly many, close and satisfying relationships between men and women in the planter class, but many women were dissatisfied.

The upper-class southern woman had to clear several barriers in the way of happiness. Making the right choice of a husband was especially important. With this decision a young woman moved from the rather narrow experience that society had permitted her into a restricted lifetime role. After spending her early years within the family circle, a planter's daughter usually attended one of the South's rapidly multiplying academies or boarding schools. There she formed friendships with other

Chapter 10: Slavery and the Growth of the South, 1800–1860

on women's health, for complications of childbirth were a major cause of death.

Moreover, a mother had to endure the loss of many of the infants she bore. Infant mortality in the first year of life exceeded 10 percent and remained high during the next few years. In the South in 1860 almost five out of ten children died before age five, and in South Carolina more than six in ten failed to reach age twenty. For those women who wanted to plan their families, methods of contraception were not always reliable. And doctors had few remedies for infection or irritation of the reproductive tract.

Slavery was another source of trouble, a source of problems that women had to endure but were not supposed to notice. "Violations of the moral law . . . made mulattoes as common as blackberries," protested a woman in Georgia, but wives had to play "the ostrich game." "A magnate who runs a hideous black harem," wrote Mrs. Chesnut, "under the same roof with his lovely white wife, and his beautiful accomplished daughters . . . poses as the model of all human virtues to these poor women whom God and the laws have given him. From the height of his awful majesty, he scolds and thunders at them, as if he never did wrong in his life."

In the early 1800s, some southern women, especially Quakers, had spoken out against slavery. Although most white women did not criticize the "peculiar institution," they often approached it differently from men, seeing it less as a system and more as a series of relationships with individuals. Perhaps southern men sensed this, for they wanted no discussion by women of the slavery issue. In the 1840s and 1850s, as national and international criticism of slavery increased, southern men published a barrage of articles stressing that women should restrict their concerns to the home. A writer in the *Southern Literary Messenger* bemoaned "these days of Women's Rights." Disapproving of women with political opinions, the *Southern Quarterly Review* declared, "The proper place for a woman is at home. One of her highest privileges, to be politically merged in the existence of her husband." Thomas Dew, one of the nineteenth century's first proslavery theorists, advised that "women are precisely what the men make them," and another writer promoted "affection, reverence, and duty" as a woman's proper attitudes.

But southern women were beginning to chafe at their customary exclusion from financial matters. A study of women in Petersburg, Virginia, has re-

vealed behavior that amounted to an implicit criticism of the institution of marriage and the loss of autonomy it entailed. During several decades before 1860 the proportion of women who had not married, or not remarried after the death of a spouse, grew to exceed 33 percent. Likewise the number of women who worked for wages, controlled their own property, or even ran businesses increased. In managing property, these women benefited from legal reforms, beginning with Mississippi's Married Women's Property Act of 1839, that were not designed to increase female independence. Rather, to offset business panics and recessions, the law gave women some property rights in order to protect families from ruin caused by the husband's indebtedness. But some women saw the resulting opportunity and took it. In the countryside southern women had fewer options, but Petersburg's women were seeking to use the talents they had and the education they had gained.

Restrictions on freedom and the use of education were not limited to upper-class women. For a large category of southern men and women, freedom was wholly denied and education in any form was not allowed. Male or female, slaves were expected to accept bondage and ignorance as their condition.

Slaves and the Conditions of Their Servitude

For African-Americans, slavery was a curse that brought no blessings other than the strengths they developed to survive it. Slaves knew a life of poverty, coercion, toil, heartbreak, and resentment. They had few hopes that were not denied; often they had to bear separation from their loved ones; and they were despised as an inferior race. That they endured and found loyalty and strength among themselves is a tribute to their courage, but it could not make up for a life without freedom or opportunity.

Southern slaves enjoyed few material comforts beyond the bare necessities. Their diet was plain and limited, although generally they had enough to eat. The basic ration was cornmeal, fat pork, molasses, and occasionally coffee. Many masters al-

Slaves' Diet, Clothing, and Housing lowed slaves to tend gardens, which provided the variety and extra nutrition of greens and sweet potatoes. Fishing and hunting benefited some slaves. "It was nothin' fine," recalled one woman, "but it was good plain eatin' what filled you up."[1] Most slaveowners were innocent of the charge that they starved their slaves, but there is considerable evidence that slaves often suffered the effects of beriberi, pellagra, and other dietary-deficiency diseases.

Clothing too was plain, coarse, and inexpensive. Children of both sexes ran naked in hot weather and wore long cotton shirts in cool. When they were big enough to go to the fields, the boys received a work shirt and a pair of breeches and the girls a simple dress. On many plantations slave women made their own clothing of osnaburg, a coarse cotton fabric known as "nigger cloth." Probably few received more than one or two changes of clothing for hot and cold seasons and one blanket each winter. Those who could earn a little money by doing extra work often bought additional clothing. Many slaves had to go without shoes until December, even as far north as Virginia. The shoes they received were frequent objects of complaint—uncomfortable brass-toed brogans or stiff wraparounds made from leather tanned on the plantation.

Summer and winter, slaves typically lived in small one-room cabins with a door and possibly a window opening but no glass. Logs chinked with mud formed the walls; dirt was the only floor; and a wattle-and-daub or stone chimney vented the fireplace, which provided heat and light. Bedding consisted of heaps of straw, straw mattresses, or wooden bedframes lashed to the walls with rope. A few crude pieces of furniture and cooking utensils completed the furnishings of most cabins. More substantial houses survive today from some of the richer plantations, but the average slave lived in crude accommodations. The gravest drawback of slave cabins was not their appearance and lack of comfort but their unhealthfulness. In each small cabin lived one or two whole families. Crowding

---

[1] Accounts by ex-slaves are quoted from *The American Slave: A Composite Autobiography,* edited by George P. Rawick (Westport, Conn.: Greenwood Press, First Reprint Edition 1972, Second Reprint Edition 1974), from materials gathered by the Federal Writers' Project and originally published in 1941. The spelling in these accounts has been standardized.

and lack of sanitation fostered the spread of infection and contagious diseases. Many slaves (and whites) carried worms and intestinal parasites picked up from fecal matter or the soil. Lice were widespread among both races, and flies and other insects spread such virulent diseases as typhoid fever, malaria, and dysentery.

Hard work was the central fact of the slaves' existence. In Gulf Coast cotton districts long hours and large work gangs suggested factories in the field rather than the small-scale, isolated work patterns of slaves in the eighteenth-century Chesapeake. Overseers rang the morning bell before dawn, so early that some slaves remembered being in the fields "before it was light enough to see clearly . . . holding their hoes and other implements—afraid to start work for fear that they would cover the cotton plants with dirt because they couldn't see clearly." And, as one woman testified when interviewed by workers in the Federal Writers' Project of the 1930s, "it was way after sundown 'fore they could stop that field work. Then they had to hustle to finish their night work in time for supper, or go to bed without it."

Slaves' Work Routines

Except in urban settings and on some rice plantations, where slaves were assigned daily tasks to complete at their own pace, working from "sun to sun" became universal in the South. These long hours and hard work were at the heart of the advantage of slave labor. As one planter put it, slaves were the best labor because "you could command them and *make* them do what was right." White workers, by contrast, were few and couldn't be *driven;* "they wouldn't stand it." Slaves who cultivated tobacco in the Upper South worked long hours picking the sticky, sometimes noxious tobacco leaves and worked under a harsh discipline that could not be applied to white labor. The slaves had to "sucker" the plants—pinch off secondary shoots to increase the size of the leaves—and remove tobacco worms by hand. According to many former slaves, workers who missed worms on the plant were forced to eat them before an angry master. No white laborers in the South faced such supervision.

Planters aimed to keep all their laborers busy all the time. Profit took precedence over paternalism's "protection" of women: slave women did heavy field work, often as much as the men and even during pregnancy. Old people—of whom there

Hard work in the fields—from first light until dark—filled the days of most slaves on cotton plantations. *The Historic New Orleans Collection.*

were few—were kept busy caring for young children, doing light chores, or carding, ginning, or spinning cotton. Children had to gather kindling for the fire, carry water to the fields, or sweep the yard. But slaves had a variety of ways to keep from being worked to death. It was impossible for the master to supervise every slave every minute, and slaves slacked off when they were not being watched. Thus travelers frequently described lackadaisical slaves who seemed "to go through the motions of labor without putting strength into them," and owners complained that slaves "never would lay out their strength freely . . . it was impossible to make them do it." Stubborn misunderstanding and literal-mindedness were another defense. One exasperated Virginia planter exclaimed, "You can make a nigger work, *but you cannot make him think.*"

Of course slaves could not slow their labor too much, because the owner enjoyed a monopoly on force and violence. Whites throughout the South believed that Negroes "can't be governed except with the whip." One South Carolinian frankly explained to a northern journalist that he had whipped his slaves occasionally, "say once a fortnight; . . . the Negroes knew they would be

> **Physical and Mental Abuse of Slaves**

whipped if they didn't behave themselves, and the fear of the lash kept them in good order." Evidence suggests that whippings were less frequent on small farms than on large plantations, but the reports of former slaves show that a large majority even of small farmers plied the lash. These beatings symbolized authority to the master and tyranny to the slaves, who made them a benchmark for evaluating a master. In the words of former slaves, a good owner was one who did not "whip too much," whereas a bad owner "whipped till he's bloodied you and blistered you."

As this testimony suggests, terrible abuses could and did occur. The master wielded virtually absolute authority on his plantation, and courts did not recognize the word of a chattel. Pregnant women were whipped, and there were burnings, mutilations, tortures, and murders. Yet the physical cruelty of slavery may have been less in the United States than elsewhere in the New World. In sugar-growing or mining regions of the Western Hemisphere in the 1800s, slaves were regarded as an expendable resource to be replaced after seven years. Treatment was so poor and families so uncommon that death rates were high and the heavily male slave population did not replace itself but instead rapidly shrank in size. In the United States, by contrast, the slave population showed a steady natu-

Coercion was the essence of slavery. To enforce their will, masters relied on whips and instruments like this pronged collar to inflict pain or restrict the slaves' movements. A slave girl in nineteenth-century New Orleans had to wear the collar shown as punishment for attempting to run away. The painting suggests that such sights were not unusual on the city's streets. *Painting: The Historic New Orleans Collection; slave collar: Massachusetts Historical Society.*

ral increase, as births exceeded deaths, and each generation grew larger.

The worst evil of American slavery was not its physical cruelty but the fact of slavery itself: coercion, loss of freedom, belonging to another person with virtually no hope for change. Recalling their days in bondage, some former slaves emphasized the physical abuse—those were "bullwhip days" to one woman; another said, "What I think 'bout slavery? Huh—nigger get back cut in slavery time, didn't he?" But their comments focused on the tyranny of whipping as much as the pain. A woman named Delia Garlic cut to the core when she said, "It's bad to belong to folks that own you soul an' body. I could tell you 'bout it all day, but even then you couldn't guess the awfulness of it." And a man named Thomas Lewis put it this way: "There was no such thing as being good to slaves. Many people were better than others, but a slave belonged to his master and there was no way to get out of it."

As these comments show, the great majority of American slaves retained their mental independence and self-respect despite their bondage. They hated their oppression, and contrary to some whites' perceptions, they were not grateful to their oppressors. Although they had to be subservient and speak honeyed words in the presence of their masters, they talked quite differently later on among themselves. The evidence of their resistant attitudes comes from their actions and from their own life stories.

Former slaves reported some kind feelings between masters and slaves, but the overwhelming picture was one of antagonism and resistance. Slaves mistrusted kindness from

Slaves' whites and suspected self-interest
Attitudes in their owners. A woman whose
Toward mistress "was good to us Niggers"
Whites said her owner was kind "'cause she was raisin' us to work for her." A man recalled that his owners "always thought lots of their niggers and Grandma Maria say, 'Why shouldn't they—it was their money.'" Christmas presents of clothing from the master did not mean anything, observed another, "'cause he was going to [buy] that anyhow."

Slaves also saw their owners as people who used human beings as beasts of burden. "Master was pretty good," said one man. "He treated us just about like you would a good mule." Another said that his master "fed us reg'lar on good, 'stantial food, just like you'd tend to your horse, if you had a real good one." A third recalled his master saying, "'A well-fed, healthy nigger, next to a mule, is the best propersition a man can invest his money in.'"

Slaves were sensitive to the thousand daily signs of their degraded status. One man recalled the general rule that slaves ate cornbread and owners ate biscuits. If blacks did get biscuits, "the flour that we made the biscuits out of was the third-grade shorts." A woman reported that on her plantation "Old Master hunted a heap, but us never did get none of what he brought in." "Us catch lots of 'possums, but mighty few of 'em us Niggers ever got a chance to eat or rabbits neither," said another. "They made Niggers go out and hunt 'em and the white folks ate 'em." If the owner took slaves' garden produce to town and sold it for them, the slaves suspected him of pocketing part of the profits.

Suspicion and resentment often grew into hatred. According to a former slave from Virginia, "the white folks treated the nigger so mean that all the slaves prayed God to punish their cruel masters." When a yellow fever epidemic struck in 1852, many slaves saw it as God's retribution. As late as the 1930s an elderly woman named Minnie Fulkes cherished the conviction that God was going to punish white people for their cruelty to blacks. She described the whippings that her mother had had to endure and then exclaimed, "Lord, Lord, I hate white people and the flood waters goin' to drown some more." A young slave girl who had suffered abuse as a house servant admitted that she took cruel advantage of her mistress when the woman had a stroke. Instead of fanning the mistress to keep flies away, the young slave struck her in the face with the fan whenever they were alone. "I done that woman bad," the slave confessed, but "she was so mean to me."

The bitterness between blacks and whites was vividly expressed by a former slave named Savilla Burrell, who visited her former master on his deathbed long after the Civil War. Sitting beside him, she reflected on the lines that "sorrow had plowed on that old face and I remembered he'd been a captain on horseback in the war. It come into my remembrance the song of Moses: 'the Lord had triumphed glorily and the horse and his rider have been throwed into the sea.'" She felt sympathy for a dying man, but she also felt satisfaction at God's revenge.

On the plantation, of course, slaves had to keep such thoughts to themselves. Often they expressed one feeling to whites, another within their own race and culture.

Slave Culture and Everyday Life

The force that helped slaves to maintain such defiance was their culture. They had their own view of the world, a body of beliefs and values born of both their past and their present, as well as the fellowship and support of their own community. With power overwhelmingly in the hands of whites, it was not possible for slaves to change their world. But drawing strength from their culture, they could resist their condition and struggle on against it.

Slave culture changed significantly after the turn of the century. Between 1790 and 1808, when Congress banned further importation of slaves, there was a rush to import Africans. After that the proportion of native-born blacks rose steadily, reaching 96 percent in 1840 and almost 100 percent in 1860. (For this reason blacks can trace their American ancestry back farther than many white Americans can.) Meanwhile, more and more slaves adopted Christianity. With time the old African culture faded farther into memory as an African-American culture matured.

In one sense African influences remained primary, for African practices and beliefs reminded the slaves that they were and ought to be different from their oppressors and thus **Remnants** encouraged them to resist. The **of African** most visible aspects of African **Culture** culture were the slaves' dress and recreation. Some slave men plaited their hair into rows and fancy designs; slave women often wore their hair "in string"—tied in small bunches with a string or piece of cloth. A few men and many women wrapped their heads in kerchiefs of the styles and colors of West Africa.

An anonymous African-American woodcarver working around 1860 created this powerful representation of a child holding a bucket. The pose and style of the piece testified to the influence of African cultural traditions among American blacks. *The Abby Aldrich Rockefeller Folk Art Collection, Williamsburg, Virginia.*

For entertainment slaves made musical instruments with carved motifs that resembled some African stringed instruments. Their drumming and dancing clearly followed African patterns; whites marveled at them. One visitor to Georgia in the 1860s described a ritual dance of African origin: "A ring of singers is formed. . . . They then utter a kind of melodious chant, which gradually increases in strength, and in noise, until it fairly shakes the house, and it can be heard for a long distance." This observer also noted the agility of the dancers and the call-and-response pattern in their chanting.

Many slaves continued to see and believe in spirits. Whites also believed in ghosts, but the belief was more widespread among slaves. It closely resembled the African concept of the living dead—the idea that deceased relatives visited the earth for many years until the process of dying was complete. Slaves also practiced conjuration, voodoo, and quasi-magical root medicine. By 1860 the most notable conjurers and root doctors were reputed to live in South Carolina, Georgia, Louisiana, and other isolated coastal areas of heavy slave importation.

These cultural survivals provided slaves with a sense of their separate past. Black achievement in music and dance was so exceptional that whites felt entirely cut off from it; in this one area some whites became aware that they did not "know" their slaves and that the slave community was a different world. Conjuration and folklore also directly fed resistance; slaves could cast a spell or direct the power of a hand (a bag of articles belonging to the person to be conjured) against the master. Not all masters felt confident enough to dismiss such a threat.

In adopting Christianity, slaves fashioned it too into an instrument of support and resistance. Theirs was a religion of justice quite unlike that of the propaganda their masters pushed at them. Former slaves scorned the preaching arranged by their masters. "You ought to have heard that preachin'," said one man. " 'Obey your master and mistress, don't steal chickens and eggs and meat,' but nary a word about havin' a soul to save." The slaves believed that Jesus cared about their souls and their present plight. They rejected the idea that in heaven whites would have "the colored folks . . . there to wait on 'em." Instead, when God's justice came, the slaveholders would be "broilin' in hell for their sin." "God is punishin' some of them ol' suckers and their children right now for the way they use to treat us poor colored folks," said one woman.

Slaves' Religion

For slaves Christianity was a religion of personal and group salvation. Devout men and women worshiped and prayed every day, "in the field or by the side of the road," or in special "prayer grounds" such as a "twisted thick-rooted muscadine bush" that afforded privacy. Beyond seeking personal guidance, these worshipers prayed "for deliverance of the slaves." Some waited "until the overseer got behind a hill" and then laid down their hoes and called on God to free them. Others held fervent secret prayer meetings that lasted far into the night. From such activities many slaves gained the unshakable belief that God would end their bondage. As one man asserted, "it was the plans of God to free us niggers." This faith and the joy and emotional

Chapter 10: Slavery and the Growth of the South, 1800–1860

Belief that God would free them sustained many slaves through the ordeal of slavery. The camp meeting depicted here occurred in 1872, but it repeated the fervor shown at many secret prayer meetings during slavery. *The Historic New Orleans Collection.*

release that accompanied their worship sustained blacks.

Slaves also developed a sense of racial identity. The whole experience of southern blacks taught them that whites despised their race. White people, as one ex-slave put it, "have been and are now and always will be against the Negro." Even "the best white woman that ever broke bread wasn't much," said another, "'cause they all hated the poor nigger." Blacks naturally drew together, helping each other in danger, need, and resistance. "We never told on each other," one woman declared. Although some slaves did tell on others, former slaves were virtually unanimous in denouncing those who betrayed the group or sought personal advantage through allegiance to whites.

Of course, different jobs and circumstances created natural variations in attitude among slaves. But for most slaves, there was no overriding class system within the black community. Only one-quarter of all slaves lived on plantations of fifty blacks or more, so few knew a wide chasm between exalted house servants and lowly field hands. Many slaves did both housework and field work, depending on their age and the season, and this fact helped to create unity rather than division among slaves.

The main source of support for individuals was the family. Slave families faced severe dangers. At any moment the master could sell a husband or wife, give a slave child away as a wedding present, or die in debt, forcing a division of his property. Many families were broken up in such ways. Others were uprooted in the trans-Appalachian expansion of the South, which caused the forced migration or sale of hundreds of thousands of slaves, often without regard to family ties. When the Union Army registered thousands of black marriages in Mississippi and Louisiana in 1864 and 1865, 25 percent of the men over forty reported that they had been forcibly separated from a previous wife. A similar proportion of former slaves later recalled that slavery had destroyed one of their marriages. Probably a substantial minority of slave families suffered disruption of one kind or another.

Slaves' Family Life

Sunday was a precious time for slaves to worship, rest, play, and spend time with the members of their families. *William Gladstone Collection.*

But this did not mean that slave families could not exist. American slaves clung tenaciously to the personal relationships that gave meaning to life, for although American law did not protect slave families, masters permitted them. In fact, slaveowners expected slaves to form families and have children. As a result, even along the rapidly expanding edge of the cotton kingdom, where the effects of the slave trade would have been most visible, there was a normal ratio of men to women, young to old.

Following African kinship taboos, African-Americans avoided marriage between cousins (a frequent occurrence among aristocratic slaveowners). Adapting other West African customs to the circumstances of their captivity, they did not condemn unwed mothers, although they did expect a young girl to form a stable marriage after one pregnancy, if not before. By naming their children after relatives of past generations, African-Americans emphasized their family histories. If they chose to bear the surname of a slaveowner, it was often not their current master's name but that of the owner under whom their family had begun in America.

Slaves abhorred interference in their family lives. Some of their strongest protests sought to prevent the breakup of a family. Indeed, some individuals refused to accept such separations and struggled for years to maintain or re-establish contact. Rape was a horror for both men and women. Some husbands faced death rather than permit their wives to be sexually abused, and women sometimes fought back. In other cases slaves seethed with anger at the injustice but could do nothing except soothe each other with human sympathy and understanding. Significantly, blacks condemned the guilty party, not the victim.

Slave men did not dominate their wives in a manner similar to white husbands, but it is misleading to say that slave women enjoyed equality of power in sex roles and family life. The larger truth is that all black people, men *and* women, were denied the opportunity to provide for or protect their families. Slavery's cruelties put black men and women in the same dilemma. Under the pressures of bondage they had to share the responsibilities of parenthood. Each might have to stand in for the other and

Chapter 10: Slavery and the Growth of the South, 1800–1860

assume extra duties. Similarly, uncles, aunts, and grandparents sometimes raised the children of those who had been sold away.

In two other respects, however, distinct gender roles remained very important in slave families and experience. First, after work in the fields was done, men's activities focused on traditional "outdoor" tasks while women did "indoor" work. Slave men hunted and fished for the family stewpot, fashioned a rough piece of furniture, or repaired implements; women cooked the food, mended garments, and cleaned house. It is clear, too, that slave families resembled white families in the fact that black men held a respected place in their homes.

Sex Roles in Slavery

Second, the life cycle and pattern of work routines frequently placed slave women in close associations with each other that heightened their sense of sisterhood. On plantations young girls worked together as house servants; nursing mothers shared opportunities to feed and care for their children; adults worked together in many common tasks from soap making to quilting; and old women were assigned to spin thread or supervise a nursery. Female slaves thus lived significant portions of their lives as part of a group of women, a fact that emphasized the gender-based element of their experience.

Although slave marriage ceremonies were often brief, usually involving jumping over a broomstick in the master's presence, partners "stuck lots closer then," in one woman's words. "[When] they marries they stay married," said another. When husbands and wives lived on neighboring plantations, visits on Wednesday and Saturday nights included big dinners of welcome and celebration. Christmas was a similarly joyous time " 'cause husbands is coming home and families is getting united again."

Slaves brought to their efforts at resistance the same common sense, determination, and practicality that characterized their family lives. American slavery produced some fearless and implacable revolutionaries. Gabriel Prosser's conspiracy apparently was known to more than a thousand slaves when it was discovered in 1800, just before it was put into motion (see page 209). A similar conspiracy in Charleston in 1822, headed by a free black named Denmark Vesey, involved many of the most trusted slaves of leading families. The

Resistance to Slavery

most famous rebel of all, Nat Turner, rose in violence in Southampton County, Virginia, in 1831.

The son of an African woman who passionately hated her enslavement, Nat was a precocious child who learned to read very young. Encouraged by his first owner to study the Bible, he enjoyed some special privileges but also knew changes of masters and hard work. His father, who successfully ran away to freedom, stood always before him as an example of defiance. In time young Nat became a preacher, an impressive orator with a reputation among whites as well as blacks. He also developed a tendency toward mysticism, and he became increasingly withdrawn. After nurturing his plan for several years, Turner led a band of rebels from house to house in the predawn darkness of August 22, 1831. The group severed limbs and crushed skulls with axes or killed their victims with guns. Before they were stopped, Nat Turner and his followers had slaughtered sixty whites of both sexes and all ages. Nat and perhaps two hundred blacks, including many innocent victims of marauding whites, lost their lives as a result of the rebellion.

But most slave resistance was not violent because the odds against revolution were especially poor in North America. The South had the highest ratio of whites to blacks in the hemisphere; at the same time, because plantations were relatively small, whites had ample opportunity to supervise the slaves' activities. There was thus literal truth to one slave's remark that "the white man was the slave's jail." Moreover, the South lacked vital geographic and demographic features that had aided revolution elsewhere. The land offered no jungles and few mountain fastnesses to which rebels could flee. And compared with South America, southern slave importations were neither large nor prolonged. The South therefore lacked a preponderance of young male slaves. Nor were its military forces weak and overtaxed like those of many Latin American nations and colonies.

Thus the scales weighed heavily against revolution, and the slaves knew it. Consequently they directed their energies toward creating means of survival and resistance within slavery. A desperate slave could run away for good, but probably in more instances slaves ran off temporarily to hide in the woods. There they were close to friends and allies who could help them escape capture in an area they knew well. Every day that a slave "lay out" in this way the master lost a day's labor. Most own-

Slave Culture and Everyday Life

ers chose not to mount an exhaustive search and sent word instead that the slave's grievances would be redressed. The runaway would then return to bargain with the master. Most owners would let the matter pass, for, like the owner of a valuable cook, they were "glad to get her back."

Other modes of resistance had the same object: to resist but survive under bondage. Appropriating food (stealing, in the master's eyes) was so common that even whites sang humorous songs about it. Blacks were also alert to the attitudes of individual whites and learned to ingratiate themselves or play off one white person against another. Field hands frequently tested a new overseer to intimidate him or win more favorable working conditions. Other blacks fought with patrollers. Some slaves engaged in verbal arguments and even physical violence to deter or resist beatings. The harshest masters were the most strongly resisted. "Good masters had good slaves 'cause they treated 'em good," but "where the old master was mean an' ornery," his slaves were ornery too.

Harmony and Tension in a Slave Society

Not only for blacks but for whites too, slave labor stood at the heart of the South's social system, and its importance grew as the century advanced. Slavery affected the organization of society, the values of individuals, and—increasingly—every aspect of politics in the region.

Ever since the seventeenth century, slavery had placed severe restrictions on black southerners, but these deepened as the 1800s advanced. In all things, from their workaday movements to Sunday worship, slaves fell under the supervision of whites. Courts held that a slave "has no civil right" and could not even hold property "except at the will and pleasure of his master." When slaves revolted, legislators tightened the legal straitjacket: after the Nat Turner insurrection of 1831, for example, they prohibited owners from teaching their slaves to read. As the sectional crisis developed, fears of slave revolt grew and restrictions on slaves increased accordingly.

Slavery imposed responsibilities on nonslaveholders as well as on slaveowners. All white male citizens bore an obligation to ride in patrols to discourage slave movements at night. Whites in strategic positions, such as ship captains and harbor masters, were required to scrutinize the papers of blacks who might be attempting to escape bondage. Urban residents who did not supervise their domestic slaves as closely as planters did found themselves subject to criticism for endangering the community. And the South's few manufacturers, instead of receiving encouragement, often felt pressure to use slave rather than free labor.

Slavery had a deep effect on southern values because it was the main determinant of wealth in the South. Ownership of slaves guaranteed the labor to **Slavery as the Basis of Wealth and Social Standing** produce cotton and other crops on a large scale—labor otherwise unavailable in a rural society. Slaves were therefore vital to the acquisition of a fortune. Beyond that, slaves were a commodity and an investment, much like gold; people bought them on speculation, hoping for a steady rise in their value. In fact, for southern society as a whole, slaveholding indicated wealth in general with remarkable precision. Important economic enterprises not based on slavery were so rare that variations in wealth from county to county followed very closely upon variations in slaveholding.

It was therefore not surprising that slaveholding was the main determinant of a white man's social position, and white women derived high status from their husband's or father's ownership of slaves. Wealth in slaves was also the foundation on which the ambitious built their reputations. Ownership of slaves brought political power: a solid majority of political officeholders were slaveholders, and the most powerful of them were generally large slaveholders. Lawyers and newspaper editors were sometimes influential, but they did not hold independent positions in the economy or society. Dependent on the planters for business and support, they served planters' interests and reflected their outlook.

Slavery's influence spread throughout the social system until even the values and mores of nonslaveholders bore its imprint. For one thing, the availability of slave labor tended to devalue free

TO HAVE AND TO HOLD the said *Slave Louisa* unto the said purchaser *his* heirs and assigns forever; the said Vendor hereby binding *himself* and *his* heirs forever to warrant and defend the *Slave Louisa* herein conveyed, against all legal claims and demands whatever. The said Vendor moreover transfer unto the said purchaser all the rights and actions of warranty to which *she is* entitled, against all the former proprietors of the *Slave Louisa* herein conveyed, hereby subrogating said purchaser to the said rights and actions to be by *him* enjoyed and exercised in the same manner as they might have been by the said Vendor.

labor. Where strenuous work under another was reserved for an enslaved race, few free people relished working "like a nigger." Nonslaveholders therefore preferred to work for themselves rather than to hire out. Whites who had to sell their labor tended to resent or reject tasks that seemed degrading. This kind of thinking engendered an aristocratic value system ill suited to a newly established democracy.

In modified form the attitudes characteristic of the planter elite gained a considerable foothold among the masses. The ideal of the aristocrat emphasized lineage, privilege, power, pride, and refinement of person and manner. Some of those qualities were in short supply in the recently settled, expanding cotton kingdom, however; they mingled with and were modified by the tradition of the frontier. In particular, independence and defense of one's honor were highly valued by planter and frontier farmer alike.

Aristocratic Values and Frontier Individualism

Fights and even duels over personal slights were not uncommon in southern communities. This custom sprang from both frontier lawlessness and aristocratic tradition. Throughout the sparsely settled regions of America in the early nineteenth century, pugnacious people took the law into their own hands. Thus it was not unusual for a southern slaveowner who had warned patrollers to stay off his property to shoot at the next group of trespassers. But instead of gradually disappearing, as it did in the North, the *code duello,* which required men to defend their honor through the rituals of a duel, hung on in the South and gained an acceptance that spread throughout the society.

A bill of sale documents that this slave woman, Louisa, was owned by the young child whom she holds on her lap. In the future her life would be subject to his wishes and decisions. *Missouri Historical Society.*

In North Carolina in 1851 a wealthy planter named Samuel Fleming responded to a series of disputes with the rising lawyer William Waightstill Avery by whipping or "cowhiding" him on a public street. According to the code, Avery had two choices: to redeem his honor through violence or to brand himself a coward through inaction. Three weeks later Avery shot Fleming dead at pointblank range during a session of Burke County Superior Court, with Judge William Battle and numerous spectators looking on. A jury took just ten minutes to find Avery not guilty, and the spectators gave him a standing ovation. Some people, including Judge Battle, were troubled by the victory of the unwritten code over the law, but most white males seemed satisfied.

Other aristocratic values that marked the planters as a class were less acceptable to the average citizen. Planters believed they were better than other people. In their pride, they expected not only to wield power but to receive special treatment. By the 1850s, some planters openly rejected the democratic creed, vilifying Thomas Jefferson for his statement that all men were equal.

Belief in their own superiority shaped the outlook of the southern elite for generations, but this attitude was never acceptable to the individualistic members of the yeoman class. Independent and proud of their position, yeomen resisted any infringement of their rights. They believed that they were as good as anyone, and many belonged to evangelical faiths that exalted values far removed from the planters' love of wealth. They were conscious, too, that they lived in a nation in which democratic ideals were gaining strength. Thus there were occasional conflicts between aristocratic pretensions and democratic zeal. As Mary Boykin Chesnut pointed out, a wealthy planter who sought public office could not announce his status too haughtily. She described the plight of Colonel John S. Preston, a South Carolinian with great ambitions. Preston, a perfect aristocrat, carried his high-flown manners too far; he refused to make the necessary gestures of respect toward the average voter—mingling with the crowd, exchanging jokes and compliments. Thus his highest aspiration, political leadership, could never be fulfilled. The voters would not accept him.

Such tensions found significant expression in the western parts of the seaboard states during the 1820s and 1830s. There yeoman farmers and citi-

Movements for Electoral Reform

zens resented their underrepresentation in state legislatures, corruption in government, and undemocratic control over local government. After vigorous debate, the reformers won most of their battles. Five southern states—Alabama, Mississippi, Tennessee, Arkansas, and Texas—adopted white manhood suffrage and other reforms, including popular election of governors, legislative apportionment based on the white population, and locally chosen county government. Kentucky enacted these measures except for elected county governments. Georgia, Florida, and Louisiana were not far behind, and reformers won significant concessions in Maryland and some adjustments in North Carolina. Only South Carolina and Virginia effectively defended property qualifications for office, legislative malapportionment, appointment of county officials, and selection of the governor by the lawmakers. The formal structure of government was more democratic than many planters would have wished.

Slaveowners knew that an open structure could permit troubling issues to arise. In Virginia nonslaveholding westerners raised a basic challenge to the slave system in the year following the Nat Turner rebellion. Advocates of gradual abolition forced a two-week legislative debate on slavery, arguing that the institution was injurious to the state and inherently dangerous. When the House of Delegates finally voted, the motion favoring abolition lost by just 73 to 58. This was the last major debate on slavery in the antebellum South.

With such tension in evidence, it was perhaps remarkable that slaveholders and nonslaveholders did not experience frequent and serious conflict. Why were class confrontations among whites so infrequent? Historians who have considered this question have given many answers. One of the most important factors was race. The South's racial ideology stressed whites' superiority to blacks and declared that race, not class, was the social dividing line. In addition, in a rural society family bonds and kinship ties are valued, and some of the poor nonslaveholding whites were related to the rich new planters. The experience of frontier living must also have created a relatively informal, egalitarian atmosphere.

The cotton boom itself had relieved tension by bringing opportunity to thousands of whites. Since the "Old" South was in fact a new and mobile soci-

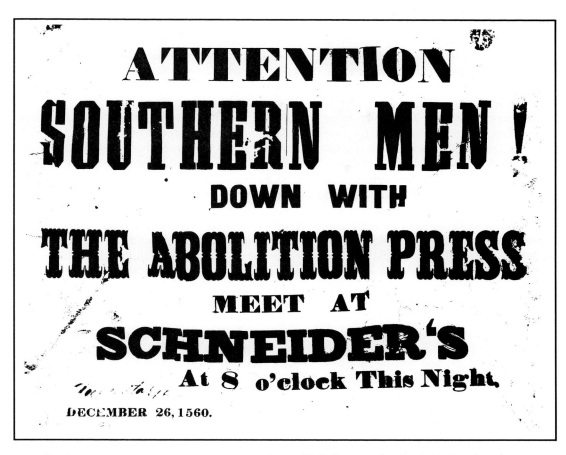

ATTENTION
SOUTHERN MEN !
DOWN WITH
THE ABOLITION PRESS
MEET AT
SCHNEIDER'S
At 8 o'clock This Night,
DECEMBER 26, 1560.

Run off in haste and anger, with a misprinted date, this handbill illustrates the determination of southern slaveholders in Augusta, Georgia, to tolerate no criticism of their peculiar institution. *Library of Congress.*

ety, many people had risen in status by acquiring land or slaves, and far more were moving about geographically. Even in cotton-rich Alabama in the 1850s, fewer than half the richest families in a county belonged to its elite category ten years later. Most had not died or lost their wealth; they had merely moved on to some new state. This constant mobility meant that southern society had not settled into a rigid, unchanging pattern.

The place yeoman farmers occupied in society, relative to slaveholders, also was critical. In the antebellum period their social and economic position normally allowed them to pursue unhindered their self-sufficient and independent style of life. Outside the market economy, most could maintain their independence free from economic competition or pressure. Socially, they lived in a region that was rural and uncrowded. Travel was difficult, and much of daily life took place within the family unit.

Consequently the yeomen lived their lives with little reference to, and no interference from, slaveholders. As long as they were able to follow their values and aspirations, the yeomen had no grievance.

Likewise, slaveholders were able to pursue their goals quite independently of the yeomen. Planters farmed for the market but also for themselves. The complementary growing patterns of corn and cotton allowed planters to raise food for their animals and laborers without lowering cotton production: from spring through December, cotton and corn needed attention alternately, but never at the same time. Thus the planter did not need to depend on the nonslaveholder, and yeomen needed nothing from the planters. In politics, too, national issues that affected planters economically often had less meaning to yeomen because they were not enmeshed in the market economy.

Harmony and Tension in a Slave Society

But suppression of dissent also played a significant, and increasing, role. White southerners who criticized the slave system out of moral conviction or class resentment were intimidated, attacked, or legally prosecuted. (Some, like James Birney, were driven from the South in the 1830s and went north to join the antislavery movement. Two sisters from Charleston, Angelina and Sarah Grimké, became leading advocates of both abolition and women's rights—see pages 352–353.) Southern cities impounded abolitionist literature and sought to bar any antislavery influences. Intellectuals developed elaborate justifications for slavery as newspapers railed at any antislavery threat. By the 1850s the defense of slavery's interests dominated discussion, and all groups in society felt pressure to uphold the slave system. Politicians vied with each other to lead an increasingly aggressive defense of the South's peculiar institution. The slavery issue exerted an ever more powerful influence on southern politics and society.

Still, there were signs that the relative lack of conflict between slaveholders and nonslaveholders was coming to an end. As the region grew older, nonslaveholders saw their opportunities beginning to narrow; meanwhile, wealthy planters enjoyed an expanding horizon. The risks of cotton production were becoming too great and the cost of slaves too high for many yeomen to rise in society. Thus from 1830 to 1860 the percentage of white southern families holding slaves declined steadily from 36 to 25 percent. At the same time, the monetary gap between the classes was widening. Although nonslaveholders were becoming more prosperous, slaveowners' wealth was increasing much faster. And although slaveowners made up a smaller portion of the population in 1860, their share of the South's agricultural wealth remained at between 90 and 95 percent. In fact, the average slaveholder was almost fourteen times as rich as the average nonslaveholder.

Hardening of Class Lines

Urban artisans and mechanics felt the pinch acutely. Their numbers were few; their place in society was hardly recognized; and in bad times they were often the first to lose work. Moreover, they faced stiff competition from urban slaves, whose masters wanted them to hire their time and bring in money by practicing a trade. White workers in Charleston, Wilmington, and elsewhere staged protests and demanded that economic competition from slaves be forbidden. This demand was always ignored—the powerful slaveowners would not tolerate interference with their property or the income they derived from it. But the angry protests of white workers resulted in harsh restrictions on *free* black workers and craftsmen, who lacked any powerful allies to stand behind them. In Charleston on the eve of the Civil War, many successful free blacks actually felt compelled to leave the city from fear of being re-enslaved.

Pre–Civil War politics reflected these tensions. Facing the prospect of a war to defend slavery, slaveowners expressed growing fear about the loyalty of nonslaveholders and discussed schemes to widen slave ownership, including reopening of the African slave trade. In North Carolina, a prolonged and increasingly bitter controversy over the combination of high taxes on land and low taxes on slaves erupted, and a class-conscious nonslaveholder named Hinton R. Helper denounced the slave system. Convinced that slavery had impoverished many whites and retarded the whole region, Helper attacked the institution in his book *The Impending Crisis,* published in New York in 1857. Discerning planters knew that such fiery controversies lay close at hand in every southern state.

But for the moment slaveowners stood secure. They held from 50 to 85 percent of the seats in state legislatures and a similarly high percentage of the South's congressional seats. In addition to their near-monopoly on political office, they had established their point of view in all the other major social institutions. Professors who criticized slavery had been dismissed from colleges and universities; school books that contained "unsound" ideas had been replaced. And almost all the Methodist and Baptist clergy, some of whom had criticized slavery in the 1790s, had given up preaching against the institution. In fact, except for a few obscure persons of conscience, southern clergy had become slavery's most vocal defenders. Society as southerners knew it seemed to be stable, with threats to the status quo under control.

In the nation generally, however, society was anything but stable. Change had become one of the major characteristics of the northern economy and society, as the rise of the market and industry produced a more diverse population. The American people were changing, and the currents of change would eventually affect the South.

Suggestions for Further Reading

Southern Society

Edward L. Ayers, *Vengeance and Justice* (1984); W. J. Cash, *The Mind of the South* (1941); Avery O. Craven, *The Growth of Southern Nationalism, 1848–1861* (1953); Clement Eaton, *The Growth of Southern Civilization, 1790–1860* (1961); Clement Eaton, *Freedom of Thought in the Old South* (1940); William W. Freehling, *Prelude to Civil War* (1965); Eugene D. Genovese, "Yeoman Farmers in a Slaveholders' Democracy," *Agricultural History,* 49 (April 1975), 331–342; Eugene D. Genovese, *The World the Slaveholders Made* (1964); William Sumner Jenkins, *Pro-Slavery Thought in the Old South* (1935); Peter Kolchin, *Unfree Labor: American Slavery and Russian Serfdom* (1987); Robert McColley, *Slavery and Jeffersonian Virginia* (1964); Donald G. Mathews, *Religion in the Old South* (1977); James Hebron Moore, *The Emergence of the Cotton Kingdom in the Old Southwest: Mississippi, 1770–1860* (1987); Frederick Law Olmsted, *The Slave States,* ed. Harvey Wish (1959); Edward Phifer, "Slavery in Microcosm: Burke County, North Carolina," *Journal of Southern History,* XXVIII (May 1962), 137–165; Frederick F. Siegel, *The Roots of Southern Distinctiveness: Tobacco and Society in Danville, Virginia, 1780–1865* (1987); Charles S. Sydnor, *The Development of Southern Sectionalism, 1819–1848* (1948); Ralph A. Wooster, *Politicians, Planters, and Plain Folk* (1975); Ralph A. Wooster, *The People in Power* (1969); Gavin Wright, *The Political Economy of the Cotton South* (1978); Bertram Wyatt-Brown, *Southern Honor* (1982).

Slaveholders and Nonslaveholders

Bennet H. Barrow, *Plantation Life in the Florida Parishes of Louisiana, as Reflected in the Diary of Bennet H. Barrow,* ed. Edwin Adams Davis (1943); Malcolm Bell, Jr., *Major Butler's Legacy: Five Generations of a Slaveholding Family* (1987); Ira Berlin, *Slaves Without Masters* (1974); Randolph B. Campbell, "Intermittent Slave Ownership: Texas as a Text Case," *Journal of Southern History,* 30, no. 1 (February 1985), 15–30; William J. Cooper, *The South and the Politics of Slavery, 1828–1856* (1978); Everett Dick, *The Dixie Frontier* (1948); Clement Eaton, *The Mind of the Old South* (1967); Drew Faust, *James Henry Hammond and the Old South* (1982); Drew Faust, *A Sacred Circle: The Dilemma of the Intellectual in the Old South* (1977); John Hope Franklin, *The Militant South, 1800–1861* (1956); John Hope Franklin, *The Free Negro in North Carolina, 1790–1860* (1943); Luther P. Jackson, *Free Negro Labor and Property Holding in Virginia, 1830–1860* (1942); Michael P. Johnson and James L. Roark, *Black Masters* (1984); Frances Anne Kemble, *Journal of a Residence on a Georgia Plantation in 1838–1839* (1863); Robert E. May, *John A. Quitman* (1985); Robert Manson Myers, ed., *The Children of Pride* (1972); James Oakes, *The Ruling Race* (1982); Frank L. Owsley, *Plain Folk of the Old South* (1949); J. Mills Thornton III, *Politics and Power in a Slave Society: Alabama, 1800–1860* (1978); C. Vann Woodward, ed., *Mary Chesnut's Civil War* (1981).

Southern Women

Carol Bleser, *The Hammonds of Redcliffe* (1981); Jane Turner Censer, *North Carolina Planters and Their Children, 1800–1860* (1984); Catherine Clinton, *The Plantation Mistress* (1982); Elizabeth Fox-Genovese, *Within the Plantation Household* (1988); Jean E. Friedman, *The Enclosed Garden* (1985); Jacqueline Jones, *Labor of Love, Labor of Sorrow* (1985); Suzanne Lebsock, *Free Women of Petersburg* (1984); Elisabeth Muhlenfeld, *Mary Boykin Chesnut* (1981); Mary D. Robertson, ed., *Lucy Breckinridge of Grove Hill* (1979); Ann Firor Scott, *The Southern Lady* (1970); Deborah G. White, *Arn'n't I a Woman?* (1985); C. Vann Woodward and Elisabeth Muhlenfeld, eds., *The Private Mary Chesnut* (1985).

Conditions of Slavery

Kenneth F. Kiple and Virginia H. Kiple, "Black Tongue and Black Men," *Journal of Southern History,* XLIII (August 1977), 411–428; Ronald L. Lewis, *Coal, Iron, and Slaves* (1979); Richard G. Lowe and Randolph B. Campbell, "The Slave Breeding Hypothesis," *Journal of Southern History,* XLII (August 1976), 400–412; Leslie Howard Owens, *This Species of Property* (1976); Willie Lee Rose, ed., *A Documentary History of Slavery in North America* (1976); Todd L. Savitt, *Medicine and Slavery* (1978); Kenneth M. Stampp, *The Peculiar Institution* (1956); Robert S. Starobin, *Industrial Slavery in the Old South* (1970).

Slave Culture and Resistance

Herbert Aptheker, *American Negro Slave Revolts* (1943); John W. Blassingame, *The Slave Community* (1979); Judith Wragg Chase, *Afro-American Art and Craft* (1971); Jeffrey J. Crow, *The Black Experience in Revolutionary North Carolina* (1977); Dena J. Epstein, *Sinful Tunes and Spirituals* (1977); Paul D. Escott, *Slavery Remembered: A Record of Twentieth-Century Slave Narratives* (1979); Eric Foner, ed., *Nat Turner* (1971); Eugene D. Genovese, *From Rebellion to Revolution* (1979); Eugene D. Genovese, *Roll, Jordan, Roll* (1974); Herbert G. Gutman, *The Black Family in Slavery and Freedom, 1750–1925* (1976); Vincent Harding, *There Is a River* (1981); Charles Joyner, *Down by the Riverside* (1984); Lawrence W. Levine, *Black Culture and Black Consciousness* (1977); Stephen B. Oates, *The Fires of Jubilee* (1975); Albert J. Raboteau, *Slave Religion* (1978); Robert S. Starobin, *Denmark Vesey* (1970); Sterling Stuckey, *Slave Culture* (1987); Peter H. Wood, *Black Majority* (1974).

In 1844, English immigrant George Martin of Rochester, New York, a carpenter, fell ill at age thirty-three and suddenly had a sense of his own mortality. Imagine "a very few years hence and not one of us will be among the living," he wrote his brother in England, "but what grieves me the most in this case is that after a wearisome and toilsome life in getting so many nice books and other things together [I] have nobody to leave them to but strangers. You cannot imagine what the feeling is," he went on, "to think that you will die, the last of your race, in a foreign land far from your kindred and home, and no friendly hand to close your eyes, that would give more than a passing sigh and then forget you."

Eight years later, in 1852, George Martin's worst fears were realized. Save for his wife, Betsy, and their children, he died among strangers, away from kin and old friends. He had maintained close contact with England—he wrote his family regularly and he visited them in 1845—and he was forever meeting fellow English immigrants in Rochester. When he died, however, only his American employer, Jonathan King, took responsibility for the widow and children.

11

DIVERSITY AND CONFLICT: PEOPLE AND COMMUNITIES, 1800–1860

The United States had changed so much and so rapidly in the decades before George Martin's death that most Americans were newcomers and strangers where they lived and where they worked. The largest cities grew to enormous size and numbered diverse ethnic, religious, and racial populations in the hundreds of thousands. Millions of immigrants settled in the expanding nation, and countless new and old Americans moved internally as the nation stretched from ocean to ocean. Most Americans probably lived a good part of their lives among strangers as they worked in shops or on farms and lived in houses that had not existed a generation before.

George and Betsy Martin came to the United States in 1834 from an agricultural hamlet twenty-two miles from London. George thought New York harbor "the most beautiful that ever was seen." That first night in New York they stayed awake, but not from visions of Eden. Their lodging at a British-run tavern was ridden with bedbugs. "My eyes and nostrils and all my body was swelled to a great size," he wrote his parents. "I was obliged to walk the rooms all night."

Canal Street Market (detail) by Henry Mosler, 1860. Oil on canvas. *The Cincinnati Historical Society.*

After two days of touring New York City, the Martins traveled by canal boat, railroad, and lake steamer to their new home on the north shore of Lake Ontario, in Upper Canada. They moved permanently to Rochester in 1838, when George found work as a carpenter. Opportunities were good in Canada, he wrote his father, but "there is more spirit of enterprise" in the United States.

His advice to those who wanted to come to the United States often shifted with the ups and downs of the business cycle. But he did write his brother, a new father, "it is about time you tried another country where you can get your children educated for nothing, and so enable them to work their way in the world. . . ." In this new country, however, "you find that folks of that country will not conform to your ways; but if you wish to succeed you must learn their ways and conform to them as soon as possible." In 1851 he complained to his brother, Peter, that visits with newcomers from England had become a burden. They were not adapting as Americans; they were refusing to leave behind their old ways.

Indeed in the last four years of his life Martin expressed anti-immigrant feelings. He lived in Rochester's Eighth Ward, among English, Irish, Swiss, French, and Canadian immigrants as well as native-born New Yorkers, and he seemed intolerant of their diversity. At the same time he became estranged from his family in England. Families often thought that emigrants had cut themselves off from inheritance rights, and George was embittered because he did not receive a full share in his father's will.

When he died in 1852, George Martin left very little. His spare time and money had gone into building his own house in Rochester, but it was unfinished at his death. His relatives in England paid $500 to complete it, so that his widow and children would have a place to live. His neighbors and fellow workmen, the butt of his anger, did nothing to help his family.

As the market economy and economic opportunity attracted immigrants and energized the native-born, the American people grew apart. In colonial days, the appearance of strangers in villages had been the exception, but in the nineteenth century, strangers were common. People were on the move, as large cities blossomed and one year's frontier became the next year's settled town. Farm families sought cohesion, and some experimented in forming new, utopian agrarian communities. More and more people, however, lived in towns and cities, where diversity became the rule. The nature of community was changing in the United States. Civic and public institutions had to offer services, like education, once provided by private families. The face of the city changed too. Opulent mansions existed within sight of notorious slums, and both wealth and poverty reached extremes unknown before in agrarian America.

Private space—the family—also experienced change. With the growth of commerce and industry, the home began to lose its function as a workplace. Especially among the middle and upper classes, the home became woman's domain, a haven from man's world. Working-class women found no such refuge. At the same time, birth control was more widely practiced and families were smaller. Recreation and leisure activity became more public as well.

Immigration further increased social diversity. Within large cities and in the countryside, whole districts became enclaves of ethnic groups. In hiring themselves out to build transportation and industry, immigrants reshaped American culture.

Free blacks and Indians struggled against a society in which their very presence was often disturbing. Free people of color were second-class citizens at best, struggling to better their lot against overwhelming legal and racial barriers. Indians, forced to abandon their lands for resettlement beyond the Mississippi River, fared no better.

To a great degree, many Americans were uncomfortable with the new direction of American life. Antipathy toward immigrants was common among native-born Americans, who feared competition for jobs. Blacks fought unceasingly for equality, and Indians tried unsuccessfully to resist forced removal. In a society growing ever more diverse and complex, conflict became common.

Although the United States remained an agricultural country, the traditional economy and society were yielding to the spreading influence of the market economy, urban growth, and immigration. This process of change would last throughout the nineteenth century and would accelerate and intensify in the last three decades. Nonetheless the path that led to the great industrial, urban, pluralist society had begun before the Civil War.

1810	New York surpasses Philadelphia in population	1837	Boston employs paid policemen
1819	Indian "civilization act"	1837–48	Horace Mann heads the Massachusetts board of education
1823	Hartford Female Seminary established by Catharine and Mary Beecher	1841–47	Brook Farm
1824	President Monroe proposes removal of Indians	1842	Knickerbocker baseball club formed
1827	*Freedom's Journal* first published	1845	Start of the Irish potato famine
1830s–1850s	Urban riots	1846–47	Mormon trek to the Great Salt Lake
1831	*Cherokee Nation* v. *Georgia*	1847–57	Peak period of immigration before the Civil War
1831–38	Trail of Tears	1848	Abortive German revolution
1835–42	Second Seminole War		

Country Life

Communities and life within them changed significantly in the first half of the nineteenth century. Within a generation many frontier settlements became sources for, rather than recipients of, migration. Villages in western New York state had lured the sons and daughters of New England in the first two decades of the century. Yet in the 1820s and 1830s, after the best land was settled and tilled and the Erie Canal opened (1825), young people moved from New York villages to the new frontier in the Old Northwest. Later, Ohio and Michigan towns and farms would send their young people farther west. Similarly, migrants from the Upper South went to Illinois and Ohio as people on the move farther south settled the Gulf states.

Widespread settlement and the development of towns rapidly overtook the frontier so that the isolated pioneers of the 1840s and 1850s—the hunter, the trapper, the homesteader—were more than one thousand miles farther west than their counterparts had been in the 1800s and 1810s. For all the romance of pioneering, many longed for a sense of community. Englishwoman Frances Trollope recorded in *Domestic Manners of the Americans* (1832) her visit to a farm family living near Cincinnati. The family grew or produced all their necessities except for coffee, tea, and whiskey, which they got by sending butter or chickens to market. But until other settlers came to live near them, they lacked the human contact that a community offered. For their inexpensive land and self-sufficiency they paid the price of isolation and loneliness. "'Tis strange to us to see company," lamented the mother. "I expect the sun may rise and set a hundred times before I shall see another human that does not belong to the family."

Although they lived in isolation on individual farms, farm families found a sense of community in the neighborhood and village. The farm village was the center of rural life—the farmers' link with religion, politics, and the outside world. But rural social life was not limited to trips to the village, with

Farm Communities

Country people looked forward to combining work and play in communal bees. In this scene of a quilting party in Virginia, young and old gathered to socialize, gossip, play, eat, court, and make quilts.
The Abby Aldrich Rockefeller Folk Art Center.

its post office, general store, and tavern; families gathered on each other's farms to do as a community what they could not do individually. Barn-raising was among the activities that regularly brought people together. In preparation for the event, the farmer and an itinerant carpenter built a platform and cut beams, posts, and joists. When the neighbors arrived by buggy and wagon, they put together the sides and raised them into position. After the roof was up, everyone celebrated with a communal meal and perhaps with singing, dancing, and folk games. Sometimes they competed in foot races, wrestling, or shooting at a mark, and on occasion they raced their horses. Similar gatherings took place at harvest time and on special occasions.

Women especially sought to counter rural isolation. Farm men had frequent opportunities to mix at general stores, markets, and taverns and in hunting and fishing. Some women too met at market, but more typically they came together at regular work and social gatherings: after-church dinners;

sewing, quilting, and corn-husking bees; and preparations for marriages and baptisms. These were times to exchange experiences and thoughts, offer each other support, and swap letters, books, and news.

Irene Hardy, who spent her childhood in rural southwestern Ohio in the 1840s, left a record of the gatherings she attended as a girl. Most vivid in her memory fifty years later were the apple bees, when neighbors gathered to make apple butter or preserves. "Usually invitations were sent about by word of mouth," she recalled. "'Married folks' came and worked all day or afternoon." A dinner feast followed, for which the visiting women made biscuits, vegetables, and coffee. After cleaning up, "the old folks went home to send their young ones for their share of work and fun." The elders gossiped to pass the time; the youngsters joked and teased each other in a comic-serious precourting ritual. "Then came supper, apple and pumpkin pies, cider, doughnuts, cakes, cold chicken and turkey," Hardy wrote, "after which games, 'Forfeits,'

Shaker meetinghouse at Pleasant Hill, Kentucky, 1820, designed by Micajah Burnett. Marked by a simplicity and beauty of design, the meetinghouse exemplifies the Shaker sense of order. Their code of behavior required separate entrances for men and women. The first floor of the building housed worship services, with its spirited songs and dances; the second floor provided separate sleeping quarters for elders and eldresses. *Linda Butler*.

'Building a Bridge,' 'Snatchability,' even 'Blind Man's Bluff' and 'Pussy Wants a Corner.' "

Traditional country bees had their town counterparts. Fredrika Bremer, a Swedish visitor to the United States, described a sewing bee in 1849 in Cambridge, Massachusetts, at which neighborhood women made clothes for "a family who had lost all their clothing by fire." Yet town bees were not the all-day family affairs typical of the countryside, and when the Hardy family moved to the town of Eaton in 1851, Irene missed the country gatherings. Life was changing: the families of Eaton seldom held bees, and they purchased their goods at the store.

Increasingly Americans were conscious of such changes. One response was an interest in utopian communities, which offered an antidote to the market economy and to the untamed growth of large urban communities and an opportunity to restore tradition and social cohesion. Whatever their particular philosophy, utopians sought order and regularity in their daily lives and a cooperative rather than competitive environment. Some experimented with communal living and nontraditional work, family, and gender roles.

The Shakers, who derived their name from the way they danced and swayed at worship services, were an early, lasting utopian experiment. Founder Ann Lee brought this offshoot of **Shakers** the English Quakers to America in 1774. Shakers believed that the end of the world was near and that sin entered the world through sexual intercourse. They regarded existing churches as too worldly and considered the Shaker family the instrument of salvation.

After the death of Mother Ann Lee in 1784, the Shakers turned to communal living to fulfill their mission. In 1787 they "gathered in" at New Lebanon, New York, to live, worship, and work communally. Other colonies soon followed. At its peak, between 1820 and 1860, the sect had about six thousand members living in twenty settlements in eight states. It was the largest and most permanent of the utopian experiments. Shaker communities emphasized agriculture and hand crafts; most managed to become self-sufficient, profitable enterprises. Shaker furniture became famous for its simplicity, excellent construction, and beauty of design.

Though economically conservative, the Shakers were social radicals. They abolished individual families, practiced celibacy, and pioneered new roles for women. Each colony was one large family. The Shaker ministry was headed by a woman, Lucy Wright, during its period of greatest growth. Celibacy, however, led to the withering away of the communities. Unable to reproduce naturally, the colonies are dying out in the twentieth century.

The most successful communitarians were the Mormons, who originated in western New York. Organized by Joseph Smith in 1830 as the Church of Jesus Christ of Latter-day Saints,

▶ **Mormon Community of Saints** the church established communities dedicated to Christian cooperation. Fleeing persecution in Ohio, Illinois, and Missouri because of their claims of continuous divine revelation and their newly adopted practice of polygyny (having more than one wife at the same time), the Mormons trekked across the continent in 1846 and 1847 to found a New Zion in the Great Salt Lake Valley. There, under Brigham Young, head of the Twelve Apostles (their governing body), they established a cohesive community of Saints—a heaven on earth. The Mormons created agricultural settlements and distributed land according to family size. An extensive irrigation system, constructed by men who contributed their labor according to the quantity of land they received and the amount of water they expected to use, transformed the arid valley into a rich oasis. As the colony developed, the church elders came to control water, trade, industry, and even the territorial government of Utah. Religious conviction carried the Mormons through persecution and over economic hurdles.

Not all utopian communities were founded by religious groups. Robert Owen's New Harmony was a well-known, short-lived attempt to found a socialist utopia in Indiana. A wealthy Scottish industrialist, Owen established the cooperative community in 1825. According to his plan, its nine hundred members were to exchange their labor for goods at a communal store. Handicrafts (hat and boot making) flourished at New Harmony, but its textile mill, the economic base of the community, failed after Owen gave it to the community to run. Turnover in membership was too great for the community to develop any cohesion, and by 1827 the experiment had ended.

More successful were the New Englanders who lived and worked at the Brook Farm cooperative in West Roxbury, Massachusetts. Inspired by the transcendental philosophy that the

▶ **Brook Farm** spiritual rises above the worldly, its members rejected materialism and sought satisfaction in a rural communal life combining spirituality, work, and play. Founded in 1841 by the Unitarian minister George Ripley, Brook Farm attracted not only farmers and craftsmen but also teachers and writers, among them Nathaniel Hawthorne. Indeed, the fame of Brook Farm rested on the intellectual achievements of its members. Its school drew students from outside the community, and its residents contributed regularly to the *Dial,* the leading transcendentalist journal. In 1845, however, Brook Farm's hundred members organized themselves into model phalanxes (units for working and living) in keeping with the philosophy of the French utopian Charles Fourier. Rigid regimentation replaced individualism, and membership dropped. After a disastrous fire in 1846, the experiment collapsed in 1847.

Though short-lived, Brook Farm played a significant part in the romantic movement in the United States. During these years Hawthorne, Ralph Waldo Emerson, and Margaret Fuller, the *Dial's* editor, joined Henry David Thoreau, James Fenimore Cooper, Herman Melville, and others in creating what is known today as the American Renaissance—the flowering of a national literature. In poetry and prose these romanticists favored faith and emotion over reason. Rebelling against convention, both social and literary, they probed and celebrated the American character and experience. Cooper, for instance, used the frontier as a backdrop, and Melville wrote of great spiritual quests as seafaring adventures. Their themes were universal; their settings and people, American.

The Lackawanna Valley (1855) by George Inness. Hired by the Lackawanna Railroad to paint a railroad scene, Inness blended landscape and machine into an organic whole. American industrialism, Inness seemed to say, belonged to the landscape; it would neither overpower nor obliterate the land. *National Gallery of Art.*

Ralph Waldo Emerson was the "high priest" of the American Renaissance at the center of the transcendental movement. He had followed his father and grandfather into the ministry but quit his Boston Unitarian pulpit in 1831. After a two-year pilgrimage in Europe, he returned to lecture and write, preaching individualism and self-reliance. His message stressed that each person could experience God directly and intuitively through the "Oversoul." What gave Emerson's writings force was his simple, direct prose. Widely admired, he influenced Thoreau, Fuller, Hawthorne, and other members of Brook Farm. They followed Emerson's advice from his first book *Nature* (1836) and his Phi Beta Kappa talk at Harvard "The American Scholar" (1837), turning to American themes and reform. Utopianism and appreciation of the American landscape went hand in hand.

Utopian communities were a reaction against contemporary society that attempted to recapture the cohesiveness associated with traditional agricul- tural and artisan life. Utopians resembled Puritan perfectionists; like the Separatists of seventeenth-century New England (see page 30), they sought to start anew in their own colonies. Communal work and life offered alternatives to the market economy and urbanizing society.

City Life

Everywhere cities were growing, especially in the North. The transportation revolution and the expansion of commerce and manufacturing, fed by immigration and internal migration, caused the population of cities to grow geometrically. Between 1800 and 1860, the number of Americans increased from 5.3 million to 31.4 million. As the population grew, the frontier receded, and small rural settlements became towns. In 1800 the nation had only

33 towns with 2,500 or more people and only 3 with more than 25,000. By 1860, 392 towns exceeded 2,500 in population and 35 had more than 25,000.

In the Northeast, the percentage of people living in urban areas grew from 9 to 35 percent between 1800 and 1860. Most of this growth occurred in northern and western communities located along the new transportation routes, where increased commerce created new jobs and opportunities. Kingston, New York, ninety miles north of New York City on the Hudson River, was one example. The Delaware and Hudson Canal, which extended south from the Hudson valley to the coalfields of Pennsylvania, rapidly transformed Kingston from a sleepy farm village of 1,000 in the 1820s to an urban community of more than 10,000 in 1850.

Urban Growth

The hundreds of small new cities like Kingston were surpassed by stars of even greater magnitude: the great metropolitan cities. In 1860 twenty-one cities exceeded 40,000 in population and nine exceeded 100,000 (see maps). By 1810, New York City had overtaken Philadelphia as the nation's most populous city and major port and commercial center. Baltimore and New Orleans dominated the South, and San Francisco became the leading West Coast city. In the Midwest the new lake cities (Chicago, Detroit, and Cleveland) began to overtake the frontier river cities (Cincinnati, Louisville, and Pittsburgh) founded a generation earlier. The largest cities formed a nationwide urban network, linked by canals, roads, and railroads, connecting the great metropolises of the North (see Chapter 9).

New York City became the nation's premier urban place. New York grew from 60,500 in 1800 to 202,600 in 1830 to 813,600 in 1860. Across the East River, Brooklyn tripled in size between 1850 and 1860, becoming the nation's third-largest city with a population of 266,700. More than 1 million people lived in New York City and Brooklyn. Many were just passing through; a majority would not stay ten years. Although contemporary bird's-eye views of New York depict an almost pastoral urban life, the city emitted energy, aromas, and sweat that make twentieth-century cities seem sanitized in comparison. It was an immigrant port city, mostly Irish and German by the 1850s, and it teemed with people.

New York City

In the 1820s New York City literally burst its boundaries. Up to that time New Yorkers could still envision the city as a village—not because they knew most of the 150,000 or so inhabitants but because an hour's walk could reach every corner. Until the 1820s nearly all New Yorkers lived within two miles of City Hall. In 1825, 14th Street had been the city's northern boundary. By 1860, 400,000 people lived beyond that divide and 42nd Street was the city's northern limit. Gone were the semirural open lots and yards of the eighteenth century, many of them cow and horse pastures, kitchen gardens, or orchards. George Templeton Strong, a New York lawyer, recorded in his diary in 1856 that he had attended a party at a Judge Hoffman's "in thirty-seventh!!!—it seems but the other day that thirty-seventh Street was an imaginary line running through a rural district and grazed over by cows." Mass transit, however, made it possible for cities to expand. Horse-drawn buses appeared in New York in 1827, and the Harlem Railroad, completed in 1832, ran the length of Manhattan. By the 1850s all big cities had horse-drawn streetcars.

Strong, like other upper-class New Yorkers, found the density and diversity of the city repugnant. He especially disliked mixing with the masses on the city railroad. One day in 1852, suffering from a "splitting headache," Strong expressed his disgust at the immigrant population that crowded the city's public transportation. In "the choky, hot railroad car," he gagged on the "stale, sickly odors from sweaty Irishmen in their shirt sleeves." He felt repelled by German-Jewish shop clerks and "fat old women, with dirty-nosed babies."

Strong's prejudices reflect one man's responses to immigration and city life in the period. Yet by twentieth-century standards, early-nineteenth-century cities certainly were disorderly, unsafe, and unhealthy. Expansion occurred so rapidly that few cities could handle the problems it brought. For example, migrants from rural areas were used to relieving themselves and throwing refuse in any vacant area. In the city, such waste spread disease, created water pollution, and gave off obnoxious odors.

New York City solved part of the problem in the 1840s by abandoning wells in favor of reservoir water piped into buildings and outdoor fountains. In some districts scavengers and refuse collectors carted away garbage and human waste, but in much of the city it just rotted on the ground. Only one-

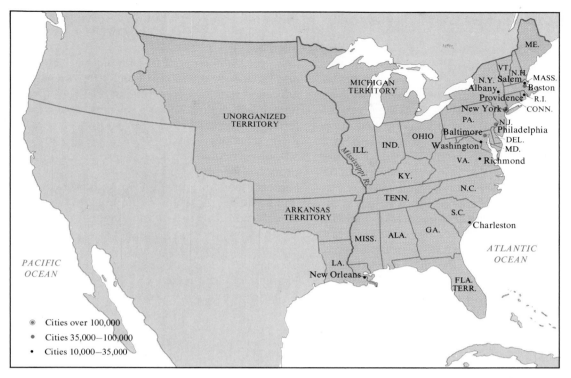

Major American Cities, 1820

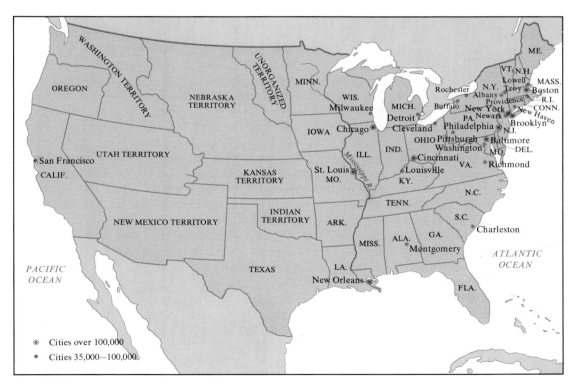

Major American Cities, 1860

City Life

quarter of New York City's streets had sewers by 1857.

New York and other cities did not have the taxing power to raise the sums needed to provide adequate services to all. The best the city could do was to charge the cost of sewers, street paving, and water mains to adjoining property. Thus the spread of new services and basic sanitation depended upon residents' ability or willingness to pay, and as a result those most in need of the services often got them last. Another solution was to depend upon private companies. This worked well with gas service. Baltimore first chartered a private gas company in 1816; New York had gas service in 1842; and by midcentury all major cities were lit by private gas suppliers. The private sector, however, failed to supply the water the cities needed. They did not have the capital to build adequate systems, and they laid pipe in commercial and well-to-do residential areas, ignoring the poor. As cities grew, water service did not keep pace. Eventually city governments had to take over.

Probably the most important and widespread service was the provision of public schools. In 1800 there were no public schools outside New England;

Horace Mann and Public Schools

by 1860 every state had some public education. Massachusetts took the lead, especially under Horace Mann, secretary of the state board of education from 1837 to 1848. Under Mann, Massachusetts established a minimum school year of six months, increased the number of high schools, formalized the training of teachers, and emphasized secular subjects and applied skills rather than religious training. In the process, teaching became a woman's profession. "Females govern with less resort to physical force," Mann believed, "and exert a more kindly, humanizing and refining influence upon the dispositions and manners of their pupils."

Horace Mann was an evangelist for public education and school reform; his preaching on behalf of free state education changed schooling throughout the nation. "If we do not prepare children to become good citizens," Mann prophesied, "if we do not develop their capacities, . . . imbue their hearts with the love of truth and duty, and a reverence for all things sacred and holy, then our republic must go down to destruction." The abolition of ignorance, Mann claimed, would end misery, crime, and suffering. "The only sphere . . . left open for our patriotism," he wrote, "is the improvement of our children—not the few, but the many; not a part of them but all."

In laying the basis of free public schools, Mann also broadened the scope of education. Previously, education had focused on literacy, religious training, and discipline. Thus most parents were indifferent to whether or not their children continued their schooling. Under Mann's leadership, the school curriculum became more secular and appropriate for future clerks, farmers, and workers. Students studied geography, American history, arithmetic, and science. Moral education was retained, but direct religious indoctrination was dropped.

Mann and others responded to the changes wrought by a market economy, urbanization, and immigration. The typical city dweller was a newcomer, whether from abroad or from a country district. The new public schools would take the nation of strangers and inculcate them with common values, ones shared by many native Protestant political leaders. The basic texts—McGuffey's readers—used the Protestant scriptures to teach children to accept their position in society. A good child, McGuffey taught, does not envy the rich: "it is God who makes some poor and others rich." McGuffey preached "that the rich have troubles which we know nothing of; and that the poor, if they are good, may be very happy." Catholics, immigrants, blacks, and working-class people sought community control of the schools, but they lost out to state control under Protestant educators. Catholics in New York responded by building their own educational system over the next half-century. When Los Angeles became a city in 1850, it attempted to establish bilingual Spanish-English instruction. Trained bilingual teachers could not be found, however, and only English was permitted when the schools opened.

Another great change in urban life was in leisure time and recreation. Urban Americans worked so hard that nearly all English visitors seemed to agree with Charles Lyell's observation

Leisure

that Americans, "whether rich or poor, were labouring from morning till night, without ever indulging in a holiday." Lyell exaggerated the situation, but the new urban work and living patterns produced different uses of leisure than had been traditional in the countryside or among European kin. Space for recreation was

New urban institutions like P. T. Barnum's American Museum in New York City drew city dwellers and created traffic jams. Much of city life took place outdoors, as this painting of the street in front of Barnum's Museum reveals. *Library of Congress.*

scarce in the expanding cities; urban life did not offer the opportunities for games and sport that agrarian society did. Gatherings at the post office or tavern or general store or the cycle of harvest festivals, fairs, and neighborly gatherings were not part of urban life. As strangers, urban dwellers found it difficult to find like-minded people to share games, sport, and recreation.

Nonetheless many city dwellers continued to enjoy traditional seventeenth-century sports and recreations. Tavern games of skill and strength, often accompanied by betting, remained popular—arm wrestling, quoits (throwing a two-pound iron or stone ring at a pin), nine pins, pitching coins. City dwellers, however, had less opportunity to ride and hunt than did those in rural areas or small towns. Fishing remained important in cities; some fished as recreation, others as a livelihood.

Theater was a major institution in American life. After a church, a theater was often the second public building constructed in town. Large cities boasted of two or more theaters that catered to different classes. In New York City the Park Theater enjoyed the patronage of the carriage trade, the Bowery drew the middle class, and the Chatham attracted workers. The opera house generally became the playhouse of the upper class. Yet some theater cut across class lines. Shakespeare was performed so often and appreciated so widely that even illiterate theatergoers knew his blank verse well.

Sports, like theater, increasingly involved city dwellers as spectators. Horse racing, boxing, pedestrianism (walking races), and, in the 1850s, base-

Sports

ball began to attract large urban crowds. Entertainment became part of specialized commerce; one purchased a ticket—to the theater, the circus, P. T. Barnum's American Museum, the racetrack, or the ball park.

In 1821, New York State legalized horse racing, and a large track was developed in Queens County across the East River from New York City. In 1823 the "race of the century" took place there, between American Eclipse representing the North and Sir Henry of Virginia representing the South. Contemporary estimates placed the crowd at from 50,000 to 100,000, and the papers reported a massive traffic jam of carriages leading from the ferry to the Union Park racecourse. American Eclipse won the match, taking two of three heats. Typically, match races took three days, and many found the betting as important as the sport. Horses and slaves, as well as money, often changed hands. After 1831, sports could be followed in the sports paper, *Spirit of the Times*. After 1845, boxing fans could read about their champions in the *National Police Gazette*. Technology kept pace with sports. In 1849, round-by-round accounts of the Hyer-Sullivan boxing match at Rock Point, Maryland, were telegraphed throughout the East.

Sport and recreation mirrored the growing divisions in American urban society. They had become less spontaneous; increasingly they relied on organization and formal rules and attracted spectators who paid an admission fee. Most importantly, they frequently depended upon exclusive associations and clubs, which advanced the interests of particular groups. The New York [Racing] Association, for instance, sponsored the match race between American Eclipse and Sir Henry of Virginia. In 1829 a group of Ohio merchants organized the Cincinnati Angling Club, with a formal constitution and by-laws, and limited the membership to twenty-five. A group of Wall Street office workers formed the Knickerbocker Club in 1842 and in 1845 set down formal rules for the game of baseball. Their written rules were widely adopted and are the basis for the game of baseball today.

Middle- and upper-class Americans formed clubs and associations to avoid being strangers to each other and to defend themselves against the culture of other groups—immigrants, migrants, blacks, and artisans—that spilled onto the city streets. Many native-born New Yorkers like George Templeton Strong felt alienated in the city of their birth. Some neighborhoods seemed dominated by foreigners, others by artisans. In the 1840s even a youth culture developed on the Bowery; the broad street came alive evenings as an urban midway with theaters, dance halls, ice-cream shops, and cafes. Older New Yorkers feared the "Bowery boy," whose ostenta-

▶ **City Life**

tious dress and behavior seemed threatening. The Bowery boy had close-cut hair in back and long locks in front, greased into a roll. He wore a broad-brimmed black hat, an open shirt collar, a black frock coat that reached below the knee, and as much jewelry as he could afford. His swaggering step, especially when he had a girl friend on his arm, frightened many in the middle class. Equally disturbing to old New Yorkers were the working women who paraded on the Bowery. They came in groups to enjoy each other's company and to meet Bowery boys. Unlike ladies who partially hid themselves beneath veils or bonnets, Bowery girls drew attention with bright, outlandish clothes and ornate hats.

Voluntary associations and clubs offered the middle and upper classes an opportunity to recapture the city. Some, like the Masonic order, provided comfort and leisure activity to middle- and upper-class members. The Masons offered everything that the bustling city did not: an elaborate hierarchy, an orderly system of deference between ranks, and harmony and shared values. Members knew each other. The Masonic order played a public role as well: Masons marched in the parades that were a regular part of the city's public and political life. Most parades contained artisan and working-class associations and societies, including the militia, and the Masons believed they too had a stake in the street life of the city.

A great deal of conflict centered on urban streets. Most working people spent much of their lives out-of-doors—they worked in the streets as laborers, shopped in open markets, paraded on special occasions, and carried out ordinary social and domestic affairs in the open. Outdoors and on the street young people courted, neighbors argued, and ethnic groups defended their turf. Urban streets served as a political arena. Extreme behavior found a home there as well; mob violence took place in the streets.

Inequality, urbanization, and immigration gave rise to urban conflict as rioting and incidents of violence became frequent. The colonial tradition of crowd action, in which disfranchised people took to the streets (see Chapter 4), had diminished in the first three decades of the nineteenth century. In the 1830s riots again became commonplace as professionals and merchants, skilled craftsmen, and ordinary laborers vented their rage against their

▶ **Urban Riots**

Chapter 11: Diversity and Conflict: People and Communities, 1800–1860

opponents. "Gentlemen of property and standing," unnerved by antislavery proponents, sacked abolitionist and antislavery organizations. In the 1840s "respectable" citizens waged war against the Mormons, driving them from Illinois and Missouri. Workers raged against new migrants to the cities and other symbols of the new industrial order. In Philadelphia, for instance, native-born workers fought Irish weavers in 1828, and whites and blacks rioted on the docks in 1834 and 1835. In North Philadelphia from 1840 to 1842, residents took to the streets continuously until the construction of a railroad through their neighborhood was abandoned. These disturbances climaxed in the great Philadelphia riots of 1844, in which mostly Protestant skilled workers fought Irish Catholics. Other cities too became battlegrounds as nativist riots peaked in the 1850s. By 1840 more than 125 people had died in urban riots, and by 1860 more than 1,000.

Public disorder spread in the city. To keep order and provide for public safety, Boston supplemented (1837) and New York replaced (1845) part-time watchmen and constables with uniformed policemen. Nonetheless, middle-class men and women did not venture out alone at night, and during the day they stayed clear of many city districts. Police controlled and suppressed street activity as did local ordinances to license and regulate street vendors and ban their cries, bells, and horns. So too did laws against disturbing the peace and vagrancy, often used against free blacks and immigrants. The influx of immigrants to the cities worsened social tensions by pitting people of different backgrounds against each other in the contest for jobs and housing. Ironically, in the midst of the dirt, the noise, the crime, and the conflict, as if to tempt those who struggled to survive, rose the opulent residences of the very rich.

Extremes of Wealth

Some observers, notably the young French visitor Alexis de Tocqueville, viewed the United States before the Civil War as a place of equality and opportunity. Over a nine-month period in 1831 and 1832, Tocqueville and his companion Gustave de Beaumont traveled four thousand miles and visited all twenty-four states. Tocqueville later introduced *Democracy in America,* his classic analysis of the American people and nation, with the statement: "No novelty in the United States struck me more vividly during my stay there than the equality of conditions."

Tocqueville believed American equality—the relative fluidity of the social order in the United States—derived from Americans' mobility. Restlessness and movement—geographic and social mobility—offered people opportunities to start anew regardless of where they came from or who they were. Prior wealth or family mattered little; a person could be known by deeds alone. And indeed, restlessness and ambition for success drove Americans on; sometimes they seemed unable to stop. "An American will build a house in which to pass his old age," Tocqueville wrote, "and sell it before the roof is on; he will plant a garden and rent it just as the trees are coming into bearing; he will clear a field and leave others to reap the harvest; he will take up a profession and leave it, settle in one place and soon go off elsewhere with his changing desires."

Talent and hard work, many Americans believed, found their just reward in such an atmosphere. According to the common wisdom, anyone could advance by working hard and saving money. A local legend from Newburyport, Massachusetts, sounded this popular theme. Tristram Dalton, a Federalist lawyer, wanted his carriage repaired. Moses Brown, an energetic mechanic, refused to wait for Dalton's servants to tow the carriage to his shop; he sought out the vehicle and fixed it on the spot. After Dalton's death his heirs squandered the family fortune, but Brown's industriousness paid off. Through hard work the humble carriage craftsman became one of Massachusetts's richest men. Eventually he bought the Dalton homestead and lived out his life there. The message was clear: "Men succeed or fail . . . not from accident or external surroundings," as the *Newburyport Herald* put it in 1856, but from "possessing or wanting the elements of success in themselves."

Other observers recorded the rise of a new aristocracy based on wealth and power and the growth of class and ethnic divisions. Among those who disagreed with the egalitarian view of American life was *New York Sun* publisher Moses Yale Beach, author of twelve editions of *Wealth and*

Differences in Wealth

The infamous Five Points section of New York City's Sixth Ward, probably the worst slum in pre–Civil War America. Immodestly dressed prostitutes cruise the streets or gaze from windows, while a pig roots for garbage in their midst. *The New-York Historical Society.*

Biography of the Wealthy Citizens of New York City. In 1845, Beach listed 750 New Yorkers with assets of $100,000 or more. John Jacob Astor led the list of 19 millionaires with a fortune of $25 million. Ten years later, in 1855, Beach reported more than 1,000 New Yorkers worth $100,000, 28 of them millionaires. Combining gossip-column tidbits with often erroneous guesses at people's wealth, Beach's editions suggest the enormous wealth of New York's upper class. Tocqueville himself, ever sensitive to the conflicting trends in American life, had described the growth of an American aristocracy based on industrial wealth. The rich and well educated "come forward to exploit industries," Tocqueville wrote, and become "more and more like the administrators of a huge empire. . . . What is this if not an aristocracy?"

Wealth throughout the United States was becoming concentrated in the hands of a relatively small number of people. In Brooklyn in 1810 two-thirds of the families owned only 10 percent of the wealth; by 1841 their share had decreased to almost nothing. In New York City between 1828 and 1845, the wealthiest 4 percent of the city's population increased their holdings from an estimated 63 percent to 80 percent of all individual wealth. By 1860 the top 5 percent of American families owned more than half the nation's wealth; the top 10 percent owned more than 70 percent.

A cloud of uncertainty hung over working men and women. Many were afraid that during hard times they would become part of the urban unemployed. They feared the competi-

Urban Poverty tion of immigrant and slave labor. They feared the insecurities and indignities of poverty, chronic illness, disability, old age, widowhood, and desertion. And they had good reason.

Poverty and squalor stalked the urban working class as cities grew. Cities were notorious for the dilapidated districts where newly arrived immigrants, indigent free blacks, the working poor, and thieves, beggars, and prostitutes lived. New York City's Five Points, a few blocks from City Hall, became the worst slum in pre–Civil War America. Dominated by the Old Brewery, which in 1837 had

A world apart from the slums and the noise of the streets were the country estates of the would-be American aristocracy. Wouterus Verschuur painted this 1854 country outing of millionaire August Belmont. *National Portrait Gallery, Smithsonian Institution, Washington, D.C., Gift of Paul Mellon.*

been converted to housing for hundreds of adults and children, the neighborhood was predominantly Irish and black. Ill suited to human habitation and lacking such amenities as running water and sewers, Five Points exemplified the worst of urban life. Contemporaries estimated that more than one thousand people lived in its rooms, cellars, and subcellars. Throughout the city, workers' housing was at a premium. Houses built for two families often held four; tenements built for six families held twelve. Many families took in lodgers to help pay the rent.

In New York and other large cities lived "street rats," children and young men who earned their living off the streets by bootblacking or petty thievery. They slept on boats, in haylofts, or in warehouses. Charles Loring Brace, a founder of the Children's Aid Society (1853), described the street rats in his *Dangerous Classes of New York* (1872): "Like the rats, they were too quick and cunning to

be often caught in their petty plunderings, so they gnawed away at the foundations of society undisturbed." To Brace and others, such rootless persons threatened American society. They represented a threat more serious than Shays's Rebellion or Burr's conspiracies. "They will vote—they will have the same rights as we ourselves," warned the first report of the Children's Aid Society in 1854, "though they have grown up ignorant of moral principle, as any savage or Indian." Moreover, "they will perhaps be embittered at the wealth and luxuries they never share. Then let society beware, when the vicious, reckless multitude of New York boys, swarming now in every foul alley and low street, come to know their power and use it!"

In a world apart from Five Points and the people of the streets lived the upper-class elite society of Philip Hone, one-time mayor of New York. Hone's diary, meticulously kept from 1826 until his death

The Urban Elite in 1851, records the activities of an American aristocrat. On February 28, 1840, for instance, Hone attended a masked ball at the Fifth Avenue mansion of Henry Breevoort, Jr., and Laura Carson Breevoort. The ball began at the fashionable hour of 10 P.M., and the five hundred ladies and gentlemen who filled the mansion wore costumes adorned with ermine and gold. For more than a week, Hone believed, the affair "occupied the minds of people of all stations, ranks, and employments." Few balls attained such grandeur, but at one time or another similar parties were held in Boston, Philadelphia, Baltimore, and Charleston.

At a less-rarefied level, Hone's social calendar was filled with elegant dinner parties featuring fine cuisine and imported wines. The New York elite who filled the pages of Hone's diary—the 1 percent of the population who owned 50 percent of the city's wealth—lived in large townhouses and mansions attended by a corps of servants. In the summer, country estates, ocean resorts, mineral spas, and grand tours of Europe offered them relief from the winter and spring social seasons.

Much of this new wealth was inherited. For every John Jacob Astor who made millions in the western fur trade, or George Law who left a farm to become a millionaire contractor and investor in railroads and banks, there were ten who used money they had inherited or married as a steppingstone to additional wealth. Andrew H. Mickle, a poor Irish immigrant, became a millionaire and mayor of New York City; his fortune came from marrying the daughter of his employer. Many of the wealthiest bore the names of the colonial commercial elite— Beekman, Breevoort, Roosevelt, Van Rensselaer, and Whitney. These rich New Yorkers were not an idle class; they devoted energy to increasing their fortunes and power. Urban capitalists like Philip Hone profited enormously from the transportation, commercial, and manufacturing revolutions; hardly a major canal, railroad, bank, or mill venture lacked the names and investments of the fashionable elite. Wealth begat wealth, and family ties through inheritance and marriage were essential in that world.

More modest in wealth, though hard working, were those in the expanding middle class. The growth and specialization of trade had rapidly increased their numbers, and they **The Middle Class** were a distinct part of the urban scene. The men were business-

men or professionals, the women homemakers. Middle-class families enjoyed the fruits of the advances in consumption. Wool carpeting, fine wallpaper, and rooms full of furniture replaced the bare floors, whitewashed walls, and emptiness of eighteenth-century middle-class homes. Houses became larger, often with four to six rooms, and were relatively cheap. Middle-class children slept one to a bed, and middle-class families used indoor toilets by the 1840s and 1850s. When Philadelphia publishing agent Joseph Engles died in 1861, his estate recorded that his parlor contained two sofas, thirteen chairs, three card tables, a fancy table, a piano, a mirror, and a fine carpet. Other rooms were similarly furnished. Middle-class families formed the backbone of the rich associational life that Tocqueville had discovered in America. They filled the family pews in church on Sundays; their children pursued whatever educational opportunities were available. If they dreamed of entering Philip Hone's world, they were mindful to keep their distance from the working class and the poor.

Women and the Family

Economic change and urbanization transformed women and families in the nineteenth century; work, class, gender roles, ethnicity, race, and religion created greater distinctions between families and among women. In the eighteenth century the range of differences among females had been much less; they had much more in common then.

Increasingly, women's and men's work grew apart. As manufacturing left the home, so did wage workers, except for those doing putting-out work. On farms, there was still an overlap between women's and men's work, but in the new stores and workshops tasks diverged. Specialization in business and production accompanied specialization in work tasks; men acquired new, narrow skills that they applied outside the home in set ways with purposefully designed tools and systems. Authority within the workplace, removed from the household, became formal and impersonal.

Some women shared these experiences for brief periods in their lives. New England farm daughters who were the first textile-mill workers performed

Working Women

new, specialized work tasks away from home. In the 1840s the new urban department stores hired young women as clerks and cash runners. Many women worked for a time as teachers, usually for two to five years. Paid employment represented a stage in their lives, a brief period before they left their paternal households and entered their marital households.

Working-class women—the poor, widows, free blacks—worked for wages to support themselves and their families. Leaving their parental homes as early as age twelve or thirteen, they earned wages most of their lives, with only short respites for bearing children and rearing infants. Unlike men and New England farm daughters, however, most of these women did not work in the new shops and factories. Instead they sold their domestic skills for wages outside of their own households. Unmarried girls and women worked as domestic servants in other women's homes; married and widowed women worked as laundresses, seamstresses, cooks, and boarding-house keepers. Some hawked food and wares on city streets; others did piecework sewing. Few of the occupations available enabled them to support themselves or a family at an acceptable level. Widowhood especially was synonymous with poverty.

Increasingly work took on greater gender meaning and segregation. Most women's work centered, as it always had, on the home. As the urban family lost its importance in the production of goods, household upkeep and child rearing grew in importance and required women's full-time attention. Interest in education, religion, morality, domestic arts, and culture began to fill the void left by the decline of the economic functions of the family. These areas came to be known as the woman's sphere. For a woman to achieve mastery in these areas was to live up to the middle-class ideal of the cult of domesticity of the nineteenth century.

Middle-class American women and men placed great importance on the family. The role of the mother was to ensure the nation's future by rearing her children and providing the home with a spiritual and virtuous environment. The family was to be a moral institution characterized by selflessness and cooperation. Thus women were idealized as the embodiment of self-sacrificing republicanism. This view was in sharp contrast to the world outside the home—a sphere increasingly identified with

A watercolor-and-ink portrait of a scrubwoman, made in 1807. Domestic work was still the most common job held by women working outside the home in the early nineteenth century. *The New-York Historical Society.*

men. The world of work—the market economy—was seen as a place of conflict dominated by base self-interest. Amid a rapidly changing world in which single men and women left their parental homes and villages, in which factories and stores replaced traditional means of production and distribution, the family was supposed to be a rock of stability and traditional values.

The domestic ideal limited the paying jobs available to middle-class women outside the home. Most paid work was viewed with disapproval because it conflicted with the ideal of domesticity. One occupation came to be recognized as consistent with the genteel female nature: teaching. In 1823 the Beecher sisters, Catharine and Mary, established the Hartford Female Seminary and added philosophy, history, and science to the traditional women's curriculum of domestic arts and religion. A decade later Catharine Beecher campaigned to establish training seminaries for female teachers. Viewing formal education as an extension of women's nurturing role, Beecher had great success in spreading her message. By the 1850s schoolteaching was a major woman's vocation, and in most

Women and the Family

large cities the majority of teachers were women, nearly all unmarried. The employment of female teachers enlarged the work opportunities open to educated women. Not only did many consider education an appropriate nurturing role for women, but men outside of the South shunned it because of the low pay. Even then, women teachers were often hired at half of the wages paid to men teachers. For society, the underpaying of women remained a bargain as long as talented, educated women had relatively limited opportunities to use their education in other occupations.

While woman's work outside the home remained limited, family size was shrinking. In 1800 American women bore, on the average, six to seven children; in 1860 they bore five and by 1900 four. This decline occurred even while many immigrants with large-family traditions were settling in the United States; thus the birthrate for native-born women declined even more. Although rural families were larger than urban ones, birthrates in both areas declined to the same degree.

Decline in the Birthrate

A number of factors reduced family size. Increasingly, small families were viewed as desirable. Children would have greater opportunities in smaller families; parents could pay more attention to them and would be better able to educate them and help them financially. Also, contemporary marriage manuals stressed the harmful effects of too many births on a woman's health; too many children weakened women physically and overworked them as mothers.

All this evidence suggests that wives and husbands made deliberate decisions to limit the size of families. In areas where farm land was relatively expensive, families were smaller than in other agricultural districts. It appears that parents who foresaw difficulty setting up their children as independent farmers chose to have fewer children. Similarly, in urban areas children were more an economic burden than an asset. As the family lost its role as a producer of goods, the length of time during which children were only consumers grew, as did the economic costs to parents.

How did men and women limit the size of their families in the early nineteenth century? Many married later, thus shortening the period of childbearing. Women had their last child at a younger age, dropping from around forty in the mid-

Birth Control

eighteenth century to around thirty-five in the mid-nineteenth century, suggesting that family planning was becoming more common. Many couples used traditional forms of birth control, such as *coitus interruptus,* or withdrawal of the male before completion of the sexual act. Medical devices, however, were beginning to compete with this ancient practice. Although animal-skin condoms imported from France were too expensive for popular use, cheap rubber condoms were widely adopted when they became available in the 1850s. Some couples used the rhythm method—attempting to confine intercourse to a woman's infertile periods. Knowledge of the "safe period," however, was uncertain even among physicians. Another method was abstinence, or less-frequent sexual intercourse.

If all else failed, abortion was widely available, especially after 1830. Ineffective folk remedies for self-induced abortion had been around for centuries, but in the 1830s surgical abortions became common. Abortionists advertised their services in large cities, and middle-class and elite women asked their doctors to perform abortions. One sign of the upswing in abortions was the increase in legislation against it. Between 1821 and 1841, ten states and one territory prohibited abortions for the first time; by 1860, twenty states had outlawed it. Only three of those twenty punished the mother, however, and the laws were rarely enforced.

Significantly, the birth-control methods women themselves controlled—douching, the rhythm method, abstinence, and abortion—were the ones that were increasing in popularity. The new emphasis on women's domesticity encouraged women's autonomy in the home and gave women greater control over their own bodies. According to the cult of domesticity, the refinement and purity of women ruled the household, including the bedroom; as one woman put it, "woman's duty was to subdue male passions, not to kindle them."

Smaller families and fewer births changed the position and living conditions of women. At one time birth and infant care had occupied the entire span of women's adult lives, and few mothers had lived to see their youngest child reach maturity. After the 1830s many women had time for other activities. Smaller families also allowed women to devote more time to their older children, and slowly childhood came to be perceived as a distinct

Chapter 11: Diversity and Conflict: People and Communities, 1800–1860

part of the life span. The expansion of public education in the 1830s and the policy of grouping school children by age tended to reinforce this trend.

Sarah Ripley of Massachusetts, a young girl in the eighteenth century and an adult in the nineteenth, revealed in her diaries the changes American society was experiencing. Daughter of

> **Sarah Ripley Stearns**

a Greenfield shopkeeper, Ripley had a privileged childhood. After completing boarding school, she returned home to work as an assistant in her father's store. In 1812, after a five-year courtship, she married Charles Stearns of Shelburn. "I have now acquitted the abode of my youth, left the protection of my parents and given up the name I have always borne," she recorded in her diary. "May the grace of God enable me to fulfill with prudence and piety the great and important duties which now dissolve [fall] on me." Yet she missed the bustle of the shop, as she confessed in her diary.

Sarah Ripley Stearns's life was not a settled one; change was everywhere. After marriage she left her parents' home and village. Motherhood occupied her, as she bore three children within four years. Her brother moved west. She moved with her family three times during her marriage, and in 1818 she became a widow. In the midst of all this, Sarah Ripley Stearns found religion an anchor. When a revival visited her village in the 1810s, Stearns declared her faith. Rather than leading to introspection, religion promoted social interaction. With her neighbors she formed a "little band of associated females" and sponsored a school society and juvenile home.

Many Protestant women, like Sarah Ripley Stearns, moved by religious concerns, entered a new arena. Visits and meetings in parlors and churches led women into a public sphere that was an extension of their domestic concerns. Stearns's benevolent society work not only aided poor children but also provided its female participants with experience in organizing and chairing meetings, raising funds, and cultivating an extended women's network. Thus religion and charity propelled women in new directions (see pages 343–345).

Women who made a conscious decision to stay single rejected the cult of domesticity and intentionally departed from the centuries-old pattern in which women moved as depen-

> **Single Women**

dents from their fathers' households to the households of their

Rebecca Lukens pioneered in an unusual role for a woman in early nineteenth-century America as she ran the Lukens Steel Company in eastern Pennsylvania from 1825 until she died in 1854. The deaths of her father in 1823 and of her husband in 1825 left her with the mill and large debts. She revived the steel company and was soon shipping its iron plates as far away as Europe. *Lukens Steel Company.*

husbands. Louisa May Alcott (1832–1888), author of the novel *Little Women* (1868), sought independence and financial security for herself. Her father, philosopher Bronson Alcott, never provided adequately for the family. Not even the family's participation in the utopian cooperative Fruitlands could put enough food on the table. Alcott worked as a seamstress, governess, teacher, housemaid, and author; her writing brought her success. "Things go smoothly, and I think I shall come out right, and prove that though an *Alcott,* I *can* support myself," she wrote her father in 1856. "I like the independent feeling; and though not an easy life, it is a free one, and I enjoy it. I can't do much with my hands; so I will make a battering-ram of my head and make a way through this rough-and-tumble world."

Louisa May Alcott had foresworn marriage, risking the opprobrium of being a spinster. She and other women took a path of independence that made them less dependent on men. They chose to pursue vocational identities outside of home and marriage, to explore their own personal growth, to follow their own abilities, and to expand their minds. With more traditional women they shared life in a mostly female world, defined by female relationships and activities. Given the difficulty women had in finding work that would allow them to be self-supporting, they undertook their independence at great risk. Nonetheless there was a significant increase in single women in the first three quarters of the nineteenth century. In Massachusetts in 1850, 17 percent of native-born women never married; in colonial days a much smaller percentage had remained single.

Independent white women helped establish new roles for women. They were responding to changes and opportunities offered by the market economy and expanding cities. Immigration, too, had an enormous impact in remaking American life; ethnic and religious diversity became a hallmark of nineteenth-century America.

Immigrant Lives in America

No less than gender, ethnic and religious differences divided Americans. In numbers alone immigrants drastically altered the United States. The 5 million strangers who came to the states between 1820 and 1860 outnumbered the entire population of the country at the first census in 1790. They came from all continents, though Europeans made up the vast majority. The peak period of pre–Civil War immigration was from 1847 through 1857; in that eleven-year period, 3.3 million immigrants entered the United States, 1.3 million from Ireland and 1.1 million from the German states. By 1860, 15 percent of the white population was foreign-born.

This massive migration had been set in motion decades earlier. In Europe around the turn of the nineteenth century, the Napoleonic wars had begun one of the greatest population shifts in history; it was to last more than a century. War, revolution, famine, industrialization, and religious persecution led many Europeans to leave home. The United States beckoned, offering them economic opportunity and religious freedom.

American institutions, both public and private, actively recruited European emigrants. Western states lured potential settlers in the interest of promoting their economies. In the 1850s, for instance, Wisconsin appointed a commissioner of emigration who advertised the state's advantages in American and European newspapers. Wisconsin also opened an office in New York and hired European agents to compete with other states and with firms like the Illinois Central Railroad for immigrants' attention.

▶ **Promotion of Immigration**

Large construction projects and mines needed strong young laborers. Textile mills and cities attracted young women workers. Europeans' awareness of the United States heightened as employers, states, and shipping companies advertised the opportunities to be found across the Atlantic. Often the message was stark: work and prosper in America or starve in Europe. With regularly scheduled sailing ships commuting across the ocean after 1848, the cost of transatlantic travel was within easy reach of millions of Europeans.

Success in America led to further emigration. "I wish, and do often say that we wish you were all in this happy land," wrote shoemaker John West of Germantown, Pennsylvania, to his kin in Corsley, England, in 1831. "A man nor woman need not stay out of employment one hour here," he advised. John Down, a weaver from Frome, England, settled in New York City without his family. Writing to his wife in August 1830, he described the bountiful meal he had shared with a farmer's family: "They had on the table puddings, pyes, and fruit of all kind that was in season, and preserves, pickles, vegetables, meats, and everything that a person would wish, and the servants [farm hands] set down at the same table with their masters." Though Down missed his family dearly, he wrote, "I do not repent of coming, for you know that there was nothing but poverty before me, and to see you and the dear children want was what I could not bear. *I would rather cross the Atlantic ten times than hear my children cry for victuals once.*" To those skeptics who claimed the United States was filling up, he advised, "There is plenty of room yet, and will be for a thousand years to come." These letters and

In 1855, New York State established Castle Garden, in the background above, as an immigrant center. There at the tip of Manhattan Island, many immigrants first touched American soil. The painting depicts immigrants ending their long sea voyage from Ireland. *Museum of the City of New York.*

others were widely circulated in Europe to advertise the success of pauper immigrants in America.

So they came, enduring the hardships of travel and of settling in a strange land. The journey was difficult. The average transatlantic crossing took six weeks; in bad weather it could take three months. Disease spread unchecked among people huddled together like cattle in steerage. More than 17,000 immigrants, mostly Irish, died from "ship fever" in 1847. On disembarking, immigrants became fair game for the con artists and swindlers who worked the docks. Agents greeted them and tried to lure them from their chosen destinations. In 1855, in response to the immigrants' plight, New York State's commissioners of emigration established Castle Garden as an immigrant center. There, at the tip of Manhattan Island, the major port for European entry, immigrants were somewhat sheltered from fraud. Authorized transportation companies

maintained offices in the large rotunda and assisted immigrants with their travel plans.

Most immigrants, like the George Martin family, gravitated toward cities, since only a minority had farming experience or the means to purchase land and equipment. Many stayed in New York itself. By 1845, 35 percent of the city's 371,000 people were of foreign birth. Ten years later 52 percent of its 623,000 inhabitants were immigrants, 28 percent from Ireland and 16 percent from the German states. Boston, an important entry port for the Irish, took on a European tone. Throughout the 1850s the city was about 35 percent foreign-born, of whom more than two-thirds were Irish. In the South, too, major cities had large immigrant populations. In 1860 New Orleans was 44 percent foreign-born, Savannah 33 percent, and the border city of St. Louis 61 percent. On the West Coast, San Francisco had a foreign-born majority.

Some immigrants, however, did settle in rural areas. In particular, German, Dutch, and Scandinavian farmers gravitated toward the Midwest. Greater percentages of Scandinavians and Netherlanders took up farming than did other nationalities; both groups came mostly as religious dissenters and migrated in family units. The Dutch who founded colonies in Michigan and Wisconsin, for instance, had seceded from the official Reformed Church of the Netherlands. Under such leaders as Albertus C. Van Raalte, they fled persecution in their native land to establish new and more pious communities—Holland and Zeeland, Michigan, among them.

Not all immigrants found success in the United States; hundreds of thousands returned to their homelands with disappointment. Before the potato blight hit Ireland, recruiters lured

> **Immigrant Disenchantment**

many Irish to swing picks and shovels on American canals and railroads and to work in construction. Among them was Michael Gaugin, who had the misfortune to arrive in New York City during the financial panic of 1837. Gaugin, for thirteen years an assistant engineer in the construction of a Dublin canal, had been attracted to the United States by the promise that "he should soon become a wealthy man." The Dublin agent for a New York firm convinced Gaugin to quit his job, which included a house and an acre of ground, and emigrate to the United States. Within two months of arriving in the United States, Gaugin became a pauper. In August 1837 he declared he was "now without means for the support of himself and his family, and has no employment, and has already suffered great deprivation since he arrived in this country; and is now soliciting means to enable him to return with his family home to Ireland." Many of those who had come with the Gaugins had already returned home.

Such experiences did not deter Irish men and women from coming to the United States. Ireland was the most densely populated European country and among the most impoverished. From 1815 on, small harvests prompted a steady stream of Irish to emigrate to America.

> **Irish Immigrants**

Then in 1845 and 1846 potatoes—the basic Irish food—rotted in the fields. From 1845 to 1849, death from starvation, malnutrition, and typhus spread. In all, 1 million died and about 1.5 million fled, two-thirds of them to the United States. People became Ireland's major export.

In the 1840s and 1850s a total of 1.7 million Irish men and women entered the United States. At the peak of Irish immigration, from 1847 to 1854, 1.2 million came. Between 1820 and 1854, except for two years, the Irish constituted the largest single group of immigrants annually. By the end of the century there would be more Irish in the United States than in Ireland.

The new Irish immigrants differed greatly from those who had left Ireland to settle in the American colonies. In the eighteenth century, the Scotch-Irish had predominated (see page 77), and their journey had involved moving from one part of the British Empire to another. The nineteenth-century Roman Catholic Irish travelers to America, however, moved from colonial Ireland to an independent republic, and the political and religious differences made their cultural adaptation that much more difficult. In comparison with the Scotch-Irish, the new immigrants from Ireland tended to be younger, increasingly female, and mostly from the rural provinces. With eldest sons heirs to family farms and with eldest daughters staying home to care for parents, the younger children who came alone to the United States were expendable in Ireland's declining economy. Farmers' daughters could find work only as domestic servants, and poverty-stricken Ireland could not absorb all of them. In American cities they found work in factories and households. If they wed, they would marry late, as did their sisters in Ireland. They helped support their families still at home, built Catholic churches and schools, and established a network of charitable and social organizations in American cities.

In the urban areas where they clustered in poverty, most Irish immigrants met growing anti-immigrant, anti-Catholic sentiment. "No Irish Need Apply" signs were common. During the colonial period, white Protestant settlers had feared "popery" as a system of tyranny

> **Anti-Catholicism**

and had discriminated against the few Catholics in America. After the Revolution, anti-Catholicism receded; but in the 1830s the trend reversed, and anti-Catholicism appeared wherever the Irish did. Attacks on the papacy and the church circulated widely in the form of libelous texts like *The Awful Disclosures of Maria Monk* (1836), which alleged sexual orgies among priests and nuns. Nowhere was anti-Catholicism more open and nasty than in Boston, though such sentiments were widespread. Anti-Catholic riots were almost commonplace. In Charlestown, Massachusetts, a mob burned a convent (1834); in Philadelphia, a crowd attacked priests and nuns and vandalized churches (1844); and in Lawrence, Massachusetts, a mob leveled the Irish neighborhood (1854).

The native-born who embraced anti-Catholicism were motivated largely by anxiety. They feared that a militant Roman church would subvert American society, that unskilled Irish workers would displace American craftsmen, and that the slums inhabited in part by the Irish were undermining the nation's values. Every American problem from immorality and alcoholism to poverty and economic upheaval was blamed on immigrant Irish Catholics. Impoverished workers complained to the Massachusetts legislature that the Irish displaced "the honest and respectable laborers of the State . . . and from their manner of living . . . work for much less per day . . . being satisfied with food to support the animal existence alone." American workers, in contrast, "not only labor for the body but for the mind, the soul, and the State." The new public schools, with their Protestant bias, represented another attack on Irish Catholics. Friction increased as Irish-American men fought back by entering politics.

In 1854, Germans replaced the Irish as the single largest group of arriving immigrants. Potato blight also sent many from the German states to the United States in the 1840s, but **German Immigrants** other hardships contributed to the steady stream. Many came from areas where small landholdings made it hard to eke out a living and to pass on land to their sons. Others were craftsmen displaced by the industrial revolution. These refugees were joined by middle-class Germans who emigrated to the United States after the abortive revolution of 1848.

Unlike the Irish, who tended to congregate in towns and cities, Germans settled everywhere. Many came on cotton boats, disembarked at New Orleans, and traveled up the Mississippi. In the South they became peddlers and merchants; in the North and West they worked as farmers, urban laborers, and businessmen. They, more than the Irish, tended to migrate in families and groups; that tendency helped maintain German culture.

Immigrants from the German states transplanted their culture and institutions in the New World. Groups of them tended to settle in small towns and rural areas, thus preserving their local and regional identities in German settlements in Pennsylvania, Ohio, Illinois, Wisconsin, Missouri, and Texas. Many American-born merchants and laborers learned German in order to do business in the settlements. In larger cities German immigrants tended to cluster in German-state groups. Their presence in great numbers transformed the tone and culture of cities like Cincinnati and Milwaukee. *Turnvereine*—German physical-culture clubs—sprouted in villages and cities; by 1853 sixty such societies were hosting exercise groups and German-language lectures.

Native-born Americans treated immigrants from the German states with greater respect than they did the Irish. Stereotypes of Germans often included such terms as "industrious," "hardworking," "self-reliant," and "intelligent." Many believed that Germans would "harmonize" better with American culture. This contrasted with the almost universal dislike of the Irish, as most Americans seemed to accept the negative British stereotypes of Irish people.

Nonetheless, Germans too met antiforeign attitudes. More than half the German immigrants were Catholic, and their Sabbath practices differed from those of Protestants. On Sundays many urban German immigrant families gathered at beer gardens to eat and drink beer, to dance, sing, and listen to band music, and sometimes to play cards. Protestants were outraged by such violations of the Lord's day. In Chicago, riots broke out when Protestants enforced the Sunday prohibition laws.

Their persistence in using the German language and their different religious beliefs set them apart. Besides the Catholic majority, a significant number of German immigrants were Jewish. And even the German Protestants—mostly Lutherans—founded their own churches and often educated their children in German-language schools. Not all Germans, however, were religious. The failure of the revolution in 1848 had sent to the United States a whole generation of liberals and freethinkers, some of whom were socialists, communists, and anarchists.

Not all immigrants came to the United States voluntarily. After the annexation of Texas, the Mexican War, and the Gadsen Purchase (see pages

Saint Isadore of Madrid, patron saint of farmers, ca. 1840, attributed to Rafael Aragon. Hispanic farmers in the Southwest sought the aid of the patron saint of agriculture as they struggled to raise crops and preserve their culture in the region. *Courtesy of Dr. and Mrs. Ward Alan Minge.*

Nueces County, Texas, at the time of the Texas Revolution (1836), Mexicans held all the land; twenty years later, they had lost it all. Commerce replaced their agricultural and ranching society and economy; rancheros and vaqueros—the cowboys—became obsolete. Although many Hispanics had fought for Texas independence, the settlers coming in tended to treat Mexicans as inferior, black people. Within two generations Hispanics became second-class citizens on land on which they had lived for generations. They became strangers in their own land.

The conflict between the immigrants and the society they joined paralleled the inner tensions experienced by most immigrants. On the one hand they felt impelled to commit themselves wholeheartedly to their new country, to learn the language and adapt themselves to American ways. On the other hand they were rooted in their own cultural traditions—the comfortable, tested customs of the society of their birth, the familiar ways and words that came intuitively and required no education.

For immigrants, conflict centered on the desire to be part of American society, albeit for some on their own terms. Once here, they claimed their right to a fair economic and political share. Indians, however, like Hispanics in the Southwest, defended what they conceived of as prior rights. Their land, their religion, their way of life came under constant attack because they were most often viewed as obstacles to expansion and economic growth.

Hispanics 367, 373), many Hispanics found themselves in the United States, some against their will, because of boundary changes. The development of Texas apart from Mexico after 1836, the discovery of gold in California, and the extension of railroads broke the linkage of the Southwest with Mexico and reoriented the Southwest toward the United States.

Hispanic culture continued in the region, but Anglos and European immigrants seized economic and political power. Anglos overwhelmed Hispanics in Texas and in California. Hispanics retained their language, Roman Catholic religion, and community through newspapers, mutual aid societies, and the church, but they lost power and status. In

Indian Resistance and Removal

The clash between Indians and the larger society was inherited from the colonial past. Population growth, westward expansion, the transportation revolution, and market orientation underlay the designs and demands on Indian land. Under the Constitution, the federal government had responsibility for dealing with Indians. For better or for worse, there had to be a federal Indian policy. Unfortunately, from the Indians' point of view, it was most often for the worse. United States territorial expansion came at the Indians' expense. The result was

Chapter 11: Diversity and Conflict: People and Communities, 1800–1860

removal of the great Indian nations to lands west of the Mississippi. Indians' resistance proved incapable of protecting their land, but it did help in preserving much of their culture.

While the population of other groups increased by leaps and bounds, the Indian population shrank. Alexis de Tocqueville noticed the contrast. "Not only have these wild tribes receded, but they are destroyed," Tocqueville concluded after personally observing the tragedy of forced removal, "and as they give way or perish, an immense and increasing people fill their place. There is no instance upon record of so prodigious a growth or so rapid a destruction." War, forced removal, disease—especially smallpox—and malnutrition reduced many tribes by half. In the 1830s alone more than half of the Pawnees, Omahas, Ottoes, Missouris, and Kansas died. Within tribes, the more traditional the family structure, the greater was the toll.

As the colonial powers in North America had done, the United States treated Indian tribes as sovereign nations, until Congress ended the practice in 1871. In its relations with tribal leaders, the government followed the ritual of international protocol. Indian chiefs and delegations who visited Washington were received with the appropriate pomp and ceremony. Leaders exchanged presents as tokens of friendship, and commemorative flags and silver medals with presidents' likenesses became prized possessions among Indian chiefs. Agreements between a tribe and the United States were signed, sealed, and ratified as was any international pact.

In practice, however, Indian sovereignty was a fiction. Protocol seemed to acknowledge independence and mutual respect, but treaty negotiations exposed the sham. Essentially, treaty making was a process used by the American government to acquire Indian land. Differences in power made it less than the bargaining of two equal nations. Treaties were often made between victors and vanquished. In a context of coercion, many old treaties gave way to new ones in which the Indians ceded their traditional holdings in return for different lands in the West. Beginning with President Jefferson, the government withheld payments due tribes for previous land cessions to pressure them to sign new treaties.

The War of 1812 snuffed out whatever realistic hopes eastern Indian leaders might have had of resisting American expansion by warfare. Armed resistance persisted and was bloody on both sides, as in the Seminole Wars (see pages 236, 333). Resistance, however, only delayed the inevitable. The Shawnee chiefs Prophet and Tecumseh led the most significant movement against the United States (see pages 228–231), but after Tecumseh's death, Prophet failed to sustain the movement.

The experiences of Prophet and other Shawnees were typical of the wanderings of an uprooted people. Until the 1870s only the Delawares and Kickapoos moved more. When **Prophet** the Shawnees gave up 17 million acres in Ohio in the 1795 Treaty of Greenville (see page 174), they scattered to Indiana and eastern Missouri. After the War of 1812, Prophet's Indiana group withdrew to Canada under British protection. In 1822 other Shawnees sought Mexican protection and moved from Missouri to present-day eastern Texas. With the United States government promoting western removal, Prophet returned from Canada and led a group to the new Shawnee lands established in eastern Kansas in 1825. When Missouri achieved statehood in 1821, the Shawnees there were forced to move to Kansas. In the 1830s Shawnees in Ohio were removed to Kansas and were joined there by others expelled from Texas. By 1854 Kansas was open to white settlement, and the Shawnees had to cede back seven-eighths of their land—1.4 million acres.

Removal had a profound impact on all Shawnees. The men had to give up their traditional role as providers; their methods of hunting and knowledge of woodland animals were useless in prairie Kansas. Shawnee women played a greater role as providers as grains became the tribe's dietary staple, supplemented by government aid under treaty provisions. Yet, remarkably, the Shawnees preserved their language and culture in the face of these drastic changes.

In the 1820s, under pressure, Indians in Ohio, southern Indiana and Illinois, southwestern Michigan, most of Missouri, central Alabama, and southern Mississippi ceded their lands. **Indian** They gave up nearly 200 million **Policy** acres for pennies an acre. But white settlers' appetites were insatiable; the expansion of commercial farming in the Midwest and of cotton plantations in the South increased the demand for Indian land and for Indians to assimilate. One instrument that served both purposes was the Indian agency system, which monopolized trade with Indians in a designated locality and paid out the rations, supplies, and annuities that Indians received in exchange for abandoning their land. With time, the tribes became dependent on these government payments—a dependency intended to make them docile in treaty negotiations.

Ever since the early days of European colonization, assimilation of Native Americans through education and Christianity had been an important goal (see page 34). It found renewed interest as the United States expanded westward. "Put into the hand of [Indian] children the primer and the hoe," the House Committee on Indian Affairs reported in 1818, "and they will naturally, in time, take hold of the plough; and, as their minds become enlightened and expand, the Bible will be their book, and they will grow up in habits of morality and industry . . . and become useful members of society." In 1819, under missionary lobbying, Congress appropriated $10,000 annually for the "civilization of the tribes adjoining the frontier settlements." This "civilization act" was a means to teach Indians to live like white settlers. Protestant missionaries administered the "civilizing fund" and established mission schools. Within five years thirty-two schools appeared. The new boarding schools, unlike earlier Christian missions, substituted English for Native Americans' languages and taught agriculture along with the Gospel. The emphasis on agriculture was intended to promote Indian interest in private property and hard work and to lay the basis for stable, Christian communities.

To settlers eyeing Indian land, assimilation through education was too slow a process, and Indians themselves questioned the instruction. At any one time in all the schools there were never more than 1,500 students; at that rate it would take centuries to assimilate all Indians. Some tribes found the missionary message repugnant. The Creek nation permitted the schools only after being assured that there would be no preaching. Zealous missionaries, however, violated the agreement, preaching to the Creeks and their black slaves. In response, a band of Creeks sacked the school. Similarly, the Passamaquoddy tribe of New England, many of whose members were Catholics, opposed teachers' efforts to make them Episcopalians. Even the vocational education seemed unpromising; graduates who returned to their tribal villages had no way of applying the commercial agricultural skills they had acquired in the schools.

Wherever Indians lived, illegal settlers plagued their lands. The federal government, though obligated by treaty to protect the integrity of treaty lands, never committed sufficient troops to keep out aggressive whites. The United States lacked the resolve to exclude settlers. The government promoted westward expansion, and legitimate Indian claims had to give way to the advance of white civilization.

It became apparent in the 1820s that not economic dependency or education or Christianity could force Indians to cede voluntarily much more land to meet the demands of expansionists. Attention focused on Cherokees, Creeks, Choctaws, Chickasaws, and Seminoles in the South because much of their land remained intact after the War of 1812 and because they aggressively resisted white encroachment. They had more formal political institutions than the northern Indians and thus were better organized to resist.

In his last annual message in December 1824, President James Monroe suggested to Congress that all Indians be moved beyond the Mississippi River.

> **Indian Removal** Three days later the president sent a special message to Congress proposing removal. Stressing the positive aspects, Monroe believed his proposal an "honorable" one that would protect Indians from invasion and provide them with independence for "improvement and civilization." Monroe felt that force would be unnecessary; the promise of a home free from white encroachment would be sufficient to win Indian acceptance.

The southern tribes unanimously rejected Monroe's offer. The Cherokee, Creek, Choctaw, and Chickasaw tribes at whom the program was directed wanted to be left alone. Between 1789 and 1825 they had negotiated a total of thirty treaties with the United States; they had reached their limits. They wished to remain on what was left of their ancestral land.

Pressure from Georgia had prompted Monroe's policy. Most Cherokees and some Creeks lived in northwestern Georgia, and in the 1820s the state accused the federal government of not fulfilling its 1802 promise to remove the Indians in return for the state's renunciation of its claim to western lands. Georgia sought complete expulsion and was satisfied neither by Monroe's removal messages nor by further Creek cessions. In 1826 the Creek nation, under federal pressure, ceded all but a small strip of its Georgia acreage. Governor George M. Troup, however, wanted all the Creek land and sent surveyors to the one remaining strip. When President John Quincy Adams threatened to send the army to protect the Indians' claims, Troup countered with his own threats. Only the eventual removal of the Georgia Creeks to the West in 1826 prevented a clash between the state and the federal government. For the Creeks the outcome was a devastating defeat. In an attempt to hold fast to the remainder of their traditional lands (in Alabama), they significantly altered their political structure. In 1829 they had centralized tribal authority, strengthening their national council at the expense of traditional village autonomy, and had forbidden any chief from ceding land.

If "civilizing" Indians was the goal, none met that test more than the Cherokees. During the Cherokee renaissance from 1819 to 1829 the tribe became economically self-sufficient and politically self-governing. The 12,000 to 15,000 adult Cherokees in the 1820s came to think of themselves as a nation and not a collection of villages. In 1821 and 1822 Sequoyah, a self-educated Cherokee, devised an eighty-six-character phonetic alphabet that led to a Cherokee-language Bible and bilingual tribal newspaper, *Cherokee Phoenix* (1828). Between 1820 and 1823 the Cherokees created a formal government with a bicameral legislature, elected representatives, a court system, and a salaried bureaucracy. In 1827 they adopted a written constitution, modeled after that of the United States. Cherokee land laws, however, differed from United States law. The tribe owned all land, and complex provisions covered the sale of land (forbidden to outsiders), abandonment of land (three years had to pass before resettlement was allowed), and proximity of farms (minimum distance was one-quarter mile apart). Nonetheless the Cherokees assimilated American cultural patterns well. By 1833 they held 1,500 black slaves whose legal status under the Cherokees was the same as that of slaves held by southern whites. Moreover, missionaries had been so successful that the Cherokees could be considered a Christian community.

Although the tribe developed a way of life similar to that of an American state, it failed to win respect or acceptance from southerners. Georgia pressed the Cherokees to sell the 7,200 square

> **Cherokees**

miles of land they held in the state. In 1822, Congress appropriated $30,000 to buy the Cherokee land in Georgia, but the tribal council refused to negotiate. Most Cherokees preferred to stay where they were and believed that their treaty rights to their land were unquestionable. Yet in 1828 and 1829, Georgia, impatient with Cherokee refusals to negotiate cession, annulled the Cherokee constitution, extended Georgia's sovereignty over the tribe, and ordered the tribal lands seized.

In 1829 the Cherokees, under Chief John Ross and backed by sympathetic whites but not by the new president, Andrew Jackson, turned to the federal courts to defend their treaty with the United States and prevent Georgia's seizure of their land. Their legal strategy reflected their maturity as a nation and their political sophistication. In *Cherokee Nation* v. *Georgia* (1831), Chief Justice John Marshall ruled that under the federal Constitution an Indian tribe was neither a foreign nation nor a state and therefore had no standing in federal courts. Nonetheless, said Marshall, the Indians had an unquestioned right to their lands; they could lose title only by voluntarily giving it up. A year later, in *Worcester* v. *Georgia,* Marshall defined the Cherokee position more clearly. The Indian nation was, he declared, a distinct political community in which "the laws of Georgia can have no force" and into which Georgians could not enter without permission or treaty privilege.

> **Cherokee Nation v. Georgia**

President Andrew Jackson, who as a general had led an expedition against the Seminoles in Spanish Florida in 1818, had little sympathy for the Indians and ignored the Supreme Court's ruling. Keen to open up new lands for settlement, he was determined to remove the Cherokees at all costs. In the Removal Act of 1830 Congress provided Jackson with the funds he needed to negotiate new treaties and resettle the resistant tribes west of the Mississippi.

The infamous Trail of Tears had begun. The Choctaws were the first to go; in the winter of 1831 and 1832, they made the forced journey from Mississippi and Alabama to the West (see map, page 332). Alexis de Tocqueville was visiting Memphis when they arrived there, "the wounded, the sick, newborn babies, and the old men on the point of death. . . . I saw them embark

> **Trail of Tears**

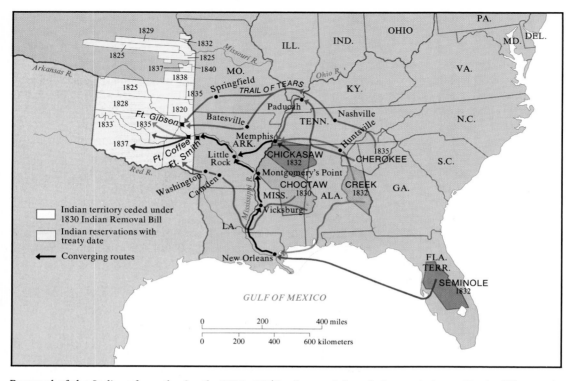

Removal of the Indians from the South, 1820–1840 *Source: Acknowledgment is due to Martin Gilbert and George Weidenfeld and Nicholson Limited for permission to reproduce the map on page 332 taken from American History Atlas.*

to cross the great river," he wrote, "and the sight will never fade from my memory. Neither sob nor complaint rose from that silent assembly. Their afflictions were of long standing, and they felt them to be irremediable."

Soon other tribes joined the trail. The Creeks in Alabama delayed removal until 1836, when the army pushed them westward. A year later the Chickasaws followed. The Cherokees, having fought through the courts to stay, found themselves divided. Some recognized the hopelessness of further resistance and accepted removal as the only chance to preserve their civilization. The leaders of this minority signed a treaty in 1835 in which they agreed to exchange their southern home for western land. Chief Ross and other antitreaty Cherokees lobbied Congress against ratification of the treaty and then against appropriating payment under its provisions. They lost. When the time for evacuation came in 1838, most Cherokees refused to move. President Martin Van Buren then sent federal troops to round up the Indians. About twenty thousand Cherokees were evicted, held in deten-

tion camps, and marched to present-day Oklahoma under military escort. Nearly one-quarter died of disease and exhaustion on the Trail of Tears. When the forced march to the West ended, the Indians had traded about 100 million acres of land east of the Mississippi for 32 million acres west of the river plus $68 million. Only a few scattered remnants of the tribes, among them the Seminoles, remained in the East and South.

What was the impact of removal, of the Trail of Tears? Change had been thrust on these tribes so suddenly and drastically that they had to transform much of their culture and societies. In the West they occupied an alien environment; they had no generational ties with the new land. Many could not be at peace with the land or get used to the strange animals and plants they found there. Many Indians became dependent upon government payments for survival. Removal brought new internal conflicts. The Cherokees struggled over the re-establishment of their government system. In 1839, followers of Chief John Ross assassinated the leaders who had negotiated the treaty. Violence continued sporadi-

The French genre painter Alfred Boisseau recorded the passage of the Choctaw through Louisiana from Mississippi to Indian Territory. With dignity they made the forced march. *New Orleans Museum of Art.*

cally for six years, until a new treaty in 1846 brought a temporary truce. In 1861 the American Civil War renewed the factionalism, forever shattering Cherokee tribal unity.

Conflict arose between western Indians and migrating tribes, and among migrants forced to share land and scarce resources. Nearly 100,000 newcomers settled west of the Mississippi, and the existing game could not support them all. The Osages and Pawnees fought the newcomers who were invading their land and homes. In the Southwest, among the Apaches and Comanches, the story was repeated, as the push of white settlement led to treaties, cession, removal and new treaties, and further cession and removal.

In the Southeast a small band of Seminoles successfully resisted removal and remained in Florida. In 1832 in the Treaty of Payne's Landing, some of the Seminole tribal leaders agreed to relocate to the West within three years. Others opposed the treaty, and some probably did not know it existed. A minority under Osceola refused to vacate their

> **Second Seminole War**

homes and fought the protreaty group. In 1835 United States troops were sent to suppress the intratribal war and impose removal. Osceola initiated a fierce guerrilla war against the federal troops.

The Florida Indians were a varied group from all over the South. They included many Creeks and Indian-blacks who were ex-slaves or descendants of runaway slaves. The American army considered them all Seminoles and subject to removal. General Thomas Jesup believed that the runaway-slave population was the key to the war. "This, you may be assured, is a Negro, not an Indian war," he wrote Ben Butler in December 1836, "and if it be not speedily put down, the South will feel the effects of it on their slave population before the end of the next season." The army intended to exterminate the Seminoles, but without success; nor did Seminole resistance provoke any slave uprisings. Osceola died in an army prison in 1838, but the Seminoles fought on until 1842, when the United States abandoned the removal effort. This Seminole war cost the lives of 1,500 soldiers and $20 million. Most of Osceola's followers agreed to move west to Indian Territory in 1858, but many Seminoles remained in the Florida Everglades, prideful that they had successfully resisted conquest.

In the West, Indians found themselves pressured to cede land. To facilitate white settlement, Commissioner of Indian Affairs William Medill in 1848 proposed gathering the western Indians into two great reservations, one northern and one southern. The Kansas and Platte valleys separated the two areas, creating a wide corridor for white settlers to use on their way westward. In 1853 and 1854, however, the government took back most of the northern reservation lands in a new round of treaties, and Kansas and Nebraska were opened to white settlement.

A complex set of attitudes drove whites to force Indian removal. Most merely wanted Indian lands; they had little or no respect for the rights or culture of the Indians. Westward territorial expansion justified pushing Indians aside. Others were aware of the injustice but believed that Indians must inevitably give way to white settlement. Some, like John Quincy Adams, believed the only way to preserve Indian civilization was to remove the tribes and establish a buffer zone between Indians and whites. Others, including Thomas Jefferson, doubted that white civilization and Indian "savagery" could coexist. Supported by missionaries and educators, they hoped to "civilize" Indians and assimilate them slowly into American culture. Whatever the source of white behavior in the United States, the outcome was the devastation of Native American peoples and their cultures. The survival of Indian life in the face of such conditions reflected the resilience and strengths of the Indians' cultures.

Another minority experienced insecurity and struggled for recognition and legal rights. Like most Indians, they too were involuntarily a part of American society. Unlike Indians, however, they wished to be fully a part of the American people.

Free People of Color

No black person was safe, wrote the abolitionist and former slave Frederick Douglass after the Philadelphia riot of 1849. "His life—his property—and all that he holds dear are in the hands of a mob, which may come upon him at any moment—at midnight or mid-day, and deprive him of his all."

Between 1832 and 1849 five major antiblack riots occurred in Philadelphia. Mobs stormed black dwellings and churches, set them on fire, and killed the people inside. The mobs intimidating free blacks could be made up of slave hunters seeking runaways but were as likely to kidnap a free black as a slave. Or they could represent civil authority. In 1829 in Cincinnati, across the Ohio River from slaveholding Kentucky, city officials, frightened by the growing black population, drove as many as two thousand blacks from the city by enforcing a law requiring cash bonds for good behavior. Free blacks faced insecurity daily. They were outsiders in the land of their birth.

Under federal law, the blacks' position was uncertain. The Bill of Rights seemed to apply to free blacks; the Fifth Amendment specified that "no person shall . . . be deprived of life, liberty, or property, without due process of law." Yet the racist theory of the eighteenth century that defined a republic as being only for whites seemed to exclude blacks (see pages 167–168). This exclusion was reflected in early federal legislation. In 1790 naturalization was limited to white aliens, and in 1792 the militia was limited to white male citizens. Moreover, Congress approved the admission to the Union of states whose constitutions restricted the rights of blacks. After the admission of Missouri in 1821, every new state admitted until the Civil War banned blacks from voting. When the Oregon and New Mexico territories were organized, public land grants were limited to whites.

In the North, blacks faced legal restrictions nearly everywhere; Massachusetts was the major exception. Many states barred entry to free blacks or required bonds of $500 to $1,000 to guarantee their good behavior, as in Ohio (1804), Illinois (1819), Michigan (1827), and Oregon (1857). Although seldom enforced, these laws clearly indicated the less-than-free status of blacks. Only in Massachusetts, New Hampshire, Vermont, and Maine could blacks vote on an equal basis with whites throughout the pre–Civil War period. Blacks gained the right to vote in Rhode Island in 1842 (though all voters faced restrictive property qualifications), but they had lost it earlier in Pennsylvania and Connecticut. No state but Massachusetts permitted blacks to serve on juries; four midwestern states and California did not allow blacks to testify against whites. In Oregon, blacks could not own real estate, make contracts, or sue in court.

Legal status was important, but practice and custom were crucial. Although Ohio repealed its law barring black testimony against whites in 1849, the exclusion persisted as custom in southern Ohio counties. Throughout the North free people of color were either excluded from or segregated in public places.

Exclusion and Segregation of Blacks

Abolitionist Frederick Douglass was repeatedly turned away from public facilities during a speaking tour of the North in 1844. A doorkeeper refused him admission to a circus in Boston, saying, "We don't allow niggers in here." He met the same reply when he tried to attend a revival meeting in New Bedford. At a restaurant in Boston and on an omnibus in Weymouth, Massachusetts, he heard the familiar words. Hotels and restaurants were closed to blacks, as were most theaters and churches.

Probably no practice inflicted greater injury than the general discrimination in hiring. Counting houses, retail stores, and factories refused to hire black men other than as janitors and general handymen. New England mills hired only whites. Except for a small professional and commercial and skilled elite, free black men in the North found steady work difficult to obtain; most toiled as unskilled daily laborers. Black women more easily found jobs because their domestic skills were in great demand in the burgeoning urban society; they worked as domestic servants, cooks, laundresses, and seamstresses. Unlike their white counterparts, however, these women did not view paid employment as a distinct period in their life cycle; around 40 percent of black women worked for wages during marriage and the child-rearing years. Given the lower wages received by black workers, not many black families could survive on one income.

Free people of color faced especially severe legal and social barriers in the southern slave states, where their presence was often viewed as an incentive to insurrection. Indeed,

Southern Free Blacks

southern states responded to fear of mass rebellion by tightening the restrictions on free blacks and forcing them to leave small towns and interior counties. After a successful slave rebellion in Haiti in the 1790s and Gabriel Prosser's slave revolt in 1800 (see page 209), southern states barred the entry of free blacks for two decades. In 1806, Virginia required newly freed blacks to leave the state.

After the Nat Turner rebellion in 1831, the position of free blacks weakened further. Within five years nearly all the southern states prohibited the freeing of any slaves without legislative or court approval, and by the 1850s Texas, Mississippi, and Georgia had banned manumission altogether.

To restrict free blacks and encourage them to migrate north, southern states adopted elaborate "black codes." Blacks, who provided most of the South's skilled labor, encountered licensing requirements and bans restricting work opportunities. Virginia and Georgia banned black river captains and pilots. Some states forbade blacks to assemble without a license; some prohibited blacks from being taught to read and write. In the late 1830s, when these black codes were enforced with vigor for the first time, free blacks increasingly moved northward, even though northern states discouraged the migration.

In spite of these obstacles, the free black population rose dramatically in the first part of the nineteenth century, from 108,000 in 1800 to almost 500,000 in 1860 (see table, page 336). Nearly half lived in the North, occasionally in rural settlements like Hammond County, Indiana, but more often in cities like Philadelphia, New York, and Cincinnati. Baltimore had the largest free black community; sizable free black populations also existed in New Orleans, Charleston, and Mobile (see pages 284–285). Social and economic divisions among blacks arose. Although occupation, wealth, education, religion, and status divided free persons of color, the common necessity of self-defense still brought them together.

The ranks of free blacks were constantly increased by ex-slaves. Some, like Frederick Douglass and Harriet Tubman, were fugitives. Douglass had hired himself out as a ship caulker in Baltimore, paying three dollars a month to his owner. Living among free workers gave him greater opportunity to escape slavery. By masquerading as a free black with the help of borrowed seaman's papers, he bluffed his way to Philadelphia and freedom. Tubman, a slave on the eastern shore of Maryland, escaped to Philadelphia in 1849 when her master's death led to rumors that she would be sold out of the state. Within the next two years she returned twice to free her two children, her sister, her mother, and her brother and his family. Other slaves were voluntarily freed by their owners. Some, like a Virginia planter named Sanders who

BLACK POPULATION OF THE UNITED STATES, 1800–1860

Year	Total Black Population	Percentage of Total U.S. Population	Free People of Color	Free Blacks as a Percentage of Black Population
1800	1,002,000	18.9	108,000	10.8
1810	1,378,000	19.0	186,000	13.5
1820	1,772,000	18.4	234,000	13.2
1830	2,329,000	18.1	320,000	13.7
1840	2,874,000	16.8	386,000	13.4
1850	3,639,000	15.7	435,000	11.9
1860	4,442,000	14.1	488,000	11.0

settled his slaves as freedmen in Michigan, sought to cleanse their souls by freeing their slaves in their wills. Some freed elderly slaves after a lifetime of service rather than support them in old age. The parents of the slave Isabella (Sojourner Truth) were freed when whites who inherited the family would not support the father, who was too old to work.

Sojourner Truth's experience in New York reveals that the gradual emancipation laws of northern states had little effect as long as slavery existed elsewhere. In 1817, New York State adopted an emancipation plan whereby all slaves over forty years old were freed and young slaves would serve ten more years. Owners tried to thwart the law by selling their slaves into other states. In 1826, fearing sale to the South, Sojourner Truth found refuge with a nearby abolitionist couple. With their help she sued successfully for the freedom of her son Peter, who had been sold unlawfully to an Alabaman. One can only guess how many blacks did not receive such help and were permanently deprived of their freedom.

In response to their oppression, free blacks founded strong, independent self-help societies to meet their unique needs and fight against their less-than-equal status. In every black

Founding of Black Institutions community African-Americans organized black churches, fraternal and benevolent associations, literary societies, and schools. In Philadelphia in the 1840s, more than half the black

population belonged to mutual beneficiary societies, and female benevolent societies and schools flourished. The black Masons grew to more than fifty lodges in seventeen states by 1860. Many leaders believed that these mutual aid societies would encourage thrift, industry, and morality and thus equip the members to improve their lot. No amount of effort could counteract white prejudice, however. Blacks remained second-class in status.

The network of societies among urban free black men and women provided a base for black protest. From 1830 to 1835, and thereafter irregularly, free blacks held national conventions with delegates drawn from city and state organizations. Under the leadership of the small black middle class, which included the Philadelphia sail manufacturer James Forten and the orator Reverend Henry Highland Garnet, the convention movement served as a forum to attack slavery and agitate for equal rights. Militant new black newspapers joined the struggle. *Freedom's Journal,* the first black weekly, appeared in March 1827; in 1837 the *Weekly Advocate* began in New York City. Both papers circulated in the North, spreading black thought and activism.

Although ending slavery and attaining equal rights remained at the top of blacks' agenda, the mood of free blacks began to shift in the late 1840s

Black Nationalism and 1850s. Many were frustrated by the failure of the abolitionist movement and by the passage of the Fugitive Slave Act of 1850 (see

In 1843, William Matthew Prior painted individual portraits of husband and wife Reverend William Lawson and Nancy Lawson. The Lawsons—New England free people of color—were active leaders in black self-help societies and as abolitionists. *Shelburn Museum.*

page 379). Some black leaders became more militant, and a few joined John Brown in his plans for rebellion (see page 387). But many more were swept up in a tide of black nationalism that stressed racial solidarity and unity, self-help, and a growing interest in Africa. Before this time, efforts to send African-Americans "back to Africa" had originated with whites seeking to solve racial problems by ridding the United States of blacks. But in the 1850s blacks held emigrationist conventions of their own under the leadership of Henry Bibb and Martin Delany. In 1859 Delany led an exploration party to the Niger Valley as the emissary of a black convention. He signed a treaty with Yoruba rulers allowing him to settle American blacks in their African kingdom (the plan was never carried out).

Nothing better illustrates the ironic position of free blacks in the United States than the flight of blacks to Canada and Africa in search of freedom while millions of European migrants were coming to the United States for liberty and opportunity. With the coming of the Civil War and emancipation, however, the status of blacks, free and slave, would move onto the national political agenda, and African-Americans would focus on their position at home.

The United States in 1860 was a far more diverse and turbulent society than it had been in 1800. The market economy, urbanization, and immigration had altered the ways people lived and worked. Economic growth not only created new jobs in towns and cities but also caused clearer distinctions in wealth and status. Inequality increased everywhere, and competition and insecurity produced resentments and conflict. Cities housed both ostentatious wealth and abject poverty, and violence and disorder became commonplace. Many Americans, both old and new, felt as if they were strangers.

In the midst of these changes, middle-class families sought to insulate their homes from the competition of the market economy. Many women found fulfillment in the domestic ideal, although others found it confining. More and more, middle-class urban women became associated with nurturing roles, first in homes and schools, then in churches and reform societies. Working-class women had more modest goals: escaping poverty and winning respect.

In Europe, famine and religious and political oppression sent millions of people across the Atlantic. They were drawn to the United States by the promise of jobs and political and religious toleration. Yet most found the going rough even though conditions were often better than in their native lands. In the process they changed the profile of the American people; Americans differed from each other more and more and shared common traditions and experiences less and less. Competition and diversity bred intolerance and prejudice. None were to feel that more painfully than Indians and free blacks, who were most often made to feel like aliens in their own land.

As the economy and society changed, conflict became commonplace and entered the public arena. The utopian communities, conflict over public space, the backlash against immigrants, urban riots, black protest, and Indian resistance were manifestations of the divisions in America. But conflict took other forms as well, as in the widespread reform movements that came to characterize American life from the 1820s through the 1850s. Through reform and politics, many Americans sought to harness and control the forces of change. Spurred on by religious revival and individualism, they turned to politics as a collective means of restoring harmony and order. In the process, divisions became even sharper.

Suggestions for Further Reading

Rural and Utopian Communities

Leonard J. Arrington and Davis Bitton, *The Mormon Experience: A History of the Latterday Saints* (1979); Priscilla J. Brewer, *Shaker Communities, Shaker Lives* (1986); R. Carlyle Buley, *The Old Northwest: Pioneer Period, 1815–1840,* 2 vols. (1950); Don H. Doyle, *The Social Order of a Frontier Community: Jacksonville, Illinois, 1825–1870* (1978); John Mack Faragher, *Sugar Creek: Life on the Illinois Prairie* (1986); Laurence Foster, *Religion and Sexuality: Three American Communal Experiments of the Nineteenth Century* (1981); Steven Hahn and Jonathan Prude, eds., *The Countryside in the Age of Capitalist Transformation* (1985); Joan M. Jensen, *Loosening the Bonds: Mid-Atlantic Farm Women, 1750–1850* (1986); Wallace Stegner, *The Gathering of Zion: The Story of the Mormon Trail* (1964); Anthony F. C. Wallace, *Rockdale: The Growth of an American Village in the Early Industrial Revolution* (1978).

Urban Communities and Inequality

Melvin A. Adelman, *A Sporting Time: New York City and the Rise of Modern Athletics, 1820–1870* (1986); Nelson M. Blake, *Water for the Cities: A History of the Urban Water Supply Problem in the United States* (1956); Stuart M. Blumin, "The Hypothesis of Middle-Class Formation in Nineteenth-Century America: A Critique and Some Proposals," *American Historical Review* 90 (April 1985), 299–338; Stuart M. Blumin, *The Urban Threshold: Growth and Change in a Nineteenth-Century American Community* (1976); Lawrence A. Cremin, *American Education: The National Experience, 1783–1876* (1980); Susan G. Davis, *Parades and Power: Street Theater in Nineteenth-Century Philadelphia* (1986); Elliott J. Gorn, *The Manly Art: Bare-Knuckle Prize Fighting in America* (1986); Karen Halttunen, *Confidence Men and Painted Women: A Study of Middle-Class Culture in America, 1830–1870* (1982); Jennie Holliman, *American Sports (1785–1835)* (1931); Alan Stanley Horlick, *Country Boys and Merchant Princes: The Social Control of Young Men in New York* (1975); Carl Kaestle, *Pillars of the Republic: Common Schools and American Society, 1780–1860* (1982); Gary B. Nash, "The Social Evolution of Preindustrial American Cities, 1700–1820: Reflections and New Directions," *Journal of Urban History,* 13 (February 1987), 115–145; Edward Pessen, *Riches, Class and Power Before the Civil War* (1973); Christine Stansell, *City of Women: Sex and Class in New York, 1789–1860* (1986); Stephen Thernstrom, *Poverty and Progress: Social Mobility in a Nineteenth Century City* (1964); Alexis de Tocqueville, *Democracy in America,* 2 vols. (1835–1840); Richard C. Wade, *The Urban Frontier: 1790–1830* (1957).

Women and the Family

Lee Virginia Chambers-Schiller, *Liberty, A Better Husband: Single Women in America: The Generations of 1780–1840* (1984); Clifford Edward Clark, Jr., *The American Family Home, 1800–1960* (1986); Nancy F. Cott, *The Bonds of Womanhood: "Woman's Sphere" in New England, 1780–1835* (1977); Carl N. Degler, *At Odds: Women and the Family in America from the Revolution to the Present* (1980); Hasia R. Diner, *Erin's Daughters in America: Irish Immigrant Women in the Nineteenth Century* (1983); Linda Gordon, *Woman's Body, Woman's Rights: A Social History of Birth Control in America* (1976); Suzanne Lebsock, *The Free Women of Petersburg: Status and Culture in a Southern Town, 1784–1860* (1984); James C. Mohr, *Abortion in America: The Origins and Evolution of National Policy, 1800–1900* (1978); James Reed, *From Private Vice to Public Virtue: The Birth Control Movement and American Society Since 1830* (1978); Mary P. Ryan, *Cradle of the Middle Class: The Family in Oneida County, New York, 1790–1865* (1981); Kathryn Kish Sklar, *Catharine Beecher: A Study in American Domesticity* (1973); Maris A. Vinovskis, *Fertility in Massachusetts from the Revolution to the Civil War* (1981); Robert V. Wells, *Revolutions in Americans' Lives* (1982); Barbara Welter, "The Cult of True Womanhood, 1820–1860," *American Quarterly,* 18 (Summer 1966), 151–174.

Immigrants

Gunther Barth, *Bitter Strength: A History of Chinese in the United States, 1850–1870* (1964); Rowland Berthoff, *British Immigrants in Industrial America* (1953); Kathleen Neils Conzen, *Immigrant Milwaukee: 1836–1860* (1976); Arnoldo De León, *The Tejano Community, 1836–1900* (1982); Jay P. Dolan, *The Immigrant Church: New York's Irish and German Catholics, 1815–1865* (1975); Charlotte Erickson, *Invisible Immigrants* (1972); Robert Ernst, *Immigrant Life in New York City, 1925–1863* (1949); Jon Gjerde, *From Peasants to Farmers: The Migration from Balestrand, Norway, to the Upper Middle West* (1985); Oscar Handlin, *Boston's Immigrants: A Study in Acculturation,* rev. ed. (1959); Walter D. Kamphoefner, *The Westfalians: From Germany to Missouri* (1987); Dale T. Knobel, *Paddy and the Republic: Ethnicity and Nationality in Antebellum America* (1986); Kerby A. Miller, *Emigrants and Exiles: Ireland and the Irish Exodus to North America* (1985); Harold Runblom and Hans Norman, *From Sweden to America* (1976); Philip Taylor, *The Distant Magnet: European Emigration to the United States of America* (1971); Mark Wyman, *Immigrants in the Valley: Irish, Germans, and Americans in the Upper Mississippi, 1830–1860* (1984).

Indians

Robert F. Berkhofer, Jr., *The White Man's Indian* (1978); Grant Foreman, *Indian Removal: The Emigration of the Five Civilized Tribes of Indians,* rev. ed. (1953); Michael D. Green, *The Politics of Indian Removal: Creek Government and Society in Crisis* (1982); Florette Henri, *The Southern Indians and Benjamin Hawkins, 1796–1816* (1986); Charles Hudson, *The Southeastern Indians* (1976); William G. McLoughlin, *Cherokee Renascence in the New Republic* (1986); William G. McLoughlin, *Cherokees and Missionaries, 1789–1839* (1984); John K. Mahon, *History of the Second Seminole War, 1835–1842* (1967); Theda Perdue, *Slavery and the Evolution of Cherokee Society, 1540–1866* (1979); Francis P. Prucha, *The Great Father: The United States Government and the American Indians,* 2 vols. (1984); Francis P. Prucha, *American Indian Policy in the Formative Years* (1967); Ronald N. Satz, *American Indian Policy in the Jacksonian Era* (1975); Bernard Sheehan, *Seeds of Extinction: Jeffersonian Philanthropy and the American Indian* (1973); Herman J. Viola, *Thomas L. McKenney: Architect of America's Early Indian Policy: 1816–1830* (1974); Wilcomb E. Washburn, *The Indian in America* (1975); Thurman Wilkin, *Cherokee Tragedy* (1970); J. Leitch Wright, Jr., *Creeks and Seminoles: The Destruction and Regeneration of the Muscogulge People* (1986).

Free People of Color

Ira Berlin, *Slaves Without Masters: The Free Negro in the Antebellum South* (1974); Leonard P. Curry, *The Free Black in Urban America, 1800–1850* (1981); James Horton and Lois Horton, *Black Bostonians: Family Life and Community Struggle in the Antebellum North* (1979); Luther Porter Jackson, *Free Negro Labor and Property Holding in Virginia, 1830–1860* (1942); David M. Katzman, *Before the Ghetto: Black Detroit in the Nineteenth Century* (1973); Rudolph M. Lapp, *Blacks in Gold Rush California* (1977); Leon Litwack, *North of Slavery: The Negro in the Free States, 1790–1860* (1961); Floyd J. Miller, *The Search for a Black Nationality: Black Colonization and Emigration, 1787–1863* (1975); Gary B. Nash, *Forging Freedom: The Formation of Philadelphia's Black Community, 1720–1840* (1988); Emma Lou Thornbrough, *The Negro in Indiana* (1957); Julie Winch, *Philadelphia's Black Elite: Activism, Accommodation, and the Struggle for Autonomy, 1787–1848* (1988); Arthur Zilversmit, *The First Emancipation: The Abolition of Slavery in the North* (1967).

The Tappan brothers amassed a fortune from the War of 1812 through the 1840s. Arthur, born in 1786, and Lewis, born in 1788, in Northampton, Massachusetts, were merchants and investors whose businesses included dry goods, textile mills, an importing house, the *New York Journal of Commerce,* and the Mercantile Agency (the first commercial-credit rating agency in the United States). Their wealth grew with the expansion of the market economy.

They lived simple lives; the balls and elaborate dinners of the urban elite were unknown to the Tappans. "A cracker and a tumbler of cold water," Lewis recalled, "sufficed for Arthur's luncheon." They lived by their mother's Calvinist tenet that this world was preparation for the next. They believed that they would have to submit their accounts to God and that "luxurious living" or "vain show" would count against them. Devoted to making money and doing benevolent work, they lived lives of "silks, feathers and piety."

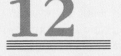

12

REFORM, POLITICS, AND EXPANSION, 1824–1844

Although they did not indulge in luxuries, they nonetheless spent large sums. Arthur was probably the most lavish giver in New York City. They contributed generously to evangelical churches and missions, to Sabbath observance, temperance, and antigambling societies, to Bible printing and distribution, to the Antimasons, and to antislavery.

At one time Lewis Tappan seemed to stray from this path. He made his first fortune during the War of 1812, married, and settled in Boston. He joined the Unitarians, the Masons, and an exclusive Federalist club. Disturbed by the perceived wasteful habits of rural migrants and Irish Catholic immigrants crowding into Boston, he believed that education and self-improvement were needed to assimilate them.

In 1828, a financial and personal religious crisis brought Lewis back to the fold. With his business in Boston failing, he joined Arthur's New York silk-importing firm and converted back to Calvinism. He quit the Masons, whom he now viewed as heathen rivals for the allegiance of the uncommitted. He threw himself into bringing about a Christian society.

The County Election, Number Two (detail) by George Caleb Bingham, 1854. Line and mezzotint engraving, hand-colored. *Collection of Mr. and Mrs. Wilson Pile. Photo by Clive Russ.*

The lives of the Tappan brothers and many other reformers were changed by one overriding issue: antislavery. Drawn to abolitionism by their religious concerns and the work of William Lloyd Garrison, Arthur and Lewis Tappan became the leaders of religious antislavery. They helped found the National Anti-Slavery Society but eventually broke with the uncompromising Garrison as they supported antislavery political parties in the 1840s. Arthur and Lewis Tappan had deservedly earned their reputations as being among the most committed reformers in the period from the 1820s through the 1850s, which became known as an age of reform.

Reform was, in part, a response to the unsettling effect of the enormous transformation that the United States experienced after the War of 1812. Population growth, immigration, internal migration, urbanization, the market economy, growing inequality, loosening family and community ties, the advancing frontier, and territorial expansion all contributed to the remaking of the United States. Many felt they were no longer masters of their own fate. Change was occurring so rapidly that people had difficulty keeping up with it. An apprentice tailor could find his trade obsolete by the time he became a journeyman; a young rural woman could find her tasks unneeded on her family's farm. Americans had fought the Revolution to make themselves independent, but poverty and obsolescent trades made them dependent. They found other changes equally disturbing. Respectable citizens felt threatened by urban mobs and paupers, and the Protestant majority feared the growing Catholic minority, with their distinctive customs and beliefs. Protestants had waged war to preserve the rights they claimed as Englishmen, not to protect alien cultures and religions. To many, all these changes seemed to undermine their traditional values.

Religious reformers like the Tappans sought to find or impose order on a society in which economic change and discord had reached a crescendo. Prompted by the evangelical ardor of the Second Great Awakening and convinced of their moral rectitude, they crusaded for individual improvement. "Americans love their country not as it is but as it will be," English visitor Francis Grund concluded in the 1830s. Everywhere benevolent and reform societies multiplied. Some sought self-improvement by renouncing alcohol and gambling. Inevitably the personal impulse to reform oneself led to the creation and reshaping of institutions. Reform soon took on a much more active role than benevolent work and became an instrument for restoring discipline and order in a changing society. Women were prominent in the reform movement, and the role of women in public life became an issue in itself.

As reform organizations spread, they turned to the government as an effective instrument of social and economic change. Temperance, institutional reform, and most notably Antimasonry and abolition brought new voters into politics. The line between social reform and politics was not always distinguishable. Opponents were no less concerned with social problems. What set them apart from reformers was their skepticism about human perfectibility and their distrust of institutions and power, both public and private. To them, coercion was the greater evil. They sought to reverse, not shape, change.

Two issues in particular provided the bridge between reform and politics: the short-lived Antimasonry frenzy and the intense, uncompromising crusade for immediate emancipation. Antimasons organized the first third-party movement, but abolition eventually overrode other concerns. No single issue evoked the depth of passion that slavery did. On a personal level it pitted neighbor against neighbor, settler against settler, section against section. Territorial expansion in the 1840s and 1850s made it even more politically explosive.

Political leaders attempted to grapple with change. In the late 1820s the opponents of religious reform found a champion in Andrew Jackson and a home in the Democratic party. Yet the Jacksonians saw themselves as reformers; they responded to change by attempting to foster individualism and to restore restraint in government. They fought special privileges and the Second Bank of the United States with the same vigor as the Tappan brothers opposed sin. President Jackson sought to restrain the national government, believing that a strong federal government restricted individual freedom by favoring one group over another. In response, reformers rallied around the new Whig party, which became the vehicle for humanitarian reform. Democrats and Whigs competed energetically in the second party system, which was marked by strong organizations, intensely loyal followings, religious and ethnic differences, and popular bases among the electorate.

IMPORTANT EVENTS

1790s–1840s	Second Great Awakening
1820s	Model penitentiaries
1825	House of Representatives elects John Quincy Adams president
1826	American Society for the Promotion of Temperance founded Morgan affair
1828	Tariff of Abominations Jackson elected president
1830	Webster-Hayne debate
1830s–1840s	Second party system
1831	*Liberator* begins publication First national Antimason Convention
1832	Veto of Second Bank of the United States recharter Jackson re-elected
1832–33	Nullification crisis
1836	Republic of Texas established Specie Circular Van Buren elected president
1837	Financial panic
1837–39	U.S.-Canada border tensions
1839–43	Hard times
1840	Whigs under Harrison win presidency
1841	Tyler assumes the presidency Oregon fever
1844	Polk elected president
1845	Texas admitted to the Union
1848	Woman's Rights Convention, Seneca Falls, New York
1851	Maine adopts prohibition

During the economically prosperous 1840s, both Democrats and Whigs eagerly promoted westward expansion to further their goals. Democrats saw the agrarian West as an antidote to urbanization and industrialization; Whigs focused on new commercial opportunities. The idea of expansion from coast to coast seemed to Americans to be the inevitable manifest destiny of the United States. The politics of territorial expansion would collide with the antislavery movement with explosive results in the 1850s and 1860s.

From Revival to Reform

The prime motivating force behind organized benevolence and reform was probably religion. Starting in the late 1790s, a tremendous religious revival, the Second Great Awakening, galvanized Protestants, especially women (see pages 206–208). The Awakening began in small villages in the East, intensified after the War of 1812, then spread over western New York, and continued to grow through the late 1840s. Under its influence, Christians in all parts of the country tried to right the wrongs of the world.

In the nineteenth century the role of churches and ministers in community life began to change. Before the Second Great Awakening, the central role of churches was declining as churches had to compete with other voluntary societies for members. A new generation of seminary-trained ministers used revivals and societies advocating benevolent works—assistance to the poor, education for youths, and pledges of temperance—to attract new members, especially women.

Revivals were the lifeblood of evangelical Christianity, and they drew converts to a religion of the heart, not the head. In 1821 Charles G. Finney, "the

Second Great Awakening

father of modern revivalism," experienced a soul-shaking conversion, which, he said, brought him "a retainer from the Lord Jesus Christ to plead his cause." Finney, a former teacher and lawyer, immediately began his career as a converter of souls, traveling from town to town for "protracted meetings," revivals lasting three to four days. He preached that salvation could be achieved through spontaneous conversion or spiritual rebirth like his own. In everyday language, he told his audiences that "God has made man a moral free agent." In other words, evil was avoidable; Christians were not doomed by original sin. Hence anyone could achieve salvation. Finney's brand of revivalism transcended sects, wealth, and race. Methodists, Presbyterians, Baptists, and Congregationalists became evangelists. The Second Great Awakening also raised people's hopes for the Second Coming of the Christian messiah and the establishment of the Kingdom of God on earth. Revivalists set out to speed the Second Coming by creating a heaven on earth. They joined the forces of good and light—reform—to combat those of evil and darkness. Some revivalists even believed that the United States had a special mission in God's design and therefore a special role in eliminating evil.

Regardless of theology, all shared a belief in individual improvement and self-reliance as moving forces. In this way the Second Great Awakening bred reform, and evangelical Protestants became missionaries for both religious and secular salvation. Wherever they preached, voluntary reform societies arose. Evangelists organized an association for each issue—temperance, education, Sabbath observance, antidueling, and later antislavery; collectively these groups formed a national web of benevolent and moral reform societies.

Beyond conversion, the great impact of the Second Great Awakening was the spread of women's involvement in benevolent activities to ameliorate the growing social ills. In Andover, Massachusetts, local revivalism began in 1814 with a male group for uplifting morals, a society to banish swearing, to observe the Sabbath, and to avoid drunkenness. In 1815, women formed the Female Charitable Society, and a year later youth were gathered into the Juvenile Bible Society. During the 1820s, without any revivals in Andover, the benevolent societies brought in new church members, of whom 70 to 80 percent were women.

Women were the earliest converts, and they tended to sustain the Second Great Awakening. When Finney led daytime prayer meetings in Rochester, New York, for instance,

Role of Women

pious middle-class women visited families while the men were away at work. Slowly they brought their families and husbands into the churches and under the influence of reform. Although many businessmen stayed and recruited their employees, churches and reform societies were influenced by women. Women more than men tended to feel personally responsible for the increasingly secular orientation of the expanding market economy. Many women felt guilty for neglecting their religious duties, and the emotionally charged conversion experience set them on the right path again.

At first, revival seemed to reinforce the cult of domesticity because piety and religious values were associated with the domestic sphere (see

From Revival to Reform

Chapter 11). In the conversion experience, women declared their submissiveness to the will of Providence, vowing to purge themselves and the world of wickedness. The organized prayer groups and female missionary societies that accompanied the Second Great Awakening were surpassed by greater organized religious and benevolent activity. Thus revival led to new public roles for women, providing a path of certainty and stability amid a rapidly changing economy and society.

In the growing, larger cities women responded both to inner voices and to the growing inequality, turbulence, and strains of change around them. They reacted to the poverty and wretched conditions found in the cities. At the turn of the nineteenth century, most of the expanding cities had women's benevolent societies to help needy women and orphans, as did Salem, Massachusetts, with its Female Charitable Society. Increasingly the spread of poverty and vice that accompanied urbanization touched the hearts of women, especially those caught up in the fervor of revival.

An 1830 exposé of prostitution in New York City revealed the diverging concerns and responses of reform men and women, on the one hand, and political organizations, on the other hand, and demonstrated the convergence of urban problems, revival, and reform. John R. McDowall, a divinity student, detailed how prostitution had taken hold on New York City. Philip Hone, one of the city's leaders (see page 319), called McDowall's Magdalen Report "a disgraceful document," and he and other New York men united to defend the city's good name against "those base slanders." Their condemnation led the male-run New York Magdalen Society to cease its work. Women, on the other hand, moved by the plight of "fallen women" and supported by the Tappans and others, responded by forming two new societies concerned with prostitutes and prostitution. In revival and reform, women and men reformers acted in the face of the opposition and the indifference of traditional political leaders.

The Female Moral Reform Society led the crusade against prostitution. During the 1830s, the New York-based association expanded its activities and geographical scope as the American Female Moral Reform Society. By 1840 it had 555 affiliated female societies among the converted across the nation. These women not only fought the evils of prostitution but also assisted poor women and orphans and entered the political sphere. In New York State in the 1840s the movement fostered public morality by successfully crusading for criminal sanctions against seducers and prostitutes.

Inevitably, reform led women and men toward public action. Evangelism demanded active Christianity because it led to working with other people. Finney's preaching of perfectionism demanded unity and active Christianity. By converting others, by ending personal corruption and dependency, and by building institutions to liberate other people, the converted confirmed their status as middle-class evangelicals. Thus wherever Finney and other evangelists held revivals in the 1820s and 1830s, they stimulated organized reform that went far beyond ameliorating social evils.

As the pace of social change increased in the 1830s and 1840s, so did efforts at reform. In western New York and Ohio, Charles G. Finney's preaching was a catalyst to reform. Western New York experienced such continuous and heated waves of revivalism that it became known as the "burned-over" district. The opening of the Erie Canal and the migration of New Englanders carried the reform ferment farther westward. There, re-

vivalist institutions—Ohio's Lane Seminary and Oberlin College were the most famous—sent committed graduates out into the world to spread the gospel of reform. Their efforts stirred nonevangelical Protestants, Catholics, and Jews as well as evangelical Christians. Evangelists also organized grassroots political movements. In the late 1830s and 1840s they rallied around the Whig party in an attempt to use government as an instrument of reform.

Temperance and Asylums

One of the most successful reform efforts was the campaign against the consumption of alcohol, which was more widespread in the early nineteenth century than it is today. As a group, American men liked to drink alcoholic spirits—whiskey, rum, and hard cider. They gathered in public houses, saloons, and rural inns to gossip, discuss politics, play cards, escape work and home pressures, and drink. Men drank on all occasions: contracts were sealed with a drink; celebrations were toasted with spirits; barn-raisings and harvests ended with liquor. Respectable women did not drink in public, but many regularly tippled alcohol-based patent medicines promoted as cure-alls. Moreover, immigration brought to America people for whom drinking was part of everyday life.

Why then did temperance become such a vital issue? And why were women especially active in the movement? Like all reform, temperance had a strong religious base. "The Holy Spirit," a temperance pamphlet proclaimed, "will not visit, much less dwell with him who is under the polluting, debasing effects of intoxicating drink." To evangelicals, the selling of whiskey was a chronic symbol of Sabbath violation, for workers commonly labored six days a week, then spent Sunday at the public house drinking and socializing. Alcohol was seen as a destroyer of families as well, since men who drank heavily either neglected their families or could not adequately support them. Temperance literature was laced with domestic images—abandoned wives, prodigal sons, drunken fathers. Outside the home, the habit of drinking could not be tolerated in the new world of the factory. Employers complained that drinkers took "St. Monday" as a

 This is to Certify

That _____ was duly elected a Member
of the above Society on the ____ day of ____ 184_; and the
pledge having been in due form administered to him he signed the same.
184_   President

This certificate of membership in a temperance society, for display, announced the virtues of the household to all visitors. In the illustration, the man signs with the support of wife and child; demon rum and its accompanying evils were banished from this home. *Library of Congress.*

holiday to recover from Sunday. Whatever they felt about other reforms, industrialists supported temperance as part of the new work habits needed for factory work. Timothy Shay Arthur dramatized all these evils in *Ten Nights in a Barroom* (1853), a classic American melodrama.

Demon rum thus became a major target of reformers. As the movement gained momentum, they shifted their emphasis from temperate use of

> **Temperance Societies**

spirits to voluntary abstinence and finally to a crusade to prohibit the manufacture and sale of spirits. The American Society for the Promotion of Temperance, organized in 1826 to urge drinkers to sign a pledge of abstinence, shortly thereafter became a pressure group for state prohibition legislation. By the mid–1830s there were some five thousand state and local temperance societies, and more than a million people had taken the pledge. By the 1840s the movement's success was reflected in a sharp decline in alcohol consumption in the United States. Between 1800 and 1830, annual per capita consumption of alcohol had risen from three to more than five gallons; by the

mid–1840s, however, it had dropped below two gallons. Success bred more victories. In 1851, Maine prohibited the manufacture and sale of alcohol except for medicinal purposes, and by 1855 similar laws had been enacted throughout New England and the Old Northwest and in New York and Pennsylvania.

Even though consumption of alcohol was declining, opposition to it did not weaken. Many reformers believed that alcohol was an evil introduced and perpetuated by Catholic immigrants. From the 1820s on, antiliquor reformers based much of their argument on this false prejudice. The Irish and Germans, the *American Protestant Magazine* complained in 1849, "bring the grog shops like the frogs of Egypt upon us." Rum and immigrants defiled the Sabbath; rum and immigrants brought poverty; rum and immigrants supported the feared papacy. Some Catholics did join with nonevangelical Protestant sects like the Lutherans to oppose temperance legislation. But other Catholics took the pledge of abstinence and formed their own temperance organizations, such as the St. Mary's Mutual Benevolent Total Abstinence Society in Boston. Even nondrinking Catholics tended to oppose state regulation of drinking, however; temperance seemed to them a question of individual choice, not state coercion. They favored self, not societal, control.

Another aspect of the temperance movement was the attack on gambling. People gathered at taverns to drink and gamble, and reformers believed that both drinking and gambling undermined independence and self-reliance. Of special concern in the nineteenth century was the spread of lotteries.

Lotteries had been brought by English colonists to the New World at the turn of the eighteenth century. England used lotteries to raise government

> **Lotteries**

revenues, and some colonists made speculative ticket purchases. In the New World, lotteries were a useful way of selling extremely valuable property in an age when few single buyers could raise the large purchase price. Hundreds of small investors could participate in a lottery for the prize, enabling a merchant to dispose of inventory or a homeowner to sell a house. Local governments used lotteries to ease the tax burden by raising money for capital improvements. The Continental Congress had hoped to use a grand lottery to raise $1.5 million to wage revolutionary war against England, but it failed to raise the anticipated revenue.

Lotteries became a target of reform, and between 1830 and 1860 every state in the Union banned them. To some, lotteries were among such vices as slavery and alcohol. Other opponents objected to the abuses inherent in the common pattern under which states delegated their lottery powers to private sponsors. For instance, a Pennsylvania investigation (1831) revealed that a state-authorized lottery to raise $27,000 a year for internal improvement, specifically for the Union Canal Company, generated enormous profits for the lottery company. On $5 million annual sales, the state received its $27,000 and the sponsors $800,000. With Protestant reformers condemning all forms of gambling, the report led to the prohibition of lotteries in Pennsylvania. The nineteenth-century experience with lotteries led states in the twentieth century, when they revived lotteries, to run their own contests.

Another important part of the reform impulse was the development of new social institutions. The age of reform prompted the establishment and construction of all sorts of asylums and other institutions to house prisoners, the insane and ill, orphans, delinquent children, and the poor. Many believed that such institutions were needed to shelter victims of instability and turbulence in society and of lack of discipline in families. Institutions would provide an environment of order, stability, and discipline, thus giving inmates an opportunity to become self-reliant and responsible.

The penitentiary movement exemplified this approach. In the 1820s New York and Pennsylvania offered competing but similar models for reforming criminals. New York's Auburn (1819–1823) and Sing-Sing (1825) prisons isolated prisoners in individual cells but brought them together in common workshops. The Pittsburgh (1826) and Philadelphia (1829) prisons isolated prisoners completely; they ate, slept, and worked in their own individual cells and had contact only with guards and visitors. Both systems sought to remove criminals from evil societal and individual influences and to place them in an ordered, disciplined regimen. It was commonly believed that criminals came from unstable families in which lack of discipline and restraint led to vice and drink. Idleness was believed to be both a symptom and a

Penitentiaries

Advertisement for the New-York Consolidated Lottery, 1826. Though lotteries were forbidden by New York State's new constitution of 1821, local operators found legal loopholes until they were suppressed in 1833, the decade in which scandals and antigambling reforms initiated the complete prohibition of lotteries. *The Metropolitan Museum of Art.*

cause of individual corruption and crime; thus the clock governed a prisoner's day, and idleness was banished.

Similar approaches were employed by societies promoting other asylums, from insane asylums and hospitals to orphanages and houses of refuge. Doctors linked mental illness, for instance, to the stress and strain of contemporary urban life. The prescribed treatment was to remove individuals from families and society, to isolate them among strangers. The asylum would impose discipline and order on patients, but in a humane fashion. In response to organized reform societies, states began to erect asylums for the insane in the 1830s. They built them in tranquil, rural settings, away from the turbulent cities. By 1860, twenty-eight of thirty-three states had public institutions for the insane.

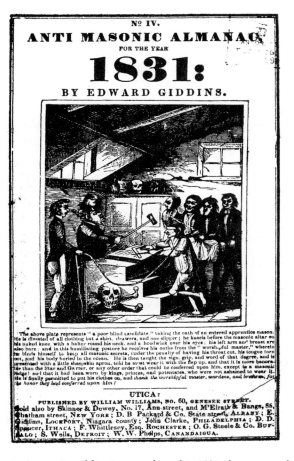

No IV.

ANTI MASONIC ALMANAC

FOR THE YEAR

1831:

BY EDWARD GIDDINS.

The above plate represents "a poor blind candidate" taking the oath of an entered apprentice mason. He is divested of all clothing but a shirt, drawers, and one slipper; he kneels before the masonic altar on his naked knee, with a halter round his neck, and a hoodwink over his eyes; his left arm and breast are also bare; and in this humiliating posture he receives his oaths from the "worshipful master," wherein he binds himself to keep all masonic secrets, under the penalty of having his throat cut, his tongue torn out, and his body buried in the ocean. He is then taught the sign, grip, and word of that degree, and is presented with a little sheepskin apron, told he must wear it with the flap up, and that it is more honorable than the Star and Garter, or any other order that could be conferred upon him, except in a masonic lodge! and that it had been worn by kings, princes, and potentates, who were not ashamed to wear it. He is finally permitted to put his clothes on, and thank the worshipful master, wardens, and brethren, for the honor they had conferred upon him!

UTICA:

PUBLISHED BY WILLIAM WILLIAMS, NO. 60, GENESEE STREET. Sold also by Skinner & Dewey, No. 17, Ann-street, and M'Elrath & Bangs, 85, Chatham street, NEW YORK; D. B Packard & Co. State-street, ALBANY; E. Giddins, LOCKPORT, Niagara county; John Clarke, PHILADELPHIA; D. D. Spencer, ITHACA; F. Whittlesey, Esq. ROCHESTER; O. G. Steele & Co. BUFFALO; S. Wells, DETROIT; W. W. Phelps, CANANDAIGUA.

Antimasonic publications, such as this 1831 almanac, made much of the allegedly sinister initiation rites that bound a new member "to keep all Masonic secrets, under the penalty of having his throat cut, his tongue torn out, and his body buried in the ocean." *The New York Public Library.*

Antimasonry

Far more intense than the asylum movement, though of shorter duration, was the crusade against Masonry. The Antimasonry movement arose overnight in the burned-over district of western New York in 1826, and it stirred political activity before virtually disappearing in the 1830s. Like other reforms, it sought political change. Indeed, foreshadowing abolitionism, it became more of a political than a reform movement. It created the first third-party movement and brought new white voters into politics at a time when male suffrage

was being extended. As temperance sought to liberate individuals from drink, Antimasons sought to liberate society from what they considered a secret, powerful, antirepublican fraternity. As asylums would restore discipline and harmony, so too, the Antimasons believed, would the abolition of Masonry re-establish moral discipline and communal harmony. The political arena quickly absorbed Antimasonry, and its short life illustrates the close tie between politics and reform from the 1820s through the 1840s.

Antimasonry was a reaction to Freemasonry, which had come to the United States from England in the eighteenth century. Freemasonry was a secret middle- and upper-class fraternity that attracted the sons of the Enlightenment, such as Benjamin Franklin and George Washington, with its emphasis on individual belief in a deity (as opposed to organized religion) and on brotherhood (as opposed to one church). In the early nineteenth century Freemasonry spread in the growing towns, attracting many commercial and political leaders. For ambitious young men, the Masons offered access to and fellowship with community leaders.

Opponents of Masonry charged that the order's secrecy was antidemocratic and antirepublican, as was its elite membership and its use of regalia and such terms as "knights" and "priests." As church leaders took up the moral crusade against Masonry, evangelicals labeled the order satanic. Antimasons argued that Masonry threatened the family because it excluded women and encouraged men to spend time at the lodges, neglecting the family for alcohol and ribald entertainments.

The Morgan affair was the catalyst for Antimasonry as an organized movement. In 1826, William Morgan, a disillusioned Mason, wrote an

Morgan Affair

exposé of Masonry, *The Illustration of Masonry, By One of the Fraternity Who Has Devoted Thirty Years to the Subject,* to which his printer David Miller added a scathing attack on the order. On September 12, 1826, prior to the book's appearance, a group of Masons abducted Morgan outside the jail in Canandaigua, New York. It was widely believed that some Masons murdered Morgan, whose body was never found.

What energized the Antimasonry crusade was that its worst fears about Masonry as a conspiracy seemed to be confirmed. Many of the officeholders in western New York, especially prosecutors, were

Chapter 12: Reform, Politics, and Expansion, 1824–1844

Masons, and they appeared to obstruct the investigation of Morgan's abduction. Public outcry and opposing political factions pressed for justice, and a series of notorious trials from 1827 through 1831 led many to suspect a conspiracy. The cover-up became as much the issue as distrust of Masonry itself, and the movement spilled over from the burned-over district to other states. In the Morgan affair, Antimason claims of a secret conspiracy seemed to be justified.

As a moral crusade, however, Antimasonry crossed over into politics almost immediately. The issue itself was a political one because the perceived obstruction of justice was a signal element. Antimasonry attracted the lower and middle classes, pitting them against higher-status Masons and exploiting the general public's distrust and envy of local political leaders. And always there were factional leaders, like Governor DeWitt Clinton of New York, willing to join the public outrage and pit his faction against others.

Unwittingly the Masons stoked the fires of Antimasonry. The silence of the order seemed to condone the murder of Morgan, and the construction of monumental lodges, like the one in Boston, advertised their determination to remain a public force. When editors who were Masons ignored the crusade against Masonry, the Antimasons started their own newspapers. The struggle aroused further public interest in politics.

Antimasonry spread as a popular movement and introduced the convention system in place of caucuses for choosing political candidates. Its electoral strength lay in New England and New York. In Vermont it became the largest party for a brief time in 1833; in Massachusetts it replaced the Democrats as the second major party. Like other reforms, however, it did not find much support in the more traditional southern society. In defense of public morality and the republic, the Antimasons held conventions in 1827 to oppose Masons running for public office. In 1828 the conventions supported the National Republican candidate, John Quincy Adams, and opposed Andrew Jackson because he was a Mason. In 1831 the Antimasons held the first national political convention in Baltimore and a year later nominated in convention William Wirt as their presidential candidate. Thus the Antimasons became one rallying point for those opposed to President Andrew Jackson.

> **Convention System**

By the mid-1830s Antimasonry had lost force as a moral and political movement. The party was a single-issue one, and as Freemasonry declined, so did the party. Yet the movement left its mark on the politics of the era. As a moral crusade concerned about public officeholders, it inspired and welcomed wider participation in the political process. In the burned-over district, wherever religious fervor appeared, and wherever families entered the market economy, Antimasonry arose. The revivalist and reform impulses in movements like Antimasonry further stimulated and awakened disagreements over values and ideology that were reinforced by conflicts over wealth, religion, and status. These differences helped polarize politics and shape parties as organizations to express those differences. The Antimasons contributed specifically to party development by pioneering the convention system and by stimulating grassroots involvement.

At the same time Antimasonry shared much in common with abolitionism. Indeed as Antimasonry waned, the abolition movement increased. William Lloyd Garrison, who at first could not fathom the frenzy over the Morgan affair, joined the ranks of Antimasons in 1832. Echoing his stand on emancipation, Garrison wrote: "I go for the immediate, unconditional and total abolition of Freemasonry." To Garrison, both slavery and Masonry undermined republican values.

Abolitionism and the Women's Movement

Abolitionism grew as an important benevolent activity in the 1820s and 1830s. But, sparked by territorial expansion, the issue of slavery eventually became so overpowering that it consumed all other reforms. Passions would become so heated that they would threaten the nation itself. Above all else, those who advocated immediate emancipation saw slavery as a moral issue—evidence of the sinfulness of the American nation. When territorial questions in the 1850s forced the issue of slavery to center stage, the abolitionist forces were well prepared (see Chapter 13).

Prior to the 1830s antislavery encompassed many different groups. Quakers had led the first antislavery movement in the eighteenth century, freeing their slaves and preaching that bondage was a sin for Christians. But in the North, where most states had begun to abolish slavery by 1800, whites took little interest in an issue that did not concern them directly. Antislavery sentiment seemed strongest in the Upper South, though northern support grew with the expansion of benevolent societies after the War of 1812. The American Colonization Society, founded in 1816 and dedicated to promoting gradual, voluntary emancipation of slaves and their resettlement in Africa, attracted a diverse group. Its ranks included evangelicals, Quakers, for a brief time some blacks, and slaveholders who found solace in the society's goal of sending free people of color to Africa. The gradualist antislavery movement remained strong, but in the 1830s the immediatists, those demanding immediate, complete, uncompensated emancipation, surpassed the gradualists as propagandists and eventually made themselves the core of abolitionism.

Through the 1820s only black people demanded an immediate end to slavery. By 1830 there were at least fifty black abolitionist societies in major

Black Antislavery Movement African-American communities. These associations assisted fugitive slaves, attacked slavery at every turn, and reminded the nation that its mission as defined in the Declaration of Independence remained unfulfilled. A free black press helped to spread their word. Black abolitionists Frederick Douglass, Sojourner Truth, and Harriet Tubman then joined forces with white reformers in the American Anti-Slavery Society. These crusaders also stirred European support for their militant and unrelenting campaign, "Brethren, arise, arise, arise!" Henry Highland Garnet commanded the 1843 National Colored Convention. "Strike for your lives and liberties. Now is the day and hour. Let every slave in the land do this and the days of slavery are numbered. Rather die freemen than live to be slaves."

In the 1830s a small minority of white reformers made immediate emancipation their primary commitment and a crusade. The most prominent and uncompromising immediatist,

William Lloyd Garrison though clearly not the most representative, was William Lloyd Garrison, who demanded "immediate and complete emancipation." Garrison had begun his career in the late 1820s editing the *National Philanthropist,* a weekly paper devoted to general reform but especially to prohibition. It was in 1828, when Benjamin Lundy recruited him to another journal, *The Genius of Universal Emancipation,* that Garrison entered the ranks of the abolitionists. Lundy supported the American Colonization Society and sought to end slavery through persuasion, a position Garrison came to reject. While preparing an article, Garrison was shocked to discover that slaveholders supported the American Colonization Society. In January 1831, Garrison broke with gradualists like Lundy and the society and, with contributions from the Tappans and others, published the first issue of the *Liberator,* which was to be his major weapon against slavery for thirty-five years. "I am in earnest—I will not equivocate—I will not excuse—I will not retreat a single inch—*and I will be heard,"* he wrote in the first issue.

Garrison's refusal to work with anyone who even indirectly delayed emancipation left him isolated from most people opposed to or uncomfortable with slavery. He even forswore political action, on the grounds that it was governments that permitted slavery. (On July 4, 1854, Garrison burned a copy of the Constitution, proclaiming, "So perish all compromises with tyranny.") Through sheer force of rhetoric, Garrison helped to make antislavery a national issue. His "immediatism" is probably best defined as tolerating no delay in ending slavery; he had no specific plan for abolishing it. In essence, Garrison called for *conversion*—all those who held slaves or cooperated with institutions supporting slavery should cast off their sins, repent, or do battle against evil.

It is impossible to say specifically why some became immediatists and others did not. Sarah Tappan raised six sons. Two (Lewis and Arthur) became immediatists; three re-

Immediatists mained in benevolent and reform activities but not abolition; and one devoted himself to drinking alcohol. Nevertheless, immediatists like Garrison, Elizabeth Chandler, Amos Phelps, Theodore Weld, and Lewis and Arthur Tappan, who left the ranks of the American Colonization Society to attack it as sinful in the 1830s, shared much in common. In the 1820s they had been young evangelicals active in benevolent societies; many became ordained ministers or flirted with the ministry as a career; and they had personal contact with free blacks and were sympathetic to black rights. Their immediatism made them more concerned about sin around them and in the United States and less concerned about converting heathens across the seas. Their concern made them more political: to abolish sin they sought to change institutions at home. Finally, they seemed to have great moral intensity; they were unwilling to compromise their beliefs. This zeal led them to be activists as they sought to realize their moral goals. Their major organizational vehicle was the American Anti-Slavery Society, organized in 1833.

Most benevolent workers and reformers kept their distance from the immediatists. Many thought the intensity of the immediatist approach was un-Christian. They shared the view that slavery was a sin, but they believed that it had to be eradicated slowly. They sought to spread Christian reform slowly, in a reasonable and patient manner. If they moved too fast, if they attacked sinners too harshly or conflicted too much with community customs and beliefs, they would destroy the harmony and order they sought to bring in benevolent and reform work. As for the American Colonization Society, they hoped to cleanse its taint.

Immediatists' greatest recruitment successes came from defending their own constitutional and natural rights, not those of slaves. Wherever they went, immediatists found their

> **Opposition to Abolitionists**

civil rights in danger, especially their right of free speech. Unruly audiences found immediatist rhetoric dangerous and a threat to the preservation of the Union. Using the new steam press, the American Anti-Slavery Society increased its distribution of antislavery propaganda tenfold between 1834 and 1835, sending out 1.1 million pieces in 1835. But southern mobs seized and destroyed much of the mail, and South Carolina (with the approval of the United States postmaster general) intercepted and burned abolitionist literature that entered the state. President Andrew Jackson even proposed a law prohibiting the mailing of antislavery tracts.

The opposition saw many dangers in abolitionism. Former Federalist Harrison Gray Otis portrayed abolitionists as subversives at an anti-abolitionist rally in Boston's Faneuil Hall in August 1835. He attacked Garrison's American Anti-Slavery Society as a "dangerous association," a "revolutionary society" with branches in every

FAIR....FAIR!!!

THE LADIES' ANTI-SLAVERY COMMITTEE are most happy to announce to the citizens of Syracuse and vicinity, that they have received very elegant additions to what has been prepared in this place, from the ladies of Rochester, Waterloo, Cazenovia, Utica, Albany, and many other places, making up in all a most desirable and splendid assortment of

USEFUL AND FANCY ARTICLES,

which will be sold at reasonable market prices. The Committee most confidently invite the patronage of the humane and philanthropic to come and buy; remembering that it is for the poorest of the poor—even the POOR SLAVE.

☞The doors will be open at 10 o'clock on Tuesday morning, August 1st, and the sales will continue two days. Admittance 12 1-2 cents.

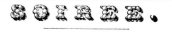

A Soiree will be given at the Fair on the evening of August 1st, in commemmoration of the WEST INDIA EMANCIPATION.

₊ Doors open at 7 o'clock—Collation at 8.— Speeches from the most accomplished orators of Boston and other places.

ELIZABETH RUSSELL, Syracuse;
P. S. WRIGHT, Utica;
MARY SPRINGSTEAD, Cazenovia;
SARAH VAN EPS, Vernon;
ABBY MOTT, Albany.

In the 1820s and 1830s, using their churches as a base, women played an activist role in reform. They organized such groups as the Ladies Anti-Slavery Committee, and entered the public arena. *American Antiquarian Society.*

community in the nation. Not only did it recruit "all men" to its "holy crusade," Otis railed, but also it asked women to "turn their sewing parties into abolition clubs." School primers would teach "that A stands for abolition." Otis predicted that the abolitionists would soon turn to politics, causing unpredictable "trouble and calamity." "What will become of the nation?" Otis asked. "What will become of the union?" Others believed that the immediatist attack on colonization undermined the best solution. Keeping blacks in America, they believed, eventually would foment slave rebellions and lead to racial amalgamation. Moreover, they charged, given the close ties of the immediatists with British abolitionists, the movement was an English plot to subvert American independence.

Another civil rights confrontation developed in Congress. Exercising their constitutional right to petition Congress, abolitionists mounted a campaign to abolish slavery and the

▶ **Gag Rule** slave trade in the District of Columbia. (Since the district was under federal rule, states' rights arguments against interfering with slavery did not apply there.) But Congress responded in 1836 by adopting the so-called gag rule, which automatically tabled abolitionist petitions, effectively preventing debate on them. Immediatists flooded Congress with nearly 700,000 petitions. In a dramatic defense of the right of petition, former president John Quincy Adams, then a Massachusetts representative, took to the floor repeatedly to defy the detested gag rule and eventually succeeded in getting it repealed in 1844.

Antislavery speakers often faced hostile crowds, and their presses were under constant threat of attack. Mobs violently defended, as they believed, American traditions. At Utica, New York, in 1835 merchants and professionals broke up the state Anti-Slavery Convention, directing their violence against the sources of evil: abolitionist conventions that mixed whites and blacks and men and women and worked with British abolitionists to plan immediatist campaigns and attacks on American traditions. Fear and hatred moved proslavery proponents to take to the streets. In 1837 a mob murdered Elijah P. Lovejoy in Alton, Illinois. Lovejoy, who had been driven out of slaveholding Missouri, had re-established his printing plant just across the river in Illinois. Rioters sacked his office, with the cooperation of local authorities, and killed the abolitionist editor. Public outrage at Lovejoy's murder, as with the gag rule and censorship of the mails, only broadened the base of antislavery support in the North.

Frustration with the federal government also fed northern support for antislavery. By and large, politicians and government officials sought to avoid the question of slavery. The Missouri Compromise of 1820 had been an effort to quarantine the issue by adopting a single formula—banning slavery north of 36°30′, Missouri's southern boundary—that would make debate on the slave or free status of new states unnecessary. Censorship of the mails and the gag rule were similar attempts to keep the issue out of the political arena. Yet the more national leaders, especially Democrats, sought to

avoid the matter, the more they hardened the resolve of the antislavery forces.

The effect of the unlawful, violent, and obstructionist tactics used by proslavery advocates and anti-immediatists cannot be overestimated. The opposition to abolition helped unify the movement by forcing the factions to work together for mutual defense. Antislavery was not at the outset a unified movement. It was splintered and factionalized, and its adherents fought each other as often as they fought the defenders of slavery. They were divided over Garrison's emphasis on "moral suasion" versus the more practical political approach of James G. Birney, the Liberty party's candidate for president in 1844 (see page 368). They were split over support of other reforms, especially the rights of women. And they disagreed over the place of free black people in American society. Even so, abolitionists eventually managed to unify and make emancipation a major issue in the politics of the 1850s.

Women had less success when it came to their own position in society. At its inception, the American Anti-Slavery Society resembled most other benevolent societies in its gender

▶ **Women Abolitionists** structure. Men established and ran the society; women supported it in their own affiliates. The early movement was gender segregated with women in a subordinate role. Slowly over time, the pattern changed among the immediatists. By the late 1840s and 1850s, women abolitionists were breaking free of woman's domestic sphere—many of them were single women—and becoming genuine colleagues to men in the movement. Men like Garrison came to accept their women colleagues' contributions in providing moral direction. Garrison worked closely with Sarah Grimké after publishing her essays on the equality of the sexes in the *Liberator*. Lydia Child, Maria Chapman, and Lucretia Mott all joined the American Anti-Slavery Society executive committee; Child edited its official organ, the *National Anti-Slavery Standard,* from 1841 to 1843, and Chapman co-edited it from 1844 until 1848.

Negative reaction to the growing involvement of women in reform movements led some women to re-examine their position in society. In 1837 two antislavery lecturers, Angelina and Sarah Grimké, became particular objects of controversy. Natives of Charleston, South Carolina, they moved north in the 1820s to speak and write more openly and forcefully against slavery. They received a hostile reception for speaking before mixed groups of men and women. Some New England Congregationalists and even abolitionists joined in the criticism; as one pastoral letter put it, women should obey, not lecture, men. This reaction turned the Grimkés' attention from slavery to women's condition. The two attacked the concept of "subordination to man," insisting that men and women had the "same rights and same duties." Sarah Grimké's *Letters on the Condition of Women and the Equality of the Sexes* (1838) and her sister's *Letters to Catharine E. Beecher,* published the same year, were the opening volleys in the war against the legal and social inequality of women.

In arguing against slavery, some women noticed the similarities between their own position and that of slaves. They saw parallels in their legal disabilities—inability to vote or control their own property, except in widowhood—and their social restrictions—exclusion from advanced schooling and from most occupations. "The investigation of the rights of the slave," Angelina Grimké confessed, "has led me to a better understanding of my own." Some of the women who worked in the Lowell mills came to the same conclusion in the 1840s.

> **Women's Rights**

Unlike other reform movements, which succeeded in building a broad base of individual and organizational support, the movement for women's rights was limited. Some men joined the ranks, notably Garrison and ex-slave Frederick Douglass, but most were actively opposed. In the 1840s the question of women's rights split the antislavery movement, the majority declaring themselves opposed. The Woman's Rights Convention at Seneca Falls, New York, in 1848, led by Elizabeth Cady Stanton and Lucretia Mott, issued a much-published indictment of the injustices suffered by women. The Seneca Falls Declaration of 1848 paralleled the 1776 Declaration of Independence, asserting "that all men and women are created equal" was a self-evident truth. The document listed the record of male tyranny against women and the inequalities and indignities that women suffered from government and the law. If women had the vote, these early advocates of women's rights argued, they could protect themselves and realize their potential as moral and spiritual leaders. Their argument won few over to their cause.

Jacksonianism and the Beginnings of Modern Party Politics

The distinction between reform and politics eroded in the 1820s and after as reform pushed its way into politics. The Antimasons and then the abolitionists appealed directly to voters. Politicians no less than reformers sought to control and direct change in an expanding, urbanizing, market-oriented nation. They too shared the unease caused by change and the corruption in private and public life. After a brief flirtation with single-party politics following the War of 1812, the United States entered a period of intense and heated political competition. The 1824 presidential election, decided by the House of Representatives, set a political barn fire that would be continuously fueled and stoked by reformers, abolitionists, and expansionists as they entered politics. By the 1830s, politics had become the great nineteenth-century American pastime.

The election of 1824, in which John Quincy Adams and Andrew Jackson faced each other for the first time, heralded the start of a new, more open political system. The Federalist party had disappeared after 1816, and James Monroe had run unopposed as the Republican candidate in 1820. From 1800 through 1820 the presidential system in which a congressional caucus chose Jefferson, Madison, and Monroe as the Republican nominees had worked well. Jefferson and Madison had both hand-picked their secretaries of state as their successors, and the caucuses had nominated them. Such a system restricted voter involvement, but this was not a drawback at first, because in 1800 only five of sixteen states selected presidential electors by popular vote. (In most, state legislators designated the electors.) In 1816, however, ten out of nineteen states chose electors by popular vote, and in 1824, eighteen out of twenty-four did so. In 1824 the caucus system fell apart.

> **End of the Caucus System**

Outgoing President James Monroe never designated an heir apparent. Without direction from the president, therefore, the caucus in 1824 chose William H. Crawford, secretary of the treasury. But

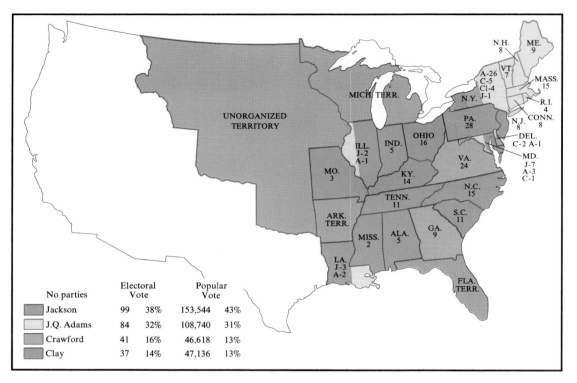

No parties	Electoral Vote		Popular Vote	
Jackson	99	38%	153,544	43%
J.Q. Adams	84	32%	108,740	31%
Crawford	41	16%	46,618	13%
Clay	37	14%	47,136	13%

Presidential Election, 1824

other Republicans, encouraged by the opportunity to appeal directly to the voters in most states, challenged Crawford as sectional candidates. Secretary of State John Quincy Adams drew support from New England, and westerners backed Speaker of the House Henry Clay of Kentucky. Secretary of War John C. Calhoun looked to the South for support and hoped to win Pennsylvania as well. Andrew Jackson, a popular military hero whose political views were unknown, was nominated by resolution of the Tennessee legislature and had the most widespread support. But Crawford, who had declined to oppose Monroe in 1816 and 1820, had the most support in Washington. Since his choice by the caucus was a foregone conclusion, the other four candidates joined in attacking the caucus system as undemocratic. When their supporters boycotted the deliberations, Crawford's victory became hollow, based on a minority vote. The role of the congressional caucus in nominating presidents ended.

Andrew Jackson led in both electoral and popular votes in the four-way presidential election of 1824, but no one received a majority in the elec-

toral college (see map). Adams finished second, and Crawford and Clay trailed far behind. (Calhoun dropped out of the race before the election.) Under the twelfth amendment to the Constitution, the House of Representatives, voting by state delegation, one vote to a state, would select the president from among the three leaders in electoral votes. Clay, who had received the fewest votes, was dropped; Crawford, a stroke victim, never received serious consideration. Clay, as Speaker of the House and leader of the Ohio Valley states, backed Adams, who received the votes of thirteen out of twenty-four state delegations. Clay became secretary of state in the Adams administration—the traditional steppingstone to the presidency.

Angry Jacksonians denounced the arrangement as a "corrupt bargain" that had stolen the office from the clear front runner. Jacksonians believed that congressional intrigue had thwarted the will of the people, and the bitterness Jackson felt at this defeat would reinforce his opposition to elitism and his emphasis on the people's will. The Republican party divided; the Adams wing emerged as the National Republicans, and the Jacksonians

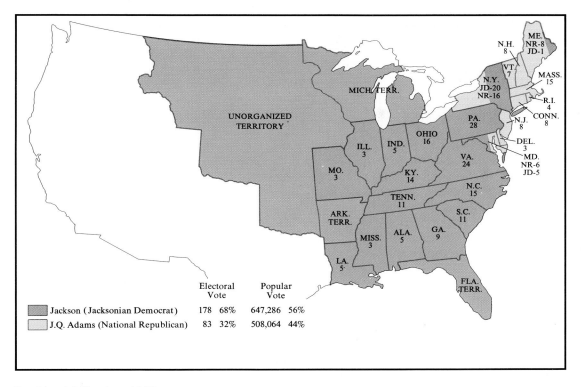

		Electoral Vote		Popular Vote	
�p)	Jackson (Jacksonian Democrat)	178	68%	647,286	56%
□	J.Q. Adams (National Republican)	83	32%	508,064	44%

Presidential Election, 1828

became the Democratic-Republicans (shortened to Democrats).

The Jacksonians immediately laid plans for 1828, while John Quincy Adams took the oath as the sixth president. Adams proposed a strong nationalist policy emphasizing Henry Clay's American System of protective tariffs, a national bank, and internal improvements (see page 234). Adams believed the federal government should take an activist role not only in the economy but in education, science, and the arts; accordingly, he proposed a national university in Washington, D.C.

Brilliant as a diplomat and secretary of state, Adams was inept as president. The political skills he had demonstrated in winning the office he could not bring to bear as president. He underestimated the lingering effects of the Panic of 1819 and the ensuing bitter opposition to a national bank and protective tariffs. Meanwhile, supporters of Andrew Jackson sabotaged Adams's administration at every opportunity.

The 1828 campaign between Adams and Jackson was an intensely personal conflict. Whatever principles the two men stood for were obscured by the

mudslinging both sides indulged in. Jackson's supporters claimed that the presidency had been stolen from the general in 1824. Adams had a similarly low opinion of General Jackson. In his diary in December 1829 he declared Jackson "incompetent both by his ignorance and by the fury of his passions." The two camps traded charges of adultery and procuring prostitutes. A month after the election, Rachel Jackson died and the president-elect attributed his wife's death to the abuse heaped upon him in the campaign. He never forgave her "murderers."

Adams won the same states as in 1824, but the opposition was unified, and Jackson swamped him (see map). Jackson polled 56 percent of the popular vote and won in the electoral college, 178 to 83. For him and his supporters, the will of the people had been served as it had not been in 1824. The intensity of the campaign, the desire to display loyalty to Jackson, and new technologies making possible the mass production of badges, medals, ceramics, and similar items introduced the widespread use of campaign material, much of it commemorating the hero of the Battle of New Orleans.

Through a lavishly financed coalition of state parties, political leaders, and newspaper editors, a popular movement elected a president. An era ended, and the Democratic party became the first truly political party in the United States. Well-organized parties became the hallmark of nineteenth-century American politics.

Andrew Jackson was nicknamed "Old Hickory," after the toughest American hardwood. A rough-and-tumble, ambitious man, he rose from humble birth to become a wealthy planter

> **Andrew Jackson**

and slaveholder. Jackson was the first American president from the West and the first not born into comfortable circumstances; he was a self-made man at ease among both frontiersmen and southern planters. He had a violent temper and was often vindictive, yet he could charm and allay the suspicions of those opposed to him. A natural leader, he inspired immense loyalty. He had an instinct for politics, and he shrewdly picked issues and supporters.

Few Americans have been as celebrated in myth and legend as Andrew Jackson. As a boy he fought in the Revolution and all his life carried scars from a redcoat attack. In the Tennessee militia General Jackson led the battle to remove Creeks from the Alabama and Georgia frontier. He burst onto the national scene as the great hero of the War of 1812 and in 1818 enhanced his glory in an expedition against Seminoles in Spanish Florida. Jackson also served as congressman and senator from Tennessee, as a judge in his home state, and as the first territorial governor of Florida (1821) before running for president in 1824. He was an active presidential aspirant until he won the office in 1828.

Jackson and his Democratic supporters offered a distinct alternative to the strong national government advocated by John Quincy Adams. The Democrats represented a wide range

> **Democrats**

of beliefs but shared some common ideals. Fundamentally, they sought to foster the Jeffersonian concept of an agrarian society, harkening back to the belief that a strong central government was the enemy of individual liberty, a tyranny to be feared. Thus, like Jefferson, they favored limited central government. The 1824 "corrupt bargain" had strengthened their suspicion of Washington politics.

Jacksonians were as fearful of the concentration of economic power as they were of political power. They saw government intervention in the economy as benefiting special-interest groups and creating corporate monopolies; thus they rejected an activist economic program as favoring the rich. Jacksonians sought to restore the independence of the individual—the artisan and the yeoman farmer—by ending federal support of banks and corporations and restricting the use of paper currency. Their concept of the proper role of government tended to be negative, and Jackson's political power was largely expressed in negative acts; he used the veto more than all previous presidents combined.

Finally, Jackson and his supporters were hostile to reform as a movement and an ideology. Reformers were increasingly calling for an activist and interventionist government as they organized to turn their programs into legislation. But Democrats tended to oppose programs like educational reform and the establishment of public education. They believed, for instance, that public schools restricted individual liberty by interfering with parental responsibility and undermined freedom of religion by replacing church schools. Nor did Jackson share reformers' humanitarian concerns. He showed little sympathy for the Indians, ordering their removal from the Southeast to make way for white agricultural settlement (see page 331).

Jackson and the Jacksonians considered themselves reformers in a different way. In following Jefferson's notion of restraint in government and in emphasizing individualism, Jackson and his followers sought to restore old republican virtues. Individual traits such as industriousness, prudence, and economy were highly prized. No less than reformers he sought to encourage self-discipline and self-reliance, to restore a harmony and unity that had been displaced by economic and social change. In doing so, he looked to Jefferson and the generation of founders as models for traditional values. "My political creed," Jackson wrote James K. Polk in 1826, "was formed in the old republican school."

Like Jefferson, Jackson strengthened the executive branch of government at the same time as he tended to weaken the federal role. Given his popularity and the strength of his personality, this concentration of power in the presidency was perhaps inevitable; but his deliberate policy of combining the roles of party leader and chief of state centralized even greater power in the White House.

Chapter 12: Reform, Politics, and Expansion, 1824–1844

Enamored of power, Jackson never hesitated to confront his opponents with all the weapons at his command. Among his followers he commanded enormous loyalty, and he rewarded them handsomely. Invoking the principle that rotating officeholders would make government more responsive to the public will, Jackson used the spoils system to reward loyal Democrats with appointments to office. He removed fewer than one-quarter of federal officeholders in his two terms, but his use of patronage nevertheless strengthened party organization and loyalty.

Jackson himself stressed his rejection of elitism and special favors, his use of rotation in office, and his belief in popular government. Time and again Jackson declared that sovereignty resided with the people. It did not rest, according to Jackson, with the states or with the courts. Summoning the electorate to support him, he confidently claimed to represent the people's will. In this view, Jackson was a reformer; he returned government to the course of liberty, to majority rule. Yet it is hard to distinguish between Jackson's belief in himself as the instrument of the people and simple egotism and demagogic arrogance. After all, his opponents too claimed to represent the people.

Among President Jackson's opponents animosity grew year by year. Daniel Webster feared the men around Jackson; Henry Clay most feared Jackson himself. Rotation in office, they contended, corrupted government. Opponents mocked Jackson as King Andrew I, charging him with abusing his presidential powers by challenging Congress on so many issues. Critics attempted to undermine his claim of restoring republican virtue and of inheriting the mantle of Jefferson. They charged him with recklessly and impulsively destroying the economy.

Jackson invigorated the philosophy of limited government. In 1830 he vetoed the Maysville, Kentucky, Road bill, which would have provided a federal subsidy to construct a sixty-mile turnpike from Maysville to Lexington, Kentucky. Jackson insisted that a federally subsidized internal improvement confined to one state was unconstitutional and that such projects were properly a state responsibility. The veto undermined Henry Clay's American System and personally embarrassed Clay because the project was in his home district. Federal-state issues would loom even larger in the nullification crisis.

Jacques Amans's 1840 oil portrait of former President Andrew Jackson. Jackson appears to look into the viewer's eyes, suggesting the directness that earned so deep a loyalty from his supporters. *The Historic New Orleans Collection.*

The Nullification and Bank Controversies

Jackson had to face more directly the question of the proper division of sovereignty between state and central government. The growing reform crusades, especially antislavery, had made the southern states fearful of federal power—and none more so than South Carolina, where the planter class was strongest and slavery most concentrated. Having watched the growth of abolitionist sentiment in Great Britain, which resulted in the 1833 emancipation of West Indian slaves, and witnessing the stridency of immediatism in the United States, South Carolinians feared the same thing would happen at home. Hard hit by the Panic of 1819, from which they never fully recovered, they also resented the high prices of imported goods created by protectionist tariffs.

To protect their interests, South Carolinian political leaders articulated the doctrine of *nullification,* according to which a state had the right to overrule, or nullify, federal legislation that conflicted with its own. In their reaction against the protectionist 1828 Tariff of Abominations (see page 257), the nullifiers expanded on the ideas expressed in the Virginia and Kentucky Resolutions of 1798 (see page 201). In his unsigned *Exposition and Protest,* John C. Calhoun argued that in any disagreement between the federal government and a state, a special state convention—like the conventions called to ratify the Constitution—would decide the conflict by either nullifying or accepting the federal law. Only the power of nullification could protect the minority against the tyranny of the majority, Calhoun asserted.

In public, Calhoun let others take the lead in advancing nullification. As Jackson's running mate in 1828, he avoided publicly identifying with nullification and thus embarrassing the ticket. As vice president, he hoped to win Jackson's support as the Democratic presidential heir apparent. Thus a silent Calhoun presided over the Senate and its packed galleries when Senators Daniel Webster of New Hampshire and Robert Y. Hayne from Calhoun's home state of South Carolina debated nullification in January 1830. The debate explored North-South frictions and the question of the nature of the Union. With Calhoun nodding agreement, Hayne charged that it was the North that threatened to bring disunity, as it had once in the Hartford Convention (see page 233). Moreover, Hayne accused reformers ("the spirit of false philanthropy") of wanting to destroy the South.

Webster-Hayne Debate

For two days Webster defended the New England states and his beloved republic in eloquent rhetoric and kept nullification on the defensive. Though debating Hayne, he aimed his remarks at Calhoun as he depicted the nation as a compact of people, not merely states. In this climax of his career as a debater, he invoked two images. One, which he hoped he would not see, was the outcome of nullification: "states dissevered, discordant, belligerent; on a land rent with civil feuds, or drenched . . . in fraternal blood!" The other was a patriotic vision of a great nation flourishing under the motto "Liberty *and* Union, now and forever, one and inseparable."

Though sympathetic to states' rights, Jackson rejected the idea of state sovereignty. His sympathy derived from his distrust of the federal government, but overriding that was his strong belief that sovereignty rested with the people. As a strong nationalist and patriot, he was deeply committed to union. Thus he shared Webster's dread and distrust of nullification. Soon after the Webster-Hayne debate, the president made his position clear at a Jefferson Day dinner with the toast: "Our Federal Union, it *must* and *shall be* preserved." Calhoun, when his turn came, offered: "The Federal Union—next to our liberty the most dear." Calhoun, torn between devotion to the Union and loyalty to his state, had revealed his preference for states' rights. Politically and personally Calhoun and Jackson grew apart, and it soon became apparent that Jackson favored Secretary of State Martin Van Buren, not Calhoun, as his successor.

South Carolina invoked its theory of nullification against the Tariff of 1832. Although this tariff had the effect of reducing some duties, it retained high taxes on imported iron, cottons, and woolens. A majority of southern representatives supported the new tariff, but South Carolinians refused to go along. In their view, their constitutional right to control their own destiny had been sacrificed to the demands of northern industrialists. They feared the consequences of accepting such an act; it could set a precedent for congressional legislation on slavery. In November 1832 a South Carolina state convention nullified the tariff, making it unlawful for officials to collect duties in the state after February 1, 1833. Immediately recruiters began to organize a volunteer army to ensure nonenforcement of the tariff.

Nullification Crisis

"Old Hickory" responded with toughness. Privately, he threatened to invade South Carolina and hang Calhoun, his vice president; publicly, he sought to avoid the use of force. On December 10, 1832, Jackson issued his own proclamation nullifying nullification. He moved troops to federal forts in South Carolina and prepared United States marshals to collect the required duties. At Jackson's request, Congress passed the Force Act, which supposedly renewed Jackson's authority to call up

Chapter 12: Reform, Politics, and Expansion, 1824–1844

Opponents of the Second Bank of the United States often depicted the bank as a serpent with many tentacles capable of strangling the economy or the interests of farmers and urban workers. Here a contemporary cartoon shows President Andrew Jackson trying to kill the bank-serpent before it strangles him. *The New-York Historical Society.*

troops; it was actually a scheme to avoid the use of force by collecting duties before ships reached South Carolina. At the same time, Jackson extended the olive branch by recommending tariff reductions. Calhoun, disturbed by South Carolina's drift toward separatism, resigned as vice president and became a United States Senator from South Carolina. In the Senate he worked with Henry Clay to draw up the compromise Tariff of 1833. Quickly passed by Congress and signed by the president, the revision lengthened the list of duty-free items and reduced duties over the next nine years. Satisfied, South Carolina's convention repealed its nullification law and in a final salvo nullified Jackson's Force Act. Jackson ignored the gesture.

Although fought over the practical issue of tariffs (and the unspoken issue of slavery), the nullification controversy did represent a genuine debate on the true nature and principles of the republic. Each side believed it was upholding the Constitution. Both sides felt they were fighting special privilege

and subversion of republican values. South Carolina was fighting the tyranny of the federal government and the manufacturers who sought tariff protection; Jackson was fighting the tyranny of South Carolina, whose refusal to bow to federal authority threatened to split the republic. Neither side won a clear victory, though both claimed to have done so. Another issue, that of a central bank, would define the powers of the federal government more clearly.

At stake was the rechartering of the Second Bank of the United States, whose twenty-year charter expired in 1836. Like its predecessor, the bank served as a depository for federal funds, on which it paid no interest; and it served the republic in many other ways. Its bank notes circulated as currency throughout the country; they could be readily exchanged for gold, and the federal government accepted them as payment in all transactions. Through its twenty-five branch

Second Bank of the United States

offices, the bank acted as a clearing-house for state banks, keeping them honest by refusing to accept their notes if they had insufficient gold in reserve.

But the bank had enemies. Most state banks resented the central bank's police role; by presenting state bank notes for redemption all at once, the Second Bank could easily ruin a state bank. Moreover, state banks, with less money in reserve, found themselves unable to compete on an equal footing with the Second Bank. Many state governments regarded the national bank, with its headquarters in Philadelphia, as unresponsive to local needs. Westerners and urban workers remembered with bitterness the bank's conservative credit policies during the Panic of 1819—and there was some truth to their complaints. Although the Second Bank served some of the functions of a central bank, it was still a private profit-making institution, and its policies reflected the self-interest of its owners. Its president, Nicholas Biddle, controlled the bank completely. An eastern patrician, Biddle symbolized all that westerners found wrong with the bank. Moreover, the bank had great political influence. Many members of Congress and business leaders were beholden to it, and its power could be checked only at rechartering time.

Rechartering was a major issue in the 1832 presidential campaign. Although the bank's charter would not expire until 1836, Biddle got Congress to approve an early rechartering. This strategy, encouraged by Henry Clay, the National Republican presidential candidate, was designed to arouse public pressure to force Jackson to sign the bill or to secure a veto override. The plan backfired when Jackson in July 1832 vetoed the rechartering bill and the Senate failed to override. Jackson's veto message was an emotional attack on the undemocratic nature of the bank. "It is to be regretted," he said, "that the rich and powerful too often bend the acts of government to their selfish purposes." Rechartering would grant "exclusive privileges, to make the rich richer and the potent more powerful." Ignoring Chief Justice John Marshall's 1819 ruling in *McCulloch* v. *Maryland* (see page 235), Jackson's veto message declared the bank unconstitutional.

The bank became the major symbol and issue in the presidential campaign of 1832. Jackson led the way by denouncing special privilege and economic power. Operating in a system in which all the states

but South Carolina now chose electors by popular vote, the Jacksonians used their effective party organization to mobilize voters by advertising the presidential election as the focal point of the political system. The Antimasons adopted a party platform, the first in the nation's history. The Democrats and the major opposition party, the National Republicans, quickly followed suit. Jackson and Martin Van Buren, Jackson's first secretary of state and then American minister to Great Britain, were nominated at the Democratic convention; Clay and John Sergeant, at the National Republican convention. John Floyd ran as South Carolina's candidate. Jackson was re-elected easily in a Democratic party triumph.

In 1833, after his sweeping victory and second inauguration, Jackson moved not only to dismantle the Second Bank of the United States but to ensure that it would not be resurrected.

Jackson's Second Term He deposited federal funds in favored state-chartered ("pet") banks; without federal money, the Second Bank shriveled. When its federal charter expired in 1836, it became just another Pennsylvania-chartered private bank. In 1841 it closed its doors.

As part of the coup de grâce delivered to the Bank of the United States, Congress, with Jackson's support, passed the Deposit Act of 1836. Under this act, the secretary of the treasury designated one bank in each state and territory to provide the services formerly performed by the Bank of the United States. The act provided that the federal surplus in excess of $5 million be distributed to the states as interest-free loans beginning in 1837, and these loans were never recalled—a fitting Jacksonian restraint on the federal purse.

Jackson was worried about more than just restraining the government. The surplus had derived from wholesale speculation in public lands. Purchasers bought public land on credit, borrowed from banks against the land to purchase additional acreage, and repeated the cycle. Between 1834 and 1836 federal receipts from land sales rose from $5 million to $25 million. Banks providing loans issued bank notes, and Jackson, an opponent of paper money, feared that the speculative craze threatened the state banks while closing the door to settlers, who could not compete with speculators in bidding for the best land.

Following his hard-money instinct and his opposition to paper currency, President Jackson ordered Treasury Secretary Levi Woodbury to issue the Specie Circular. It provided that after August 15, 1836, only specie—gold or silver—or Virginia land scrip would be accepted as payment for federal lands. The circular stated that it sought to end "the monopoly of the public lands in the hands of speculators and capitalists" and the "ruinous extension" of bank notes and credit. By ending credit sales, the circular reduced significantly public land purchases and the budget surplus. As a result the government suspended the loan payments to the states soon after they were begun.

> **Specie Circular**

The policy was a disaster on many fronts. Although federal land sales were sharply reduced, speculation continued as available land for sale became a scarce commodity. The ensuing increased demand for specie squeezed banks, and many suspended specie payment (the redemption of bank notes for specie). This led to further credit contraction as banks issued fewer notes and gave less credit. Equally damaging was the way Jackson attacked the problem. He instinctively pursued a tight money policy and was indifferent to the impact of his policies. More important, the Specie Circular, issued in July 1836, was similar to a bill defeated in the Senate nearly three months earlier. His opponents saw King Andrew at work. In the waning days of Jackson's administration, Congress voted to repeal the circular, but the president pocket-vetoed the bill. Finally in May 1838, a joint resolution of Congress overturned the circular. Restrictions on land sales ended, but the speculative fervor was over. The federal government did not revive loans to states.

From George Washington to John Quincy Adams, presidents had vetoed nine bills; Jackson vetoed twelve. Previous presidents believed that vetoes were justified only on constitutional grounds, but Jackson, as in the veto of the Second Bank of the United States, stressed policy disagreement as well. He made the veto an important weapon in controlling Congress, since representatives and senators had to consider the possibility of a presidential veto on any bill. In effect he made the executive a rival branch of government equal to Congress.

The Whig Challenge and the Second Party System

Once historians described the 1830s and 1840s as the Age of Jackson, and the personalities of the leading political figures dominated historical accounts. Increasingly, however, historians have viewed these years as an age of popularly based political parties and reformers, for only when the passionate concerns of reformers and abolitionists spilled into politics did party differences become paramount and party loyalties solidify. For the first time grassroots political groups, organized from the bottom up, set the tone of political life.

In the 1830s the Democrats' opponents, including remnants of what had been the National Republican party, found shelter under a common umbrella, the Whig party. Resentful of Jackson's domination of Congress, the Whigs borrowed their name from the British party that had opposed the tyranny of Hanoverian monarchs in the eighteenth century. From the congressional elections of 1834 through the 1840s, they and the Democrats competed nearly equally; only a few percentage points separated the two parties in national elections. They fought at every level—city, county, and state—and achieved a stability previously unknown in American politics. Both parties built strong organizations, commanded the loyalty of legislators, and attracted mass popular followings. The rise of political party competition in this period—commonly called the Second Party System—was a renewal of the organized political competition that had marked the First Party System of the Republicans and Federalists.

The two parties emphasized responsiveness to their supporters—a priority that reflected significant changes in the electoral process. Although many states still permitted only taxpayers to vote in local elections, by the 1830s only a handful of states significantly restricted adult white male suffrage in nonlocal elections. Some even allowed immigrants who had taken out their first citizenship papers to vote. Moreover, contested elections for the presidency inspired greater political interest. The effect of these changes was a sharp increase in the number of votes cast in presidential elections. Between

1824 and 1828 the number of votes cast for president increased threefold, from 360,000 to over 1.1 million. In 1840, 2.4 million men cast votes. The proportion of eligible voters who cast ballots also increased. In 1824 an estimated 27 percent of those eligible voted; from 1828 through 1836, about 55 percent; in 1840, more than 80 percent.

On the political agenda during these years were numerous fundamental issues. At the national level, officials struggled with the question of the proper constitutional roles of the federal and state governments, national expansion, and Indian policy. Also, many state conventions drafted new constitutions and deliberated over such basic issues as the rights of individuals and corporations; the rights of labor and capital; government aid to business; currency and sources of revenue; and public education, temperance, and abolition.

Increasingly the two parties differed in their approaches to these issues. Both favored economic expansion, but the Whigs sought it through an activist government, the Democrats

> **Whigs** through limited central government. Thus the Whigs supported corporate charters, a national bank, and paper currency; the Democrats were opposed. The Whigs favored more humanitarian reforms than did the Democrats—public schools, abolition of capital punishment, temperance, prison and asylum reform.

In general, Whigs were more optimistic than Democrats and more enterprising. They did not hesitate to help one group if doing so would promote the general welfare. The chartering of corporations, they argued, expanded economic opportunity for everyone, providing work for laborers and increasing demand for food from farmers. Meanwhile the Democrats, distrustful of the concentration of economic power and of moral and economic coercion, held fast to their Jeffersonian principle of limited government.

For all the economic inequality that characterized the era, it was not the major issue that divided the parties. Nor did the conflicts over the Second Bank or corporate charters divide the haves and have-nots. Although the Whigs attracted more of the upper and middle class, both sides drew support from manufacturers, merchants, laborers, and farmers. Instead, religion and ethnicity determined party membership. In the North, the Whigs' concern for energetic government and humanitarian and moral reform won the favor of native-born and

British-American evangelical Protestants, especially those involved in religious revival. These Presbyterians, Baptists, and Congregationalists were overwhelmingly Whigs, as were the relatively small number of free black voters. Democrats, on the other hand, tended to be foreign-born Catholics and nonevangelical Protestants, both groups that preferred to keep religious and secular affairs separate.

The Whig party thus became the vehicle of revivalist Protestantism. In many locales, the membership of reform societies overlapped that of the

> **Whigs and Reformers** party. Indeed, Whigs practiced a kind of political revivalism. Their rallies resembled camp meetings; their speeches echoed evangelical rhetoric; their programs embodied the perfectionist beliefs of reformers. This potent blend of religion and politics—which, as Tocqueville noted, were "intimately united" in America—greatly intensified political loyalties.

In unifying evangelicals, the Whigs alienated members of other faiths. The evangelicals' ideal Christian state had no room for Catholics, Mormons, Unitarians, Universalists, or religious freethinkers. Sabbath laws and temperance legislation threatened the religious freedom and individual liberty of these groups, which generally opposed state interference in moral and religious questions. As a result, more than 95 percent of Irish Catholics, 90 percent of Reformed Dutch, and 80 percent of German Catholics voted Democratic.

Vice President Martin Van Buren headed the Democratic ticket in the presidential election of 1836. Hand-picked by Jackson, Van Buren was a shrewd politician who had built a political machine—the Albany Regency—in New York; he had left that state's government to join Jackson's cabinet in 1829. He had helped found the Democratic party and was among a new generation who made their careers in party politics. The opposition Whigs, who in 1836 had not yet coalesced into a national party, entered three sectional candidates: Daniel Webster of New England, Hugh White of the South, and William Henry Harrison of the West. By splintering the vote, they hoped to throw the election into the House, but Van Buren comfortably captured the electoral college even though he held only a 25,000-vote edge out of a total of 1.5 million votes cast. No vice-presidential candidate received a majority of electoral votes, though, and for the only time in American history the Senate decided a vice-presidential race; it selected Democratic candidate Richard M. Johnson.

Van Buren took office just weeks before the American credit system collapsed. The economic boom of the 1830s was over. In May 1837 New York banks stopped redeeming paper currency with gold, responding to the impact of the Specie Circular. Soon all banks suspended payments in hard coin. Suspension of specie began a cycle that led to banks curtailing loans and reduced business confidence. The credit contraction only made things worse; after a brief recovery, hard times set in and persisted from 1839 to 1843.

Martin Van Buren and Hard Times

Not surprisingly, economic issues were paramount during these years. Unfortunately, Van Buren followed Jackson's hard-money policies. He curtailed federal spending, thus accelerating deflation, and opposed the Whigs' advocacy of a national bank, which would have expanded credit. Even worse, Van Buren proposed a new regional treasury system for holding government deposits, replacing banks; Van Buren wanted to prevent further government losses from failing banks. The treasury branches would accept and pay out only gold and silver coin; they would not accept paper currency or checks drawn on state banks. Van Buren's independent treasury bill was passed in 1840. By creating a constant demand for hard coin, it deprived banks of gold and added to the general deflation.

The Whigs fought the Democrats at the state level over these issues. The Whigs favored new banks, more paper currency, and more corporations. As the party of hard money, the Democrats favored eliminating paper currency altogether and using only gold or silver coin. Increasingly the Democrats became distrustful even of state banks, and by the mid-1840s a majority favored eliminating all bank corporations. The Whigs, riding the wave of economic distress into office, made banking and corporate charters more readily available.

With the nation in hard times, the Whigs confidently prepared for the election of 1840. Their strategy was simple: keep their loyal supporters and win over independents distressed by hard times. The Democrats renominated President Van Buren in a somber convention. The Whigs rallied behind the military hero General William

Election of 1840

Henry Harrison, conqueror of Prophet Town, or Tippecanoe Creek, in 1811. Harrison and his running mate, John Tyler of Virginia, ran a "log cabin and hard cider" campaign—a people's crusade against the aristocratic president in the Palace. Though depicted as an ordinary farmer, Harrison came from a Virginia plantation family. Using huge rallies, parades, songs, posters, and campaign hats, the Whigs wooed supporters and independents alike. Harrison stayed carefully above the issues, earning the nickname "General Mum," but party hacks bluntly blamed the hard times on the Democrats. In a huge turnout in which 80 percent of eligible voters cast ballots, Harrison won the popular vote by a narrow margin but swept the electoral college 234 to 60.

Immediately after taking office in 1841, President Harrison called a special session of Congress to enact the Whig economic program: repeal of the independent treasury system, a new national bank, and a higher protective tariff. The Whigs had gambled on the health of the sixty-eight-year-old Harrison but lost. Harrison died within a month of his inauguration. His successor, John Tyler, a former Democrat who had left the party in opposition to Jackson's nullification proclamation, turned out to be more a Democrat than a Whig. He was as critical of the Whigs' economic nationalism as he had been of Jackson's use of executive power. Tyler consistently opposed the Whig congressional program. He repeatedly vetoed Henry Clay's protective tariffs, bills promoting internal improvements, and bills aimed at reviving the Bank of the United States. The only important measures that became law under his administration were the repeal of the independent treasury and passage of a higher tariff. Two days after Tyler's second veto of a bank bill, the entire cabinet except Secretary of State Daniel Webster resigned. Webster, involved in negotiating a new treaty with Great Britain, left shortly thereafter. Tyler became a president without a party, and the Whigs lost the presidency without an election. Whigs referred to Tyler as "His Accidency."

Hard times in the late 1830s and early 1840s deflected attention from the renewal of Anglo-American tensions. Northern commercial rivalry with Britain, the default of state governments and corporations on British-held debts during the Panic of 1837, rebellion in Canada, boundary disputes, Southern alarm over West

Anglo-American Tensions

Using many of the techniques of twentieth-century politics, General William Henry Harrison ran a "log cabin and hard cider" campaign—a popular crusade—against Jackson heir, President Martin Van Buren. This campaign handkerchief shows Harrison welcoming two of his comrades to his log cabin, with a barrel of cider outside. *The New-York Historical Society.*

Indian emancipation, and American expansionism—all caused Anglo-American conflict.

One of the most troublesome of these disputes arose from the *Caroline* affair, in which a United States citizen, Amos Durfee, had been killed when Canadian militia set the privately owned steamer *Caroline* afire in the Niagara River. (The *Caroline* had supported an unsuccessful uprising against Great Britain in Upper Canada in 1837.) Britain refused to apologize and American newspapers called for revenge. Fearing that popular support for the Canadian rebels would ignite war, President Van Buren had posted troops at the border to discourage border raids. Tensions subsided in November 1840 when Alexander McLeod, a Canadian deputy sheriff, was arrested in New York for the murder of Durfee. McLeod was eventually acquitted. If he had been found guilty and executed, Lord Palmerston, the British foreign minister, might have sought war.

At about the same time another quarrel threatened Anglo-American relations. The Treaty of Ghent, which ended the War of 1812, had not solved the boundary dispute between Maine and New Brunswick. Moreover, although Great Britain had accepted an 1831 arbitration decision fixing a new boundary, the United States Senate had rejected it in 1832. Thus when Canadians began to log the disputed region in the winter of 1838 and 1839, the citizens of Maine attempted to expel them. The lumbermen soon captured the Maine land agent and posse; both sides mobilized their militia; and Congress authorized a call-up of fifty thousand men. No blood was spilled, however. General Winfield Scott, who had patrolled the border during the *Caroline* affair, was dispatched to Aroostook, Maine. Scott arranged a truce between the warring state and province, and the two sides compromised on their conflicting claims in the Webster-Ashburton Treaty (1842).

These border disputes with Great Britain prefigured an issue that became prominent in national politics in the mid- to late 1840s: the westward expansion of the United States. Tyler's succession to power in 1841 and a Democratic victory in the presidential election of 1844 ended an activist federal government in the domestic sphere for the rest of the decade. Attention turned to the debate over territorial expansion. Reform, however, was not dead. Its passions would resurface in the 1850s in the debate over slavery in the territories.

Manifest Destiny

The belief that American expansion westward and southward was inevitable, divinely ordained, and just was first called *manifest destiny* by a Democrat, the newspaperman John L. O'Sullivan. The annexation of Texas, O'Sullivan wrote in 1845, was "the fulfillment of our manifest destiny to overspread the continent allotted by Providence for the free development of our yearly multiplying millions." Americans had thought similarly for decades, but during the 1840s they used such rhetoric to hurry the inexorable process along and to justify war and threats of war in the quest for more territory.

Americans had been hungry for new lands ever since the colonists first turned their eyes westward. There lay fertile soil, valuable minerals, and the chance for a better life or a new beginning. Acquisition of the Louisiana Territory and Florida had set the process in motion (see map, page 366). Agrarian Democrats saw the West as an antidote to urbanization and industrialization. Enterprising Whigs looked to the new commercial opportunities the West offered. Both parties reflected the popular mood as the proportion of Americans living west of the Appalachians grew from one-quarter to one-half between 1830 and 1860.

A fierce national pride also spurred the quest for western land. Dampened during times of depression, it reasserted itself during recoveries and booms, as in the 1840s. North or South, Whig or Democrat, Americans were convinced that theirs was the greatest country on earth, with a special role to play in the world. What better evidence of such a role could there be than expansion from coast to coast?

Americans also idealistically believed that westward expansion would extend American freedom and democracy. The acquisition of new territory, they reasoned, would bring the benefits of America's republican system of government to less fortunate people. Of course such idealism was self-serving, and it contained an undercurrent of racism as well. Indians were perceived as savages best removed from their homes east of the Mississippi and confined to small areas in the West. Mexicans and Central and South Americans were also seen as inferior peoples, fit to be controlled or conquered. Thus the same racism that justified slavery in the South and discrimination in the North supported expansion in the West.

Finally, the expansionist fever of the 1840s was fed by the desire to secure the nation from perceived external threats. The internal enemies of the 1830s—a monster bank, corporations, paper currency, alcohol, Sabbath violation—seemed to pale before the threats Americans found on their borders in the 1840s. Expansion, some believed, was necessary to preserve American independence.

Among the long-standing objectives of expansionists was the Republic of Texas, which included parts of present-day Oklahoma, Kansas, Colorado, Wyoming, and New Mexico, as well as all of Texas. This territory was originally part of Mexico. After winning its independence from Spain in 1821, the government of Mexico encouraged the development of these rich but remote northern provinces, offering large tracts of land to settlers called *empresarios*, who agreed to bring two hundred or more families into the area. Americans like Moses and Stephen Austin, who had helped to formulate the policy, responded eagerly, for Mexico was offering land virtually free in return for settlers' promises to become Mexican citizens and adopt the Catholic religion.

> **Republic of Texas**

By 1835, thirty-five thousand Americans, including many slaveholders, lived in Texas. These new settlers ignored local laws and oppressed native Mexicans, and when the Mexican government attempted to tighten its control over the region, Anglos and insurgent Hispanics rebelled. At the

Manifest Destiny

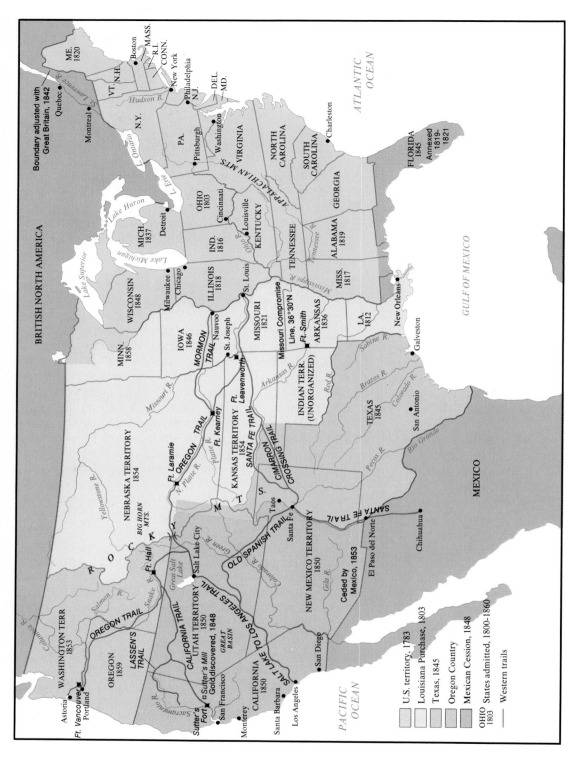

Westward Expansion, 1800–1860

BRITISH NORTH AMERICA

Boundary adjusted with Great Britain, 1842

ATLANTIC OCEAN

ME. 1820

MASS.
R.I.
CONN.
VT. N.H.
Boston
New York

Quebec
Montreal

N.Y.

Hudson R.
Philadelphia
N.J.
DEL.
MD.

PA.
Pittsburgh
Washington

L. Ontario
L. Erie

APPALACHIAN MTS.

VIRGINIA

NORTH CAROLINA

SOUTH CAROLINA

Charleston

GEORGIA

FLORIDA 1845
Annexed 1819–1821

St. Lawrence R.

Lake Huron

Lake Superior

Lake Michigan

MICH. 1837
Detroit

OHIO 1803
Cincinnati
Louisville
Ohio R.

IND. 1816

KENTUCKY

TENNESSEE
Tennessee R.

ALABAMA 1819

WISCONSIN 1848
Milwaukee
Chicago

ILLINOIS 1818
St. Louis

MISS. 1817

GULF OF MEXICO

MINN. 1858

IOWA 1846
Nauvoo
St. Joseph

MORMON TRAIL

MISSOURI 1821
Missouri Compromise Line, 36°30′N

ARKANSAS 1836
Ft. Smith

LA. 1812
New Orleans

Galveston

Missouri R.

NEBRASKA TERRITORY 1854

Ft. Kearney
Platte R.
N. Platte R.
Ft. Laramie
OREGON TRAIL

BIG HORN MTS.

Yellowstone R.

KANSAS TERRITORY 1854

Ft. Leavenworth

SANTA FE TRAIL

Arkansas R.

Red R.

INDIAN TERR. (UNORGANIZED)

Sabine R.

TEXAS 1845

San Antonio

Brazos R.

Colorado R.

CIMARRON CROSSING TRAIL

ROCKY MTS.

Green R.

Salt Lake City
Great Salt Lake

Ft. Hall

OLD SPANISH TRAIL

Taos
Santa Fe

NEW MEXICO TERRITORY 1850

SANTA FE TRAIL

El Paso del Norte

Chihuahua

Ceded by Mexico, 1853

Pecos R.
Rio Grande

Gila R.

MEXICO

Columbia R.
Salmon R.
Snake R.

WASHINGTON TERR. 1853

OREGON 1859

CALIFORNIA TRAIL 1850
UTAH TERRITORY 1850

GREAT BASIN

LASSEN'S TRAIL

Sutter's Mill Gold discovered, 1848
Sutter's Fort
Sacramento R.
San Francisco
Monterey

CALIFORNIA 1850

SALT LAKE TO LOS ANGELES TRAIL

Santa Barbara
Los Angeles
San Diego

Astoria
Ft. Vancouver
Portland

PACIFIC OCEAN

Legend:
- U.S. territory, 1783
- Louisiana Purchase, 1803
- Texas, 1845
- Oregon Country
- Mexican Cession, 1848
- OHIO 1803 — States admitted, 1800–1860
- Western trails

Alamo in San Antonio in 1836, fewer than two hundred Texans made a heroic stand against three thousand Mexicans under General Antonio López de Santa Anna. All the defenders of the mission, including Davy Crockett and Colonel James Bowie, died in the battle, and "Remember the Alamo" became the Texans' rallying cry. By the end of the year the Texans had won independence, delighting most Americans, some of whom saw the victory as a triumph of white Protestantism over Catholic Mexico. Others noted that proslavery Texas had defeated antislavery Mexicans.

Although they established an independent republic, Texans soon sought annexation to the United States. To many white Texans, an independent republic was but a means to joining the Union. Sam Houston, President of Texas, opened negotiations with Washington, but the issue became politically explosive. Southerners favored annexing proslavery Texas; antislavery forces, many northerners, and most Whigs opposed annexation. In view of the political dangers, President Jackson delayed recognition of Texas until after the election of 1836, and President Van Buren ignored annexation.

Rebuffed by the United States, Texans talked about developing close ties with the British and extending their republic all the way to the Pacific Coast. Faced with the specter of a rival republic to the south, and with British colonies already entrenched to the north, some Americans feared encirclement. If Texas reached the ocean and became an English ally, would not American independence be threatened?

President Tyler—committed to expansion, fearful of Texan ties with the British, and eager to build political support in the South—pushed for annexation. But in April 1844 the Senate rejected a treaty of annexation. A letter from Secretary of State Calhoun to the British minister justifying annexation as a step in protecting slavery so outraged senators that the treaty was defeated 16 to 35.

Just as southerners sought expansion to the Southwest, northerners looked to the Northwest. In 1841 "Oregon fever" struck thousands. Avoiding Mexican-held California and lured

> **Oregon Fever**

by the glowing reports of missionaries who seemed to show as much interest in the Northwest's richness and beauty as in the conversion of Indians, migrants organized hundreds of wagon trains and embarked on the Oregon Trail. The 2,000-mile

To Texans, their War for Independence paralleled the American Revolution. This banner of a lady of liberty, similar to images used during the American Revolution, was carried by Texans in 1836. *Archives Division, Texas State Library.*

journey took six months or more, but within a few years five thousand settlers had arrived in the fertile Willamette Valley south of the Columbia River.

Since the Anglo-American convention of 1818, Britain and the United States had jointly occupied the disputed Oregon Territory (see page 236). Beginning with the administration of President John Quincy Adams, the United States had tried to fix the boundary at the 49th parallel, but Britain was determined to maintain access to Puget Sound and the Columbia River. Time only increased the American appetite. In 1843 a Cincinnati convention demanded that the United States obtain the entire Oregon Country, up to its northernmost border of 54°40'. Soon "Fifty-four Forty or Fight" had become the rallying cry of American expansionists.

The expansion into Oregon and the rejection of the annexation of Texas, both favored by antislavery forces, heightened southern pessimism. Southern

> **Election of 1844**

leaders became anxious about their diminishing ability to control the debate over slavery. They persuaded the 1844 Democratic convention to adopt a rule that the presidential nominee had to receive two-thirds of the convention votes. In effect, the southern states acquired a veto, and they used it to block Van Buren as the nominee; most southerners objected to Van Buren's antislavery stance and opposition to Texas annexation. The party chose instead "Young Hickory," House Speaker James K. Polk, a hard-money Jacksonian and avid expansionist from Tennessee. The Whig leader Henry Clay, who opposed annexation, won his party's unanimous designation. The main plank of the Democratic platform called for occupation of the entire Oregon Territory and annexation of Texas. The Whigs, though they favored expansion, argued that the Democrats' belligerent nationalism would lead the nation to war with Great Britain or Mexico or both. Clay favored expansion through negotiation, not force.

With a well-organized campaign, Polk and the Democrats captured the executive mansion by 170 electoral votes to 105 (they won the popular vote by just 38,000 out of 2.7 million votes cast). Polk carried New York's 36 electoral votes by just 6,000 votes; abolitionist James G. Birney, the Liberty party candidate, drew almost 16,000 votes away from Clay, handing New York and the election to Polk. Thus abolitionist forces unwittingly influenced the choice of a slaveholder as president, but they viewed Polk as more moderate than Clay and the lesser of two evils.

Interpreting Polk's victory as a mandate for annexation, President Tyler proposed in his last days in office that Texas be admitted by joint resolution of Congress. (The usual method of annexation, by treaty negotiation, required a two-thirds vote in the Senate—which expansionists clearly did not have. Joint resolution required only a simple majority in both houses.) Proslavery and antislavery congressmen debated the extension of slavery into the territory, and the resolution passed the House 120 to 98 and the Senate 27 to 25. Three days before leaving office, Tyler signed the measure. Mexico immediately broke relations with the United States; war loomed.

Politics, the reform spirit, and expansionism commingled in the 1830s and 1840s. Reform imbued with revivalism sought to bring order in a rapidly changing society. But reformers had no monopoly on claims of republican virtue; their opponents too claimed descent from the revolutionary values that held individual liberty dear. Once reform forced itself into politics, it sparked a broader-based interest and brought with it an intensity that would remake the political system. Political organi-

zation and conflict stimulated even greater interest in campaigns and political issues. Expansion and territorial questions further intensified conflict. Eventually, however, one issue absorbed nearly all attention and created a crisis in the Union: slavery.

Suggestions for Further Reading

Religion, Revivalism, and Reform

Michael Barkun, *Crucible of the Millennium: The Burned-over District of New York in the 1840s* (1986); Terry Bilhartz, *Urban Religion and the Second Great Awakening: Church and Society in Early National Baltimore* (1986); Paul S. Boyer, *Urban Masses and Moral Order in America, 1820–1920* (1978); Whitney R. Cross, *The Burned-Over District* (1950); Clifford S. Griffen, *Their Brother's Keepers: Moral Stewardship in the United States, 1800–1865* (1960); Keith J. Hardman, *Charles Grandison Finney, 1792–1875: Revivalist and Reformer* (1987); Leon A. Jick, *The Americanization of the Synagogue, 1820–1870* (1976); Charles A. Johnson, *The Frontier Camp Meeting* (1955); Paul E. Johnson, *A Shopkeeper's Millennium: Society and Revivals in Rochester, New York, 1815–1837* (1978); William G. McLoughlin, *Revivals, Awakenings, and Reform: An Essay on Religion and Social Change in America, 1607–1977* (1978); Perry Miller, *The Life of the Mind in America: From the Revolution to the Civil War* (1966); Russel B. Nye, *Society and Culture in America, 1830–1860* (1974); Randolph A. Roth, *The Democratic Dilemma: Religion, Reform, and the Social Order in the Connecticut Valley of Vermont, 1791–1850* (1987); Richard D. Shiels, "The Scope of the Second Great Awakening: Andover, Massachusetts, as a Case Study," *Journal of the Early Republic,* 5 (Summer 1985), 223–246; Timothy L. Smith, *Revivalism and Social Reform in Mid-Nineteenth Century America* (1957); William W. Sweet, *Revivalism in America* (1949); Alice Felt Tyler, *Freedom's Ferment* (1944); Ronald G. Walters, *American Reformers, 1815–1860* (1978).

Temperance, Asylums, and Antimasonry

Ronald P. Formisano and Kathleen S. Kutolowski, "Antimasonry and Masonry: The Genesis of Protest, 1826–1827," *American Quarterly,* 29 (1977), 139–165; Paul Goodman, *Towards a Christian Republic: Antimasonry and the Great Transition in New England, 1826–1836* (1988); Gerald N. Grob, *Mental Institutions in America: Social Policy to 1875* (1973); Michael S. Hindus, *Prison and Plantation: Crime, Justice, and Authority in Massachusetts and South Carolina, 1767–1878* (1980); Kathleen Smith Kutolowski, "Antimasonry Reexamined: Social Bases of the Grass-Roots Party," *Journal of American History,* 71 (September 1984), 269–293; W. David Lewis, *From Newgate to Dannemora: The Rise of the Penitentiary in New York, 1796–1948* (1965); W. J.

Rorabaugh, *The Alcoholic Republic: An American Tradition* (1979); Charles E. Rosenberg, *The Care of Strangers: The Rise of America's Hospital System* (1987); David J. Rothman, *The Discovery of the Asylum: Social Order and Disorder in the New Republic* (1971); Ian R. Tyrrell, *Sobering Up: From Temperance to Prohibition in Antebellum America, 1800–1860* (1979); William Preston Vaughn, *The Antimasonic Party in the United States, 1826–1843* (1983)

Women and Reform

Barbara J. Berg, *The Remembered Gate: Origins of American Feminism: The Woman and the City, 1800–1860* (1977); Anne M. Boylan, "Women in Groups: An Analysis of Women's Benevolent Organizations in New York and Boston, 1797–1840," *Journal of American History,* 71 (December 1984), 497–523; Catherine Clinton, *The Other Civil War: American Women in the Nineteenth Century* (1984); Ellen C. Du Bois, *Feminism and Suffrage: The Emergence of an Independent Woman's Movement in America, 1848–1869* (1978); Barbara Leslie Epstein, *The Politics of Domesticity: Women, Evangelism, and Temperance in Nineteenth-Century America* (1981); Lori D. Ginzberg, " 'Moral Suasion Is Moral Balderdash': Women, Politics, and Social Activism in the 1850s," *Journal of American History,* 73 (December 1986), 601–622; Elisabeth Griffith, *In Her Own Right: The Life of Elizabeth Cady Stanton* (1984); Nancy A. Hewitt, *Women's Activism and Social Change: Rochester, New York, 1822–1872* (1984); Gerda Lerner, The *Grimké Sisters of South Carolina* (1967); Mary P. Ryan, *Cradle of the Middle Class: The Family in Oneida County, New York, 1790–1865* (1981); Ian R. Tyrrell, "Women and Temperance in Antebellum America, 1830–1860," *Civil War History,* 28 (June 1982), 128–152.

Antislavery and Abolitionism

David Brion Davis, *Slavery and Human Progress* (1984); Frederick Douglass, *Life and Times of Frederick Douglass* (1881); George M. Fredrickson, *The Black Image in the White Mind: The Debate on Afro-American Character and Destiny, 1817–1914* (1971); Lawrence J. Friedman, *Gregarious Saints: Self and Community in American Abolitionism, 1830–1870* (1982); Aileen S. Kraditor, *Means and Ends in American Abolitionism: Garrison and His Critics on Strategy and Tactics* (1967); William H. Pease and Jane H. Pease, *They Who Would Be Free: Blacks' Search for Freedom, 1830–1861* (1974); Lewis Perry and Michael Fellman, eds., *Antislavery Reconsidered* (1979); Benjamin Quarles, *Black Abolitionists* (1969); Leonard L. Richards, *The Life and Times of Congressman John Quincy Adams* (1986); Leonard L. Richards, *"Gentlemen of Property and Standing": Anti-Abolition Mobs in Jacksonian America* (1970); James Brewer Stewart, *Holy Warriors: The Abolitionists and American Slavery* (1976); John L. Thomas, *The Liberator: William Lloyd Garrison* (1963); Ronald G. Walters, *The Antislavery Appeal: American Abolitionism After 1830* (1976); Bertram Wyatt-Brown, *Lewis Tappan and the Evangelical War Against Slavery* (1969).

Andrew Jackson and the Jacksonians

Lee Benson, *The Concept of Jacksonian Democracy: New York as a Test Case* (1964); Donald B. Cole, *Martin Van Buren and the American Political System* (1984); Mary W. M. Hargreaves, *The Presidency of John Quincy Adams* (1985); Richard B. Latner, *The Presidency of Andrew Jackson* (1979); Marvin Meyers, *The Jacksonian Persuasion* (1960); John Niven, *Martin Van Buren* (1983); Edward Pessen, *Jacksonian America: Society, Personality, and Politics,* rev. ed. (1979); Robert V. Remini, *The Legacy of Andrew Jackson: Essays on Democracy, Indian Removal, and Slavery* (1988); Robert V. Remini, *The Life of Andrew Jackson* (1988); Robert V. Remini, *Andrew Jackson and the Bank War* (1967); Arthur M. Schlesinger, Jr., *The Age of Jackson* (1945); John William Ward, *Andrew Jackson: Symbol for an Age* (1955); Harry L. Watson, *Jacksonian Politics and Community Conflict: The Emergence of the Second American Party System in Cumberland County, North Carolina* (1981); Major L. Wilson, *The Presidency of Martin Van Buren* (1984).

Democrats and Whigs

William J. Cooper, *The South and the Politics of Slavery, 1828–1856* (1978); Roger A. Fischer, *Tippecanoe and Trinkets Too: The Material Culture of American Presidential Campaigns, 1828–1984* (1988); Ronald P. Formisano, *The Transformation of Political Culture: Massachusetts Parties, 1790s–1840s* (1983); Ronald P. Formisano, *The Birth of Mass Political Parties: Michigan, 1827–1861* (1971); William W. Freehling, *Prelude to Civil War: The Nullification Controversy in South Carolina* (1966); Daniel Walker Howe, *The Political Culture of the American Whigs* (1979); Richard P. McCormick, *The Second American Party System: Party Formation in the Jacksonian Era* (1966); Merrill D. Peterson, *The Great Triumvirate: Webster, Clay, and Calhoun* (1987); James Roger Sharp, *The Jacksonians Versus the Banks: Politics in the States After the Panic of 1837* (1970).

Manifest Destiny and Foreign Policy

John M. Belohlavek, *"Let the Eagle Soar!" The Foreign Policy of Andrew Jackson* (1985); Norman B. Graebner, ed., *Manifest Destiny* (1968); Thomas R. Hietala, *Manifest Design: Anxious Aggrandizement in Late Jacksonian America* (1985); Reginald Horsman, *Race and Manifest Destiny* (1981); Frederick Merk, *Manifest Destiny and Mission in American History* (1963); David M. Pletcher, *The Diplomacy of Annexation: Texas, Oregon, and the Mexican War* (1973); Charles G. Sellers, Jr., *James K. Polk: Continentalist, 1843–1846* (1966); Paul A. Varg, *United States Foreign Relations, 1820–1860* (1979); Albert K. Weinberg, *Manifest Destiny* (1935).

He was free at last. Escaping from slavery in Virginia, Anthony Burns had stowed away on a ship and made his way safely to Boston. Breathing the free air in a city well known for its abolitionists, Burns seemed safe. He found a job in a clothing store, and his future for once looked bright.

Then Anthony Burns made an understandable but serious mistake. He wrote a letter and tried to route it to his brother, still enslaved in Virginia. Their master intercepted the letter and left for Boston, intending to seize his wayward human property. In so doing, he counted on the support of the American government and American law. In May 1854, a deputy marshal arrested Burns by authority of the Fugitive Slave Act and placed him under guard in Boston's Federal Courthouse.

Dramatic events followed, with repercussions that were unexpected by many of those most deeply affected. Predictably, Boston's abolitionists went into action, organizing public protests at Faneuil Hall and later attacking the courthouse in an attempt to free Burns by force. A prominent white clergyman and a black man broke through the door but were beaten back by deputy marshals armed with clubs. Someone fired a shot, and one deputy fell dead.

President Franklin Pierce then decided on emphatic enforcement of federal law. "Incur any expense," Pierce telegraphed officials, "to insure the execution of the law." To demonstrate his determination, he sent marines, cavalry, and artillery to Boston and ordered a federal ship to stand ready to return Burns to Virginia. Legal maneuvers before the federal commissioner who would hear the case stood little chance of success, but Burns's owner seemed willing to sell his property. The United States attorney, however, prevented this solution and instead won a decision that Anthony Burns must return to slavery. On June 2, a formidable contingent of troops marched Burns to the harbor through streets draped in black and hung with American flags at half mast. At a cost of $100,000, equivalent to roughly $2,000,000 today, a single black man was sent back into slavery under the terms and through the power of federal law.

13

SLAVERY AND AMERICA'S FUTURE: THE ROAD TO WAR, 1845–1861

The Assault in the U.S. Senate Chamber on Senator Sumner (detail) from *Frank Leslie's Illustrated Newspaper,* June 7, 1856. Hand-colored by Karla Cinquanta.

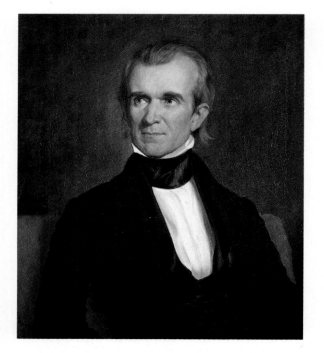
James K. Polk was an effective president who achieved his goals. But territorial expansion led to sectional conflict. *Corcoran Gallery of Art.*

The polarizing effects of this demonstration of federal support for slavery reached far and wide. In Boston, conservatives found that the spectacle of the national government enforcing bondage had radicalized them. "I put my face in my hands and wept. I could do nothing less," wrote one man, and textile manufacturer Amos A. Lawrence observed that "we went to bed one night old fashioned, conservative, Compromise Union Whigs & waked up stark mad Abolitionists." Juries refused to convict the prominent abolitionists who had stormed the courthouse, and New England states passed personal liberty laws designed to impede or block federal power. The southern states, in turn, reacted with outrage at every sign of northern "faithlessness" about the Fugitive Slave Act. The slavery issue was driving the sections apart. Although black Bostonians later raised enough money to purchase freedom for Anthony Burns, the nation's agony steadily deepened. Northerners feared that the Slave Power was dominating American government, and white southerners demanded that their rights be upheld.

What brought these issues to center stage, more than anything else, was territorial expansion. Be-

tween 1845 and 1853 the United States added Texas, the West Coast, and the Southwest to its domain and launched the settlement of the Great Plains. But each time the nation expanded, it confronted a thorny issue—whether new territories and states should be slave or free. Over this question there were disagreements too violent for compromise. Sensing that fact, John C. Calhoun called Mexico "the forbidden fruit; the penalty of eating it would be to subject our institutions to political death." A host of political leaders, including Henry Clay, Lewis Cass, Stephen A. Douglas, and Presidents Jackson and Van Buren, tried from the 1830s through the 1850s to postpone or compromise disagreements about slavery in the territories. But repeatedly these disputes injected into national politics the bitterness surrounding slavery. If slavery was the sore spot in the body politic, territorial disputes were salt rubbed into the sore.

As Americans fought over slavery in the territories, the conflict broadened to encompass many other issues. The United States had always been a heterogeneous, diverse society, not a cohesive unit, but now various concerns became linked to one divisive issue instead of balancing each other. Battles over slavery in the territories broke the second party system apart and then shaped a realigned system that emphasized sectional enmity. Sectional parties replaced nationwide organizations that had tried to compromise differences.

As parties clamored for support and as citizens reflected on events, the feeling grew in both North and South that America's future was at stake. The new Republican party charged that southerners were taking over the federal government and trying to make slavery legal in every part of the Union. Republicans believed that America's future depended on the free labor of free men, whose rights were protected by a government devoted to liberty. By contrast, southern leaders of every party united in defense of slavery. They charged the North with lawless behavior and failure to respect the Constitution. To these southerners slavery was the foundation of white equality and republicanism, and a government that failed to protect slavery seemed un-American and unworthy of their loyalty.

Not all citizens were obsessed with these conflicts. In fact, the results of the 1860 presidential election indicated that most voters hoped for neither disunion nor civil war. Yet within six months they had both, for the passions that slavery

IMPORTANT EVENTS

1846	War with Mexico Oregon Treaty Wilmot Proviso		**1856**	Preston Brooks attacks Charles Sumner in Senate chamber "Bleeding Kansas" Buchanan elected president
1847	Lewis Cass proposes idea of popular sovereignty		**1857**	*Dred Scott* v. *Sanford* Lecompton Constitution
1848	Taylor elected president Free-Soil party formed		**1858**	Voters reject Lecompton Constitution Lincoln-Douglas debates Freeport Doctrine
1849	California applies for admission to Union as free state		**1859**	John Brown raids Harpers Ferry
1850	Compromise of 1850		**1860**	Democratic party splits in half Lincoln elected president Crittenden Compromise fails South Carolina secedes from Union
1851	Mob rescues fugitive slave in Boston			
1852	Publication of *Uncle Tom's Cabin,* by Harriet Beecher Stowe Pierce elected president		**1861**	Six more southern states secede Confederacy established Attack on Fort Sumter
1854	Publication of "Appeal of the Independent Democrats" Kansas-Nebraska Act Republican party formed Democrats lose ground in congressional elections			

unleashed could not be contained or resolved. What had begun as a dark cloud over the territories grew into a storm. Both sections felt threatened and anxious and believed that the future hung in the balance. At the last minute neither the victorious Republican party nor defensive southern slaveholders could agree on any of the desperate compromises proposed and thus a vast civil war began.

Conflict Begins: The Mexican War

Territorial expansion surged forward under the leadership of President James K. Polk. The annexa-

tion of Texas just before his inauguration (see page 368) had not cooled Polk's interest in acquiring California and the Southwest, and he desired Oregon as well. But, though Polk was an effective president who reached most of his goals, he was unaware of the price that expansion would exact in domestic harmony. The addition of a huge domain to the nation's boundaries had major side effects. It divided the Whig party, drove southern Whigs into a full embrace of slavery, and brought into the open an aggressive new southern theory about slavery's position in the territories. It also elicited northern protests and proposals that revealed profound disagreement between the sections.

Although his supporters had belligerently demanded all of the Oregon Territory, Polk found as president that diplomacy had its advantages. Congress's annexation of Texas had outraged Mexican

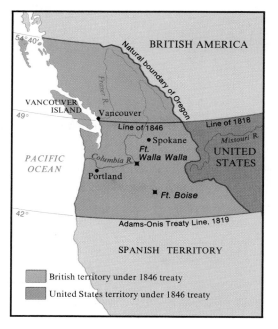

American Expansion in Oregon

leaders, who severed relations with the United States. Knowing that war with Mexico could break out at any time, Polk decided to try to avoid a conflict with Great Britain in the Northwest, where America and Britain had jointly occupied disputed territory since 1818. Dropping the demand for a boundary at 54°40′, he kept up pressure on the British to accept the 49th parallel. Eventually, in 1846 Great Britain agreed. In the Oregon Treaty, the United States gained all of present-day Oregon, Washington, and Idaho and parts of Wyoming and Montana (see map).

Toward Mexico, Polk was much more aggressive. He ordered American troops to defend the border claimed by Texas—but contested by Mexico—and offered to buy a huge tract of land in the Southwest from the resentful Mexicans. After purchase failed, Polk resolved to ask Congress for a declaration of war and set to work compiling a list of grievances. This task became unnecessary when word arrived that Mexican forces had engaged a body of American troops in disputed territory. American blood had been shed. Eagerly Polk declared that "war exists by the act of Mexico itself" and summoned the nation to arms.

Congress voted to recognize a state of war between Mexico and the United States in May 1846,

but controversy grew. Public opinion about the war was sharply divided, with southwesterners enthusiastic and New Englanders strenuously opposed. In Congress Whigs charged that Polk had "literally provoked" an unnecessary war and "usurped the power of Congress by making war upon Mexico." The aged John Quincy Adams passionately opposed the war, dying after delivery of a powerful speech against it, and a tall young Whig from Illinois named Abraham Lincoln questioned its justification. Moreover, a small minority of antislavery Whigs agreed with abolitionists—the war was no less than a plot to extend slavery. Joshua Giddings of Ohio charged on the floor of the House that Polk's purpose was "to render slavery secure in Texas" and to extend slavery's domain to vast expanses of new territory.

In the North these charges fed fear of the Slave Power. Abolitionists long had warned that there was a Slave Power—a slaveholding oligarchy in control of the South and intent

Idea of a Slave Power

on controlling the nation. These dangerous aristocrats had gained power in their region by persecuting critics of slavery and suppressing their ideas. The Slave Power's assault on northern liberties, abolitionists argued, had begun in 1836, when Congress passed the gag rule (see page 352). Many white northerners, even those who saw nothing wrong with slavery, had viewed John Quincy Adams's stand against the rule as a valiant defense of free speech and the right to petition. The battle over free speech first made the idea of a Slave Power credible.

Now the Mexican War increased fears of this sinister power. Antislavery northerners asked why claims to all of Oregon had been abandoned but a questionable war begun for slave territory. Steadily these arguments had an effect on northern opinion. But the impact of events on southern opinion and southern leaders was even more dramatic.

At first many southern leaders criticized the war with Mexico. Southern Whigs attacked the Democratic president for causing the war, and southern congressmen did not immediately see defense of slavery as the paramount issue. In 1845 Alexander H. Stephens of Georgia had declared, "I am no defender of slavery in the abstract," and even John C. Calhoun, despite his earlier schemes to annex Texas for slavery, strongly opposed the seizure of large amounts of land from Mexico. A Whig editor in Georgia argued that "we have territory enough, especially if every province, like Texas, is to bring in its train war and debt and death."

But the war proved generally popular with southern voters, and no southern Whig could oppose it once slavery became the central issue. That happened in August 1846, when a Democratic representative from Pennsylvania, David Wilmot, offered an amendment to a military appropriations bill. Wilmot attached a condition, or proviso, to the bill: that "neither slavery nor involuntary servitude shall ever exist" in any territory gained from Mexico. His proviso did not pass both houses of Congress, but it immediately transformed the debate.

Wilmot Proviso

Alexander H. Stephens, recently "no defender of slavery," now declared that slavery was based on the Bible and beyond moral criticism. John C. Calhoun drew up resolutions on the territories that staked out a radical, new southern position. According to these resolutions, the territories belonged to all the states, and the federal government could do nothing to limit the spread of slavery there. Southern slaveholders had a constitutional *right,* Calhoun claimed, to take their slaves anywhere in the territories. This position, which quickly became orthodox for every southern politician, was a radical reversal of history. The founding fathers, under the Articles of Confederation, had excluded slavery from the Northwest Territory (see page 174). Article IV, Section 3, of the Constitution authorized Congress to make "all needful rules and regulations" for the territories, and the Missouri Compromise had barred slavery from most of the Louisiana Purchase. But southern leaders now demanded protection for slavery.

In the North, meanwhile, the Wilmot Proviso soon became a rallying cry for abolitionists and Free-Soilers. Eventually the legislatures of fourteen northern states endorsed it—and not because all its supporters were abolitionists. David Wilmot, significantly, was neither an abolitionist nor a Free-Soiler. He denied having any "squeamish sensitiveness upon the subject of slavery" or "morbid sympathy for the slave" and explained that his goal was to defend "the rights of white freemen." Wilmot wanted California "for free white labor"; he was fighting for opportunity for "the sons of toil, of my own race and own color." His involvement in antislavery controversy showed the remarkable

ANTI-TEXAS MEETING
AT FANEUIL HALL!

Friends of Freedom!

A proposition has been made, and will soon come up for consideration in the United States Senate, to annex Texas to the Union. This territory has been wrested from Mexico by violence and fraud. Such is the character of the leaders in this enterprise that the country has been aptly termed "that valley of rascals." It is large enough to make *nine* or *ten* States as large as Massachusetts. It was, under Mexico, a free territory. The freebooters have made it a slave territory. The design is to annex it, with its load of infamy and oppression, to the Union. The immediate result may be a war with Mexico—the ultimate result *will be* some 18 or 20 more slaveholders in the Senate of the United States, a still larger number in the House of Representatives, and the balance of power in the hands of the South! And if, when in a minority in Congress, slaveholders browbeat the North, demand the passage of gag laws, trample on the Right of Petition, and threaten, in defiance of the General Government, to hang every man, caught at the South, who dares to speak against their "domestic institutions,"what limits shall be set to their intolerant demands and high handed usurpations, when they are in the majority?

All opposed to this scheme, of whatever sect or party, are invited to attend the meeting at the Old Cradle of Liberty, to-morrow, (Thursday Jan. 25,)at 10 o'clock, A. M., at which time addresses are expected from several able speakers.

Bostonians! Friends of Freedom!! Let your voices be heard in loud remonstrance against this scheme, fraught with such ruin to yourselves and such infamy to your country.
January 24, 1838.

As this broadside shows, suspicion that the Slave Power sought additional territory and influence preceded the Mexican War and was deeply rooted. *Library of Congress.*

ability of the slavery issue to absorb other concerns in the North.

Like Wilmot, most white northerners were racists, not abolitionists, but it was possible to be racist *and* an opponent of slavery. Fear of the Slave Power was building a potent antislavery movement that united abolitionists and antiblack voters. The latter's concern was to protect themselves, not southern blacks, from the Slave Power. As the issues of the day broadened from abolitionism to slavery's extension and then to the Slave Power, they excited growing numbers of people. And as northerners became antislavery, southern slaveholders became deeply alarmed.

Despite profound disagreement at home, events on the battlefield went well for American troops, who as in previous wars were mainly volunteers furnished by the states. General Zachary Taylor's forces attacked and occupied Monterrey, securing northeastern Mexico (see map, page 376). Polk then ordered Colonel Stephen Kearny and a small detachment to invade the remote and relatively unpopulated provinces of New Mexico and California. Taking Santa Fe without opposition, Kearny pushed into California, where he joined forces with rebellious American settlers, led by Captain John C. Frémont, and a couple of United States naval units. A quick victory was followed by reverses, but

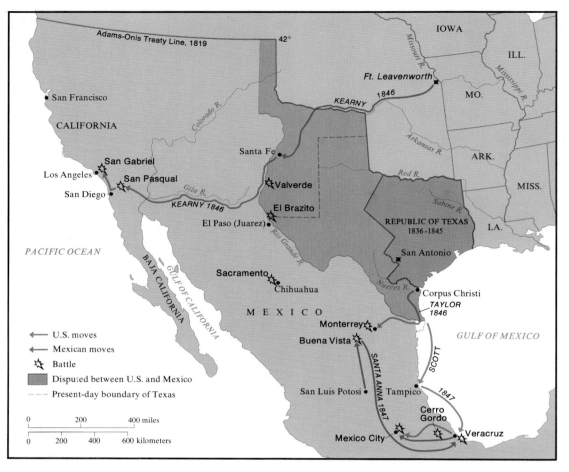

The Mexican War

American soldiers soon re-established their dominance in distant and thinly populated California.

Meanwhile, General Winfield Scott led fourteen thousand men from Veracruz, on the Gulf of Mexico, toward Mexico City. This daring invasion was the decisive campaign of the war. After a series of hard-fought battles, Scott's men captured the Mexican capital and brought the war to an end. On February 2, 1848, representatives of both countries signed the Treaty of Guadalupe Hidalgo. The United States gained California and New Mexico (including present-day Nevada, Utah, and Arizona) and recognition of the Rio Grande as the southern boundary of Texas. In return, the American government agreed to settle the claims of its citizens against Mexico and to pay Mexico a mere $15 million.

> **Treaty of Guadalupe Hidalgo**

The cost of the war included thirteen thousand Americans and fifty thousand Mexicans dead, plus Mexican-American enmity lasting into the twentieth century. But the domestic cost was even higher. As sectional distrust and bitterness grew, party unity for both Democrats and Whigs began to loosen. Although Polk sought to unify his party by renouncing a second term early in his administration and following traditional Jacksonian economic policies, he could not prevent dissension among Democrats. The territorial status of slavery was beyond solution by him or anyone else.

In the presidential election of 1848 slavery in the territories was the one overriding issue. Both parties tried to push this question into the background, but it dominated the conventions, the campaign, and the election. The Democrats tried to avoid sectional conflict by nominating General Lewis Cass of Michigan for

> **Election of 1848 and Popular Sovereignty**

General Winfield Scott, wearing a broad-brimmed hat to shield his face from the Mexican sun, reviews some of the 14,000 troops whose march to Mexico City was the decisive campaign of the war. *Decatur House, National Trust for Historical Preservation.*

president and General William Butler of Kentucky for vice president. Cass devised the idea of "popular sovereignty" for the territories—letting residents in the territories decide the question of slavery for themselves. His party's platform declared that Congress did not have the power to interfere with slavery and criticized those who pressed the question. The Whigs nominated General Zachary Taylor, who was a southern slaveholder as well as a military hero, with Congressman Millard Fillmore of New York as his running mate. Their convention similarly refused to assert that Congress had power over slavery in the territories. But the issue would not stay in the background.

Many southern Democrats distrusted Cass and eventually abandoned their party to vote for Taylor because he was a slaveholder. In the North concern over slavery led to the formation of a new party (see table, page 384). First New York Democrats devoted to the Wilmot Proviso rebelled and nominated former president Van Buren. Antislavery Whigs and former supporters of the Liberty party then joined them to organize the Free-Soil Party, with Van Buren as its candidate. This party, whose slogan was "Free soil, free speech, free labor, and free men," won almost 300,000 northern votes. Taylor polled 1,360,000 votes to Cass's

1,220,000 and won the White House, but the results were more ominous than decisive. Sectional concerns were fragmenting the parties, and the influence of antislavery forces clearly was growing. Slavery in the territories posed a dangerous threat to the party system.

The election of 1848 and the conflict over slavery in the territories shaped politics in the 1850s. At the national level, all issues would be seen though the prism of sectional conflict over slavery in the territories. The nation's uncertain attempts to deal with economic and social change would give way to more pressing questions about the nature of the Union itself. And the second party system would succumb to crisis over slavery and the future.

Territorial Problems Are Compromised but Re-emerge

The first sectional battle of the decade involved the territory of California. More than eighty thousand Americans flooded into California in 1849. With

Congress unable to agree on a formula to govern the territories, President Taylor urged these settlers to apply directly for admission to the Union. They promptly did so, submitting a proposed state constitution that did not allow for slavery. Because California's admission as a free state would upset the sectional balance of power in the Senate, southern politicians wanted to make California a slave territory or at least to extend the Missouri Compromise line west through California. Representatives from nine southern states, meeting in Nashville, asserted the South's right to part of the territory.

Sensing that the Union was in peril, the venerable Whig leader Henry Clay marshalled his energies once more. Twice before, in 1820 and 1833, the "Great Pacificator" had taken the lead in shaping sectional compromise; now he labored one last time to preserve the nation. To hushed Senate galleries Clay presented a series of compromise measures. Over the weeks that followed, Clay and Senator Stephen A. Douglas of Illinois steered their omnibus bill, or package of compromises, through debate and amendment.

The problems to be solved were thorny indeed. Would California or a part of it become a free state? How should the land acquired from Mexico be organized? Texas, which allowed slavery, claimed large portions of the new land as far west as Santa Fe, so that claim too had to be settled. And in addition to southern complaints that fugitive slaves were not being returned as the Constitution required, and northern objections to the sale of human beings in the nation's capital, the lawmakers had to deal with the most troublesome issue: conflicting theories of settlers' rights in the territories.

Clay and Douglas hoped to avoid a specific formula and preserve the ambiguity that existed about settlers' rights in the territories. Lewis Cass's idea of popular sovereignty, for example, had both an attractive ring to it and a useful vagueness. Cass had observed that Congress could stay out of the territorial wrangle. Ultimately it would have to approve statehood for a territory, but Congress should "in the meantime," Cass said, allow the people living there "to regulate their own concerns in their own way." These few words, seemingly clear, proved highly ambiguous.

When could settlers bar slavery? Southerners claimed that neither Congress nor a territorial legislature could bar slavery. Only when settlers framed a state constitution could they take that step.

Northerners, meanwhile, argued that Americans living in a territory were entitled to local self-government and thus could outlaw slavery at any time, if they allowed it at all. To avoid dissension within their party, northern and southern Democrats explained Cass's statement to their constituents in these two incompatible ways. Northern and southern Whigs, too, were divided over the territorial issue.

The cause of compromise gained a powerful supporter when Senator Daniel Webster committed all his prestige and eloquence to Clay's bill. "I wish to speak today," Webster declaimed, "not as a Massachusetts man, nor as a Northern man, but as an American. I speak today for the preservation of the Union. Hear me for my cause." Turning away from his earlier support for the Wilmot Proviso, Webster urged northerners not to "taunt or reproach" the South with antislavery measures. To southern firebrands he issued a warning that disunion could no more take place "without convulsion" than "the heavenly bodies [could] rush from their spheres, and jostle each other in the realms of space, without causing the wreck of the universe!"

Yet even Webster's influence was not enough. After months of labor, when Clay and Douglas finally brought their package to a vote, they met defeat. But the determined Douglas had not given up. With Clay sick and absent from Washington, Douglas brought the compromise measures up again, one at a time. Congress lacked a majority to approve the package, but Douglas shrewdly realized that different majorities might be created for each of the measures. Congressmen divided on sectional, not party, lines; the strategy worked; and Douglas's resourcefulness salvaged a positive result from more than eight months of congressional effort. The Compromise of 1850, as it was called, became law.

Under the terms of its various measures, California was admitted as a free state, and the Texas boundary was set at its present limits (see map). The United States paid Texas $10 million in consideration of the boundary agreement. The territories of New Mexico and Utah were organized with power to legislate on "all rightful subjects . . . consistent with the Constitution." A stronger fugitive slave law and an act to suppress the slave trade in the District of Columbia completed the compromise.

Compromise of 1850

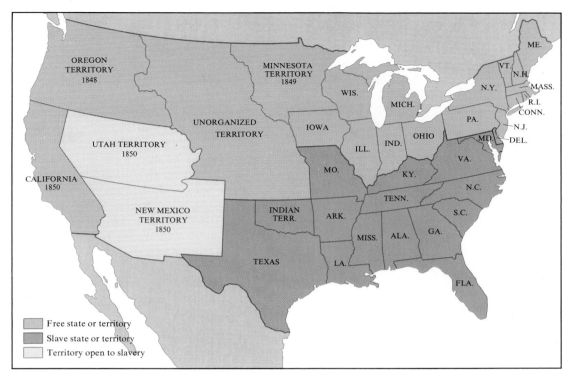

The Compromise of 1850

Jubilation greeted passage of the Compromise of 1850; in Washington, crowds celebrated the happy news. "On one glorious night," records a modern historian, "the word went abroad that it was the duty of every patriot to get drunk. Before the next morning many a citizen had proved his patriotism," and several prominent senators "were reported stricken with a variety of implausible maladies—headaches, heat prostration, or overindulgence in fruit."

In reality, there was less cause for celebration than citizens thought. Fundamentally, the Compromise of 1850 was not a settlement of sectional disputes. It was at best an artful evasion. Douglas had found a way to pass his proposals without getting northerners and southerners to come to agreement on them; neither side had given up anything. This compromise bought time for the nation, but it did not create guidelines for the settlement of future territorial questions. It merely put them off.

Furthermore, the compromise had two basic flaws. The first pertained to popular sovereignty. What were "rightful subjects of legislation, consistent with the Constitution"? During debate, south-

erners asserted that this meant there would be no prohibition of slavery during the territorial stage; northerners declared that settlers could bar slavery whenever they wished. After passage of the compromise, legislators from the two sections went home and explained the act in these different ways, as if there were two different compromises. (In fact, the compromise admitted the disagreement by providing for the appeal of a territorial legislature's action to the Supreme Court. But no such case ever arose.) Thus, in the controversy over popular sovereignty, nothing had been settled. In one politician's words, the legislators seemed to have enacted a lawsuit instead of a law.

The second flaw lay in the Fugitive Slave Act, which laid bare the anomalies of protecting slavery in a land of freedom. The new law empowered slaveowners to go into court in **Fugitive** their own states and present evi- **Slave Act** dence that a slave who owed them service had escaped. The transcript of such a proceeding, including a description of the fugitive, was to be taken as conclusive proof of a person's slave status, even in free states and

The Webb family toured the North, presenting dramatic readings of *Uncle Tom's Cabin*. Performances by the Webbs and others deepened the already powerful impact of Harriet Beecher Stowe's novel.   *Stowe-Day Foundation, Hartford, Conn.*

United States marshal and sent him to safety in Canada.

At this point a relatively unknown writer dramatized the plight of the slave in a way that captured the sympathies of millions of northerners.

> **Uncle Tom's Cabin**

Harriet Beecher Stowe, daughter of a religious New England family that had produced many prominent ministers, wrote *Uncle Tom's Cabin* out of deep moral conviction. Her book, serialized in 1851 and then published in 1852, showed how slavery brutalized the men and women who suffered under it. Stowe also portrayed slavery's evil effects on slaveholders, indicting the institution itself more harshly than the southerners caught in its web. In nine months the book sold over 300,000 copies; by mid-1853, over a million. Countless people saw *Uncle Tom's Cabin* performed as a stage play or read similar novels inspired by it. Stowe brought slavery home to many who had never before given it much thought.

The popularity of *Uncle Tom's Cabin* alarmed and appalled white southerners sensitive about slavery. In the territorial controversies, and now in popular literature, they saw threats to their way of life, a way of life based on slavery. Behind the South's aggressive claims about territorial rights lay fear—fear that if nearby areas became free soil, they would be used as bases from which to spread abolitionism into the slave states. Jefferson Davis of Mississippi voiced this concern when he wrote in 1855 that "abolitionism would gain but little in excluding slavery from the territories, if it were never to disturb that institution in the States." To defend slavery against political threats, southern leaders relied on Calhoun's territorial theories and on the dogma of states' rights and strict construction.

To protect slavery in the arena of ideas it was vital to counter indictments of the institution as a moral wrong. Accordingly proslavery theorists elaborated

> **Proslavery Theories**

numerous arguments based on partially scientific or pseudoscientific data. Southern writers or politicians readily discussed anthropological evidence for the separate origin of the races or physicians' views on the inferiority of the black body. Other proslavery spokesmen expounded the new "science" of phrenology. Its data on the external dimensions of human skulls and the volume of the cranial cavity "proved" that blacks were a separate and inferior race.

territories. Legal authorities had to decide only whether the black person brought before them was the person described, not whether he or she was indeed a slave. Fees and penalties encouraged United States marshals to assist in apprehending fugitives and discouraged citizens from harboring them. (Authorities were paid ten dollars if the alleged fugitive was turned over to the slaveowner, five dollars if he or she was not.)

Abolitionist newspapers quickly attacked the fugitive slave law as a violation of the Bill of Rights. Why were alleged fugitives denied a trial by jury before being sent into bondage? Why did suspected fugitives have no right to present evidence or cross-examine witnesses? Did not the law give authorities a financial incentive to turn prisoners over to slaveowners? These arguments convinced some northerners that free blacks could be sent into slavery, mistakenly or otherwise, with no means to defend themselves. Protest meetings were held in Massachusetts, New York, Pennsylvania, northern Ohio, northern Illinois, and elsewhere. In Boston in 1851, a mob grabbed a runaway slave from a

Chapter 13: Slavery and America's Future: The Road to War, 1845–1861

One southern sociologist, a Virginian named George Fitzhugh, focused on relations between management and labor and compared free labor unfavorably to slavery. To Fitzhugh, wage labor in northern industry was more inhumane than slavery because northern employers cared nothing about wage laborers as people. The factory owner, Fitzhugh argued, turned workers out when they grew old or sick, whereas paternalistic slaveowners cared responsibly for their aged slaves. From these points Fitzhugh drew a startling conclusion: slavery ought to be practiced in all societies, whatever their racial composition. His notions, extreme even for the South, illustrated well how southern defenses often deepened fears of the Slave Power.

Yet in private and in their hearts most southern leaders fell back on two rationales for slavery: the belief that blacks were inferior and biblical accounts of slaveholding. Among friends, Jefferson Davis ignored all the latest racist theories and reverted to the eighteenth-century argument that southerners were doing the best they could with a situation they had inherited. "Is it well to denounce an evil for which there is no cure?" he asked. On another occasion, repeating the widespread belief that living with a sizable free black population was impossible, he protested to a friend that Congress never discussed "any thing but that over which we have no control, slavery of the negro."

Davis was troubled but far from despair in 1852. He and other southerners had reason to hope that slavery would be secure and allowed to expand under the administration of a new president. Franklin Pierce, a Democrat from New Hampshire, won a smashing victory that year over the Whig presidential nominee, General Winfield Scott. Pierce's victory derived less from his strengths than from his opponents' weaknesses. The Whigs had been a congressional party, competitive with the Democrats in the states but lacking commanding presidents in an era of strong leaders like Jackson and Polk. Sectional discord was steadily splitting the party into southern and northern wings that cooperated less and less. The deaths of President Taylor (1850), Daniel Webster (1852), and Henry Clay (1852) deprived the party of the few dominant personalities it had, and no new leaders emerged to solve its problems. The Whig party in 1852 ran on little but its past reputation, and many politicians were predicting its demise.

> **Election of 1852**

But southerners were pleased that Pierce made no secret of his belief that the defense of each section's rights was essential to the nation's unity. Americans generally hoped that Pierce's firm support for the Compromise of 1850 might end sectional divisions. By comparison Scott's views on the compromise were unknown, and the Free-Soil candidate, John P. Hale of New Hampshire, openly rejected it. Thus Pierce's victory seemed to confirm most Americans' support for the compromise.

But Pierce did not seem able to avoid sectional conflict. His proposal for a transcontinental railroad ran into congressional dispute over where it should be built, North or South. His vigorous enforcement of the fugitive slave law appalled and alarmed many northerners. His attempts to acquire foreign territory stirred up more trouble. An annexation treaty with Hawaii failed because southern senators would not vote for another free state, and Pierce's efforts to annex Cuba angered antislavery northerners. After he tried to purchase Cuba from Spain in 1854, publication of a government document, the Ostend Manifesto, revealed that three administration officials had rashly talked of "wresting" Cuba from Spain. Some northerners concluded that Pierce was determined to acquire more slave territory. Then another territorial bill threw Congress and the nation into a bitter conflict that had significant results.

Territorial Problems Shatter the Party System

The new controversy began in a surprising way. Stephen A. Douglas, one of the architects of the Compromise of 1850, introduced a bill to establish the Kansas and Nebraska territories. Although Douglas had no reason to attack the compromise, which lent him fame, he did have other concerns and goals. Douglas was from Illinois, a state whose economy benefited from settlement on the Great Plains. A midwestern transcontinental railroad would accelerate this process, but a necessary precondition for such a railroad was the organization of the territory it would cross. Thus it was probably in the interest of building such a railroad that Douglas introduced a bill that inflamed sectional

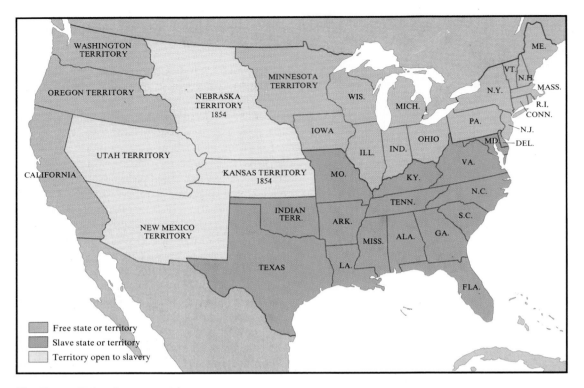

The Kansas-Nebraska Act, 1854

passions, completed the destruction of the Whig party, damaged the northern Democrats, gave birth to the Republican party, and thwarted his own ambitions for national office.

The Kansas-Nebraska bill exposed the first flaw of the Compromise of 1850—the conflicting interpretations of popular sovereignty. Douglas's bill left

> **Kansas-Nebraska Bill**
"all questions pertaining to slavery in the Territories . . . to the people residing therein," but northerners and southerners still disagreed violently over what territorial settlers could constitutionally do. Moreover, the Kansas-Nebraska bill opened another Pandora's box. The new territories lay within the Louisiana Purchase, and under the Missouri Compromise all that land from 36°30′ north to the Canadian border was off-limits to slavery. Thus, if popular sovereignty were to mean anything in Kansas or Nebraska, it had to mean that the Missouri Compromise was no longer in force and that settlers could establish slavery there.

Southern congressmen, anxious to establish the slaveholders' right to take their slaves into any territory, pressed Douglas to concede this point. They demanded an explicit repeal of the 36°30′ limitation as the price of their support. During a carriage ride with Senator Archibald Dixon of Kentucky, Douglas debated the point at length. Finally he made an impulsive decision, "By God, Sir, you are right. I will incorporate it in my bill, though I know it will raise a hell of a storm."

In Douglas's mind this change did not make his bill a proslavery measure, for he believed that conditions of climate and soil would effectively keep slavery out of Kansas and Nebraska. But the fact remained that his bill threw land open to slavery where it had been prohibited before. This fact immediately generated opposition from Free-Soilers and antislavery forces. The struggle in Congress was titanic and lasted three and one-half months. Douglas obtained the support of President Pierce, and eventually he prevailed: the bill became law in May 1854 (see map).

Unfortunately the storm—far more violent than Douglas had imagined—was just beginning. Abolitionists charged a sinister aggression by the Slave Power, and northern fears about slavery's influence deepened. Opposition to the fugitive slave law grew dramatically; between 1855 and 1859 Connecticut, Rhode Island, Massachusetts, Michigan, Maine, Ohio, and Wisconsin passed personal liberty laws. These laws interfered with the fugitive slave law by providing counsel for alleged fugitives and requiring trial by jury. They enraged southern leaders, who saw them as a refusal to honor the Compromise of 1850. Even more important, however, was the devastating impact of the Kansas-Nebraska Act on political parties.

The Kansas-Nebraska Act broke the weakened Whig party into northern and southern wings that could no longer cooperate as a national organization. One of the two great parties in the second party system was now gone. The Democrats survived, but their support in the North fell drastically in the 1854 elections. Northern Democrats lost sixty-six of the ninety-one congressional seats they had won in free states in 1852 and lost control of all but two free-state legislatures.

Moreover, anger over the territorial issue created a new political party. During debate on the Kansas-Nebraska bill, six congressmen had published an "Appeal of the Independent Democrats." Joshua Giddings, Salmon Chase, and Charles Sumner were the principal authors of this bitter protest against the Kansas-Nebraska bill. They attacked Douglas's legislation as a "gross violation of a sacred pledge" (the Missouri Compromise) and a "criminal betrayal of precious rights" that would make free territory a "dreary region of despotism." Their appeal tapped a reservoir of deep concerns in the North, concerns that Illinois's Abraham Lincoln cogently expressed.

The New Republican Party

Although he did not condemn southerners— "They are just what we would be in their situation"—Lincoln exposed the moral bankruptcy and significance of the Kansas-Nebraska Act. Denying "that there CAN be MORAL RIGHT in the enslaving of one man by another," Lincoln argued that the founding fathers had banned slavery from the Northwest Territory, avoided explicit use of the word, and treated it overall as a "cancer" that must eventually be removed. The Kansas-Nebraska Act, on the other hand, opened territory that had been closed to slavery. Rather than encouraging liberty, Douglas's bill put slavery "on the high road to extension and perpetuity," and that constituted a "moral wrong and injustice." America's future, Lin-

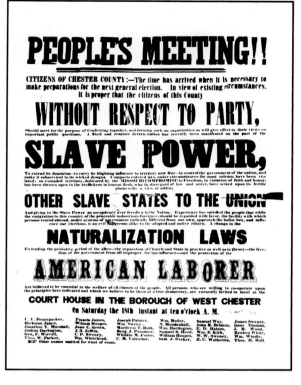

Throughout the North the Kansas-Nebraska Act kindled fires of alarm over the Slave Power's "determination . . . to extend its dominion" and "control the government of the nation." Meetings like this one in West Chester, Pennsylvania, aided the new Republican party. *American Antiquarian Society.*

coln warned, was being mortgaged to slavery, whereas the nation should "readopt the Declaration of Independence" and commit itself to freedom.

Thousands agreed. During the summer and fall of 1854, antislavery Whigs and Democrats, Free-Soilers, and other reformers throughout the Northwest met to form a new Republican party, dedicated to keeping slavery out of the territories. The Republicans' influence rapidly spread to the East, and they won a stunning victory in the 1854 elections. In the party's first appearance on the ballot, Republicans captured a majority of House seats in the North. Antislavery fears had created a new party and caused roughly a quarter of northern Democrats to desert their party.

For the first time, too, a sectional party had gained significant power in the political system. When Whigs and Democrats had competed

NEW POLITICAL PARTIES

Party	Period of Influence	Area of Influence	Outcome
Liberty party	1839–1848	North	Merged with other antislavery groups to form Free-Soil party
Free-Soil party	1848–1854	North	Merged with Republican party
Know-Nothings (American party)	1853–1856	Nationwide	Disappeared, freeing some northern voters to join Republican party
Republican party	1854–present	North (later nationwide)	Became rival of Democratic party in third party system

throughout the country, the national base of each had moderated sectional conflict. Party leaders compromised to achieve unity and subordinated sectional differences to partisan needs. But now the Whigs were gone, and politics in the 1850s would never be the same. Henceforth, Democrats would struggle to maintain a national following while the new Republican party grew rapidly in the North by addressing emotional, moral concerns.

Nor were Republicans the only new party. An anti-immigrant organization, the American party, also seemed likely for a few years to replace the Whigs. This party, popularly known as the Know-Nothings (because its members at first kept their purposes secret, answering all queries with the words "I know nothing"), exploited nativist fear of foreigners. Between 1848 and 1860, nearly 3.5 million immigrants came to the United States—proportionally the heaviest influx of foreigners in American history (see pages 324–328). The Democratic party courted these new citizens and relied on their votes in elections. But native-born Americans harbored serious misgivings about them. The temperance movement also gained new strength early in these years, promising to stamp out the evils associated with liquor and immigrants. It was in this context that the Know-Nothings became prominent, campaigning to reinforce Protestant morality and restrict voting and office holding to the native-born.

> **Know-Nothings**

> **Realignment of Political System**

> **Republican Appeals**

By the mid-1850s the American party was powerful and growing; in 1854 so many new congressmen won office with anti-immigrant as well as antislavery support that Know-Nothings could claim they outnumbered Republicans. But like the Whigs, the Know-Nothings could not keep their northern and southern wings together, and they melted away after 1856. That left the field to the Republicans, who wooed the nativists and in several states passed temperance ordinances and laws postponing suffrage for naturalized citizens (see table).

Republicans, Know-Nothings, and Democrats were all scrambling to attract former Whig voters. The demise of that party ensured a major realignment of the political system, with nearly half the old electorate up for grabs. To woo these homeless Whigs, the remaining parties stressed a variety of issues chosen to appeal for one reason or another. Immigration, temperance, homestead bills, the tariff, internal improvements—all played an important role in attracting voters during the 1850s.

The Republicans appealed strongly to groups interested in the economic development of the West. Commercial agriculture was booming in the Ohio–Mississippi–Great Lakes area, but residents of that region needed more canals, roads, and river and harbor improvements to reap the full benefit of their labors. Because credit was

Republican support for roads, canals, river and harbor improvements, and free homesteads appealed powerfully to those who were settling the thriving states of the upper Middle West. This painting by Arthur F. Tait, entitled "Arguing the Point, Settling the Presidency" (1854), captures the spirit of the times. *Copyright © 1971, The R. W. Norton Art Gallery, Shreveport, La. Used by permission.*

scarce, there was also widespread interest in a federal land-grant program: its proponents argued that western land should be made available free to those who would use it. The Whigs had favored all these things before their party collapsed, but the Democrats resolutely opposed them. Following long-standing party principles, Democratic presidents vetoed internal improvements bills and a homestead bill as late as 1859. Seizing their opportunity, the Republicans added internal improvements and land-grant planks to their platform. They also backed higher tariffs as an enticement to industrialists and businessmen, whose interest in tariffs was quickened by a panic in 1857.

Another major feature of the realigned political system was ideology, and ideological appeals had a significant impact on the sectional crisis. In the North, Republicans attracted many voters through effective use of ideology. They spoke to the image that northerners had of themselves, their society, and their future when they preached "Free Soil, Free Labor, Free Men." These phrases resonated

with traditional ideals of equality, liberty, and opportunity under self-government—the heritage of republicanism. Use of that heritage also undercut charges that the Republican party was radical and unreliable.

"Free Soil, Free Labor, Free Men" seemed to fit with a northern economy that was energetic, expanding, and prosperous. Untold thousands of farmers had moved west to establish productive farms and growing communities. Midwestern farmers were using machines that multiplied their yields. Railroads were carrying their crops to market. And industry was beginning to perform wonders of production, making available goods that had hitherto been beyond the reach of the average person. As northerners surveyed the general growth and prosperity, they thought they saw a reason for it.

The key to progress seemed, in the eyes of many, to be free labor. People believed in the dignity of labor and the incentive of opportunity. Any hardworking, virtuous person, it was thought, could

Republican Ideology

improve his condition and gain economic independence by applying himself to opportunities that the country had to offer. Republicans pointed out that the South, which relied on slave labor and had little industry, appeared backward and retrograde in comparison. Praising both laborers and opportunity, the Republicans captured much of the spirit of the age in the North.

In the tradition of republicanism the virtuous common man was the backbone of the country. Republicans pointed to Abraham Lincoln as a contemporary symbol of that tradition, a person of humble origins who had risen to be a successful lawyer and political leader. They portrayed their party as the guardian of economic opportunity, fighting to ensure that individuals had a chance to work, acquire land, and attain success. In the words of an Iowa Republican, the United States was thriving because its "door is thrown open to all, and even the poorest and humblest in the land, may, by industry and application, gain a position which will entitle him to the respect and confidence of his fellow-men."

Thus the Republican party attracted support from a variety of sources. Opposition to the extension of slavery had brought the party together, but party members carefully broadened their appeal by adopting the causes of other groups. They were wise to do so. As the newspaper editor Horace Greeley wrote in 1856, "It is beaten into my bones that the American people are not yet anti-slavery." Four years later Greeley again judged that "an Anti-Slavery man *per se* cannot be elected." But, he added, "a Tariff, River-and-Harbor, Pacific Railroad, Free Homestead man, *may* succeed *although* he is Anti-Slavery." As these elements joined the Republican party, they also learned more about the dangers of slavery, and thus the process of party building deepened the sectional conflict.

A similar process was under way in the South. The disintegration of the Whig party had left many southerners at loose ends politically, including a good number of wealthy plant-

Southern Democrats

ers, small-town businessmen, and slaveholders. Some of these people gravitated to the American party, but not for long. In the increasingly tense atmosphere of sectional crisis, they were highly susceptible to strong states' rights positions, which provided a handy defense for slavery. Democratic

leaders emphasized such appeals during the 1850s and managed to convert most of the formerly Whig slaveholders. Democrats spoke to the class interests of slaveholders, and the slaveholders responded.

Most Democrats south of the Mason-Dixon line, however, were not slaveholders. Since Andrew Jackson's day, small farmers had been the heart of the Democratic party. Democratic politicians, though often slaveowners themselves, had lauded the common man and argued that their policies advanced his interests. According to the southern version of republicanism, white citizens in a slave society enjoyed liberty and social equality because the black race was enslaved. Slavery supposedly prevented the evil of aristocracy by making all white men equal. As Jefferson Davis put it in 1851, other societies undermined the status of the common white because in them social distinctions were drawn "by property, between the rich and the poor." In the South, however, slavery elevated every white person's status and allowed the non-slaveholder to "*stand upon the broad level of equality with the rich man.*" To retain the support of ordinary whites, southern Democrats emphasized this argument and appealed to racism. The issue in the sectional crisis, they warned, was "shall negroes govern white men, or white men govern negroes?"

Southern leaders also portrayed sectional controversies as matters of injustice and insult to all southerners. The rights of all southern whites, they argued, were in jeopardy because antislavery and Free-Soil forces were destroying constitutional government. Northern agitators, by attacking an institution protected in the Constitution, were damaging rights precious to southerners. The stable, well-ordered South was the true defender of constitutional principles, but runaway change in the North was threatening to subvert the nation.

These arguments had their effect, and racial fears and traditional political loyalties helped keep the political alliance between yeoman farmers and planters intact through the 1850s. No viable party emerged in the South to replace the Whigs. The result was a one-party system there that emphasized sectional issues. No one raised potential conflicts of interest between slaveholders and non-slaveholders. Instead, in the South as in the North, political realignment sharpened sectional divisions.

In both sections political leaders argued that opportunity was threatened by racial change or by slavery. The *Montgomery* (Alabama) *Mail* warned southern whites that the Republicans intended "to free the negroes and force amalgamation between them and the children of the poor men of the South. The rich will be able to keep out of the way of the contamination." Republicans warned northern workers that if slavery entered the territories, the great reservoir of opportunity for decent people without means would be poisoned. The North's free labor system had to be extended to the territories if coming generations were to prosper. These charges aroused fears and anxieties in both sections.

But events in Kansas, coming like repeated hammer blows, did even more to deepen the conflict. Put into practice, the Kansas-Nebraska Act spawned hatreds and violence, for among the settlers in the territory were claim jumpers and partisans in the sectional struggle. Abolitionists and religious groups sent armed, Free-Soil settlers to make Kansas free; southerners sent their reinforcements to establish slavery and prevent "northern hordes" from stealing Kansas away. Clashes between the two groups caused bloodshed, and soon the whole nation was talking about "Bleeding Kansas."

Politics in the territory resembled war more than democracy. When elections for a territorial legislature were held in 1855, thousands of proslavery

Bleeding Kansas Missourians invaded the polls and ran up a large but unlawful majority for slavery candidates. The legislature that resulted promptly legalized slavery, and in response Free-Soilers called an unauthorized convention and created their own government and constitution. A proslavery posse sent to arrest the Free-Soil leaders sacked the town of Lawrence; in revenge, John Brown, an antislavery zealot who saw himself as God's instrument to destroy slavery, murdered five proslavery settlers. Soon armed bands of guerrillas roamed the state, battling over land claims as well as slavery.

The passion generated by this conflict erupted in the chamber of the United States Senate in May 1856, when Charles Sumner of Massachusetts denounced "the Crime against Kansas." Radical in his antislavery views, Sumner bitterly assailed the president, the South, and Senator Andrew P. Butler of South Carolina. Soon thereafter Butler's nephew, Representative Preston Brooks, approached Sumner at the latter's Senate desk, raised his arm, and began to beat Sumner over the head with a cane.

The earliest known photograph of John Brown, probably taken in 1846 in Massachusetts, shows him pledging his devotion to an unidentified flag, possibly an abolitionist banner. Already Brown was aiding runaway slaves and pondering ways to strike at slavery. *Ohio Historical Society.*

Trapped behind his desk, which was screwed to the floor, Sumner tried to rise, eventually wrenching the desk free before he collapsed, bloody upon the floor. Violence had invaded the halls of Congress. Shocked northerners recoiled from what they saw as another southern assault on free speech and the South's readiness to use violence to have its way. William Cullen Bryant, editor of the *New York Evening Post* asked, "Has it come to this, that we must speak with bated breath in the presence of our southern masters?" As if in reply, the *Richmond Enquirer* denounced "vulgar Abolitionists in the Senate" who "have been suffered to run too long without collars. They must be lashed into submission." Popular opinion in Massachusetts strongly supported Sumner, while South Carolina voters reelected Brooks and sent him dozens of new canes. The country was becoming polarized.

The election of 1856 showed how far the polarization had gone. When Democrats met to select a nominee, they shied away from prominent leaders whose views on the territories were well known. Instead they chose James Buchanan of Pennsylvania, whose chief virtue was that he had been in Britain for four years, serving as ambassador, and thus had not been involved in territorial controversies. This anonymity and superior party organization helped Buchanan win 1.8 million votes and the election, but he owed his victory to southern support. Eleven of sixteen free states voted against him, and Democrats did not regain power in those states for decades. The Republican candidate, John C. Frémont, won those eleven free states and 1.3 million votes; Republicans had become the dominant party in the North. The Know-Nothing candidate, Millard Fillmore, won almost 1 million votes, but this election was his party's last hurrah. The future battle was between a sectional Republican party and an increasingly divided Democratic party.

Slavery and the Nation's Future

For years the issue of slavery in the territories had convulsed Congress, and for years the members of Congress had tried to settle the issue with vague formulas. In 1857 a different branch of government stepped onto the scene with a different approach. The Supreme Court addressed this emotion-charged subject and attempted to lay controversy to rest with a definitive verdict.

A Missouri slave named Dred Scott had sued his owner for his freedom. Dred Scott based his suit on the fact that his former owner, an army surgeon, had taken him for several years into Illinois, a free state, and into the Wisconsin Territory, from which slavery had been barred by the Missouri Compromise. Scott first won and then lost his case as it moved on appeal through the state courts, into the federal system, and finally after eleven years to the Supreme Court.

Dred Scott Case

Normally this was the type of case that the Supreme Court avoided. Its justices were reluctant, as a rule, to inject themselves into political battles, and it seemed likely that the Court would stay out of this one. An 1851 decision had declared that state courts had the last word in determining the status of Negroes who lived within their jurisdiction. The Supreme Court had only to follow this precedent to avoid ruling on substantive, and very controversial, matters.

Was a black person like Dred Scott a citizen and eligible to sue? Had residence in free territory made him free? Did Congress have the power to prohibit slavery in a territory or to delegate that power to a territorial legislature? All these issues were raised by the case, and behind the last question lay all the disagreement that Lewis Cass, Henry Clay, Stephen Douglas, and others had for years tried to obscure.

Initially it appeared that the Supreme Court would dispose of *Dred Scott* v. *Sanford* by following the 1851 precedent. At its conference the Court even assigned one justice the task of writing such an opinion. Then the Court decided to rule on the Missouri Compromise after all. This change occurred for a number of reasons. Two northerners on the Court indicated that they would dissent from the planned ruling and argue for Scott's freedom and for the constitutionality of the Missouri Compromise. Their decision emboldened southerners on the Court, who on their own were growing anxious to declare the 1820 compromise unconstitutional. Southern sympathizers in Washington were pressing for a proslavery verdict; moreover, many justices felt they should try to resolve an issue whose uncertainties had caused so much strife.

Thus on March 6, 1857, Chief Justice Roger B. Taney delivered the majority opinion of a divided Court. Taney declared that Scott was not a citizen of either the United States or Missouri; that residence in free territory did not make Scott free; and that Congress had no power to bar slavery from a territory, as it had done in the Missouri Compromise. Not only did the decision overturn a sectional compromise that had been venerated for years, it also said that the basic ideas of the Wilmot Proviso, and probably popular sovereignty, were invalid.

The Slave Power seemed to have gained vital constitutional ground. Black Americans were especially dismayed, for Taney's decision also declared that at the nation's founding blacks had been regarded "as beings of an inferior order" with "no rights which the white man was bound to respect." The founding fathers, he asserted, had never intended for black people to be citizens. Though historically erroneous (black people had been citizens in several of the original states), the Dred Scott decision seemed to shut the door permanently on black people's hopes for justice and equal rights.

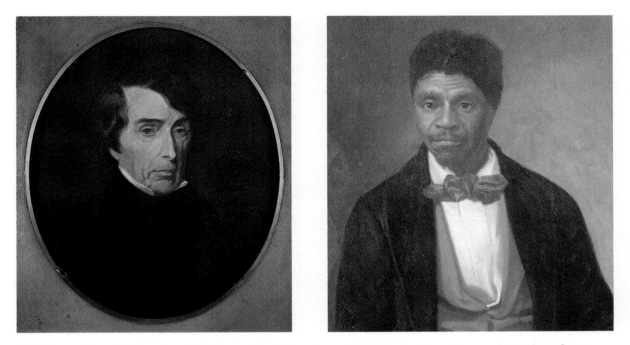

Dred Scott, a slave who brought suit in Missouri for his freedom, and Chief Justice Roger Taney, a descendant of Maryland's slaveholding elite, were principal figures in the most controversial Supreme Court decision of the century. *Roger Taney: Maryland Historical Society; Dred Scott: Missouri Historical Society.*

Northern whites who rejected the decision's content also noted that the circumstances surrounding it aroused sectional suspicions. Five of the nine justices were southern; only one northerner had agreed with their united stand. Three northern justices actively dissented or refused to concur in crucial parts of the decision. President Buchanan, who supported southern positions, was known to have influence with Justice Robert Grier of Pennsylvania, the one northerner who supported Taney's opinion. In fact, Buchanan had secretly brought improper but effective influence to bear.

A storm of angry reaction broke in the North. The decision alarmed a wide variety of northerners—abolitionists, would-be settlers in the West, and those who hated black people but feared the influence of the South. Every charge against the aggressive Slave Power seemed now to be confirmed. "There is such a thing as THE SLAVE POWER," warned the *Cincinnati Daily Commercial.* "It has marched over and annihilated the boundaries of the states. We are now one great homogenous slaveholding community." And the *Cincinnati Freeman* asked, "What security have the Germans and the Irish that their children will not,

within a hundred years, be reduced to slavery in this land of their adoption?" Echoed the *Atlantic Monthly,* "Where will it end? Is the success of this conspiracy to be final and eternal?" The poet James Russell Lowell both stimulated and expressed the anxieties of poor northern whites when he had his Yankee narrator, Ezekiel Biglow, say,

> Wy, it's just ez clear ez figgers,
>   Clear ez one an' one make two,
> Chaps thet make black slaves o' niggers,
>   Want to make wite slaves o' you.

Republican politicians capitalized on these fears, building their coalition of abolitionists, who opposed slavery on moral grounds, and other (even racist) northerners, who feared that slavery jeopardized their interests. Abraham Lincoln stressed that the territorial question affected every citizen. "The whole nation," he declared as early as 1854, "is interested that the best use shall be made of these Territories. We want them for homes of free white people. This they cannot be, to any considerable extent, if slavery shall be planted within

Abraham Lincoln on the Slave Power

them." The territories must be reserved, he insisted, "as an outlet for *free white people everywhere*" so immigrants could come to America and "find new homes and better their condition in life."

More importantly, Lincoln warned of slavery's increasing control over the nation. In language of biblical majesty, he painted prospects that chilled thousands of voters and asked what kind of nation America was becoming. The founding fathers, Lincoln insisted, had created a government dedicated to freedom. To be sure, they had admitted slavery's existence, but "this Government has endured eighty-two years," he argued in 1858, "because, during all that time, until the introduction of the Nebraska Bill, the public mind did rest . . . in the belief that slavery was in course of ultimate extinction." After the Dred Scott decision it was clear that slavery's advocates, including highly placed government officials, were trying to "push it forward, till it shall become lawful in *all* the states . . . *North* as well as *South*."

Lincoln charged that the next step in the unfolding Slave Power conspiracy would be a Supreme Court decision "declaring that the Constitution does not permit a State to exclude slavery from its limits. . . . We shall lie down pleasantly, dreaming that the people of Missouri are on the verge of making their State free; and we shall awake to the reality instead, that the Supreme Court has made Illinois a slave State." This charge was not mere imagination, for cases soon were in the courts challenging state laws that gave freedom to slaves brought within their borders.

Lincoln's most eloquent statement against the Slave Power was his famous "House Divided" speech. In it Lincoln declared: "I do not expect the Union to be dissolved—I do not expect the House to fall—but I do expect it to cease to be divided. It will become all one thing or all the other. Either the opponents of slavery will arrest the further spread of it, and place it where the public mind shall rest in the belief that it is in the course of ultimate extinction; or its advocates will push it forward, till it shall become alike lawful in all the States, old as well as new, North as well as South." Lincoln warned repeatedly that the latter possibility was well on the way to realization, and events convinced countless northerners that slaveholders were close to their goal of making slavery a national institution.

Politically, the force of Republican arguments off-set the difficulties that the Dred Scott decision posed for party leaders. By endorsing southern constitutional theories, the Court had invalidated the central position of the Republican party: no extension of slavery. Republicans could only repudiate the decision, appealing to a "higher law," or hope to change the personnel of the Court. They did both and probably gained politically as public fear of the Slave Power increased.

For northern Democrats like Stephen Douglas, the Court's decision posed an awful dilemma. Northerners were alarmed by the prospect that the territories would be opened to slavery. To retain support in the North, therefore, Douglas had to find some way to hedge, to reassure voters. Yet he had to do so without alienating southern Democrats. Douglas's task was problematic even at best; given the emotions of the time, it proved impossible.

Douglas chose to stand by his principle of popular sovereignty, which encountered a second test in Kansas in 1857. There, after Free-Soil settlers boycotted an election, proslavery forces met at Lecompton and wrote a constitution that permitted slavery. New elections to the territorial legislature, however, returned an antislavery majority, and the legislature promptly called for a popular vote on the new constitution, which was defeated by more than ten thousand votes. The evidence was overwhelming that Kansans did not want slavery, yet President Buchanan tried to force the Lecompton Constitution through Congress.

Debates on the Lecompton Constitution underlined the fact that southerners and the Buchanan administration were demanding a proslavery result, contrary to the desires of the people of Kansas. Never had the Slave Power's influence over the government seemed more blatant. Breaking with the administration, Douglas threw his weight against a document the people had rejected. He gauged their feelings correctly, for in 1858 Kansas voters rejected the constitution a third time. But his action infuriated southern Democrats. After the Dred Scott decision, southerners like Senator Albert G. Brown of Mississippi believed that slavery was *protected* in the territories. "The Constitution as expounded by the Supreme Court awards it. We demand it; we mean to have it."

In his well-publicized debates with Abraham Lincoln, his challenger for the Illinois Senate seat in 1858, Douglas further alienated the southern wing of his party. Speaking at Freeport, Illinois, he

Stephen Douglas Proposes the Freeport Doctrine

attempted to revive the notion of popular sovereignty with some tortured extensions of his old arguments. Asserting that the Supreme Court had not ruled on the powers of a *territorial* legislature, Douglas claimed that a territorial legislature could bar slavery either by passing a law against it or by doing nothing. Without the patrol laws and police regulations that support slavery, he reasoned, the institution could not exist. This argument, called the Freeport Doctrine, temporarily shored up Douglas's crumbling position in the North. But it gave southern Democrats further evidence that Douglas was unreliable, and many turned viciously against him. Some, like William L. Yancey of Alabama, studied the trend in northern opinion and concluded that southern rights would be safe only in a separate nation.

A growing number of slaveholders were deciding that slavery could not be safe within the Union. Such concern was not new. As early as 1838, the Louisiana planter Bennet Barrow had written in his diary, "Northern States meddling with slavery . . . openly speaking of the sin of Slavery in the southern states . . . must eventually cause a separation of the Union." And in 1856, a calmer, more polished Georgian named Charles Colcock Jones, Jr., rejoiced at the Democrat James Buchanan's defeat of Republican John C. Frémont for the presidency. The result guaranteed four more years of peace and prosperity, wrote Jones, but "beyond that period . . . we scarce dare expect a continuance of our present relations." Increasingly slaveowners agreed with Jones and Barrow.

The immediate consequence for politics, however, was the likelihood of division in the Democratic party. Northern Democrats could not support the territorial protection for slavery that southern Democrats insisted was their constitutional right. Thus the territories continued to generate wider conflict, even though the issue had little immediate, practical significance. In territories outside Kansas the number of settlers was small, and everywhere the number of blacks was negligible—less than 1 percent of the population in Kansas and New Mexico. By 1858 even Jefferson Davis had given up on agricultural development in the Southwest and admitted his uncertainty that slavery could succeed in Kansas. Nevertheless, men like Davis and Douglas spent many hours attacking each other on the floor

of the Senate. And the general public in both North and South moved from anxiety to alarm and anger. The situation had become explosive.

The Breakup of the Union

One year before the 1860 presidential election, violence inflamed passions further when John Brown led a small band of whites and blacks in an attack on Harpers Ferry, Virginia. Hoping to trigger a slave rebellion, Brown failed miserably and was quickly captured, tried, and executed. Yet his attempted insurrection struck fear into the South. Then it came to light that Brown had financial backing from several prominent abolitionists, and northern intellectuals such as Emerson and Thoreau praised him as a hero and a martyr. These disclosures and northern praise of Brown multiplied southerners' fears and anger many times over. The unity of the nation was now in peril.

Many observers feared that the election of 1860 would decide the fate of the Union. Divisions in the Democratic party did nothing to reassure them. For several years, the Democratic party had been the only remaining organization that was truly national in scope. Even religious denominations had split into northern and southern wings during the 1840s and 1850s. "One after another," wrote a Mississippi newspaper editor, "the links which have bound the North and South together, have been severed . . . [but] the Democratic party looms gradually up, its nationality intact, and waves the olive branch over the troubled waters of politics." At its 1860 convention, however, the Democratic party broke in two.

Stephen A. Douglas wanted the party's presidential nomination, but he could not afford to alienate northern opinion by accepting the southern position on the territories.

Splintering of the Democratic Party

Southern Democrats like William L. Yancey, on the other hand, were determined to have their rights—as Roger Taney had defined them—recognized, and they moved to block Douglas's nomination. When Douglas nevertheless marshalled a majority for his version of the platform, delegates from the five Gulf states plus South Carolina, Georgia, and Arkansas walked out of the convention hall in Charleston. Efforts at com-

These soldiers, photographed in 1859, were helping the Federal government protect slavery. The Richmond Grays, a militia company in the 1st Regiment, Virginia Volunteers, helped suppress John Brown's raid. Eighteen months later many of these men were wearing gray for the Confederacy. *The Valentine Museum.*

promise failed, so the Democrats presented two nominees: Douglas for the northern wing, Vice President John C. Breckinridge of Kentucky for the southern. The Republicans nominated Abraham Lincoln. A Constitutional Union party, formed to preserve the nation but strong only in the Upper South, nominated John Bell of Tennessee.

In the ensuing campaign three of the candidates stressed their support for the Union. Bell's only issue was the need to preserve the Union intact. Douglas clearly preferred saving the Union to endangering it, and Breckinridge quickly backed away from any appearance of extremism. His supporters in several states declared that he was not a threat to the Union. Then the *New Orleans Bee* charged that every disunionist in the land was enthusiastic for Breckinridge, and a Texas paper made an earthy reference to his association with radicals: "Mr. Breckinridge claims that he isn't a disunionist. An animal not willing to pass for a pig shouldn't stay in the stye." Frightened by such criticism, Breckinridge went even further to disavow secession. He altered his plan to do no speaking during the campaign and delivered one address in which he flatly denied that his aim was secession. Thereafter his supporters stressed his loyalty and even went so far as to ridicule the possibility of secession in case of a Republican victory. Lincoln and the Republicans denied any intention of interfering with slavery in the states where it existed but stood firm against any extension of slavery into the territories.

The results of the balloting were sectional in character, with Lincoln the winner but with Douglas, Breckinridge, and Bell together receiving most of the votes. Douglas had broad-based support but won few states; Breckinridge carried nine southern states, with his strength concentrated in the Deep South; Bell won pluralities in Virginia, Kentucky, and Tennessee. Lincoln prevailed in the North, but in the states that ultimately remained loyal to the Union he won only a plurality, not a majority (see table, page 394). Lincoln's victory was won in the electoral college.

> **Election of 1860**

Given the heterogeneous nature of Republican voters, it is likely that many of them did not view the issue of slavery in the territories as paramount. But opposition to slavery's extension was the core issue of the Republican party, and Lincoln's alarm over slavery's growing power in the nation was genuine. The slavery issue would not go away. While abolitionists and Free-Soilers in the North worked to keep the Republicans from compromising on their territorial stand, proslavery advocates and secessionists whipped up public opinion in the South and shrewdly manipulated state conventions.

Chapter 13: Slavery and America's Future: The Road to War, 1845–1861

During the 1860 presidential campaign these framed pictures of Abraham Lincoln and Stephen Douglas—widely recognized as rivals since their 1858 debates—were distributed by their supporters. *Museum of American Political Life, West Hartford, Conn. Photo by Sally Andersen-Bruce.*

Lincoln made the crucial decision not to soften his party's position on the territories. He wrote of the necessity of maintaining the bond of faith between voter and candidate, of declining to set "the minority over the majority." But Lincoln's party had not won a majority of votes. His refusal to compromise probably derived both from his convictions and his concern for the unity of the Republican party. Although many conservative Republicans—eastern businessmen and former Whigs who did not feel strongly about slavery—hoped for a compromise, the original and strongest Republicans—antislavery voters and "conscience Whigs"—would not abandon free soil. Lincoln chose to preserve the unity of his party and to take a stand against slavery.

Southern leaders in the Senate were willing, conditionally, to accept a compromise formula drawn up by Senator John J. Crittenden of Kentucky. Crittenden, hoping to don the mantle of Henry Clay and avert disunion, had suggested that the two sections divide the territories between them at 36°30′. But the southerners would agree to this *only* if the Republicans did too, for they wanted no less and knew that extremists in the South would demand much more. When Lincoln ruled out concessions on the territorial issue, Crittenden's peacemaking effort collapsed. Virginians called for a special convention in Washington, to which several states sent representatives. But this gathering, too, failed to find a suitable formula or to reach unanimity on disputed questions.

Political leaders in the North and the South had communicated clearly with each other about the Crittenden proposal, but in another sense they misjudged each other. As the historian David Potter has shown, Lincoln and other prominent Republicans believed that southerners were bluffing when they threatened secession; they expected a pro-Union majority in the South to assert itself. Therefore Lincoln determined not to yield to threats but to call the southerners' bluff. On their side, moderate southern leaders had become convinced, with more accuracy, that northern leaders were not taking them seriously and that a posture of strength was necessary to win respect for their position. "To rally the men of the North, who would preserve the government as our fathers found it, we . . . should offer no doubtful or divided front," wrote Jefferson Davis. Thus southern leaders who hoped to preserve the Union did not offer compromise, for fear of inviting aggression. Nor did northern leaders who loved the Union, believing compromise would be unnecessary and unwise. With such attitudes controlling leaders' actions, the prospects for a solution were dim.

Meanwhile the Union was being destroyed. On December 20, 1860, South Carolina passed an ordinance of secession amid jubilation and cheering. This step marked the inauguration of a strategy

The Breakup of the Union

▶

PRESIDENTIAL VOTE IN 1860		
	Lincoln	Other Candidates
Entire United States	1,866,452	2,815,617
North plus border and southern states that rejected secession prior to war[1]	1,866,452	2,421,752
North plus border states that fought for union[2]	1,864,523	1,960,842

Note the large vote for other candidates in the righthand column.
[1] Kentucky, Missouri, Maryland, Delaware, Virginia, North Carolina, Tennessee, Arkansas
[2] Kentucky, Missouri, Maryland, Delaware

Source: From David Potter, Lincoln and His Party in the Secession Crisis. *Copyright 1942, 1967 by Yale University Press. Reprinted by permission.*

> **Secession of South Carolina**

known as separate-state secession. Foes of the Union, knowing the difficulty of persuading all the southern states to challenge the federal government simultaneously, had concentrated their hopes on the most extreme proslavery state. With South Carolina out of the Union, they hoped other states would follow and build momentum toward disunion.

The strategy proved effective. By reclaiming its independence, South Carolina had raised the stakes in the sectional confrontation. No longer was secession an unthinkable step; the Union was broken. Extremists now argued that other states should secede to support South Carolina and that those who favored compromise could make a better deal outside the Union than in it. Moderates found it difficult to dismiss such arguments, since most of them—even those who felt deep affection for the Union—were committed to defending southern rights and the southern way of life.

In these circumstances, southern extremists soon got their way. Overwhelming their opposition, they quickly called conventions and passed secession ordinances in six other states: Mississippi, Florida, Alabama, Georgia, Louisiana, and Texas. By February 1861 these states had joined with South Carolina to form a new government in Montgomery, Alabama: the Confederate States of America. Choosing Jefferson Davis as their president, they began to function independently of the United States.

> **Confederate States of America**

Yet this apparent unanimity of action was deceiving. Confused and dissatisfied with the alternatives, many voters who had cast a ballot for president stayed home rather than vote for delegates who would consider secession. In some conventions the vote to secede had been close, the balance tipped by the overrepresentation of plantation districts. Furthermore, the conventions were noticeably reluctant to seek ratification of their acts by the people. Four states in the Upper South—Virginia, North Carolina, Tennessee, and Arkansas—flatly rejected secession and did not join the Confederacy until after the fighting had started. In Kentucky and Missouri popular sentiment was too divided for decisive action; these slave states remained under Union control, along with Maryland and Delaware (see map).

Misgivings about secession were not surprising, since it posed new and troubling issues for southerners, not the least of them the possibility of war and the question of who would be sacrificed. A careful look at election returns indicates that slaveholders and nonslaveholders were beginning to part company politically. Heavily slaveholding counties gave strong support to secession. But nonslaveholding areas that had been willing to support Breckinridge proved far less willing to support secession. Many counties with few slaves took an antisecession position or were staunchly Unionist. Large numbers of yeomen also sat out the election. In other words, nonslaveholders were beginning to consider their class interests, as planters had been doing for some time. With the threat of war on the

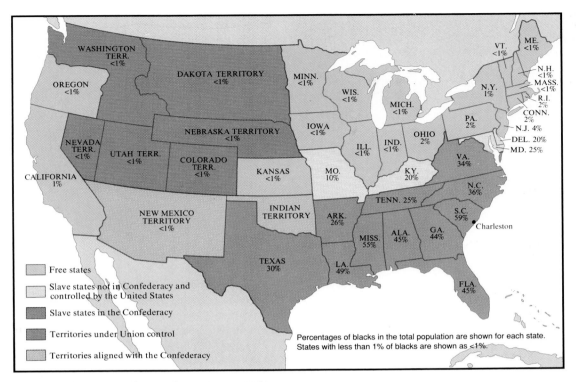

The Divided Nation—Slave and Free Areas, 1861

Legend:
- Free states
- Slave states not in Confederacy and controlled by the United States
- Slave states in the Confederacy
- Territories under Union control
- Territories aligned with the Confederacy

Percentages of blacks in the total population are shown for each state. States with less than 1% of blacks are shown as <1%.

horizon, nonslaveholders began to ask how far they would go to support slavery and slaveowners.

Some opposition to secession was fervently pro-Union, as is apparent in the comment of a northern Alabama delegate after his convention had approved secession: "Here I set & from my window see the nasty little thing flaunting in the breeze which has taken the place of that glorious banner which has been the pride of millions of Americans and the boast of freemen the wide world over." Such sentiments presented problems for the Confederacy, though they were not sufficiently developed to prevent secession.

The dilemma facing President Lincoln on inauguration day in March 1861 was how to maintain the authority of the federal government without provoking war in the states that had left the Union. He decided to proceed cautiously; by holding onto federal fortifications, he reasoned, he could assert federal sovereignty while waiting for a restoration of relations. But Jefferson Davis, who could not claim to lead a sovereign nation if its ports and military facilities were under foreign control, would not cooperate. A collision was inevitable.

It came in the early morning hours of April 12, 1861, at Fort Sumter in Charleston harbor. A federal garrison there was running low on food.

Attack on Fort Sumter

Lincoln notified the South Carolinians that he was sending a ship to resupply the fort. For the Montgomery government, the alternatives were to attack the fort or to acquiesce in Lincoln's authority. Accordingly, orders were sent to obtain surrender or attack the fort. Under heavy bombardment for two days, the federal garrison finally surrendered. Confederates then permitted the soldiers, none of whom had been killed, to sail away on unarmed vessels while the residents of Charleston celebrated. The bloodiest war in America's history thus began in a deceptively gala spirit.

Throughout the 1840s and 1850s many able leaders had worked diligently to avert this outcome. North and South, most had hoped to keep the nation together. As late as 1858 even Jefferson Davis had declared, "This great country will continue united." He had explained sincerely that the United States "is my country and to the innermost fibers of my heart I love it all, and every part." Secession

The Breakup of the Union

▶ 395

The tracks of shells illuminate the night sky as Fort Sumter undergoes bombardment by Confederate batteries on April 12, 1861. The nation's bloodiest war had begun. *Library of Congress.*

dismayed northern editors and voters, but it also plunged some planters into depression. Paul Cameron, the largest slaveowner in North Carolina, confessed that he was "very unhappy. I love the Union." Why, then, had the war occurred? Why had all the efforts to prevent it failed?

Slavery was an issue that could not be compromised. The conflict over slavery was fundamental and beyond adjustment. Too many powerful emotions were engaged in attacking or defending it. Too many important interests and principles were involved in maintaining or destroying it. It was deeply entwined with almost every major policy question of the present and the future. Ultimately each section regarded slavery as too important to ignore.

Even after extreme views were put aside, the North and the South had fundamentally different attitudes toward the institution. The logic of Republican ideology tended in the direction of abolishing slavery, though Republicans denied any such intention. Similarly, the logic of arguments by southern leaders led toward establishing slavery everywhere, though southern leaders denied that they sought any such thing. Lincoln put the problem succinctly. Soon after the 1860 election he assured his old friend Alexander Stephens of Georgia that the Re-

publican party would not attack slavery in the states where it existed. But Lincoln continued, "You think slavery is *right* and ought to be expanded; while we think it is *wrong* and ought to be restricted. That I suppose is the rub."

Fundamental disagreements have not always led to war. A nation may face unresolvable issues yet manage to get past them. New events can capture people's attention; time can alter interests and attitudes, if in the intervening years conflict is contained or restricted. That is precisely what America's compromisers sought to achieve. They tried to soothe passions and buy time for the nation, to avoid a conflict that could not be settled and conserve the many areas of consensus among Americans. Their efforts were well intentioned and patriotic, but they were doomed to failure.

The issue of slavery in the territories made conflict impossible to avoid. Territorial expansion generated disputes so frequently that the nation never gained a breathing space. And as the conflict recurred it deepened its influence on policy and its effect on the government. Every southern victory increased fear of the Slave Power, and each increase in Free-Soil sentiment made alarmed slaveholders more insistent in their demands. The slavery issue cast dark clouds over the future. Even

Chapter 13: Slavery and America's Future: The Road to War, 1845–1861

those opposed to war could offer no way to avoid it.

In the profoundest sense, slavery was tied up with the war. Concerns about slavery had driven all the other conflicts, but the fighting began with this, its central issue, shrouded in confusion. How would the Civil War affect slavery, its place in the law, and black people's place in society? The answers to those questions, and the degree to which answers were sought, would be of fateful import.

Suggestions for Further Reading

Politics: General

Thomas B. Alexander, *Sectional Stress and Party Strength* (1967); Maurice G. Baxter, *One and Inseparable: Daniel Webster and the Union* (1984); Paul Bergeron, *The Presidency of James K. Polk* (1987); Ray Allen Billington, *The Protestant Crusade, 1800–1860* (1938 and 1964); Frederick J. Blue, *The Free Soilers: Third Party Politics, 1848–1854* (1973); Stanley W. Campbell, *The Slave Catchers* (1968); Avery O. Craven, *The Coming of the Civil War* (1942); Don E. Fehrenbacher, *The Dred Scott Case* (1978); George M. Fredrickson, *The Black Image in the White Mind* (1971); Holman Hamilton, *Prologue to Conflict: The Crisis and Compromise of 1850* (1964); Michael F. Holt, *The Political Crisis of the 1850s* (1978); James M. McPherson, *Battle Cry of Freedom* (1988); Stephen E. Maizlish and John J. Kushma, eds., *Essays on American Antebellum Politics, 1840–1860* (1982); Chaplain W. Morrison, *Democratic Politics and Sectionalism: The Wilmot Proviso Controversy* (1967); Paul D. Nagle, *One Nation Indivisible* (1964); Roy F. Nichols, *The Disruption of American Democracy* (1948); Russell B. Nye, *Fettered Freedom* (1949); Merrill D. Peterson, *The Great Triumvirate: Webster, Clay, and Calhoun* (1987); David M. Potter, *The Impending Crisis, 1848–1861* (1976); James A. Rawley, *Race and Politics* (1969); Charles G. Sellers, *James K. Polk: Continentalist, 1843–1846* (1966); Joel H. Silbey, *The Transformation of American Politics, 1840–1960* (1967); Elbert B. Smith, *The Presidency of James Buchanan* (1975); Kenneth M. Stampp, *And the War Came* (1950); Gerald W. Wolff, *The Kansas-Nebraska Bill* (1977).

The South and Slavery

William L. Barney, *The Secessionist Impulse* (1974); Steven A. Channing, *A Crisis of Fear: Secession in South Carolina* (1970); William J. Cooper, Jr., *The South and the Politics of Slavery, 1828–1856* (1978); Daniel W. Crofts, *Reluctant Confederates: Upper South Unionists in the Secession Crisis* (1989); Drew G. Faust, *The Ideology of Slavery* (1981); Drew G. Faust, *A Sacred Circle: The Dilemma of the Intellectual in the Old South* (1978); Eugene D. Genovese, *The World the Slaveholders Made* (1969); Eugene D. Genovese, *The Political Economy of Slavery* (1967); William Sumner Jenkins, *Pro-Slavery Thought in the Old South* (1935); Michael P. Johnson, *Toward a Patriarchal Republic: The Secession of Georgia* (1977); John Niven, *John C. Calhoun and the Price of Union* (1988); David M. Potter, *The South and the Sectional Conflict* (1968); Thomas E. Schott, *Alexander H. Stephens of Georgia* (1988); William R. Stanton, *The Leopard's Spots* (1960); J. Mills Thornton III, *Politics and Power in a Slave Society* (1978); Ralph Wooster, *The Secession Conventions of the South* (1962).

The North and Antislavery

Eugene H. Berwanger, *The Frontier Against Slavery* (1967); Frederick J. Blue, *Salmon P. Chase* (1987); David Donald, *Charles Sumner and the Coming of the Civil War* (1960); Louis Filler, *The Crusade Against Slavery, 1830–1860* (1960); Eric Foner, *Free Soil, Free Labor, Free Men* (1970); William E. Gienapp, *The Origins of the Republican Party, 1852–1856* (1986); Henry V. Jaffa, *Crisis of the House Divided* (1959); Robert W. Johannsen, *The Frontier, the Union, and Stephen A. Douglas* (1989); Robert W. Johannsen, *Stephen A. Douglas* (1973); Aileen S. Kraditor, *Means and Ends in American Abolitionism* (1969); Stephen B. Oates, *To Purge This Land with Blood,* 2nd ed. (1984); Lewis Perry and Michael Fellman, eds., *Antislavery Reconsidered* (1979); Jeffrey Rossbach, *Ambivalent Conspirators* (1982); Richard Sewell, *Ballots for Freedom: Antislavery Politics in the United States, 1837–1860* (1976); Alice Felt Tyler, *Freedom's Ferment* (1944); Ronald G. Walters, *American Reformers* (1978).

The Mexican War and Foreign Policy

K. Jack Bauer, *Zachary Taylor* (1985); Gene M. Brack, *Mexico Views Manifest Destiny, 1821–1846* (1976); Neal Harlow, *California Conquered* (1982); Reginald Horsman, *Race and Manifest Destiny* (1981); Robert W. Johannsen, *To the Halls of the Montezumas: The Mexican War and the American Imagination* (1985); Ernest M. Lander, Jr., *Reluctant Imperialists: Calhoun, the South Carolinians, and the Mexican War* (1980); Robert E. May, *The Southern Dream of a Caribbean Empire, 1854–1861* (1973); Frederick Merk, *The Oregon Question* (1967); Frederick Merk, *The Monroe Doctrine and American Expansion, 1843–1849* (1966); Frederick Merk, *Manifest Destiny and Mission in American History* (1963); David M. Pletcher, *The Diplomacy of Annexation: Texas, Oregon, and the Mexican War* (1973); John H. Schroeder, *Mr. Polk's War: American Opposition and Dissent* (1973); Otis A. Singletary, *The Mexican War* (1960); David J. Weber, *The Mexican Frontier, 1821–1846* (1982).

They came from many different places. They held many different points of view. Perhaps the only thing that united them was the fact that they were caught in a gigantic struggle. Each felt dwarfed by the immense force of the Civil War, a vast and complex event beyond any individual's control.

Moncure Conway, a Virginian who had converted to abolitionism and settled in New England, saw the Civil War as a momentous opportunity to bring justice to human affairs. The progress of reform in the North, Conway wrote in an earnest pamphlet, heralded the dawn of "Humanity's advancing day." Before this dawn, "Slavery, hoary tyrant of the ages," cried out " 'Back! back . . . into the chambers of Night!' " Conway urged northerners to accept slavery's challenge and defeat it, so that "the rays of Freedom and Justice" could shine throughout America. Then the United States would stand as a beacon not only of commercial power but of moral righteousness.

14

TRANSFORMING FIRE: THE CIVIL WAR, 1861–1865

Conway's lofty idealism was far removed from the motives that drove most federal soldiers to march grimly to their death. Although slaves believed they were witnessing God's "Holy War for the liberation of the poor African slave people," Union troops often took a different perspective. When a Yankee soldier ransacked a slave family's cabin and stole the best quilts, the mother exclaimed, "Why you nasty, stinkin' rascal. You say you come down here to fight for the niggers, and now you're stealin' from 'em." The soldier replied, "You're a G-- D--- liar, I'm fightin' for $14 a month and the Union."

Southerners too acted from limited and pragmatic motives, fighting in self-defense or out of regional loyalty. A Union officer interrogating Confederate prisoners noticed the poverty of one captive. Clearly the man was no slaveholder, so the officer asked him why he was fighting. "Because y'all are down here," replied the Confederate.

The great suffering and frustration of the war were apparent in the bitter words of another southerner, a civilian. Impoverished by the conflict, this farmer had endured inflation, taxes, and shortages to support the Confederacy. Then an impressment agent arrived to take from him still more—grain and meat, horses and

A Rainy Day in Camp (detail) by Winslow Homer, 1871. Oil on canvas. *Metropolitan Museum of Art, Gift of Mrs. William F. Milton.*

Head Quarters, Virginia Forces,
STAUNTON, VA.

MEN OF VIRGINIA, TO THE RESCUE !

Your soil has been invaded by your Abolition foes, and we call upon you to rally at once, and drive them back. We want Volunteers to march immediately to Grafton and report for duty. Come one! Come ALL! and render the service due to your State and Country. Fly to arms, and succour your brave brothers who are now in the field.

The Volunteers from the Counties of Pendleton, Highland, Bath, Alleghany, Monroe, Mercer, and other Counties convenient to that point, will immediately organize, and report at Monterey, in Highland County, where they will join the Companies from the Valley, marching to Grafton. The Volunteers from the Counties of Hardy, Hampshire, Randolph, Pocahontas, Greenbrier, and other Counties convenient, will in like manner report at Beverly. And the Volunteers from the Counties of Upshur, Lewis, Barbour, and other Counties, will report at Philippi, in Barbour County. The Volunteers, as soon as they report at the above points, will be furnished with arms, rations, &c., &c.

Action! Action! should be our rallying motto, and the sentiment of Virginia's inspired Orator, "Give me Liberty or give me Death," animate every loyal son of the Old Dominion! Let us drive back the invading foot of a brutal and desperate foe, or leave a record to posterity that we died bravely defending our homes and firesides,—the honor of our wives and daughters,—and the sacred graves of our ancestors!

[Done by Authority.]
M. G. HARMAN, Maj. Commd'g
at Staunton.
J. M. HECK, Lt. Col. Va. Vol.
R. E. COWAN, Maj. Va. Vol.
May 30, 1861.

The voters of the Upper South were reluctant to secede and wanted the Union to be preserved, but the outbreak of war established their loyalty to the Confederacy. *Library of Congress.*

mules and wagons. In return the agent offered only a certificate promising repayment sometime in the future. Angry and fed up, the farmer bluntly declared, "The sooner this damned Government falls to pieces, the better it will be for us."

In contrast, many northern businessmen looked forward to the economic effects of the war with optimism and anticipation. The conflict ensured vast government expenditures, a heavy demand for products, and lucrative government contracts. *Harper's Monthly* reported that an eminent financier expected a long war, the kind of war that would mean huge purchases, paper money, active speculation, and rising prices. "The battle of Bull Run," predicted the financier, "makes the fortune of every man in Wall Street who is not a natural idiot."

For each of these people and millions of others, the Civil War was a life-changing event. It obliterated the normal circumstances of life, sweeping millions of men into training camps and battle units. Armies numbering in the hundreds of thousands marched over the South, devastating once-peaceful countrysides. Families struggled to survive without their men; businesses tried to cope with the loss of workers. Women in both North and South faced added responsibilities in the home and moved into new jobs in the work force. Nothing seemed untouched.

Change was the most drastic in the South, where the leaders of the secession movement had launched a revolution for the purpose of keeping things unchanged. Never were men more mistaken: their revolutionary means were fundamentally incompatible with their conservative purpose. Southern whites had feared that a peacetime government of Republicans would interfere with slavery and upset the routine of plantation life. Instead their own actions led to a war that turned southern life upside-down and imperiled the very existence of slavery. The Civil War forced changes in every phase of southern society, and the leadership of Jefferson Davis, president of the Confederate States of America, resulted in policies more objectionable to the elite than any proposed by President Lincoln. Life in the Confederacy proved to be a shockingly unsouthern experience.

War altered the North as well, but not as deeply. Because most of the fighting took place on southern soil, most northern farms and factories remained physically unscathed. The drafting of workers and the changing needs for products slowed the pace of industrialization somewhat, but factories and businesses remained busy. Workers lost ground to inflation, but the economy hummed. A new probusiness atmosphere dominated the United States Congress, where the seats of southern representatives were empty. To the discomfort of many, the powers of the federal government and the president increased during the war.

The war strained society in both North and South. Disaffection was strongest in the Confederacy, where the sufferings of ordinary citizens were greatest. There poverty and class resentment fed a lower-class antagonism to the war that threatened the Confederacy from within as federal armies assailed it from without. But dissent also flourished in the North, where antiwar sentiment occasionally erupted into violence.

Ultimately, the Civil War forced new social and racial arrangements on the nation. Its greatest effect

1861	Four more southern states secede from Union Battle of Bull Run General McClellan organizes Union Army Union blockade begins First confiscation act	**1864**	Battle of Cold Harbor Lincoln requests party plank abolishing slavery General Sherman enters Atlanta Lincoln re-elected Jefferson Davis proposes Confederate emancipation Sherman marches through Georgia
1862	Capture of Fort Henry and Fort Donelson Capture of New Orleans Battle of Shiloh Confederacy enacts conscription McClellan attacks Virginia Second confiscation act Confederacy mounts offensive Battle of Antietam	**1865**	Sherman marches through Carolinas Congress approves Thirteenth Amendment Hampton Roads Conference Lee surrenders at Appomattox Lincoln assassinated
1863	Emancipation Proclamation National Banking Act Union enacts conscription Black soldiers join Union Army Food riots in southern cities Battle of Chancellorsville Battle of Gettysburg and surrender of Vicksburg Draft riots in New York City		

was to compel leaders and citizens to deal with an issue they had often tried to avoid: slavery. This issue had, in complex and indirect ways, given rise to the war; now the scope and demands of the war forced reluctant Americans to grapple with it.

The South Goes to War

In the first bright days of the southern nation, few foresaw the changes that were in store. Lincoln's call for troops to put down the Confederate insurrection stimulated an outpouring of regional loyalty that unified the classes. Four border slave states—

Missouri, Kentucky, Maryland, and Delaware—and western Virginia refused to secede, but the rest of the Upper South joined the Confederacy. From every quarter southerners flocked to defend their region against Yankee aggression. In the first few months of the war half a million men volunteered to fight; there were so many would-be soldiers that the Confederate government could not arm them all.

The ground swell of popular support for the Confederacy generated a mood of optimism and gaiety. Women sewed dashing, colorful uniforms for men who would before long be lucky to wear drab gray or butternut homespun. Confident recruits boasted of whipping the

Battle of Bull Run

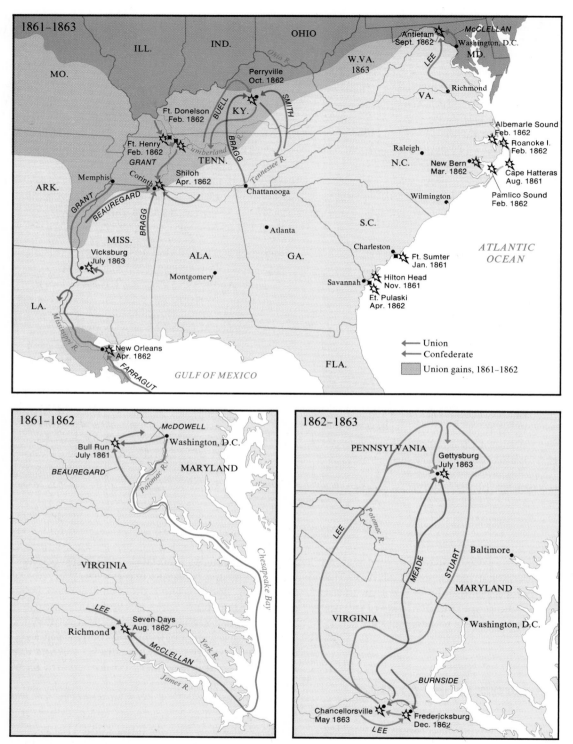

1861–1863

ILL. IND. OHIO

MO.

W.VA. 1863

McCLELLAN

Antietam Sept. 1862

Washington, D.C. MD.

LEE

Richmond

VA.

Perryville Oct. 1862

BUELL KY. *SMITH*

Ft. Donelson Feb. 1862

BRAGG

Ft. Henry Feb. 1862

Cumberland R.

GRANT TENN. *Tennessee R.*

Albemarle Sound Feb. 1862

Roanoke I. Feb. 1862

Raleigh N.C.

New Bern Mar. 1862

Cape Hatteras Aug. 1861

Pamlico Sound Feb. 1862

Memphis

ARK. *GRANT* Corinth Shiloh Apr. 1862

Chattanooga

BEAUREGARD *BRAGG*

Wilmington

MISS.

Vicksburg July 1863

ALA. GA.

Atlanta

S.C.

Charleston

ATLANTIC OCEAN

Montgomery

Ft. Sumter Jan. 1861

Savannah Hilton Head Nov. 1861

Ft. Pulaski Apr. 1862

LA.

Mississippi R.

New Orleans Apr. 1862

FARRAGUT

GULF OF MEXICO

FLA.

→ Union
→ Confederate
▨ Union gains, 1861–1862

1861–1862

McDOWELL

Bull Run July 1861

Washington, D.C.

BEAUREGARD

MARYLAND

Potomac R.

VIRGINIA

Chesapeake Bay

LEE

Seven Days Aug. 1862

Richmond

McCLELLAN

York R.

James R.

1862–1863

PENNSYLVANIA

Gettysburg July 1863

LEE *Potomac R.*

Baltimore

MEADE *STUART*

MARYLAND

VIRGINIA

Washington, D.C.

BURNSIDE

Chancellorsville May 1863

Fredericksburg Dec. 1862

LEE

The Civil War, 1861–1863

Yankees and returning home in time for dinner, and the first major battle of the war only increased such cockiness. On July 21, 1861, General Irvin McDowell and thirty thousand federal troops attacked General P. G. T. Beauregard's twenty-two thousand southerners at a stream called Bull Run, near Manassas Junction, Virginia. Both armies were ill trained, and confusion reigned on the battlefield. But nine thousand Confederate reinforcements and a timely stand by General Thomas Jackson (thereafter known as "Stonewall" Jackson) won the day for the South. Union troops fled back to Washington in disarray, and shocked northern congressmen and spectators, who had been watching the battle from a point two miles away, suddenly feared their capital would be taken.

In the wake of Bull Run, the North undertook a massive build-up of troops in northern Virginia. Lincoln gave command of the army to General George B. McClellan, an officer who proved to be better at organization and training than at fighting. McClellan devoted the fall and winter of 1861 to readying a formidable force of a quarter of a million men. "The vast preparation of the enemy," wrote one Confederate soldier, produced a "feeling of despondency" among southerners.

The North also moved to blockade southern ports in order to choke off the Confederacy's avenues of commerce and supply. At first the handful of available steamers proved woefully inadequate to the task of patrolling 3,550 miles of coastline. But the Union Navy gradually increased the blockade's effectiveness, though it never bottled up southern commerce completely.

In the late summer and fall of 1861 Union naval power came ashore in the South. Federal squadrons captured Cape Hatteras and Hilton Head, part of the Sea Islands off Port Royal, South Carolina. A few months later, similar operations secured Albemarle and Pamlico sounds, Roanoke Island, and New Bern in North Carolina, as well as Fort Pulaski, which defended Savannah. Federal naval operations were biting into the Confederate coastline (see map).

Union Naval Campaign

The coastal victories off South Carolina foreshadowed another major development in the unraveling of the southern status quo. At the gunboats' approach, frightened planters abandoned their lands and fled. Their slaves, who thus became the first to escape slavery through military action, greeted what they hoped to be freedom with rejoicing and destruction of the cotton gins, symbols of their travail. Their jubilation and the constantly growing stream of runaways who poured into the Union lines removed any doubt about which side the slaves would support, given the opportunity. Ironically the federal government, unwilling at first to wage a war against slavery, did not acknowledge the slaves' freedom—though it did set to work finding ways to use them in the Union cause.

With the approach of spring 1862, the military outlook for the Confederacy darkened again. In April 1862 ships commanded by Admiral David Farragut smashed through log booms on the Mississippi River and fought their way upstream to capture New Orleans. In northern Tennessee land forces won significant victories for the Union. A hard-drinking, hitherto unsuccessful general named Ulysses S. Grant recognized the strategic importance of Fort Henry and Fort Donelson, the Confederate outposts guarding the Tennessee and Cumberland rivers. Grant saw that if federal troops could capture these forts, two prime routes into the heartland of the Confederacy would lie open. In the space of ten days he seized the forts, using his forces so well that he was able to demand unconditional surrender of Fort Donelson's defenders. A path into Tennessee, Alabama, and Mississippi now lay open before the Union Army.

Grant's Campaign in Tennessee

On April 6, Confederate General Albert Sidney Johnston caught Grant's army in an undesirable position at Pittsburg Landing in southern Tennessee. The Confederates inflicted heavy damage in fierce fighting. Close to victory, General Johnston was struck by a ball that severed an artery in his thigh; within minutes he was dead. Deprived of their leader, southern troops faced a reinforced Union Army the next day, and the tide of battle turned. After ten hours of heavy combat, Grant's men forced the Confederates to withdraw to Corinth, Mississippi. There was no clear victor in the Battle of Shiloh, but destruction reigned. Northern troops lost 13,000 of 63,000 men; southerners sacrificed 11,000 out of 40,000.

The losses at Shiloh foreshadowed the enormous costs of the war. Never before in Europe or America had such massive forces pummeled each other with weapons of such destructive power. Yet

Slaves at Hilton Head, on the South Carolina coast, were among the first black southerners to come under Federal authority in November 1861. Although their masters had fled, these slaves were not yet free. *The William Gladstone Collection.*

the armies in the Civil War seemed virtually indestructible. Even in the bloodiest engagements the losing army was never destroyed, even though thousands of men died. Many citizens, like soldier (later Supreme Court Justice) Oliver Wendell Holmes, wondered at "the butcher's bill." The improved range of modern rifles multiplied casualties, and because medical knowledge was rudimentary, minor wounds often led to death through infection. The slaughter was most vivid to the soldiers themselves, who saw the blasted bodies of their friends and comrades. "Any one who goes over a battlefield after a battle," wrote one Confederate, "never cares to go over another . . . again. . . . It is a sad sight to see the dead and if possible more sad to see the wounded—shot in every possible way you can imagine."

Troops learned the hard way that soldiering was far from glorious. "The dirt of a camp life knocks all its poetry into a cocked hat," wrote a North Carolina volunteer in 1862. One year later he marveled at his earlier innocence. Fighting had taught him "the realities of a soldier's life. We had no tents after the 6th of August, but slept on the ground, in the woods or open fields, without regard to the weather. . . . I learned to eat fat bacon raw, and to

like it. . . . Without time to wash our clothes or our persons, and sleeping on the ground all huddled together, the whole army became lousy more or less with body lice. It was a necessary and unavoidable incident to our arduous campaign."

The scope and duration of the conflict began to have unexpected effects. Tens of thousands of Confederate soldiers had volunteered for just one year's service, planning to return home in the spring of 1862 to plant their crops. To keep southern armies in the field, the War Department of the Confederacy offered bounties and furloughs to all who would re-enlist. Officials then called for new volunteers; but, as one official admitted, "the spirit of volunteering had died out." Three states threatened or instituted a draft. Finally, faced with a critical shortage of troops, the Confederate government enacted the first national conscription, or draft, law in American history. Thus the war forced an unprecedented change on the states that had seceded out of fear of change.

Confederacy Resorts to a Draft

With their ranks reinforced, southern armies moved into heavier fighting. The Confederacy had relocated its capital from Montgomery, Alabama, to

Antietam was the bloodiest day of the war. Nearly 6,000 men died—far more than in the War of 1812 and the Mexican War combined—and another 17,000 were wounded. The northern victory helped prevent European recognition of the Confederacy. *Kennedy Galleries, N.Y.C.*

Richmond, Virginia. General McClellan sailed his troops to the York peninsula and advanced on Richmond from the east. By May and June the sheer size of the federal armies outside the South's capital was highly threatening. But General Stonewall Jackson and General Robert E. Lee managed to stave off the attacks of McClellan's legions. First, Jackson maneuvered into the Shenandoah Valley, behind Union forces, and threatened Washington, drawing some of the federals away from Richmond to protect their own capital. Then, in a series of engagements culminating in the Seven Days' battles, Lee held McClellan off. On August 3, McClellan withdrew to the Potomac, and Richmond was safe for almost two more years.

Buoyed by these results, Jefferson Davis conceived an ambitious plan to turn the tide of the war and compel the United States to recognize the **Davis Orders an Offensive** Confederacy. He ordered a general offensive, sending Lee north to Maryland and General Kirby Smith and General Braxton Bragg to Kentucky. The South would go on the offensive and take the war north. Davis and his commanders issued a proclamation to the people of Maryland and Kentucky, asserting that the Confederates sought only the right of self-government. Lincoln's refusal to grant them independence forced them to attack "those who persist in their refusal to make peace." Davis urged invaded states to make a separate peace with his government and invited the Northwest, whose trade

followed the Mississippi to New Orleans, to leave the Union.

The plan was promising, and Davis rejoiced that his outnumbered forces were ready to take the initiative. Every part of the offensive failed, however. In the bloodiest single day of fighting, September 17, 1862, McClellan turned Lee back in the Battle of Antietam near Sharpsburg, Maryland. Smith and Bragg had to withdraw from Kentucky just one day after Bragg had attended the inauguration of a provisional Confederate governor. The entire effort collapsed.

But southern armies were not exhausted. General James E. B. ("Jeb") Stuart executed a daring cavalry raid into Pennsylvania on October 10 through 12, and Lee decimated General Ambrose Burnside's soldiers as they charged his fortified positions at Fredericksburg, Virginia, on December 13. The Confederate Army of Northern Virginia performed so bravely and controlled the engagement so thoroughly that Lee, a restrained and humane man, was moved to say, "It is well that war is so terrible. We should grow too fond of it."

Nevertheless, the Confederacy had marshaled all its strength for a breakthrough, but it had failed to achieve one. Outnumbered and disadvantaged in resources (see figure, page 406), the South could not continue its offensive. The North, in contrast, had reserves of every kind on which to draw. Profoundly disappointed, Davis admitted to a committee of Confederate representatives that southerners had entered "the darkest and most dangerous

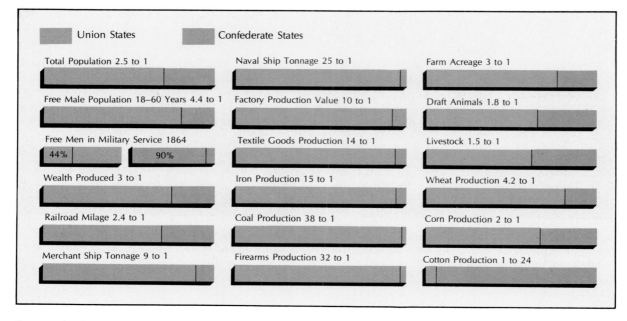

Union States		Confederate States			

Total Population 2.5 to 1

Free Male Population 18–60 Years 4.4 to 1

Free Men in Military Service 1864

44%   90%

Wealth Produced 3 to 1

Railroad Milage 2.4 to 1

Merchant Ship Tonnage 9 to 1

Naval Ship Tonnage 25 to 1

Factory Production Value 10 to 1

Textile Goods Production 14 to 1

Iron Production 15 to 1

Coal Production 38 to 1

Firearms Production 32 to 1

Farm Acreage 3 to 1

Draft Animals 1.8 to 1

Livestock 1.5 to 1

Wheat Production 4.2 to 1

Corn Production 2 to 1

Cotton Production 1 to 24

Comparative Resources, Union and Confederate States, 1861. *Source: From* Times Atlas of World History. *Times Books, London, 1978. Used with permission.*

period we have yet had." Tenacious defense and stoical endurance now seemed the South's only long-range hope. Perceptive southerners shared their president's despair.

War Transforms the South

Even more than the fighting, changes in civilian life robbed southerners of their gaiety and nonchalance. The war altered southern society beyond all expectations and with astonishing speed. One of the first traditions to fall was the southern preference for local government.

The South had been an area of limited government. States' rights had been its motto, but by modern standards the state governments were weak and sketchy affairs. To withstand the massive power of the North, the South had to centralize; like the colonial revolutionaries, southerners faced a choice of join or die. No one saw the necessity of centralization more clearly than Jefferson Davis. If the states insisted on fighting separately, said Davis, "we had better make terms as soon as we can."

From the outset, Davis pressed to bring all arms, supplies, and troops under his control. He advocated conscription when the states failed to enroll enough new soldiers. He took a strong leadership role toward the Confederate congress, which raised taxes and later passed a tax-in-kind—a tax paid not in money but in wheat, corn, oats, rye, cotton, peas, and other farm products. Almost three thousand agents dispersed to collect the tax, assisted by almost fifteen hundred appraisers. Where opposition arose, the government suspended the writ of habeas corpus and imposed martial law. In the face of a political opposition that cherished states' rights, Davis proved unyielding.

Centralization of Power in the South

To replace the food that soldiers would have grown, Davis exhorted farmers to switch from cash crops to food crops, and he encouraged the states to require that they do so. But the army was still short of food and labor. In emergencies the War Department resorted to impressing slaves for labor on fortifications, and after 1861 the government relied heavily on the impressment of food to feed the troops. Officers swooped down on farms in the line of march and carted away grain, meat, and other food, plus wagons and draft animals.

Soon the Confederate administration in Richmond was taking virtually complete control of the southern economy. Because it controlled the supply of labor through conscription, the administration could regulate industry, compelling factories to work on government contracts to supply government needs. In addition, the Confederate congress passed laws giving the central government almost full control of the railroads; in 1864 shipping, too, came under extensive regulation. New statutes even limited corporate profits and dividends. A large bureaucracy sprang up to administer these operations: over seventy thousand civilians were needed to staff the Confederate administration. By the war's end the southern bureaucracy was proportionally larger than its northern counterpart.

The mushrooming bureaucracy expanded the cities. Clerks and subordinate officials, many of them women, crowded the towns and cities where Confederate departments had their offices. These sudden population booms stretched the existing housing supply and stimulated new construction. The pressure was especially great in Richmond, whose population increased two-and-a-half times. Before the war's end Confederate officials were planning the relocation of entire departments to diminish crowding in Richmond. Mobile's population jumped from 29,000 to 41,000; Atlanta began to grow; and 10,000 people poured into war-related industries in little Selma, Alabama.

Effects of War on Southern Cities and Industry

Another prime cause of urban growth was industrialization. Because of the Union blockade, which disrupted imports of manufactured products, the traditionally agricultural South became interested in industry. Davis exulted that southerners were manufacturing their own goods, thus "becoming more and more independent of the rest of the world." Many planters shared his expectations, remembering their battles against tariffs and hoping that their agrarian nation would industrialize enough to win "deliverance, full and unrestricted, from all commercial dependence" on the North. Indeed, though the Confederacy started almost from scratch, it achieved tremendous feats of industrial development. Chief of Ordnance Josiah Gorgas was able to increase the capacity of the Tredegar Iron Works and other factories to the point that his Ordnance Bureau was supplying all Confederate small arms and ammunition by 1865.

As a result of these changes southerners adopted new ways. Women, sheltered in the patriarchal antebellum society, gained substantial new responsibilities. The wives and mothers of soldiers became heads of households and undertook what had previously been considered men's work. To them fell the added tasks of raising crops and tending animals. Although wives of nonslaveowners had a harder time cultivating their fields than did women whose families owned slaves, the latter suddenly had to deal with field hands unaccustomed to feminine oversight. Only among the very rich were there enough servants to take up the slack and leave a woman's routine undisturbed. In the cities, white women, who had been virtually excluded from the labor force, found a limited number of new, respectable, paying jobs. Clerks had always been males, but the war changed that, too. "Government girls" staffed the Confederate bureaucracy, and female schoolteachers became a familiar sight for the first time in the South. Such experiences, though restricted, undermined the image of the omnipotent male and gave thousands of women new confidence in their abilities.

Change in the Southern Woman's Role

One of those who acquired such confidence as a result of the war was a young North Carolinian named Janie Smith. Raised in a rural area by prosperous parents, she had faced few challenges or grim realities. Then suddenly the war reached her farm, and troops turned her home into a hospital. "It makes me shudder when I think of the awful sights I witnessed that morning," she wrote to a friend. "Ambulance after ambulance drove up with our wounded. . . . Under every shed and tree, the tables were carried for amputating the limbs. . . . The blood lay in puddles in the grove; the groans of the dying and complaints of those undergoing amputation were horrible." But Janie Smith learned to cope with crisis. She helped to nurse the wounded and ended her account with the proud words, "I can dress amputated limbs now and do most anything in the way of nursing wounded soldiers."

The Confederate experience introduced and sustained many other new values. Legislative bodies yielded power to the executive branch of government, which could act more decisively in time of war. The traditional emphasis on aristocratic lineage gave way to respect for achievement and bravery under fire. Thus many men of ordinary background, such as Josiah Gorgas, Stonewall Jackson, and General Nathan Bedford Forrest, gained distinction in industry and on the battlefield that would have been beyond their grasp in time of peace. Finally, sacrifice for the cause discouraged the pursuit of pleasure; hostesses gave "cold water parties" (at which water was the only refreshment) to demonstrate their patriotism.

For the elite such sacrifice was symbolic, but for millions of ordinary southerners it was terrifyingly real. Mass poverty descended on the South, afflicting for the first time a large minority of the white population. Many yeoman families had lost their breadwinners to the army. As a South Carolina newspaper put it, "The duties of war have called away from home the sole supports of many, many families. . . . Help must be given, or the poor will suffer." The poor sought help from relatives, neighbors, friends, anyone. Sometimes they took their cases to the Confederate government, as did an elderly Virginian who pleaded, "If you dount send [my son] home I am bound to louse my crop and cum to suffer. I am eaighty one years of adge." One woman wrote: "I ask in the name of humanity to discharge my husband he is not able to do your government much good and he might do his children some good and thare is no use in keeping a man thare to kill and leave widows and poor little orphan children to suffer . . . my poor children have no home nor no Father."

> **Human Suffering in the South**

Other factors aggravated the effect of the labor shortage. The South was in many places so sparsely populated that the conscription of one skilled craftsman could work a hardship on the people of an entire county. Often they begged in unison for the exemption or discharge of the local miller or the neighborhood tanner, wheelwright, or potter. Physicians were also in short supply. Most serious, however, was the loss of a blacksmith. As a petition from Alabama explained, "our Section of County [is] left entirely Destitute of any man that is able to keep in order any kind of Farming Tules, Such as the few aged Farmers and families of Those that is gone to defend their rites is Compeled to have to make a Support With."

The blockade created shortages of common but important items—salt, sugar, coffee, nails—and speculation and hoarding made the shortages worse. Greedy businessmen moved to corner

> **Hoarding and Runaway Inflation in the South**

the supply of some commodities; prosperous citizens tried to stock up on food. The *Richmond Enquirer* criticized one man for hoarding seven hundred barrels of flour; another man, a planter, purchased so many wagonloads of supplies that his "lawn and paths looked like a wharf covered with a ship's loads." Some people bought up the entire stock of a store and held the goods to sell later at higher prices. "This disposition to speculate upon the yeomanry of the country," lamented the *Richmond Examiner,* "is the most mortifying feature of the war." North Carolina's Governor Zebulon Vance asked where it would all stop: "the cry of distress comes up from the poor wives and children of our soldiers. . . . What will become of them?"

Inflation, fueled by the Confederate government's inadequate financial policies, raged out of control until prices had increased almost 7,000 percent. Inflation imperiled urban dwellers and the many who could no longer provide for themselves. As early as 1861 and 1862, newspapers were reporting that "the poor of our . . . country will be unable to live at all" and that "want and starvation are staring thousands in the face." Officials warned of "great suffering next year," predicting that "women and children are bound to come to suffering if not starvation."

Some concerned citizens tried to help. "Free markets," which dispersed goods as charity, sprang up in various cities; some families came to the aid of their neighbors. But other citizens would not cooperate: "It is folly for a poor mother to call on the rich people about here," raged one woman. "Their hearts are of steel they would sooner throw what they have to spare to the dogs than give it to a starving child." The need was so vast that it overwhelmed private charity. A rudimentary relief program organized by the Confederacy offered hope but was soon curtailed to supply the armies. Southern yeomen sank into poverty and suffering.

As their fortunes declined, people of once-modest means looked around them and found abundant evidence that all classes were not sacrificing equally. They saw that the wealthy gave up only their luxuries, while many poor families went without necessities. They saw that the government contrib-

> **Inequities of the Confederate Draft**

uted to these inequities through policies that favored the upper class. Until the last year of the war, for example, prosperous southerners could avoid military service by hiring substitutes. Prices for substitutes skyrocketed, until it was common for a man of means to pay $5,000 or $6,000 to send someone to the front. Well over fifty thousand upper-class southerners purchased such substitutes. Mary Boykin Chesnut knew of one young aristocrat who had "spent a fortune in substitutes. Two have been taken from him [when *they* were conscripted], and two he paid to change with him when he was ordered to the front. He is at the end of his row now, for all able-bodied men are ordered to the front. I hear he is going as some general's courier."

As Chesnut's last remark indicates, the rich also traded on their social connections to avoid danger. "It is a notorious fact," complained an angry Georgian, that "if a man has influential friends—or a little money to spare he will never be enrolled." The Confederate senator from Mississippi, James Phelan, informed Jefferson Davis that apparently "nine tenths of the youngsters of the land whose relatives are conspicuous in society, wealthy, or influential obtain some safe perch where they can doze with their heads under their wings."

Anger at such discrimination exploded in October 1862 when the Confederate congress exempted from military duty anyone who was supervising at least twenty slaves. "Never did a law meet with more universal odium," observed one representative. "Its influence upon the poor is most calamitous." Immediately protests arose from every corner of the Confederacy, and North Carolina's legislators formally condemned the law. Its defenders argued, however, that the exemption preserved order and aided food production, and the statute remained on the books.

Dissension spread as growing numbers of citizens concluded that the struggle was "a rich man's war and a poor man's fight." Alert politicians and newspaper editors warned that class resentment was building to a dangerous level; letters to Confederate officials during this period contained a bitterness that suggested the depth of the people's anger. "If I and my little children suffer [and] die while there Father is in service," threatened one woman, "I invoke God Almighty that our blood rest upon the South." Another woman swore to the secretary of war that

Confederate Colonel Vannoy H. Manning poses in uniform with his wife. As the death toll mounted and suffering increased, southern women grew less willing to urge their men into battle. *Lawrence T. Jones Collection.*

an allwise god . . . will send down his fury and judgment in a very grate manar [on] all those our leading men and those that are in power if thare is no more favors shone to . . . the wives and mothers of those who in poverty has with patrootism stood the fence Battles. . . . I tell you that with out some grate and speadly alterating in the conduckting of afares in this our little nation god will frown on it.

War was magnifying social tensions in the Confederacy.

The Northern Economy Copes with War

With the onset of war, the tidal wave of change rolled over the North just as it had over the South. Factories and citizens' associations geared up to support the war, and the federal government and its executive branch gained power they had never had before. The energies of an industrializing, capitalist society were harnessed to serve the cause of the Union. Idealism and greed flourished together, but the northern economy proved its awesome productivity.

The war did not destroy the North's prosperity. Northern factories ran overtime, and unemployment was low. Furthermore, northern farms and factories came through the war unharmed, whereas most areas of the South suffered extensive damage. To Union soldiers on the battlefield, sacrifice was a grim reality, but northern civilians experienced only the bustle and energy of wartime production.

At first, the war was a shock to business. With the sudden closing of southern markets, firms could no longer predict the demand for their goods, and many companies had to redirect their activities in order to remain open. Southern debts became uncollectible, jeopardizing not only northern merchants but many western banks. In farming regions, families struggled with an aggravated shortage of labor. For reasons such as these, the war initially caused an economic slump.

Initial Slump in Northern Business

A few enterprises never pulled out of the tailspin: cotton mills lacked cotton; construction declined; shoe manufacturers sold fewer of the cheap shoes that planters had bought for their slaves. Overall the war slowed industrialization in the North, but its economic impact was not all negative. Certain entrepreneurs, such as wool producers, benefited from shortages of competing products, and soaring demand for war-related goods swept some businesses to new heights of production. To feed the hungry war machine the federal government pumped unprecedented amounts of money into the economy. The treasury issued $3.2 billion in bonds and paper money called greenbacks, while the War Department spent over $360 million in revenues from new taxes (including a broad excise tax and the nation's first income tax). Government contracts soon came to a total of more than $1 billion.

Secretary of War Edwin M. Stanton's list of supplies needed by the Ordnance Department indicates the scope of government demand: "7,892 cannon, 11,787 artillery carriages, 4,022,130 small-arms, . . . 1,022,176,474 cartridges for small-arms, 1,220,555,435 percussion caps, . . . 14,507,682 cannon primers and fuses, 12,875,294 pounds of artillery projectiles, 26,440,054 pounds of gunpowder,

6,395,152 pounds of niter, and 90,416,295 pounds of lead." Stanton's list covered only weapons; the government also purchased huge quantities of uniforms, boots, food, camp equipment, saddles, ships, and other necessities.

War-related spending revived business in many northern states. In 1863, a merchants' magazine examined the effects of the war in Massachusetts: "Seldom, if ever, has the business of Massachusetts been more active or profitable than during the past year. . . . Labor has been in great demand . . . trade is again in a high state of prosperity. Wealth has flowed into the State in no stinted measure, despite war and heavy taxes. In every department of labor the government has been, directly or indirectly, the chief employer and paymaster." Government contracts had a particularly beneficial impact on the state's wool, metal, and shipbuilding industries, and they saved Massachusetts shoe manufacturers from ruin.

Nothing revealed the wartime partnership between business and government better than the work of Jay Cooke for himself and the U.S. Treasury. A wealthy New York financier, Cooke threw himself into the marketing of government bonds to finance the war effort. With great imagination and energy, Cooke convinced both large investors and ordinary citizens to place enormous sums at the disposal of the war effort. In the process he earned commissions for himself, but the financier's profit greatly benefited the Union cause as the interests of capitalism and government, finance and patriotism, merged.

War production promoted the development of heavy industry in the North. The output of coal rose substantially. Iron makers improved the quality of their product while boosting the production of pig iron from 920,000 tons in 1860 to 1,136,000 tons in 1864. Although new railroad construction slowed, the manufacture of rails increased. Of considerable significance for the future were the railroad industry's adoption of a standard gauge for track and foundries' development of new and less-expensive ways to make steel.

Effects of War on Northern Industry and Agriculture

Another strength of the northern economy was the complementary relationship between agriculture and industry. The mechanization of agriculture had begun before the war. Wartime recruitment

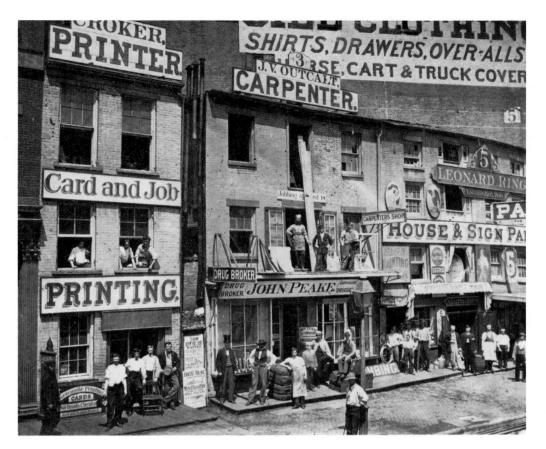

Despite initial problems, the task of supplying a vast war machine kept the northern economy humming. This photograph shows the west side of Hudson Street, New York City, in 1865. *The New-York Historical Society.*

and conscription, however, gave western farmers an added incentive to purchase labor-saving machinery. The shift from human labor to machines created new markets for industry and expanded the food supply for the urban industrial work force.

The boom in the sale of agricultural tools was tremendous. Cyrus and William McCormick built an industrial empire in Chicago from the sale of their reapers. Between 1862 and 1864 the manufacture of mowers and reapers doubled to 70,000 yearly; manufacturers could not supply the demand. By the end of the war, 375,000 reapers were in use, triple the number in 1861. Large-scale commercial agriculture became a reality. As a result, farm families whose breadwinners went to war did not suffer as they did in the South. "We have seen," one magazine observed, "a stout matron whose sons are in the army, cutting hay with her team . . .

and she cut seven acres with ease in a day, riding leisurely upon her cutter."

Northern industrial and urban workers did not fare as well. Jobs were plentiful following the initial slump, but inflation took much of a worker's paycheck. By 1863 nine-cent-a-pound beef was selling for eighteen cents. The price of coffee had tripled; rice and sugar had doubled; and clothing, fuel, and rent had all climbed. Studies of the cost of living indicate that between 1860 and 1864 consumer prices rose at least 76 percent, while daily wages rose only 42 percent. Consequently, workers' families suffered a substantial decline in their standard of living.

As their real wages shrank, industrial workers also lost job security. To increase production, some employers were replacing workers with labor-saving machines. Other employers urged the gov-

New Militancy Among Northern Workers ernment to liberalize immigration procedures so they could import cheap labor. Workers responded by forming unions and sometimes by striking. Skilled craftsmen organized to combat the loss of their jobs and status to machines; women and unskilled workers, excluded by the craftsmen, formed their own unions. In recognition of the increasingly national scope of business activity, thirteen occupational groups—including tailors, coal miners, and railway engineers—formed national unions during the Civil War. Because of the tight labor market, unions were able to win many of their demands without striking, but still the number of strikes rose steadily.

Employers reacted negatively to this new spirit among workers—a spirit that William H. Sylvis, leader of the iron molders, called a "feeling of manly independence." Manufacturers viewed labor activism as a threat to their property rights and freedom of action, and accordingly they too formed statewide or craft-based associations to cooperate and pool information. These employers compiled blacklists of union members and required new workers to sign "yellow dog" contracts, or promises not to join a union. To put down strikes, they hired strikebreakers from the ranks of the poor and desperate—blacks, immigrants, and women—and sometimes received additional help from federal troops.

Troublesome as unions were, they did not prevent many employers from making a profit. The highest profits were made from profiteering on government contracts. Unscrupulous businessmen took advantage of the sudden immense demand for goods for the army by selling clothing and blankets made of "shoddy"—wool fibers reclaimed from rags or worn cloth. Shoddy goods often came apart in the rain; most of the shoes purchased in the early months of the war were worthless too. Contractors sold inferior guns for double the usual price and tainted meat for the price of good. Corruption was so widespread that it led to a year-long investigation by the House of Representatives. A group of contractors that demanded $50 million for their products had to reduce their claims to $17 million as a result of the findings of the investigation.

Legitimate enterprises also made healthy profits. The output of woolen mills increased so dramatically that dividends in the industry nearly tripled.

Wartime Benefits to Northern Business Some cotton mills made record profits on what they sold, even though they reduced their output. Brokerage houses worked until midnight and earned unheard-of commissions. Railroads carried immense quantities of freight and passengers, increasing their business to the point that railroad stocks doubled or even tripled in value. The price of Erie Railroad stock rose from $17 to $126 a share.

In fact, railroads were a leading beneficiary of government largesse. Congress had failed in the 1850s to resolve the question of a northern versus a southern route for the first transcontinental railroad. With the South out of Congress, the northern route quickly prevailed. In 1862 and 1864 Congress chartered two corporations, the Union Pacific Railroad and the Central Pacific Railroad, and assisted them financially in connecting Omaha, Nebraska, with Sacramento, California. For each mile of track laid, the railroads received a loan ranging from $16,000 to $48,000 plus twenty square miles of land along a free 400-foot-wide right of way. Overall, the two corporations gained approximately 20 million acres of land and nearly $60 million in loans.

Other businessmen benefited handsomely from the Morrill Land Grant Act (1862). To promote public education in agriculture, engineering, and military science, Congress granted each state 30,000 acres of public land for each of its congressional representatives. The states were free to sell the land as they saw fit, as long as they used the income for the purposes Congress had intended. The law eventually fostered sixty-nine colleges and universities, but one of its immediate effects was to enrich a few prominent speculators. Hard-pressed to meet wartime expenses, some states sold their land cheaply to wealthy entrepreneurs. Ezra Cornell, for example, purchased 500,000 acres in the Midwest.

Higher tariffs also pleased many businessmen. Northern businesses did not uniformly favor high import duties; some manufacturers desired cheap imported raw materials more than they feared foreign competition. But northeastern congressmen traditionally supported higher tariffs, and after southern lawmakers left Washington, they had their way: the Tariff Act of 1864 raised tariffs generously. According to one scholar, manufacturers had only to mention the rate they considered necessary and that rate was declared. Some healthy industries made artificially high profits by raising their prices to a level just below that of the foreign competition. By the end of the war, tariff increases averaged 47 percent, and rates were more than double those of 1857.

Wartime Society in the North

The outbreak of war stimulated patriotism in the North, just as it initially had in the South. Northern society, which had felt the stresses associated with increasing industrialization, immigration, and widespread social change, found a unifying cause in the preservation of the nation and the American form of government. Throughout thousands of towns and communities, northern citizens had participated in local government and local office-holding. They worked in their government and felt it worked for them. Secession threatened to destroy this American system of representative government, and northerners rallied to its defense. Secular and church leaders supported the cause, and even ministers who preferred to separate politics and pulpit denounced "the iniquity of causeless rebellion."

But there were other aspects of the northern response to war. The frantic wartime activity, the booming economy, and the Republican alliance with business combined to create a new atmosphere in Washington. The balance of opinion shifted against wage earners and toward large corporations; the notion spread that government should aid businessmen but not interfere with them. Noting the favorable atmosphere, railroad builders and industrialists—men such as Leland Stanford, Collis P. Huntington, John D. Rockefeller, John M. Forbes, and Jay Gould—took advantage of it. Their enterprises grew with the aid of government loans, grants, and tariffs.

As long as the war lasted, the powers of the federal government and the president continued to grow. Abraham Lincoln, like Jefferson Davis, found

Wartime Powers of the U.S. Executive

that war required active presidential leadership. At the beginning of the conflict, Lincoln launched a major shipbuilding program without waiting for Con-

gress to assemble. The lawmakers later approved his decision, and Lincoln continued to act in advance of Congress when he deemed it necessary. In one striking exercise of executive power, Lincoln suspended the writ of habeas corpus for all people living between Washington and Philadelphia. There was scant legal justification for this act, but Lincoln's motive was practical: to ensure the loyalty of Maryland. Later in the war, with congressional approval, Lincoln repeatedly suspended the writ and invoked martial law. Between ten and twenty thousand United States citizens were arrested on suspicion of disloyal acts (though some of these arrests were aimed at suppressing petty crime rather than dissent).

On occasion Lincoln used his wartime authority to bolster his political power. He and his generals proved adept at arranging furloughs for soldiers who could vote in close elections. Needless to say, the citizens in arms whom Lincoln helped to vote usually voted Republican. In another instance, when the Republican governor of Indiana found himself short of funds because of Democratic opposition, Lincoln generously supplied eight times the amount of money that the governor needed to get through the emergency situation.

Among the clearest examples of the wartime expansion of federal authority were the National Banking Acts of 1863, 1864, and 1865. Prior to the Civil War the nation did not have a uniform currency, for the federal government had never exercised its authority in this area. Banks operating under state charters issued no fewer than seven thousand different kinds of notes, which had to be distinguished from a variety of forgeries. Now, acting on the recommendations of Secretary of the Treasury Salmon Chase, Congress established a national banking system empowered to issue a maximum number of national bank notes. At the close of the war in 1865, Congress laid a prohibitive tax on state bank notes and forced most major state institutions to join the national system. This process led to a sounder currency and a simpler monetary system—but also to inflexibility in the money supply and an eastern-oriented financial structure.

Soldiers may have sensed the increasing scale of things better than anyone else. Most federal troops were young; eighteen was the most common age, followed by twenty-one. Many soldiers went straight from small towns and farms into large armies supplied by extensive bureaucracies. By December 1861 there were 640,000 volunteers in arms, a stupendous increase over the regular army of 20,000 men. The increase occurred so rapidly that it is remarkable the troops were supplied and organized as well as they were. Many soldiers' first experiences with large organizations, however, were unfortunate.

Soldiers benefited from certain new products, such as Gail Borden's canned condensed milk, but blankets, clothing, and arms were often of poor quality. Vermin were commonplace. Hospitals were badly managed at first. Rules of hygiene in large camps were badly written or unenforced; latrines were poorly made or carelessly used. One investigation turned up "an area of over three acres, encircling the camp as a broad belt, on which is deposited an almost perfect layer of human excrement." Water supplies were unsafe and typhoid fever epidemics common. About 57,000 army men died from dysentery and diarrhea.

The situation would have been much worse but for the U.S. Sanitary Commission. A voluntary civilian organization, the commission worked to improve conditions in camps and to aid sick and wounded soldiers. Still, 224,000 Union troops died from disease or accidents, far more than the 140,000 who died in battle.

Such conditions would hardly have predisposed the soldier to sympathize with changing social attitudes on the home front. Amid the excitement of moneymaking, a gaudy culture of vulgar display flourished in the largest cities. A visitor to Chicago commented that "so far as lavish display is concerned, the South Side in some portions has no rival in Chicago, and perhaps not outside New York." Its new residences boasted "marble fronts and expensive ornamentation" that created "a glittering, heartless appearance." William Cullen Bryant, the distinguished editor of the *New York Evening Post,* observed sadly, "Extravagance, luxury, these are the signs of the times. . . . What business have Americans at any time with such vain show, with such useless magnificence? But especially how can they justify it . . . in this time of war?"

Self-Indulgence Versus Sacrifice in the North

The newly rich did not bother to justify it. *Harper's Monthly* reported that "the suddenly enriched contractors, speculators, and stock-jobbers . . . are spending money with a profusion never before witnessed in our country, at no time remarkable for its frugality. . . . The ordinary sources of expenditure seem to have been exhausted, and these ingenious prodigals have invented new ones. The men button their waistcoats with diamonds . . . and the women powder their hair with gold and silver dust." The *New York Herald* summarized that city's atmosphere:

> All our theatres are open . . . and they are all crowded nightly. . . . The most costly accommodations, in both hotels and theatres, are the first and most eagerly taken. . . . The richest silks, laces and jewelry are the soonest sold. . . . Not to keep a carriage, not to wear diamonds, not to be attired in a robe which cost a small fortune, is now equivalent to being a nobody. This war has entirely changed the American character. . . . The individual who makes the most money—no matter how—and spends the most—no matter for what—is considered the greatest man. . . .
>
> The world has seen its iron age, its silver age, its golden age, and its brazen age. This is the age of shoddy.

Yet strong elements of idealism coexisted with ostentation. Many churches supported the Union cause as God's cause. One Methodist paper described the war as a contest between "equalizing, humanizing Christianity" and "disunion, war, selfishness, [and] slavery." Abolitionists, after initial uncertainty over whether to let the South go, campaigned to turn the war into a war against slavery. Free black communities and churches both black and white responded to the needs of slaves who flocked to the Union lines. They sent clothing, ministers, and teachers in generous measure to aid the runaways.

Northern women, like their southern counterparts, took on new roles. Those who stayed home organized over ten thousand soldiers' aid societies, rolled innumerable bandages, and raised $3 million. Thousands served as nurses in front-line hospitals, where they pressed for better care of the wounded. The professionalization of medicine since the Revolution had created a medical system dominated by men; thus dedicated and able female nurses had to fight both military regulations and professional hostility to win the chance to make their contribution. In the hospitals they quickly proved their worth, but only the wounded welcomed them. Even Clara Barton, the most famous female nurse, was ousted from her post during the winter of 1863.

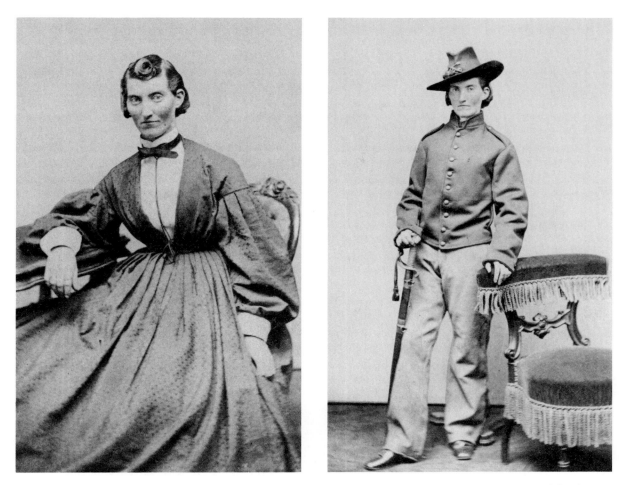

The restrictions of gender roles often frustrated women who longed to contribute to the war effort. Frances Clalin disguised her identity in order to fight with Federal forces in Missouri. *Trustees of the Boston Public Library.*

The poet Walt Whitman, who became a daily visitor to wounded soldiers in Washington, D.C., left a record of his experiences as a volunteer nurse. As

Walt Whitman

he dressed wounds and tried to comfort suffering and lonely men, Whitman found "the marrow of the tragedy concentrated in those Army Hospitals." But despite "indescribably horrid wounds . . . the groan that could not be repress'd . . . [the] emaciated face and glassy eye," he also found in the hospitals inspiration and a deepening faith in American democracy. Whitman admired the "incredible dauntlessness" and sacrifice of the common soldier who fought for the Union. "The genius of the United States is not best or most in its executives or legislatures," he had written in the

Preface to his great work *Leaves of Grass* (1855), "but always most in the common people." Whitman worked this idealization of the common man into his poetry, rejecting the lofty meter and rhyme of European verse and striving instead for a "genuineness" that would appeal to the masses.

Thus northern society embraced strangely contradictory tendencies. Materialism and greed flourished alongside idealism, religious conviction, and self-sacrifice. While wealthy men purchased 118,000 substitutes and almost 87,000 commutations at $300 each to avoid service in the Union Army, other soldiers risked their lives out of a desire to preserve the Union or extend freedom. It was as if several different wars were under way, each of them serving different motives.

Lincoln, shown here in a portrait by Peter Baumgras from the spring of 1865, formulated complex, studied positions on slavery and emancipation. *McLellan Lincoln Collection, The John Hay Library, Brown University. Photo by John Miller.*

The Strange Advent of Emancipation

At the very highest levels of government there was a similar lack of clarity about the purpose of the war. Through the first several months of the struggle, both Davis and Lincoln studiously avoided references to slavery, the crux of the matter. Davis realized that emphasis on the issue might increase class conflict in the South. Earlier in his career he had struggled to convince nonslaveholders that defense of the planters' slaves was in their interest. Rather than face that challenge again, Davis articulated a conservative ideology. He told southerners they were fighting for constitutional liberty: northern betrayal of the founding fathers' legacy had necessitated secession. As long as Lincoln also avoided making slavery an issue, Davis's line seemed to work.

Lincoln had his own reasons for not mentioning slavery. For some time he clung to the hopeful but mistaken idea that a pro-Union majority would assert itself in the South. Perhaps it would be possible, he thought, to coax the South back into the Union and stop the fighting. Raising the slavery issue would effectively end the possibility of any such compromise.

Powerful political considerations also dictated that Lincoln remain silent. The Republican party was a young and unwieldy coalition. Some Republicans burned with moral outrage over slavery; others were frankly racist, dedicated to protecting free whites from the Slave Power and the competition of cheap slave labor; still others saw the tariff or immigration or some other issue as paramount. A forthright stand by Lincoln on the subject of slavery could split the party, pleasing some groups and alienating others. Until a consensus developed among the party's various wings, or until Lincoln found a way to appeal to all the elements of the party, silence was the best approach.

The president's hesitancy ran counter to some of his personal feelings. Lincoln was a sensitive and compassionate man whose self-awareness, humility, and moral anguish during the war were evident in his speeches and writings. But as a politician, Lincoln kept his moral convictions to himself. He distinguished between the personal and the official; he would not let his feelings determine his political acts. As a result, his political positions were studied and complex, calculated for maximum advantage. Frederick Douglass, the astute and courageous black protest leader, sensed that Lincoln the man was without prejudice toward black people. Yet Douglass judged him "pre-eminently the white man's president."

Lincoln first broached the subject of slavery in a major way in March 1862, when he proposed that the states consider emancipation on their own. He asked Congress to pass a resolution promising aid to any state that decided to emancipate, and he appealed to border-state representatives to give the idea of emancipation serious consideration. What Lincoln was talking about was gradual emancipation, with compensation for slaveholders and colonization of the freed slaves outside the United States. To a delegation of free blacks he explained that "it is better for us both . . . to be separated."

Lincoln's Plan for Gradual Emancipation

Until well into 1864 Lincoln steadfastly promoted an unpromising and in national terms wholly impractical scheme to colonize blacks in some region like Central America. Despite Secretary of State William H. Seward's care to insert phrases such as "with their consent," the word *deportation* crept into one of Lincoln's speeches in place of *colonization*. Thus his was as conservative a scheme as could be devised. Moreover, since the states would make the decision voluntarily, no responsibility for it would attach to Lincoln.

Others wanted to go much further. A group of congressional Republicans known as the Radicals dedicated themselves to seeing that the war was prosecuted vigorously. They were instrumental in creating a joint committee on the conduct of the war, which investigated Union reverses, sought to increase the efficiency of the war effort, and prodded the executive to take stronger measures. Early in the war these Radicals, with support from other representatives, turned their attention to slavery.

In August 1861, at the Radicals' instigation, Congress passed its first confiscation act. Designed to punish the Confederate rebels, the law confiscated

▶ **Confiscation Acts**

all property used for "insurrectionary purposes"—that is, if the South used slaves in a hostile action, those slaves were declared seized and liberated from their owners' possession. A second confiscation act (July 1862) was much more drastic: it confiscated the property of all those who supported the rebellion, even those who merely resided in the South and paid Confederate taxes. Their slaves were "forever free of their servitude, and not again [to be] held as slaves." The logic behind these acts was that the insurrection—as Lincoln always termed it—was a serious revolution requiring strong measures. Let the government use its full powers, free the slaves, and crush the revolution, urged the Radicals.

Lincoln chose not to go that far. He stood by his proposal of voluntary gradual emancipation by the states and made no effort to enforce the second confiscation act. His stance brought a public protest from Horace Greeley, editor of the powerful *New York Tribune*. In an open letter to the president entitled "The Prayer of Twenty Millions," Greeley wrote, "We require of you. . . that you execute the laws. . . . We think you are strangely and disastrously remiss . . . with regard to the emancipating

provisions of the new Confiscation Act. . . . We complain that the Union cause has suffered from mistaken deference to Rebel Slavery." Reaching the nub of the issue, the influential editor went on, "On the face of this wide earth, Mr. President, there is not one disinterested, determined, intelligent champion of the Union cause who does not feel that all attempts to put down the Rebellion and at the same time uphold its inciting cause are preposterous and futile."

Lincoln's letter in reply was an explicit statement of his complex and calculated approach to the question. He disagreed, he said, with all those who would make the saving or destroying of slavery the paramount issue of the war. "I would save the Union," announced Lincoln. "If I could save the Union without freeing *any* slave I would do it, and if I could save it by freeing *all* the slaves I would do it; and if I would save it by freeing some and leaving others alone I would also do that. What I do about slavery, and the colored race, I do because I believe it helps to save the Union." Lincoln closed with a personal disclaimer: "I have here stated my purpose according to my view of *official* duty; and I intend no modification of my oft-expressed *personal* wish that all men every where could be free."

When he wrote those words, Lincoln had already decided to take a new step: issuance of the Emancipation Proclamation. On the advice of the cabinet, however, he was waiting for a Union victory before announcing it, so that the proclamation would not appear to be an act of desperation. Yet the letter to Greeley was not simply an effort to stall; it was an integral part of Lincoln's approach to the future of slavery, as the text of the Emancipation Proclamation would show.

On September 22, 1862, shortly after the Battle of Antietam, Lincoln issued the first part of his two-part proclamation. Invoking his powers as com-

▶ **Emancipation Proclamations**

mander-in-chief of the armed forces, he announced that on January 1, 1863, he would emancipate the slaves in states whose people "shall then be in rebellion against the United States." The January proclamation would designate the areas in rebellion based on the presence or absence of bona fide representatives in Congress.

The September proclamation was less a declaration of the right of slaves to be free than it was a threat to southerners to end the war. "Knowing the value that was set on the slaves by the rebels," said Garrison Frazier, a black Georgian, "the President thought that his proclamation would stimulate them to lay down their arms . . . and their not doing so has now made the freedom of the slaves a part of the war." Lincoln may not actually have expected southerners to give up their effort, but he was careful to offer them the option, thus putting the onus of emancipation on them.

Lincoln's designation of the areas in rebellion on January 1 is worth noting. He excepted from his list every Confederate county or city that had fallen under Union control. Those areas, he declared, "are, for the present, left precisely as if this proclamation were not issued." Lincoln also did not liberate slaves in the border slave states that remained in the Union.

"The President has purposely made the proclamation inoperative in all places where . . . the slaves [are] accessible," complained the anti-administration *New York World*. "He has proclaimed emancipation only where he has notoriously no power to execute it." The exceptions, said the paper, "render the proclamation not merely futile, but ridiculous." Partisanship aside, even Secretary of State Seward, a moderate Republican, said sarcastically, "We show our sympathy with slavery by emancipating slaves where we cannot reach them and holding them in bondage where we can set them free." A British official, Lord Russell, commented on the "very strange nature" of the document, noting that it did not declare "a principle adverse to slavery."

Furthermore, by making the liberation of the slaves "a fit and necessary war measure," Lincoln raised a variety of legal questions. How long did a war measure have force? Did its power cease with the suppression of a rebellion? The proclamation did little to clarify the status or citizenship of the freed slaves. And a reference to garrison duty in one of the closing paragraphs suggested that slaves would have inferior duties and rank in the army. For many months, in fact, their pay and treatment were inferior.

Thus the Emancipation Proclamation was a puzzling and ambiguous document that said less than it seemed to say. It freed no bondsmen, and major limitations were embedded in its language. But if as a moral and legal document it was wanting, as a political document it was nearly flawless. Because the proclamation defined the war as a war against slavery, radicals could applaud it. Yet at the

same time it protected Lincoln's position with conservatives, leaving him room to retreat if he chose and forcing no immediate changes on the border slave states. The president had not gone as far as Congress, and he had taken no position that he could not change later if necessary.

In June 1864, however, Lincoln gave his support to the constitutional end of slavery. Reformers such as Elizabeth Cady Stanton and Susan B. Anthony had petitioned and pressured for an amendment that would write emancipation into the Constitution. On the eve of the Republican national convention, he called the party's chairman to the White House and instructed him to have the party "put into the platform as the keystone, the amendment of the Constitution abolishing and prohibiting slavery forever." It was done; the party called for a new amendment, the thirteenth. Although Republican delegates probably would have adopted such a plank without his urging, Lincoln showed his commitment by lobbying Congress for quick approval of the measure. He succeeded, and the proposed amendment went to the states for ratification or rejection. Lincoln's strong support for the Thirteenth Amendment—an unequivocal prohibition of slavery—constitutes his best claim to the title Great Emancipator.

Yet Lincoln soon clouded that clear stand, for in 1865 the newly re-elected president considered allowing the defeated southern states to re-enter the Union and delay or defeat the amendment. In February he and Secretary of State Seward met with three Confederate commissioners at Hampton Roads, Virginia. The end of the war was clearly in sight, and southern representatives angled vainly for an armistice that would allow southern independence. But Lincoln was doing some political maneuvering of his own, apparently contemplating the creation of a new and broader party based on a postwar alliance with southern Whigs and moderates. The cement for the coalition would be concessions to planter interests.

Pointing out that the Emancipation Proclamation was only a war measure, Lincoln predicted that the courts would decide whether it had granted all, some, or none of the slaves their freedom. Seward observed that the Thirteenth Amendment, which would be definitive, was not yet ratified; re-entry into the Union would allow the southern states to vote against it and block it. Lincoln did not con-

Hampton Roads Conference

Nearly 180,000 black men fought in the Union army, providing a vital infusion of strength for the northern cause. These soldiers in the 2nd U.S. Colored Light Artillery participated in the Battle of Nashville in December 1864. *Chicago Historical Society.*

tradict him but spoke in favor of "prospective" ratification—ratification with a five-year delay. He also promised to seek $400 million in compensation for slaveholders and to consider their position on such related questions as confiscation. Such financial aid would provide an economic incentive for planters to rejoin the Union and capital to ease the transition to freedom for both races.

These were startling propositions from a president who was on the verge of military victory. Most northerners opposed them, and only the opposition of Jefferson Davis, who set himself against anything short of independence, prevented discussion of the proposals in the South. They indicated that even at the end of the war, Lincoln was keeping his options open, maintaining the line he had drawn between *"official* duty" and *"personal* wish." Contrary to legend, then, Lincoln did not attempt to lead public opinion on race, as did advocates of equality in one direction and racist Democrats in the other. Instead he moved cautiously, constructing complex and ambiguous positions. He avoided the great risks inherent in challenging, educating, or inspiring the nation's conscience.

Before the war was over, the Confederacy too addressed the issue of emancipation. Ironically, a strong proposal in favor of liberation came from Jefferson Davis. Though emancipation was far less popular in the South than in the North, Davis did not flinch or conceal his purpose.

> **Davis's Plan for Emancipation**

He was dedicated to independence, and he was willing to sacrifice slavery to achieve that goal. After considering the alternatives for some time, Davis concluded in the fall of 1864 that it was necessary to act.

Reasoning that the military situation of the Confederacy was desperate and that independence with emancipation was preferable to defeat with emancipation, Davis proposed that the central government purchase and train forty thousand male Negro laborers. The men would work for the army under a promise of emancipation and future residence in the South. Later Davis upgraded his proposal, calling for the recruitment and arming of slave soldiers. The wives and children of these soldiers, he made plain, must also receive freedom from the states. Davis and his advisers did not favor full equality—they envisioned "an intermediate state of serfage or peonage." Thus they shared with Lincoln and their generation a racial blindness that tried to ignore the massive changes under way.

The Strange Advent of Emancipation

Still, Davis had proposed a radical change for the conservative, slaveholding South. Bitter debate resounded through the Confederacy, but Davis stood his ground. When the Confederate congress approved enlistments without the promise of freedom, Davis insisted on more. He issued an executive order to guarantee that owners would cooperate with the emancipation of slave soldiers, and his allies in the states started to work for emancipation of the soldiers' families. Some black troops started to drill as the end of the war approached.

Confederate emancipation began too late to revive southern armies or win diplomatic advantages with antislavery Europeans. But Lincoln's Emancipation Proclamation stimulated a vital infusion of forces into the Union armies. Beginning in 1863 slaves shouldered arms for the North. Before the war was over, 134,000 slaves (and 52,000 free blacks) had fought for freedom and the Union. Their participation was crucial to northern victory, and it discouraged recognition of the Confederacy by foreign governments. Lincoln's policy, despite its limitations and its lack of clarity, had great practical effect.

The Disintegration of Confederate Unity

During the final two years of fighting, both northern and southern governments waged the war in the face of increasing opposition at home. Dissatisfaction that had surfaced earlier grew more intense and sometimes even violent. The unrest was connected to the military stalemate: neither side was close to victory in 1863, though the war had become gigantic in scope and costly in lives. But protest also arose from fundamental stresses in the social structures of the North and the South.

The Confederacy's problems were both more serious and more deeply rooted than the North's. Vastly disadvantaged in terms of industrial capacity, natural resources, and labor, southerners felt the cost of the war more quickly, more directly, and more painfully than northerners. But even more fundamental were the Confederacy's internal problems; crises that were integrally connected with the

southern class system threatened the Confederate cause.

One ominous development was the increasing opposition of planters to their own government, whose actions often had a negative effect on them. Not only did the Richmond government impose high taxes and a tax-in-kind, Confederate military authorities also impressed slaves to build fortifications. And when Union forces advanced on plantation areas, Confederate commanders sent detachments through the countryside to burn stores of cotton that lay in the enemy's path. Such interference with plantation routines and financial interests was not what planters had expected of their government, and they resisted. Many taxes went unpaid, and many planters continued to grow and ship cotton, despite the government's desire to withhold it from world markets as a diplomatic weapon.

Nor were the centralizing policies of the Davis administration popular. Many planters agreed with the *Charleston Mercury* that the southern states had seceded because the federal government had grown and "usurped powers not granted—progressively trenched upon State Rights." The increasing size and power of the Richmond administration therefore startled and alarmed them.

The Confederate constitution, drawn up by the leading political thinkers of the South, had in fact granted substantial powers to the central government, especially in time of war. But for many planters, states' rights had become virtually synonymous with complete state sovereignty. R. B. Rhett, editor of the *Charleston Mercury,* wishfully (and inaccurately) described the Confederate constitution: "[It] leaves the States untouched in their Sovereignty, and commits to the Confederate Government only a few simple objects, and a few simple powers to enforce them." Governor Joseph E. Brown of Georgia took a similarly exalted view of the importance of the states. During the brief interval between Georgia's secession from the Union and its admission to the Confederacy, Brown sent an ambassador to Europe to seek recognition for the sovereign republic of Georgia from Queen Victoria, Napoleon III, and the king of Belgium. His mentality harkened back to the 1770s and the Articles of Confederation, not to the Constitution of 1789 or the Confederate constitution.

In effect, years of opposition to the federal government within the Union had frozen southerners

A southern family flees its home as the battle lines draw near. The war forced many Confederates to become refugees. Photographed by Mathew Brady. *National Archives.*

in a defensive posture. Now they erected the barrier of states' rights as a defense against change, hiding behind it while their capacity for creative statesmanship atrophied. Planters sought a guarantee that their plantations and their lives would remain untouched; they were deeply committed neither to building a southern nation nor to winning independence. If the Confederacy had been allowed to depart from the Union in peace and continue as a semideveloped cotton-growing region, they would have been content. When secession revolutionized their world, they could not or would not adjust to it.

Confused and embittered, southerners struck out at Jefferson Davis. Conscription, thundered Governor Brown, was "subversive of [Georgia's] sovereignty, and at war with all the principles for the support of which Georgia entered into this revolution." Searching for ways to frustrate the law, Brown bickered over draft exemptions and ordered local enrollment officials not to cooperate with the Confederacy. The *Charleston Mercury* told readers that "conscription . . . is . . . the very embodiment of Lincolnism, which our gallant armies are today fighting." In a gesture of stubborn selfishness, planter Robert Toombs of Georgia, a former United States senator, defied the government, the newspapers, and his neighbors' petitions by continuing to grow large amounts of cotton. His action bespoke

the inflexibility and frustration of the southern elite at a crucial point in the Confederacy's struggle to survive.

The southern courts ultimately upheld Davis's power to conscript. He continued to provide strong leadership and drove through the legislature measures that gave the Confederacy a fighting chance. Despite his cold formality and inability to disarm critics, Davis possessed two important virtues: iron determination and total dedication to independence. These qualities kept the Confederacy afloat, for he implemented his measures and enforced them. But his actions earned him the hatred of most influential and elite citizens.

Meanwhile, at the bottom of southern society, there were other difficulties. Food riots occurred in the spring of 1863 in Atlanta, Macon, Columbus, and Augusta, Georgia, and in **Food** Salisbury and High Point, North **Riots in** Carolina. On April 2, a crowd as- **Southern** sembled in the Confederate capi- **Cities** tal of Richmond to demand relief from Governor Letcher. A passerby, noticing the excitement, asked a young girl, "Is there some celebration?" "There is," replied the girl. "We celebrate our right to live. We are starving. As soon as enough of us get together we are going to the bakeries and each of us will take a loaf of bread." Soon they did just that, sparking a riot that

The Disintegration of Confederate Unity

Davis himself had to quell at gunpoint. Later that year, another group of angry rioters ransacked a street in Mobile, Alabama.

Throughout the rural South, ordinary people resisted more quietly—by refusing to cooperate with impressments of food, conscription, or tax collection. "In all the States impressments are evaded by every means which ingenuity can suggest, and in some openly resisted," wrote a high-ranking commissary officer. Farmers who did provide food refused to accept certificates of credit or government bonds in lieu of cash, as required by law. Conscription officers increasingly found no one to draft— men of draft age were hiding out in the forests. "The disposition to avoid military service," observed one of Georgia's senators in 1864, "is general." In some areas tax agents were killed in the line of duty.

Davis was ill equipped to deal with such discontent. Austere and private by nature, he failed to communicate with the masses. For long stretches of time he buried himself in military affairs or administrative details, until a crisis forced him to rush off on a speaking tour to revive the spirit of resistance. His class perspective also distanced him from the sufferings of the common people. While his social circle in Richmond dined on duck and oysters, ordinary southerners leached salt from the smokehouse floor and went hungry. State governors who saw to the common people's needs won the public's loyalty, but Davis failed to reach out to them and thus lost the support of the plain folk.

Such civil discontent was certain to affect the Confederate armies. "What man is there that would stay in the army and no that his family is sufring at home?" an angry citizen wrote

> **Desertions from the Confederate Army**

anonymously to the secretary of war. An upcountry South Carolina newspaper agreed, asking, "What would sooner make our soldiers falter than the cry from their families?" Spurred by concern for their loved ones and resentment of the rich man's war, large numbers of men did indeed leave the armies, supported by their friends and neighbors. Mary Boykin Chesnut observed a man being dragged back to the army as his wife looked on. "Desert again, Jake!" she cried openly. "You desert again, quick as you kin. Come back to your wife and children."

Desertion did not become a serious problem for the Confederacy until the summer of 1862, and stif-fer policing solved the problem that year. But from 1863 on, the number of men on duty fell rapidly as desertions soared. By the summer of 1863, John A. Campbell, the South's assistant secretary of war, wondered whether "so general a habit" as desertion could be considered a crime. Campbell estimated that 40,000 to 50,000 troops were absent without leave and that 100,000 were evading duty in some way. Liberal furloughs, amnesty proclamations, and appeals to return had little effect; by November 1863, Secretary of War James Seddon admitted that one-third of the army could not be accounted for. The situation was to worsen.

The gallantry of those who stayed on in Lee's army and the daring of their commander made for a deceptively positive start to the 1863 campaign.

> **Battle of Chancellors-ville**

On May 2 and 3 at Chancellorsville, Virginia, 130,000 members of the Union Army of the Potomac bore down on fewer than 60,000 Confederates. Acting as if they enjoyed being outnumbered, Lee and Stonewall Jackson boldly divided their forces, ordering 30,000 men under Jackson on a day-long march westward and to the rear for a flank attack. Jackson arrived at his position late in the afternoon to witness unprepared Union troops "laughing, smoking," playing cards, and waiting for dinner. "Push right ahead," Jackson said, and his weary but excited corps swooped down on the federals and drove their right wing back in confusion. The Union forces left Chancellorsville the next day defeated. Although Stonewall Jackson had been fatally wounded, it was a remarkable southern victory.

But two critical battles in July 1863 brought crushing defeats for the Confederacy and a turning point for the war. General Ulysses S. Grant, after months of searching through swamps and bayous, had succeeded in finding an advantageous approach to Vicksburg and promptly laid siege to that vital western fortification. If Vicksburg fell, United States forces would control the Mississippi, cutting the Confederacy in half and gaining an open path into its interior (see map, page 402). Meanwhile, with no serious threat to Richmond, General Robert E. Lee proposed a Confederate invasion of the North. Both movements drew toward conclusion early in July.

In the North, Lee's troops streamed through western Maryland and into Pennsylvania, threatening both Washington and Baltimore. The possibility of a major victory near the Union capital became more and more likely. But along the Mississippi, Confederate prospects darkened. Davis and Secretary of War Seddon repeatedly wired General Joseph E. Johnston to concentrate his forces and attack Grant's army. "Vicksburg must not be lost, at least without a struggle," they insisted. Johnston, however, either failed in imagination or did not understand the possibilities of his command. "I consider saving Vicksburg hopeless," he telegraphed at one point, and despite prodding he did nothing to relieve the garrison. In the meantime, Grant's men were supplying themselves by drawing on the agricultural riches of the Mississippi River valley. With such provisions, they could continue their siege indefinitely. In fact, their rich meat-and-vegetables diet became so tiresome that one day, as Grant rode by, a private looked up and muttered, "Hardtack" (pilot biscuit). Soon a line of soldiers was shouting "Hardtack! Hardtack!" demanding respite from turkey and sweet potatoes.

In such circumstances the fall of Vicksburg was inevitable, and on July 4, 1863, its commander surrendered. On the same day a battle that had been raging since July 1 concluded at

> **Battle of Gettysburg**

Gettysburg, Pennsylvania. On July 1 and 2, Union and Confederate forces had both made gains in furious fighting. Then on July 3 Lee ordered a direct assault on Union fortifications atop Cemetery Ridge. Full of foreboding, General James Longstreet warned Lee that "no 15,000 men ever arrayed for battle can take that position." But Lee, hoping success might force the Union to accept peace with independence, stuck to his plan. His brave troops rushed the position, and a hundred momentarily breached the enemy's line. But most fell in heavy slaughter. On July 4 Lee had to withdraw, having suffered almost 4,000 killed and approximately 24,000 missing and wounded. The Confederate general reported to Jefferson Davis that "I am alone to blame" and offered to resign. Davis replied that to find a more capable commander was "an impossibility."

Although southern troops displayed a courage and dedication at Gettysburg that would never be forgotten, the results of the battles on July 4 were disastrous. Josiah Gorgas, the genius of Confederate ordnance operations, confided to his diary, "Today absolute ruin seems our portion. The Confederacy totters to its destruction." In desperation

President Davis and several state governors resorted to threats and racial scare tactics to drive southern whites to further sacrifice. Defeat, Davis warned, would mean "extermination of yourselves, your wives, and children." Governor Charles Clark of Mississippi predicted "elevation of the black race to a position of equality—aye, of superiority, that will make them your masters and rulers." Abroad, British officials held back the delivery of badly needed warships, and diplomats postponed recognition of the Confederate government.

From this point on, the internal disintegration of the Confederacy quickened. A few newspapers and a few bold publications began to call openly for peace. "We are for peace," admitted the *Raleigh* (North Carolina) *Daily Progress*, "because there has been enough of blood and carnage, enough of widows and orphans." A neighboring journal, the *North Carolina Standard,* vowed to "tell the truth," tacitly admitted that defeat was inevitable, and called for negotiations. Similar proposals were made in several state legislatures, though they were presented as plans for independence on honorable terms. Confederate leaders began to realize that they were losing the support of the common people. A prominent Texan noted in his diary that secession had been the work of political leaders operating without the firm support of "the mass of the people without property." Governor Zebulon Vance of North Carolina, who agreed, wrote privately that independence would require more "blood and misery . . . and our people will not pay this price I am satisfied for their independence. . . . The great popular heart is not now & never has been in this war."

In North Carolina a peace movement grew under the leadership of William W. Holden, a popular Democratic politician and editor. In the summer of

> **Southern Peace Movements**

1863 over one hundred public meetings took place in support of peace negotiations; many established figures believed that Holden had the majority of the people behind him. In Georgia early in 1864, Governor Brown and Alexander H. Stephens, vice president of the Confederacy, led a similar effort. Ultimately, however, these movements came to naught. The lack of a two-party system threw into question the legitimacy of any criticism of the government; even Holden and Brown could not entirely escape the taint of dishonor and disloyalty. That the movement existed despite the risks suggested deep disaffection.

The results of the 1863 Confederate congressional elections continued the tendency toward dissent. Everywhere secessionists and supporters of the Confederate administration lost seats to men who were not identified with the government. Many of the new representatives, who were often former Whigs, openly opposed the administration or publicly favored peace. In the last years of the war, Davis depended heavily on support from Union-occupied districts to maintain a majority in the congress. Having secured the legislation he needed, he used the bureaucracy and the army to enforce his unpopular policies. Ironically, as the South's situation grew desperate, former critics such as the *Charleston Mercury* became supporters of the administration. They and a core of courageous, determined soldiers kept the Confederacy alive in spite of disintegrating popular support.

By 1864 much of the opposition to the war had moved entirely outside politics. Southerners were simply giving up the struggle, withdrawing their cooperation from the government, and forming a sort of counter-society. Deserters joined with ordinary citizens who were sick of the war to dominate whole towns and counties. Secret societies dedicated to reunion, such as the Heroes of America and the Red Strings, sprang up. Active dissent spread throughout the South but was particularly common in upland and mountain regions. "The condition of things in the mountain districts of North Carolina, South Carolina, Georgia, and Alabama," admitted Assistant Secretary of War John A. Campbell, "menaces the existence of the Confederacy as fatally as either of the armies of the United States." Confederate officials tried using the army to round up deserters and compel obedience, but this approach was only temporarily effective. The government was losing the support of its citizens.

Antiwar Sentiment in the North

In the North opposition to the war was similar in many ways, but not as severe. There was concern over the growing centralization of government, and war-weariness was a frequent complaint. Discrimination and injustice in the draft sparked protest among poor citizens, just as they did in the South. But the Union was so much richer than the South in human resources that none of these problems ever threatened the stability of the government. Fresh recruits were always available, and food and other necessities were not subject to severe shortages.

Moreover, Lincoln possessed a talent that Davis lacked: he knew how to stay in touch with the ordinary citizen. Through letters to newspapers and to soldiers' families, he reached the common people and demonstrated that he had not forgotten them. Their grief was his also, for the war was his personal tragedy. After scrambling to the summit of political ambition, Lincoln had seen the glory of the presidency turn to horror. The daily carnage, the tortuous political problems, and the ceaseless criticism weighed heavily on him. In moving language, this president—a self-educated man of humble origins—was able to communicate his suffering. His words helped to contain northern discontent, though they could not remove it.

Much of this wartime protest sprang from politics. The Democratic party, though nudged from its dominant position by the Republican surge of the late 1850s, remained strong. Its **Peace Democrats** leaders were determined to regain power, and they found much to criticize in Lincoln's policies: the carnage and length of the war, the expansion of federal powers, inflation and the high tariff, and the improved status of blacks. Accordingly, running as the party of tradition, they attacked the continuation of the war and called for reunion on the basis of "the Constitution as it is and the Union as it was." The Democrats denounced conscription and martial law and defended states' rights and the interests of agriculture. They charged repeatedly that Republican policies were designed to flood the North with blacks, depriving white males of their status, jobs, and women. Their stand appealed to southerners who had settled north of the Ohio River, to conservatives, to many poor people, and to some eastern merchants who had lost profitable southern trade. In the 1862 congressional elections, the Democrats made a strong comeback, and during the war, peace Democrats influenced New York State and won majorities in the legislatures of Illinois and Indiana.

Led by outspoken men like Clement L. Vallan-

Mobs in the New York City draft riots directed much of their anger at blacks. This woodcut from *Leslie's Illustrated* shows rioters burning an orphanage for black children. *Anne S. K. Brown Military Collection, John Hay Library, Brown University.*

digham of Ohio, the peace Democrats were highly visible. Vallandigham criticized Lincoln as a dictator who had suspended the writ of habeas corpus without congressional authority and arrested thousands of innocent citizens. Like other Democrats, he condemned both conscription and emancipation and urged voters to use their power at the polling place to depose "King Abraham." Vallandigham stayed carefully within legal bounds, but his attacks were so damaging to the war effort that military authorities arrested him after Lincoln suspended habeas corpus. Fearing that Vallandigham might gain the stature of a martyr, the president decided against a jail term and exiled him to the Confederacy. Thus Lincoln rid himself of a troublesome critic, in the process saddling puzzled Confederates with a man who insisted on talking about "our country." Eventually Vallandigham returned to the North through Canada.

Lincoln believed that antiwar Democrats were linked to secret organizations, such as the Knights of the Golden Circle and the Order of American Knights, that harbored traitorous ideas. These societies, he feared, stimulated draft resistance, discouraged enlistment, sabotaged communications, and plotted to aid the Confederacy. Likening such

groups to a poisonous snake striking at the government, Republicans sometimes branded them—and by extension the peace Democrats—as Copperheads. Though Democrats were connected with these organizations, most engaged in politics rather than treason. And though some saboteurs and Confederate agents were active in the North, they never brought about any major demonstration of support for the Confederacy. Whether Lincoln overreacted in arresting his critics and suppressing opposition is still a matter of debate, but it is certain that he acted with a heavier hand and with less provocation than Jefferson Davis.

More violent opposition to the government came from ordinary citizens facing the draft, especially the urban poor. Conscription was a massive but poorly organized affair. Federal enrolling officers made up the list of eligibles, a procedure open to personal favoritism and ethnic or class prejudice. Lists of those conscripted reveal that poor men were called more often than rich and that disproportionate numbers of immigrants were called. (Approximately 200,000 men born in Germany and 150,000 born in Ireland served in the Union Army.) Rich men could furnish substitutes or pay a commutation to avoid service.

As a result, there were scores of disturbances and melees. Enrolling officers received rough treatment in many parts of the North, and riots occurred in Ohio, Indiana, Pennsylvania, Illinois, and Wisconsin, and in such cities as Troy, Albany, and Newark. By far the most serious outbreak of violence occurred in New York City in July 1863. The war was unpopular in that Democratic stronghold, and ethnic and class tensions ran high. Shippers had recently broken a longshoremen's strike by hiring black strikebreakers to work under police protection. Working-class New Yorkers feared an influx of black labor from the South and regarded blacks as the cause of an unpopular war. Irish workers, often recently arrived and poor themselves, resented being forced to serve in the place of others. And indeed, local draft lists provide evidence that the poor and foreign-born had to bear the burden of service.

> **New York City Draft Riot**

The provost marshal's office came under attack first; then mobs crying "Down with the rich" looted wealthy homes and stores. But blacks proved to be the rioters' special target. Luckless blacks who happened to be in the rioters' path were beaten; soon the mob rampaged through black neighborhoods, destroying even an orphans' asylum. At least seventy-four people died during the violence, which raged out of control for three days. Only the dispatch of army units fresh from Gettysburg ended the episode.

Once inducted, northern soldiers felt many of the same anxieties and grievances as their southern counterparts. Federal troops too had to cope with loneliness and concern for their loved ones, disease, and the tedium of camp life. Thousands of men slipped away from authorities. Given the problems plaguing the draft and the discouragement in the North over lack of progress in the war, it is not surprising that the Union Army struggled with a desertion rate as high as the Confederates'.

Discouragement and war-weariness neared their peak during the summer of 1864. At that point the Democratic party nominated the popular General George B. McClellan for president and put a qualified peace plank into its platform. The plank, written by Vallandigham, condemned "four years of failure to restore the Union by the experiment of war" and called for an armistice. Lincoln, running with Tennessee's Andrew Johnson on a "National Union" ticket, concluded that it was "exceedingly

probable that this Administration will not be re-elected."

Then, during a publicized interchange with Confederate officials sent to Canada, Lincoln insisted that the terms for peace include reunion and "the abandonment of slavery." A wave of protest rose in the North, for many voters were weary of war and not ready to demand terms beyond preservation of the Union. Lincoln quickly backtracked, denying that his offer meant "that nothing *else* or *less* would be considered, if offered." He would insist on freedom only for those slaves (about 134,000) who had joined the Union Army under his promise of emancipation. Thus Lincoln in effect acknowledged the danger that he would not be re-elected. The fortunes of war, however, soon changed the electoral situation.

Northern Pressure and Southern Will

The year 1864 brought to fruition the North's long-term diplomatic strategy. From the outset, the North had pursued one paramount diplomatic goal: to prevent recognition of the Confederacy by European nations. Foreign recognition would damage the North's claim that it was fighting not a separate nation but an illegal rebellion. More important, recognition would open the way to the foreign military and financial aid that could assure Confederate independence.

> **Northern Diplomatic Strategy**

Among members of the British elite, there was considerable sympathy for southern planters, whose aristocratic values were similar to their own. In terms of power politics, both England and France stood to benefit from a divided America, which would necessarily be a weakened rival. Thus Lincoln and Secretary of State Seward faced a difficult task. To achieve their goal, they needed to avoid both major military defeats and unnecessary controversies with the European powers. Southerners aided them by an overconfident reliance on "King Cotton" diplomacy. Knowing that the textile industry, directly or indirectly, employed one-fifth of the British population, southern leaders declared that "Cotton is King." They believed that the

British government, concerned about obtaining cotton for the country's mills, would have to recognize the Confederacy.

Cotton was a good card to play, but it was not a trump. At the beginning of the war British mills had a 50 percent surplus of cotton on hand. New sources of supply in India, Egypt, and Brazil helped to fill their needs later on, and some southern cotton continued to reach Europe, despite the Confederacy's recommendation that its citizens plant and ship no cotton. The British government, refusing to be stampeded into recognition, kept its eye on the battlefield. France, though sympathetic to the South, was unwilling to act without the British. Confederate agents were able to purchase valuable arms and supplies in Europe and obtained some loans from European financiers, but they never achieved a diplomatic breakthrough.

More than once the Union strategy nearly broke down. A major crisis occurred in 1861 when the overzealous commander of an American frigate stopped the British steamer *Trent* and abducted two Confederate ambassadors. The British reacted strongly, but Lincoln and Seward were able to delay until public opinion cooled and they could back down and return the ambassadors. In a series of confrontations, the United States protested against the building and sale of warships to the Confederacy. A few ships built in Britain, notably the *Alabama,* reached open water to serve the Confederacy. Over twenty-two months, without entering a southern port, the *Alabama* destroyed or captured more than sixty northern ships. But soon the British government began to bar delivery to the Confederacy of warships such as the Laird rams, formidable vessels whose pointed prows were designed to break the Union blockade.

Back on American battlefields, the northern victory was far from won. Most engagements had demonstrated the advantages enjoyed by the defense and the extreme difficulty of destroying an opposing army. As General William Tecumseh Sherman recognized, the North had to "keep the war South until they are not only ruined, exhausted, but humbled in pride and spirit." Yet the world's recognized military authorities agreed that deep invasion was extremely difficult and risky. The farther an army penetrated enemy territory, the more vulnerable its own communications and support became. Moreover, noted the Prussian expert Karl von Clausewitz, if the invader encountered a "truly national" resistance, his troops would be "everywhere exposed to attacks by an insurgent population." Thus, if southerners were determined enough to mount a "truly national" resistance, their defiance and the vast size of their country would make a northern victory virtually impossible.

General Grant decided to test these obstacles—and southern will—with an innovation of his own: the strategy of raids. Raids were nothing new, but what Grant had in mind was raids on a massive scale. He proposed to use whole armies, not just cavalry, to destroy Confederate railroads, thus denying the enemy rail transportation and damaging the South's economy. Federal armies, abandoning their lines of support, would live off the land while they laid waste all resources useful to the Confederacy. After General George H. Thomas's troops won the Battle of Chattanooga in November 1863 by ignoring orders and charging up Missionary Ridge, the heartland of the South lay open. Moving to Virginia, Grant entrusted General Sherman with 100,000 men for a raid deep into the South, toward Atlanta.

Jefferson Davis countered by placing the army of General Johnston in Sherman's path. Davis's entire political strategy for 1864 depended on the demonstration of Confederate military strength and a successful defense of Atlanta. With the federal elections of 1864 approaching, Davis hoped that a display of strength and resolution by the South would defeat Lincoln and elect a president who would sue for peace. When Johnston slowly but steadily fell back toward Atlanta, Davis grew anxious and pressed his commander for information and assurances that Atlanta would be held. From a purely military point of view, Johnston was conducting the defense skillfully, but Jefferson Davis could not take a purely military point of view. When Johnston remained uninformative and continued to drop back, Davis replaced him with the one-legged General John Hood, who knew his job was to fight. "Our all depends on that army at Atlanta," wrote Mary Boykin Chesnut. "If that fails us, the game is up."

For southern morale, the game was up. Hood attacked but was beaten, and Sherman's army occupied Atlanta on September 2, 1864. The victory buoyed northern spirits and assured Lincoln's re-election. Mary Chesnut moaned, "There is no hope," and a government clerk in Richmond wrote, "Our fondly-cherished visions of peace have van-

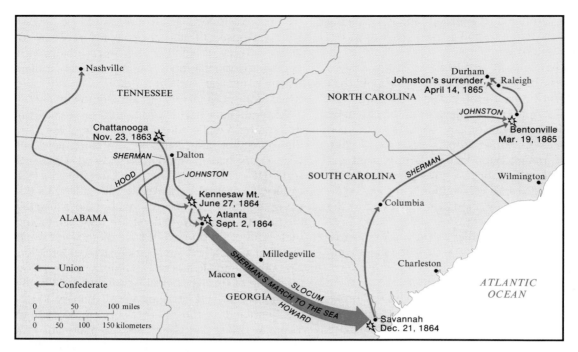

Sherman's March to the Sea

ished like a mirage of the desert." Davis exhorted southerners to fight on and win new victories before the federal elections, but he had to admit that "two-thirds of our men are absent . . . most of them absent without leave." Hood's army marched north to cut Sherman's supply lines and force him to retreat, but Sherman, planning to live off the land, marched the greater part of his army straight to the sea, destroying Confederate resources as he went (see map).

As he moved across Georgia, Sherman cut a path fifty to sixty miles wide; the totality of the destruction was awesome. A Georgia woman described the "Burnt Country" this way: "The fields were trampled down and the road was lined with carcasses of horses, hogs, and cattle that the invaders, unable either to consume or to carry with them, had wantonly shot down to starve our people and prevent them from making their crops. The stench in some places was unbearable." Such devastation diminished the South's material resources, and, more importantly, it was bound to damage the faltering southern will to resist.

After reaching Savannah in December, Sherman turned north and marched his armies into the Carolinas. Wreaking great destruction as he moved through South Carolina into North Carolina, Sherman encountered little resistance. The opposing army of General Johnston was small, but Sherman's men should have been prime targets for guerrilla raids and harassing attacks by local defense units. The absence of both led South Carolina's James Chesnut, Jr., to write that his state "was shamefully and unnecessarily lost. . . . We had time, opportunity and means to destroy him. But there was wholly wanting the energy and ability required by the occasion." Southerners were reaching the limit of their endurance.

Sherman's march brought additional human resources to the Union cause. In Georgia alone as many as nineteen thousand slaves gladly took the opportunity to escape bondage and join the Union Army as it passed through the countryside. Others held back to await the end of the war on the plantations, either from an ingrained wariness of whites or from negative experiences with the federal soldiers. The destruction of food harmed slaves as well as white rebels, and many blacks lost blankets, shoes, and other valuables to their liberators. In fact, the brutality of Sherman's troops shocked

Chapter 14: Transforming Fire: The Civil War, 1861–1865

These photographs capture the very different personal styles of Generals Grant (left) and Lee (right). Their bloody battles in 1864 caused revulsion to the war but ultimately brought its end in sight. *National Archives*.

these veterans of the whip. "I've seen them cut the hams off of a live pig or ox and go off leavin' the animal groanin'," recalled one man. "The master had 'em kilt then, but it was awful."

It was awful, too, in Virginia, where the preliminaries to victory proved to be protracted and ghastly. Throughout the spring and summer of 1864 Grant hurled his troops at Lee's army and suffered appalling losses: almost 18,000 casualties in the Battle of the Wilderness, more than 8,000 at Spotsylvania, and 12,000 in the space of a few hours at Cold Harbor (see map, page 430). Before the last battle, Union troops pinned scraps of paper bearing their names and addresses to their backs, certain that they would be mowed down as they rushed Lee's trenches. In four weeks in May and June, Grant lost as many men as were enrolled in Lee's entire army. Undaunted, Grant remarked, "I propose to fight it out along this line if it takes all summer." The heavy fighting prepared the way for eventual victory: Lee's army shrank until offensive action was no longer possible, while at the same time the Union Army kept replenishing its forces with new recruits.

The end finally came in the spring of 1865. Grant kept battering at Lee, who tried but failed to break through the federal line east of Petersburg on

Heavy Losses Force Lee's Surrender

March 25. With the numerical superiority of Grant's army now upward of two to one, Confederate defeat was inevitable. On April 2 Lee abandoned Richmond and Petersburg. On April 9, hemmed in by federal troops, short of rations, and with fewer than 30,000 men left, Lee surrendered to Grant. At Appomattox Courthouse the Union general treated his rival with respect and paroled the defeated troops. Within weeks Jefferson Davis was captured, and the remaining Confederate forces laid down their arms and surrendered. The war was over at last.

Lincoln did not live to see the last surrenders. On the evening of Good Friday, April 14, he went to Ford's Theatre in Washington, where an assassin named John Wilkes Booth shot him at pointblank range. Lincoln died the next day. The Union lost its wartime leader and, for many, relief at the war's end was tempered by uncertainty about the future.

Northern Pressure and Southern Will

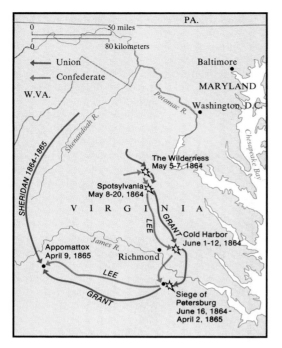

The War in Virginia, 1864–1865

Costs and Effects

The costs of the Civil War were enormous. The total number of casualties on both sides exceeded 1 million—a frightful toll for a nation of 31 million people. Approximately 364,222 federal soldiers died, 140,070 of them from wounds suffered in battle. Another 275,175 Union soldiers were wounded but survived. On the Confederate side, an estimated 258,000 lost their lives, and almost as many suffered wounds. More men died in the Civil War than in all other American wars before Vietnam combined. Fundamental disagreements, which would continue to trouble Reconstruction, caused unprecedented loss of life.

> **Casualties**

Although precise figures on enlistments are impossible to obtain, it appears that during the course of the conflict the Confederate armies claimed the services of 700,000 to 800,000 men. Far more, possibly 2.3 million, served in the Union armies. All these men were taken from home, family, and personal goals and had their lives disrupted in ways that were not easily repaired.

Property damage and financial costs were also enormous, though difficult to tally. Federal loans and taxes during the conflict totaled almost $3 billion, and interest on the war debt was $2.8 billion. The Confederacy borrowed over $2 billion but lost far more in the destruction of homes, fences, crops, livestock, and other property. To give just one example of the wreckage that attended four years of conflict on southern soil, the number of hogs in South Carolina plummeted from 965,000 in 1860 to approximately 150,000 in 1865. Scholars have noted that small farmers lost just as much, proportionally, as planters whose slaves were emancipated.

> **Financial Cost of the War**

Estimates of the total cost of the war exceed $20 billion—five times the total expenditure of the federal government from its creation to 1861. The northern government increased its spending by a factor of seven in the first full year of the war; by the last year its spending had soared to twenty times the prewar level. By 1865 the federal government accounted for over 26 percent of the gross national product.

These changes were more or less permanent. In the 1880s, interest on the war debt still accounted for approximately 40 percent of the federal budget and Union soldiers' pensions for as much as 20 percent. Thus, although many southerners had hoped to separate government from the economy, the war made such separation an impossibility. Although federal expenditures shrank after the war, they stabilized at twice the prewar level, or at 4 percent of the gross national product. Wartime emergency measures had brought the banking and transportation systems under federal control, and the government had put its power behind manufacturing and business interests through tariffs, loans, and subsidies. Industrialization and large organizations arrived to stay, and in political terms national power increased permanently. Extreme forms of the states' rights controversy were dead, though Americans continued to favor a state-centered federalism.

Despite all these changes, one crucial question remained unanswered: what was the place of black men and women in American life? The Union victory provided a partial answer: slavery as it had existed before the war could not persist. But what would replace it? About 186,000 black soldiers had rallied to the Union cause, infusing it with new

Lincoln's death caused a vast outpouring of grief in the North. His funeral train stopped at several cities on its way to Illinois to allow local services to be held. *Anne S. K. Brown Military Collection, John Hay Library, Brown University.*

strength. Did their sacrifice entitle them to full citizenship? They and other former slaves eagerly awaited an answer, which would have to be found during Reconstruction.

Suggestions for Further Reading

The War and the South

Thomas B. Alexander and Richard E. Beringer, *The Anatomy of the Confederate Congress* (1972); Richard E. Beringer et al., *Why the South Lost the Civil War* (1986); Robert F. Durden, *The Gray and the Black: The Confederate Debate on Emancipation* (1972); Clement Eaton, *A History of the Southern Confederacy* (1954); Paul D. Escott, *Many Excellent People* (1985); Paul D. Escott, *After Secession: Jefferson Davis and the Failure of Confederate Nationalism* (1978); Paul D. Escott, " 'The Cry of the Sufferers': The Problem of Poverty in the Confederacy," *Civil War History,* XXIII (September 1977), 228–240; Eli N. Evans, *Judah P. Benjamin* (1987); J. B. Jones, *A Rebel War Clerk's Diary,* 2 vols., ed. Howard Swiggett (1935); Stanley Lebergott, "Why the South Lost," *Journal of American History,* 70 (June, 1983), 58–74; Ella Lonn, *Desertion During the Civil War* (1928); Malcolm C. McMillan, *The Disintegration of a Confederate State* (1986); Mary Elizabeth Massey, *Refugee Life in the Confederacy* (1964); Larry E. Nelson, *Bullets, Ballots, and Rhetoric: Confederate Policy for the United States Presidential Contest of 1864* (1980); Harry P. Owens and James J. Cooke, eds., *The Old South in the Crucible of War* (1983); Frank L. Owsley, *State Rights in the Confederacy* (1925); Charles W. Ramsdell, *Behind the Lines in the Southern Confederacy,* ed. Wendell H. Stephenson (1944); James L. Roark, *Masters Without Slaves* (1977); Georgia Lee Tatum, *Disloyalty in the Confederacy* (1934); Emory M. Thomas, *The Confederate Nation* (1979); Emory M. Thomas, *The Confederacy as a Revolutionary Experience* (1971); Emory M. Thomas, *The Confederate State of Richmond* (1971); William A. Tidwell, *Come Retribution: The Confederate Secret Service and the Assassination of Lincoln* (1989); Bell Irvin Wiley, *The Life of Johnny Reb* (1943); Bell Irvin Wiley, *The Plain People of the Confederacy* (1943); W. Buck Yearns, ed., *The Confederate Governors* (1985); W. Buck Yearns and John G. Barrett, *North Carolina Civil War Documentary* (1980).

The War and the North

Ralph Andreano, ed., *The Economic Impact of the American Civil War* (1962); Robert Cruden, *The War That Never Ended* (1973); David Donald, ed., *Why the North Won the Civil War* (1960); David Gilchrist and W. David Lewis, eds., *Economic Change in the Civil War Era* (1965); Wood Gray, *The Hidden Civil War* (1942); Randall C. Jimerson, *The Private Civil War* (1988); Frank L. Klement, *The Copperheads in the Middle West* (1960); Susan Previant Lee and Peter Passell, *A New Economic View of American History* (1979); James M. Mc-

Pherson, *Battle Cry of Freedom* (1988); James H. Moorhead, *American Apocalypse* (1978); Phillip S. Paludan, *"A People's Contest": The Union and the Civil War, 1861–1865* (1989); George Winston Smith and Charles Burnet Judah, *Life in the North During the Civil War* (1966); George Templeton Strong, *Diary,* 4 vols., ed. Allan Nevins and Milton Hasley Thomas (1952); Paul Studenski, *Financial History of the United States* (1952); Bell Irvin Wiley, *The Life of Billy Yank* (1952).

Women

John R. Brumgardt, ed., *Civil War Nurse: The Diary and Letters of Hannah Ropes* (1980); Beth Gilbert Crabtree and James W. Patton, eds., *"Journal of a Secesh Lady": The Diary of Catherine Ann Devereux Edmondston, 1860–1866* (1979); Jacqueline Jones, *Labor of Love, Labor of Sorrow* (1985); Mary Elizabeth Massey, *Bonnet Brigades* (1966); George C. Rable, *Civil Wars: Women and the Crisis of Southern Nationalism* (1989); Mary D. Robertson, ed., *Lucy Breckinridge of Grove Hill: The Journal of a Virginia Girl, 1862–1864* (1979); C. Vann Woodward and Elisabeth Muhlenfeld, ed., *Mary Chesnut's Civil War* (1981); Agatha Young, *Women and the Crisis* (1959).

Blacks

Ira Berlin, ed., *Freedom: A Documentary History of Emancipation, 1861–1867,* Series I, *The Destruction of Slavery* (1979), and Series II, *The Black Military Experience* (1982); David W. Blight, *Frederick Douglass' Civil War* (1989); Dudley Cornish, *The Sable Arm* (1956); Barbara Jeanne Fields, *Slavery and Freedom on the Middle Ground* (1985); Leon Litwack, *Been in the Storm So Long* (1979); James M. McPherson, *The Negro's Civil War* (1965); James M. McPherson, *The Struggle for Equality* (1964); Clarence L. Mohr, *On the Threshold of Freedom* (1986); Benjamin Quarles, *The Negro in the Civil War* (1953).

Military History

Bern Anderson, *By Sea and by River* (1962); Nancy Scott Anderson and Dwight Anderson, *The Generals: Ulysses S. Grant and Robert E. Lee* (1987); Richard E. Beringer et al., *Why the South Lost the Civil War* (1986); Bruce Catton, *Grant Takes Command* (1969); Bruce Catton, *Grant Moves South* (1960); Thomas L. Connelly and Archer Jones, *The Politics of Command* (1973); Benjamin Franklin Cooling, *Forts Henry and Donelson* (1988); Burke Davis, *Sherman's March* (1980); William C. Davis, ed., *The Image of War,* multivolume (1983–1985); Walter T. Durham, *Nashville: The Occupied City* (1985); Shelby Foote, *The Civil War, a Narrative,* 3 vols. (1958–1974); William A. Frassanito, *Grant and Lee: The Virginia Campaigns, 1864–1865* (1983); Douglas Southall Freeman, *Lee's Lieutenants,* 3 vols. (1942–1944); Douglas Southall Freeman, *R. E. Lee,* 4 vols. (1934–1935); Joseph T. Glatthaar, *The March to the Sea and Beyond* (1985); Herman Hattaway and Archer Jones, *How the North Won* (1983); Lawrence Lee Hewitt, *Port Hudson, Confederate Bastion on the Mississippi* (1988); Archer Jones, *Confederate Strategy from Shiloh to Vicksburg* (1961); Gerald F. Linderman, *Embattled Courage: The Experience of Combat in the American Civil War* (1989); Thomas L. Livermore, *Numbers and Losses in the Civil War in America* (1957); James Lee McDonough, *Chattanooga* (1984); Grady McWhiney and Perry D. Jamieson, *Attack and Die* (1982); J. B. Mitchell, *Decisive Battles of the Civil War* (1955); Reid Mitchell, *Civil War Soldiers* (1988); Harry W. Pfanze, *Gettysburg: The Second Day* (1988); Robert Garth Scott, *Into the Wilderness with the Army of the Potomac* (1987); Stephen W. Sears, *George B. McClellan* (1988); Stephen Z. Starr, *The Union Cavalry in the Civil War,* 3 vols. (1985); Emory M. Thomas, *Bold Dragoon: The Life of J.E.B. Stuart* (1987); Frank E. Vandiver, *Rebel Brass* (1956).

Diplomatic History

Stuart L. Bernath, *Squall Across the Atlantic: American Civil War Prize Cases and Diplomacy* (1970); Kinley J. Brauer, "The Slavery Problem in the Diplomacy of the American Civil War," *Pacific Historical Review,* XLVI, no. 3 (1977), 439–469; David P. Crook, *The North, the South, and the Powers, 1861–1865* (1974); Charles P. Cullop, *Confederate Propaganda in Europe* (1969); Norman A. Graebner, "Northern Diplomacy and European Neutrality," in David Donald, ed., *Why the North Won the Civil War* (1960); Frank J. Merli, *Great Britain and the Confederate Navy* (1970); Frank L. Owsley and Harriet Owsley, *King Cotton Diplomacy* (1959); Gordon H. Warren, *Fountain of Discontent: The Trent Affair and Freedom of the Seas* (1981); Gordon H. Warren, "The King Cotton Theory," in Alexander DeConde, ed., *Encyclopedia of American Foreign Policy,* 3 vols. (1978).

Abraham Lincoln and the Union Government

Allan G. Bogue, *The Earnest Men: Republicans of the Civil War Senate* (1981); Gabor S. Borit, ed., *The Historian's Lincoln* (1989); Fawn Brodie, *Thaddeus Stevens* (1959); LaWanda Cox, *Lincoln and Black Freedom* (1981); Richard N. Current, *The Lincoln Nobody Knows* (1958); Leonard P. Curry, *Blueprint for Modern America: Non-Military Legislation of the First Civil War Congress* (1968); Christopher Dell, *Lincoln and the War Democrats* (1975); David Donald, *Charles Sumner and the Rights of Man* (1970); Ludwell H. Johnson, "Lincoln's Solution to the Problem of Peace Terms, 1864–1865," *Journal of Southern History,* XXXIV (November 1968), 441–447; Peyton McCrary, *Abraham Lincoln and Reconstruction: The Louisiana Experiment* (1978); Stephen B. Oates, *Our Fiery Trial* (1979); Stephen B. Oates, *With Malice Toward None* (1977); James G. Randall, *Mr. Lincoln* (1957); Joel Silbey, *A Respectable Minority: The Democratic Party in the Civil War Era* (1977); Benjamin P. Thomas, *Abraham Lincoln* (1952); Hans L. Trefousse, *The Radical Republicans* (1969); Glyndon G. Van Deusen, *William Henry Seward* (1967); T. Harry Williams, *Lincoln and His Generals* (1952); T. Harry Williams, *Lincoln and the Radicals* (1941).

Saturday, May 16, was a beautiful spring day in 1868. Sunlight and balmy weather bathed the nation's capital, but few people paused to relax or enjoy their surroundings. Washington was tense with excitement. Professional gamblers had flooded into the city, outnumbered perhaps only by the reporters who leaped upon every rumor or scrap of information. As the morning passed, a crowd gathered around the Senate chamber. Foreign dignitaries filled the diplomatic box, and spectators packed the Senate galleries. Outside the chamber thousands milled about, choking the hallways and spilling onto the terraces and streets.

Precisely at noon the chief justice of the United States entered the Senate. Managers and counsel stood ready. Soon two senators who were seriously ill slowly made their way into the chamber, bringing the number of senators present to the full complement of fifty-four. All principals in this solemn drama were present before the High Court of Impeachment except the accused: Andrew Johnson, president of the United States. Johnson, who never appeared to defend himself in person, waited anxiously at the White House as Chief Justice Salmon Chase ordered the calling of the roll. To each senator he put the questions, "How say you? Is the respondent, Andrew Johnson, President of the United States, guilty or not guilty of a high misdemeanor, as charged in this article?" Thirty-five senators answered, "Guilty"; nineteen, "Not guilty." The thirty-five votes for conviction were one short of the required two-thirds majority. The United States had come within one vote of removing the president from office.

15

RECONSTRUCTION BY TRIAL AND ERROR, 1865–1877

How had this extraordinary event come about? What had brought the executive and legislative branches of government into such severe conflict? An unprecedented problem—the reconstruction of the Union—furnished the occasion; deepening differences over the proper policy to pursue had led to the confrontation. By 1868 president and Congress had reached a point of bitter antagonism; some congressmen were charging that the president was siding with traitors.

In 1865, at the end of the war, such an event seemed most unlikely. Although he was a southerner from Tennessee, Johnson had built his career upon criticizing the wealthy planters and championing the South's small farmers. When an assassin's

The Shackle Broken by the Genius of Freedom (detail of Hon. Robert B. Elliott of South Carolina delivering his great speech on civil rights in the House of Representatives, January 6, 1874). Color lithograph published by E. Sachs & Company, Baltimore, 1874. *Chicago Historical Society.*

bullet thrust him into the presidency, many former slaveowners shared the worries of a North Carolina lady who wrote, "Think of Andy Johnson [as] the president! What will become of us—'the aristocrats of the South' as we are termed?" Northern Radicals who sounded out the new president on his views also felt confident that he would deal sternly with the South. When one of them suggested the exile or execution of ten or twelve leading rebels to set an example, Johnson had vigorously replied, "How are you going to pick out so small a number? Robbery is a crime; rape is a crime; *treason* is a crime; and *crime* must be punished."

Moreover, fundamental change was already under way in the South. During his army's last campaign, General William T. Sherman had issued Special Field Order No. 15, which set aside for Negro settlement the Sea Islands and all abandoned coastal lands thirty miles to the interior, from Charleston to the Saint John's River in northern Florida. Black refugees quickly poured into these lands; by the middle of 1865, forty thousand freed people were living in their new homes. One former slaveowner who visited his old plantation in Beaufort, South Carolina, received friendly and courteous treatment, but his ex-slaves "firmly and respectfully" informed him that "we own this land now. Put it out of your head that it will ever be yours again."

Before the end of 1865, however, these signs of change were reversed. Although Jefferson Davis was imprisoned for two years, no Confederate leaders were executed, and southern aristocrats soon came to view Andrew Johnson not as their enemy but as their friend and protector. Johnson pardoned rebel leaders liberally, allowed them to take high offices, and ordered government officials to reclaim the freedmen's land and give it back to the original owners. One man in South Carolina expressed blacks' dismay: "Why do you take away our lands? You take them from us who have always been true, always true to the Government! You give them to our all-time enemies! That is not right!"

The unexpected outcome of Johnson's program led Congress to examine his policies and design new plans for Reconstruction. Out of negotiations in Congress and clashes between the president and the legislators, there emerged first one, and then two, new plans for Reconstruction. Before the process was over, the nation had adopted the Fourteenth and Fifteenth Amendments and impeached its president.

Racism did not disappear. During the war the federal government had been reluctant to give even black troops fair treatment, and in Congress northern Democrats continued to oppose equality. Republicans were often divided among themselves, but a mixture of idealism and party purposes drove them forward. Ultimately, fear of losing the peace proved decisive with northern voters. The United State enfranchised the freedmen and gave them a role in reconstructing the South.

Blacks benefited from greater control over their personal lives and took the risks of voting and participating in politics. But they knew that the success of Reconstruction also depended on the determination and support of the North. Southern opposition to Reconstruction grew steadily. By 1869 a secret terrorist organization known as the Ku Klux Klan had added large-scale violence to southern whites' repertoire of resistance. Despite federal efforts to protect them, black people were intimidated at the polls, robbed of their earnings, beaten, or murdered. Prosecution of Klansmen rarely succeeded, and Republicans lost their offices in an increasing number of southern states. By the early 1870s the failure of Reconstruction was apparent. Republican leaders and northern voters had to decide how far they would persist in their efforts to reform the South.

As the 1870s advanced, other issues drew attention away from Reconstruction. Industrial growth accelerated, creating new opportunities and raising new problems. Interest in territorial expansion revived. Political corruption became a nationwide scandal and bribery a way of doing business. North Carolina's Jonathan Worth, an old-line Whig who had opposed secession as strongly as he now fought Reconstruction, deplored the atmosphere of greed. "Money has become the God of this country," he wrote in disgust, "and men, otherwise good men, are almost compelled to worship at her shrine." Eventually these other forces triumphed; politics moved on to new concerns; and the courts turned their attention away from civil rights. Even northern Republicans gave up on racial reforms in 1877.

Thus the nation stumbled, by trial and error, toward a policy that attempted to reconstruct the South. Congress insisted on equality before the law for black people and gave black men the right to vote. It took the unprecedented step of impeaching the president. But more far-reaching measures to advance black freedom never had much support in

1865	Johnson begins Reconstruction
	Confederate leaders regain power
	Black codes
	Congress refuses to seat southern representatives
	Thirteenth Amendment ratified
1866	Civil Rights Act
	Congress approves Fourteenth Amendment
	Freedmen's Bureau renewed
	Most southern states reject Fourteenth Amendment
	Ex parte Milligan
1867	Military Reconstruction Act; Tenure of Office Act
	Purchase of Alaska
	Constitutional conventions called in southern states
1868	House impeaches Johnson; Senate acquits him
	Most southern states readmitted
	Fourteenth Amendment ratified
	Ulysses S. Grant elected president
1869	Congress approves Fifteenth Amendment (ratified in 1870)
1870	Enforcement Act
1871	Enforcement Act of 1871
	Ku Klux Klan Act
	Treaty with England settles *Alabama* claims
1872	Amnesty Act
	Liberal Republicans organize
	Debtors urge government to keep greenbacks in circulation
	Grant re-elected
1873	*Slaughter-House* cases
	Panic of 1873
1874	Grant vetoes increase in paper money
	Democrats win House
1875	Several Grant appointees indicted for corruption
	Civil Rights Act
	Congress requires that after 1878 greenbacks be convertible into gold
1876	*U.S.* v. *Cruikshank*; *U.S.* v. *Reese*
	Presidential election disputed
1877	Congress elects Hayes
	Black Exodusters migrate to Kansas

Congress, and when suffrage alone proved insufficient to remake the South, the nation soon lost interest. Reconstruction proclaimed anew the American principle of human equality but failed to secure it in reality.

Equality: The Unresolved Issue

For America's former slaves, Reconstruction had one paramount meaning: a chance to explore freedom. A southern white woman admitted in her diary that the black people "showed a natural and exultant joy at being free." Former slaves remembered rejoicing and singing far into the night after federal troops reached their plantations. The slaves on one Texas plantation jumped up and down and clapped their hands as one man shouted, "We is free—no more whippings and beatings."

A few blacks gave in to the natural desire to do what had been impossible before. One grandmother who had long resented her treatment "dropped her hoe" and ran to confront the mistress. "I'm free!" she yelled at her. "Yes, I'm free! Ain't got to work for you no more! You can't put me in your pocket [sell me] now!" Another man recalled that he and others "started on the move" and

To escape the plantation and seek new opportunities, many blacks migrated to southern cities. In Jacksonville, Florida, some found work on the docks. *Library of Congress.*

left the plantation, either to search for family members or oftentimes just to exercise their new-found freedom of movement. As he traveled, one man sang about being free as a frog, " 'cause a frog had freedom to get on a log and jump off when he pleases."

Most freedmen reacted more cautiously and shrewdly, taking care to test the boundaries of their new condition. "After the war was over," explained one man, "we was afraid to move. Just like tarpins or turtles after emancipation. Just stick our heads out to see how the land lay." As slaves they had learned to expect hostility from white people, and they did not presume it would instantly disappear. Life in freedom, they knew, might still be a matter of what was allowed, not what was right. "You got to say master?" asked a freedman in Georgia. "Naw," answered his fellows, but "they said it all the same. They said it for a long time."

One sign of this shrewd caution was the way freedmen evaluated potential employers. "Most all the niggers that had good owners stayed with 'em, but the others left. Some of 'em come back and some didn't," explained one man. If a white person had been relatively considerate to blacks in bondage, blacks reasoned that he might prove a desirable employer in freedom. Other blacks left their plantation all at once, for, as one put it, "that master am sure mean and if we doesn't have to stay we shouldn't, not with that master."

In addition to a fair employer, the freedmen wanted opportunity through education and especially through land of their own. Land represented

> **Blacks' Desire for Land**

their chance to farm for themselves, to have an independent life. It represented compensation for their generations of travail in bondage. A northern observer noted that freedmen made "plain, straight-forward" inquiries as they settled the land set aside for them by Sherman. They wanted to be sure the land "would be theirs after they had improved it." Not just in the Sea Island region but everywhere, blacks young and old thirsted for homes of their own. One white southerner noted with surprise in her diary that

Uncle Lewis, the pious, the honored, the venerated, gets his poor old head turned with false notions of freedom and independence, runs off to the Yankees with a pack of lies against his mistress, and sets up a claim to part of her land!

Lewis simply wanted a new beginning. Like other freedmen, he hoped to leave slavery behind.

No one could say how much of a chance the whites, who were in power, would give to blacks. During the war the federal government had refused at first to arm black volunteers. Many whites agreed with Corporal Felix Brannigan of the Seventy-fourth New York Regiment. "We don't want to fight side and side with the nigger," he said. "We think we are a too superior race for that." In September 1862, Abraham Lincoln said, "If we were to arm [the Negroes], I fear that in a few weeks the arms would be in the hands of the rebels."

Necessity forced a change in policy; because the war was going badly, the administration authorized black enlistments. By spring 1863, black troops were proving their value. One general reported that his "colored regiments" possessed "remarkable aptitude for military training," and another observer said, "They fight like fiends." Lincoln came to see "the colored population" as "the great *available* and yet *unavailed of* force for restoring the Union," and recruitment proceeded rapidly.

Black leaders hoped that military service would secure equal rights for their people. Once the black soldier had fought for the Union, wrote Frederick Douglass, "there is no power on earth which can deny that he has earned the right of citizenship in the United States." If black soldiers turned the tide, asked another man, "Would the nation refuse us our rights . . . ? Would it refuse us our vote?"

Wartime experience seemed to prove that it would. Despite their valor, black soldiers faced persistent discrimination. In Ohio, for example, a mob shouting "Kill the nigger" attacked an off-duty soldier; on duty, blacks did most of the "fatigue duty," or heavy labor. Moreover, black soldiers were expected to accept inferior pay as they risked their lives. The government paid white privates $13 per month plus a clothing allowance of $3.50. Black troops earned $10 per month less $3 deducted for clothing. Blacks resented this injustice so deeply that in protest two regiments refused to accept any pay, and eventually Congress remedied the discrimination. Still, that was only a small victory over prejudice.

The general attitude of northerners on racial questions was mixed. Abolitionists and many Re-publicans helped black Americans fight for equal rights, and they won some victories. In 1864 the federal courts accepted black testimony, and New York City desegregated its streetcars. The District of Columbia did the same in 1865, the year the Thirteenth Amendment won ratification. One state, Massachusetts, enacted a comprehensive public accommodations law. Nevertheless, there were many signs of resistance to racial equality. The Democratic party fought hard against equality, charging that Republicans favored race-mixing and were undermining the status of the white worker. Voters in three states—Connecticut, Minnesota, and Wisconsin—rejected black suffrage in 1865.

The fact that the racial attitudes of northerners seemed mixed and uncertain was significant, for the history of emancipation in the British Caribbean indicated that, if equality were to be won, the North would have to take a strong and determined stand. In 1833 Great Britain had abolished slavery in its possessions, providing slaveowners with £20 million in compensation and requiring all former agricultural slaves to work the land for six more years as apprentices. Despite such generosity to the slaveowners, the transition to free labor had not been easy.

Everywhere in the British Caribbean planters fought tenaciously to maintain control over their laborers. Retaining control of local government, the planters fashioned laws, taxes, and administrative decisions with an eye to keeping freedmen on the plantations. With equal determination, the former slaves attempted to move onto small plots of land and raise food crops instead of sugar. They wanted independence and were not interested in raising export crops for the world market. The British, even abolitionists, however, judged the success of emancipation by the volume of production for the market. Their concern for the freedmen soon faded, and before long the authorities assisted planters further by allowing the importation of indentured "coolie" labor from India.

In the United States, some of the same tendencies had appeared on the Sea Islands long before the war ended. The planters had fled and therefore were not present to try to control their former slaves. The freedmen, however, showed a strong desire to leave the plantations and establish small, self-sufficient farms of their own. Northern soldiers, officials, and missionaries of both races brought education and aid to the freedmen but also wanted them to grow cotton. They disapproved of charity and emphasized the values of competitive capitalism. "The danger to the Negro," wrote one worker in the Sea Islands, was "too high wages." Indeed it would be "most unwise and injurious," declared another worker, to give former slaves free land.

"The Yankees preach nothing but cotton, cotton!" complained one Sea Island black. "We wants land," wrote another, "this very land that is rich with the sweat of we face and the blood of we back." Asking only for a chance to buy land, this man complained that "they make the lots too big, and cut we out." Indeed, the government did sell thousands of acres in the Sea Islands for nonpayment of taxes, but 90 percent of the land went to wealthy investors from the North. Even after blacks pooled their earnings, they were able to buy less than 2,000 of the 16,749 acres sold in March 1863. Thus even from their northern supporters, the former slaves had received only partial support. How much opportunity would freedom bring? That was a major question to be answered during Reconstruction, and the answer depended on the evolution of policy in Washington.

Johnson's Reconstruction Plan

Through 1865 the formation of Reconstruction policy rested solely with Andrew Johnson, for shortly before he became president Congress recessed and did not reconvene until December. In the nearly eight months that intervened, Johnson devised his own plan and put it into operation. He decided to form new state governments in the South by using his power to grant pardons.

Johnson had a few precedents to follow in Lincoln's wartime plans for Reconstruction. In December 1863 Lincoln had proposed a "10-percent" plan for a government being organized in captured portions of Louisiana. According **Lincoln's** to this plan, a state government **Reconstruc-** could be established as soon as 10 **tion Plan** percent of those who had voted in 1860 took an oath of future loyalty. Only high-ranking Confederate officials would be denied a chance to take the oath, and Lincoln urged that at least a few well-qualified blacks be given the ballot. Radicals bristled, however, at such a mild plan, and a majority of Congress (in the Wade-Davis bill, which Lincoln pocket-vetoed) favored stiffer requirements and stronger proof of loyalty.

Later, in 1865, Lincoln suggested but then abandoned more lenient terms. At Hampton Roads, where he raised questions about the extent of emancipation (see page 418), Lincoln discussed compensation and restoration to the Union, with full rights, of the very state governments that had tried to leave it. Then in April he considered allowing the Virginia legislature to convene in order to withdraw its support from the Confederate war effort. Faced with strong opposition in his cabinet, however, Lincoln reversed himself, denying that he had intended to confer legitimacy on a rebel government. At the time of his death, Lincoln had given general approval to a plan drafted by Secretary of War Stanton that would have imposed military authority and the appointment of provisional governors as steps toward the creation of new state governments. Beyond these general outlines, it is impossible to say what Lincoln would have done had he survived.

Johnson began with the plan Stanton had drafted for consideration by the cabinet. At a cabinet meeting on May 9, 1865, Johnson's advisers split evenly on the question of voting rights for freedmen in the South. Johnson said that he favored black suffrage, but only if the southern states adopted it voluntarily. A champion of states' rights, he regarded this decision as too important to be taken out of the hands of the states.

Such conservatism had an enduring effect on Johnson's policies, but at first it appeared that his old enmity toward the planters might produce a plan for radical changes in class relations among whites. As he appointed provisional governors in the South, Johnson also proposed rules that would keep the wealthy planter class out of power. He required every southern voter to swear an oath of loyalty as a condition of gaining amnesty or pardon. Some southern whites, however, would face special difficulties in regaining their rights.

Johnson barred certain classes of southerners from taking the oath and gaining amnesty. Former federal officials who had violated their oaths to sup-

Oaths of Amnesty and New State Governments

port the United States and had aided the Confederacy could not take the oath. Nor could graduates of West Point or Annapolis who had resigned their commissions to fight for the South. The same was true for high-ranking Confederate officers and Confederate political leaders. To this list Johnson added another important group: all southerners who aided the rebellion and whose taxable property was worth more than $20,000. Such individuals had to apply personally to the president for pardon and restoration of political rights; otherwise, they risked legal penalties, which included confiscation of their land.

Thus it appeared that the leadership class of the Old South would be removed from power, for virtually all the rich and powerful whites of prewar days needed Johnson's special pardon. Many observers in both South and North sensed that the president meant to take his revenge on the haughty aristocrats whom he had always denounced and to raise up a new leadership of deserving yeomen.

Johnson's provisional governors began the Reconstruction process by calling constitutional conventions. The delegates chosen for these conventions had to draft new constitutions eliminating slavery and invalidating secession. After ratification of these constitutions, new governments could be elected, and the states would be restored to the Union with full congressional representation. But no southerners could participate in this process who had not taken the oath of amnesty or who had been ineligible to vote on the day the state seceded. Thus freedmen could not participate in the conventions. It was theoretically possible for the white delegates to enfranchise them, but unlikely.

If Johnson intended to end the power of the old elite, his plan did not work out as he hoped. The old white leadership proved resilient and influential; prominent Confederates (a few with pardons, but many without) won elections and turned up in various appointive offices. Then, surprisingly, Johnson helped to subvert his own plan. He started pardoning aristocrats and chief rebels, who should not have been in office. By the fall of 1865 the clerks at the pardon office were straining under the burden, and additional staff had to be hired to churn out the necessary documents. These pardons, plus the return of planters' abandoned lands, put the old elite back in power.

Combative and inflexible, President Andrew Johnson contributed greatly to the failure of his own reconstruction program. *Brady photograph, National Portrait Gallery, Smithsonian Institution, Washington, D.C.*

Why did Johnson issue so many pardons? Perhaps vanity betrayed his judgment. Scores of gentlemen of the type who had previously scorned him now waited on him for an appointment. Too long a lonely outsider, Johnson may have succumbed to the attention and flattery of the pardon seekers. Whether he did or not, he clearly had allowed himself too little time. It took months for the constitution making and elections to run their course; by the time the process was complete and Confederate leaders had emerged in powerful positions, the reconvening of Congress was near. Johnson faced a choice between admitting failure and scrapping his entire effort or swallowing hard and supporting what had resulted. The choice was not difficult for someone who believed in white supremacy and wanted southern support in the next election. Johnson decided to stand behind his new governments and declare Reconstruction completed. Thus in December 1865 many Confederate congressmen traveled to Washington to claim seats in the United States Congress, and Alexander Stephens, vice president of the Confederacy, returned to the capital as senator-elect.

Johnson's Reconstruction Plan

Many northerners frowned on the election of such prominent rebels, and other results of Johnson's program also sparked negative comment in the North. Some of the state con-

> **Black Codes** ventions were slow to repudiate secession; others only grudgingly admitted that slavery was dead. Two refused to take any action to repudiate the large Confederate debt. Even Johnson admitted that these acts showed "something like defiance, which is all out of place at this time." Furthermore, to define the status of freedmen, some legislatures merely revised large sections of the slave codes by substituting the word *freedmen* for *slave,* and new laws written from scratch were also very restrictive. According to the new black codes, former slaves who were supposed to be free were compelled to carry passes, observe a curfew, live in housing provided by a landowner, and give up hope of entering many desirable occupations. Stiff vagrancy laws and restrictive labor contracts bound supposedly free laborers to the plantation, and "anti-enticement" laws punished anyone who tried to lure these workers to other employment. Finally, observers noted that the practice in state-supported institutions, such as schools and orphanages, was to exclude blacks altogether. It seemed to northerners that the South was intent on returning black people to a position of servility.

Thus it was not surprising that a majority of northern congressmen decided to take a close look at the results of Johnson's plan. On reconvening, they voted not to admit the newly elected southern representatives, whose credentials were subject under the Constitution to congressional scrutiny. The House and Senate established an important joint committee to examine Johnson's policies and advise on new ones. Reconstruction entered a second phase, one in which Congress would play a strong role.

The Congressional Reconstruction Plan

Northern congressmen disagreed on what to do, but they did not doubt their right to play a role in Reconstruction. The Constitution mentioned neither secession nor reunion, but it did assign a great many major responsibilities to Congress. Among them was the injunction to guarantee to each state a republican government. Under this provision, the legislators thought, they could devise policies for Reconstruction, just as Johnson had used his power to pardon for the same purpose.

They soon found that other constitutional questions had a direct bearing on the policies they followed. What, for example, had rebellion done to the relationship between southern states and the Union? Lincoln had always insisted that the Union remained unbroken, but not even Andrew Johnson accepted the southern view that the wartime state governments of the South could merely re-enter the nation. Johnson argued that the Union had endured, though individuals had erred—thus the use of his power to grant or withhold pardons. In contrast, congressmen who favored vigorous Reconstruction measures tended to argue that war *had* broken the Union. The southern states had committed legal suicide and reverted to the status of territories, they argued, or the South was a conquered nation subject to the victor's will. Moderate congressmen held that the states had forfeited their rights through rebellion and had thus come under congressional supervision.

These diverse theories mirrored the diversity of Congress itself. Northern legislators fell into four major categories: Democrats, conservative Republicans, moderate Republicans, and

> **The Radicals** other Republicans called Radicals. No one of these groups had decisive power. In terms of ideology the majority of congressmen were conservative. In terms of partisan politics the Republican party had a majority; but there was considerable distance between conservative Republicans, who desired a limited federal role in Reconstruction and were fairly happy with Johnson's actions, and the Radicals. The Radicals, led by Thaddeus Stevens, Charles Sumner, and George Julian, were a minority within their party, but they had the advantage of a clearly defined goal. They believed that it was essential to democratize the South, establish public education, and ensure the rights of freedmen. They favored black suffrage, often supported land confiscation and redistribution, and were willing to exclude the South from the Union for several years if necessary to achieve their goals. Between the conservative Republicans and the Radicals lay the moderates, who held the balance of power.

One overwhelming political reality faced all the groups in Congress: the 1866 elections were approaching in the fall. Since Congress had questioned Johnson's program, its members had to develop some modification or alternative program before the elections. The northern public expected the legislators to develop a new Reconstruction plan, and as politicians they knew better than to go before their constituents empty-handed. Thus they had to forge a majority coalition composed either of Democrats and Republicans or of various elements of the Republican party. The kind of coalition that formed would determine the kind of plan that Congress developed.

Ironically, Johnson and the Democrats eliminated the possibility of a conservative coalition. The president and the Democrats in Congress refused to cooperate with conservative or moderate Republicans. They insisted, despite evidence of widespread northern concern, that Reconstruction was over, that the new state governments were legitimate, and that southern representatives should be admitted to Congress. These unrealistic, intransigent positions threw away the Democrats' potential influence and blasted any possibility of bipartisan compromise. Republicans found themselves all lumped together by Democrats; to form a new program, conservative Republicans had to work with the Radicals. Thus bargaining over changes in the Johnson program went on almost entirely within the Republican party. This development and subsequent events enhanced the influence of the Radicals. In 1865, however, Republican congressmen were reluctant to break with the president; he was, for better or worse, the titular head of their party, so they made one last effort to work with him.

Early in 1866 many lawmakers thought a compromise had been reached. Under its terms Johnson would agree to two modifications of his program. Under one bill the life of the Freedmen's Bureau, which Congress established in March 1865 to feed the hungry, negotiate labor contracts, and start schools, would be extended; second, a civil rights bill would be passed to counteract the black codes. This bill, drawn up by a conservative Republican, was designed to force southern courts to practice equality before the law by giving federal judges the power to move cases in which blacks were treated unfairly from state courts into federal

Congress Struggles for a Compromise

courts. Its provisions applied to discrimination by private persons as well as by government officials. As the first major bill to enforce the Thirteenth Amendment's abolition of slavery, it was a significant piece of legislation, and it became very important in the twentieth century (see page 944).

But in spring 1866, Johnson destroyed the compromise by vetoing both bills (they were later repassed). Denouncing any change in his program, the president condemned Congress's action. In inflammatory language he questioned the legitimacy of congressional involvement in policymaking and revealed his own racism. Because the civil rights bill defined United States citizens as native-born persons who were taxed, Johnson pronounced it discriminatory toward "large numbers of intelligent, worthy, and patriotic foreigners . . . in favor of the negro." The bill, he said, would "operate in favor of the colored and against the white race."

All hope of working with the president was now gone. But Republican congressmen sensed that their constituents remained dissatisfied with the results of Reconstruction. Newspapers reported the daily violations of blacks' rights in the South and carried troubling accounts of anti-black violence—notably in Memphis and New Orleans, where police aided brutal riots against black citizens. Such violence convinced Republicans, and the northern public, that more needed to be done. The Republican lawmakers therefore pushed on, and from bargaining among their various factions there emerged a plan. It took the form of a proposed amendment to the Constitution—the fourteenth—and it represented a compromise between radical and conservative elements of the party. The Fourteenth Amendment was Congress's alternative to Johnson's program of Reconstruction.

Fourteenth Amendment

Of four points in the amendment, there was nearly universal agreement on one: the Confederate debt was declared null and void, the war debt of the United States guaranteed. Northerners uniformly rejected the notion of paying taxes to reimburse those who had financed a rebellion, and business groups agreed on the necessity of upholding the credit of the United States government. There was also fairly general support for altering the personnel of southern governments. In language that harkened back to Johnson's proclamations on amnesty or pardon, the Fourteenth Amendment prohibited political power

Police joined rioters in New Orleans to shoot down and kill thirty-four blacks and three white Republicans. At this time President Johnson was insisting that Reconstruction was over. *The Historic New Orleans Collection.*

for prominent Confederates. Only at the discretion of Congress, by a two-thirds vote of each house, could these political penalties be removed.

The section of the Fourteenth Amendment that would have by far the greatest legal significance in later years was the first (see the Appendix). On its face, this section was an effort to strike down the black codes and guarantee basic rights to freedmen. It conferred citizenship on freedmen and prohibited states from abridging their constitutional "privileges and immunities." Similarly, the amendment barred any state from taking a person's life, liberty, or property "without due process of law" and from denying "equal protection of the laws." These clauses were phrased broadly enough to become powerful guarantees in the twentieth century of black Americans' civil rights—indeed, of the rights of all citizens. They also took on added meaning with court rulings that corporations were legally "persons" (see page 504).

The second section of the amendment, which dealt with representation, revealed the compromises and political motives that had produced the document. Northerners, in Congress and out, disagreed about whether black citizens should have

the right to vote. Commenting on the ambivalence of northern opinion, a citizen of Indiana wrote that there was strong feeling in favor of "humane and liberal laws for the government and protection of the colored population." But he admitted to a southern relative that there was prejudice, too. "Although there is a great deal [of] profession among us for the relief of the darkey yet I think much of it is far from being sincere. I guess we want to compel you to do right by them while we are not willing ourselves to do so."

Republican congressmen shied away from confronting this ambivalence, but political reality required them to do something. Under the Constitution, representation was based on population. During slavery each black slave had counted as three-fifths of a person for purposes of congressional representation. Republicans feared that emancipation, which made every former slave five-fifths of a person, might increase the South's power in Congress. If it did, and if blacks were not allowed to vote, the former secessionists would gain seats in Congress.

What a strange result that would seem to most northerners. They had never planned to reward the South for rebellion, and Republicans in Congress were determined not to hand over power to their political enemies. So they offered the South a choice. According to the second section of the Fourteenth Amendment, states did not have to give black men the right to vote. But if they did not do so, their representation would be reduced proportionally (this clause has never been invoked, despite the clear intent of the amendment). If they did enfranchise black men, their representation would be increased proportionally—but Republicans would be able to appeal to the new black voters. This compromise protected northern interests and gave Republicans a chance to compete if freedmen gained the ballot.

The Fourteenth Amendment dealt with the voting rights of black men but ignored female citizens, black and white. For this reason it provoked a strong reaction from the women's rights movement. Advocates of equal rights for women had worked with abolitionists for decades, often subordinating their cause to that of the slaves. During the drafting of the Fourteenth Amendment, however, female activists demanded to be heard. When legislators defined them as nonvoting citizens, prominent women's leaders such as Elizabeth Cady

Stanton and Susan B. Anthony decided that it was time to end their alliance with abolitionists. Thus the independent women's rights movement grew.

In 1866, however, the major question in Reconstruction politics was how the public would respond to the amendment. Would the northern public support Congress's plan or the president's? Johnson did his best to block the Fourteenth Amendment and to convince northerners to reject it. Condemning Congress for its refusal to seat southern representatives, the president urged state legislatures in the South to vote against ratification. Every southern legislature except Tennessee's rejected the amendment by a large margin. It did best in Alabama, where it failed by a vote of 69 to 8 in the assembly and 27 to 2 in the senate. In three states the amendment received no support at all.

Southern Rejection of the Fourteenth Amendment

To present his case to northerners, Johnson arranged a National Union convention to publicize his program. The chief executive also took to the stump himself. In an age when active personal campaigning was rare for a president, Johnson boarded a special train for a "swing around the circle" that carried his message far into the Midwest and then back to Washington. In cities such as Cleveland and St. Louis, Johnson criticized the Republicans in a ranting, undignified style. But increasingly audiences rejected his views and hooted and jeered at him.

The election of 1866 was a resounding victory for Republicans in Congress. Men whom Johnson had denounced won re-election by large margins, and the Republican majority increased as some new candidates defeated incumbent Democrats. Everywhere Radical and moderate Republicans gained strength. The section of the country that had won the war had spoken clearly: Johnson's policies, people feared, were giving the advantage to rebels and traitors. Thus Republican congressional leaders received a mandate to continue with their Reconstruction plan.

But, thanks largely to Johnson, that plan had reached an impasse. All but one of the southern governments created by the president had turned their backs on the Fourteenth Amendment, determined to resist. Nothing could be accomplished as long as those governments existed and as long as the southern electorate was constituted as it was. The newly elected northern Republicans were not going to ignore their constituents' wishes and surrender to the South. To break the deadlock, Republicans had little choice but to form new governments in the South and enfranchise the freedmen. They therefore decided to do both. The unavoidable logic of the situation had forced the majority toward the Radical plan.

The Radicals hoped Congress would do much more. Thaddeus Stevens, for example, argued that economic opportunity was essential to the freedmen. "If we do not furnish them with homesteads from forfeited and rebel property, and hedge them around with protective laws; if we leave them to the legislation of their late masters, we had better left them in bondage," Stevens declared. To provide that opportunity, Stevens drew up a plan for extensive confiscation and redistribution of land. Significantly, only one-tenth of the land affected by his plan was earmarked for freedmen, in 40-acre plots. All the rest was to be sold to generate money for veterans' pensions, compensation to loyal citizens for damaged property, and payment of the federal debt. By these means Stevens hoped to win support for a basically unpopular measure. But he failed, and in general the Radicals were not able to command the support of the majority of the public. Northerners of that era were accustomed to a limited role for government, and the business community staunchly opposed any interference in private property.

As a result, the Military Reconstruction Act that was passed in 1867 incorporated only a small part of the Radical program. The act called for new governments in the South and a return to military authority until they were set up. It barred from political office the Confederate leaders listed in the Fourteenth Amendment. It guaranteed freedmen the right to vote in elections for state constitutional conventions and for subsequent state governments. In addition, each southern state was required to ratify the Fourteenth Amendment; to ratify its new constitution; and to submit its new constitution to Congress for approval. Thus black people gained an opportunity to fight for a better life through the political process, but the only weapon put into their hands was the ballot. The law required no redistribution of land and guaranteed no basic changes in southern social structure. It also permitted an early return to the Union.

Military Reconstruction Act of 1867

The confrontation between Congress and Andrew Johnson culminated in the president's impeachment. Here the Senate conducts his trial, which ended in acquittal by a margin of one vote.
Library of Congress; colored by Karla Cinquanta.

Congress's role as the architect of Reconstruction was not quite over, for its quarrels with Andrew Johnson grew more bitter. To restrict Johnson's influence and safeguard its plan, Congress passed a number of controversial laws. First it set the date for its own reconvening—an unprecedented act, for the president traditionally summoned the legislature to Washington. Then it limited Johnson's power over the army by requiring the president to issue military orders through the General of the Army, Ulysses S. Grant, who could not be sent from Washington without the Senate's consent. Finally, Congress passed the Tenure of Office Act, which gave the Senate power to interfere with changes in the president's cabinet. Designed to protect Secretary of War Stanton, who sympathized with the Radicals, this law violated the tradition that a president controlled his own cabinet.

Johnson took several belligerent steps of his own. He issued orders to military commanders in the South limiting their powers and increasing the powers of the civil governments he had created in 1865. Then he removed any officers who conscientiously enforced Congress's new law, preferring commanders who allowed disqualified Confederates to vote. Finally, in August 1867 he tried to remove Secretary of War Stanton. With that attempt the confrontation reached its climax.

Twice before, the House Judiciary Committee had considered impeachment, rejecting the idea once and then recommending it by only a 5-to-4 vote. The recommendation had been decisively defeated by the House. After Johnson's last action, however, a third attempt to impeach the president carried easily.

Impeachment of President Johnson

In 1868, the angry House was so determined to indict Johnson that it voted before drawing up specific charges. The indictment concentrated on Johnson's violation of the Tenure of Office Act, though modern scholars regard his systematic efforts to impede enforcement of the Military Reconstruction Act as a far more serious offense.

Johnson's trial in the Senate lasted more than three months. The prosecution, led by such Radicals as Thaddeus Stevens and Benjamin Butler, argued that Johnson was guilty of "high crimes and misdemeanors." But they also advanced the novel idea that impeachment was a political matter, not a judicial trial of guilt or innocence. The Senate ultimately rejected such reasoning, which would have

Chapter 15: Reconstruction by Trial and Error, 1865–1877

This lithograph celebrates the passage of the Fifteenth Amendment, which was important but fell short of an outright guarantee of the right to vote. *Library of Congress.*

transformed impeachment into a political weapon against any chief executive who disagreed with Congress. Although a majority of senators voted to convict Johnson, the prosecution fell one vote short of the necessary two-thirds majority. Johnson remained in office for the few months left in his term, and his acquittal established the precedent that only serious misdeeds merited removal from office.

In 1869, in an effort to write democratic principles and colorblindness into the Constitution, the Radicals succeeded in presenting the Fifteenth Amendment for ratification. This

> **Fifteenth Amendment**

measure forbade states to deny the right to vote "on account of race, color, or previous condition of servitude." The wording fell short of an outright guarantee of the right to vote because many northern states denied the suffrage to women and certain groups of men—Chinese immigrants, illiterates, those too poor to pay taxes. Ironically, the votes of four uncooperative southern states—compelled by Congress to approve the amendment as an added condition to rejoining the Union—proved necessary to impose even this language on parts of the North. Although several states outside the South refused to ratify, the Fifteenth Amendment became law in 1870.

Reconstruction Politics in the South

From the start, Reconstruction encountered the resistance of white southerners. Their opposition to change appeared in the black codes and other

> **White Resistance**

policies of the Johnson governments as well as in private attitudes. Many whites set their faces against emancipation, and—as was true in the British Caribbean—the former planter class proved especially unbending. In 1866 a Georgia newspaper frankly declared, "Most of the

Thomas Nast, in this 1868 cartoon, pictured the combination of forces—southern opposition and northern racism and indifference—that threatened the success of Reconstruction. *Library of Congress.*

white citizens believe that the institution of slavery was right, and . . . they will believe that the condition, which comes nearest to slavery, that can now be established will be the best." Unwillingness to accept black freedom would have been a major problem in any circumstances; Andrew Johnson's encouragement of southern whites actively to resist Congress only intensified the problem.

Fearing the end of their control over slaves, some planters attempted to postpone freedom by denying or misrepresenting events. Former slaves reported that their owners "didn't tell them it was freedom" or "wouldn't let [them] go." Agents of the Freedmen's Bureau agreed. One agent in Georgia concluded, "I find the old system of slavery working with even more rigor than formerly at a few miles distant from any point where U.S. troops are stationed." To hold onto their workers some landowners claimed control over black children and used guardianship and apprentice laws to bind black families to the plantation.

Whites also blocked blacks from acquiring land. A few planters divided up plots among their slaves, but most condemned the idea of making blacks landowners. One planter in South Carolina refused to sell as little as an acre and a half to each family. Even a Georgian whose family was known for its concern for the slaves was outraged that two property owners planned to "rent their lands to the Negroes!" Such action was "injurious to the best interest of the community." The son of a free black landowner in Virginia who sold nearly two hundred acres to former slaves explained, "White folks wasn't lettin' Negroes have nothing." These realities severely limited for blacks the rewards of a supposedly free labor system.

Adamant resistance by propertied whites soon manifested itself in other ways, including violence. In one North Carolina town a local magistrate clubbed a black man on a public street, and bands of "Regulators" terrorized blacks in parts of that state and Kentucky. Such incidents were predictable in a society in which many planters believed, as a South Carolinian put it, that blacks "can't be governed except with the whip."

After President Johnson encouraged the South to resist congressional Reconstruction, many white conservatives worked hard to capture the new state governments. Elsewhere, large numbers of whites boycotted the polls in an attempt to defeat Congress's plans. Since the new constitutions had to be approved by a majority of registered voters, registered whites could defeat them by sitting out the elections. This tactic was tried in North Carolina and succeeded in Alabama, forcing Congress to base ratification on a majority of those voting.

Very few black men stayed away from the polls. Enthusiastically and hopefully they seized the opportunity to participate in politics, voting solidly Republican. Most agreed with one man who felt that he should "stick to the end with the party that freed me." Illiteracy did not prohibit blacks (or uneducated whites) from making intelligent choices. Although William Henry could read only "a little," he testified that he and his friends had no difficulty selecting the Republican ballot. "We stood around and watched," he explained. "We saw D. Sledge vote; he owned half the country. We knowed he voted Democratic so we voted the other ticket so it would be Republican."

Zeal for voting spread through the entire black community. Women, who could not vote, encouraged their husbands and sons, and preachers exhorted their congregations to use the franchise. Such community spirit helped to counter white pressure tactics, and the freedmen's enthusiasm showed their hunger for equal rights.

With a large black turnout, and with prominent Confederates barred from politics under the Fourteenth Amendment, a new southern Republican party came to power in the constitutional conventions. Among Republican delegates were some blacks (265 out of the total of just over 1,000 delegates throughout the South), northerners who had moved to the South, and native southern whites who favored change. Together these Republicans brought the South's fundamental law into line with progressive reforms that had been adopted in the rest of the nation. The new constitutions were more democratic. They eliminated property qualifications for voting and holding office, and they made elective state and local offices that had been appointive. They provided for public schools and institutions to care for the mentally ill, the blind, the deaf, the destitute, and the orphaned, and they ended imprisonment for debt and barbarous punishments such as branding.

The conventions also broadened women's rights in possession of property and divorce. Usually, the main goal was not to make women equal with men but to provide relief to thousands of suffering debtors. In families left poverty-stricken by the war and weighed down by debt, the husband had usually contracted the debts. Thus, giving women legal control over their own property provided some protection to their families. There were some delegates, however, whose goal was to elevate women. Blacks in particular called for laws to provide for women's suffrage, but they were ignored by their white colleagues.

Under these new constitutions the southern states elected new governments. Again the Republican party triumphed, bringing new men into positions of power. The ranks of state

Triumph of Republican Governments

legislators in 1868 included some black southerners for the first time in history. Congress's second plan for Reconstruction was well under way. It remained to be seen what these new governments would do and how much change they would bring to society.

There was one possibility of radical change through these new governments. That possibility depended on the disfranchisement of substantial numbers of Confederate leaders. If the Republican regimes used their new power to exclude many whites from politics as punishment for rebellion, they would have a solid electoral majority based on black voters and their white allies. Land reform and the assurance of racial equality would be possible. But none of the Republican governments did this, or even gave it serious consideration.

Why did the new legislators shut the door on the possibility of deep and thoroughgoing reform? First, they appreciated the realities of power and the depth of racial enmity. In most states whites were the majority of the population, and former slaveowners controlled the best land and other sources of economic power. James Lynch, a leading black politician from Mississippi, candidly explained why Negroes shunned "the folly of" disfranchisement. Unlike northerners who "can leave when it becomes too uncomfortable," former slaves "must be in friendly relations with the great body of the whites in the state. Otherwise . . . peace can be maintained only by a standing army." Despised and lacking in economic or social power, southern Republicans saw mere acceptance and legitimacy as ambitious goals.

Second, blacks believed in the principle of universal suffrage and the Christian goal of reconciliation. Far from being vindictive toward the race that had enslaved them, they treated leading rebels with generosity and appealed to white southerners to adopt a spirit of fairness and cooperation. Henry McNeil Turner, like other Negro ministers, urged black Georgians to "love whites . . . soon their prejudice would melt away, and with God for our father, we will all be brothers." (Years later Turner criticized his own naiveté, saying that in the constitutional convention his motto had been "Anything to please the white folks.") Therefore southern Republicans quickly (in some cases immediately) restored the voting rights of former Confederates, as Congress steadily released more individuals from the penalties of the Fourteenth Amendment.

Thus the South's Republican party committed itself to a strategy of winning white support. To put the matter another way, the Republican party condemned itself to defeat if white voters would not cooperate. In just a few years Republicans were reduced to the embarrassment of making futile appeals to whites while ignoring the claims of their strongest supporters, blacks.

But for a time both Republicans and their opponents, who called themselves Conservatives or Democrats, moved to the center and appealed for support from a broad range of groups. Some propertied whites accepted congressional Reconstruction as a reality and declared that they would try to compete under the new rules. As these Democrats angled for some black votes, Republicans sought to attract more white voters. Both parties found an area of agreement in economic policies.

The Reconstruction governments devoted themselves to stimulating industry. This policy reflected northern ideals, but it also sprang from a growing southern interest in industrialization. Confederates had learned how vital industry was, and many postwar southerners were eager to build up the manufacturing capacity of their region. Accordingly, Reconstruction legislatures designed many tempting inducements to investment. Loans, subsidies, and exemptions from taxation for periods up to ten years helped to bring new industries into the region. The southern railroad system was rebuilt and expanded, coal and iron mining laid the basis for Birmingham's steel plants, and the number of manufacturing establishments nearly doubled between 1860 and 1880. This emphasis on big business interests, however, produced higher state debts and taxes, took money from schools and other programs, and multiplied possibilities for corruption. It also locked Republicans into a conservative strategy. They were appealing to elite whites who never responded, and the alternate possibility of making a strong, class-based appeal to poorer whites was lost.

> **Industrial-ization**

Policies appealing to black voters never went beyond equality before the law. In fact, the whites who controlled the southern Republican party were reluctant to allow blacks a share of offices proportionate to their electoral strength. Black leaders, aware of their weakness, did not push for revolutionary economic or social change. In every southern state blacks led efforts to establish public schools, but most did not press for integrated facilities. Having a school to attend was the most important thing at the time, for the Johnson governments had excluded

> **Other Republican Policies**

blacks from schools and other state-supported institutions. As a result, virtually every public school organized during Reconstruction was racially segregated, and these separate schools established a precedent for segregation. By the 1870s segregation was becoming a common, but not universal, practice in theaters, trains, and other public accommodations in the South.

A few black politicians did fight for civil rights and integration. Most were mulattos from cities such as New Orleans or Mobile, where large populations of light-skinned free blacks had existed before the war. Their experience in such communities had made them sensitive to issues of status, and they spoke out for open and equal public accommodations. Laws requiring equal accommodations won passage throughout the Deep South, but they often went unenforced or required the injured party to bring legal action for enforcement.

Economic progress was uppermost in the minds of most freed people and black representatives from agricultural districts. Land, above all else, had the potential to benefit the former slave, but few black state legislators promoted confiscation. Some hoped that high taxes on large landowners would force portions of these estates onto the market (small farmers' lands were protected by homestead exemptions). And in fact, much land fell into state hands for nonpayment of taxes and was offered for sale in small lots. But most freedmen had too little cash to bid against investors or speculators, and few gained land in this way. South Carolina established a land commission, but its purpose was to assist in the purchase of land. Any widespread redistribution of land had to arise from Congress, which never supported such action.

Within a few years, as centrists in both parties met with failure, the other side of white reaction to congressional Reconstruction began to dominate. Some conservatives had always favored fierce opposition to Reconstruction through pressure and racist propaganda. They put economic and social pressure on blacks: one black Republican complained that "my neighbors will not employ me, nor sell me a farthing's worth of anything." Charging that the South had been turned over to ignorant blacks, conservatives deplored "black domination." The cry of "Negro rule" now became constant.

Such attacks were gross distortions. Blacks participated in politics but did not dominate or control events. They were a minority in eight out of ten

Chapter 15: Reconstruction by Trial and Error, 1865–1877

One notable success in Reconstruction efforts to stimulate industry was Birmingham, Alabama. Here workers cast iron into blocks called pigs. *Birmingham Public Library.*

state conventions (transplanted northerners were a minority in nine out of ten). Of the state legislatures, only in the lower house in South Carolina did blacks ever constitute a majority; generally their numbers among officials were far inferior to their proportion in the population. Sixteen blacks won seats in Congress before Reconstruction was over, but none was ever elected governor, and only eighteen served in a high state office such as lieutenant governor, treasurer, superintendent of education, or secretary of state. Freedmen were participating in government, to be sure, but there was no justification for racist denunciations of "Ethiopian minstrelsy, Ham radicalism in all its glory."

Conservatives also stepped up their propaganda against the allies of black Republicans. "Carpetbagger" was a derisive name for whites who had come

Carpet-baggers and Scalawags
from the North. It suggested an evil and greedy northern politician, recently arrived with a carpetbag into which he planned to stuff ill-gotten gains before fleeing. The stranger's carpetbag, a popular travel bag whose frame was covered with heavy carpet material, was presumably deep enough to hold loot stolen from southern treasuries and filched from hapless, trusting former slaves. Immigrants from the North, who held the largest share of Republican offices, were all tarred with this brush.

In fact most northerners who settled in the South had arrived before Congress gave blacks the right to vote. They had come seeking business opportunities or a warmer climate, and most never entered politics. Those who did generally wanted to democratize the South and to introduce northern ways, such as industry, public education, and the spirit of enterprise. Hard times and ostracism by white southerners made many of these men dependent on officeholding for a living, a fact that increased Republican factionalism and damaged the party. Although carpetbaggers supported black suffrage and educational opportunities, most opposed social equality and integration.

Conservatives invented the term "scalawag" to stigmatize and discredit any native white southerner who cooperated with the Republicans. A substantial number of southerners did so, including some wealthy and prominent men. Most scalawags, however, were representatives of the yeoman class, men from mountain areas and small farming districts—average white southerners who saw that

Reconstruction Politics in the South

Throughout the South, black people welcomed the opportunity to participate in democratic governments. Here a convention of blacks assembles in Washington, D.C., to discuss Reconstruction problems.

they could benefit from the education and opportunities promoted by Republicans. Banding together with freedmen, they pursued common class interests and hoped to make headway against the power of long-dominant planters. Cooperation even convinced a few scalawags that "there is but little if any difference in the talents of the two races" and that all should have "an equal start."

Yet this black-white coalition was usually vulnerable to the issue of race, and scalawags shied away from support for racial equality. Republican tax policies also cut into upcountry, yeoman support, because reliance on the property tax hit some small landholders hard. In addition, poll taxes (whose proceeds were often earmarked for education) endangered the independence of other small farmers, forcing them toward participation in the market in order to obtain cash.

Taxation was a major problem for the Reconstruction governments. Financially the Republicans, despite their achievements, were doomed to be unpopular. Republicans wanted to continue prewar services, repair war's destruction, stimulate industry, and support important new ventures such as public schools. But the Civil War had destroyed much of the South's tax base. One category of valuable property—slaves—was entirely gone. Hundreds of thousands of citizens had lost much of the rest of their real and personal property—money, livestock, fences, and buildings—to the war. Thus an increase in taxes was necessary even to maintain traditional services, and new ventures required even higher taxes. Eventually and inevitably, Republican tax policies aroused much opposition.

Corruption was another powerful charge levied against the Republicans. Unfortunately, it was true. Many carpetbaggers and black politicians sold their votes, taking part in what scholars recognize was a nationwide surge of corruption (see page 545). Although white Democrats often shared in the guilt, and despite the efforts of some Republicans to stop it, Democrats convinced many voters that scandal was the inevitable result of a foolish Reconstruction program based on blacks and carpetbaggers.

All these problems damaged the Republicans, but in many southern states the deathblow came through violence: the murders, whippings, and intimidation of terrorist groups who most often used the name Ku Klux Klan. Terrorism against blacks occurred throughout Reconstruction, but after 1867 white violence became more

Ku Klux Klan

organized and purposeful. The Ku Klux Klan rode to frustrate Reconstruction and keep the freedmen in subjection. Nighttime visits, whippings, beatings, and murder became common, and in some areas virtually open warfare developed despite the authorities' efforts to keep the peace.

Although the Klan persecuted blacks who stood up for their rights as laborers or people, its main purpose was political. Lawless nightriders made active Republicans the target of their attacks. Prominent white Republicans and black leaders were killed in several states. After blacks who worked for a South Carolina scalawag started voting, terrorists visited the plantation and "whipped every nigger man they could lay their hands on." Klansmen also attacked Union League Clubs (Republican organizations that mobilized the black vote) and schoolteachers who were aiding the freedmen.

Klan violence was not spontaneous; certain social forces gave direction to racism. In North Carolina, for example, Alamance and Caswell counties were the sites of the worst Klan violence. They were in the Piedmont, where slim Republican majorities rested on cooperation between black voters and whites of the yeoman class, particularly yeomen whose Unionism or discontent with the Confederacy had turned them against local Democratic officials. Together these black and white Republicans had ousted officials long entrenched in power. But the Republican majority was a small one, and it would fail if either whites or blacks faltered in their support.

In Alamance and Caswell counties the wealthy and powerful men who had lost their accustomed political control organized a campaign of terror. They brought it into being and used it for their purposes. They were the secret organization's county officers and local chieftains; they recruited members and planned atrocities. They used the Klan to regain political power: by whipping up racism or frightening enough Republicans, the Ku Klux Klan could split the Republican coalition and restore a Democratic majority.

Klan violence injured Republicans across the South. No fewer than one-tenth of black leaders who had been delegates to the 1867–1868 constitutional conventions were attacked, seven fatally. In one judicial district of North Carolina the Ku Klux Klan was responsible for twelve murders, over seven hundred beatings, and other acts of violence including rape and arson. A single attack on Ala-

The Ku Klux Klan aimed to terrorize and intimidate its victims by violence and other methods. Mysterious regalia, such as the pointed hood (which was held up by a stick inside) contributed to a menacing atmosphere. The miniature coffin, typically left on a Republican's doorstep, conveyed a more direct threat. *KKK hood: Old Court House Museum, Vicksburg, Miss. Photo by Bob Pickett; KKK coffin: Collection of State Historical Museum, Mississippi Department of Archives and History. Photo by Gib Ford.*

bama Republicans at the town of Eutaw left four blacks dead and fifty-four wounded. In South Carolina five hundred masked Klansmen lynched eight black prisoners at the Union County jail, and nearby in York County the Klan committed "at least eleven murders and hundreds of whippings." According to historian Eric Foner, the Klan "made it virtually impossible for Republicans to campaign or vote in large parts of Georgia." Clearly, "violence had a profound effect on Reconstruction politics."

Thus a combination of difficult fiscal problems, Republican mistakes, racial hostility, and terror brought down the Republican regimes, and in most southern states so-called Radical Reconstruction was over after only a few years. The most lasting failure of Reconstruction governments, however, was not political; it was social. The new governments failed to alter the South's social structure or its distribution of wealth and power. Exploited as slaves, freedmen remained vulnerable to exploitation during Reconstruction. Without land of their own, they were dependent on white landowners, who could use their economic power to compromise blacks' political freedom. Armed only with the ballot, southern blacks had little chance to effect major changes.

> **Failure of Reconstruction**

To reform the southern social order, Congress would have had to redistribute land, but never did a majority of congressmen favor such a plan. Radical Republicans like Albion Tourgée condemned Congress's timidity. Turning the freedman out on his own without protection, said Tourgée, constituted "cheap philanthropy." Indeed, freedmen who had to live with the consequences of Reconstruction considered it a failure. The North should have "fixed some way for us," said former slaves, but instead it "threw all the Negroes on the world without any way of getting along."

Freedom had come, but blacks knew they "still had to depend on the southern white man for work, food, and clothing," and it was clear that most whites were hostile. Unless Congress exercised careful supervision over the South, the situation of the freedmen was sure to deteriorate. Whenever the North lost interest, Reconstruction would collapse.

The Social and Economic Meaning of Freedom

Black southerners entered upon life after slavery hopefully, determinedly, but not naively. They had too much experience with white people to assume that all would be easy. As one man in Texas advised his son, even before the war was over, "Our forever was going to be spent living among the Southerners, after they got licked." Expecting to meet with hostility, black people tried to gain as much as they could from their new circumstances. Often the most valued changes were personal ones—alterations in location, employer, or surroundings that could make an enormous difference to individuals or families.

One of the first decisions that many made was whether to leave the old plantation or remain. This meant making a judgment about where the chances of liberty and progress would be greatest. Former slaves drew upon their experiences in bondage to assess the whites with whom they had to deal. "Most all the Negroes that had good owners stayed with them," said one man, "but the others left." Not surprisingly, cruel slaveholders usually saw their former chattels walk off en masse. "And let me tell you," added one man who abandoned a harsh planter, "we sure cussed ole master out before we left there."

On new farms or old, the newly freed men and women reached out for valuable things in life that had been denied them. One of these was education. Whatever their age, blacks hungered for the knowledge in books that had been permitted only to whites. With freedom they started schools and filled classrooms both day and night. On "log seats" or "a dirt floor," many freedmen studied their letters in old almanacs, discarded dictionaries, or whatever was available. Young children brought infants to school with them, and adults attended at night or after "the crops were laid by." Many a teacher had "to make herself heard over three other classes reciting in concert" in a small room, but the scholars kept coming. The desire to escape slavery's ignorance was so great that many blacks paid tuition, typically $1.00 or $1.50 a month, despite their poverty. These seemingly small amounts constituted one-tenth of many people's agricultural wage and added up to more than $1 million by 1870.

> **Education for Blacks**

The federal government and northern reformers of both races assisted this search for education. In its brief life the Freedmen's Bureau founded over four thousand schools, and idealistic men and women from the North established others and staffed them ably. The Yankee schoolmarm—dedicated, selfless, and religious—became an

Freed from slavery, blacks of all ages filled the schools to seek the educations that had been denied to them in bondage. *William Gladstone Collection.*

agent of progress in many southern communities. Thus, with the aid of religious and charitable organizations throughout the North, blacks began the nation's first assault on the problems created by slavery. The results included the beginnings of a public school system in each southern state and the enrollment of over 600,000 blacks in elementary school by 1877.

Blacks and their white allies also realized that higher education was essential—colleges and universities to train teachers and equip ministers and professionals for leadership. The American Missionary Association founded seven colleges, including Fisk and Atlanta universities, between 1866 and 1869. The Freedmen's Bureau helped to establish Howard University in Washington, D.C., and northern religious groups such as Methodists, Baptists, and Congregationalists supported dozens of seminaries, colleges, and teachers' colleges. By the late 1870s black churches had joined in the effort, founding numerous colleges despite their smaller

financial resources. Although some of the new institutions did not survive, they brought knowledge to those who would educate others and laid a foundation for progress.

Even in Reconstruction, blacks were choosing many highly educated individuals as leaders. Many blacks who won public office during Reconstruction came from the prewar elite of free people of color. This group had benefited from its association with wealthy whites, who were often blood relatives. Some planters had given their mulatto children outstanding educations. Francis Cardozo, who served in South Carolina's constitutional convention and was later that state's secretary of the treasury and secretary of state, had attended universities in Scotland and England. P. B. S. Pinchback, who became lieutenant governor of Louisiana, was the son of a planter who had sent him to school in Cincinnati at age nine. The two black senators from Mississippi, Blanche K. Bruce and Hiram Revels, were both privileged in their educations. Bruce was the son of a planter who had provided tutoring on his plantation; Revels was the son of free North Carolina mulattos who had sent him to Knox College in Illinois. These men and many self-educated former slaves brought experience as artisans, businessmen, lawyers, teachers, and preachers to political office.

While elected officials wrestled with the political tasks of Reconstruction, millions of former slaves concentrated on improving life at home, on their farms, and in their neighborhoods. A major goal of black men and women was to gain some living space for themselves and their families. Surrounded by an unfriendly white population, they sought to insulate themselves from white interference and to strengthen the bonds of their own community. Throughout the South they devoted themselves to reuniting their families, moving away from the slave quarters, and founding black churches. Given the eventual failure of Reconstruction, the practical gains that blacks made in their daily lives often proved the most enduring.

The search for long-lost family members was awe inspiring. With only shreds of information to guide them, thousands of black people embarked on

Reunification of Black Families

odysseys in search of a husband, wife, child, or parent. By relying on the black community for help and information, many succeeded in their quest, sometimes almost miraculously. Others walked through several states and never found loved ones.

Husbands and wives who had belonged to different masters established homes together for the first time, and parents asserted the right to raise their own children. Saying "You took her away from me and didn' pay no mind to my cryin', so now I'm takin' her back home," one mother reclaimed a child whom the mistress had been raising in her own house. Another woman bristled when her old master claimed a right to whip her children, promptly informing him that "he warn't goin' to brush none of her chilluns no more." One girl recalled that her mistress had struck her soon after freedom. As if to clarify the new ground rules, this girl "grabbed her leg and would have broke her neck." The freedmen were too much at risk to act recklessly, but as one man put it, they were tired of punishment, and "they sure didn't take no more foolishment off of white folks."

Many black people wanted to minimize all contact with whites. "There is a prejudice against us . . . that will take years to get over," Reverend Garrison Frazier told General Sherman in January 1865. To avoid contact with intrusive whites, who were used to supervising and controlling them, blacks abandoned the slave quarters and fanned out into distant corners of the land they worked. Some moved away to build new homes in the woods. "After the war my stepfather come," recalled Annie Young, "and got my mother and we moved out in the piney woods." Others described moving "across the creek to [themselves]" or building a "saplin house . . . back in the woods" or "'way off in the woods." Some rural dwellers established small all-black settlements that still can be found today along the backroads of the South.

Even once-privileged slaves shared this desire for independence and social separation. One man turned down the master's offer of the overseer's house as a residence and moved instead to a shack in "Freetown." He also declined to let the former owner grind his grain for free, because it "make him feel like a free man to pay for things just like anyone else." One couple, a carriage driver and trusted house servant during slavery, passed up the fine cooking of the "big house" so that they could move "in the colored settlement."

The other side of this movement away from whites was closer communion within the black community. Freed from the restrictions and regulations of slavery, blacks could build

Founding of Black Churches

their own institutions as they saw fit. The secret church of slavery now came out into the open; in countless communities throughout the South, "some of the niggers started a brush arbor." A brush arbor was merely "a sort of . . . shelter with leaves for a roof," but the freedmen worshiped in it enthusiastically. "Preachin' and shouting sometimes lasted all day," ex-slaves recalled, for there were "glorious times then" when black people could worship together in freedom. Within a few years independent black branches of the Methodist and Baptist churches had attracted the great majority of black Christians in the South.

The desire to gain as much independence as possible carried over into the freedmen's economic arrangements. Since most former slaves lacked money to buy land, they preferred the next best thing—renting the land they worked. But many whites would not consider renting land to blacks; there was strong social pressure against it. Because few blacks had the means to rent a farm, other alternatives had to be tried.

Northerners and officials of the Freedmen's Bureau favored contracts between owners and laborers. To northerners who believed in "free soil, free labor, free men," contracts and wages seemed the key to progress. For a few years the Freedmen's Bureau helped to draw up and enforce such contracts, but they proved unpopular with both blacks and whites. Owners often filled the contracts with detailed requirements that reminded blacks of their circumscribed lives under slavery. Disputes frequently arose over efficiency, lost time, and other matters. Besides, cash was not readily available in the early years of Reconstruction; times were hard and the failure of Confederate banks had left the South with a shortage of credit facilities.

Black farmers and white landowners therefore turned to a system of sharecropping: black families worked for part of the crop while living on the landowner's property. The land-**Rise of the Share-cropping System** lord or a merchant "furnished" food and supplies needed before the harvest, and the sharecropper, landowner, and furnishing merchant all received payment from the crop. Republican laws gave laborers a first lien, or legal first claim, on the crop, increasing their feeling of ownership. Naturally, landowners tried to set the laborers' share at a low level, but blacks had some bargaining power. By holding out and refusing to make contracts at the end of the year, sharecroppers succeeded in lowering the owners' share to around one-half during Reconstruction.

The sharecropping system originated as a desirable compromise. It eased landowners' problems with cash and credit; blacks accepted it because it gave them a reasonable amount of freedom from daily supervision. Instead of working under a white overseer as in slavery, they were able to farm a plot of land on their own in family groups. Sharecropping later proved to be a disaster, both for blacks and for the South. Unscrupulous owners in a discriminatory society had many opportunities to cheat sharecroppers. Owners and merchants frequently paid less for blacks' cotton than they paid for whites'. Greedy men could overcharge or ma-

nipulate records so that the sharecropper always stayed in debt. The problem, however, was even more fundamental than that.

Southern farmers were concentrating on cotton, a crop with a bright past and a dim future. During the Civil War, India, Brazil, and Egypt had begun to **Overdependence on Cotton** supply cotton to Britain, and not until 1878 did the South recover its prewar share of British cotton purchases. This temporary loss of markets reduced per capita income, as did a decline in the amount of labor invested by the average southern farmer. Part of the exploitation of slavery had been the sending of black women and children into the fields. In freedom these people like their white counterparts stayed at home when possible. Black families valued human dignity more highly than the levels of production that had been achieved under the lash.

But even as southerners grew more cotton, matching and eventually surpassing prewar totals, their reward diminished. Cotton prices began a long decline whose causes merely coincided with the Civil War. From 1820 to 1860 world demand for cotton had grown at a rate of 5 percent per year, but from 1866 to 1895 the rate of growth was only 1.3 percent per year. By 1860 the English textile industry, world leader in production, had penetrated all the major new markets, and from that point on increases in demand were slight. As a result, when southern farmers planted more cotton they tended to depress the price.

In these circumstances overspecialization in cotton was a mistake, but for most southern farmers there was no alternative. Landowners required sharecroppers to grow the prime cash crop, whose salability was sure. Because of the shortage of banks and credit in the South, white farmers often had to borrow from a local merchant, who insisted on cotton production to secure his loan. Thus southern agriculture slipped deeper and deeper into depression. Black sharecroppers struggled under a growing burden of debt that reduced their independence and bound them to landowners almost as oppressively as slavery had bound them to their masters. Many white farmers became debtors too and gradually lost their land. These were serious problems, but few people in the North were paying attention.

The End of Reconstruction

The North's commitment to racial equality had never been total, and by the early 1870s it was evident that even the North's partial commitment was weakening. New issues were capturing people's attention, and soon voters began to look for reconciliation with southern whites. In the South, Democrats won control of one state after another, and they threatened to defeat Republicans in the North as well. Before long the situation had returned to "normal" in the eyes of southern whites.

The Supreme Court, after first re-establishing its power, participated in the northern retreat from Reconstruction. During the Civil War the Court had been cautious and reluctant to assert itself. Reaction to the *Dred Scott* decision had been so violent, and the Union's wartime emergency so great, that the Court had refrained from blocking or interfering with government actions. The justices, for example, had breathed a collective sigh of relief when legal technicalities prevented them from reviewing the case of Clement Vallandigham, who had been convicted of aiding the enemy by a military court when regular civil courts were open (see page 425).

But in 1866 a similar case, *Ex parte Milligan,* reached the Court through proper channels. Lambdin P. Milligan of Indiana had participated in a plot to free Confederate prisoners of war and overthrow state governments; for these acts a military court had sentenced Milligan, a civilian, to death. Milligan challenged the authority of the military tribunal, claiming that he had a right to a civil trial. In sweeping language the Supreme Court declared that military trials were illegal when civil courts were open and functioning, thus indicating that it intended to reassert itself as a major force in national affairs. This decision could have led to a direct clash with Congress, which in 1867 established military districts and military courts in the initial phase of its Reconstruction program. But Congress altered part of the Court's jurisdiction; it was constitutionally empowered to do so but had never taken such action before (and has not taken it since). By altering the Court's jurisdiction, Congress protected its Reconstruction policy and avoided a confrontation.

In the 1870s, interpretations by the Supreme Court drastically narrowed the meaning and effectiveness of the Fourteenth Amendment. In 1873 the **Supreme Court Decisions on Reconstruction** Court decided *Bradwell v. Illinois,* a case in which Myra Bradwell, a female attorney, had been denied the right to practice law in Illinois on account of her gender. Pointing to the Fourteenth Amendment, Bradwell's attorneys contended that the state had unconstitutionally abridged her "privileges and immunities" as a citizen. The Supreme Court rejected her claim, alluding to women's traditional role in the home.

The next day, in the *Slaughter-House* cases, the Court made its restrictive reading of the Fourteenth Amendment even more clear. The *Slaughter-House* cases had begun in 1869, when the Louisiana legislature granted one company a monopoly on the slaughtering of livestock in New Orleans. Rival butchers in the city promptly sued. Their attorney, former Supreme Court Justice John A. Campbell, pointed out that Louisiana had discriminated, violating the rights of some of its citizens to favor others. More fundamentally, Campbell argued that the Fourteenth Amendment had revolutionized the constitutional system by bringing individual rights under federal protection. Campbell thus expressed an original and central goal of the Republican party: to nationalize civil rights and guard them from state interference. Over the years his argument would win acceptance, offering shelter from government regulation to corporate "persons" in the nineteenth century and providing protection for blacks and other minorities in the twentieth.

But in the *Slaughter-House* decision, the Supreme Court dealt a stunning blow to the scope and vitality of the Fourteenth Amendment and to the hopes of blacks. Refusing to accept Campbell's argument, it interpreted the "privileges and immunities" of citizens so narrowly that it reduced them almost to trivialities. Although the Fourteenth Amendment clearly protected citizens' rights, the Court declared that state citizenship and national citizenship were separate. National citizenship involved only such things as the right to travel freely from state to state and to use the navigable waters of the nation, and only these narrow rights were protected by the Fourteenth Amendment. With this interpretation, the words "No state shall make or enforce any law which shall abridge the privileges or immunities of citizens of the United States" disappeared, for decades, as a meaningful or effective part of the Constitution.

The Supreme Court also concluded that the butchers who sued had not been deprived of their rights or property in violation of the "due process" clause of the amendment. Thus the justices dismissed Campbell's central contention: that the Fourteenth Amendment guaranteed the great basic rights of the Bill of Rights against state action. In so doing, the Court limited severely the amendment's potential for securing and protecting the rights of black citizens.

In 1876 the Court weakened the Reconstruction-era amendments even further by emasculating the enforcement clause of the Fourteenth Amendment and revealing deficiencies inherent in the Fifteenth Amendment. In *United States* v. *Cruikshank* the Court dealt with Louisiana whites who were indicted for attacking a meeting of blacks and conspiring to deprive them of their rights. The justices ruled that the Fourteenth Amendment did not empower the federal government to redress the misdeeds of private individuals against other citizens; only flagrant discrimination by the states was covered. In *United States* v. *Reese* the Court noted that the Fifteenth Amendment did not guarantee a citizen's right to vote but merely listed certain impermissible grounds for denying suffrage. Thus a path lay open for southern states to disfranchise blacks for supposedly nonracial reasons—lack of education, lack of property, or lack of descent from a grandfather qualified to vote before the Military Reconstruction Act. (So-called grandfather clauses became a way of including illiterate whites in the electorate yet excluding blacks, because the grandfathers of most blacks had been slaves before Reconstruction and unable to vote.)

The retreat from Reconstruction continued steadily in politics as well. In 1868 Ulysses S. Grant, running as a Republican, defeated Horatio Seymour, a Democrat of New York,

> **Election of 1868**

in a presidential campaign that revived sectional divisions. Although he was not a Radical, Grant realized that Congress's program represented the wishes of northerners, and he supported a platform that praised congressional Reconstruction and endorsed Negro suffrage in the South. (The platform stopped short of endorsing black suffrage in the North.) The Democrats went in the opposite direction; their platform vigorously denounced Reconstruction. By associating themselves with rebellion and with Johnson's repudiated program, the Democrats went down to defeat in all but eight states, though the popular vote was fairly close.

In office Grant sometimes called out federal troops to stop violence or enforce acts of Congress, but only when he had to. He hoped to avoid confrontation with the South, to erase the image of dictatorship that his military background summoned up. In fact, neither he nor Johnson imposed anything approaching a military occupation on the South. Rapid demobilization reduced a federal army of more than 1 million to 57,000 within a year of the surrender at Appomattox. Thereafter the number of troops in the South continued to fall, until in 1874 there were only 4,082 in the southern states outside Texas. Throughout Reconstruction, the strongest federal units were in Texas and the West, fighting Indians, not white southerners.

In 1870 and 1871 the violent campaigns of the Ku Klux Klan moved Congress to pass two Enforcement Acts and an anti-Klan law. These laws, for the first time, made acts by *individuals* against the civil and political rights of others a federal offense. They permitted martial law and suspension of the writ of habeas corpus to combat murders, beatings, and threats by the Klan. Federal troops and prosecutors used them vigorously but with only partial success. Out of hundreds of indictments, a few dozen Klansmen were convicted, more confessed, and many others (roughly two thousand in South Carolina alone) fled their states to avoid prosecution. A conspiracy of silence frustrated some prosecutions: frightened witnesses were unwilling to testify and juries unwilling to convict. After the passage of anti-Klan legislation, the Klan disbanded officially and went underground. Paramilitary organizations known as Rifle Clubs and Red Shirts often took the Klan's place.

Klan terrorism tested Republicans' resolve to change things in the South in an especially clear-cut way. Yet even on this issue there were ominous signs that the North's commitment to racial justice was fading. Some conservative but influential Republicans opposed the anti-Klan laws, basing their opposition on the charge that the laws infringed on states' rights. It was striking that some Republicans were echoing an old and standard line of the Democrats. This opposition foreshadowed a more general revolt within Republican ranks in 1872.

Disenchanted with Reconstruction, in 1872 a group calling itself the Liberal Republicans bolted the party and nominated Horace Greeley, the well-

Liberal Republicans Revolt

known editor of the *New York Tribune,* for president. The Liberal Republicans were a varied group, including civil service reformers, foes of corruption, and advocates of a lower tariff. Normally such disparate elements would not cooperate with each other, but they were united by two popular, widespread attitudes: distaste for federal intervention in the South and a desire to let market forces and the "best men" determine events in the South. The Democrats also gave their nomination to Greeley in 1872. The combination was not enough to defeat Grant, but it reinforced his desire to avoid confrontation with white southerners. Grant continued to use troops sparingly and in 1875 refused a desperate request from the governor of Mississippi.

The Liberal Republican challenge reflected growing dissatisfaction with Grant's administration. Strong-willed but politically naive, Grant made a series of poor appointments. His secretary of war, his private secretary, and officials in the Treasury and Navy departments were all involved in bribery or tax-cheating scandals. Instead of exposing the corruption, Grant defended some of the culprits. As the clamor against dishonesty in government grew, Grant's popularity and his party's popularity declined. In the 1874 elections Democrats recaptured the House of Representatives.

Congress's resolve on southern issues weakened steadily. By joint resolution it had removed the political disabilities of the Fourteenth Amendment from many former Confederates.

Amnesty Act

In 1872 it adopted a sweeping Amnesty Act, which pardoned most of the remaining rebels and left only five hundred excluded from political participation. A Civil Rights Act passed in 1875 purported to guarantee black people equal accommodations in public places, such as inns and theaters, but it was weak and contained no effective provisions for enforcement. (The law was later struck down by the Supreme Court; see page 490.)

Democrats regained power in the South rather quickly, winning four states before 1872 and a total of eight by the start of 1876 (see map). As they did so, northern Republicans worried about their opponents' stress on the failure and scandals of Reconstruction governments. Many Republicans sensed that their constituents were tiring of the same old issues.

In fact, new concerns were catching the public's eye. Industrialization and immigration had surged forward, hastening the changes in national life. Only eight years after the war, industrial production had increased by an impressive 75 percent. For the first time, nonagricultural workers outnumbered farmers, and only Britain had a greater industrial output. Government financial policies had done much to bring this rapid growth about. Soon after the war Congress had shifted some of the government's tax revenues to pay off the interest-bearing war debt. The debt fell from $2.33 billion in 1866 to only $587 million in 1893, and every dollar repaid was a dollar injected into the economy for potential reinvestment. Thus approximately 1 percent of the gross national product was pumped back into the economy from 1866 to 1872 and only slightly less than that during the rest of the 1870s. Low taxes on investment and high tariffs on manufactured goods also aided industrialists. With such help the northern economy quickly recovered its prewar rate of growth.

In the same period 3 million new immigrants had entered the country, most of them joining the labor force of industrial cities in the North and West. As the number of immigrants began to rise again, there was a corresponding revival of ingrained suspicions and hostilities among native-born Americans. The Mormon question too—how Utah's growing Mormon community, which practiced polygamy, could be reconciled to American law—became prominent.

Then the Panic of 1873 occurred, which ushered in over five years of continuing economic contraction. The panic threw 3 million people out of work and focused attention on economic and monetary problems. The clash between labor and capital became the major issue of the day, and class attitudes diverged, especially in the larger cities. Debtors and the unemployed sought easy-money policies to spur economic expansion. Businessmen, disturbed by the strikes and industrial violence that accompanied the panic, became increasingly concerned about the defense of property.

The monetary issue aroused strong controversy. Civil War greenbacks had the potential to expand the money supply and lift prices if

Greenbacks Versus Sound Money

they were kept in circulation. In 1872, Democratic farmers and debtors had urged such a policy, but they were overruled by

Chapter 15: Reconstruction by Trial and Error, 1865–1877

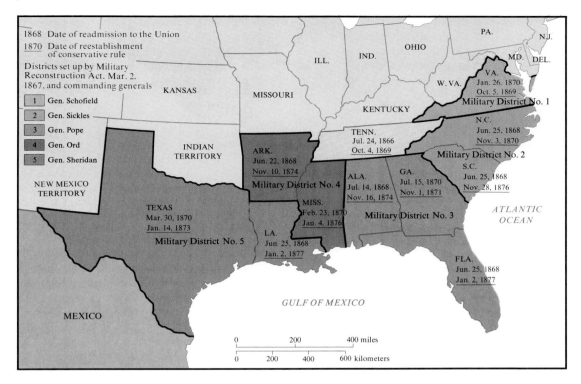

The Reconstruction

"sound money" men. Now hard times swelled the ranks of "greenbackers"—voters who favored greenbacks and easy money. In 1874, Congress voted to increase the number of greenbacks in circulation, but Grant vetoed the bill in deference to the opinions of financial leaders. The next year sound-money interests prevailed in Congress, winning passage of a law requiring that after 1878 greenbacks be convertible into gold. The law limited the inflationary impact of the greenbacks and aided creditors, not debtors such as hard-pressed farmers.

In international affairs there was renewed pressure for, and controversy about, expansion. Secretary of State William H. Seward accomplished a major addition of territory to the national domain in 1867. Through negotiation with the Russian government, he arranged the purchase of Alaska for $7.2 million dollars. Opponents ridiculed Seward's venture, calling Alaska Frigidia, the Polar Bear Garden, and Walrussia. But Seward convinced important congressmen of Alaska's economic potential, and other lawmakers favored the dawning of friendship with Russia. In the same year the United States took control of the Midway Islands, a

thousand miles from Hawaii; they were scarcely mentioned again until the Second World War. In 1870 President Grant tried to annex the Dominican Republic, but Senator Charles Sumner blocked the attempt. Seward and his successor, Hamilton Fish, used diplomacy to arrange a financial settlement of claims against Britain for permitting the sale of the *Alabama* and other Confederate cruisers (see page 427).

By 1876 it was obvious to most political observers that the North was no longer willing to pursue the goals of Reconstruction. The results of a disputed presidential election confirmed this fact. Samuel J. Tilden, Democratic governor of New York, ran strongly in the South and took a commanding lead in both the popular vote and the electoral college over Rutherford B. Hayes, the Republican nominee. Tilden won 184 electoral votes and needed only one more for a majority. Nineteen votes from Louisiana, South Carolina, and Florida were disputed; both Democrats and Republicans claimed to have won in those states despite fraud on the part of their opponents. One vote

Election of 1876

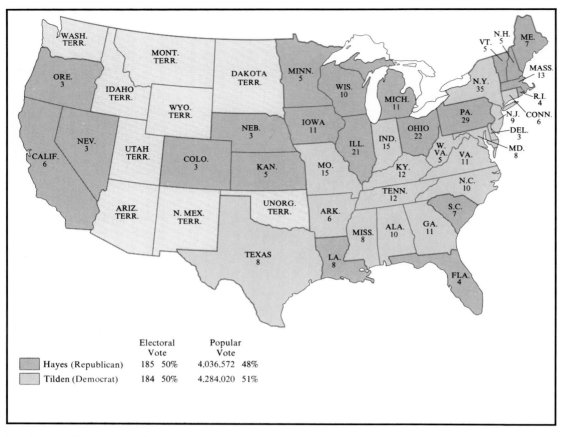

Presidential Election, 1876

	Electoral Vote		Popular Vote	
Hayes (Republican)	185	50%	4,036,572	48%
Tilden (Democrat)	184	50%	4,284,020	51%

from Oregon was undecided due to a technicality (see map).

To resolve this unprecedented situation, on which the Constitution gave no guidance, Congress established a fifteen-member electoral commission. In the interest of impartiality, membership on the commission was to be balanced between Democrats and Republicans. But one independent Republican, Supreme Court Justice David Davis, refused appointment in order to accept his election as a senator. A regular Republican took his place, and the Republican party prevailed 8 to 7 on every decision, a strict party vote. Hayes would become the winner if Congress accepted the commission's findings.

Congressional acceptance, however, was not certain. Democrats controlled the House and had the power to filibuster to block action on the vote. Many citizens worried that the nation had entered a major constitutional crisis and was slipping once

again into civil war. The crisis was resolved when Democrats acquiesced in the election of Hayes. Scholars have found that negotiations went on between some of Hayes's supporters and southerners who were interested in federal aid to railroads, internal improvements, federal patronage, and removal of troops from southern states. But the most recent studies suggest that these negotiations did not have a deciding effect on the outcome. Neither party was well enough organized to implement and enforce a bargain between the sections. Northern and southern Democrats decided they could not win and failed to contest the election. Thus Hayes became president, and southerners looked forward to the withdrawal of federal troops from the South. Reconstruction was unmistakably over.

Southern Democrats rejoiced, but black Americans grieved over the betrayal of their hopes for equality. Tens of thousands of blacks pondered leaving the South, where freedom was no longer

Exodusters, southern blacks dismayed by the failure of Reconstruction, left the South by the thousands for Kansas or states farther west in the late 1870s. This photo shows one of the leaders of the movement to Kansas, Benjamin "Pap" Singleton. *Kansas State Historical Society.*

Black Exodusters

a real possibility. "[We asked] whether it was possible we could stay under a people who had held us in bondage," said Henry Adams, who led a migration to Kansas. "[We] appealed to the President . . . and to Congress . . . to protect us in our rights and privileges," but "in 1877 we lost all hopes." Thereafter many southern blacks "wanted to go to a territory by ourselves." In South Carolina, Louisiana, Mississippi, and other southern states, thousands gathered up their possessions and migrated to Kansas. They were known as Exodusters, disappointed people still searching for their share in the American dream. Even in Kansas they met disillusionment, as the welcome extended by the state's governor soon gave way to hostile public reactions.

Thus the nation ended over fifteen years of bloody civil war and controversial reconstruction without establishing full freedom for black Americans. Their status would continue to be a major issue. A host of other issues would arise from industrialization. How would the country develop its immense resources in a growing and increasingly interconnected national economy? How would farmers, industrial workers, immigrants, and capitalists fit into the new social system? Industrialization promised not just a higher standard of living but also a different lifestyle in both urban and rural areas. Moreover, it increased the nation's power and laid the foundation for an enlarged American role in international affairs. Again Americans turned their thoughts to expansion and the conquest of new frontiers. As the United States entered its second hundred years of existence, it confronted these serious challenges. The experiences of the 1860s and 1870s suggested that the solutions, if any, might be neither clear nor complete.

Suggestions for Further Reading

National Policy, Politics, and Constitutional Law

Richard H. Abbott, *The Republican Party and the South, 1855–1877* (1986); Herman Belz, *Emancipation and Equal*

Rights (1978); Herman Belz, *A New Birth of Freedom* (1976); Herman Belz, *Reconstructing the Union* (1969); Michael Les Benedict, *A Compromise of Principle: Congressional Republicans and Reconstruction, 1863–1869* (1974); Michael Les Benedict, *The Impeachment and Trial of Andrew Johnson* (1973); David W. Bowen, *Andrew Johnson and the Negro* (1989); Charles S. Campbell, *The Transformation of American Foreign Relations, 1865–1900* (1976); Adrian Cook, *The Alabama Claims* (1975); Michael Kent Curtis, *No State Shall Abridge* (1987); David Donald, *Charles Sumner and the Rights of Man* (1970); Harold M. Hyman, *A More Perfect Union* (1973); Ronald J. Jensen, *The Alaska Purchase and Russian-American Relations* (1975); William S. McFeely, *Grant* (1981); William S. McFeely, *Yankee Stepfather: General O. O. Howard and the Freedmen* (1968); Eric L. McKitrick, *Andrew Johnson and Reconstruction* (1966); James M. McPherson, *The Abolitionist Legacy* (1975); Kenneth M. Stampp, *The Era of Reconstruction* (1965); Mark W. Summers, *Railroads, Reconstruction, and the Gospel of Prosperity* (1984); Glyndon C. Van Deusen, *William Henry Seward* (1967).

The Freed Slaves

Roberta Sue Alexander, *North Carolina Faces the Freedmen* (1985); Ira Berlin, ed., *Freedom: A Documentary History of Emancipation, 1861–1867* (1984); Edmund L. Drago, *Black Politicians and Reconstruction in Georgia* (1982); Paul D. Escott, *Slavery Remembered* (1979); Eric Foner, "Reconstruction and the Crisis of Free Labor," in Eric Foner, ed., *Politics and Ideology in the Age of the Civil War* (1980); Peter Kolchin, *First Freedom* (1972); Leon Litwack, *Been in the Storm So Long* (1979); Howard Rabinowitz, ed., *Southern Black Leaders in Reconstruction* (1982); C. Peter Ripley, *Slaves and Freedmen in Civil War Louisiana* (1976); Willie Lee Rose, *Rehearsal for Reconstruction* (1964); Emma Lou Thornbrough, ed., *Black Reconstructionists* (1972); Okon Uya, *From Slavery to Public Service* (1971); Clarence Walker, *A Rock in a Weary Land* (1982).

Politics and Reconstruction in the South

Richard N. Current, *Those Terrible Carpetbaggers* (1988); Jonathan Daniels, *Prince of Carpetbaggers* (1958); W. E. B. Du Bois, *Black Reconstruction* (1935); Paul D. Escott, *Many Excellent People: Power and Privilege in North Carolina, 1850–1900* (1985); W. McKee Evans, *Ballots and Fence Rails: Reconstruction on the Lower Cape Fear* (1966); Eric Foner, *Reconstruction: America's Unfinished Revolution, 1863–1877* (1988); Eric Foner, *Nothing but Freedom* (1983); William C. Harris, *William Woods Holden, Firebrand of North Carolina Politics* (1988); William C. Harris, *The Day of the Carpetbagger* (1979); Thomas Holt, *Black over White: Negro Political Leadership in South Carolina During Reconstruction* (1977); Robert Manson Myers, ed., *The Children of Pride* (1972); Elizabeth Studley Nathans, *Losing the Peace* (1968); Lillian A. Pereyra, *James Lusk Alcorn* (1966); Michael Perman, *The Road to Redemption* (1984); Michael Perman, *Reunion Without Compromise* (1973); Lawrence N. Powell, "The Politics of Livelihood," in J. Morgan Kousser and James M. McPherson, eds., *Region, Race and Reconstruction* (1982); Lawrence N. Powell, *New Masters* (1980); George C. Rable, *But There Was No Peace* (1984); James Roark, *Masters Without Slaves* (1977); James Sefton, *The United States Army and Reconstruction, 1865–1877* (1967); Mark W. Summers, *Railroads, Reconstruction, and the Gospel of Prosperity* (1984); J. Mills Thornton III, "Fiscal Policy and the Failure of Radical Reconstruction," in J. Morgan Kousser and James M. McPherson, eds., *Region, Race and Reconstruction* (1982); Albion W. Tourgée, *A Fool's Errand* (1979); Allen Trelease, *White Terror* (1967); Ted Tunnell, *Carpetbagger from Vermont* (1989); Ted Tunnell, *Crucible of Reconstruction* (1984); Michael Wayne, *The Reshaping of Plantation Society* (1983); Sarah Woolfolk Wiggins, *The Scalawag in Alabama Politics, 1865–1881* (1977).

Women, Family, and Social History

Ellen Carol Dubois, *Feminism and Suffrage* (1978); Herbert G. Gutman, *The Black Family in Slavery and Freedom, 1750–1925* (1976); Elizabeth Jacoway, *Yankee Missionaries in the South* (1979); Jacqueline Jones, *Labor of Love, Labor of Sorrow* (1985); Jacqueline Jones, *Soldiers of Light and Love* (1980); Robert C. Kenzer, *Kinship and Neighborhood in a Southern Community* (1987); Rebecca Scott, "The Battle over the Child," *Prologue,* 10, no. 2 (Summer 1978), 101–113.

The End of Reconstruction

Michael Les Benedict, "Southern Democrats in the Crisis of 1876–1877," *Journal of Southern History,* LXVI, no. 4 (November 1980), 489–524; William Gillette, *Retreat from Reconstruction, 1869–1879* (1980); William Gillette, *The Right to Vote* (1969); Keith Ian Polakoff, *The Politics of Inertia* (1973); John G. Sproat, *"The Best Men": Liberal Reformers in the Gilded Age* (1968); C. Vann Woodward, *Reunion and Reaction* (1951).

Reconstruction's Legacy for the South

Robert G. Athearn, *In Search of Canaan* (1978); Norman L. Crockett, *The Black Towns* (1979); Stephen J. DeCanio, *Agriculture in the Postbellum South* (1974); Steven Hahn, *The Roots of Southern Populism* (1983); Susan Previant Lee and Peter Passell, *A New Economic View of American History* (1979); Jay R. Mandle, *The Roots of Black Poverty* (1978); Nell Irvin Painter, *Exodusters* (1976); Howard Rabinowitz, *Race Relations in the Urban South, 1865–1890* (1978); Roger L. Ransom and Richard Sutch, *One Kind of Freedom* (1977); Laurence Shore, *Southern Capitalists* (1986); Peter Wallenstein, *From Slave South to New South* (1987); Jonathan M. Wiener, *Social Origins of the New South* (1978); Joel Williamson, *After Slavery* (1966); C. Vann Woodward, *Origins of the New South* (1951).

Appendix

Historical Reference Books by Subject:
Encyclopedias, Dictionaries, Atlases, Chronologies, and Statistics

American History: General

Concise Dictionary of American History (1983); *Dictionary of American History* (1976–1978); Robert H. Ferrell and John S. Bowman, eds., *The Twentieth Century: An Almanac* (1984); John D. Buenker and Edward R. Kantowicz, eds., *Historical Dictionary of the Progressive Era, 1890–1920* (1988); George H. Gallup, *The Gallup Poll: Public Opinion, 1935–1971* (1972) and *1972–1977* (1978); Bernard Grun, *The Timetables of History* (1975); Stanley Hochman, *Yesterday and Today* (1979); *International Encyclopedia of the Social Sciences* (1968–); R. Alton Lee, ed., *Encyclopedia USA* (1983–); Michael Martin and Leonard Gelber, *Dictionary of American History* (1981); Richard B. Morris, *Encyclopedia of American History* (1982); James S. Olson, ed., *Historical Dictionary of the New Deal* (1985); James S. Olson, *Historical Dictionary of the 1920s* (1988); Thomas Parker and Douglas Nelson, *Day by Day: The Sixties* (1983); Harry Ritter, *Dictionary of Concepts in History* (1986); Arthur M. Schlesinger, Jr., ed., *The Almanac of American History* (1983); *Scribner Desk Dictionary of American History* (1984); U.S. Bureau of the Census, *Historical Statistics of the United States* (1975); *Webster's New Geographical Dictionary* (1984); Philip P. Wiener, ed., *Dictionary of the History of Ideas* (1973).

American History: General Atlases

Geoffrey Barraclough, ed., *The Times Atlas of World History* (1979); W. P. Cumming et al., *The Discovery of North America* (1972); Robert H. Ferrell and Richard Natkiel, *Atlas of American History* (1987); Edward W. Fox, *Atlas of American History* (1964); Kenneth T. Jackson and James T. Adams, *Atlas of American History* (1978); Adrian Johnson, *America Explored* (1974); National Geographic Society, *Historical Atlas of the United States* (1988); Charles O. Paullin, *Atlas of the Historical Geography of the United States* (1932); U.S. Department of the Interior, *National Atlas of the United States* (1970). Other atlases are listed under specific categories.

American History: General Biographies

Concise Dictionary of American Biography (1980); *Dictionary of American Biography* (1928–); John A. Garraty, ed., *Encyclopedia of American Biography* (1974); *National Cyclopedia of American Biography* (1898–). Other biographical works appear under specific categories.

African-Americans

Rayford W. Logan and Michael R. Winston, eds., *The Dictionary of American Negro Biography* (1983); W. A. Low and Virgil A. Clift, eds., *Encyclopedia of Black America* (1981); Bruce Kellner, *The Harlem Renaissance* (1984); Randall M. Miller and John D. Smith, eds., *Dictionary of Afro-American Slavery* (1988); Edgar A. Toppin, *A Biographical History of Blacks in America* (1971).

American Revolution

Mark M. Boatner III, *Encyclopedia of the American Revolution* (1974); Lester J. Cappon, ed., *Atlas of Early American History: The Revolutionary Era, 1760–1790* (1976); Douglas W. Marshall and Howard H. Peckham, *Campaigns of the American Revolution* (1976); Gregory Palmer, ed., *Biographical Sketches of Loyalists of the American Revolution* (1984); *Rand-McNally Atlas of the American Revolution* (1974).

Architecture

William D. Hunt, Jr., ed., *Encyclopedia of American Architecture* (1980).

Business and the Economy

Christine Ammer and Dean S. Ammer, *Dictionary of Business and Economics* (1983); Douglas Auld and Graham Bannock, *The American Dictionary of Economics* (1983); Douglas Greenwald, *Encyclopedia of Economics* (1982); John N. Ingham, *Biographical Dictionary of American Business Leaders* (1983); William H. Mulligan, Jr., ed., *A Historical Dictionary of American Industrial Language* (1988); Glenn G. Munn, *Encyclopedia of Banking and Finance* (1973); David W. Pearce, *Dictionary of Modern Economics* (1983); Glenn Porter, ed., *Encyclopedia of American Economic History* (1980).

Cities and Towns

Charles Abrams, *The Language of Cities: A Glossary of Terms* (1971); John L. Androit, ed., *Township Atlas of the United States* (1979); Ory M. Nergal, ed., *The Encyclopedia of American Cities* (1980); David D. Van Tassel and John J.

Grabowski, eds., *The Encyclopedia of Cleveland History* (1987). See also "Politics and Government."

Civil War

Mark M. Boatner III, *The Civil War Dictionary* (1988); Patricia L. Faust, *Historical Times Encyclopedia of the Civil War* (1986); E. B. Long, *The Civil War Day by Day* (1971); Mark E. Neely, Jr., *The Abraham Lincoln Encyclopedia* (1982); Craig L. Symonds, *A Battlefield Atlas of the Civil War* (1983); U.S. War Department, *The Official Atlas of the Civil War* (1958); Jon L. Wakelyn, ed., *Biographical Dictionary of the Confederacy* (1977); Ezra J. Warner and W. Buck Yearns, *Biographical Register of the Confederate Congress* (1975). See also "The South."

Conservation

Forest History Society, *Encyclopedia of American Forest and Conservation History* (1983).

Constitution and Supreme Court

Congressional Quarterly, *Guide to the Supreme Court* (1979); Leon Friedman and Fred I. Israel, eds., *The Justices of the United States Supreme Court, 1789–1978* (1980); Richard F. Hixson, *Mass Media and the Constitution* (1989); Robert J. Janosik, ed., *Encyclopedia of the American Judicial System* (1987); *Judges of the United States* (1980); Leonard W. Levy et al., eds., *Encyclopedia of the American Constitution* (1986).

Crime and Police

William G. Bailey, *Encyclopedia of Police Science* (1987); Sanford H. Kadish, ed., *Encyclopedia of Crime and Justice* (1983); Carl Sifakis, *The Encyclopedia of American Crime* (1982).

Culture and Folklore

Hennig Cohen and Tristram Potter Coffin, eds., *The Folklore of American Holidays* (1987); Richard M. Dorson, ed., *Handbook of American Folklore* (1983); M. Thomas Inge, ed., *Handbook of American Popular Culture* (1979–1981); J. F. Rooney, Jr., Wilbur Zelinsky, and Dean R. Louder, eds., *This Remarkable Continent: An Atlas of United States and Canadian Society and Cultures* (1982); Marjorie Tallman, *Dictionary of American Folklore* (1959); Justin Wintle, ed., *Makers of Nineteenth Century Culture, 1800–1914* (1982). See also "Entertainment," "Mass Media and Journalism," "Music," and "Sports."

Education

Lee C. Deighton, ed., *The Encyclopedia of Education* (1971); Joseph C. Kiger, ed., *Research Institutions and Learned Societies* (1982); John F. Ohles, ed., *Biographical Dictionary of American Educators* (1978).

Entertainment

Tim Brooks and Earle Marsh, *The Complete Directory to Prime Time Network TV Shows, 1946–Present* (1979); Barbara N. Cohen-Stratyner, *Biographical Dictionary of Dance* (1982); John Dunning, *Tune in Yesterday* [radio] (1967); Stanley Green, *Encyclopedia of the Musical Film* (1981); *Notable Names in the American Theater* (1976); *New York Times Encyclopedia of Television* (1977); Andrew Sarris, *The American Cinema: Directors and Directions, 1929–1968* (1968); Anthony Slide, *The American Film Industry* (1986); Evelyn M. Truitt, *Who Was Who on Screen* (1977). See also "Culture and Folklore," "Mass Media and Journalism," "Music," and "Sports."

Foreign Policy and International Relations

Alexander DeConde, ed., *Encyclopedia of American Foreign Policy* (1978); John E. Findling, *Dictionary of American Diplomatic History* (1980); *International Geographic Encyclopedia and Atlas* (1979); Warren F. Kuehl, ed., *Biographical Dictionary of Internationalists* (1983); George T. Kurian, *Encyclopedia of the Third World* (1981); Jack C. Plano and Roy Olton, eds., *The International Relations Dictionary* (1988); Jack E. Vincent, *A Handbook of International Relations* (1969). See also "Peace Movements and Pacifism," "Wars and the Military," and specific wars.

Immigration and Ethnic Groups

American Jewish Yearbook (1899–); Stephanie Bernardo, *The Ethnic Almanac* (1981); Hyung-Chan Kim, ed., *Dictionary of Asian American History* (1986); Matt S. Meier, *Mexican American Biographies* (1988); Matt S. Meier and Feliciano Rivera, *Dictionary of Mexican American History* (1981); Sally M. Miller, ed., *The Ethnic Press in the United States* (1987); Stephan Thernstrom, ed., *Harvard Encyclopedia of American Ethnic Groups* (1980).

Labor

Gary M. Fink, ed., *Biographical Dictionary of American Labor Leaders* (1984); Gary M. Fink, ed., *Labor Unions* (1977); Philip S. Foner, *First Facts of American Labor* (1984).

Literature

James T. Callow and Robert J. Reilly, *Guide to American Literature* (1976–1977); *Dictionary of Literary Biography* (1978–); Eugene Ehrlich and Gorton Carruth, *The Oxford Illustrated Literary Guide to the United States* (1982); Jon Tuska and Vicki Piekarski, *Encyclopedia of Frontier and Western Fiction* (1983). See also "Culture and Folklore," "The South," and "Women."

Mass Media and Journalism

Robert V. Hudson, *Mass Media* (1987); William H. Taft, ed., *Encyclopedia of Twentieth-Century Journalists* (1986).

Medicine and Nursing

Vern L. Bullough et al., eds., *American Nursing: A Biographical Dictionary* (1988); Martin Kaufman et al., eds., *Dictionary of American Medical Biography* (1984); Martin Kaufman et al., eds., *Dictionary of American Nursing Biography* (1988); George L. Maddox, ed., *The Encyclopedia of Aging* (1987).

Music

John Chilton, *Who's Who of Jazz* (1972); Edward Jablonski, *The Encyclopedia of American Music* (1981); Roger Lax and Frederick Smith, *The Great Song Thesaurus* (1984). See also "Culture and Folklore" and "Entertainment."

Native Americans

Michael Coe et al., *Atlas of Ancient America* (1986); Frederick J. Dockstader, *Great North American Indians* (1977); *Handbook of North American Indians* (1978–); Barry Klein, ed., *Reference Encyclopedia of the American Indian* (1978); Paul Stuart, *Nation Within a Nation: Historical Statistics of American Indians* (1987); Helen H. Tanner, ed., *Atlas of Great Lakes Indian History* (1987); Carl Waldman, *Atlas of the North American Indian* (1985).

Peace Movements and Pacifism

Harold Josephson et al., eds., *Biographical Dictionary of Modern Peace Leaders* (1985); Ervin Laszlo and Jong Y. Yoo, eds., *World Encyclopedia of Peace* (1986); Robert S. Meyer, *Peace Organizations Past and Present* (1988). See also "Wars and the Military" and specific wars.

Politics and Government: General

Erik W. Austin, *Political Facts of the United States Since 1789* (1986); Congressional Quarterly, *Congress and the Nation, 1945–1976* (1965–1977); Jack P. Greene, ed., *Encyclopedia of American Political History* (1984); Leon Hurwitz, *Historical Dictionary of Censorship in the United States* (1985); Bernard K. Johnpoll and Harvey Klehr, eds., *Biographical Dictionary of the American Left* (1986); Kenneth C. Martis, *Historical Atlas of Political Parties in the United States Congress, 1789–1989* (1989); Kenneth C. Martis, *Historical Atlas of United States Congressional Districts, 1789–1983* (1982); Edwin V. Mitchell, *An Encyclopedia of American Politics* (1968); William Safire, *Safire's Political Dictionary* (1978); Edward L. and Frederick H. Schapsmeier, eds., *Political Parties and Civic Action Groups* (1981); Arthur M. Schlesinger, Jr., and Fred I. Israel, eds., *History of American*

Presidential Elections, 1789–1968 (1971); Robert Scruton, *A Dictionary of Political Thought* (1982); Jay M. Shafritz, *The Dorsey Dictionary of American Government and Politics* (1988); Hans Sperber and Travis Trittschuh, *American Political Terms* (1962). See also "Constitution and Supreme Court," "States and the West," and the following sections.

Politics and Government: Statistics

Erik W. Austin and Jerome C. Clubb, *Political Facts of the United States Since 1789* (1986); Congressional Quarterly, *Guide to U.S. Elections* (1975); Svend Peterson, *A Statistical History of the American Presidential Elections* (1963); Richard M. Scammon et al., eds., *America Votes* (1956–); G. Scott Thomas, *The Pursuit of the White House: A Handbook of Presidential Election Statistics and History* (1987).

Politics and Government: Leaders

Roy R. Glashan, comp., *American Governors and Gubernatorial Elections, 1775–1978* (1979); Henry F. Graff, *The Presidents* (1984); Otis L. Graham, Jr., and Meghan R. Wander, eds., *Franklin D. Roosevelt: His Life and Times* (1985); Melvin G. Holli and Peter d'A. Jones, eds., *Biographical Dictionary of American Mayors, 1820–1980: Big City Mayors* (1981); Joseph E. Kallenback and Jessamine S. Kallenback, *American State Governors, 1776–1976* (1977); Thomas A. McMullin and David Walker, *Biographical Directory of American Territorial Governors* (1984); Marie Mullaney, *Biographical Directory of the Governors of the United States, 1983–1987* (1988); Merrill D. Peterson, ed., *Thomas Jefferson: A Reference Biography* (1986); John W. Raimo, ed., *Biographical Directory of American Colonial and Revolutionary Governors, 1607–1789* (1980); John W. Raimo, ed., *Biographical Directory of the Governors of the United States, 1978–1983* (1985); Robert Sobel, ed., *Biographical Directory of the United States Executive Branch, 1774–1977* (1977); Robert Sobel and John W. Raimo, eds., *Biographical Directory of the Governors of the United States, 1789–1978* (1978); U.S. Congress, *Biographical Directory of the United States Congress, 1774–1989* (1989).

Religion and Cults

Henry Bowden, *Dictionary of American Religious Biography* (1977); John T. Ellis and Robert Trisco, *A Guide to American Catholic History* (1982); Edwin S. Gaustad, *Historical Atlas of Religion in America* (1976); Samuel S. Hill, Jr., ed., *Encyclopedia of Religion in the South* (1984); Charles H. Lippy and Peter W. Williams, eds., *Encyclopedia of the American Religious Experience* (1988); J. Gordon Melton, *Biographical Dictionary of American Cult and Sect Leaders* (1986); J. Gordon Melton, *The Encyclopedia of American Religions* (1987); J. Gordon Melton, *The Encyclopedic Handbook of Cults in America* (1986); Mark A. Noll and Nathan O. Hatch, eds., *Eerdmans Handbook to Christianity in America* (1983); Arthur C. Piepkorn, *Profiles in Brief: The*

Religious Bodies of the United States and Canada (1977–1979).

Science and Technology

James W. Cortada, *Historical Dictionary of Data Processing* (1987); Charles C. Gillispie, ed., *Dictionary of Scientific Biography* (1970–); National Academy of Sciences, *Biographical Memoirs* (1877–).

Social Issues, Organizations, and Reform

Louis Filler, *A Dictionary of American Social Reform* (1963); Louis Filler, *Dictionary of American Social Change* (1982); Robert S. Fogarty, *Dictionary of American Communal and Utopian History* (1980); Harold M. Keele and Joseph C. Kiger, eds., *Foundations* (1984); Mark E. Lender, *Dictionary of American Temperance Biography* (1984); Patricia M. Melvin, ed., *American Community Organizations* (1986); Alvin J. Schmidt, *Fraternal Organizations* (1980); Walter I. Trattner, *Biographical Dictionary of Social Welfare in America* (1986). See also "Crime."

The South

Robert Bain et al., eds., *Southern Writers: A Biographical Dictionary* (1979); Kenneth Coleman and Charles S. Gurr, eds., *Dictionary of Georgia Biography* (1983); William C. Ferris and Charles R. Wilson, eds., *Encyclopedia of Southern Culture* (1986); David C. Roller and Robert W. Twyman, eds., *The Encyclopedia of Southern History* (1979); Walter P. Webb et al., eds., *The Handbook of Texas* (1952, 1976). See also "Politics and Government" and "States and the West."

Sports

Ralph Hickok, *New Encyclopedia of Sports* (1977); Ralph Hickok, *Who Was Who in American Sports* (1971); Zander Hollander, *The NBA's Official Encyclopedia of Pro Basketball* (1981); Frank G. Menke and Suzanne Treat, *The Encyclopedia of Sports* (1977); *The NFL's Official Encyclopedic History of Professional Football* (1977); David L. Porter, *Biographical Dictionary of American Sports: Baseball* (1987), *Football* (1987), and *Outdoor Sports* (1988); Paul Soderberg et al., *The Big Book of Halls of Fame in the United States and Canada* (1977); David Wallechinsky, *The Complete Book of the Olympics* (1984). See also "Culture and Folklore."

States and the West

John Clayton, ed., *The Illinois Fact Book and Historical Almanac, 1673–1968* (1970); Doris O. Dawdy, *Artists of the American West* (1974–1984); Howard R. Lamar, ed., *The Reader's Encyclopedia of the American West* (1977); James W. Scott and Ronald L. De Lorme, *Historical Atlas of Washington* (1988); *The Worldmark Encyclopedia of the States* (1986). See also "Politics and Government" and "The South."

Vietnam War

John S. Bowman, ed., *The Vietnam War: An Almanac* (1986); James S. Olson, ed., *Dictionary of the Vietnam War* (1988); Harry G. Summers, Jr., *Vietnam War Almanac* (1985). Also see the next section.

Wars and the Military

R. Ernest Dupuy and Trevor N. Dupuy, *The Encyclopedia of Military History* (1977); Holger H. Herwig and Neil M. Heyman, *Biographical Dictionary of World War I* (1982); Michael Kidrow and Dan Smith, *The War Atlas: Armed Conflict, Armed Peace* (1983); Roger J. Spiller and Joseph G. Dawson III, eds., *Dictionary of American Military Biography* (1984); U.S. Military Academy, *The West Point Atlas of American Wars, 1689–1953* (1959); *Webster's American Military Biographies* (1978). See also "American Revolution," "Civil War," "Vietnam War," and "World War II."

Women

Edward T. James et al., *Notable American Women, 1607–1950* (1971); Lina Mainiero, ed., *American Women Writers* (1979–1982); Barbara G. Shortridge, *Atlas of American Women* (1987); Barbara Sicherman and Carol H. Green, eds., *Notable American Women, The Modern Period* (1980); Angela H. Zophy and Frances M. Kavenik, eds., *Dictionary of American Women's History* (1989).

World War II

Marcel Baudot et al., eds., *The Historical Encyclopedia of World War II* (1980); Simon Goodenough, *War Maps: Great Land Battles of World War II* (1983); Robert Goralski, *World War II Almanac, 1931–1945* (1981); John Keegan, ed., *The Rand-McNally Encyclopedia of World War II* (1977); Thomas Parrish, ed., *The Simon and Schuster Encyclopedia of World War II* (1978); Louis L. Snyder, *Louis L. Snyder's Historical Guide to World War II* (1982); U.S. Military Academy, *Campaign Atlas to the Second World War: Europe and the Mediterranean* (1980); Peter Young, ed., *The World Almanac Book of World War II* (1981). See also "Wars and the Military."

Declaration of Independence in Congress, July 4, 1776

The unanimous declaration of the thirteen United States of America

When, in the course of human events, it becomes necessary for one people to dissolve the political bonds which have connected them with another, and to assume, among the powers of the earth, the separate and equal station to which the laws of nature and of nature's God entitle them, a decent respect to the opinions of mankind requires that they should declare the causes which impel them to the separation.

We hold these truths to be self-evident: That all men are created equal; that they are endowed by their Creator with certain unalienable rights; that among these are life, liberty, and the pursuit of happiness; that, to secure these rights, governments are instituted among men, deriving their just powers from the consent of the governed; that whenever any form of government becomes destructive of these ends, it is the right of the people to alter or to abolish it, and to institute new government, laying its foundation on such principles, and organizing its powers in such form, as to them shall seem most likely to effect their safety and happiness. Prudence, indeed, will dictate that governments long established should not be changed for light and transient causes; and accordingly all experience hath shown that mankind are more disposed to suffer, while evils are sufferable, than to right themselves by abolishing the forms to which they are accustomed. But when a long train of abuses and usurpations, pursuing invariably the same object, evinces a design to reduce them under absolute despotism, it is their right, it is their duty, to throw off such government, and to provide new guards for their future security. Such has been the patient sufferance of these colonies; and such is now the necessity which constrains them to alter their former systems of government. The history of the present King of Great Britain is a history of repeated injuries and usurpations, all having in direct object the establishment of an absolute tyranny over these states. To prove this, let facts be submitted to a candid world.

He has refused his assent to laws, the most wholesome and necessary for the public good.

He has forbidden his governors to pass laws of immediate and pressing importance, unless suspended in their operation till his assent should be obtained; and, when so suspended, he has utterly neglected to attend to them.

He has refused to pass other laws for the accommodation of large districts of people, unless those people would relinquish the right of representation in the legislature, a right inestimable to them, and formidable to tyrants only.

He has called together legislative bodies at places unusual, uncomfortable, and distant from the depository of their public records, for the sole purpose of fatiguing them into compliance with his measures.

He has dissolved representative houses repeatedly, for opposing, with manly firmness, his invasions on the rights of the people.

He has refused for a long time, after such dissolutions, to cause others to be elected; whereby the legislative powers, incapable of annihilation, have returned to the people at large for their exercise; the state remaining, in the mean time, exposed to all the dangers of invasions from without and convulsions within.

He has endeavored to prevent the population of these states; for that purpose obstructing the laws for naturalization of foreigners; refusing to pass others to encourage their migration hither, and raising the conditions of new appropriations of lands.

He has obstructed the administration of justice, by refusing his assent to laws for establishing judiciary powers.

He has made judges dependent on his will alone, for the tenure of their offices, and the amount and payment of their salaries.

He has erected a multitude of new offices, and sent hither swarms of officers to harass our people and eat out their substance.

He has kept among us, in times of peace, standing armies, without the consent of our legislatures.

He has affected to render the military independent of, and superior to, the civil power.

He has combined with others to subject us to a jurisdiction foreign to our constitution, and unacknowledged by our laws, giving his assent to their acts of pretended legislation:

For quartering large bodies of armed troops among us;

For protecting them, by a mock trial, from punishment for any murders which they should commit on the inhabitants of these states;

For cutting off our trade with all parts of the world;

For imposing taxes on us without our consent;

For depriving us, in many cases, of the benefits of trial by jury;

For transporting us beyond seas, to be tried for pretended offenses;

For abolishing the free system of English laws in a neighboring province, establishing therein an arbitrary government, and enlarging its boundaries, so as to render it at once an example and fit instrument for introducing the same absolute rule into these colonies;

For taking away our charters, abolishing our most valuable laws, and altering fundamentally the forms of our governments;

For suspending our own legislatures, and declaring themselves invested with power to legislate for us in all cases whatsoever.

He has abdicated government here, by declaring us out of his protection and waging war against us.

He has plundered our seas, ravaged our coasts, burned our towns, and destroyed the lives of our people.

He is at this time transporting large armies of foreign mercenaries to complete the works of death, desolation, and tyranny already begun with circumstances of cruelty and perfidy scarcely paralleled in the most barbarous ages, and totally unworthy the head of a civilized nation.

He has constrained our fellow-citizens, taken captive on

the high seas, to bear arms against their country, to become the executioners of their friends and brethren, or to fall themselves by their hands.

He has excited domestic insurrection among us, and has endeavored to bring on the inhabitants of our frontiers the merciless Indian savages, whose known rule of warfare is an undistinguished destruction of all ages, sexes, and conditions.

In every stage of these oppressions we have petitioned for redress in the most humble terms; our repeated petitions have been answered only by repeated injury. A prince, whose character is thus marked by every act which may define a tyrant, is unfit to be the ruler of a free people.

Nor have we been wanting in our attentions to our British brethren. We have warned them, from time to time, of attempts by their legislature to extend an unwarrantable jurisdiction over us. We have reminded them of the circumstances of our emigration and settlement here. We have appealed to their native justice and magnanimity; and we have conjured them, by the ties of our common kindred, to disavow these usurpations, which would inevitably interrupt our connections and correspondence. They, too, have been deaf to the voice of justice and of consanguinity. We must, therefore, acquiesce in the necessity which denounces our separation, and hold them, as we hold the rest of mankind, enemies in war, in peace friends.

We, therefore, the representatives of the United States of America, in General Congress assembled, appealing to the Supreme Judge of the world for the rectitude of our intentions, do, in the name and by the authority of the good people of these colonies, solemnly publish and declare, that these United Colonies are, and of right ought to be, FREE AND INDEPENDENT STATES; that they are absolved from all allegiance to the British crown, and that all political connection between them and the state of Great Britain is, and ought to be, totally dissolved; and that, as free and independent states, they have full power to levy war, conclude peace, contract alliances, establish commerce, and do all other acts and things which independent states may of right do. And for the support of this declaration, with a firm reliance on the protection of Divine Providence, we mutually pledge to each other our lives, our fortunes, and our sacred honor.

JOHN HANCOCK
and fifty-five others

Articles of Confederation

Whereas the Delegates of the United States of America in Congress assembled did on the fifteenth day of November in the Year of our Lord One Thousand Seven Hundred and Seventy seven, and in the Second Year of the Independence of America agree to certain articles of Confederation and perpetual Union between the States of Newhampshire, Massachusetts-bay, Rhodeisland and Providence Plantations, Connecticut, New York, New Jersey, Pennsylvania, Delaware, Maryland, Virginia, North-Carolina, South-Carolina and Georgia in the Words following, viz. "Articles of Confederation and perpetual Union between the states of Newhamp-

shire, Massachusetts-bay, Rhodeisland and Providence Plantations, Connecticut, New-York, New-Jersey, Pennsylvania, Delaware, Maryland, Virginia, North-Carolina, South-Carolina and Georgia.

Article I The Stile of this confederacy shall be "The United States of America."

Article II Each state retains its sovereignty, freedom and independence, and every Power, Jurisdiction and right, which is not by this confederation expressly delegated to the United States, in Congress assembled.

Article III The said states hereby severally enter into a firm league of friendship with each other, for their common defence, the security of their Liberties, and their mutual and general welfare, binding themselves to assist each other, against all force offered to, or attacks made upon them, or any of them, on account of religion, sovereignty, trade, or any other pretence whatever.

Article IV The better to secure and perpetuate mutual friendship and intercourse among the people of the different states in this union, the free inhabitants of each of these states, paupers, vagabonds and fugitives from Justice excepted, shall be entitled to all privileges and immunities of free citizens in the several states; and the people of each state shall have free ingress and regress to and from any other state, and shall enjoy therein all the privileges of trade and commerce, subject to the same duties, impositions and restrictions as the inhabitants thereof respectively, provided that such restriction shall not extend so far as to prevent the removal of property imported into any state, to any other state of which the Owner is an inhabitant; provided also that no imposition, duties or restriction shall be laid by any state, on the property of the united states, or either of them.

If any Person guilty of, or charged with treason, felony, or other high misdemeanor in any state, shall flee from Justice, and be found in any of the united states, he shall upon demand of the Governor or executive power, of the state from which he fled, be delivered up and removed to the state having jurisdiction of his offence.

Full faith and credit shall be given in each of these states to the records, acts and judicial proceedings of the courts and magistrates of every other state.

Article V For the more convenient management of the general interests of the united states, delegates shall be annually appointed in such manner as the legislature of each state shall direct, to meet in Congress on the first Monday in November, in every year, with a power reserved to each state, to recal its delegates, or any of them, at any time within the year, and to send others in their stead, for the remainder of the Year.

No state shall be represented in Congress by less than two, nor by more than seven Members; and no person shall be capable of being a delegate for more than three years in any term of six years; nor shall any person, being a delegate, be capable of holding any office under the united states, for which he, or another for his benefit receives any salary, fees or emolument of any kind.

Each state shall maintain its own delegates in a meeting of the states, and while they act as members of the committee of the states.

In determining questions in the united states, in Congress assembled, each state shall have one vote.

Freedom of speech and debate in Congress shall not be impeached or questioned in any Court, or place out of Congress, and the members of congress shall be protected in their persons from arrests and imprisonments, during the time of their going to and from, and attendance on congress, except for treason, felony, or breach of the peace.

Article VI   No state without the Consent of the united states in congress assembled, shall send any embassy to, or receive any embassy from, or enter into any conference, agreement, or alliance or treaty with any King, prince or state; nor shall any person holding any office of profit or trust under the united states, or any of them, accept of any present, emolument, office or title of any kind whatever from any king, prince or foreign state; nor shall the united states in congress assembled, or any of them, grant any title of nobility.

No two or more states shall enter into any treaty, confederation or alliance whatever between them, without the consent of the united states in congress assembled, specifying accurately the purposes for which the same is to be entered into, and how long it shall continue.

No state shall lay any imposts or duties, which may interfere with any stipulations in treaties, entered into by the united states in congress assembled, with any king, prince or state, in pursuance of any treaties already proposed by congress, to the courts of France and Spain.

No vessels of war shall be kept up in time of peace by any state, except such number only, as shall be deemed necessary by the united states in congress assembled, for the defence of such state, or its trade; nor shall any body of forces be kept up by any state, in time of peace, except such number only, as in the judgment of the united states, in congress assembled, shall be deemed requisite to garrison the forts necessary for the defence of such state; but every state shall always keep up a well regulated and disciplined militia, sufficiently armed and accoutred, and shall provide and constantly have ready for use, in public stores, a due number of field pieces and tents, and a proper quantity of arms, ammunition and camp equipage.

No state shall engage in any war without the consent of the united states in congress assembled, unless such state be actually invaded by enemies, or shall have received certain advice of a resolution being formed by some nation of Indians to invade such state, and the danger is so imminent as not to admit of a delay, till the united states in congress assembled can be consulted: nor shall any state grant commissions to any ships or vessels of war, nor letters of marque or reprisal, except it be after a declaration of war by the united states in congress assembled, and then only against the kingdom or state and the subjects thereof, against which war has been so declared, and under such regulations as shall be established by the united states in congress assembled, unless such state be infested by pirates, in which case vessels of war may be fitted out for that occasion, and kept so long as the danger shall continue, or until the united states in congress assembled shall determine otherwise.

Article VII   When land-forces are raised by any state for the common defence, all officers of or under the rank of colonel, shall be appointed by the legislature of each state respectively by whom such forces shall be raised, or in such manner as such state shall direct, and all vacancies shall be filled up by the state which first made the appointment.

Article VIII   All charges of war, and all other expences that shall be incurred for the common defence or general welfare, and allowed by the united states in congress assembled, shall be defrayed out of a common treasury, which shall be supplied by the several states, in proportion to the value of all land within each state, granted to or surveyed for any Person, as such land and the buildings and improvements thereon shall be estimated according to such mode as the united states in congress assembled, shall from time to time direct and appoint. The taxes for paying that proportion shall by laid and levied by the authority and direction of the legislatures of the several states within the time agreed upon by the united states in congress assembled.

Article IX   The united states in congress assembled, shall have the sole and exclusive right and power of determining on peace and war, except in the cases mentioned in the sixth article—of sending and receiving ambassadors—entering into treaties and alliances, provided that no treaty of commerce shall be made whereby the legislative power of the respective states shall be restrained from imposing such imposts and duties on foreigners, as their own people are subjected to, or from prohibiting the exportation or importation of any species of goods or commodities whatsoever—of establishing rules for deciding in all cases, what captures on land or water shall be legal, and in what manner prizes taken by land or naval forces in the service of the united states shall be divided or appropriated.—of granting letters of marque and reprisal in times of peace—appointing courts for the trial of piracies and felonies committed on the high seas and establishing courts for receiving and determining finally appeals in all cases of captures, provided that no member of congress shall be appointed a judge of any of the said courts.

The united states in congress assembled shall also be the last resort on appeal in all disputes and differences now subsisting or that herafter may arise between two or more states concerning boundary, jurisdiction or any other cause whatever; which authority shall always be exercised in the manner following. Whenever the legislative or executive authority or lawful agent of any state in controversy with another shall present a petition to congress, stating the matter in question and praying for a hearing, notice thereof shall be given by order of congress to the legislative or executive authority of the other state in controversy, and a day assigned for the appearance of the parties by their lawful agents, who shall then be directed to appoint by joint consent, commissioners or judges to constitute a court for hearing and determining the matter in question: but if they cannot agree, congress shall name three persons out of each of the united states, and from the list of such persons each party shall alternately strike out one, the petitioners beginning, until the number shall be reduced to thirteen; and from that number not less than seven, nor more than nine names as congress shall direct, shall in the presence of congress be drawn out by lot, and the persons whose names shall be so drawn or any five of them, shall be commissioners or judges, to hear and finally determine the controversy, so always as a major part of the judges who shall hear the cause shall agree in the determination: and if either party shall neglect to attend at the day appointed, without shewing reasons, which congress shall judge sufficient, or being present shall refuse to strike, the congress shall proceed to nominate three persons out of each state, and the secretary of congress shall strike in behalf of such party absent or refusing; and the judgment and sentence of the court to be appointed, in the manner before prescribed, shall be final and conclusive; and if any of the parties shall refuse to submit to the authority of such court, or to appear to defend their claim or cause, the court shall nevertheless proceed to pronounce sentence, or judgment, which shall in like manner be final and decisive, the judgment or sentence and other proceedings being in either case transmitted to congress, and lodged among the acts of congress for the security of the parties concerned: provided that every commissioner, before he sits in judgment, shall take an oath to be administered by one of the judges of the supreme or superior court of the state, where the cause shall be tried, "well and truly to hear and determine the matter in question, according to the best of his judgment, without favour, affection or hope of reward:" provided also that no state shall be deprived of territory for the benefit of the united states.

All controversies concerning the private right of soil claimed under different grants of two or more states, whose jurisdictions as they may respect such lands, and the states which passed such grants are adjusted, the said grants or either of them being at the same time claimed to have originated antecedent to such settlement of jurisdiction, shall on the petition of either party to the congress of the united states, be finally determined as near as may be in the same manner as is before prescribed for deciding disputes respecting territorial jurisdiction between different states.

The united states in congress assembled shall also have the sole and exclusive right and power of regulating the alloy and value of coin struck by their own authority, or by that of the respective states—fixing the standard of weights and measures throughout the united states.—regulating the trade and managing all affairs with the Indians, not members of any of the states, provided that the legislative right of any state within its own limits be not infringed or violated—establishing and regulating post-offices from one state to another, throughout all the united states, and exacting such postage on the papers passing thro' the same as may be requisite to defray the expences of the said office—appointing all officers of the land forces, in the service of the united states, excepting regimental officers.—appointing all the officers of the naval forces, and commissioning all officers whatever in the service of the united states—making rules for the government and regulation of the said land and naval forces, and directing their operations.

The united states in congress assembled shall have authority to appoint a committee, to sit in the recess of congress, to be denominated "A Committee of the States," and to consist of one delegate from each state; and to appoint such other committees and civil officers as may be necessary for managing the general affairs of the united states under their direction—to appoint one of their number to preside, provided that no person be allowed to serve in the office of president more than one year in any term of three years; to ascertain the necessary sums of Money to be raised for the service of the united states, and to appropriate and apply the same for

defraying the public expences—to borrow money, or emit bills on the credit of the united states, transmitting every half year to the respective states an account of the sums of money so borrowed or emitted,—to build and equip a navy—to agree upon the number of land forces, and to make requisitions from each state for its quota, in proportion to the number of white inhabitants in such state; which requisition shall be binding, and thereupon the legislature of each state shall appoint the regimental officers, raise the men and cloath, arm and equip them in a soldier like manner, at the expence of the united states, and the officers and men so cloathed, armed and equipped shall march to the place appointed, and within the time agreed on by the united states in congress assembled: But if the united states in congress assembled shall, on consideration of circumstances judge proper that any state should not raise men, or should raise a smaller number than its quota, and that any other state should raise a greater number of men than the quota thereof, such extra number shall be raised, officered, cloathed, armed and equipped in the same manner as the quota of such state, unless the legislature of such state shall judge that such extra number cannot be safely spared out of the same, in which case they shall raise officer, cloath, arm and equip as many of such extra number as they judge can be safely spared. And the officers and men so cloathed, armed and equipped, shall march to the place appointed, and within the time agreed on by the united states in congress assembled.

The united states in congress assembled shall never engage in a war, nor grant letters of marque and reprisal in time of peace, nor enter into any treaties or alliances, nor coin money, nor regulate the value thereof, nor ascertain the sums and expences necessary for the defence and welfare of the united states, or any of them, nor emit bills, nor borrow money on the credit of the united states, nor appropriate money, nor agree upon the number of vessels of war, to be built or purchased, or the number of land or sea forces to be raised, nor appoint a commander in chief of the army or navy, unless nine states assent to the same: nor shall a question on any other point, except for adjourning from day to day be determined, unless by the votes of a majority of the united states in congress assembled.

The congress of the united states shall have power to adjourn to any time within the year, and to any place within the united states, so that no period of adjournment be for a longer duration than the space of six Months, and shall publish the Journal of their proceedings monthly, except such parts thereof relating to treaties, alliances or military operations as in their judgment require secresy; and the yeas and nays of the delegates of each state on any question shall be entered on the Journal, when it is desired by any delegate; and the delgates of a state, or any of them, at his or their request shall be furnished with a transcript of the said Journal, except such parts as are above excepted, to lay before the legislatures of the several states.

Article X The committee of the states, or any nine of them, shall be authorised to execute, in the recess of congress, such of the powers of congress as the united states in congress assembled, by the consent of nine states, shall from time to time think expedient to vest them with; provided that no power be delegated to the said committee, for the exercise of which, by the articles of confederation, the voice of nine states in the congress of the united states assembled is requisite.

Article XI Canada acceding to this confederation, and joining in the measures of the united states, shall be admitted into, and entitled to all the advantages of this union: but no other colony shall be admitted into the same, unless such admission be agreed to by nine states.

Article XII All bills of credit emitted, monies borrowed and debts contracted by, or under the authority of congress, before the assembling of the united states, in pursuance of the present confederation, shall be deemed and considered as a charge against the united states, for payment and satisfaction whereof the said united states, and the public faith are hereby solemnly pledged.

Article XIII Every state shall abide by the determinations of the united states in congress assembled, on all questions which by this confederation are submitted to them. And the Articles of this confederation shall be inviolably observed by every state, and the union shall be perpetual; nor shall any alteration at any time hereafter be made in any of them; unless such alteration be agreed to in a congress of the united states, and be afterwards confirmed by the legislatures of every state.

AND WHEREAS it hath pleased the Great Governor of the World to incline the hearts of the legislatures we respectively represent in congress, to approve of, and to authorize us to ratify the said articles of confederation and perpetual union. KNOW YE that we the under-signed delegates, by virtue of the power and authority to us given for that purpose, do by these presents, in the name and in behalf of our respective constituents, fully and entirely ratify and confirm each and every of the said articles of confederation and perpetual union, and all and singular the matters and things therein contained: And we do further solemnly plight and engage the faith of our respective constituents, that they shall abide by the determinations of the united states in congress assembled, on all questions, which by the said confederation are submitted to them. And that the articles thereof shall be inviolably observed by the states we respectively represent, and that the union shall be perpetual. In Witness whereof we have hereunto set our hands in Congress. Done at Philadelphia in the state of Pennsylvania the ninth Day of July in the Year of our Lord one Thousand seven Hundred and Seventy-eight, and in the third year of the independence of America.

Constitution of the United States of America and Amendments

Preamble

We the people of the United States, in order to form a more perfect union, establish justice, insure domestic tranquillity, provide for the common defense, promote the general welfare, and secure the blessings of liberty to ourselves and our posterity, do ordain and establish this Constitution for the United States of America.

Article I

Section 1 All legislative powers herein granted shall be vested in a Congress of the United States, which shall consist of a Senate and a House of Representatives.

Section 2 The House of Representatives shall be composed of members chosen every second year by the people of the several States, and the electors in each State shall have the qualifications requisite for electors of the most numerous branch of the State Legislature.

No person shall be a Representative who shall not have attained to the age of twenty-five years, and been seven years a citizen of the United States, and who shall not, when elected, be an inhabitant of that State in which he shall be chosen.

Representatives and direct taxes shall be apportioned among the several States which may be included within this Union, according to their respective numbers, *which shall be determined by adding to the whole number of free persons, including those bound to service for a term of years and excluding Indians not taxed, three-fifths of all other persons.* The actual enumeration shall be made within three years after the first meeting of the Congress of the United States, and within every subsequent term of ten years, in such manner as they shall by law direct. The number of Representatives shall not exceed one for every thirty thousand, but each State shall have at least one Representative; *and until such enumeration shall be made, the State of New Hampshire shall be entitled to choose three, Massachusetts eight, Rhode Island and Providence Plantations one, Connecticut five, New York six, New Jersey four, Pennsylvania eight, Delaware one, Maryland six, Virginia ten, North Carolina five, South Carolina five, and Georgia three.*

When vacancies happen in the representation from any State, the Executive authority thereof shall issue writs of election to fill such vacancies.

The House of Representatives shall choose their Speaker and other officers; and shall have the sole power of impeachment.

Section 3 The Senate of the United States shall be composed of two Senators from each State, *chosen by the legislature thereof,* for six years; and each Senator shall have one vote.

Immediately after they shall be assembled in consequence of the first election, they shall be divided as equally as may be into three classes. The seats of the Senators of the first class shall be vacated at the expiration of the second year, of the second class at the expiration of the fourth year, and of the third class at the expiration of the sixth year, so that one-third may be chosen every second year; *and if vacancies happen by resignation or otherwise, during the recess of the legislature of any State, the Executive thereof may make temporary*

Passages no longer in effect are printed in italic type.

appointments until the next meeting of the legislature, which shall then fill such vacancies.

No person shall be a Senator who shall not have attained to the age of thirty years, and been nine years a citizen of the United States, and who shall not, when elected, be an inhabitant of that State for which he shall be chosen.

The Vice-President of the United States shall be President of the Senate, but shall have no vote, unless they be equally divided.

The Senate shall choose their other officers, and also a President *pro tempore*, in the absence of the Vice-President, or when he shall exercise the office of President of the United States.

The Senate shall have the sole power to try all impeachments. When sitting for that purpose, they shall be on oath or affirmation. When the President of the United States is tried, the Chief Justice shall preside: and no person shall be convicted without the concurrence of two-thirds of the members present.

Judgment in cases of impeachment shall not extend further than to removal from the office, and disqualification to hold and enjoy any office of honor, trust or profit under the United States: but the party convicted shall nevertheless be liable and subject to indictment, trial, judgment and punishment, according to law.

Section 4   The times, places and manner of holding elections for Senators and Representatives shall be prescribed in each State by the legislature thereof; but the Congress may at any time by law make or alter such regulations, except as to the places of choosing Senators.

The Congress shall assemble at least once in every year, and such meeting *shall be on the first Monday in December, unless they shall by law appoint a different day.*

Section 5   Each house shall be the judge of the elections, returns and qualifications of its own members, and a majority of each shall constitute a quorum to do business; but a smaller number may adjourn from day to day, and may be authorized to compel the attendance of absent members, in such manner, and under such penalties, as each house may provide.

Each house may determine the rules of its proceedings, punish its members for disorderly behavior, and with the concurrence of two-thirds, expel a member.

Each house shall keep a journal of its proceedings, and from time to time publish the same, excepting such parts as may in their judgment require secrecy; and the yeas and nays of the members of either house on any question shall, at the desire of one-fifth of those present, be entered on the journal.

Neither house, during the session of Congress, shall, without the consent of the other, adjourn for more than three days, nor to any other place than that in which the two houses shall be sitting.

Section 6   The Senators and Representatives shall receive a compensation for their services, to be ascertained by law and paid out of the treasury of the United States. They shall in all cases except treason, felony and breach of the peace, be privileged from arrest during their attendance at the session

of their respective houses, and in going to and returning from the same; and for any speech or debate in either house, they shall not be questioned in any other place.

No Senator or Representative shall, during the time for which he was elected, be appointed to any civil office under the authority of the United States, which shall have been created, or the emoluments whereof shall have been increased, during such time; and no person holding any office under the United States shall be a member of either house during his continuance in office.

Section 7   All bills for raising revenue shall originate in the House of Representatives; but the Senate may propose or concur with amendments as on other bills.

Every bill which shall have passed the House of Representatives and the Senate, shall, before it become a law, be presented to the President of the United States; if he approve he shall sign it, but if not he shall return it with objections to that house in which it originated, who shall enter the objections at large on their journal, and proceed to reconsider it. If after such reconsideration two-thirds of that house shall agree to pass the bill, it shall be sent, together with the objections, to the other house, by which it shall likewise be reconsidered, and, if approved by two-thirds of that house, it shall become a law. But in all such cases the votes of both houses shall be determined by yeas and nays, and the names of the persons voting for and against the bill shall be entered on the journal of each house respectively. If any bill shall not be returned by the President within ten days (Sundays excepted) after it shall have been presented to him, the same shall be a law, in like manner as if he had signed it, unless the Congress by their adjournment prevent its return, in which case it shall not be a law.

Every order, resolution, or vote to which the concurrence of the Senate and House of Representatives may be necessary (except on a question of adjournment) shall be presented to the President of the United States; and before the same shall take effect, shall be approved by him, or being disapproved by him, shall be repassed by two-thirds of the Senate and House of Representatives, according to the rules and limitations prescribed in the case of a bill.

Section 8   The Congress shall have power

To lay and collect taxes, duties, imposts, and excises, to pay the debts and provide for the common defense and general welfare of the United States; but all duties, imposts and excises shall be uniform throughout the United States;

To borrow money on the credit of the United States;

To regulate commerce with foreign nations, and among the several States, and with the Indian tribes;

To establish an uniform rule of naturalization, and uniform laws on the subject of bankruptcies throughout the United States;

To coin money, regulate the value thereof, and of foreign coin, and fix the standard of weights and measures;

To provide for the punishment of counterfeiting the securities and current coin of the United States;

To establish post offices and post roads;

To promote the progress of science and useful arts by securing for limited times to authors and inventors the exclusive right to their respective writings and discoveries;

To constitute tribunals inferior to the Supreme Court;

To define and punish piracies and felonies committed on the high seas and offenses against the law of nations;

To declare war, grant letters of marque and reprisal, and make rules concerning captures on land and water;

To raise and support armies, but no appropriation of money to that use shall be for a longer term than two years;

To provide and maintain a navy;

To make rules for the government and regulation of the land and naval forces;

To provide for calling forth the militia to execute the laws of the Union, suppress insurrections, and repel invasions;

To provide for organizing, arming, and disciplining the militia, and for governing such part of them as may be employed in the service of the United States, reserving to the States respectively the appointment of the officers, and the authority of training the militia according to the discipline prescribed by Congress;

To exercise exclusive legislation in all cases whatsoever, over such district (not exceeding ten miles square) as may, by cession of particular States, and the acceptance of Congress, become the seat of government of the United States, and to exercise like authority over all places purchased by the consent of the legislature of the State, in which the same shall be, for erection of forts, magazines, arsenals, dockyards, and other needful buildings;—and

To make all laws which shall be necessary and proper for carrying into execution the foregoing powers, and all other powers vested by this Constitution in the government of the United States, or in any department or officer thereof.

Section 9 The migration or importation of such persons as any of the States now existing shall think proper to admit shall not be prohibited by the Congress prior to the year 1808; but a tax or duty may be imposed on such importation, not exceeding $10 for each person.

The privilege of the writ of habeas corpus shall not be suspended, unless when in cases of rebellion or invasion the public safety may require it.

No bill of attainder or ex post facto law shall be passed.

No capitation, or other direct, tax shall be laid, unless in proportion to the census or enumeration herein before directed to be taken.

No tax or duty shall be laid on articles exported from any State.

No preference shall be given by any regulation of commerce or revenue to the ports of one State over those of another; nor shall vessels bound to, or from, one State, be obliged to enter, clear, or pay duties in another.

No money shall be drawn from the treasury, but in consequence of appropriations made by law; and a regular statement and account of the receipts and expenditures of all public money shall be published from time to time.

No title of nobility shall be granted by the United States: and no person holding any office of profit or trust under them, shall, without the consent of the Congress, accept of any present, emolument, office, or title, of any kind whatever, from any king, prince, or foreign state.

Section 10 No State shall enter into any treaty, alliance, or confederation; grant letters of marque and reprisal; coin money; emit bills of credit; make anything but gold and silver coin a tender in payment of debts; pass any bill of attainder, ex post facto law, or law impairing the obligation of contracts, or grant any title of nobility.

No State shall, without the consent of Congress, lay any imposts or duties on imports or exports, except what may be absolutely necessary for executing its inspection laws: and the net produce of all duties and imposts, laid by any State on imports or exports, shall be for the use of the treasury of the United States; and all such laws shall be subject to the revision and control of the Congress.

No State shall, without the consent of Congress, lay any duty of tonnage, keep troops or ships of war in time of peace, enter into any agreement or compact with another State, or with a foreign power, or engage in war, unless actually invaded, or in such imminent danger as will not admit of delay.

Article II

Section 1 The executive power shall be vested in a President of the United States of America. He shall hold his office during the term of four years, and, together with the Vice-President, chosen for the same term, be elected as follows:

Each State shall appoint, in such manner as the legislature thereof may direct, a number of electors, equal to the whole number of Senators and Representatives to which the State may be entitled in the Congress; but no Senator or Representative, or person holding an office of trust or profit under the United States, shall be appointed an elector.

The electors shall meet in their respective States, and vote by ballot for two persons, of whom one at least shall not be an inhabitant of the same State with themselves. And they shall make a list of all the persons voted for, and of the number of votes for each; which list they shall sign and certify, and transmit sealed to the seat of government of the United States, directed to the President of the Senate. The President of the Senate shall, in the presence of the Senate and House of Representatives, open all the certificates, and the votes shall then be counted. The person having the greatest number of votes shall be the President, if such number be a majority of the whole number of electors appointed; and if there be more than one who have such majority, and have an equal number of votes, then the House of Representatives shall immediately choose by ballot one of them for President; and if no person have a majority, then from the five highest on the list said house shall in like manner choose the President. But in choosing the President the votes shall be taken by States, the representation from each State having one vote; a quorum for this purpose shall consist of a member or members from two-thirds of the States, and a majority of all the States shall be necessary to a choice. In every case, after the choice of the President, the person having the greatest number of votes of the electors shall be the Vice-President. But if there should remain two or more who have equal votes, the Senate shall choose from them by ballot the Vice-President.

The Congress may determine the time of choosing the electors and the day on which they shall give their votes; which day shall be the same throughout the United States.

No person except a natural-born citizen, *or a citizen of the United States at the time of the adoption of this Constitution*, shall be eligible to the office of President; neither shall any person be eligible to that office who shall not have attained to the age of thirty-five years, and been fourteen years a resident within the United States.

In cases of the removal of the President from office or of his death, resignation, or inability to discharge the powers and duties of the said office, the same shall devolve on the Vice-President, and the Congress may by law provide for the case of removal, death, resignation, or inability, both of the President and Vice-President, declaring what officer shall then act as President, and such officer shall act accordingly, until the disability be removed, or a President shall be elected.

The President shall, at stated times, receive for his services a compensation, which shall neither be increased nor diminished during the period for which he shall have been elected, and he shall not receive within that period any other emolument from the United States, or any of them.

Before he enter on the execution of his office, he shall take the following oath or affirmation:—"I do solemnly swear (or affirm) that I will faithfully execute the office of the President of the United States, and will to the best of my ability preserve, protect and defend the Constitution of the United States."

Section 2 The President shall be commander in chief of the army and navy of the United States, and of the militia of the several States, when called into the actual service of the United States; he may require the opinion, in writing, of the principal officer in each of the executive departments, upon any subject relating to the duties of their respective offices, and he shall have power to grant reprieves and pardons for offenses against the United States, except in cases of impeachment.

He shall have power, by and with the advice and consent of the Senate, to make treaties, provided two-thirds of the Senators present concur; and he shall nominate, and by and with the advice and consent of the Senate, shall appoint ambassadors, other public ministers and consuls, judges of the Supreme Court, and all other officers of the United States, whose appointments are not herein otherwise provided for, and which shall be established by law: but Congress may by law vest the appointment of such inferior officers, as they think proper, in the President alone, in the courts of law, or in the heads of departments.

The President shall have power to fill up all vacancies that may happen during the recess of the Senate, by granting commissions which shall expire at the end of their next session.

Section 3 He shall from time to time give to the Congress information of the state of the Union, and recommend to their consideration such measures as he shall judge necessary and expedient; he may, on extraordinary occasions, convene both houses, or either of them, and in case of disagreement between them, with respect to the time of adjournment, he may adjourn them to such time as he shall think proper; he shall receive ambassadors and other public ministers; he shall take care that the laws be faithfully executed, and shall commission all the officers of the United States.

Section 4 The President, Vice-President and all civil officers of the United States shall be removed from office on impeachment for, and on conviction of, treason, bribery, or other high crimes and misdemeanors.

Article III

Section 1 The judicial power of the United States shall be vested in one Supreme Court, and in such inferior courts as the Congress may from time to time ordain and establish. The judges, both of the Supreme and inferior courts, shall hold their offices during good behavior, and shall, at stated times, receive for their services a compensation which shall not be diminished during their continuance in office.

Section 2 The judicial power shall extend to all cases, in law and equity, arising under this Constitution, the laws of the United States, and treaties made, or which shall be made, under their authority;—to all cases affecting ambassadors, other public ministers and consuls;—to all cases of admiralty and maritime jurisdiction;—to controversies to which the United States shall be a party;—to controversies between two or more States;—*between a State and citizens of another State;*—between citizens of different States;—between citizens of the same State claiming lands under grants of different States, and between a State, or the citizens thereof, and foreign states, citizens or subjects.

In all cases affecting ambassadors, other public ministers and consuls, and those in which a State shall be party, the Supreme Court shall have original jurisdiction. In all the other cases before mentioned, the Supreme Court shall have appellate jurisdiction, both as to law and fact, with such exceptions, and under such regulations, as the Congress shall make.

The trial of all crimes, except in cases of impeachment, shall be by jury; and such trial shall be held in the State where said crimes shall have been committed; but when not committed within any State, the trial shall be at such place or places as the Congress may by law have directed.

Section 3 Treason against the United States shall consist only in levying war against them, or in adhering to their enemies, giving them aid and comfort. No person shall be convicted of treason unless on the testimony of two witnesses to the same overt act, or on confession in open court.

The Congress shall have power to declare the punishment of treason, but no attainder of treason shall work corruption of blood, or forfeiture except during the life of the person attainted.

Article IV

Section 1 Full faith and credit shall be given in each State to the public acts, records, and judicial proceedings of every other State. And the Congress may by general laws prescribe the manner in which such acts, records, and proceedings shall be proved, and the effect thereof.

Section 2 The citizens of each State shall be entitled to all privileges and immunities of citizens in the several States.

A person charged in any State with treason, felony, or other crime, who shall flee from justice, and be found in another State, shall on demand of the executive authority of the State from which he fled, be delivered up, to be removed to the State having jurisdiction of the crime.

No person held to service or labor in one State, under the laws thereof, escaping into another, shall, in consequence of any law or regulation therein, be discharged from such service or labor, but shall be delivered up on claim of the party to whom such service or labor may be due.

Section 3 New States may be admitted by the Congress into this Union; but no new State shall be formed or erected within the jurisdiction of any other State; nor any State be formed by the junction of two or more States, or parts of States, without the consent of the legislatures of the States concerned as well as of the Congress.

The Congress shall have power to dispose of and make all needful rules and regulations respecting the territory or other property belonging to the United States; and nothing in this Constitution shall be so construed as to prejudice any claims of the United States, or of any particular State.

Section 4 The United States shall guarantee to every State in this Union a republican form of government, and shall protect each of them against invasion; and on application of the legislature, or of the executive (when the legislature cannot be convened), against domestic violence.

Article V

The Congress, whenever two-thirds of both houses shall deem it necessary, shall propose amendments to this Constitution, or, on the application of the legislatures of two-thirds of the several States, shall call a convention for proposing amendments, which, in either case, shall be valid to all intents and purposes, as part of this Constitution, when ratified by the legislatures of three-fourths of the several States, or by conventions in three-fourths thereof, as the one or the other mode of ratification may be proposed by the Congress; provided *that no amendments which may be made prior to the year one thousand eight hundred and eight shall in any manner affect the first and fourth clauses in the ninth section of the first article;* and that no State, without its consent, shall be deprived of its equal suffrage in the Senate.

Article VI

All debts contracted and engagements entered into, before the adoption of this Constitution, shall be as valid against the United States under this Constitution, as under the Confederation.

This Constitution, and the laws of the United States which shall be made in pursuance thereof; and all treaties made, or which shall be made, under the authority of the United States, shall be the supreme law of the land; and the judges in every State shall be bound thereby, anything in the Constitution or laws of any State to the contrary notwithstanding.

The Senators and Representatives before mentioned, and the members of the several State legislatures, and all executive and judicial officers, both of the United States and of the several States, shall be bound by oath or affirmation to support this Constitution; but no religious test shall ever be required as a qualification to any office or public trust under the United States.

Article VII

The ratification of the conventions of nine States shall be sufficient for the establishment of this Constitution between the States so ratifying the same.

Done in Convention by the unanimous consent of the States present, the seventeenth day of September in the year of our Lord one thousand seven hundred and eighty-seven and of the Independence of the United States of America the twelfth. In witness whereof we have hereunto subscribed our names.

GEORGE WASHINGTON
and thirty-seven others

Amendments to the Constitution*

Amendment I

Congress shall make no law respecting an establishment of religion, or prohibiting the free exercise thereof; or abridging the freedom of speech, or of the press; or the right of the people peaceably to assemble, and to petition the government for a redress of grievances.

Amendment II

A well-regulated militia being necessary to the security of a free State, the right of the people to keep and bear arms shall not be infringed.

Amendment III

No soldier shall, in time of peace, be quartered in any house without the consent of the owner, nor in time of war, but in a manner to be prescribed by law.

Amendment IV

The right of the people to be secure in their persons, houses, papers, and effects, against unreasonable searches and seizures, shall not be violated, and no warrants shall issue but upon probable cause, supported by oath or affirmation, and particularly describing the place to be searched, and the persons or things to be seized.

---

*The first ten Amendments (the Bill of Rights) were adopted in 1791.

Amendment V

No person shall be held to answer for a capital, or otherwise infamous crime, unless on a presentment or indictment of a grand jury, except in cases arising in the land or naval forces, or in the militia, when in actual service in time of war or public danger; nor shall any person be subject for the same offense to be twice put in jeopardy of life or limb; nor shall be compelled in any criminal case to be a witness against himself, nor be deprived of life, liberty, or property, without due process of law; nor shall private property be taken for public use without just compensation.

Amendment VI

In all criminal prosecutions, the accused shall enjoy the right to a speedy and public trial, by an impartial jury of the State and district wherein the crime shall have been committed, which district shall have been previously ascertained by law, and to be informed of the nature and cause of the accusation; to be confronted with the witnesses against him; to have compulsory process for obtaining witnesses in his favor, and to have the assistance of counsel for his defense.

Amendment VII

In suits at common law, where the value in controversy shall exceed twenty dollars, the right of trial by jury shall be preserved, and no fact tried by a jury shall be otherwise reexamined in any court of the United States, than according to the rules of the common law.

Amendment VIII

Excessive bail shall not be required, nor excessive fines imposed, nor cruel and unusual punishments inflicted.

Amendment IX

The enumeration in the Constitution, of certain rights, shall not be construed to deny or disparage others retained by the people.

Amendment X

The powers not delegated to the United States by the Constitution, nor prohibited by it to the States, are reserved to the States respectively, or to the people.

Amendment XI

[Adopted 1798]

The judicial power of the United States shall not be construed to extend to any suit in law or equity, commenced or prosecuted against one of the United States by citizens of another State, or by citizens or subjects of any foreign state.

Amendment XII

[Adopted 1804]

The electors shall meet in their respective States, and vote by ballot for President and Vice-President, one of whom, at least, shall not be an inhabitant of the same State with themselves; they shall name in their ballots the person voted for as President, and in distinct ballots the person voted for as Vice-President, and they shall make distinct lists of all persons voted for as President, and of all persons voted for as Vice-President, and of the number of votes for each, which lists they shall sign and certify, and transmit sealed to the seat of government of the United States, directed to the President of the Senate;—the President of the Senate shall, in the presence of the Senate and House of Representatives, open all the certificates and the votes shall then be counted;—the person having the greatest number of votes for President shall be the President, if such number be a majority of the whole number of electors appointed; and if no person have such majority, then from the persons having the highest numbers not exceeding three on the list of those voted for as President, the House of Representatives shall choose immediately, by ballot, the President. But in choosing the President, the votes shall be taken by States, the representation from each State having one vote; a quorum for this purpose shall consist of a member or members from two-thirds of the States, and a majority of all the States shall be necessary to a choice. And if the House of Representatives shall not choose a President whenever the right of choice shall devolve upon them, before *the fourth day of March* next following, then the Vice-President shall act as President, as in the case of the death or other constitutional disability of the President.

The person having the greatest number of votes as Vice-President shall be the Vice-President, if such number be a majority of the whole number of electors appointed; and if no person have a majority, then from the two highest numbers on the list the Senate shall choose the Vice-President; a quorum for the purpose shall consist of two-thirds of the whole number of Senators, and a majority of the whole number shall be necessary to a choice. But no person constitutionally ineligible to the office of President shall be eligible to that of Vice-President of the United States.

Amendment XIII

[Adopted 1865]

Section 1 Neither slavery nor involuntary servitude, except as a punishment for crime whereof the party shall have been duly convicted, shall exist within the United States, or any place subject to their jurisdiction.

Section 2 Congress shall have power to enforce this article by appropriate legislation.

Amendment XIV

[Adopted 1868]

Section 1   All persons born or naturalized in the United States, and subject to the jurisdiction thereof, are citizens of the United States and of the State wherein they reside. No State shall make or enforce any law which shall abridge the privileges or immunities of citizens of the United States; nor shall any State deprive any person of life, liberty, or property, without due process of law; nor deny to any person within its jurisdiction the equal protection of the laws.

Section 2   Representatives shall be apportioned among the several States according to their respective numbers, counting the whole number of persons in each State, excluding Indians not taxed. But when the right to vote at any election for the choice of Electors for President and Vice-President of the United States, Representatives in Congress, the executive and judicial officers of a State, or the members of the legislature thereof, is denied to any of the male inhabitants of such State, being twenty-one years of age and citizens of the United States, or in any way abridged, except for participation in rebellion, or other crime, the basis of representation therein shall be reduced in the proportion which the number of such male citizens shall bear to the whole number of male citizens twenty-one years of age in such State.

Section 3   No person shall be a Senator or Representative in Congress, or Elector of President and Vice-President, or hold any office, civil or military, under the United States, or under any State, who, having previously taken an oath, as a member of Congress, or as an officer of the United States, or as a member of any State legislature, or as an executive or judicial officer of any State, to support the Constitution of the United States, shall have engaged in insurrection or rebellion against the same, or given aid or comfort to the enemies thereof. Congress may, by a vote of two-thirds of each house, remove such disability.

Section 4   The validity of the public debt of the United States, authorized by law, including debts incurred for payment of pensions and bounties for services in suppressing insurrection or rebellion, shall not be questioned. But neither the United States nor any State shall assume or pay any debt or obligation incurred in aid of insurrection or rebellion against the United States, or any claim for the loss of emancipation of any slave; but all such debts, obligations, and claims shall be held illegal and void.

Section 5   The Congress shall have power to enforce, by appropriate legislation, the provisions of this article.

Amendment XV

[Adopted 1870]

Section 1   The right of citizens of the United States to vote shall not be denied or abridged by the United States or by any State on account of race, color, or previous condition of servitude.

Section 2   The Congress shall have power to enforce this article by appropriate legislation.

Amendment XVI

[Adopted 1913]

The Congress shall have power to lay and collect taxes on incomes, from whatever source derived, without apportionment among the several States, and without regard to any census or enumeration.

Amendment XVII

[Adopted 1913]

Section 1   The Senate of the United States shall be composed of two Senators from each State, elected by the people thereof, for six years; and each Senator shall have one vote. The electors in each State shall have the qualifications requisite for electors of [voters for] the most numerous branch of the State legislatures.

Section 2   When vacancies happen in the representation of any State in the Senate, the executive authority of such State shall issue writs of election to fill such vacancies: Provided, that the Legislature of any State may empower the executive thereof to make temporary appointments until the people fill the vacancies by election as the Legislature may direct.

Section 3   This amendment shall not be so construed as to affect the election or term of any Senator chosen before it becomes valid as part of the Constitution.

Amendment XVIII

[Adopted 1919; Repealed 1933]

Section 1   After one year from the ratification of this article the manufacture, sale, or transportation of intoxicating liquors within, the importation thereof into, or the exportation thereof from the United States and all territory subject to the jurisdiction thereof, for beverage purposes, is hereby prohibited.

Section 2   The Congress and the several States shall have concurrent power to enforce this article by appropriate legislation.

Section 3   This article shall be inoperative unless it shall have been ratified as an amendment to the Constitution by the legislatures of the several States, as provided by the Constitution, within seven years from the date of the submission thereof to the States by the Congress.

Amendment XIX

[Adopted 1920]

Section 1   The right of citizens of the United States to vote shall not be denied or abridged by the United States or by any State on account of sex.

Section 2 The Congress shall have power to enforce this article by appropriate legislation.

Amendment XX

[Adopted 1933]

Section 1 The terms of the President and Vice-President shall end at noon on the 20th day of January, and the terms of Senators and Representatives at noon on the 3d day of January, of the years in which such terms would have ended if this article had not been ratified; and the terms of their successors shall then begin.

Section 2 The Congress shall assemble at least once in every year, and such meeting shall begin at noon on the 3d day of January, unless they shall by law appoint a different day.

Section 3 If, at the time fixed for the beginning of the term of the President, the President-elect shall have died, the Vice-President-elect shall become President. If a President shall not have been chosen before the time fixed for the beginning of his term, or if the President-elect shall have failed to qualify, then the Vice-President-elect shall act as President until a President shall have qualified; and the Congress may by law provide for the case wherein neither a President-elect nor a Vice-President-elect shall have qualified, declaring who shall then act as President, or the manner in which one who is to act shall be selected, and such persons shall act accordingly until a President or Vice-President shall have qualified.

Section 4 The Congress may by law provide for the case of the death of any of the persons from whom the House of Representatives may choose a President whenever the right of choice shall have devolved upon them, and for the case of the death of any of the persons from whom the Senate may choose a Vice-President whenever the right of choice shall have devolved upon them.

Section 5 Sections 1 and 2 shall take effect on the 15th day of October following the ratification of this article.

Section 6 This article shall be inoperative unless it shall have been ratified as an amendment to the Constitution by the Legislatures of three-fourths of the several States within seven years from the date of its submission.

Amendment XXI

[Adopted 1933]

Section 1 The eighteenth article of amendment to the Constitution of the United States is hereby repealed.

Section 2 The transportation or importation into any State, Territory, or Possession of the United States for delivery or use therein of intoxicating liquors, in violation of the laws thereof, is hereby prohibited.

Section 3 This article shall be inoperative unless it shall have been ratified as an amendment to the Constitution by conventions in the several States, as provided in the Constitution, within seven years from the date of submission thereof to the States by the Congress.

Amendment XXII

[Adopted 1951]

Section 1 No person shall be elected to the office of President more than twice, and no person who has held the office of President, or acted as President, for more than two years of a term to which some other person was elected President shall be elected to the office of President more than once. But this article shall not apply to any person holding the office of President when this article was proposed by the Congress, and shall not prevent any person who may be holding the office of President, or acting as President, during the term within which this article becomes operative from holding the office of President or acting as President during the remainder of such term.

Section 2 This article shall be inoperative unless it shall have been ratified as an amendment to the Constitution by the legislatures of three-fourths of the several States within seven years from the date of its submission to the States by the Congress.

Amendment XXIII

[Adopted 1961]

Section 1 The District constituting the seat of Government of the United States shall appoint in such manner as the Congress may direct:
A number of electors of President and Vice-President equal to the whole number of Senators and Representatives in Congress to which the District would be entitled if it were a State, but in no event more than the least populous State; they shall be in addition to those appointed by the States, but they shall be considered for the purposes of the election of President and Vice-President, to be electors appointed by a State; and they shall meet in the District and perform such duties as provided by the twelfth article of amendment.

Section 2 The Congress shall have the power to enforce this article by appropriate legislation.

Amendment XXIV

[Adopted 1964]

Section 1 The right of citizens of the United States to vote in any primary or other election for President or Vice-President, for electors for President or Vice-President, or for Senator or Representative in Congress, shall not be denied or abridged by the United States or any State by reason of failure to pay any poll tax or other tax.

Section 2 The Congress shall have the power to enforce this article by appropriate legislation.

Amendment XXV

[Adopted 1967]

Section 1 In case of the removal of the President from office or of his death or resignation, the Vice-President shall become President.

Section 2 Whenever there is a vacancy in the office of the Vice-President, the President shall nominate a Vice-President who shall take office upon confirmation by a majority vote of both Houses of Congress.

Section 3 Whenever the President transmits to the President pro tempore of the Senate and the Speaker of the House of Representatives his written declaration that he is unable to discharge the powers and duties of his office, and until he transmits to them a written declaration to the contrary, such powers and duties shall be discharged by the Vice-President as Acting President.

Section 4 Whenever the Vice-President and a majority of either the principal officers of the executive departments or of such other body as Congress may by law provide, transmit to the President pro tempore of the Senate and the Speaker of the House of Representatives their written declaration that the President is unable to discharge the powers and duties of his office, the Vice-President shall immediately assume the powers and duties of the office as Acting President.

Thereafter, when the President transmits to the President pro tempore of the Senate and the Speaker of the House of Representatives his written declaration that no inability exists, he shall resume the powers and duties of his office unless the Vice-President and a majority of either the principal officers of the executive department[s] or of such other body as Congress may by law provide, transmit within four days to the President pro tempore of the Senate and the Speaker of the House of Representatives their written declaration that the President is unable to discharge the powers and duties of his office. Thereupon Congress shall decide the issue, assembling within forty-eight hours for that purpose if not in session. If the Congress, within twenty-one days after receipt of the latter written declaration, or, if Congress is not in session, within twenty-one days after Congress is required to assemble, determines by two-thirds vote of both Houses that the President is unable to discharge the powers and duties of his office, the Vice-President shall continue to discharge the same as Acting President; otherwise, the President shall resume the powers and duties of his office.

Amendment XXVI

[Adopted 1971]

Section 1 The right of citizens of the United States, who are eighteen years of age or older, to vote shall not be denied or abridged by the United States or by any State on account of age.

Section 2 The Congress shall have power to enforce this article by appropriate legislation.

The American People and Nation: A Statistical Profile

POPULATION OF THE UNITED STATES

Year	Number of States	Population	Percent Increase	Population Per Square Mile	Percent Urban/ Rural	Percent Male/ Female	Percent White/ Nonwhite	Persons Per House- hold	Median Age
1790	13	3,929,214		4.5	5.1/94.9	NA/NA	80.7/19.3	5.79	NA
1800	16	5,308,483	35.1	6.1	6.1/93.9	NA/NA	81.1/18.9	NA	NA
1810	17	7,239,881	36.4	4.3	7.3/92.7	NA/NA	81.0/19.0	NA	NA
1820	23	9,638,453	33.1	5.5	7.2/92.8	50.8/49.2	81.6/18.4	NA	16.7
1830	24	12,866,020	33.5	7.4	8.8/91.2	50.8/49.2	81.9/18.1	NA	17.2
1840	26	17,069,453	32.7	9.8	10.8/89.2	50.9/49.1	83.2/16.8	NA	17.8
1850	31	23,191,876	35.9	7.9	15.3/84.7	51.0/49.0	84.3/15.7	5.55	18.9
1860	33	31,443,321	35.6	10.6	19.8/80.2	51.2/48.8	85.6/14.4	5.28	19.4
1870	37	39,818,449	26.6	13.4	25.7/74.3	50.6/49.4	86.2/13.8	5.09	20.2
1880	38	50,155,783	26.0	16.9	28.2/71.8	50.9/49.1	86.5/13.5	5.04	20.9
1890	44	62,947,714	25.5	21.2	35.1/64.9	51.2/48.8	87.5/12.5	4.93	22.0
1900	45	75,994,575	20.7	25.6	39.6/60.4	51.1/48.9	87.9/12.1	4.76	22.9
1910	46	91,972,266	21.0	31.0	45.6/54.4	51.5/48.5	88.9/11.1	4.54	24.1
1920	48	105,710,620	14.9	35.6	51.2/48.8	51.0/49.0	89.7/10.3	4.34	25.3
1930	48	122,775,046	16.1	41.2	56.1/43.9	50.6/49.4	89.8/10.2	4.11	26.4
1940	48	131,669,275	7.2	44.2	56.5/43.5	50.2/49.8	89.8/10.2	3.67	29.0
1950	48	150,697,361	14.5	50.7	64.0/36.0	49.7/50.3	89.5/10.5	3.37	30.2
1960	50	179,323,175	18.5	50.6	69.9/30.1	49.3/50.7	88.6/11.4	3.33	29.5
1970	50	203,302,031	13.4	57.4	73.5/26.5	48.7/51.3	87.6/12.4	3.14	28.0
1980	50	226,545,805	11.4	64.0	73.7/26.3	48.6/51.4	86.0/14.0	2.76	30.0
1988	50	245,110,000	7.6	69.2	NA/NA	48.7/51.3*	84.7/15.3*	2.67*	31.8*

*1986 figure.
NA = Not available.

VITAL STATISTICS

| Year | Birth Rate* | Death Rate* | Life Expectancy in Years | | | | | Marriage Rate | Divorce Rate |
			Total Population	White Females	Nonwhite Females	White Males	Nonwhite Males		
1790	NA	NA	NA	NA	NA	NA	NA	NA	NA
1800	55.0	NA	NA	NA	NA	NA	NA	NA	NA
1810	54.3	NA	NA	NA	NA	NA	NA	NA	NA
1820	55.2	NA	NA	NA	NA	NA	NA	NA	NA
1830	51.4	NA	NA	NA	NA	NA	NA	NA	NA
1840	51.8	NA	NA	NA	NA	NA	NA	NA	NA
1850	43.3	NA	NA	NA	NA	NA	NA	NA	NA
1860	44.3	NA	NA	NA	NA	NA	NA	NA	NA
1870	38.3	NA	NA	NA	NA	NA	NA	NA	NA
1880	39.8	NA	NA	NA	NA	NA	NA	NA	NA
1890	31.5	NA	NA	NA	NA	NA	NA	NA	NA
1900	32.3	17.2	47.3	48.7	33.5	46.6	32.5	NA	NA
1910	30.1	14.7	50.0	52.0	37.5	48.6	33.8	NA	NA
1920	27.7	13.0	54.1	55.6	45.2	54.4	45.5	12.0	1.6
1930	21.3	11.3	59.7	63.5	49.2	59.7	47.3	9.2	1.6
1940	19.4	10.8	62.9	66.6	54.9	62.1	51.5	12.1	2.0
1950	24.1	9.6	68.2	72.2	62.9	66.5	59.1	11.1	2.6
1960	23.7	9.5	69.7	74.1	66.3	67.4	61.1	8.5	2.2
1970	18.4	9.5	70.9	75.6	69.4	68.0	61.3	10.6	3.5
1980	15.9	8.8	73.7	78.1	73.6	70.7	65.3	10.6	5.2
1985	15.5	8.7	74.7	78.7	75.0	71.9	67.2	10.0	4.8

Data per one thousand for Birth, Death, Marriage, and Divorce rates.
NA = Not available.
*Data for 1800, 1810, 1830, 1850, 1870, and 1890 for whites only.

Immigration Totals by Decade

Years	Number	Years	Number
1820–1830	151,824	1911–1920	5,735,811
1831–1840	599,125	1921–1930	4,107,209
1841–1850	1,713,251	1931–1940	528,431
1851–1860	2,598,214	1941–1950	1,035,039
1861–1870	2,314,824	1951–1960	2,515,479
1871–1880	2,812,191	1961–1970	3,321,677
1881–1890	5,246,613	1971–1980	4,493,000
1891–1900	3,687,546	1980–1990 (projected)	8,500,000
1901–1910	8,795,386	Total	58,155,620

Sources: U.S. Bureau of the Census, Historical Statistics of the United States, Colonial Times to 1970 (1975); U.S. Bureau of the Census, Statistical Abstract of the United States, 1988 (1987).

Major Sources of Immigrants by Country (in thousands)

Period	Germany	Italy	Britain (UK)	Ireland	Austria-Hungary	Canada	Russia (USSR)[a]	Mexico	Denmark, Norway, Sweden,[b]	Caribbean (West Indies)
1820–1830	8	—	27	54	—	2	—	5	—	4
1831–1840	152	2	76	207	—	14	—	7	2	12
1841–1850	435	2	267	781	—	42	—	3	14	14
1851–1860	952	9	424	914	—	59	—	3	25	11
1861–1870	787	12	607	436	8	154	3	2	126	9
1871–1880	718	56	548	437	73	384	39	5	243	14
1881–1890	1,453	307	807	655	354	393	213	2[c]	656	29
1891–1900	505	652	272	388	593	3	505	—	372	—[d]
1901–1910	341	2,046	526	339	2,145	179	1,597	50	505	108
1911–1920	144	1,110	341	146	896	742	922	219	203	123
1921–1930	412	455	330	221	64	925	89	459	198	75
1931–1940	114	68	29	13	11	109	7	22	11	16
1941–1950	227	58	132	28	28	172	4	61	27	50
1951–1960	478	185	192	57	104	378	6	300	57	123
1961–1970	200	207	231	42	31	287	22	443	45	520
1971–1980	66	130	124	14	16	115	46	637	15	760
1981–1986	42	21	85	7	7	67	44	402	11	473
Total	6,974	5,320	5,018	4,739	4,330	4,025	3,497	2,620	2,510	2,341

Notes: Numbers are rounded. Dash indicates less than one thousand.
[a] Includes Finland, Latvia, Estonia, and Lithuania.
[b] Includes Iceland.
[c] Figure for 1881–1885 only.
[d] Figure for 1894–1900 only.

Sources: U.S. Bureau of the Census, Historical Statistics of the United States: Colonial Times to 1970 (1975); U.S. Bureau of the Census, Statistical Abstract of the United States, 1988 (1987).

THE AMERICAN FARM

Year	Farm Population (in thousands)	Percent of Total Population	Number of Farms (in thousands)	Total Acres (in thousands)	Average Acreage Per Farm	Corn Production (millions of bushels)	Wheat Production (millions of bushels)
1850	NA	NA	1,449	293,561	203	592[a]	100[a]
1860	NA	NA	2,044	407,213	199	839[b]	173[b]
1870	NA	NA	2,660	407,735	153	1,125	254
1880	21,973	43.8	4,009	536,082	134	1,707	502
1890	24,771	42.3	4,565	623,219	137	1,650	449
1900	29,875	41.9	5,740	841,202	147	2,662	599
1910	32,077	34.9	6,366	881,431	139	2,853	625
1920	31,974	30.1	6,454	958,677	149	3,071	843
1930	30,529	24.9	6,295	990,112	157	2,080	887
1940	30,547	23.2	6,102	1,065,114	175	2,457	815
1950	23,048	15.3	5,388	1,161,420	216	3,075	1,019
1960	15,635	8.7	3,962	1,176,946	297	4,314	1,355
1970	9,712	4.8	2,949	1,102,769	374	4,200	1,370
1980	6,051	2.7	2,428	1,042,000	427	6,600	2,400
1986	5,226	2.2	2,212	1,008,000	456	8,253	2,087

[a] Figure for 1849.
[b] Figure for 1859.
NA = Not available.

THE AMERICAN WORKER

Year	Total Number of Workers	Males as Percent of Total Workers	Females as Percent of Total Workers	Married Women as Percent of Female Workers	Female Workers as Percent of Female Population	Percent of Labor Force Unemployed	Percent of Workers in Labor Unions
1870	12,506,000	85	15	NA	NA	NA	NA
1880	17,392,000	85	15	NA	NA	NA	NA
1890	23,318,000	83	17	13.9	18.9	4 (1894 = 18)	NA
1900	29,073,000	82	18	15.4	20.6	5	3
1910	38,167,000	79	21	24.7	25.4	6	6
1920	41,614,000	79	21	23.0	23.7	5 (1921 = 12)	12
1930	48,830,000	78	22	28.9	24.8	9 (1933 = 25)	7
1940	53,011,000	76	24	36.4	27.4	15 (1944 = 1)	27
1950	59,643,000	72	28	52.1	31.4	5	25
1960	69,877,000	68	32	59.9	34.8	5.4	26
1970	82,049,000	63	37	63.4	42.6	4.8	25
1980	108,544,000	58	42	59.7	51.1	7.0	23
1986	117,834,000	56	44	58.5	54.7	6.9 (1983 = 9.5)	20

NA = Not available.

Year	Gross National Product (GNP) (in $ billions)	Steel Production (in tons)	Automobiles Registered	New Housing Starts	Foreign Trade Exports (in millions of dollars)	Foreign Trade Imports (in millions of dollars)
1790	NA	NA	NA	NA	20	23
1800	NA	NA	NA	NA	71	91
1810	NA	NA	NA	NA	67	85
1820	NA	NA	NA	NA	70	74
1830	NA	NA	NA	NA	74	71
1840	NA	NA	NA	NA	132	107
1850	NA	NA	NA	NA	152	178
1860	NA	13,000	NA	NA	400	362
1870	7.4[a]	77,000	NA	NA	451	462
1880	11.2[b]	1,397,000	NA	NA	853	761
1890	13.1	4,779,000	NA	328,000	910	823
1900	18.7	11,227,000	8,000	189,000	1,499	930
1910	35.3	28,330,000	458,300	387,000 (1918 = 118,000)	1,919	1,646
1920	91.5	46,183,000	8,131,500	247,000 (1925 = 937,000)	8,664	5,784
1930	90.7	44,591,000	23,034,700	330,000 (1933 = 93,000)	4,013	3,500
1940	100.0	66,983,000	27,465,800	603,000 (1944 = 142,000)	4,030	7,433
1950	286.5	96,836,000	40,339,000	1,952,000	10,816	9,125
1960	506.5	99,282,000	61,682,300	1,365,000	19,600	15,046
1970	1,016.0	131,514,000	89,279,800	1,469,000	42,700	40,189
1980	2,732.0	111,800,000	121,600,000	1,313,000	220,783	244,871
1986	4,235.0	81,600,000	135,700,000	1,807,000	217,300	370,000

[a]Figure is average for 1869–1878.
[b]Figure is average for 1879–1888.
NA = Not available.

Year	Defense[a]	Veterans Benefits and Services[a]	Income Security[ad]	Health[a]	Education and Manpower[a]	Interest on Public Debt[a]	Federal Debt (dollars)
1790	14.9	4.1[b]	NA	NA	NA	55.0	75,463,000[c]
1800	55.7	.6	NA	NA	NA	31.3	82,976,000
1810	48.4 (1814 = 79.7)	1.0	NA	NA	NA	34.9	53,173,000
1820	38.4	17.6	NA	NA	NA	28.1	91,016,000
1830	52.9	9.0	NA	NA	NA	12.6	48,565,000
1840	54.3 (1847 = 80.7)	10.7	NA	NA	NA	.7	3,573,000
1850	43.8	4.7	NA	NA	NA	1.0	63,453,000
1860	44.2 (1865 = 88.9)	1.7	NA	NA	NA	5.0	64,844,000
1870	25.7	9.2	NA	NA	NA	41.7	2,436,453,000
1880	19.3	21.2	NA	NA	NA	35.8	2,090,909,000
1890	20.9 (1899 = 48.6)	33.6	NA	NA	NA	11.4	1,222,397,000
1900	36.6	27.0	NA	NA	NA	7.7	1,263,417,000
1910	45.1 (1919 = 59.5)	23.2	NA	NA	NA	3.1	1,146,940,000
1920	37.1	3.4	NA	NA	NA	16.0	24,299,321,000
1930	25.3	6.6	NA	NA	NA	19.9	16,185,310,000
1940	15.7 (1945 = 85.7)	6.5	15.2	.5	.8	10.5	42,967,531,000
1950	30.4 (1953 = 59.4)	20.5	10.9	.6	.5	13.4	257,357,352,000
1960	49.0	5.9	20.6	.9	1.1	10.0	286,330,761,000
1970	41.8	4.4	8.0	3.0	4.4	9.9	370,918,707,000
1980	22.7	3.6	14.6	3.9	5.4	12.7	907,700,000,000
1986	27.6	2.7	12.1	3.6	3.1	18.9	2,125,300,000,000

[a] Figures represent percentage of total federal spending for each category.
[b] 1789–1791 figure.
[c] 1791 figure.
[d] Includes Social Security and Medicare.
NA = Not available.

Territorial Expansion of the United States

Territory	Date Acquired	Square Miles	How Acquired
Original states and territories	1783	888,685	Treaty with Great Britain
Louisiana Purchase	1803	827,192	Purchase from France
Florida	1819	72,003	Treaty with Spain
Texas	1845	390,143	Annexation of independent nation
Oregon	1846	285,580	Treaty with Great Britain
Mexican Cession	1848	529,017	Conquest from Mexico
Gadsden Purchase	1853	29,640	Purchase from Mexico
Alaska	1867	589,757	Purchase from Russia
Hawaii	1898	6,450	Annexation of independent nation
The Philippines	1899	115,600	Conquest from Spain (granted independence in 1946)
Puerto Rico	1899	3,435	Conquest from Spain
Guam	1899	212	Conquest from Spain
American Samoa	1900	76	Treaty with Germany and Great Britain
Panama Canal Zone	1904	553	Treaty with Panama (returned to Panama by treaty in 1978)
Corn Islands	1914	4	Treaty with Nicaragua (returned to Nicaragua by treaty in 1971)
Virgin Islands	1917	133	Purchase from Denmark
Pacific Islands Trust (Micronesia)	1947	8,489	Trusteeship under United Nations (some granted independence)
All others (Midway, Wake, and other islands)		42	

Admission of States into the Union

State	Date of Admission	State	Date of Admission
1. Delaware	December 7, 1787	26. Michigan	January 26, 1837
2. Pennsylvania	December 12, 1787	27. Florida	March 3, 1845
3. New Jersey	December 18, 1787	28. Texas	December 29, 1845
4. Georgia	January 2, 1788	29. Iowa	December 28, 1846
5. Connecticut	January 9, 1788	30. Wisconsin	May 29, 1848
6. Massachusetts	February 6, 1788	31. California	September 9, 1850
7. Maryland	April 28, 1788	32. Minnesota	May 11, 1858
8. South Carolina	May 23, 1788	33. Oregon	February 14, 1859
9. New Hampshire	June 21, 1788	34. Kansas	January 29, 1861
10. Virginia	June 25, 1788	35. West Virginia	June 20, 1863
11. New York	July 26, 1788	36. Nevada	October 31, 1864
12. North Carolina	November 21, 1789	37. Nebraska	March 1, 1867
13. Rhode Island	May 29, 1790	38. Colorado	August 1, 1876
14. Vermont	March 4, 1791	39. North Dakota	November 2, 1889
15. Kentucky	June 1, 1792	40. South Dakota	November 2, 1889
16. Tennessee	June 1, 1796	41. Montana	November 8, 1889
17. Ohio	March 1, 1803	42. Washington	November 11, 1889
18. Louisiana	April 30, 1812	43. Idaho	July 3, 1890
19. Indiana	December 11, 1816	44. Wyoming	July 10, 1890
20. Mississippi	December 10, 1817	45. Utah	January 4, 1896
21. Illinois	December 3, 1818	46. Oklahoma	November 16, 1907
22. Alabama	December 14, 1819	47. New Mexico	January 6, 1912
23. Maine	March 15, 1820	48. Arizona	February 14, 1912
24. Missouri	August 10, 1821	49. Alaska	January 3, 1959
25. Arkansas	June 15, 1836	50. Hawaii	August 21, 1959

Presidential Elections

Year	Number of States	Candidates	Parties	Popular Vote	% of Popular Vote	Electoral Vote	% Voter Participation[b]
1789	11	**George Washington**	No party			69	
		John Adams	designations			34	
		Other candidates				35	
1792	15	**George Washington**	No party			132	
		John Adams	designations			77	
		George Clinton				50	
		Other candidates				5	
1796	16	**John Adams**	Federalist			71	
		Thomas Jefferson	Democratic-Republican			68	
		Thomas Pinckney	Federalist			59	
		Aaron Burr	Democratic-Republican			30	
		Other candidates				48	
1800	16	**Thomas Jefferson**	Democratic-Republican			73	
		Aaron Burr	Democratic-Republican			73	
		John Adams	Federalist			65	
		Charles C. Pinckney	Federalist			64	
		John Jay	Federalist			1	
1804	17	**Thomas Jefferson**	Democratic-Republican			162	
		Charles C. Pinckney	Federalist			14	
1808	17	**James Madison**	Democratic-Republican			122	
		Charles C. Pinckney	Federalist			47	
		George Clinton	Democratic-Republican			6	
1812	18	**James Madison**	Democratic-Republican			128	
		DeWitt Clinton	Federalist			89	
1816	19	**James Monroe**	Democratic-Republican			183	
		Rufus King	Federalist			34	
1820	24	**James Monroe**	Democratic-Republican			231	
		John Quincy Adams	Independent Republican			1	

Year	Number of States	Candidates	Parties	Popular Vote	% of Popular Vote	Electoral Vote	% Voter Participation[b]
1824	24	**John Quincy Adams**	Democratic-Republican	108,740	30.5	84	26.9
		Andrew Jackson	Democratic-Republican	153,544	43.1	99	
		Henry Clay	Democratic-Republican	47,136	13.2	37	
		William H. Crawford	Democratic-Republican	46,618	13.1	41	
1828	24	**Andrew Jackson**	Democratic	647,286	56.0	178	57.6
		John Quincy Adams	National Republican	508,064	44.0	83	
1832	24	**Andrew Jackson**	Democratic	688,242	54.5	219	55.4
		Henry Clay	National Republican	473,462	37.5	49	
		William Wirt	Anti-Masonic	101,051	8.0	7	
		John Floyd	Democratic			11	
1836	26	**Martin Van Buren**	Democratic	765,483	50.9	170	57.8
		William H. Harrison	Whig			73	
		Hugh L. White	Whig	739,795	49.1	26	
		Daniel Webster	Whig			14	
		W. P. Mangum	Whig			11	
1840	26	**William H. Harrison**	Whig	1,274,624	53.1	234	80.2
		Martin Van Buren	Democratic	1,127,781	46.9	60	
1844	26	**James K. Polk**	Democratic	1,338,464	49.6	170	78.9
		Henry Clay	Whig	1,300,097	48.1	105	
		James G. Birney	Liberty	62,300	2.3		
1848	30	**Zachary Taylor**	Whig	1,360,967	47.4	163	72.7
		Lewis Cass	Democratic	1,222,342	42.5	127	
		Martin Van Buren	Free Soil	291,263	10.1		
1852	31	**Franklin Pierce**	Democratic	1,601,117	50.9	254	69.6
		Winfield Scott	Whig	1,385,453	44.1	42	
		John P. Hale	Free Soil	155,825	5.0		
1856	31	**James Buchanan**	Democratic	1,832,955	45.3	174	78.9
		John C. Frémont	Republican	1,339,932	33.1	114	
		Millard Fillmore	American	871,731	21.6	8	
1860	33	**Abraham Lincoln**	Republican	1,865,593	39.8	180	81.2
		Stephen A. Douglas	Democratic	1,382,713	29.5	12	
		John C. Breckinridge	Democratic	848,356	18.1	72	
		John Bell	Constitutional Union	592,906	12.6	39	
1864	36	**Abraham Lincoln**	Republican	2,206,938	55.0	212	73.8
		George B. McClellan	Democratic	1,803,787	45.0	21	
1868	37	**Ulysses S. Grant**	Republican	3,013,421	52.7	214	78.1
		Horatio Seymour	Democratic	2,706,829	47.3	80	
1872	37	**Ulysses S. Grant**	Republican	3,596,745	55.6	286	71.3
		Horace Greeley	Democratic	2,843,446	43.9	[a]	
1876	38	**Rutherford B. Hayes**	Republican	4,036,572	48.0	185	81.8
		Samuel J. Tilden	Democratic	4,284,020	51.0	184	

Year	Number of States	Candidates	Parties	Popular Vote	% of Popular Vote	Electoral Vote	% Voter Participation[b]
1880	38	**James A. Garfield**	Republican	4,453,295	48.5	214	79.4
		Winfield S. Hancock	Democratic	4,414,082	48.1	155	
		James B. Weaver	Greenback-Labor	308,578	3.4		
1884	38	**Grover Cleveland**	Democratic	4,879,507	48.5	219	77.5
		James G. Blaine	Republican	4,850,293	48.2	182	
		Benjamin F. Butler	Greenback-Labor	175,370	1.8		
		John P. St. John	Prohibition	150,369	1.5		
1888	38	**Benjamin Harrison**	Republican	5,477,129	47.9	233	79.3
		Grover Cleveland	Democratic	5,537,857	48.6	168	
		Clinton B. Fisk	Prohibition	249,506	2.2		
		Anson J. Streeter	Union Labor	146,935	1.3		
1892	44	**Grover Cleveland**	Democratic	5,555,426	46.1	277	74.7
		Benjamin Harrison	Republican	5,182,690	43.0	145	
		James B. Weaver	People's	1,029,846	8.5	22	
		John Bidwell	Prohibition	264,133	2.2		
1896	45	**William McKinley**	Republican	7,102,246	51.1	271	79.3
		William J. Bryan	Democratic	6,492,559	47.7	176	
1900	45	**William McKinley**	Republican	7,218,491	51.7	292	73.2
		William J. Bryan	Democratic; Populist	6,356,734	45.5	155	
		John C. Wooley	Prohibition	208,914	1.5		
1904	45	**Theodore Roosevelt**	Republican	7,628,461	57.4	336	65.2
		Alton B. Parker	Democratic	5,084,223	37.6	140	
		Eugene V. Debs	Socialist	402,283	3.0		
		Silas C. Swallow	Prohibition	258,536	1.9		
1908	46	**William H. Taft**	Republican	7,675,320	51.6	321	65.4
		William J. Bryan	Democratic	6,412,294	43.1	162	
		Eugene V. Debs	Socialist	420,793	2.8		
		Eugene W. Chafin	Prohibition	253,840	1.7		
1912	48	**Woodrow Wilson**	Democratic	6,296,547	41.9	435	58.8
		Theodore Roosevelt	Progressive	4,118,571	27.4	88	
		William H. Taft	Republican	3,486,720	23.2	8	
		Eugene V. Debs	Socialist	900,672	6.0		
		Eugene W. Chafin	Prohibition	206,275	1.4		
1916	48	**Woodrow Wilson**	Democratic	9,127,695	49.4	277	61.6
		Charles E. Hughes	Republican	8,533,507	46.2	254	
		A. L. Benson	Socialist	585,113	3.2		
		J. Frank Hanly	Prohibition	220,506	1.2		
1920	48	**Warren G. Harding**	Republican	16,143,407	60.4	404	49.2
		James M. Cox	Democratic	9,130,328	34.2	127	
		Eugene V. Debs	Socialist	919,799	3.4		
		P. P. Christensen	Farmer-Labor	265,411	1.0		
1924	48	**Calvin Coolidge**	Republican	15,718,211	54.0	382	48.9
		John W. Davis	Democratic	8,385,283	28.8	136	
		Robert M. La Follette	Progressive	4,831,289	16.6	13	
1928	48	**Herbert C. Hoover**	Republican	21,391,993	58.2	444	56.9
		Alfred E. Smith	Democratic	15,016,169	40.9	87	

Year	Number of States	Candidates	Parties	Popular Vote	% of Popular Vote	Electoral Vote	% Voter Participation[b]
1932	48	**Franklin D. Roosevelt**	Democratic	22,809,638	57.4	472	56.9
		Herbert C. Hoover	Republican	15,758,901	39.7	59	
		Norman Thomas	Socialist	881,951	2.2		
1936	48	**Franklin D. Roosevelt**	Democratic	27,752,869	60.8	523	61.0
		Alfred M. Landon	Republican	16,674,665	36.5	8	
		William Lemke	Union	882,479	1.9		
1940	48	**Franklin D. Roosevelt**	Democratic	27,307,819	54.8	449	62.5
		Wendell L. Wilkie	Republican	22,321,018	44.8	82	
1944	48	**Franklin D. Roosevelt**	Democratic	25,606,585	53.5	432	55.9
		Thomas E. Dewey	Republican	22,014,745	46.0	99	
1948	48	**Harry S Truman**	Democratic	24,179,345	49.6	303	53.0
		Thomas E. Dewey	Republican	21,991,291	45.1	189	
		J. Strom Thurmond	States' Rights	1,176,125	2.4	39	
		Henry A. Wallace	Progressive	1,157,326	2.4		
1952	48	**Dwight D. Eisenhower**	Republican	33,936,234	55.1	442	63.3
		Adlai E. Stevenson	Democratic	27,314,992	44.4	89	
1956	48	**Dwight D. Eisenhower**	Republican	35,590,472	57.6	457	60.6
		Adlai E. Stevenson	Democratic	26,022,752	42.1	73	
1960	50	**John F. Kennedy**	Democratic	34,226,731	49.7	303	62.8
		Richard M. Nixon	Republican	34,108,157	49.5	219	
1964	50	**Lyndon B. Johnson**	Democratic	43,129,566	61.1	486	61.7
		Barry M. Goldwater	Republican	27,178,188	38.5	52	
1968	50	**Richard M. Nixon**	Republican	31,785,480	43.4	301	60.6
		Hubert H. Humphrey	Democratic	31,275,166	42.7	191	
		George C. Wallace	American Independent	9,906,473	13.5	46	
1972	50	**Richard M. Nixon**	Republican	47,169,911	60.7	520	55.2
		George S. McGovern	Democratic	29,170,383	37.5	17	
		John G. Schmitz	American	1,099,482	1.4		
1976	50	**Jimmy Carter**	Democratic	40,830,763	50.1	297	53.5
		Gerald R. Ford	Republican	39,147,793	48.0	240	
1980	50	**Ronald Reagan**	Republican	43,899,248	50.8	489	52.6
		Jimmy Carter	Democratic	35,481,432	41.0	49	
		John B. Anderson	Independent	5,719,437	6.6	0	
		Ed Clark	Libertarian	920,859	1.1	0	
1984	50	**Ronald Reagan**	Republican	54,455,075	58.8	525	53.1
		Walter Mondale	Democratic	37,577,185	40.6	13	
1988	50	**George Bush**	Republican	48,901,046	53.4	426	50.2
		Michael Dukakis	Democratic	41,809,030	45.6	111[c]	

Candidates receiving less than 1 percent of the popular vote have been omitted. Thus the percentage of popular vote given for any election year may not total 100 percent.

Before the passage of the Twelfth Amendment in 1804, the Electoral College voted for two presidential candidates; the runner-up became vice president.

Before 1824, most presidential electors were chosen by state legislatures, not by popular vote.

[a] Greeley died shortly after the election; the electors supporting him then divided their votes among minor candidates.

[b] Percent of voting-age population casting ballots.

[c] One elector from West Virginia cast her Electoral College presidential ballot for Lloyd Bentsen, the Democratic party's vice presidential candidate.

Presidents, Vice Presidents, and Cabinet Members

The Washington Administration

President	George Washington	1789–1797
Vice President	John Adams	1789–1797
Secretary of State	Thomas Jefferson	1789–1793
	Edmund Randolph	1794–1795
	Timothy Pickering	1795–1797
Secretary of Treasury	Alexander Hamilton	1789–1795
	Oliver Wolcott	1795–1797
Secretary of War	Henry Knox	1789–1794
	Timothy Pickering	1795–1796
	James McHenry	1796–1797
Attorney General	Edmund Randolph	1789–1793
	William Bradford	1794–1795
	Charles Lee	1795–1797
Postmaster General	Samuel Osgood	1789–1791
	Timothy Pickering	1791–1794
	Joseph Habersham	1795–1797

The John Adams Administration

President	John Adams	1797–1801
Vice President	Thomas Jefferson	1797–1801
Secretary of State	Timothy Pickering	1797–1800
	John Marshall	1800–1801
Secretary of Treasury	Oliver Wolcott	1797–1800
	Samuel Dexter	1800–1801
Secretary of War	James McHenry	1797–1800
	Samuel Dexter	1800–1801
Attorney General	Charles Lee	1797–1801
Postmaster General	Joseph Habersham	1797–1801
Secretary of Navy	Benjamin Stoddert	1798–1801

The Jefferson Administration

President	Thomas Jefferson	1801–1809
Vice President	Aaron Burr	1801–1805
	George Clinton	1805–1809
Secretary of State	James Madison	1801–1809
Secretary of Treasury	Samuel Dexter	1801
	Albert Gallatin	1801–1809
Secretary of War	Henry Dearborn	1801–1809
Attorney General	Levi Lincoln	1801–1805
	Robert Smith	1805
	John Breckinridge	1805–1806
	Caesar Rodney	1807–1809

Postmaster General	Joseph Habersham	1801
	Gideon Granger	1801–1809
Secretary of Navy	Robert Smith	1801–1809

The Madison Administration

President	James Madison	1809–1817
Vice President	George Clinton	1809–1813
	Elbridge Gerry	1813–1817
Secretary of State	Robert Smith	1809–1811
	James Monroe	1811–1817
Secretary of Treasury	Albert Gallatin	1809–1813
	George Campbell	1814
	Alexander Dallas	1814–1816
	William Crawford	1816–1817
Secretary of War	William Eustis	1809–1812
	John Armstrong	1813–1814
	James Monroe	1814–1815
	William Crawford	1815–1817
Attorney General	Caesar Rodney	1809–1811
	William Pinkney	1811–1814
	Richard Rush	1814–1817
Postmaster General	Gideon Granger	1809–1814
	Return Meigs	1814–1817
Secretary of Navy	Paul Hamilton	1809–1813
	William Jones	1813–1814
	Benjamin Crowninshield	1814–1817

The Monroe Administration

President	James Monroe	1817–1825
Vice President	Daniel Tompkins	1817–1825
Secretary of State	John Quincy Adams	1817–1825
Secretary of Treasury	William Crawford	1817–1825
Secretary of War	George Graham	1817
	John C. Calhoun	1817–1825
Attorney General	Richard Rush	1817
	William Wirt	1817–1825
Postmaster General	Return Meigs	1817–1823
	John McLean	1823–1825
Secretary of Navy	Benjamin Crowninshield	1817–1818
	Smith Thompson	1818–1823
	Samuel Southard	1823–1825

The John Quincy Adams Administration

President	John Quincy Adams	1825–1829
Vice President	John C. Calhoun	1825–1829
Secretary of State	Henry Clay	1825–1829
Secretary of Treasury	Richard Rush	1825–1829
Secretary of War	James Barbour	1825–1828
	Peter Porter	1828–1829
Attorney General	William Wirt	1825–1829
Postmaster General	John McLean	1825–1829
Secretary of Navy	Samuel Southard	1825–1829

The Jackson Administration

President	Andrew Jackson	1829–1837
Vice President	John C. Calhoun	1829–1833
	Martin Van Buren	1833–1837
Secretary of State	Martin Van Buren	1829–1831
	Edward Livingston	1831–1833
	Louis McLane	1833–1834
	John Forsyth	1834–1837
Secretary of Treasury	Samuel Ingham	1829–1831
	Louis McLane	1831–1833
	William Duane	1833
	Roger B. Taney	1833–1834
	Levi Woodbury	1834–1837
Secretary of War	John H. Eaton	1829–1831
	Lewis Cass	1831–1837
	Benjamin Butler	1837
Attorney General	John M. Berrien	1829–1831
	Roger B. Taney	1831–1833
	Benjamin Butler	1833–1837
Postmaster General	William Barry	1829–1835
	Amos Kendall	1835–1837
Secretary of Navy	John Branch	1829–1831
	Levi Woodbury	1831–1834
	Mahlon Dickerson	1834–1837

The Van Buren Administration

President	Martin Van Buren	1837–1841
Vice President	Richard M. Johnson	1837–1841
Secretary of State	John Forsyth	1837–1841
Secretary of Treasury	Levi Woodbury	1837–1841
Secretary of War	Joel Poinsett	1837–1841
Attorney General	Benjamin Butler	1837–1838
	Felix Grundy	1838–1840
	Henry D. Gilpin	1840–1841
Postmaster General	Amos Kendall	1837–1840
	John M. Niles	1840–1841
Secretary of Navy	Mahlon Dickerson	1837–1838
	James Paulding	1838–1841

The William Harrison Administration

President	William H. Harrison	1841
Vice President	John Tyler	1841
Secretary of State	Daniel Webster	1841
Secretary of Treasury	Thomas Ewing	1841
Secretary of War	John Bell	1841
Attorney General	John J. Crittenden	1841
Postmaster General	Francis Granger	1841
Secretary of Navy	George Badger	1841

The Tyler Administration

President	John Tyler	1841–1845
Vice President	None	
Secretary of State	Daniel Webster	1841–1843
	Hugh S. Legaré	1843
	Abel P. Upshur	1843–1844
	John C. Calhoun	1844–1845
Secretary of Treasury	Thomas Ewing	1841
	Walter Forward	1841–1843
	John C. Spencer	1843–1844
	George Bibb	1844–1845
Secretary of War	John Bell	1841
	John C. Spencer	1841–1843
	James M. Porter	1843–1844
	William Wilkins	1844–1845
Attorney General	John J. Crittenden	1841
	Hugh S. Legaré	1841–1843
	John Nelson	1843–1845
Postmaster General	Francis Granger	1841
	Charles Wickliffe	1841
Secretary of Navy	George Badger	1841
	Abel P. Upshur	1841
	David Henshaw	1843–1844
	Thomas Gilmer	1844
	John Y. Mason	1844–1845

The Polk Administration

President	James K. Polk	1845–1849
Vice President	George M. Dallas	1845–1849
Secretary of State	James Buchanan	1845–1849
Secretary of Treasury	Robert J. Walker	1845–1849
Secretary of War	William L. Marcy	1845–1849
Attorney General	John Y. Mason	1845–1846
	Nathan Clifford	1846–1848
	Isaac Toucey	1848–1849
Postmaster General	Cave Johnson	1845–1849
Secretary of Navy	George Bancroft	1845–1846
	John Y. Mason	1846–1849

The Taylor Administration

President	Zachary Taylor	1849–1850
Vice President	Millard Fillmore	1849–1850
Secretary of State	John M. Clayton	1849–1850
Secretary of Treasury	William Meredith	1849–1850
Secretary of War	George Crawford	1849–1850
Attorney General	Reverdy Johnson	1849–1850
Postmaster General	Jacob Collamer	1849–1850
Secretary of Navy	William Preston	1849–1850
Secretary of Interior	Thomas Ewing	1849–1850

The Fillmore Administration

President	Millard Fillmore	1850–1853
Vice President	None	
Secretary of State	Daniel Webster	1850–1852
	Edward Everett	1852–1853
Secretary of Treasury	Thomas Corwin	1850–1853
Secretary of War	Charles Conrad	1850–1853
Attorney General	John J. Crittenden	1850–1853
Postmaster General	Nathan Hall	1850–1852
	Sam D. Hubbard	1852–1853
Secretary of Navy	William A. Graham	1850–1852
	John P. Kennedy	1852–1853
Secretary of Interior	Thomas McKennan	1850
	Alexander Stuart	1850–1853

The Pierce Administration

President	Franklin Pierce	1853–1857
Vice President	William R. King	1853–1857
Secretary of State	William L. Marcy	1853–1857
Secretary of Treasury	James Guthrie	1853–1857
Secretary of War	Jefferson Davis	1853–1857
Attorney General	Caleb Cushing	1853–1857
Postmaster General	James Campbell	1853–1857
Secretary of Navy	James C. Dobbin	1853–1857
Secretary of Interior	Robert McClelland	1853–1857

The Buchanan Administration

President	James Buchanan	1857–1861
Vice President	John C. Breckinridge	1857–1861
Secretary of State	Lewis Cass	1857–1860
	Jeremiah S. Black	1860–1861
Secretary of Treasury	Howell Cobb	1857–1860
	Philip Thomas	1860–1861
	John A. Dix	1861
Secretary of War	John B. Floyd	1857–1861
	Joseph Holt	1861
Attorney General	Jeremiah S. Black	1857–1860
	Edwin M. Stanton	1860–1861
Postmaster General	Aaron V. Brown	1857–1859
	Joseph Holt	1859–1861
	Horatio King	1861
Secretary of Navy	Isaac Toucey	1857–1861
Secretary of Interior	Jacob Thompson	1857–1861

The Lincoln Administration

President	Abraham Lincoln	1861–1865
Vice President	Hannibal Hamlin	1861–1865
	Andrew Johnson	1865
Secretary of State	William H. Seward	1861–1865
Secretary of Treasury	Samuel P. Chase	1861–1864
	William P. Fessenden	1864–1865
	Hugh McCulloch	1865
Secretary of War	Simon Cameron	1861–1862
	Edwin M. Stanton	1862–1865
Attorney General	Edward Bates	1861–1864
	James Speed	1864–1865
Postmaster General	Horatio King	1861
	Montgomery Blair	1861–1864
	William Dennison	1864–1865
Secretary of Navy	Gideon Welles	1861–1865
Secretary of Interior	Caleb B. Smith	1861–1863
	John P. Usher	1863–1865

The Andrew Johnson Administration

President	Andrew Johnson	1865–1869
Vice President	None	
Secretary of State	William H. Seward	1865–1869
Secretary of Treasury	Hugh McCulloch	1865–1869
Secretary of War	Edwin M. Stanton	1865–1867
	Ulysses S. Grant	1867–1868
	Lorenzo Thomas	1868
	John M. Schofield	1868–1869
Attorney General	James Speed	1865–1866
	Henry Stanbery	1866–1868
	William M. Evarts	1868–1869
Postmaster General	William Dennison	1865–1866
	Alexander Randall	1866–1869
Secretary of Navy	Gideon Welles	1865–1869
Secretary of Interior	John P. Usher	1865
	James Harlan	1865–1866
	Orville H. Browning	1866–1869

The Grant Administration

President	Ulysses S. Grant	1869–1877
Vice President	Schuyler Colfax	1869–1873
	Henry Wilson	1873–1877
Secretary of State	Elihu B. Washburne	1869
	Hamilton Fish	1869–1877
Secretary of Treasury	George S. Boutwell	1869–1873
	William Richardson	1873–1874
	Benjamin Bristow	1874–1876
	Lot M. Morrill	1876–1877
Secretary of War	John A. Rawlins	1869
	William T. Sherman	1869
	William W. Belknap	1869–1876
	Alphonso Taft	1876
	James D. Cameron	1876–1877
Attorney General	Ebenezer Hoar	1869–1870
	Amos T. Ackerman	1870–1871
	G. H. Williams	1871–1875
	Edwards Pierrepont	1875–1876
	Alphonso Taft	1876–1877
Postmaster General	John A. J. Creswell	1869–1874
	James W. Marshall	1874
	Marshall Jewell	1874–1876
	James N. Tyner	1876–1877
Secretary of Navy	Adolph E. Borie	1869
	George M. Robeson	1869–1877
Secretary of Interior	Jacob D. Cox	1869–1870
	Columbus Delano	1870–1875
	Zachariah Chandler	1875–1877

The Hayes Administration

President	Rutherford B. Hayes	1877–1881
Vice President	William A. Wheeler	1877–1881
Secretary of State	William B. Evarts	1877–1881
Secretary of Treasury	John Sherman	1877–1881
Secretary of War	George W. McCrary	1877–1879
	Alex Ramsey	1879–1881
Attorney General	Charles Devens	1877–1881
Postmaster General	David M. Key	1877–1880
	Horace Maynard	1880–1881
Secretary of Navy	Richard W. Thompson	1877–1880
	Nathan Goff, Jr.	1881
Secretary of Interior	Carl Schurz	1877–1881

The Garfield Administration

President	James A. Garfield	1881
Vice President	Chester A. Arthur	1881
Secretary of State	James G. Blaine	1881
Secretary of Treasury	William Windom	1881
Secretary of War	Robert T. Lincoln	1881
Attorney General	Wayne MacVeagh	1881
Postmaster General	Thomas L. James	1881
Secretary of Navy	William H. Hunt	1881
Secretary of Interior	Samuel J. Kirkwood	1881

The Arthur Administration

President	Chester A. Arthur	1881–1885
Vice President	None	
Secretary of State	F. T. Frelinghuysen	1881–1885
Secretary of Treasury	Charles J. Folger	1881–1884
	Walter Q. Gresham	1884
	Hugh McCulloch	1884–1885
Secretary of War	Robert T. Lincoln	1881–1885
Attorney General	Benjamin H. Brewster	1881–1885
Postmaster General	Timothy O. Howe	1881–1883
	Walter Q. Gresham	1883–1884
	Frank Hatton	1884–1885
Secretary of Navy	William H. Hunt	1881–1882
	William E. Chandler	1882–1885
Secretary of Interior	Samuel J. Kirkwood	1881–1882
	Henry M. Teller	1882–1885

The Cleveland Administration

President	Grover Cleveland	1885–1889
Vice President	Thomas A. Hendricks	1885–1889
Secretary of State	Thomas F. Bayard	1885–1889
Secretary of Treasury	Daniel Manning	1885–1887
	Charles S. Fairchild	1887–1889
Secretary of War	William C. Endicott	1885–1889
Attorney General	Augustus H. Garland	1885–1889
Postmaster General	William F. Vilas	1885–1888
	Don M. Dickinson	1888–1889
Secretary of Navy	William C. Whitney	1885–1889
Secretary of Interior	Lucius Q. C. Lamar	1885–1888
	William F. Vilas	1888–1889
Secretary of Agriculture	Norman J. Colman	1889

The Benjamin Harrison Administration

President	Benjamin Harrison	1889–1893
Vice President	Levi P. Morton	1889–1893
Secretary of State	James G. Blaine	1889–1892
	John W. Foster	1892–1893
Secretary of Treasury	William Windom	1889–1891
	Charles Foster	1891–1893
Secretary of War	Redfield Proctor	1889–1891
	Stephen B. Elkins	1891–1893
Attorney General	William H. H. Miller	1889–1891
Postmaster General	John Wanamaker	1889–1893
Secretary of Navy	Benjamin F. Tracy	1889–1893
Secretary of Interior	John W. Noble	1889–1893
Secretary of Agriculture	Jeremiah M. Rusk	1889–1893

The Cleveland Administration

President	Grover Cleveland	1893–1897
Vice President	Adlai E. Stevenson	1893–1897
Secretary of State	Walter Q. Gresham	1893–1895
	Richard Olney	1895–1897
Secretary of Treasury	John G. Carlisle	1893–1897
Secretary of War	Daniel S. Lamont	1893–1897
Attorney General	Richard Olney	1893–1895
	James Harmon	1895–1897
Postmaster General	Wilson S. Bissell	1893–1895
	William L. Wilson	1895–1897
Secretary of Navy	Hilary A. Herbert	1893–1897
Secretary of Interior	Hoke Smith	1893–1896
	David R. Francis	1896–1897

Secretary of Agriculture	Julius S. Morton	1893–1897

The McKinley Administration

President	William McKinley	1897–1901
Vice President	Garret A. Hobart	1897–1901
	Theodore Roosevelt	1901
Secretary of State	John Sherman	1897–1898
	William R. Day	1898
	John Hay	1898–1901
Secretary of Treasury	Lyman J. Gage	1897–1901
Secretary of War	Russell A. Alger	1897–1899
	Elihu Root	1899–1901
Attorney General	Joseph McKenna	1897–1898
	John W. Griggs	1898–1901
	Philander C. Knox	1901
Postmaster General	James A. Gary	1897–1898
	Charles E. Smith	1898–1901
Secretary of Navy	John D. Long	1897–1901
Secretary of Interior	Cornelius N. Bliss	1897–1899
	Ethan A. Hitchcock	1899–1901
Secretary of Agriculture	James Wilson	1897–1901

The Theodore Roosevelt Administration

President	Theodore Roosevelt	1901–1909
Vice President	Charles Fairbanks	1905–1909
Secretary of State	John Hay	1901–1905
	Elihu Root	1905–1909
	Robert Bacon	1909
Secretary of Treasury	Lyman J. Gage	1901–1902
	Leslie M. Shaw	1902–1907
	George B. Cortelyou	1907–1909
Secretary of War	Elihu Root	1901–1904
	William H. Taft	1904–1908
	Luke E. Wright	1908–1909
Attorney General	Philander C. Knox	1901–1904
	William H. Moody	1904–1906
	Charles J. Bonaparte	1906–1909
Postmaster General	Charles E. Smith	1901–1902
	Henry C. Payne	1902–1904
	Robert J. Wynne	1904–1905
	George B. Cortelyou	1905–1907
	George von L. Meyer	1907–1909
Secretary of Navy	John D. Long	1901–1902
	William H. Moody	1902–1904
	Paul Morton	1904–1905
	Charles J. Bonaparte	1905–1906
	Victor H. Metcalf	1906–1908
	Truman H. Newberry	1908–1909

Secretary of Interior	Ethan A. Hitchcock	1901–1907
	James R. Garfield	1907–1909
Secretary of Agriculture	James Wilson	1901–1909
Secretary of Labor and Commerce	George B. Cortelyou	1903–1904
	Victor H. Metcalf	1904–1906
	Oscar S. Straus	1906–1909
	Charles Nagel	1909

The Taft Administration

President	William H. Taft	1909–1913
Vice President	James S. Sherman	1909–1913
Secretary of State	Philander C. Knox	1909–1913
Secretary of Treasury	Franklin MacVeagh	1909–1913
Secretary of War	Jacob M. Dickinson	1909–1911
	Henry L. Stimson	1911–1913
Attorney General	George W. Wickersham	1909–1913
Postmaster General	Frank H. Hitchcock	1909–1913
Secretary of Navy	George von L. Meyer	1909–1913
Secretary of Interior	Richard A. Ballinger	1909–1911
	Walter L. Fisher	1911–1913
Secretary of Agriculture	James Wilson	1909–1913
Secretary of Labor and Commerce	Charles Nagel	1909–1913

The Wilson Administration

President	Woodrow Wilson	1913–1921
Vice President	Thomas R. Marshall	1913–1921
Secretary of State	William J. Bryan	1913–1915
	Robert Lansing	1915–1920
	Bainbridge Colby	1920–1921
Secretary of Treasury	William G. McAdoo	1913–1918
	Carter Glass	1918–1920
	David F. Houston	1920–1921
Secretary of War	Lindley M. Garrison	1913–1916
	Newton D. Baker	1916–1921
Attorney General	James C. McReynolds	1913–1914
	Thomas W. Gregory	1914–1919
	A. Mitchell Palmer	1919–1921
Postmaster General	Albert S. Burleson	1913–1921
Secretary of Navy	Josephus Daniels	1913–1921
Secretary of Interior	Franklin K. Lane	1913–1920
	John B. Payne	1920–1921
Secretary of Agriculture	David F. Houston	1913–1920
	Edwin T. Meredith	1920–1921

Secretary of Commerce	William C. Redfield	1913–1919
	Joshua W. Alexander	1919–1921
Secretary of Labor	William B. Wilson	1913–1921

The Harding Administration

President	Warren G. Harding	1921–1923
Vice President	Calvin Coolidge	1921–1923
Secretary of State	Charles E. Hughes	1921–1923
Secretary of Treasury	Andrew Mellon	1921–1923
Secretary of War	John W. Weeks	1921–1923
Attorney General	Harry M. Daugherty	1921–1923
Postmaster General	Will H. Hays	1921–1922
	Hubert Work	1922–1923
	Harry S. New	1923
Secretary of Navy	Edwin Denby	1921–1923
Secretary of Interior	Albert B. Fall	1921–1923
	Hubert Work	1923
Secretary of Agriculture	Henry C. Wallace	1921–1923
Secretary of Commerce	Herbert C. Hoover	1921–1923
Secretary of Labor	James J. Davis	1921–1923

The Coolidge Administration

President	Calvin Coolidge	1923–1929
Vice President	Charles G. Dawes	1925–1929
Secretary of State	Charles E. Hughes	1923–1925
	Frank B. Kellogg	1925–1929
Secretary of Treasury	Andrew Mellon	1923–1929
Secretary of War	John W. Weeks	1923–1925
	Dwight F. Davis	1925–1929
Attorney General	Henry M. Daugherty	1923–1924
	Harlan F. Stone	1924–1925
	John G. Sargent	1925–1929
Postmaster General	Harry S. New	1923–1929
Secretary of Navy	Edwin Derby	1923–1924
	Curtis D. Wilbur	1924–1929
Secretary of Interior	Hubert Work	1923–1928
	Roy O. West	1928–1929
Secretary of Agriculture	Henry C. Wallace	1923–1924
	Howard M. Gore	1924–1925
	William M. Jardine	1925–1929
Secretary of Commerce	Herbert C. Hoover	1923–1928
	William F. Whiting	1928–1929
Secretary of Labor	James J. Davis	1923–1929

The Hoover Administration

President	Herbert C. Hoover	1929–1933
Vice President	Charles Curtis	1929–1933
Secretary of State	Henry L. Stimson	1929–1933
Secretary of Treasury	Andrew Mellon	1929–1932
	Ogden L. Mills	1932–1933
Secretary of War	James W. Good	1929
	Patrick J. Hurley	1929–1933
Attorney General	William D. Mitchell	1929–1933
Postmaster General	Walter F. Brown	1929–1933
Secretary of Navy	Charles F. Adams	1929–1933
Secretary of Interior	Ray L. Wilbur	1929–1933
Secretary of Agriculture	Arthur M. Hyde	1929–1933
Secretary of Commerce	Robert P. Lamont	1929–1932
	Roy D. Chapin	1932–1933
Secretary of Labor	James J. Davis	1929–1930
	William N. Doak	1930–1933

The Franklin D. Roosevelt Administration

President	Franklin D. Roosevelt	1933–1945
Vice President	John Nance Garner	1933–1941
	Henry A. Wallace	1941–1945
	Harry S Truman	1945
Secretary of State	Cordell Hull	1933–1944
	Edward R. Stettinius, Jr.	1944–1945
Secretary of Treasury	William H. Woodin	1933–1934
	Henry Morgenthau, Jr.	1934–1945
Secretary of War	George H. Dern	1933–1936
	Henry A. Woodring	1936–1940
	Henry L. Stimson	1940–1945
Attorney General	Homer S. Cummings	1933–1939
	Frank Murphy	1939–1940
	Robert H. Jackson	1940–1941
	Francis Biddle	1941–1945
Postmaster General	James A. Farley	1933–1940
	Frank C. Walker	1940–1945
Secretary of Navy	Claude A. Swanson	1933–1940
	Charles Edison	1940
	Frank Knox	1940–1944
	James V. Forrestal	1944–1945
Secretary of Interior	Harold L. Ickes	1933–1945
Secretary of Agriculture	Henry A. Wallace	1933–1940
	Claude R. Wickard	1940–1945
Secretary of Commerce	Daniel C. Roper	1933–1939
	Harry L. Hopkins	1939–1940
	Jesse Jones	1940–1945
	Henry A. Wallace	1945
Secretary of Labor	Frances Perkins	1933–1945

The Truman Administration

President	Harry S Truman	1945–1953
Vice President	Alben W. Barkley	1949–1953
Secretary of State	Edward R. Stettinius, Jr.	1945
	James F. Byrnes	1945–1947
	George C. Marshall	1947–1949
	Dean G. Acheson	1949–1953
Secretary of Treasury	Fred M. Vinson	1945–1946
	John W. Snyder	1946–1953
Secretary of War	Robert P. Patterson	1945–1947
	Kenneth C. Royall	1947
Attorney General	Tom C. Clark	1945–1949
	J. Howard McGrath	1949–1952
	James P. McGranery	1952–1953
Postmaster General	Frank C. Walker	1945
	Robert E. Hannegan	1945–1947
	Jesse M. Donaldson	1947–1953
Secretary of Navy	James V. Forrestal	1945–1947
Secretary of Interior	Harold L. Ickes	1945–1946
	Julius A. Krug	1946–1949
	Oscar L. Chapman	1949–1953
Secretary of Agriculture	Clinton P. Anderson	1945–1948
	Charles F. Brannan	1948–1953
Secretary of Commerce	Henry A. Wallace	1945–1946
	W. Averell Harriman	1946–1948
	Charles W. Sawyer	1948–1953
Secretary of Labor	Lewis B. Schwellenbach	1945–1948
	Maurice J. Tobin	1948–1953
Secretary of Defense	James V. Forrestal	1947–1949
	Louis A. Johnson	1949–1950
	George C. Marshall	1950–1951
	Robert A. Lovett	1951–1953

The Eisenhower Administration

President	Dwight D. Eisenhower	1953–1961
Vice President	Richard M. Nixon	1953–1961
Secretary of State	John Foster Dulles	1953–1959
	Christian A. Herter	1959–1961
Secretary of Treasury	George M. Humphrey	1953–1957
	Robert B. Anderson	1957–1961
Attorney General	Herbert Brownell, Jr.	1953–1958
	William P. Rogers	1958–1961
Postmaster General	Arthur E. Summerfield	1953–1961
Secretary of Interior	Douglas McKay	1953–1956
	Fred A. Seaton	1956–1961
Secretary of Agriculture	Ezra T. Benson	1953–1961
Secretary of Commerce	Sinclair Weeks	1953–1958
	Lewis L. Strauss	1958–1959
	Frederick H. Mueller	1959–1961

Secretary of Labor	Martin P. Durkin	1953
	James P. Mitchell	1953–1961
Secretary of Defense	Charles E. Wilson	1953–1957
	Neil H. McElroy	1957–1959
	Thomas S. Gates, Jr.	1959–1961
Secretary of Health, Education, and Welfare	Oveta Culp Hobby	1953–1955
	Marion B. Folsom	1955–1958
	Arthur S. Flemming	1958–1961

The Kennedy Administration

President	John F. Kennedy	1961–1963
Vice President	Lyndon B. Johnson	1961–1963
Secretary of State	Dean Rusk	1961–1963
Secretary of Treasury	C. Douglas Dillon	1961–1963
Attorney General	Robert F. Kennedy	1961–1963
Postmaster General	J. Edward Day	1961–1963
	John A. Gronouski	1963
Secretary of Interior	Stewart L. Udall	1961–1963
Secretary of Agriculture	Orville L. Freeman	1961–1963
Secretary of Commerce	Luther H. Hodges	1961–1963
Secretary of Labor	Arthur J. Goldberg	1961–1962
	W. Willard Wirtz	1962–1963
Secretary of Defense	Robert S. McNamara	1961–1963
Secretary of Health, Education, and Welfare	Abraham A. Ribicoff	1961–1962
	Anthony J. Celebrezze	1962–1963

The Lyndon Johnson Administration

President	Lyndon B. Johnson	1963–1969
Vice President	Hubert H. Humphrey	1965–1969
Secretary of State	Dean Rusk	1963–1969
Secretary of Treasury	C. Douglas Dillon	1963–1965
	Henry H. Fowler	1965–1969
Attorney General	Robert F. Kennedy	1963–1964
	Nicholas Katzenbach	1965–1966
	Ramsey Clark	1967–1969
Postmaster General	John A. Gronouski	1963–1965
	Lawrence F. O'Brien	1965–1968
	Marvin Watson	1968–1969
Secretary of Interior	Stewart L. Udall	1963–1969
Secretary of Agriculture	Orville L. Freeman	1963–1969
Secretary of Commerce	Luther H. Hodges	1963–1964
	John T. Connor	1964–1967
	Alexander B. Trowbridge	1967–1968
	Cyrus R. Smith	1968–1969

Secretary of Labor	W. Willard Wirtz	1963–1969
Secretary of Defense	Robert F. McNamara	1963–1968
	Clark Clifford	1968–1969
Secretary of Health, Education, and Welfare	Anthony J. Celebrezze	1963–1965
	John W. Gardner	1965–1968
	Wilbur J. Cohen	1968–1969
Secretary of Housing and Urban Development	Robert C. Weaver	1966–1969
	Robert C. Wood	1969
Secretary of Transportation	Alan S. Boyd	1967–1969

The Nixon Administration

President	Richard M. Nixon	1969–1974
Vice President	Spiro T. Agnew	1969–1973
	Gerald R. Ford	1973–1974
Secretary of State	William P. Rogers	1969–1973
	Henry A. Kissinger	1973–1974
Secretary of Treasury	David M. Kennedy	1969–1970
	John B. Connally	1971–1972
	George P. Shultz	1972–1974
	William E. Simon	1974
Attorney General	John N. Mitchell	1969–1972
	Richard G. Kleindienst	1972–1973
	Elliot L. Richardson	1973
	William B. Saxbe	1973–1974
Postmaster General	Winton M. Blount	1969–1971
Secretary of Interior	Walter J. Hickel	1969–1970
	Rogers Morton	1971–1974
Secretary of Agriculture	Clifford M. Hardin	1969–1971
	Earl L. Butz	1971–1974
Secretary of Commerce	Maurice H. Stans	1969–1972
	Peter G. Peterson	1972–1973
	Frederick B. Dent	1973–1974
Secretary of Labor	George P. Shultz	1969–1970
	James D. Hodgson	1970–1973
	Peter J. Brennan	1973–1974
Secretary of Defense	Melvin R. Laird	1969–1973
	Elliot L. Richardson	1973
	James R. Schlesinger	1973–1974
Secretary of Health, Education, and Welfare	Robert H. Finch	1969–1970
	Elliot L. Richardson	1970–1973
	Casper W. Weinberger	1973–1974
Secretary of Housing and Urban Development	George Romney	1969–1973
	James T. Lynn	1973–1974
Secretary of Transportation	John A. Volpe	1969–1973
	Claude S. Brinegar	1973–1974

The Ford Administration

President	Gerald R. Ford	1974–1977
Vice President	Nelson A. Rockefeller	1974–1977
Secretary of State	Henry A. Kissinger	1974–1977
Secretary of Treasury	William E. Simon	1974–1977
Attorney General	William Saxbe	1974–1975
	Edward Levi	1975–1977
Secretary of Interior	Rogers Morton	1974–1975
	Stanley K. Hathaway	1975
	Thomas Kleppe	1975–1977
Secretary of Agriculture	Earl L. Butz	1974–1976
	John A. Knebel	1976–1977
Secretary of Commerce	Frederick B. Dent	1974–1975
	Rogers Morton	1975–1976
	Elliot L. Richardson	1976–1977
Secretary of Labor	Peter J. Brennan	1974–1975
	John T. Dunlop	1975–1976
	W. J. Usery	1976–1977
Secretary of Defense	James R. Schlesinger	1974–1975
	Donald Rumsfeld	1975–1977
Secretary of Health, Education, and Welfare	Casper Weinberger	1974–1975
	Forrest D. Mathews	1975–1977
Secretary of Housing and Urban Development	James T. Lynn	1974–1975
	Carla A. Hills	1975–1977
Secretary of Transportation	Claude Brinegar	1974–1975
	William T. Coleman	1975–1977

The Carter Administration

President	Jimmy Carter	1977–1981
Vice President	Walter F. Mondale	1977–1981
Secretary of State	Cyrus R. Vance	1977–1980
	Edmund Muskie	1980–1981
Secretary of Treasury	W. Michael Blumenthal	1977–1979
	G. William Miller	1979–1981
Attorney General	Griffin Bell	1977–1979
	Benjamin R. Civiletti	1979–1981
Secretary of Interior	Cecil D. Andrus	1977–1981
Secretary of Agriculture	Robert Bergland	1977–1981
Secretary of Commerce	Juanita M. Kreps	1977–1979
	Philip M. Klutznick	1979–1981
Secretary of Labor	F. Ray Marshall	1977–1981
Secretary of Defense	Harold Brown	1977–1981
Secretary of Health, Education, and Welfare	Joseph A. Califano	1977–1979
	Patricia R. Harris	1979
Secretary of Health and Human Services	Patricia R. Harris	1979–1981
Secretary of Education	Shirley M. Hufstedler	1979–1981
Secretary of Housing and Urban Development	Patricia R. Harris	1977–1979
	Moon Landrieu	1979–1981
Secretary of Transportation	Brock Adams	1977–1979
	Neil E. Goldschmidt	1979–1981
Secretary of Energy	James R. Schlesinger	1977–1979
	Charles W. Duncan	1979–1981

The Reagan Administration

President	Ronald Reagan	1981–1989
Vice President	George Bush	1981–1989
Secretary of State	Alexander M. Haig	1981–1982
	George P. Shultz	1982–1989
Secretary of Treasury	Donald Regan	1981–1985
	James A. Baker III	1985–1988
	Nicholas F. Brady	1988–1989
Attorney General	William F. Smith	1981–1985
	Edwin A. Meese III	1985–1988
	Richard L. Thornburgh	1988–1989
Secretary of Interior	James G. Watt	1981–1983
	William P. Clark, Jr.	1983–1985
	Donald P. Hodel	1985–1989
Secretary of Agriculture	John Block	1981–1986
	Richard E. Lyng	1986–1989
Secretary of Commerce	Malcolm Baldrige	1981–1987
	C. William Verity, Jr.	1987–1989
Secretary of Labor	Raymond J. Donovan	1981–1985
	William E. Brock	1985–1987
	Ann Dore McLaughlin	1987–1989
Secretary of Defense	Casper Weinberger	1981–1987
	Frank C. Carlucci	1987–1989
Secretary of Health and Human Services	Richard S. Schweiker	1981–1983
	Margaret Heckler	1983–1985
	Otis R. Bowen	1985–1989
Secretary of Education	Terrel H. Bell	1981–1984
	William J. Bennett	1985–1988
	Lauro F. Cavazos	1988–1989

Secretary of Housing and Urban Development	Samuel R. Pierce, Jr.	1981–1989
Secretary of Transportation	Drew Lewis	1981–1982
	Elizabeth Hanford Dole	1983–1987
	James H. Burnley IV	1987–1989
Secretary of Energy	James B. Edwards	1981–1982
	Donald P. Hodel	1982–1985
	John S. Herrington	1985–1989

The Bush Administration

President	George Bush	1989–
Vice President	Dan Quayle	1989–
Secretary of State	James A. Baker III	1989–
Secretary of Treasury	Nicholas F. Brady	1989–
Attorney General	Richard L. Thornburgh	1989–
Secretary of Interior	Manuel Lujan, Jr.	1989–

Secretary of Agriculture	Clayton K. Yeutter	1989–
Secretary of Commerce	Robert A. Mosbacher	1989–
Secretary of Labor	Elizabeth Hanford Dole	1989–
Secretary of Defense	Richard B. Cheney	1989–
Secretary of Health and Human Services	Louis W. Sullivan	1989–
Secretary of Education	Lauro F. Cavazos	1989–
Secretary of Housing and Urban Development	Jack F. Kemp	1989–
Secretary of Transportation	Samuel K. Skinner	1989–
Secretary of Energy	James D. Watkins	1989–
Secretary of Veterans Affairs	Edward J. Derwinski	1989–

Party Strength in Congress

Period	Congress	House Majority Party		House Minority Party		Others	Senate Majority Party		Senate Minority Party		Others	Party of President	
1789–91	1st	Ad	38	Op	26		Ad	17	Op	9		F	Washington
1791–93	2nd	F	37	DR	33		F	16	DR	13		F	Washington
1793–95	3rd	DR	57	F	48		F	17	DR	13		F	Washington
1795–97	4th	F	54	DR	52		F	19	DR	13		F	Washington
1797–99	5th	F	58	DR	48		F	20	DR	12		F	J. Adams
1799–1801	6th	F	64	DR	42		F	19	DR	13		F	J. Adams
1801–03	7th	DR	69	F	36		DR	18	F	13		DR	Jefferson
1803–05	8th	DR	102	F	39		DR	25	F	9		DR	Jefferson
1805–07	9th	DR	116	F	25		DR	27	F	7		DR	Jefferson
1807–09	10th	DR	118	F	24		DR	28	F	6		DR	Jefferson
1809–11	11th	DR	94	F	48		DR	28	F	6		DR	Madison
1811–13	12th	DR	108	F	36		DR	30	F	6		DR	Madison
1813–15	13th	DR	112	F	68		DR	27	F	9		DR	Madison
1815–17	14th	DR	117	F	65		DR	25	F	11		DR	Madison
1817–19	15th	DR	141	F	42		DR	34	F	10		DR	Monroe
1819–21	16th	DR	156	F	27		DR	35	F	7		DR	Monroe
1821–23	17th	DR	158	F	25		DR	44	F	4		DR	Monroe
1823–25	18th	DR	187	F	26		DR	44	F	4		DR	Monroe
1825–27	19th	Ad	105	J	97		Ad	26	J	20		C	J. Q. Adams
1827–29	20th	J	119	Ad	94		J	28	Ad	20		C	J. Q. Adams
1829–31	21st	D	139	NR	74		D	26	NR	22		D	Jackson
1831–33	22nd	D	141	NR	58	14	D	25	NR	21	2	D	Jackson
1833–35	23rd	D	147	AM	53	60	D	20	NR	20	8	D	Jackson
1835–37	24th	D	145	W	98		D	27	W	25		D	Jackson
1837–39	25th	D	108	W	107	24	D	30	W	18	4	D	Van Buren
1839–41	26th	D	124	W	118		D	28	W	22		D	Van Buren
1841–43	27th	W	133	D	102	6	W	28	D	22	2	W	W. Harrison
												W	Tyler
1843–45	28th	D	142	W	79	1	W	28	D	25	1	W	Tyler
1845–47	29th	D	143	W	77	6	D	31	W	25		D	Polk
1847–49	30th	W	115	D	108	4	D	36	W	21	1	D	Polk
1849–51	31st	D	112	W	109	9	D	35	W	25	2	W	Taylor
												W	Fillmore
1851–53	32nd	D	140	W	88	5	D	35	W	24	3	W	Fillmore
1853–55	33rd	D	159	W	71	4	D	38	W	22	2	D	Pierce
1855–57	34th	R	108	D	83	43	D	40	R	15	5	D	Pierce
1857–59	35th	D	118	R	92	26	D	36	R	20	8	D	Buchanan
1859–61	36th	R	114	D	92	31	D	36	R	26	4	D	Buchanan

Period	Congress	House Majority Party		House Minority Party		Others	Senate Majority Party		Senate Minority Party		Others	Party of President	
1861–63	37th	R	105	D	43	30	R	31	D	10	8	R	Lincoln
1863–65	38th	R	102	D	75	9	R	36	D	9	5	R	Lincoln
1865–67	39th	U	149	D	42		U	42	D	10		R	Lincoln
												R	Johnson
1867–69	40th	R	143	D	49		R	42	D	11		R	Johnson
1869–71	41st	R	149	D	63		R	56	D	11		R	Grant
1871–73	42nd	R	134	D	104	5	R	52	D	17	5	R	Grant
1873–75	43rd	R	194	D	92	14	R	49	D	19	5	R	Grant
1875–77	44th	D	169	R	109	14	R	45	D	29	2	R	Grant
1877–79	45th	D	153	R	140		R	39	D	36	1	R	Hayes
1879–81	46th	D	149	R	130	14	D	42	R	33	1	R	Hayes
1881–83	47th	D	147	R	135	11	R	37	D	37	1	R	Garfield
												R	Arthur
1883–85	48th	D	197	R	118	10	R	38	D	36	2	R	Arthur
1885–87	49th	D	183	R	140	2	R	43	D	34		D	Cleveland
1887–89	50th	D	169	R	152	4	R	39	D	37		D	Cleveland
1889–91	51st	R	166	D	159		R	39	D	37		R	B. Harrison
1891–93	52nd	D	235	R	88	9	R	47	D	39	2	R	B. Harrison
1893–95	53rd	D	218	R	127	11	D	44	R	38	3	D	Cleveland
1895–97	54th	R	244	D	105	7	R	43	D	39	6	D	Cleveland
1897–99	55th	R	204	D	113	40	R	47	D	34	7	R	McKinley
1899–1901	56th	R	185	D	163	9	R	53	D	26	8	R	McKinley
1901–03	57th	R	197	D	151	9	R	55	D	31	4	R	McKinley
												R	T. Roosevelt
1903–05	58th	R	208	D	178		R	57	D	33		R	T. Roosevelt
1905–07	59th	R	250	D	136		R	57	D	33		R	T. Roosevelt
1907–09	60th	R	222	D	164		R	61	D	31		R	T. Roosevelt
1909–11	61st	R	219	D	172		R	61	D	32		R	Taft
1911–13	62nd	D	228	R	161	1	R	51	D	41		R	Taft
1913–15	63rd	D	291	R	127	17	D	51	R	44	1	D	Wilson
1915–17	64th	D	230	R	196	9	D	56	R	40		D	Wilson
1917–19	65th	D	216	R	210	6	D	53	R	42		D	Wilson
1919–21	66th	R	240	D	190	3	R	49	D	47		D	Wilson
1921–23	67th	R	301	D	131	1	R	59	D	37		R	Harding
1923–25	68th	R	225	D	205	5	R	51	D	43	2	R	Coolidge
1925–27	69th	R	247	D	183	4	R	56	D	39	1	R	Coolidge
1927–29	70th	R	237	D	195	3	R	49	D	46	1	R	Coolidge
1929–31	71st	R	267	D	167	1	R	56	D	39	1	R	Hoover
1931–33	72nd	D	220	R	214	1	R	48	D	47	1	R	Hoover
1933–35	73rd	D	310	R	117	5	D	60	R	35	1	D	F. Roosevelt
1935–37	74th	D	319	R	103	10	D	69	R	25	2	D	F. Roosevelt
1937–39	75th	D	331	R	89	13	D	76	R	16	4	D	F. Roosevelt
1939–41	76th	D	261	R	164	4	D	69	R	23	4	D	F. Roosevelt

Period	Congress	House Majority Party		House Minority Party		Others	Senate Majority Party		Senate Minority Party		Others	Party of President	
1941–43	77th	D	268	R	162	5	D	66	R	28	2	D	F. Roosevelt
1943–45	78th	D	218	R	208	4	D	58	R	37	1	D	F. Roosevelt
1945–47	79th	D	242	R	190	2	D	56	R	38	1	D	Truman
1947–49	80th	R	245	D	188	1	R	51	D	45		D	Truman
1949–51	81st	D	263	R	171	1	D	54	R	42		D	Truman
1951–53	82nd	D	234	R	199	1	D	49	R	47		D	Truman
1953–55	83rd	R	221	D	211	1	R	48	D	47	1	R	Eisenhower
1955–57	84th	D	232	R	203		D	48	R	47	1	R	Eisenhower
1957–59	85th	D	233	R	200		D	49	R	47		R	Eisenhower
1959–61	86th	D	284	R	153		D	65	R	35		R	Eisenhower
1961–63	87th	D	263	R	174		D	65	R	35		D	Kennedy
1963–65	88th	D	258	R	117		D	67	R	33		D	Kennedy
												D	Johnson
1965–67	89th	D	295	R	140		D	68	R	32		D	Johnson
1967–69	90th	D	246	R	187		D	64	R	36		D	Johnson
1969–71	91st	D	245	R	189		D	57	R	43		R	Nixon
1971–73	92nd	D	254	R	180		D	54	R	44	2	R	Nixon
1973–75	93rd	D	239	R	192	1	D	56	R	42	2	R	Nixon
1975–77	94th	D	291	R	144		D	60	R	37	3	R	Ford
1977–79	95th	D	292	R	143		D	61	R	38	1	D	Carter
1979–81	96th	D	276	R	157		D	58	R	41	1	D	Carter
1981–83	97th	D	243	R	192		R	53	D	46	1	R	Reagan
1983–85	98th	D	267	R	168		R	55	D	45		R	Reagan
1985–87	99th	D	253	R	182		R	53	D	47		R	Reagan
1987–89	100th	D	258	R	177		D	55	R	45		R	Reagan
1989–91	101st	D	259	R	174		D	54	R	46		R	Bush

AD = Administration; AM = Anti-Masonic; C = Coalition; D = Democratic; DR = Democratic-Republican; F = Federalist; J = Jacksonian; NR = National Republican; Op = Opposition; R = Republican; U = Unionist; W = Whig. Figures are for the beginning of first session of each Congress, except the 93rd, which are for the beginning of the second session.

Justices of the Supreme Court

	Term of Service	Years of Service	Life Span		Term of Service	Years of Service	Life Span
John Jay	1789–1795	5	1745–1829	Stephen J. Field	1863–1897	34	1816–1899
John Rutledge	1789–1791	1	1739–1800	Salmon P. Chase	1864–1873	8	1808–1873
William Cushing	1789–1810	20	1732–1810	William Strong	1870–1880	10	1808–1895
James Wilson	1789–1798	8	1742–1798	Joseph P. Bradley	1870–1892	22	1813–1892
John Blair	1789–1796	6	1732–1800	Ward Hunt	1873–1882	9	1810–1886
Robert H. Harrison	1789–1790	—	1745–1790	Morrison R. Waite	1874–1888	14	1816–1888
James Iredell	1790–1799	9	1751–1799	John M. Harlan	1877–1911	34	1833–1911
Thomas Johnson	1791–1793	1	1732–1819	William B. Woods	1880–1887	7	1824–1887
William Paterson	1793–1806	13	1745–1806	Stanley Matthews	1881–1889	7	1824–1889
John Rutledge*	1795	—	1739–1800	Horace Gray	1882–1902	20	1828–1902
Samuel Chase	1796–1811	15	1741–1811	Samuel Blatchford	1882–1893	11	1820–1893
Oliver Ellsworth	1796–1800	4	1745–1807	Lucius Q. C. Lamar	1888–1893	5	1825–1893
Bushrod Washington	1798–1829	31	1762–1829	Melville W. Fuller	1888–1910	21	1833–1910
Alfred Moore	1799–1804	4	1755–1810	David J. Brewer	1890–1910	20	1837–1910
John Marshall	1801–1835	34	1755–1835	Henry B. Brown	1890–1906	16	1836–1913
William Johnson	1804–1834	30	1771–1834	George Shiras, Jr.	1892–1903	10	1832–1924
H. Brockholst Livingston	1806–1823	16	1757–1823	Howell E. Jackson	1893–1895	2	1832–1895
Thomas Todd	1807–1826	18	1765–1826	Edward D. White	1894–1910	16	1845–1921
Joseph Story	1811–1845	33	1779–1845	Rufus W. Peckham	1895–1909	14	1838–1909
Gabriel Duval	1811–1835	24	1752–1844	Joseph McKenna	1898–1925	26	1843–1926
Smith Thompson	1823–1843	20	1768–1843	Oliver W. Holmes	1902–1932	30	1841–1935
Robert Trimble	1826–1828	2	1777–1828	William R. Day	1903–1922	19	1849–1923
John McLean	1829–1861	32	1785–1861	William H. Moody	1906–1910	3	1853–1917
Henry Baldwin	1830–1844	14	1780–1844	Horace H. Lurton	1910–1914	4	1844–1914
James M. Wayne	1835–1867	32	1790–1867	Charles E. Hughes	1910–1916	5	1862–1948
Roger B. Taney	1836–1864	28	1777–1864	Willis Van Devanter	1911–1937	26	1859–1941
Philip P. Barbour	1836–1841	4	1783–1841	Joseph R. Lamar	1911–1916	5	1857–1916
John Catron	1837–1865	28	1786–1865	Edward D. White	1910–1921	11	1845–1921
John McKinley	1837–1852	15	1780–1852	Mahlon Pitney	1912–1922	10	1858–1924
Peter V. Daniel	1841–1860	19	1784–1860	James C. McReynolds	1914–1941	26	1862–1946
Samuel Nelson	1845–1872	27	1792–1873	Louis D. Brandeis	1916–1939	22	1856–1941
Levi Woodbury	1845–1851	5	1789–1851	John H. Clarke	1916–1922	6	1857–1945
Robert C. Grier	1846–1870	23	1794–1870	William H. Taft	1921–1930	8	1857–1930
Benjamin R. Curtis	1851–1857	6	1809–1874	George Sutherland	1922–1938	15	1862–1942
John A. Campbell	1853–1861	8	1811–1889	Pierce Butler	1922–1939	16	1866–1939
Nathan Clifford	1858–1881	23	1803–1881	Edward T. Sanford	1923–1930	7	1865–1930
Noah H. Swayne	1862–1881	18	1804–1884	Harlan F. Stone	1925–1941	16	1872–1946
Samuel F. Miller	1862–1890	28	1816–1890	Charles E. Hughes	1930–1941	11	1862–1948
David Davis	1862–1877	14	1815–1886	Owen J. Roberts	1930–1945	15	1875–1955

	Term of Service	Years of Service	Life Span		Term of Service	Years of Service	Life Span
Benjamin N. Cardozo	1932–1938	6	1870–1938	William J. Brennan, Jr.	1956–	—	1906–
Hugo L. Black	1937–1971	34	1886–1971	Charles E. Whittaker	1957–1962	5	1901–1973
Stanley F. Reed	1938–1957	19	1884–1980	Potter Stewart	1958–1981	23	1915–1985
Felix Frankfurter	1939–1962	23	1882–1965	Byron R. White	1962–	—	1917–
William O. Douglas	1939–1975	36	1898–1980	Arthur J. Goldberg	1962–1965	3	1908–
Frank Murphy	1940–1949	9	1890–1949	Abe Fortas	1965–1969	4	1910–1982
Harlan F. Stone	1941–1946	5	1872–1946	Thurgood Marshall	1967–	—	1908–
James F. Byrnes	1941–1942	1	1879–1972	*Warren C. Burger*	1969–1986	17	1907–
Robert H. Jackson	1941–1954	13	1892–1954	Harry A. Blackmun	1970–	—	1908–
Wiley B. Rutledge	1943–1949	6	1894–1949	Lewis F. Powell, Jr.	1971–1987	16	1907–
Harold H. Burton	1945–1958	13	1888–1964	*William H. Rehnquist*	1971–	—	1924–
Fred M. Vinson	1946–1953	7	1890–1953	John P. Stevens III	1975–	—	1920–
Tom C. Clark	1949–1967	18	1899–1977	Sandra Day O'Connor	1981–	—	1930–
Sherman Minton	1949–1956	7	1890–1965	Antonin Scalia	1986–	—	1936–
Earl Warren	1953–1969	16	1891–1974	Anthony M. Kennedy	1988–	—	1936–
John Marshall Harlan	1955–1971	16	1899–1971				

*Appointed and served one term, but not confirmed by the Senate.
Note: Chief justices are in italics.

French Revolution: American opinion concerning, 185, 194–195, 197; influence on blacks, 209
Frontenac, Louis de Buade de, 59
Fruitlands cooperative, 323
Fugitive Slave Act (1850), 336, 371–372, 378, 379–380, 381, 383
Fulkes, Minnie, 293
Fuller, Margaret, 162, 310, 311
Fulton, Robert, 245, 252
"Fundamental Constitutions of Carolina" (Locke), 48
Fundamental Orders of Connecticut (1639), 33

Gabriel's Rebellion, 209, 297, 335
Gadsden Purchase, 267, 327
Gage, Gen. Thomas, 137, 139, 140
Gallatin, Albert, 216
Galloway, Joseph, 133, 135, 136, 145, 148
Gama, Vasco de, 15
Gambia, 12
Gambling, as object of reformers, 346–347
Garlic, Delta, 292
Garnet, Rev. Henry Highland, 336, 350
Garrison, William Lloyd, 342, 349, 350, 351, 352, 353
Gaspée (ship), 123
Gates, Horatio, 148, 151
Gaugin, Michael, 326
General Court (Massachusetts Bay), 33, 37
Genêt, Citizen Edmond, 195, 219
The Genius of Universal Emancipation (journal), 350
George I (King of England), 78
George II (King of England), 112
George III (King of England): succession to throne, 112; and British debt crisis, 112; loyalty of American colonists to, 124, 133, 136; as villain of Declaration of Independence, 143
Georgia, 150, 151, 152, 236, 275, 356; founding of, 58; population growth in, 77; slavery in, 89, 166, 294; fear of slave uprisings in, 138; white settlement of, 139; debts of, 191; western migration in, 203; promotion of economic growth by, 253; agricultural economy of, 278; population density of, 281; planter society in, 289; political reforms in, 300; Indian land concessions in, 330–331; ban on manumission in, 335; racism in, 335; secessionist sentiment in, 391; secession of, 394; states' rights sentiment in, 420, 421; disillusionment with Civil War in, 422, 423, 424; Civil War military campaigns in, 427–428; Reconstruction period in, 438, 447–448, 453–454
Germain, Lord George, 140–141, 147, 150
Germans: emigration to American colonies, 76, 77, 78, 79; and growth of American cities, 312, 326, 327; migration to American countryside, 326, 327; bigotry against, 346
Germantown, Pennsylvania, 148
Germany, 15
Gerry, Elbridge, 177, 180, 199
Gerstier, Chevalier de, 247
Gettysburg, Pennsylvania, 423
Gibbons v. Ogden, 236, 252
Giddings, Joshua, 374, 383
Gilbert, Sir Humphrey, 20–21
Girls, inclusion in education system, 162
Glorious Revolution (1688–89), 42, 67, 68, 96, 114
Gnadenhuetten, Ohio, 152
Gold, discovery in California, 269–270
Gordon, Thomas, 113
Gould, Jay, 413
Governor's Club (Philadelphia), 73
Grant, Ulysses S., 446; military campaigns of Civil War, 403, 422, 423, 427, 429; Lee's surrender to, 429; election to presidency, 459; Reconstruction policy, 459, 460; re-election of, 460; political corruption under, 460; and monetary policy, 461; foreign policy of, 461
Grasse, Comte de, 152
Great Awakening (1730s–60s), 74, 98–100; Second (1800s–40s), 187, 205–210, 229–230, 238–239, 342, 343–345
Great Basin, 6, 10
Great Britain, see England
Great Lakes campaigns (War of 1812), 228, 231
Great Meadows, Pennsylvania, 108
Great Plains, 6, 8, 9, 10, 20, 372, 381; exploration of, 251
Great Salt Lake, 251, 267
Great Salt Lake Valley, 310
Greece, ancient, republicanism in, 160
Greeley, Horace, 386, 417, 459–460
Greene, Gen. Nathanael, 151–152
Green River, Wyoming, 268 & ill.
Greenwood, John, 62 (ill.), 88 (ill.)
Grenville, George, 112–113, 114, 118
Grier, Robert, 389
Grimké, Angelina, 302, 352–353
Grimké, Sarah, 162, 302, 352–353
Growth, economic: and movement toward market economy, 249; government promotion of, 251–253; slavery as fuel of, 275, 276, 278–280, 298, 300–301. See also Market economy
Grund, Francis, 342
Guatemala, 9, 10
Guilford Court House, North Carolina, 152
Guinea: culture of, 10, 12; importation of slaves from, 49–50, 52
Gulf of Mexico, British blockade of, 231
Gullah language, 53
Gustavus, Ohio, 266

The Hague, the Netherlands, 216
Haitian Revolution, 208, 209, 335
Hale, John P., 381
Halfway Covenant, 61

Halifax, Nova Scotia, 113, 142
Hallam, Nancy, 87 (ill.)
Hamilton, Alexander, 210, 216, 234, 236; concept of republicanism, 160; on treaty obligations, 172; and ratification of Constitution, 182; profile of, 190–191; fiscal policy of, 191–194; view of French Revolution, 194; and partisan politics, 194, 195, 197; and foreign policy, 195, 201; authorship of Washington's farewell address, 198; domination of J. Adams administration, 199; duel with Burr, 222. Works: Defense of the Constitutionality of the Bank, 192; The Federalist, 182, 190; Report on Manufactures, 193, 257
Hamilton, Dr. Alexander, 73–74, 94
Hamilton, Elizabeth Schuyler, 190
Hamilton Corporation, 256
Hammond County, Indiana, 335
Hampton Roads Conference, 418–419, 440
Hancock, John, 103, 122, 123
Hancock, Thomas, 82
Handsome Lake, 210
Hard Labor Creek, South Carolina, 138
Hardy, Irene, 308–309
Harlem Railroad, 312
Harmar, Gen. Josiah, 174
Harpers Ferry, Virginia, 254, 391
Harper's Monthly, 400, 414
Harrison, William Henry: military campaigns of War of 1812, 227, 228, 232; and election of 1836, 362; death of, 363; election to presidency, 363, 364 (ill.)
Hartford, Connecticut, 68
Hartford Convention, 233–234, 358
Hartford Female Seminary, 321
Harvard University, 93, 94, 176–177, 311
Hawaii, proposed annexation of, 381
Hawkins, John, 20
Hawthorne, Nathaniel, 310, 311
Hayes, Rutherford B., 461, 462
Hayne, Robert Y., 358
"Headright" system, 26–27, 28
Helper, Hinton R., 302
Hemingway, Eliza R., 261
Henry VII (King of England), 15
Henry VIII (King of England), 21, 22
Henry the Navigator (Prince of Portugal), 15
Henry, Patrick, 115, 133, 182
Henry, William, 448
Heroes of America, 424
Hessian mercenaries, in American Revolution, 141, 145, 146, 148
Higher education: colonial, 93, 94; black institutions, 455
High Point, North Carolina, 421
Highways: and transformation of trade routes, 245; government support for, 357
Hill, John William, 246 (ill.)
Hillsborough, Lord, 120
Hilton Head, South Carolina, 403, 404 (ill.)

Locke, John, 48, 94, 113
London, England, overpopulation of, 22, 23 (ill.)
London Crystal Palace Exhibition (1851), 254
Long, Maj. Stephen, 251
Long Island, New York, 43, 45, 85–86, 145, 231
Longstreet, Gen. James, 423
Lord Dunmore's War, 139
Los Angeles, California, educational system of, 314
Lotteries, 346–347
Louis XIV (King of France), 68
Louis XVI (King of France), 150, 194
Louisbourg, 82, 109
Louisiana, 59, 60 (ill.), 458; admission to statehood, 238; agricultural economy of, 278; population density of, 281; migration to, 283; slavery in, 286, 295; political reform in, 300; secession of, 394; Reconstruction period in, 440, 455, 459; 1876 vote disputed, 461; exodus of disaffected blacks, 463
Louisiana Purchase, 214, 218–219, 220, 222, 235, 251, 263, 267, 365, 375, 382
Louisiana Territory, 222; Spain gains control of, 109; division between free and slave states, 239
Louisville, Kentucky, 312; as center of commerce, 259, 271–272
L'Ouverture, Toussaint, 208
Lovejoy, Elijah P., 352
Lowell, Francis Cabot, 256
Lowell, James Russell, 389
Lowell, Massachusetts, textile factories, 256, 257, 261, 262, 263 (ill.), 353
Lowell Offering (newspaper), 262
Loyalists: opposition to American patriots, 135–137; return of confiscated property to, 172
Loyal Nine, 116, 117, 125
Lucas, Eliza, 54
Lukens, Rebecca, 323 (ill.)
Lundy, Benjamin, 350
Luther, Martin, 21
Lutherans, 246
Lyell, Charles, 314
Lynch, James, 449
Lynn, Massachusetts, 250
Lyon, Matthew, 200 (ill.), 201

McClellan, Gen. George P., 403, 426
McCormick, Cyrus, 254, 266, 411
McCormick, William, 411
McCulloch v. Maryland, 235–236, 360
McDonald, Archibald, 268
McDowall, John P., 345
McDowell, Gen. Irvin, 403, 405
McGillivray, Alexander, 173
McGuffey's Readers, 314
MacIntosh, Ebenezer, 116
McLeod, Alexander, 364
Macon, Georgia, 421
Macon's Bill Number 2 (1810), 226
Madison, James, 191, 214, 353; and drafting of Constitution, 177–178, 179–180; and ratification of Constitution, 181, 182; and Constitutional amendments, 188; and passage of national tax law, 188; and national fiscal policy, 192, 194; view of French Revolution, 194; and partisan politics, 194, 197; and foreign policy, 195; opposition to Alien and Sedition Acts, 201; and certification of Marbury appointment, 217, 218; on importance of Mississippi navigation, 218; election to presidency, 225; foreign policy as president, 226, 232; Indian policy of, 231; military reforms under, 232–233; reelection of, 233; economic nationalism of, 234–235

Magdalen Report (McDowall), 345
Magic, in slave society, 294
Maine, 61, 68; political reorganization of, 67; War of 1812 enlistees from, 228; admission to statehood, 239; black political rights in, 334; reform movements in, 346; border dispute with New Brunswick, 364–365; abolitionist sentiment in, 383
Maison Carrée, 162
Mali, 10, 12
Manhattan Island, New York, 43, 45, 64, 145, 312, 325
Manifest Destiny, 365–368; and conflict with Mexico, 373–376
Mann, Horace, 314
Manning, Col. Vannoy H., 409 (ill.)
Manufacturing: and colonial economic development, 79–80, 82; post-Revolutionary development of, 176; government protection of, 193, 234, 235, 238, 251, 252, 253, 257; growth of, 233, 460; and development of market economy, 244, 245, 249 (see also Market economy); mass production in, 254–257; and specialization of trade, 257, 259; financing of, 259; working conditions in, 260–264; frontier, 271–272; impact of Civil War on, 407, 409–412; in Reconstruction South, 450, 451 (ill.)
Manumission, 166, 335
Marbury, William, 217–218
Marbury v. Madison, 217–218
Marietta, Ohio, 174, 203
Market economy: infrastructure of, 244–249; specialization of labor in, 249, 250–251; cyclical nature of, 249–250; government participation in, 251–253; role of mass production in, 254–257; specialization of trade in, 257, 259; credit system of, 259–260; working conditions in, 260–264; role of commercial agriculture in, 264–266; and westward expansion, 266–272; social consequences of, 306; utopian communes as response to, 309–311; and urban growth, 311–317; distribution of wealth in, 317–320; transformation of family life by, 320–324; demand for immigrant labor, 324–325, 326; expansion of, 341, 342, 344; impact of Civil War on, 400, 409–413

Marquette, Father Jacques, 59
Marriage: changing role of women in, 163, 164; in planter society, 287–289; in slave society, 295, 296, 297
Married Women's Property Act (1839), 289
Marshall, James, 269
Marshall, John, 360; and American-French trade negotiations, 199; brings prestige to Supreme Court, 217; establishes principle of judicial review, 217–218; and trial of Burr, 222; asserts supremacy of federal government, 235–236; on federal authority over interstate commerce, 252; on sanctity of contracts, 252; on Indian nationality, 331
Martha's Vineyard, 61
Martin, Betsy, 305–306
Martin, George, 305–306, 325
Martin, Josiah, 134–135
Martin, Luther, 179
Martin, Nabby, 93 (ill.)
Martin, Peter, 306
Mary II (Queen of England), 67–68
Maryland, 43; colonization of, 27–28; colonial economy of, 28–29; political organization of, 29–30; and imperial trading system, 66; and colonial reorganization of, 67–68; population growth in, 77; slavery in, 91; resistance to British taxation in, 121; fear of slave uprisings in, 137, 138; free black population of, 166; manumission law of, 166; and ratification of Articles of Confederation, 169; debts of, 191, 192; unrest over whiskey tax, 193; and national partisan alignments, 197; grassroots campaigning in, 222; taxation of national bank, 235; political reform in, 300; alignment with Union, 394, 401, 413; Civil War engagements in, 405, 422–423
Mason, George, 177, 179, 180
Masonic order, 316; black lodges, 336; opposition to, 341, 342, 348–349
Massachusetts: slavery in, 49; European-Indian trade relations in, 60–61; changing religious mores in, 61; and imperial trading system, 63; political organization of, 66, 67; political reorganization of, 67, 68, 127; economic development in, 82, 253; religious revivalism in, 98; resentment against British army in, 110; resistance to British taxation in, 120, 125; representation in First Continental Congress, 132; loyalist sentiment in, 134, 136; organization of revolutionary militias in, 141; agrarian uprising in, 157–158; educational reform in, 162, 314; emancipation of slaves in, 165; state constitution of, 168; state currency of, 171 (ill.); representation in Constitutional Convention, 177; ratification of Constitution by, 182; debts of, 191; state-supported religion in, 207; and national partisan alignments, 235;

Native Americans (*Continued*)
pean diseases, 19–20; exchange of plants and animals with Old World, 20; cultural clash with English colonists, 25–26, 33–35, 37; assistance to Puritan colonists, 31; relations with Pennsylvania Quakers, 47–48; enslavement of, 49, 56–58; and manipulation of racial antagonisms, 79; exploitation of antagonisms between European powers, 104, 105, 107; alliances in Seven Years' War, 108, 109; warfare in British colonial possessions, 110–112; territorial concessions to in Quebec, 127; role in American Revolution, 132, 148–149, 151–152; loyalties vis-a-vis American Revolution, 138–139; toll of American Revolution on, 152, 153; land claims of, 172–173, 174–175, 218, 226; religious revival among, 209–210, 229–230; assistance to Lewis and Clark expedition, 219; resistance to westward expansion broken, 227–228, 228–231, 232; role in frontier life, 267, 268; forced resettlement of, 306, 328–334, 356, 365

Naturalization Act (1798), 200, 216
Nature (Emerson), 311
Navigation, technological advances in, 15, 245, 246, 248
Navigation Acts, 64–65, 66, 67, 69, 113, 119
Nebraska: integration into national market economy, 249; migration to, 334; political organization of, 381, 382
Netherlands, the: exploratory voyages of, 16, 18; sojourn of Puritans in, 30–31; colonialism of, 37; cedes New Netherland to England, 43, 45; and slave trade, 45, 51; trade relations with Indians, 55, 56, 58; American trade with, 172; war with France, 194
Nevada, 6; acquisition from Mexico, 267; American expansion into, 376
Nevis, 49
New Amsterdam, 19, 46 (ill.). *See also* New York City
Newark, New Jersey, 426
New Bedford, Massachusetts, 335
New Bern, North Carolina, 57, 135, 403
New Brunswick, 137, 364–365
Newburyport, Massachusetts, 317
Newburyport Herald, 317
New England: migration of Puritans to, 30–31; political organization of, 31, 33, 66, 67; European-Indian relations in, 31, 33–35, 60–61; communal ideals of, 32–33; land settlement patterns in, 33; economy of, 35; role of family in, 35–36; religious orthodoxy of, 36–37; inhospitability toward Quakers, 46; changing religious mores in, 61; population increases in, 61; and imperial trading system, 62–66; political reorganization of, 67; witchcraft panic in, 68–69; regional trading patterns, 81 (ill.); economic development in, 82, 233; civic rituals

in, 92; religious rituals in, 92; religious revivalism in, 98, 207–208; resentment against British army in, 110; resistance to British taxation in, 122; and national partisan alignments, 197, 198, 220, 226, 354; migration from, 202, 203, 307, 345; grassroots campaigning in, 222; proposed secession of, 222, 225, 233, 234; War of 1812 enlistees from, 228; British blockade of, 231; opposition to protective tariff, 235; integration into national market economy, 244, 245, 250–251; promotion of economic growth in, 253; textile manufacturing in, 256–257, 260–262, 263, 320–321; commercial farming in, 264, 265, 266; abolitionist sentiment in, 275, 372; racial discrimination in, 335; reform movements in, 346, 349; opposition to westward expansion in, 374

Newfoundland, 16, 18, 21, 109, 153; British gain control of, 105
New Hampshire, 33, 61, 236; political reorganization of, 67; slavery in, 165–166; ratification of Constitution by, 182; textile manufacturing in, 262; black political rights in, 334
New Harmony, Indiana, commune, 310
New Haven, Connecticut, 33, 62
New Jersey, 43, 145–146, 171, 222; founding of, 46; political reorganization of, 67; economic development in, 83; land riots in, 97–98; loyalist sentiment in, 136; extent of franchise in, 162–163; emancipation of slaves in, 165; slavery in, 166; and ratification of Articles of Confederation, 169; representation in Constitutional Convention, 177; migration from, 202
New Jersey Plan, 178
New Lebanon, New York, 310
New Mexico, 365, 391; colonizing of, 55, 56 (ill.); acquisition from Mexico, 267; racial discrimination in, 334; American expansion into, 375, 376; political organization of, 378
New Netherland, 19, 34, 37, 43, 45–46. *See also* New York
New Orleans, Louisiana, 59, 218, 220, 232, 245, 282, 286, 327; clothing manufacture in, 256; as center of cotton trade, 276 (ill.); free black population of, 285 & ill., 335; slavery in, 292 (ill.); growth of, 312, 325; capture by Union forces, 403; Reconstruction period in 443, 444, 450; butcher monopoly in, 458–459
New Orleans Bee (newspaper), 392
Newport, Rhode Island, 55, 62, 79
Newspapers, role in colonial urban life, 87
Newton, Connecticut, 33
New York, 57, 61, 151, 171, 362, 364; founding of, 43, 45–46; complicity with pirates, 64; political organization of, 66, 96; political reorganization of, 67–68; economic development in, 83;

domestic life in, 88; slave revolt in, 97; land riots in, 98; resistance to British taxation in, 117, 118, 122; resistance to Quartering Act, 119; representation in First Continental Congress, 132–133; emancipation of slaves in, 165, 336; resistance to centralized government, 172; purchase of Indian lands, 175; representation in Constitutional Convention, 177; ratification of Constitution by, 182; and national partisan alignments, 197, 220, 226, 368, 377, 424; westward migration in, 202; grassroots campaigning in, 222; proposed secession of, 222; War of 1812 enlistees from, 228; railroads in, 247; promotion of economic growth by, 252; credit system of, 259; industrialization of, 260; labor politics in, 263; commercial farming in, 265, 266; migration from, 307; culture and recreation in, 315–316; migration to, 325; religious revival in, 343, 345; reform movements in, 345, 346, 347, 348–349; abolitionist sentiment in, 380
New York Central rail system, 248
New York City, 46, 126, 142, 148, 189, 305–306, 341; slaves in, 55; growth of, 78, 79, 312, 314, 324, 325, 326; economic development of, 83; life style of, 87; religious revivalism in, 99; loyalist sentiment in, 135–136; British siege of, 144–145; celebration of Constitutional ratification in, 181 (ill.), 186 (ill.); British blockade of, 226; water system for, 243; integration into national market economy, 244, 245, 249; poverty in, 250; clothing manufacture in, 256; as center of commerce, 259, 265, 266; population density of, 281; educational system of, 314; culture and recreation in, 315, 316; public disorders in, 317, 425 (ill.), 426; class society in, 317–320; free black population of, 335, 336; reform movements in, 344–345; civilian life in Civil War, 411 (ill.), 414; racial equality in, 439
New York Consolidated Lottery, 347 (ill.)
New York Evening Post, 387, 414
New York Herald, 414
New York Journal, 121 (ill.)
New York Journal of Commerce, 341
New York Magdalen Society, 345
New York Racing Association, 316
New York Society of Pewterers, 186 (ill.)
New York Tribune, 417
New York World, 418
Niagra, New York, 111, 148–149
Nickel Plate Railroad, 243
Nigeria, 12, 41
Niña (ship), 16
Ninth Amendment, U.S. Constitution, 188
Nipmucks, 60–61
Non-Importation Act (1806), 223, 225, 233

Tulane, Paul, 256
Tunis, 223
Turner, Henry McNeil, 449
Turner, Nat, 297, 298, 300, 335
Turnvereine, 327
Tuscaroras, 58; settlement in Pennsylvania, 48; trade relations with Europeans, 57; role in American Revolution, 149
Twelfth Amendment, U.S. Constitution, 202, 354
Two Treatises of Civil Government (Locke), 94
Tyler, John, 363, 365, 367, 368
Tyler, Royall, 161 & ill.

Union Army, 295; reorganization of, 403; living conditions of troops, 413–414; care for wounded soldiers, 414–415; black soldiers in, 419 (ill.), 420, 430–431, 439; desertions from, 426; total enlistments in, 430
Union Canal Company, 347
Union County, South Carolina, 453
Union League Clubs, 453
Union Navy, blockade of Southern ports, 403
Union Pacific Railroad, 412
United Provinces of the Río de la Plata, 237
United States (U.S.S.), 228
United States Military Academy, 251
U.S. Sanitary Commission, 414
United States v. *Cruikshank,* 459
United States v. *Reese,* 459
Universities, *see* Higher education
University of Georgia, 281 (ill.)
University of Pennsylvania, 95, 188
Urbanization: and poverty, 81; in frontier West, 271–272; and slave economy, 282; and growth of Confederate bureaucracy, 407
Urban life: colonial, 87–88; and growth of cities, 311–317; culture and leisure in, 314–316; distribution of wealth in, 317–320; impact of immigrants on, 325, 326–327
Utah, 6; acquisition from Mexico, 267; Mormon settlement of, 310, 460; American expansion into, 376; political organization of, 378
Utica, New York, 352
Utopian communities, 309–311

Vallandigham, Clement L., 424–425, 426
Van Buren, Martin, 358, 367, 368; Indian policy of, 332; election to vice-presidency, 360; election to presidency, 362–363; credit policy of, 363; and election of *1840,* 363; foreign policy of, 364; and debate over slavery, 372; and election of *1848,* 377
Vance, Zebulon, 408, 423
Van Huffel, Pieter, 237 (ill.)
Van Raalte, Albertus C., 326
Vermont: land riots in, 98; emancipation of slaves in, 165; and national partisan alignments, 226; black political rights in, 334; reform movements in, 349

Verrazano, Giovanni da, 16
Verschuur, Wouterus, 319 (ill.)
Vesey, Denmark, 297
Vespucci, Amerigo, 16
Veto, in system of checks and balances, 361
"Vices of the Political System of the United States" (Madison), 177
Vicksburg, Mississippi, 278, 422, 423
Virginia, 47, 152, 176, 185, 361, 363, 393, 401, 403; colonizing of, 21, 23, 25; political organization of, 26–27, 29–30, 66, 67, 96, 300; slavery in, 42, 89, 90, 91, 290, 291, 293, 300, 371; ties to North Carolina, 48; European-Indian trade relations in, 59–60; and imperial trading system, 66; population growth in, 77; domestic life in, 88; religious rituals in, 92; religious revivalism in, 98, 99–100; western land claims of, 107–108, 169; Indian warfare in, 110, 111, 139; resistance to British taxation in, 115; representation in First Continental Congress, 133; opposition to American resistance in, 134; fear of slave uprisings in, 138; free black population of, 166; manumission laws of, 166; representation in Constitutional Convention, 177; ratification of Constitution by, 182; debts of, 191, 192; unrest over whiskey tax, 193; and national partisan alignments, 197, 392; migration from, 203; state-supported religion in, 207; black insurrection in, 209; agricultural economy of, 277, 278, 280; population density of, 281; planter society in, 288, 289; abolitionist sentiment in, 300; rural life in, 308 (ill.); racial discrimination in, 335; rejection of secession, 394; hardships of Civil War in, 408; Civil War engagements in, 429, 430 (ill.); readmission to Union, 440; Reconstruction period in, 448
Virginia Agricultural Society, 238
Virginia Company, 22–23, 26, 31
Virginia Plan, 178, 179
Virginia Resolution, 201, 358
Virginia Stamp Act Resolves, 115
Virtual representation theory, 113, 114
Voice of Industry (newspaper), 262
Voting, *see* Franchise (voting); Presidential elections

Wade-Davis bill, 440
Waltham textile manufacturing system, 256, 257
Waltham watches, 254
Wampanoag and Operatives' Journal, 262
Ware v. *Hylton,* 189
War of 1812, 214, 234, 235, 240, 244, 249, 257, 271, 329, 330, 341, 342, 343, 356, 364; declaration of, 226; recruitment of soliders for, 226–228; military campaigns of, 228–232; settlement of, 232; consequences of, 232–242
War of the Austrian Succession, 82

War of the League of Augsburg, 68
War of the Spanish Succession, 69
Washington, George, 131, 150, 151, 153 (ill.), 213, 215; action against French in Ohio country, 108; military campaigns of American Revolution, 132, 144–145, 146, 148, 152; participation in First Continental Congress, 133; leadership of American Revolution, 141–142; as symbol of virtue, 161; as slaveholder, 164–165; and drafting of Constitution, 177; election to presidency, 189–190; selection of cabinet, 191; fiscal policy of, 192–193, 194; and partisan politics, 194, 195, 197, 198; foreign policy of, 195–197, 198, 201; farewell address of, 198, 201; and Freemasonry, 348
Washington, Martha Custis, 141
Washington, D.C., 355, 393, 415, 435, 455; relocation of nation's capital to, 213–214; Adams's "midnight appointments," 215, 217; British occupation of, 231; suppression of slave trade in, 352, 378; threatened by Confederate forces, 403, 405, 422–423; racial equality in, 439
"Washington at Verplanck's Point" (Trumbull), 190 (ill.)
Washington State, 6, 374
Wasp (U.S.S.), 228
Watson, James, 142 (ill.)
Wayne, Gen. Anthony, 174, 175 (ill.)
Wayne, Pennsylvania, 131
Wealth, distribution of, 317–320
Wealth and Biography of the Wealthy Citizens of New York City (Beach), 317–318
The Wealth of Nations (Smith), 251
Weatherwise's Federal Almanack, 177 (ill.)
Webb family, 380
Webster, Daniel, 357, 363; defense of federal union, 358, 378; and election of *1836,* 362; death of, 381
Webster-Ashburton Treaty (1842), 365
Weehawken, New Jersey, 222
Weekly Advocate, 336
Weems, Mason Locke, 161
Weld, Theodore, 350
West, Benjamin, 111 (ill.), 161
West Chester, Pennsylvania, 383 (ill.)
Westchester County, New York, 145
West Indies: slavery in, 49; New England's trade with, 62–63; European trade rivalries in, 82, 150; exile of loyalists in, 137; relations with England, 137–138; American trade with, 172, 176, 196, 223; American-French trade rivalry in, 199
West Point, 131
West Roxbury, Massachusetts, 310
Wethersfield, Connecticut, 34
Weymouth, Massachusetts, 335
Whig party: as reformist vehicle, 342, 345, 362; and revival of political parties, 342–343, 361–362; and election of *1836,* 362; promotion of activist